D1172518

## TALES FROM SPANDAU

Sentenced to long prison terms at the Trial of the Major War Criminals at Nuremberg, seven of Adolf Hitler's closest associates – Rudolf Hess, Albert Speer, Karl Dönitz, Erich Raeder, Walther Funk, Konstantin von Neurath, and Baldur von Schirach – were to have become forgotten men at Berlin's Spandau Prison. Instead, they became the focus of a bitter four-decade tug-of-war between the Soviet Union and the Western Allies – a dispute on the fault line of the Cold War itself that drew in heads of state, military strategists, powerful businessmen, vocal church leaders, old-world aristocrats, international spies, and neo-Nazis. Drawing on long-secret records from four countries, Norman J. W. Goda provides a new perspective on the terrifying shadow thrown by Nazi Germany on the Cold War years and how that shadow helped to influence the Cold War itself.

Norman J. W. Goda is Professor of History at Ohio University. He is the author of *Tomorrow the World: Hitler, Northwest Africa, and the Path toward America* (1998) and coauthor of *U.S. Intelligence and the Nazis* (Cambridge, 2005).

# Tales from Spandau

## NAZI CRIMINALS AND THE COLD WAR

**Norman J. W. Goda**
Ohio University

CAMBRIDGE
UNIVERSITY PRESS

CAMBRIDGE UNIVERSITY PRESS
Cambridge, New York, Melbourne, Madrid, Cape Town, Singapore, São Paulo

Cambridge University Press
32 Avenue of the Americas, New York, NY 10013-2473, USA

www.cambridge.org
Information on this title: www.cambridge.org/9780521867207



First published 2007

Printed in the United States of America

*A catalog record for this publication is available from the British Library.*

*Library of Congress Cataloging in Publication Data*

Goda, Norman J. W., 1961–
Tales from Spandau : Nazi criminals and the Cold War / Norman J. W. Goda.
p. cm.
Includes bibliographical references and index.
ISBN 0-521-86720-7
1. War criminals – Germany. 2. Spandau Prison (Berlin, Germany) 3. Cold War.
4. Germany – History – 1945–1955. 5. Criminal justice, Administration of – Germany – Berlin – History. 6. National socialism and justice. I. Title.
DD244.G63 2006
365′.48092243155 2006005656

ISBN-13 978-0-521-86720-7 hardback
ISBN-10 0-521-86720-7 hardback

*For*

*Gwyneth*

# Contents

# Acknowledgments

I incurred more debts in writing this book than I can ever repay, so sincerely heartfelt thanks will have to do. But they are indeed heartfelt.

As all historians, I could have done nothing without able, helpful, professional archivists. At the National Archives and Records Administration in College Park, Maryland, William Cunliffe, David Van Tassel, Dick Myers, Robert Wolfe, Amy Schmidt, Eric Van Slander, Fidel Taperra, Sean Morris, and Michael Peterson located hard-to-find records on the history of Spandau Prison. In the Amherst College Library's Archives and Special Collections department, Peter Nelson located key files in John J. McCloy's papers. In the Ministère des Affaires étrangères, Bureau des Archives de l'occupation française en Allemagne et en Autriche in Colmar, I am indebted to Nathalie Moreau, Pascal Penot, Valérie Flury, Odile Dufour, and especially Michel Chauffeton for their painstaking search through partly classified records. As always, the entire staff of The National Archives in Kew was as professional and as helpful as could be.

At the Politisches Archiv des Auswärtigen Amtes in Berlin, my friend Knud Piening was of tremendous assistance as always. Manuela Vack helped me to navigate the massive collection of Albert Speer's personal papers at the Bundesarchiv in Koblenz. Frau Hartmann helped me with East German Communist Party records at the Stiftung Archiv der Parteien und Massenorganisationen der DDR im Bundesarchiv in Berlin. In the Allied Museum of Berlin, Florian Weiss provided important help, locating lost British Kommandatura records as well as a trove of photos of Spandau. The staff of the Landesarchiv Berlin was also of great assistance. In the ThyssenKrupp Konzernarchiv in Duisburg, Dr. Manfred Rasch and staff generously helped me with Walter Rohland's papers. Michael Bing of the Landeskirchliches Archiv Stuttgart helped me to locate key sections of the Theophil Wurm papers.

Closer to home, I am grateful to Ohio University's master bibliographer, Dan Olsen, who procured microfilms for me over the course of some five years. Large sections of this book were written at the Hannah McCauley

Library at Ohio University at Lancaster, and I am indebted to the professional librarians there: Sharon Huge, Julia Robinson, Tami Walker, and Joyce Mohler for graciously allowing me to monopolize desk space, their printer, and their microfilm reader. Members of the Berlin United States Military Veterans Association, particularly those who served as sentries at Spandau Prison, shared their memories with me and some, including Don Galuoppo and Joseph Gnoffo, generously shared their photos of the prison. Arsen Djatej at Ohio University located and translated Russian-language memoir sources that also add to Spandau Prison's history.

My friends Gerhard L. Weinberg, Steven M. Miner, Richard Breitman, and Charles Sydnor read the manuscript as a whole and made invaluable comments, as did my father, Herbert L. Goda. Jeffrey Herf, Frank Buscher, Dick de Mildt, Robert Hertzstein, Peter Hoffmann, Francis Nicosia, Robert Gellately, Ronald Zweig, Michael Marrus, Peter Hayes, Agnes Petersen, Timothy Naftali, Carole Fink, Günther Heydemann, Robert Wolfe, John Brobst, Mark Ruff, Jonathan Wiesen, Geoffrey Megargee, and JonDavid Wynecken either commented on parts of the manuscript or gave me different angles to think about. Lewis Bateman and Ciara McLaughlin at Cambridge University Press immediately had faith in this project, and my production editor Camilla Knapp and copy editor Sara Black made the manuscript far better than it otherwise would have been.

This book could not have been completed without the generous financial support of Ohio University's College of Arts and Sciences, its International Studies Program, and its Office of the Vice President for Research, which financed my travels to Europe and photographic reproduction costs. I am also indebted to Ohio University for the leave time they generously provided in the fall of 2004.

Last and most importantly: My wonderful, wonderful boys, Grant and Lucas, put up with my absences in Europe, disappearances into the library, and the occasionally missed youth hockey game. And my loving wife and best friend Gwyneth put up with much, much more. For all she has given me, here as always, I gratefully and lovingly dedicate what follows to her.

Lancaster, Ohio
2006

# Abbreviations and Terms

| | |
|---|---|
| AA | Auswärtiges Amt (Foreign Ministry, Federal Republic of Germany) |
| *AAP-BRD* | *Akten zur auswärtigen Politik der Bundesrepublik Deutschland* |
| AAPS | Archives of the Allied Prison Spandau (NARA, RG 84, Berlin Mission, Records Relating to Spandau Prison, 1947–1987, Microfilm Publication A33520) |
| ACA | Allied Control Authority |
| ACC | Allied Control Council |
| AEG | Allgemeine Elekricitäts-Gesellschaft |
| AFS | American Field Service |
| AHC | Allied High Commission |
| AK | Allied Kommandatura |
| AMB/SlgD | Alliierten Museum Berlin, Sammlung Dokumenten |
| BA-B | Bundesarchiv (Berlin) (the letter "B" afterwards denotes Bestand [Record Group]) |
| BA-K | Bundesarchiv (Koblenz) (the letter "B" afterwards denotes Bestand [Record Group]) |
| BASC | Berlin Air Safety Center |
| Bd. | Band (volume) – for German archival citations |
| BKA | Bundeskanzleramt (Office of the Federal Chancellor) |
| BRD | Bundesrepublik Deutschland (Federal Republic of Germany) |
| CDU | Christian Democratic Union |
| CSU | Christian Social Union |
| DAF | *Deutsche Arbeitsfront* (German Labor Front) |
| DDR | Deutsche Demokratische Republik (German Democratic Republic) |
| DM | Deutschmark |
| *DzD* | Germany, Bundesministerium des Innern, *Dokumente zur Deutschlandpolitik* |
| EDC | European Defense Community |
| FRG | Federal Republic of Germany |
| GBI | *Generalbauinspektorat* |

| | |
|---|---|
| GDR | German Democratic Republic |
| GMFB | Gouvernement militaire français de Berlin |
| GSFG | Group Soviet Forces Germany |
| *FAZ* | *Frankfurter Allgemeine Zeitung* |
| FO | Foreign Office |
| FCO | Foreign and Commonwealth Office |
| FDGB | *Freie Deutsche Gewerkschaftsbund* (Free German Federation of Trade Unions) |
| FDP | Free Democratic Party |
| *FRUS* | *Foreign Relations of the United States* |
| HC | Cabinet du Haut-Commissariat de la République française en Allemagne |
| HFRH | *Hilfsgemeinschaft Freiheit für Rudolf Hess* (Freedom for Rudolf Hess Aid Society) |
| HICOG | U.S. High Commissioner for Germany |
| HICOM | Allied High Commission, Germany |
| ICC | International Criminal Court |
| ICTR | International Criminal Tribunal for Rwanda |
| ICTY | International Criminal Tribunal for the Former Yugoslavia |
| KPD | Communist Party of Germany |
| LAB | Landesarchiv Berlin |
| LKA-S | Landeskirchliches Archiv Stuttgart |
| LCO | Lord Chancellor's Office (London) |
| LF | Lot File |
| LPD | Liberal Democratic Party of Germany |
| MAE-AOFAA | Ministère des Affaires étrangères, Bureau des Archives de l'occupation française en Allemagne et Autriche (Colmar) |
| MGFA | Militärgeschichtliches Forschungsamt |
| MP | Member of Parliament |
| NARA | National Archives and Records Administration, College Park, Maryland |
| NATO | North Atlantic Treaty Organization |
| NKFD | *Nationalkomitee Freies Deutschland* (National Committee for a Free Germany) |
| NKVD | People's Commissariat for Internal Affairs (includes Soviet State Security Police) |
| NL | Nachlaß (Personal Papers) |
| NPD | National Democratic Party of Germany |
| OCCWC | Office of the Chief of Counsel for War Crimes |
| OMGUS | Office of Military Government, U.S. Zone (Germany) |
| OPC | Office of Policy Coordination |
| OSS | Office of Strategic Services |
| PA-AA | Politisches Archiv des Auswärtigen Amtes (Berlin) (the letter "B" afterwards denotes Bestand [Record Group]) |
| POW | prisoner of war |
| PREM | Records of the Prime Minister's Office |

| | |
|---|---|
| RAF | Royal Air Force |
| RG | Record Group (relates to NARA records-entry numbers in bibliography) |
| RM | Reichsmark |
| SA | *Sturmabteilung* |
| SAPMO | Stiftung Archiv der Parteien und Massenorganisationen der DDR im Bundesarchiv (Berlin) |
| SD | *Sicherheitsdienst* |
| SED | Socialist Unity Party of Germany |
| SIB | Special Investigations Branch |
| Sig. | Signatur (Archival designation for Speer and Wolters Nachlaß) |
| SMERSH | Soviet Military Counterintelligence, 1943–1946, the acronym of which means “Death to Spies” |
| SPD | Social Democratic Party of Germany |
| SRP | Socialist Reich Party |
| SS | *Schutzstaffel*<br>SS-Obergruppenführer (rank comparable to U.S. Army Lieutenant General)<br>SS-Gruppenführer (rank comparable to U.S. Army Major General)<br>SS-Obersturmbannführer (rank comparable to U.S. Army Lieutenant Colonel)<br>SS-Sturmbannführer (rank comparable to U.S. Army Major)<br>SS-Hauptsturmführer (rank comparable to U.S. Army Captain) |
| *SSD* | Speer, Albert. *Spandau: The Secret Diaries*. Translated by Richard Winston and Clara Winston. New York: Macmillan, 1976 |
| TKA | ThyssenKrupp Konzernarchiv (Duisburg) |
| *TMWC* | International Military Tribunal, *Trial of the Major War Criminals before the International Military Tribunal, Nuremberg, 14 November 1945–1 October 1946*. 42 vols. Nuremberg: International Military Tribunal, 1949 |
| TNA | The National Archives (U.K.), Kew |
| *TWC-CC10* | United States. *Trials of War Criminals before the Nuremberg Military Tribunals under Control Council Law No. 10, Nuremberg, October 1946–April 1949*. 13 vols. Washington, DC: GPO, 1949–1953 |
| *UdSSR* | Jochen P. Laufer and Georgij P. Kynin, *Die UdSSR und die deutsche Frage, 1941–1948: Dokumente aus dem Archiv für Außenpolitik der Russischen Föderation*. 3 vols. Berlin: Duncker und Humblot, 2004. |
| VdS | *Verband deutscher Soldaten* |

# Introduction

> "If we are ever all out, none of us will ever see each other again; most certainly we shall never laugh about Spandau."
>
> Rudolf Hess

No death in history had been planned so meticulously as that of Rudolf Hess, who turned 93 years old in April 1987 and whose demise was expected at any moment. In another time, Hess had been in the inner circle of Adolf Hitler himself and the third most important man in Nazi Germany. He had tried with Hitler to seize power in Munich in November 1923, he had devotedly served jail time with Hitler in 1924, and as deputy leader of the Nazi Party his signature was on numerous major state documents dated before and after 1939 when Hitler set the world ablaze. Now Hess was the sole remaining inmate of Spandau Allied Military Prison in the British sector of West Berlin. For the past four decades at this imposing Prussian nineteenth-century structure, the four major powers that had defeated Nazism – the United States, the United Kingdom, France, and the Soviet Union – had held Hitler's closest living associates who had received prison terms at the famous Trial of the Major War Criminals at Nuremberg. And for more than two decades, Hess had been Spandau's lone prisoner.

Hess was diagnosed as paranoid, convinced from time to time that his Allied captors were trying to poison him. He was also a hypochondriac who had spent his first years in Spandau keeping his fellow inmates (and the Allied guards) awake moaning with imaginary stomach pains. By now he was constantly irritable and every bit the Nazi that he had been in 1924 when he had in Landsberg prison taken Hitler's dictations for what would become *Mein Kampf*. When given a private female nurse by the Americans only months before his death, Hess had her removed from the prison because she was black.[1] In his final testament to posterity discovered by the Soviets in 1986, Hess claimed that Hitler never wanted war with the Western powers. Somehow, Hess believed, Hitler was forced into it by a secret force working on his subconscious – a force controlled by Germany's greatest nemesis, the Jews. For the rest, Hess mused about West German unemployment, which he thought might bring Nazism, or something like it, back into power.[2]

Yet despite his lack of capacity for much beyond fantasy and complaining, Hess had by the 1980s become a symbol for many things. His remaining presence as Spandau's only prisoner reflected the Soviets' unforgiving stance toward Nazism, their fear that Nazism was not completely dead, and their conviction that Communists were the only true anti-Nazis. It was the Kremlin specifically that again and again refused to allow Hess to leave. The various Allied attempts to have Hess remanded to a sanitarium or to the custody of his family reflected the self-assurance in Western capitals that Nazism could no longer rise in West Germany and that even for a man such as Hess, humanitarian instincts had their place. For the West German government and for the government of West Berlin, Hess represented the absurdity of the Cold War machinery there. It was West Berliners who met the financial burdens of Spandau for the sake of an incarceration arrangement that was poorly thought out even by the confused standards of the early Cold War. Keeping Hess in Spandau also ran counter to the West German desire to move beyond Nazism's long shadow. And to Hess's family and his ultra–right wing supporters, Hitler's former deputy represented all the supposed injustices of Nuremberg – from the victors sitting in judgment of the vanquished to the bits of evidence, supposedly ignored, that might have turned the Nuremberg judgment on its head.

Thus, Hess's death had to be managed very carefully. In October 1982, when Hess was 88, the Four Powers had agreed that on his death, the body, following an official autopsy, would be secretly flown to Hess's home state of Bavaria and handed over to his family there. It was a generous step. In the thirty-five years that the Allies had run Spandau, the Soviets had refused to allow anyone – even family – to receive the remains of a major war criminal whose death might come in prison. Moscow feared that releasing the body would result in a loud political funeral or even a shrine to the Nazi dead. Indeed, the governing agreement up to 1982 was that Hess's body would be cremated under the watch of the prison authorities. By now the Soviets were willing to allow the family to have the remains, but only under certain conditions. The Western Allies had to use their influence with the West German authorities to ensure that a Hess funeral would not become an occasion for neo-Nazi rallies. The funeral also had to occur within the family circle only. Hess's property, from his Luftwaffe uniform to his pocket watch to his denture plates, would be destroyed so as not to become holy Nazi relics.[3] Hess's son Wolf Rüdiger Hess agreed in a written contract that, on his honor, a quiet funeral would be held with only the closest family members present.[4] Everything was set to minimize the commotion. And on August 17, 1987, Rudolf Hess committed the one act that could possibly have ruined these carefully laid plans. He hanged himself.

Conspiracy theories that Hess had been murdered by his captors immediately flew out from Bavaria with the help of the Hess family itself. And while the Allied powers struggled amongst themselves to understand how the most heavily guarded prisoner in the world could commit suicide – at age 93 yet – the question of what to do with Spandau Prison itself remained. The last prisoner was dead. Back in 1982 it was agreed that the prison would be destroyed as soon as possible after Hess's death so that it could not become a pilgrimage site for Germans sympathetic to Hess or nostalgic for the Nazi years.[5] Demolition had also been discussed for years by the West Berlin municipal government, which worried that controversy over Spandau prison would damage the city's image.[6] The delay in demolition resulting from the Hess suicide investigation brought anxious inquiries to the British authorities from the Governing Mayor of West Berlin, who complained that "opposition to pulling the prison down is growing daily, and . . . the longer we wait, the more difficult the situation will become."[7]

The British military authorities in West Berlin hired a German contractor to perform the demolition with cranes and wrecking balls (after studying three bids) but in the meantime, to appease the Governing Mayor, they quickly brought in 100 British army personnel with axes to destroy the windows and roofs in order to begin the demolition process publicly as per a West German request to demonstrate that the prison would not remain standing.[8] The British also hurriedly built a new security fence around the prison property so that souvenirs could not be stolen.[9] A convoy of army trucks transported scrap lumber and metal from the prison to the British Army Ordnance depot in West Berlin, where it was mixed with other scrap so as to lose its Spandau identity before reentering the private construction sector.[10] Once selected, the German contractor received threatening telephone calls, but under British supervision the company demolished Spandau Prison in September 1987. The bricks were taken to Gatow Air Base in the British sector, where they were buried and covered with dirt and trees and made inaccessible to those who offered the demolition crew up to 800 Deutschmark (DM) per brick.[11] The prison was buried shortly after its last inmate.

And thus ended the story of history's most bizarre prison. There has never been a place like Spandau Prison, and there has never been a serious historical study of the prison itself or the contentious politics surrounding its notorious inmates.[12] Spandau was the only prison for Nazi war criminals that was ever governed internationally. It was the only prison for war criminals where most of the prisoners served out their full terms ranging from ten years to twenty years to life. And it was the living legacy of the one postwar trial with which most people in the Western world were familiar, the Trial of the Major War Criminals before the International Military Tribunal at Nuremberg. This Nuremberg trial became the model for future international criminal proceedings from the subsequent U.S. military trials in Nuremberg itself to the trial of Adolf Eichmann in Jerusalem in 1961 to the trials of Yugoslav war criminals at The Hague and of Rwanda's Hutu murderers in Arusha from the mid-1990s. But for better or worse, a piece of Nuremberg's legitimacy would depend on Spandau.

The prison had many incongruous facets that cannot be replicated. After the Nuremberg trial it housed only seven prisoners, then six, then five, then four, then three, then for more than two decades, one. It was under the control of uneasy allies who never trusted one another's motives, particularly where the fate of Germany was concerned. It employed a set of regulations concerning feeding, letter writing, visits, and overall secrecy that were, at the very least, odd. It had no governing body after 1948 and could not adapt itself to change without torturous international negotiations. It had no machinery for paroles, pardons, hospital visits, or the handling of prisoners' deaths. A prison regime such as Spandau could no longer be created today.

Yet the story of Spandau and its high-profile prisoners is worth a close look. We can do so now as never before. Soviet official records on the prison remain closed; British records can only be released to the public thirty years after their generation (meaning that records from 1987 will become available in 2017); and while some French records on Spandau are available, others are closed until the mid-twenty-first century. But there are a variety of available sources. These records include long-open British, U.S., and French military government records from 1945 to 1949 and diplomatic records from the 1950s to the mid-1970s. West and East German records up to this time are available, too. Also available since 2001 are the personal papers of Albert Speer, arguably Spandau's most controversial inmate and surely its most verbose.[13] Speer's voluminous papers are especially interesting. Together with other records, they provide needed corrective to his famous *Spandau Diaries*, selectively compiled after his release in 1966 from thousands of notes smuggled out of the prison over the course of his twenty-year sentence. Speer's *Spandau Diaries* has for more than three decades been the only available look inside the prison. Though accurate concerning the day-to-day occurrences that Speer mentions, its limited perspective leaves much untouched, while deliberately misrepresenting Speer's famous introspection concerning his guilt.[14]

Also recently available are the records of Spandau Prison itself, including the often-contentious weekly meetings of the prison directors. With the decision to liquidate Spandau came the Soviet insistence that the prison records be destroyed. All documents generated in the prison had an official stamp from Spandau Prison itself, and Moscow was afraid that the documents themselves, like Hess's belongings, could become souvenirs. The Four Powers agreed, however, that the records could be microfilmed, and after extensive archiving, eight copies of the Archives of the Allied Prison Spandau (nearly 84,000 pages) were photographed onto thirty-six rolls of microfilm, two sets for each of the governing powers. The British, French, and Russian sets are still classified, but the American set in the National Archives outside of Washington, D.C., is available to scholars.[15] Finally, the Nazi War Crimes Disclosure Act of 1998, by which all U.S. records concerning Nazi war criminals are to be opened to the public, triggered the release of close to ten thousand pages of previously classified State Department records from the 1970s and 1980s concerning international discussions and agreements concerning Rudolf Hess.[16] In many ways, then, one does not have to wait for others to release their records a decade or more hence.

But is a story about seven prison sentences important? Yes, it is for a number of reasons. Spandau adds to the study, undertaken over the last fifteen years or so, on the postwar German confrontation with the Nazi past and on other national memories of history's most terrible conflict.[17] Much of this literature gives both postwar Germanys mixed reviews for the honesty and forthrightness with which they accepted German responsibility. Most Germans who lived through the war preferred to see themselves as victims of the Nazis, Allied bombs, or the Red Army rather than as active or passive accomplices with their own government. The German reaction to foreign war crimes trials was generally negative. The reaction to long-term imprisonment of Germans by other powers, whether in West Germany, Italy, the Netherlands, Poland, Yugoslavia, the U.S.S.R., or elsewhere, was overwhelmingly negative, too. Such men were viewed as political prisoners rather than as criminals. Vigorous national debates over reparations to Jews, extension of the West German statute of limitations for murder, the use of former concentration camps as sites of national memory, and, most recently, the public display of photographs of German crimes have been a staple of German public discourse.[18]

Spandau adds to this picture. West German governments conducted tireless bilateral negotiations for the release of Germans found guilty by American, French, British, Dutch, Italian, and other national tribunals and imprisoned by one or another of these countries. But they were more careful with the Spandau prisoners. The West German public, from the press to churches to veterans' groups to the Red Cross, pressed for the release of the Nuremberg criminals with the additional argument that they were mistreated by the Soviets. But the government in Bonn understood the more explosive nature of these men. For one thing, they were convicted in the trial of the century. For another, they were held by four powers, not one. And one of the four was the Soviet Union, which could turn official efforts on behalf of major war criminals against West German society itself, which the Soviets argued was unreconstructed, revanchist, and another variant of Nazism.

Indeed, Spandau was different because it was a focal point not just of German memory of the war but of many others as well. British and American trials, even beyond Nuremberg, were the only proceedings in which the prosecutors tried Germans for crimes committed against other nationals. Though

Anglo-American prosecutors dove into the Nuremberg trial with the hope that it would serve a variety of universal judicial and historical ends, British and American recollections of World War II became more forgiving toward the Germans with time.[19] Most German war crimes (with some important exceptions) were not committed against Anglo-American soldiers. Moreover, though England had been bombed, neither country had been occupied by foreign troops.[20] In the years ahead, British memory of the war focused on the heroism of Royal Air Force pilots during the Battle of Britain and the duel in the desert between Montgomery's Eighth Army and Rommel's Afrika Korps rather than crimes against British prisoners.[21] For Americans, the defining moment of the war in Europe was and continues to be the Normandy landings of June 1944. Though the massacre of U.S. prisoners at Malmédy in December 1944 by Waffen-SS troops provoked outrage, and indeed American momentum for war crimes trials, it was the hard-fought D-Day landings that lodged most in American memory. France suffered invasion and occupation, but French memories of German war crimes focused mostly on those committed in France, preferably without the participation of French collaborators.[22] All three, moreover, quickly came to see the Soviets as a greater threat in the postwar years than a resurgent Germany.

Soviet memory of the war was another matter. Despite the wanton and paranoid brutality of the Stalinist system against the U.S.S.R.'s own citizens and despite Stalin's collaboration with Hitler until mid-1941, the war was officially remembered in terms of the surprise German invasion in June of that year and the German policy of annihilation that followed. The German murder of millions of Jews and other civilians as well as Soviet POWs through shooting, systematic starvation, and gassing meant that, from the start, official Soviet statements defined the war entirely in terms of German atrocities. From the spring of 1942, an Extraordinary State Commission collected tens of thousands of documents and more than a quarter-million witness statements and examined forensic evidence while the government released numerous international calls for judicial retribution.[23] Soviet war crimes trials were held as early as December 1943 at Kharkov for the German mass murder of civilians (though Jewish victims were not distinguished from Soviet citizens at large).[24] Despite Soviet atrocities against Polish civilians and Polish army officers before the German invasion and despite Soviet crimes against civilians during the advances into Poland, Romania, Hungary, and Germany in 1944 and 1945, this would be remembered as the most just of all wars – a war of liberation against an imperialist and murderous invader. And there could be no forgiving. Critics of the International Military Tribunal pointed to the irony of one brutal dictatorship sitting in judgment of another. Thanks in part to the scale of Soviet suffering and in part to the Communist dialectic wherein all wars launched by Communists were wars of liberation, the Soviets claimed to see no such inconsistencies.[25]

And the variant perceptions of the war and its meaning converged at Spandau Prison, which also sat at the very fault line of the ensuing Cold War. Spandau thus contained a strategic element. Defeated Germany was divided into four military occupation zones after the war, and Berlin itself, located 110 miles within the Soviet occupation zone, was itself divided into four occupation sectors. The city of Berlin, like Germany as a whole, was to have been governed through Four-Power cooperation, but if this cooperation were to end, so would joint governance of Berlin and perhaps even Western access to the city should the Soviets choose to use force. In the summer of 1948, the Soviets challenged Allied access to the western Berlin sectors. Angered by democratic and free-market reforms in the areas of Allied control, the Soviet delegations walked out from the Four-Power bodies that governed Germany and Berlin itself. Soviet forces then blockaded the road and rail routes across the Soviet occupation zone to western Berlin. Four-Power cooperation in the city was at an end thanks to the Berlin blockade, the subsequent Allied airlift of food and medicine to West Berlin's two million residents, and the creation of two separate German states in 1949. Since the Soviet-sponsored East German state, the German Democratic Republic, needed a united Berlin as its capital to ensure its own legitimacy, the Soviets would try for much of the Cold War to eliminate the Allied presence from the western half of the city.

Yet Spandau was an anomaly in East–West struggle. As Four-Power relations in Berlin broke down in nearly every imaginable way, Spandau survived – along with the Berlin Air Safety Center – as the lone remaining establishment where the Four Powers worked together. The Soviets, obsessed with the punishment of the major war criminals, would never surrender their right to help guard them in Britain's sector of Berlin just as the Western Allies, determined to hold on to their rights in West Berlin, would not surrender access to their sectors as a whole. Spandau Prison was thus emblematic of what would become a four-decade Allied assertion – that Berlin would remain under Four-Power governance until all four powers, not just the Soviets, decided otherwise. The Allies could not leave their Four-Power duties at Spandau or move the German prisoners out of Berlin without legitimizing broader Soviet efforts to push the Western powers out of the city. The Soviets, who resisted any attempt to release the major war criminals and most attempts to make life easier for them, understood this, constantly referring to the sanctity of Four-Power agreements over Berlin, even though Moscow had rejected Four-Power rule as such. The West Germans too came to understand that Spandau was a linchpin that helped keep West Berlin's citizens under Allied military protection. In a bizarre sense, the lengthy incarceration of Hitler's closest living associates had a role in protecting West Berliners from Communist rule. Even the tortuous negotiations over Hess's death in the 1970s and 1980s were conducted for fear that a Four-Power breakdown at Spandau might trigger a latter-day Berlin crisis.

Yet Spandau's significance is not just historical. It is also contemporary. The world is discussing what to do with high-level criminals from recent conflicts. In 1993 and 1994, the United Nations created two ad hoc tribunals, the International Criminal Tribunal for the Former Yugoslavia (ICTY) and the International Criminal Tribunal for Rwanda (ICTR) to punish the perpetrators from the genocidal conflicts in those regions. In 1998, the UN established a permanent International Criminal Court (ICC) for current and future mass crimes. Yet what is the aim of such tribunals? Is it simply to dispense justice? Is it to create a historical record of the crimes in question? Is it to provide historical remembrance so that such crimes shall not be repeated? Is it to provide deterrence for future dictators? Is it to help foster reconciliation between societies once at war with one another? Given the magnitude of genocidal crimes, can something as finite as law even address them properly? Commentators have disagreed on these points.[26]

Perhaps, as Hannah Arendt said while observing the stirring trial of Adolf Eichmann in Jerusalem in 1961, a trial is on safest ground when it aims at legal judgment alone. A trial aimed at shaping national identity through the dramatic narrative of the past, which the Eichmann trial attempted to do, risks turning a legal proceeding into something more akin to a show trial.[27] Or perhaps, as many others have argued, a different kind of trial is in order for a different kind of criminal, whose acts destroy the lives of thousands or even millions. The bar of history may demand nothing less.[28] Perhaps the trial of such figures is such a huge job with so many aims and so many problems (grandstanding by the defense, possible acquittal) that international trials cannot help but spawn skepticism.[29] Perhaps British Prime Minister Winston Churchill was right – it is far easier to shoot the perpetrators summarily than to risk the possible embarrassments and failures that go with such an immense legal undertaking.[30]

And these debates, complicated though they are, rarely consider the role of punishment and its effect. For many, the punishment is irrelevant. Italian Jewish leader Tullia Zevi said of the 1996 trial of SS-Hauptsturmführer Erich Priebke, who had been extradited from Argentina at age 82 to stand trial for helping to direct the infamous Ardeatine Caves massacre of 335 men and boys near Rome, "The verdict is in some ways irrelevant.... What is important is the trial.... What do I care if Priebke ends up under house arrest, or in prison for life?"[31] For others, the punishment can never fit the crime anyway. If a common murderer is executed, then what of the man who ordered the deaths of thousands or even millions? Arendt wrote during the Nuremberg trial that "for these crimes, no punishment is severe enough.... [Their] guilt shatters any and all legal systems."[32] Despite what he once said over lunch at Nuremberg, Hermann Göring could not really die ten deaths.[33] And if hanging a man convicted of crimes against humanity pales in comparison to the crimes themselves, then a prison sentence may fall far shorter of the mark.

The UN tribunals do not employ the death penalty on principle. Rather they assign prison terms that are to correspond as closely as possible with the acts and stature of the accused. Jean Kambanda, the former Hutu Premier of Rwanda, is serving a life sentence in Mali for the crime of genocide committed against Rwandan Tutsis in 1994. The infamous Serb leader Slobodan Milosević would surely have received a life sentence for the crimes he ordered and facilitated in Croatia, Bosnia, and Kosovo had he not died during his trial at The Hague in March 2006. Many criminals from the Yugoslav wars of the 1990s are already imprisoned with shorter terms ranging from years to decades. It is too early to say what results will emerge from the Iraqi Special Tribunal trying Saddam Hussein and his top deputies, but those not receiving the death penalty (which the Special Tribunal may impose) will surely receive long prison sentences. If such sentences are to be served in their entirety then those convicted will surely become regional and even global political problems as they age in jail.

To their victims, such men remain as unpardonable as the major Nazi criminals were to the Soviets – living reminders of the mass suffering they helped to direct. To their advocates, whether unreconstructed Serb nationalists, anti-American Iraqis, or others gripped by a nostalgia for the past, such criminals become imprisoned martyrs, especially as memories of their crimes fade. And to the mass of well-meaning yet uninformed, such men will become humanitarian causes as they become aged and infirm.[34] Indeed the post-1945 period shows that advocates of imprisoned war criminals sidestep the bulk of trial evidence. In virtually all cases concerning Nazi and Japanese perpetrators after the war, nationalist advocates for revision, mercy, or an end to foreign trials either looked past the evidence or locked on to insignificant quirks in the trial that in their view should have led to a revision of the sentence. And those who saw injustice at Nuremberg viewed the tough punishments imposed by foreign judges as confirmations of that injustice.[35] Within a surprisingly brief time, the "humanitarian" subjects at hand became not the victims of Nazi crimes but rather the Nazi criminals themselves, now aging under strict prison conditions far from their families.

The issue here is not whether Hitler's closest associates deserved long prison sentences. They deserved far worse. The question is how punishment affects the aims of the trial itself. Hermann Göring, sentenced to hang at Nuremberg, predicted that within fifty years German towns and villages would build statues in his honor. None have been built. Yet Konstantin von Neurath, sentenced to fifteen years at Nuremberg, became a martyr in the eyes of many West Germans, as did Rudolf Hess. Those hanged at Nuremberg were only discussed afterward as historical figures. The others became subjects of heated discussions concerning the nature of the verdicts and the memory of the past.

But war criminals also become factors in international relations. Trials of international criminals cannot help but be political and thus necessarily have political repercussions. The Israeli kidnapping of Eichmann from Argentina in May 1960, for instance, complicated the American response to the U-2 incident of the same month in which Francis Gary Powers was shot down while conducting reconnaissance over Soviet territory. The United States understood the Israeli step, but it also needed Argentina's continued backing against the Soviets in the UN Security Council. Since both incidents were violations of national sovereignty, Washington had to smooth the waters between Buenos Aires and Tel Aviv.[36] The timing of the ICTY's indictment of Slobodan Milosević in May 1999 was based partly on preserving the tribunal's own integrity lest Milosević cut an immunity deal with the NATO powers during the war over Kosovo. Milosević's handover to UN authorities by the Serb government in June 2001 was based partly on Serbia's need to secure U.S. financial aid and caused long-term resentment in Belgrade.[37]

And while Eichmann passed into history with his execution, Milosević, who served nearly five years of presentencing custody while staring at a life sentence, became precisely what his captors did not want him to be – a political prisoner, as were German and Japanese war criminals incarcerated after World War II. Certainly no properly convicted war criminal is a political prisoner in the accepted sense, like Nelson Mandela or Alexander Solzhenitsyn who were arrested and confined by repressive regimes owing to their conscience or politics. Rather they are political prisoners who also happen to be bona fide criminals. The international discussion over the conditions of their imprisonment, the significance of their imprisonment, their supposed martyrdom, and ultimately their release is entirely political in nature though couched in legal terms. And political prisoners, guilty or not, sympathetic or not, are never easy matters. They occupy the diplomats as well as the intellectuals.

Hitler and his very closest associates helped the issue in 1945 by never making it to trial. Hitler, Reichsführer-SS Heinrich Himmler, and Propaganda Chief Josef Goebbels all committed suicide to avoid capture. Reinhard Heydrich, Hitler's ruthless security chief, was assassinated in May 1942 by Czech partisans in Prague. Hitler's party secretary Martin Bormann and his Gestapo chief Heinrich Müller were killed in Berlin in the final days of fighting there.[38] All would have stood trial at Nuremberg had they lived long enough, and all would have been hanged. Winston Churchill, who had wanted them all quietly shot from the beginning, surely felt relieved.

There were still enough high-level Nazi figures, however, for the Americans to hold, with the British, the Soviets, and the French, what Americans policymakers believed was a necessary legal innovation – an international trial of the major war criminals who had helped to set the world afire. The prisoners would not simply be shot as many had suggested. Such would have lowered the victors to the thuggish level of the vanquished. They would not receive Soviet-style show trials, since such ran counter to the Western legal tradition in which even the most heinous criminal had the right of defense. They would receive a trial that would conform as closely as possible to the liberal legal practice that the Nazis themselves had tried to destroy.[39] The International Military Tribunal at Nuremberg thus tried twenty-two of the highest level Nazi officials that were left on four criminal counts. These counts, defined by the London Charter of August 1945 (which established the Tribunal) and introduced via formal indictment against the defendants, were as follows:

- Conspiracy (Count I) – a common plan to commit crimes against peace, which came to embrace war crimes and crimes against humanity. Prosecutors thus argued that the preparation for such crimes was a crime in itself and that all crimes from war-making to the murder of civilians were linked.
- Crimes against Peace (Count II) – the planning and launching of aggressive war in violation of international agreements and treaties.
- War Crimes (Count III) – violations of the laws and customs of war as defined by international accord in The Hague Conventions of 1899 and 1907 and the Geneva Convention of 1929. These violations include plunder and the use of slave labor in occupied areas, the mistreatment of prisoners of war, the murder of civilians or prisoners on land or on the high seas, and the wanton destruction of cities, towns, and villages.
- Crimes against Humanity (Count IV) – the murder, enslavement, deportation, or extermination of civilian populations either before or during the war, and the persecution of civilians before or during the war on political, religious, or ethnic grounds. This new legal concept allowed for the illegality of German governmental acts toward Jews even within Germany and its annexed territories before the outbreak of war.[40]

From November 1945 to October 1946, the world could follow what was surely the trial of the century. But the trial had its problems. The desire of U.S. trial advocates to condemn the full span of the Nazi state from its prewar persecution of German Jews to the planning for war to the concentration camp system meant that the International Military Tribunal had legal imperfections. American advocates of the trial hoped to use Count I, Conspiracy, as an umbrella charge by which all Nazi acts from 1933 forward could be viewed legally as a foundation of aggressive war and atrocity. Yet conspiracy had no basis in European continental law, and it was difficult to prove that all Nazi plans and acts were tied together. Count II, Crimes against Peace, predicated on Germany's breaking of international treaties en route to rearmament and war, had no firm basis in international law either and has not been precisely defined to this day. Count IV, Crimes against Humanity,

1. The major war criminals on trial at Nuremberg. Photograph courtesy of Harry S. Truman Museum and Presidential Library.

by which government officials could be tried for acts of persecution against their own nationals whether or not a state of war exists, is ensconced legal precedent today, but it was a new concept in 1945. Only Count III of the indictment – War Crimes as per The Hague Conventions of 1907 and the Geneva Convention of 1929 – had firm basis in international legal consensus before 1945. The Tribunal was thus subject to the charge of applying ex post facto law to its defeated enemies.

In fact, German nationals had already been tried more than two decades earlier for the traditional war crimes they had committed against prisoners and civilians during World War I. The post–World War II argument that no one had quite known the rules was thus fallacious. A clear documentary case could also be made – and in fact was made at Nuremberg – for a conscious German design for rearmament and war after 1933 in violation of signed agreements. And the Tribunal in its own judgment limited the impact of Count IV by ruling (based on the arcane language of the London Charter itself) that no official German act of persecution before the start of war in September 1939 could be considered legally criminal. Partly for this reason, the Tribunal itself, though hearing much on the murderous Nazi treatment of Europe's Jews, missed that millennial antisemitism stood at the center of German policies from 1933 forward while crippling for a decade the historical understanding of how fundamental the notion of an all-encompassing Jewish conspiracy was to Hitler and his followers. The ex post facto argument, on the other hand, stuck. Right, wrong, or just confused, it was an oft-heard complaint in postwar West German legal circles and even in the U.S. and British legal communities during and after the trial.[41]

There were political problems at Nuremberg as well. The Soviet government was part of the Tribunal despite its own extensive guilt under all four counts of the indictment. Partly, this irony resulted in transparent fabrications. Joseph Stalin's effort to deny the 1940 murder by Soviet State Security Police (NKVD) units of more than 20,000 Polish army officers and civilians – a Soviet war crime the Germans partially unearthed in Katyn Forest near Smolensk in 1943 – led to Moscow's insistence that the Nuremberg indictment accuse the Germans of killing and burying 11,000 Polish officers at Katyn.[42] The Soviets even postdated the massacre from spring 1940 to fall 1941 so that the Germans could plausibly have committed it. The Soviets also wrested U.S. agreement that self-incriminating evidence concerning their own crimes against peace be suppressed, such as the Secret Protocol to the Nazi-Soviet Non-Aggression Pact of August 1939, in which the Germans and Soviets quietly agreed to partition Poland.[43] In addition, Soviet participation prompted the presumption of guilt characteristic of the Soviet judicial system. The Soviet judge at Nuremberg, Ion T. Nikitschenko, had been an integral part of the Stalinist show trials of the 1930s; he had headed the Soviet prosecution team at Nuremberg before becoming judge; and he was on record before the trial as stating that the defendants as far as he was concerned had "already been convicted."[44]

And there were procedural problems. The German defense attorneys were hastily chosen, had little time to prepare their cases, and often received translated documents and affidavits after the documents were entered into evidence. The four justices – Sir Geoffrey Lawrence of Great Britain, Francis Biddle of the United States, Henri Donnedieu de Vabres of France, and Nikitschenko of the Soviet Union – reached verdicts and sentences in horse trading sessions, which brought strange inconsistencies between punishments. There was no machinery for appeal and not much of one for clemency petitions so that the death sentences pronounced were carried out within two weeks. Thus, there were aspects of Nuremberg that did not live up to the Western legal tradition, and its flaws meant that Nuremberg would be viewed by a growing percentage of Germans with certain skepticism. The victors, it could be said, sat in judgment of the vanquished in a stilted trial. Postwar justice was imperfect from its initial conception.

On the other hand, Nuremberg was based on mountains of evidence – so much of it presented in documentary form that it bored many journalists

2. Lord Geoffrey Lawrence of Great Britain, the president of the International Military Tribunal, hears testimony. Photograph courtesy of the National Archives and Records Administration.

to tears, while later convincing the Israeli government that the Eichmann trial would need more oral testimony if only for drama's sake.[45] Nuremberg bared the secrets of one of history's most criminal regimes in nauseating and chilling detail. The guilty, despite flawed and cumbersome procedure, were indeed guilty. At the end of the trial on October 1, 1946 – its 220th day – twelve of the defendants were sentenced to death by hanging. These included Nazi jack-of-all-trades Hermann Göring; military chiefs Wilhelm Keitel and Alfred Jodl; and Minister for the Eastern Occupied Territories Alfred Rosenberg, each of whom was found guilty on all four counts of the indictment. They also included Foreign Minister Joachim von Ribbentrop; Security Chief Ernst Kaltenbrunner; Governor-General of Poland Hans Frank; Labor Plenipotentiary Fritz Sauckel; Interior Minister Wilhelm Frick; Reich Commissar of the Netherlands Arthur Seyss-Inquart; and Jew-baiting newspaperman Julius Streicher. Nazi Party Secretary Martin Bormann was tried and sentenced to hang in absentia (unbeknownst to all he was killed in the war's final days), and Göring would cheat the noose by poisoning himself in his cell the night before his execution.

The death sentences were not surprising to either the condemned men or the Soviets, who had assumed all along that all twenty-two defendants would be so sentenced. The three acquittals were thus a surprise. An astonished hum in the packed courtroom accompanied the acquittal of former Reichsbank President and Economics Minister Hjalmar Schacht, whom Hitler had dismissed in 1937 owing to differences on rearmament policy. Also walking free would be the former Chancellor and Ambassador Franz von Papen, who in 1933 had helped Hitler come to power and who in 1938 had helped end Austrian independence. Hans Fritzsche, who as a third-level propaganda official was simply not a major figure and who was tried only because the Soviets had captured him, was acquitted, too. The Soviets would protest the acquittal of all three, as did an angry crowd outside Nuremberg's Palace of Justice. No one was appeased by Schacht's subsequent arrest and denazification procedure by western German authorities, especially since Schacht appealed and was acquitted again in 1948. Von Papen was subjected to denazification as well and served brief time in western German detention from 1947 to 1949. Fritzsche served a brief imprisonment in West Germany until his release in 1950.

There was also disappointment and controversy over the seven unexpected prison terms. Three of the defendants were sentenced to life imprisonment. One was Rudolf Hess, Hitler's deputy chief of the Nazi Party from 1933 to 1941. The Soviets had badly wanted to hang Hess, but he was convicted only on Counts I and II. The feeling that he was mentally unbalanced also earned him sympathy with Biddle and Donnedieu de Vabres. One was Erich Raeder, the commander-in-chief of the German Navy from 1928 to 1943, convicted on Counts I, II, and III. The third was Walther Funk, Schacht's replacement as minister of economics and president of the Reichsbank from 1938 to 1945, convicted on Counts II, III, and IV. The Tribunal passed what seemed to be a fourth de facto life sentence – fifteen years – on the 73-year-old Konstantin von Neurath, Hitler's foreign minister from 1933 to 1938 and Reichsprotektor of Bohemia and Moravia from 1939 to 1941. Von Neurath was still fortunate. He was the only defendant found guilty on all four counts who was not hanged.

There were also three lesser, though still substantial sentences. Albert Speer, Hitler's minister for armaments and munitions from 1942 to 1945, was convicted on Counts III and IV and sentenced to twenty years' imprisonment. The Western judges were impressed with Speer's faux contrition at the trial and thus spared his life. Had all the evidence on Speer been available in 1946, he might well have hanged. Joining Speer for twenty years was Baldur von Schirach, the head of the Hitler Youth from 1933 to 1940 and Nazi Party district leader (Gauleiter) of Vienna from 1938 to 1945. The Tribunal convicted von Schirach on Count IV, thanks primarily to the deportation of Jews from Vienna, and sentenced him to twenty years' imprisonment.

Karl Dönitz, the commander of the German submarine force from 1935 to 1943, the commander-in-chief of the navy from 1943 to 1945, and Hitler's designated successor after the latter's suicide in April 1945, received the lightest prison term. His orders to sink unarmed merchant ships without warning and his use of forced labor for naval construction meant that the Tribunal found him guilty on Counts II and III and sentenced him to ten years' imprisonment.

Given the fact that Nuremberg's legal innovators, prosecutorial teams, and justices had saddled their governments with the burden of implementing these prison sentences for what turned out to be more than forty years, it is astonishing how little thought the judges gave to the incarceration. The Tribunal discussed neither the location of the prison nor the prison regulations, and it did not even provide standard committal papers to note the official start date of the prison sentences. No one gave any thought to the possibility of later parole or clemency even though several of the defendants were already aging and sick men. Nor did anyone consider that as the years and the decades progressed, the prisoners themselves would become politically explosive figures. The judges and prosecutors simply went home after the reading of the sentences, not even assuming the role of considering the clemency petitions allowed each defendant.[46] Germany in the fall of 1946 was an unnerving place with a variety of issues that seemed far more pressing than the fate of seven men sentenced to prison.

And the joint prosecution of Nazi war criminals was at an end. The international judicial undertaking at Nuremberg had been difficult, particularly when it came to dealings between the Western Allies and the Soviets, whose governments were becoming increasingly estranged over the future of Germany and Europe itself. From this point forward each of the occupation powers would hold its own trials within its own occupation zone. The United States held twelve subsequent trials at Nuremberg as well as 489 proceedings at Dachau in which a total of 1,941 German defendants were indicted for crimes ranging from the Nazi euthanasia program to the mass shootings of Jews in occupied Soviet territories. Three-hundred-twenty-four received death sentences, 247 received sentences of life imprisonment, 946 received shorter prison terms.[47] British military courts held trials of Germans in their occupation zone and also in Italy and the Netherlands, trying a variety of figures ranging from German Field Marshals (Albert Kesselring, Erich von Manstein) to concentration camp guards. Of 1,085 defendants, the British sentenced 240 to death with most of the remainder receiving prison terms, including Kesselring and von Manstein themselves. French military courts in Germany, meanwhile, convicted 2,107 Germans, sentencing 104 to death.[48]

Since one state or another was responsible for the men convicted at these subsequent trials, the state in question could fix legal inconsistencies and adjust to changing political constellations as it saw fit in the years ahead.

The issue of sentence revision became most acute after 1950. By now there was a West German state – the Federal Republic of Germany – whose government in Bonn was highly critical of the postwar trials and obliged to listen to German church figures, large veterans' groups, and others who viewed postwar Allied justice as fundamentally unjust. The West Germans seemingly gained additional leverage as a result of the North Korean attack on South Korea in June 1950, which triggered fears of a similar Communist adventure in Central Europe and brought discussion of a West German defense contribution to the new NATO alliance. Germans would not fight, so the argument went, especially among West German veterans' groups, for an alliance that held its former military commanders in prison.[49]

After 1949, the Allied powers created a variety of review boards to examine the cases of Germans convicted by American, British, and French military courts. The worst offenders, such as SS-Gruppenführer Otto Ohlendorf, under whose command 90,000 Jews in the southern Ukraine were shot between June 1941 and June 1942, and SS-Obergruppenführer Oswald Pohl, the chief of the SS Economic Administration Main Office, which ruthlessly exploited millions of concentration camp laborers, were executed by U.S. authorities in January 1951, despite a storm of protest from within the new West German state and death threats against the U.S. high commissioner, John J. McCloy.[50] But other Germans convicted of war crimes received generous credits of prison time for good behavior and adjustments relating to judicial inconsistencies between sentences. Most Germans sentenced by U.S., British, and French military tribunals and held in Allied military prisons in West Germany had their sentences revised. The populations in Allied war crimes prisons in West Germany dropped dramatically in the 1950s, and among the first released were Field Marshals Kesselring and von Manstein, partly on the realization in London that their deaths in prison would be a political disaster.

*Prison Populations in Allied War Crimes Prisons in West Germany*[51]

| | Landsberg (U.S.) | Werl (U.K.) | Wittlich (FR) | Total |
|---|---|---|---|---|
| April 1950 | 663 | 379 | 273 | 1315 |
| August 1952 | 338 | 132 | 105 | 575 |
| November 1953 | 290 | 79 | 74 | 443 |
| July 1955 | 50 | 25 | 20 | 95 |

In 1957 and 1958, the last inmates walked free from all three Allied war crimes prisons in West Germany. No one served their sentence in its entirety. The longest anyone served at the British war crimes prison at Werl, for example, was a little more than twelve years.

Despite their bitterness toward the Germans, the Soviets also understood that the timely release of those convicted of war crimes by Soviet tribunals had its political uses. By January 1950, the Soviets held about 31,000 German POWs, some hardened criminals, some convicted on minor offenses, and some not tried at all.[52] In part, their freedom could be used to purchase some semblance of legitimacy for the new Communist government in East Germany, which had done nothing right thus far. After an uprising by East German workers against the East German regime in June 1953, the Soviets allowed the release of prisoners who had been held in the U.S.S.R. as war criminals on the hope that their homecoming might somehow scotch the bitterness many in the East felt toward their new rulers.[53] In part, convicted war criminals could be used to build relations with the West German state. Despite the comment by Soviet Minister President Nikolai Bulganin to West German Chancellor Konrad Adenauer in September 1955 that there were no more POWs in the U.S.S.R., only war criminals, those 9,155 Germans were freed after Adenauer's Moscow trip as the price of relations with Bonn.

The men condemned by the International Military Tribunal, on the other hand, were a different story. They were conspicuous Nazi leaders convicted at the most well-known of all postwar trials. Unlike lesser proceedings, "Nuremberg" had become a catchword for what had by now become unique international consensus on the issue of warlike aggression and violations of international law. For the Soviets especially, Nuremberg validated Soviet suffering on an international scale while justifying Soviet foreign policy in Europe and Germany. Its lessons could never be discounted, and its condemned could never legitimately be freed. Despite Western Allied concerns that the Nuremberg prisoners had become a political burden, no one in the West was willing to challenge the Soviets on the issue. At the very least, the Western advocacy of convicted major war criminals would prove embarrassing if the Soviets chose to make it so. At the most, the Soviets could react by endangering the security of West Berlin, which housed the prison but sat deep in East German territory. So it remained for four decades.

Spandau thus became a macabre symbol for the Nazi past but also for the following problem. The discussion concerning war criminals and their place in the memory of the past is not national but international. And it becomes most contentious not during the trial but afterward. The years and even decades of punishment must thus receive the same careful thought from the advocates of international justice as do the months of trial. Otherwise, the punishment can erode some of the foundations on which the trial itself was built. International justice, it would seem, demands a thick skin indeed.

CHAPTER ONE

# "To the Gallows with All of Them"

"Bravo for the death sentences. But why only twelve?"
*Neues Deutschland*, October 2, 1946

"Death, death," whispered Joachim von Ribbentrop to himself in his prison cell on the afternoon of October 1, 1946. Moments earlier Sir Geoffrey Lawrence, the British president of the International Military Tribunal at Nuremberg, had read the sentences of the guilty Nuremberg defendants. "Now," Ribbentrop whispered to himself, "I won't be able to write my beautiful memoirs." Hans Frank, the former head of the General Government in Poland, the slaughterhouse region where millions of Jews had been gassed, was more resigned. "I deserved it," he sighed. Hitler's top military officers, Field Marshal Wilhelm Keitel and Generaloberst Alfred Jodl accepted their death sentences but not the pedestrian execution method of hanging. Each asked to be executed by firing squad as befitted an officer. Their requests were denied. Hermann Göring, Hitler's one-time successor, was pale. He asked to be left alone in his cell, perhaps already considering his suicide by a hidden cyanide capsule.

Though the Tribunal acquitted three of the defendants – Franz von Papen, Hjalmar Schacht, and Hans Fritzsche – the seven men sentenced to prison terms could still count themselves fortunate. Execution did not await them. Hitler's deputy Rudolf Hess feigned indifference. He did not listen to his sentence when it was pronounced and professed not to know what it was afterward. Albert Speer, Hitler's arms and munitions minister, had saved his skin through a staged repentance before the Tribunal. Though Labor Plenipotentiary Fritz Sauckel would face the gallows for providing slave workers to German industries, Speer, who had demanded the slave labor, received but twenty years. He began the act that he would maintain the rest of his life with the comment, "Well, that is fair enough. I can't complain."

The others were less relieved. Erich Raeder, the commander-in-chief of the German Navy from 1928 to 1943, asked to be left alone. He preferred death by hanging "by way of mercy," instead of his life sentence. Hitler Youth leader Baldur von Schirach agreed. "Better a quick death than a slow one," he mused about his twenty-year sentence. Hitler's designated successor, Karl Dönitz, received the shortest sentence of all – ten years' imprisonment – but he was convinced afterward, and would remain so, that he had been judged unfairly. Walther Funk, the German minister of economics, moaned that he hoped his life sentence would not really amount to life. "Life imprisonment," he said. "What does that mean? They won't keep me in prison all my life, will they? They don't mean that do they?" Hitler's first foreign minister, the aristocratic Konstantin Freiherr von Neurath, could only stammer to himself. His fifteen-year sentence was generous. But at age 73 and with heart trouble besides, von Neurath knew that it amounted to a life sentence.[1]

Ironically, the Four Powers that governed occupied Germany and that had held the Nuremberg trial were thinking little about these seven men. The Allied judges left the courtroom for good after the sentences; the prosecutors already had planes to catch from the half-ruined city. The Allied military authorities who assumed responsibility for the sentences were too busy implementing the twelve death sentences to worry about prison terms. A prison had not been prepared, nor had prison regulations been agreed. The entire prison arrangement would be improvised over the following months with no realization that the decisions made in 1946 and 1947 would last for decades. Thus, the Allies overlooked numerous issues that would come back to haunt them in the years ahead.

## THE NUREMBERG SENTENCES

The International Military Tribunal's job ended on October 1, 1946, when it pronounced sentence. Thereafter the convicted prisoners were bound over to the Four-Power military government in Germany. From June 1945 until the division into two German states in October 1949, this government was the Four-Power Allied Control Authority (ACA), headquartered in Berlin. The ACA's executive body was the Allied Control Council, which consisted of the four military governors from the United States, Great Britain, France, and the Soviet Union. It provided general governance by Four-Power directives. The Control Council was aided in its work by the Coordinating Committee headed by the four deputy military governors, who thrashed out policy differences, and an array of other committees that covered everything from legal to cultural to economic affairs.[2]

The International Military Tribunal was a court created by separate international agreement – the London Charter of August 1945 – and so the Allied Control Council had no jurisdiction over it.[3] The military government took up the issue of the Nuremberg sentences only slowly, having to occupy itself throughout 1945 and 1946 with practical issues in Germany such as demobilization, reparations, infrastructure, and the provision of food and fuel to the German population.

The governing written agreement on implementing the Nuremberg sentences was Control Council Directive Number 35.[4] Serious discussion within the Control Council on the directive began on February 21, 1946, with the submission of a British draft nearly seven months before the Tribunal actually pronounced sentence. The major issue was the carrying out of the anticipated death sentences, which were to be performed either by hanging or guillotine, and the impact the executions might have on public opinion in Germany and the rest of the world. These discussions, which would continue into September 1946, demonstrate how far prison sentences were from the minds of the top Allied authorities that year. It also shows that the Control Council correctly viewed itself not as an appellate court that could overturn or interpret verdicts but solely as a body to carry out or alter the sentences passed down from the Tribunal.

There were arguments from the start. Soviet and American legal officers protested the original British suggestion that defendants not be executed until thirty days after sentencing. Such was far too generous to the Nazis who would be condemned, especially for the Soviets, whose own war crimes trials in 1945 and 1946 were characterized by public hangings literally moments after sentencing.[5] Two months of discussion produced new proposals. The Western Allies called for a twenty-day interval between sentencing and execution, while the Soviets called for a week. The Western Allies insisted that the condemned be allowed to file petitions for clemency. The American and British were willing to allow defense councils four to five days to submit mercy petitions to the Control Council, while the Soviets and French, both of whom saw in clemency the threat of overturned sentences, felt that no more than twenty-four hours should be allowed.[6]

In the Control Council itself, none of the four military governors had any legal training. This shortcoming mattered little to their task, which was to govern a defeated nation. And indeed, neither the British governor, Air Chief Marshal Sir Sholto Douglas, nor the American governor, General Joseph T. McNarney, were interested in overturning the verdicts of the Tribunal, which would have heard testimony for more than a year and examined thousands of documents by the time of the verdicts. Yet neither governor wished to appear savagely vindictive either. Douglas, who had succeeded Field Marshal Bernard Law Montgomery in May 1946 and who felt the full weight of Nuremberg's importance, viewed clemency as a humanitarian rather than a judicial problem, and thus one to be taken seriously. McNarney, who had replaced General Dwight D. Eisenhower in November 1945, agreed and even suggested that "it would be advisable for the [clemency question] to be carefully examined as to whether the purposes of the occupation of

Germany might not be served by acts of grace toward some of those who had been tried by the International Military Tribunal."[7]

The Soviets, and to a lesser degree the French, were moved far less by such concerns. But as Charles Fahy, the director of the U.S. military government's Legal Division told Deputy Military Governor Lieutenant General Lucius D. Clay, "The longer [review] periods proposed . . . are definitely necessary . . . for petitions to be drawn with care . . . and to give the Control Commission . . . time to study them without haste and disorderly pressure. The seven-day period of review favored by the Soviet delegation would reduce this judicial process to a mere formality."[8] The Control Council compromised. Defense counsel would have four days to submit clemency petitions, and the condemned would have fifteen days to live following sentence.

Though Directive Number 35 was made official on September 7, 1946, the Control Council had animated discussions concerning clemency down to the very eve of the verdicts. French Military Governor Pierre Koenig wanted to set up a special Four-Power commission to advise the Control Council in considering clemency petitions. But on insistence of Soviet Military Governor Marshal Vasily Sokolovsky (the victor of Smolensk and Marshal Georgy Zhukov's successor in Germany), the Control Council would make clemency decisions on its own without binding input from a special ad hoc commission. Those condemned to death would not escape their fate. "I do not intend," Sokolovsky said, "to share the responsibility with any other agency."[9]

He need not have worried. Douglas himself was under strong pressure from Prime Minister Clement Attlee's Labour cabinet in London to reject any mitigation or alteration of sentences proposed from within the Control Council.[10] And as matters turned out, none of the clemency petitions filed – and one was filed for each defendant save Ernst Kaltenbrunner and Albert Speer – brought much sympathy anyway when considered by the Control Council on October 9 and 10, 1946. Pleading everything from weakness in the face of Hitler's gaze (Ribbentrop) to the soldierly obligation to follow Hitler's orders (Göring, Keitel, Jodl) to the nonsensical idea that the forced emigration of 90,000 Jews from Austria before the war had saved Jewish lives (Seyss-Inquart), the petitions were all rejected with haste. Alfred Seidl, the attorney for Frank and Hess, ignored the nature of clemency and the mood of the Control Council. Rather than conveying his clients' contrition, either real or feigned, Seidl challenged the legality of the Tribunal and its verdicts. "An unrepentant Nazi," wrote the British legal analyst of Seidl, "I can scarcely contain my indignation. Denazify that chap."[11] Sokolovsky went further. "If the Control Council has the right to increase the punishment," he said of Hess's life sentence, "I would vote for the increase."[12] Thirty-five years later, with Hess aging alone in prison, Seidl was making the same unhelpful arguments.[13]

A specially created Quadripartite Commission for the Detention of Major War Criminals with its seat in Nuremberg had already been appointed by the Control Council on September 17, 1946, to detain the condemned after the verdicts and to arrange for their hangings, a grisly process that included the construction of gallows in the prison at Nuremberg. Yet even with the members of this commission appointed and the clemency petitions considered and rejected, the Control Council still had several issues to decide. Animated discussion over the degree of press coverage to be allowed resulted in decisions to permit limited press presence at the hangings themselves, to allow limited (and supposedly tasteful) publication of official photos of the bodies, and to keep Control Council Directive Number 35 a secret from the public at large. The last was an ironic decision, since, as the U.S. Deputy Military Governor Lucius Clay pointed out, everything about the trial had thus far been conducted in the light of day.[14] Given the legitimate concern that the executions of former major government figures could cause public unrest if not handled with skill, such discussion was understandable.

The headaches did not end there. Hermann Göring's improbable and sensational suicide in his cell by cyanide poisoning on the night of October 15, 1946, prompted an extensive investigation by the Quadripartite Commission. The suicide also triggered recriminations in the Control Council that the notification of the prisoners on October 11 that their clemency appeals had been rejected had been a mistake. The French, who had wanted to withhold the bad news until the moment before execution for precisely this reason, made sure that upon being proven right, their statements were on the record. The Göring investigation meanwhile strongly suggested that Göring had managed to hide the cyanide capsule since his arrest despite diligent American countermeasures.[15]

In the early morning of October 16, 1946, the hangings of the remaining ten men condemned to death finally took place amidst some nationalistic theatrics by the condemned men themselves, especially Julius Streicher, who claimed he was being murdered by Jews, but the arguments within the Control Council about the publication of the graphic photographs went on for another week.[16] And within this busy and macabre context, it is understandable that the Control Council viewed the seven guilty men sentenced by the Tribunal to prison as lucky fellows indeed. Walther Funk, who received a life sentence, "got off quite easily," according to both Sokolovsky and Douglas, the latter of whom added that Karl Dönitz, who received a ten-year sentence, was "left with a relatively mild punishment."[17] It is ironic that the Control Council considered least the cases of the men who would live the longest and whose cases would torment the Allies the most.

The fates of these seven men were left to the Allied Kommandatura in Berlin, a Four-Power military city government headed by the four army commandants, one from each of the four Berlin sectors. Control Council

Directive 35 called for the Kommandatura to select a prison in Berlin for the incarceration of those receiving prison sentences. That the imprisonment was to be a Four-Power responsibility was never questioned during the Control Council discussions on the directive throughout 1946. The Kommandatura simply went to work after receiving the finished directive in September.

First, the Berlin commandants had to choose a prison building, and it is a measure of the grim nature of Berlin in 1946 that there was practically no discussion of the issues of symbolism and martyrdom that would inevitably accompany a prison in which leading Nazis could conceivably spend many years. These issues were obvious with regard to the hangings, but with the trial winding down in Nuremberg, the Kommandatura simply had to find a functional prison building as quickly as it could. Availability and security were the uppermost criteria.

Allied and Soviet officials determined in 1946 and early 1947 that whatever site was chosen in Berlin would be a temporary solution since, at the time, more international trials of major criminals were still a possibility and a new, absolutely secure prison building was desirable. A prison that could hold up to fifty major war criminals was the governing criteria, and unlike the Nuremberg trial itself, which was conducted in the clear air of public analysis, the prison that held its captives was to be removed from public consciousness while any attempted escape by the prisoners was to be made impossible either from within or with the help of outsiders.

But there were not many choices. Greater Berlin contained thirteen functioning prisons excluding small police lockups. Four small prisons were in the American sector, five were in the British, one large modern prison was in the French sector, and two smaller prisons were in the Soviet sector. All of Berlin's prisons suffered from overcrowding thanks to denazification programs in Berlin and to the large number of Germans sentenced for petty crimes relating to theft, black marketeering, and so forth. By mid-1946, the sanitation and food situation in Berlin's prisons was deplorable. No one wanted to add to the problem by requisitioning a functioning prison for the major war criminals while displacing hundreds of ordinary prisoners, possibly across sector lines.[18]

Initial discussions raised practical and symbolic difficulties. The Kommandatura's Legal Committee in September 1946 recommended the partially destroyed antiaircraft tower near the Tiergarten in central Berlin as a temporary holding area for the major war criminals, but the conversion work necessary to turn the tower into a secure prison was estimated at three months. In the meantime, the Legal Committee suggested that the prisoners could remain in U.S. custody at Nuremberg, or that perhaps they could be held in the old military prison in Spandau, located in the British sector. The Legal Committee helpfully added that Spandau had an execution chamber complete with a guillotine plus facilities for eight simultaneous nondrop strangulations should the major war criminals receiving death sentences be executed in Berlin.[19]

But where would the permanent prison be? Plötzensee, the site at which the accomplices of the July 20, 1944, assassination plot against Hitler had their bodies mangled at Hitler's behest, was discussed but quickly dropped. The British legal representative Colonel C. W. Harris rejected it "due to the association with the many victims of fascism who had been placed there." Harris added that Plötzensee carried the danger of escape, since it was close to the center of Berlin and to the river Spree.[20] The Soviet commandant, Major General Alexander G. Kotikov, agreed that the prison had to be removed from public view and should preclude all possibility of escape. Ironic symbolism, on the other hand, had its appeals. Kotikov suggested use of the former Gestapo prison at Moabit (also near the Spree in central Berlin) since its name, he reasoned, was a "by-word" for Nazi terror. Ernst Thälman, the chairman of the Communist Party of Germany (KPD) before 1933, had been held there for four years before his murder in 1944. The suggestion, however, was not pursued by the other commandants.[21]

The speedy construction of a new building far from the city center with no symbolic significance was another option, but it was not practical given the shortage of building materials. The U.S. commandant in Berlin, Major General Frank Keating recommended constructing a new prison on the Pfaueninsel – a picturesque lake island in western Berlin once favored by Prussian King Frederick William II – as a sort of German Alcatraz. The British suggested the conversion of a castle on the outskirts of the Soviet sector. Time was running out, however, since the Tribunal pronounced sentence on October 1, 1946. A new prison could not be constructed quickly, and as for renovation projects such as the antiaircraft tower or a castle, Kotikov made clear that for reasons of time limits and security, he preferred a prison that was already in existence to one that would have to be converted.[22] Thus, by October 2, after having visited most of the facilities available in Berlin, the Allies and Soviets settled on the military prison in Spandau as a temporary solution. The aim now centered on readying Spandau prison to receive high-profile prisoners.

Spandau Prison was built between 1878 and 1881 as a Prussian military prison in what was then not an incorporated part of Berlin, but a separate garrison town for the Prussian army. It remained a military prison until 1919, after which time it came under the control of civilian authorities. During World War II, the Germans used it for both military detention and the detention of civilians awaiting transport to the concentration camps at Brandenburg and Sonnenburg. Members of the "Red Orchestra," the famous Soviet spy ring, were held and interrogated there. Execution by strangulation and guillotine proceeded during the war years, though it is not possible to say how many victims were executed at Spandau.[23] Given the heavy fighting in and around Berlin in the latter stages of the war, Spandau was in the best repair of any working prison. And with 132 cells in all, each with toilet facilities, it seemed to have enough space "to satisfy the need for the probable number of persons which will be sentenced by the International Military Tribunal plus the required staff and guard."[24]

Repair work on the prison began immediately. Located in the outer reaches of the British sector of Berlin, the prison, like all others in the city, functioned under the immediate supervision and expense of the local German municipal authority, the Berlin *Magistrat* (municipal council) created by the Allies in August 1946, and specifically the public prosecutors' office (*Generalstaatsanwalt*).[25] In October 1946 there were about 665 prisoners at Spandau, virtually all of them sharing cells. Bombardment had reduced the buildings to a state of ill repair so that, in the closing days of the Nazi regime, prisoners had escaped simply by lowering ropes out their windows.[26] Overcrowded and lacking basic medical facilities and enough food for their populations, prisons in 1946 had prisoners grow their own vegetables.[27]

One of the first oddities of Spandau was that, thanks to its "temporary" nature as a holding area for the major war criminals, its legal status was never precisely defined. The Kommandatura order, which placed the administration and costs of Berlin's regular prisons under the *Generalstaatsanwalt* also said that prisons established by the occupation forces in Berlin for their own needs were not to be included in the *Generalstaatsanwalt* prison budget.[28] But the British military government, strapped financially as it was, determined immediately that the costs of repairing and maintaining the prison would be borne by the Berlin city government. Since the prison complex was never formally requisitioned, it would remain German property and a German financial responsibility under a sort of British trusteeship with the repair and operating funds coming out of the normal prison operating budget of the Berlin *Magistrat* rather than occupation costs, reparations, or the Allied budget. Whether this was accidental or deliberate is hard to say, but as late as 1950, the chief British legal adviser in Berlin lamented that "[Spandau's] precise status from that time [1946] has, so far as this Office is aware, never been clearly defined."[29] As the relationship between the Allies and the West Berlin authorities evolved into something friendlier than it had been in 1946, it was this imprecise status that kept the prison in place, since West Berlin's municipal government would repeatedly refuse to increase its prison budget to accommodate the expensive structural changes that would make Spandau less of a waste.

But this was in the future. For now there was no negotiation. The *Magistrat* received orders in the third week of October 1946 to evacuate all prisoners from Spandau to other prisons at its own expense by the first week of November 1946.[30] Since the city had no prison trucks, the Berlin government had to contract with more than fifty private businesses that owned trucks in order to move the prisoners as best they could at a cost of more than 6,000 Reichsmark (RM).[31] This only worsened the overcrowding problem in Berlin's prisons. A Christmas amnesty awarded by the Allies in Berlin at the end of 1946 aided the problem somewhat as did the allocation of more than RM 800,000 to repair Berlin's other prisons besides Spandau. Food for the general prison population, however, to say nothing of heat, remained a pressing need.[32]

In addition, Spandau needed repairs. After an inspection of October 10, 1946, by the Kommandatura's building and housing subcommittees, the determination was that Spandau Prison needed 670 square meters of glass, 330 square meters of roofing materials together with 125 kilograms of plastic for the roof, and more articles of a like nature, which, counting the manpower necessary to make the repairs, was estimated at RM 13,000.[33] The lord mayor of Berlin, Otto Ostrowski, thus received an order from the Kommandatura dated November 25, 1946, that would provide the legal basis for the city's financing of the prison for the next forty-one years: "You will immediately fill all orders submitted by the management of the Allied Prison in Spandau for supplies and equipment necessary for the preparation and operation of the prison."[34] In practice, this meant that the *Magistrat* would have to pay German contractors and laborers for the basic construction work, which would be conducted under Allied supervision. It also meant that, to save on costs, the *Magistrat* would use some of the prison labor already available in Spandau. By the first week of December, construction costs amounted to RM 7,200.[35]

And this would not be nearly enough, which meant a delay in transferring the prisoners from Nuremberg to Berlin. By the time the four prison governors of Spandau held their first meeting, the Allies had been surprised by Göring's suicide in his Nuremberg cell on the night of October 15, 1946. Göring's ingestion of cyanide the night before his execution spared him the hangman's noose and thus his judicial punishment, while constituting a major topic of discussion among ordinary Germans. "Psychologically," lamented American authorities, "[Göring's suicide] undoubtedly constitutes one of the 'Lost Battles' in the overall endeavor to prevent a new myth arising around the Nazi leaders."[36] To prevent suicides in Spandau, additional security measures were taken immediately. All protruding objects in the cells had to be removed, and all electrical outlets had to be covered. Sick wards had to be set up because the prison cell bloc had no such facilities. And the kitchen had to be refurbished so that not a morsel of food would be prepared outside the prison.[37]

All these measures did not even touch the issues of external security, which were hamstrung by overall shortages in postwar Berlin. Timber and barbed wire were in such short supply in the British sector of Berlin that the Soviets ordered a search for material in the Soviet sector of the city. This rare offer

3. An aerial photograph of Spandau Prison, probably from 1982. Building 1 is the cell bloc building and building 2 is the infirmary, which was in complete decay by that time. The other marked buildings beyond the prison walls included the governor's mess, living quarters for the warders and staff, and barracks for the external guard. Photograph courtesy of the National Archives and Records Administration.

for goods to flow from the Soviet area of control to the West foreshadowed how important Spandau would be to the Soviets. After all, the Soviets had insisted since joint occupation of Berlin began that the Western democracies supply Berlin with food and coal from their own German zones.[38] There were no materials at all for an electric fence between the prison wall and the outer perimeter fence, so the Spandau governors decided to use a plain six-foot barbed wire fence in the meantime with a sign that said "Trespassers are warned that it is very dangerous." The Allies also debated whether the electrical fence, once installed, should carry a lethal current. It eventually carried a current of 4,000 volts. Landmines near the fence were briefly considered as well.

Finally, the British lacked the materials and the expertise to install a prison alarm system, and because they did not trust German contractors to install one (engineers from Siemens were briefly considered but rejected as unreliable), this measure too was delayed to the point where the Soviets became suspicious of British motives. The Soviets suggested that German contractors simply be watched closely during the alarm installation while also insisting that the windows of the guard towers be expanded for greater visibility. A simple alarm system, the Soviet authorities caustically noted, was less complicated to build than an atom bomb.[39] In any event, the Berlin *Magistrat* would have to pay for all of these alterations out of pocket as well as the yearly expenses of running the prison itself including staff salaries. In 1949 it was determined that these costs for the preceding year (this under the Berlin blockade) exceeded 450,000 of the new West German Deutschmark (DM) for the maintenance of seven prisoners. The *Magistrat* would complain in that year that the maintenance of seven ordinary prisoners cost the city only DM 8,000 per annum.[40]

These physical problems explain some of the delay in moving the prisoners to Spandau from Nuremberg. But they were not essential. After all, Colonel Burton Andrus, who commanded the U.S. Army prison at Nuremberg in late 1946, told Albert Speer on November 30 that he and the other prisoners would be transferred on December 15.[41] Thanks to poor weather and a shortage of materials, all repairs to Spandau had not yet been completed, but, at the most, this would have delayed the transfer by two months. The unusual length of the delay (October 1946 to July 1947) arose over the nature of the prisoners' incarceration as written in the prison regulations themselves.

Control Council Directive Number 35 said nothing regarding the prison regulations. The Allied Kommandatura's Legal Committee took up the issue of prison regulations and submitted a preliminary draft in January 1947. The regulations would not be approved by the commandants themselves until June of that year, for reasons that are explained later. But, as amended, the essentials of the Spandau regulations were these.[42] The prison was under Four-Power control. Supreme Authority lay with the Kommandatura itself, while Executive Authority lay with the Kommandatura's Legal Committee. Within the prison itself, day-to-day authority lay with a board of prison governors or directors, one from each of the Four Powers, each of whom would serve as chair of the governorate on the same rotating monthly basis as used by the Kommandatura itself. Thus, January, May, and September would be British months in the chair; February, June, and October would be the French months; March, July, and November, the Soviet months; and April, August, and December, the American months. German was the official language within the prison. In reality, the chairmanship of the prison governorate conferred little more than the right to preside over weekly governors' meetings. All governors' decisions concerning the operation of Spandau Prison had to be unanimous, which gave any one governor veto power over the rest.

As for the internal prison staff, each power would have a team of civilian warders, or internal prison guards, including one chief and one assistant warder, making for a Four-Power warder staff of thirty-two warders in all.[43]

Warders were to wear a standard uniform of dark blue with black boots and ties, along with a peaked hat with chinstrap.[44] The warders would work in eight-hour mixed-nationality shifts of seven men during the day and five at night, each shift having the chief and assistant warder from a different nation. For the health of the prisoners, each power also had to supply a medical officer so that there would be a board of four, again with a rotating chair. Medical recommendations also had to be unanimous, and the governors could countermand medical orders, though unanimity among the medical officers would signal that the Soviets had already decided not to veto a given recommendation.[45] A single cleric as well as cooks, waiters, and other civilian prison staff such as electricians and stokers could come from any of the United Nations (there were seventy-two such staff members in 1947), but they had to be carefully screened before hiring for the sake of security. In fact, no German (save the prisoners themselves) could enter the actual prison walls.[46] The Danish Evangelical pastor, H. W. Engdahl Thygesen, who had been working in internment camps in the U.S. zone for a year by 1947 and who had volunteered for the Spandau position, was rejected despite the fact that all of Spandau's inmates were Evangelical. The appointment of a Lutheran, the Legal Committee decided, was "inadvisable" for political and security reasons because this was the prisoners' own denomination. Likewise, the first hired wave of prison staff was fired before the prisoners even arrived thanks to their black market ties and general unreliability.[47]

Finally, the nation in the governor's chair was to provide the exterior guard for the prison, and these would be armed troops from that power's military detachment in Berlin. By February 12, 1947, it was determined that each power would provide a minimum of two commissioned officers, two sergeants, six corporals, and forty-four sentries. They would rotate in shifts. Six civilian homes around the prison would be demolished together with attendant trees to widen the security belt, which would be surrounded by a ten-foot barbed wire fence. Between the barbed wire perimeter and the prison wall would be the aforementioned electrified fence of six feet.[48] The number of troops was later reduced so that by 1949 the Four Powers together had a combined seventy-five to eighty troops comprising the military guard. For three-quarters of each year then, another power would guard a facility in the British sector of Berlin, and for three months out of every year, it would be the Soviets, though it was unanimously decided that the governors would call on British sector troops in an emergency.[49] In the meantime, as one member of the U.S. military government pointed out in 1949, Spandau had a ratio of twenty-five exterior and interior guards to each single prisoner, while the famously secure U.S. prison at Alcatraz in California had a staff-to-prisoner ratio of just one man to 1.8 inmates.[50] At the outset, the British called it all "a shocking waste of manpower," but an unavoidable one owing to the politics of the matter.[51]

In early 1947 though, more prisoners were expected, and it was still understood that Spandau was a temporary solution. It bothered no one at the time that the Berlin city government would pay the costs. On the other hand, the treatment of the prisoners themselves was far more contentious. Generally speaking, neither the Allies nor the Soviets were in a charitable mood toward Hess, Speer, and the others in 1947, and there was unanimous agreement that the basis for the regulations concerning the treatment of the prisoners would be the German Prison Regulations of 1943, though in some aspects the Spandau regulations were more generous. Prisoners were to be admitted with a number, strip-searched for poisons or weapons, and then dressed in prison-issued clothing. Each would be called thereafter by his convict number and never by name. To prevent suicide attempts, prisoners could have no food that was not prepared within the prison, they could not keep their spectacles at night, and they would have their sparsely outfitted cells searched twice daily. To this the prison governors would add for a time that prisoners would not even possess the original copies of personal letters for fear that they may be laced with poison for suicide attempts. The prisoners would only receive copies of personal letters.[52] Food each day would be of the same caloric value as normal German prison fare, with more food possible should it be considered medically necessary. Later, the governors would specify that when the prisoners worked, they would be fed according to Berlin Ration Card Number 2 (1,167 grams at 2,202 Calories) and that when they did not they would be fed in accordance with Berlin Ration Card Number 3 (1,032 grams, 1,887 Calories).[53]

Additional privileges were sparse. The prisoners could read selected and approved material from the prison library, which included religious, technical, and literary but not political or recent historical material. The prisoners could send and receive a single letter every four weeks of four-page length and 1,200 words. Letters had to be in clear German with no signals or shorthand, and the prison authorities would censor incoming and outgoing mail. Prisoners could receive a single visitor every two calendar months for a fifteen-minute visit. Discussions had to be conducted in German in the presence of a representative of each governor with no hand signals allowed and with prohibition against visitors handing the prisoners anything. A wire mesh grate would separate the prisoners and their visitors. Mail and visitation privileges could be broadened with approval of the governors for exceptional circumstances, though in practice this would never be easy.

These privileges, albeit limited, were more extensive than in the 1943 German regulations for those serving penal servitude, wherein one letter was allowed only every eight weeks and one visitor every twelve.[54] And at no time were the prisoners to suffer physical abuse. Reading privileges and rations could be curtailed for violations of the regulations, but such punishment would not be administered if the medical board determined that it would result in a health detriment. Prisoners could be fettered hand and foot if necessary, but in Spandau's forty-year history, no such punishment ever occurred.

In the meantime, care was taken early to ensure internal security while prohibiting the prison from becoming a shrine to Nazi martyrs-in-waiting. The absolute secrecy of everything transpiring within the prison was paramount. Even before the regulations were drafted, the Kommandatura prohibited the taking of photographs inside the prison for publication in newspapers.[55] And the regulations strictly prohibited staff from revealing any details concerning the prisoners, from having any relationship with prisoners' families, or from profiting in any way from their unique positions. Even health-related information could only be revealed to prisoners' families by the governors themselves. The photographs and stories that would appear in West German magazines and other journalistic enterprises in the 1950s and after were technically illegal. Given the fact that the Four Powers viewed the criminals it sentenced to prison as major war criminals, there was little argument concerning the preceding regulations at the time of their drafting. After all, Spandau was a prison. It was not supposed to be especially pleasant, and the men there were fortunate that they were not hanged or decapitated.

## ENTOMBED ALIVE: THE BATTLE OVER SOLITARY CONFINEMENT

There was indeed a far larger argument amongst the Western Allies and the Soviets in 1947. It was over the issue of solitary confinement of the prisoners, and it threatened to wreck the entire Four-Power enterprise at Spandau. The dispute, carried out primarily between the British and the Soviets, is worth a close look because it helps establish an understanding of what the Soviets and their Communist allies in Europe believed that Nuremberg and Spandau were to achieve while showing the limits of vengeance deemed appropriate by the Western democracies.

It would be simplistic to say that the Soviets viewed the Trial of the Major War Criminals as nothing more than another Stalinist show trial. But surely they viewed postwar justice as having a powerful political component. A lengthy study on Soviets aims in war crimes trials by the U.S. Office of Strategic Services (OSS) in April 1945 argued that "In punishing war criminals [the Soviets] will be guided by legal principles, yet . . . motivated by political considerations."[56] This did not mean the punishment of everyone. Those of political use, such as German army commanders who as POWs had been enlisted into the Soviet-sponsored National Committee for a Free Germany (NKFD), would be spared.[57] But with regard to German leaders, OSS had predicted, based on Soviet statements, that nothing less than the

physical elimination of such men would do, and primarily for reasons of politics and security. The U.S.S.R., said the report "intends to eliminate the German leaders, not because they broke a law, but because they launched this war, and because, if left unpunished, they might precipitate a future aggression."

There was a broader political aim, too. As the Nuremberg trials progressed, the Soviets were holding a wave of concurrent trials in Smolensk, Briansk, Leningrad, Riga, Minsk, Kiev, Nikolaev, and Velike Luki, all from December 1945 to February 1946. The trials, which attracted large crowds, were reported in the Soviet press alongside the news from Nuremberg. Soviet prosecutors did not link individual defendants to individual crimes, but such was never the point. In the Soviet worldview, the entire fascist system was guilty. Thus, evidence against individuals came from physical pretrial interrogations. Defendants then confessed to their crimes in court and their defense attorneys, disallowed from cross-examining witnesses, simply tried to get mercy for their clients. Soviet judges sentenced virtually all senior figures to death by hanging, and sentences were implemented in public immediately. The trials in the U.S.S.R. were to exact retribution but also to reconsolidate Soviet society after the war by pointing to the suffering caused by the invaders.[58]

The Soviets were more magnanimous at Nuremberg. Decades later, Soviet jurists would point to the great accommodation to Anglo-American justice in allowing the defendants' attorneys to cross-examine witnesses.[59] To a point, the Soviets had to compromise because the Americans and British held most of the high-profile prisoners (the Soviets supplied only Raeder and Fritzsche to Nuremberg). But the Soviets still fully expected each of the defendants to receive the death penalty. Back in 1942, Moscow called for trials and executions of the top German leaders. In a note to the Allied governments of October 14, 1942, Stalin's foreign minister Vyacheslav M. Molotov mentioned Hitler, Göring, Hess, Ribbentrop, Himmler, and Goebbels by name, and, because Hess was in British custody after his flight to Great Britain in May 1941, the Soviets wanted him tried immediately.[60] During the Four-Power negotiations in London in 1945 that produced the Charter for the Tribunal, the Soviet negotiator, Ion Nikitschenko (then vice chairman of the Soviet Supreme Court), insisted that "We are dealing here with the chief war criminals who have already been condemned and whose conviction has already been announced."[61] Shortly before the Nuremberg trial, Soviet publications had called for the leading members of Hitler's government to receive "the hangman's noose." On the evening of November 26, 1945 – just as the trial was opening – Soviet show trial prosecutor and deputy foreign minister Andrei Vishinsky raised a glass to the Tribunal's judges with the toast, "I propose a toast to the defendants. May their paths lead straight from the courthouse to the grave."[62]

The opening statement to the Tribunal by Justice Robert H. Jackson, the chief U.S. prosecutor, focusing on Count I of the Nuremberg indictment, has rightly been cited as a rhetorical masterpiece. It balanced the historic importance of the trial, the heinousness of the crimes to be discussed, the necessity to avoid the theory of collective guilt with regard to the German people, and the requirement of the victors to "stay the hand of vengeance."[63] Similar assessments have been made regarding the opening of the British case, which focused on Count II, by British chief prosecutor Sir Hartley Shawcross.[64] The French and Soviet cases, which focused on war crimes and crimes against humanity in Western and Eastern Europe, respectively, have received far less attention. The Soviet case, which began on February 8, 1946, with a dramatic opening statement by the Soviet chief prosecutor General Roman Rudenko, had much that was wrong with it. The Soviets had already insisted that their own murder of thousands of Polish army officers in 1940 be included in the indictment against the German defendants.[65] In addition, the Soviets made sure that their cooperation with Hitler's Germany, which included the Soviet attacks on eastern Poland and Finland in the fall and winter of 1939, be banned from the body of evidence. These were legacies that Nuremberg would never live down.

But even bona fide Soviet evidence had its flaws. Rudenko's opening correctly noted that the main target of Hitler's war was the Soviet Union and the case that followed included gruesome detail on the German spoliation in the U.S.S.R. But his statement that the Germans were defeated by the heroic resistance of the Red Army and the Soviet people while the whole world watched in admiration was a political argument that emphasized problematic Soviet unity during the war and a skewed notion of what the Soviet liberation of "freedom-loving nations" such as Poland, Romania, and Hungary really meant.[66] And though the Soviet case discussed a long list of horrific German crimes from mass shootings of Jews at Babi Yar, to the murder of Soviet POWs, to the leveling of Ukrainian villages, to the death camps at Auschwitz to Treblinka, there were flaws to these elements as well. The Soviets introduced general evidence from state forensic teams and survivor testimonies without tying much of it to most of the specific defendants.[67]

Still, the Soviets' case revealed their expectations for the trial. Rudenko and his team employed a style similar to that of Soviet trials at Leningrad, Minsk, Kiev, and elsewhere. It was enough to argue that the entire German state apparatus had been guilty of all crimes because the state itself had implemented them.[68] Besides, the U.S. and British prosecutors had already entered evidence against the individual defendants. When the judges deliberated their verdicts and sentences, Nikitschenko received specific instructions from Moscow to argue and vote for the death penalty for each defendant.[69] Thus, Moscow was clearly disappointed with the acquittals, partial acquittals, and prison terms. Nikitschenko's written dissent, published as part of the Nuremberg record, might have been prompted by Stalin himself, and, for all intents and purposes, it was the true verdict according to later Soviet jurists.[70]

Nikitschenko's dissent opened with the "unfounded acquittal" of Hjalmar Schacht, Franz von Papen, and Hans Fritzsche and then moved to the partial acquittal and life sentence assigned to Rudolf Hess. The entire issue of Hess will be examined in Chapter 6, but for the moment it is noteworthy that the Soviets had badly wanted to hang Hess for the past four years. Hess was, aside from Göring, the closest surviving member of Hitler's inner circle. He had flown to Britain in May 1941 in search of a peace arrangement between Berlin and London shortly before the Germans in June launched Operation *Barbarossa*, the assault on the Soviet Union. Thus, to the Soviets, Hess was one of the chief figures responsible for the crimes that took place in the U.S.S.R. The British press in 1942 reported that Hess was a prisoner of war (under which status Hess was theoretically eligible for repatriation to Germany), which triggered suspicion by Stalin himself that the British might use the Nazis to the long-term detriment of the Soviet Union. Stalin's anger led to official Soviet calls in 1942 for Hess's immediate trial by an international body and some tense moments between British and Soviet diplomats.[71] At Nuremberg in 1945, the Soviets rejected the notion that Hess was mentally deranged, and they were surely galled by the contempt he displayed for the Soviet prosecution effort by removing his translation headset during Rudenko's opening statement.[72] Lawrence voted with Nikitschenko that Hess was guilty on all four counts of the indictment. But Hess's absence from Germany after May 1941 and his seeming mental inability to defend himself at trial justified, in the view of Judges Biddle and Donnedieu de Vabres, acquittal on Counts III and IV of the indictment and a sentence more merciful than hanging.[73]

Nikitschenko argued in his dissent that Hess's hands were coated with blood. The Soviets generally deemphasized Jewish wartime suffering in their effort to paint the war as an attack on the working class and the Soviet Union as such. Nikitschenko's instructions from Moscow before the Nuremberg judges' deliberations thus emphasized Hess's place in the Nazi hierarchy and his flight to Great Britain without mentioning Nazi antisemitism at all. Now the Soviet judge pointed out that Hess had signed one of the Nuremberg Laws (the Law for the Protection of German Blood and Honor of September 15, 1935), which formed the legal basis for Nazi crimes against Jews and that Hess also signed the decree of May 10, 1938, extending the Nuremberg Laws to Austria. Hess, Nikitschenko noted, also signed the decree of October 12, 1939, creating the administrative setup of the Polish territories annexed to Germany while giving Hans Frank (who would indeed hang) dictatorial powers in the General Government.

Most conspicuously, however, Nikitschenko repeated that Hess's mission to Britain was directed against the U.S.S.R. "Hess," the Soviet judge argued,

> was an active supporter of Hitler's aggressive policy. The crimes against peace committed by him are dealt with in sufficient detail in the Judgment. The mission undertaken by Hess in flying to England should be considered as the last of these crimes, as it was undertaken in the hope of facilitating the realization of aggression against the Soviet Union.

"[Among] political leaders of Hitlerite Germany Hess was third in significance and played a decisive role in the crimes of the Nazi regime," wrote Nikitschenko, "[and] I consider the only justified sentence in his case can be – death." Thus, even though twelve of the twenty-two defendants at Nuremberg received the death penalty, the Nuremberg trial as a whole had not ended the way that the Soviets had wanted.

Soviet clients elsewhere, particularly in the Soviet occupation zone of Germany, agreed. In the Soviet sector of Berlin, the leadership of the Soviet-sponsored Socialist Unity Party (SED) had also followed the Nuremberg trial with great interest. The German Communist leaders who had fled to Moscow in the 1930s and who survived Stalin's purges by being faithful party hacks had been rewarded in April 1945 by being flown into Berlin by the Soviets to assume control of what Stalin hoped would be a new German government. Because Wilhelm Pieck (the SED chairman), Walter Ulbricht (the deputy chairman), and the other German Communist leaders winked at the excesses of the Soviet occupation, which included mass rape of German women and the plundering of everything from rolling stock to art treasures, one can assume that they were on the same page as Moscow when it came to the punishment of major war criminals, too.

Unlike many other Germans, who over time saw Nuremberg as an episode of victors' justice, or who were too preoccupied with the uncertainties of daily life to care one way or the other about the progress of the trial, German Communists saw vital importance in it all.[74] In December 1945 Wilhelm Pieck headed a delegation of what was then the Democratic Bloc of antifascist parties from the Soviet sector of Berlin in petitioning the Allied Control Council. Acknowledging that the Nuremberg trial was of "immense importance" but that many Germans viewed it as nothing more than Allied propaganda, Pieck asked that more German observers be allowed to witness the trials, and particularly those from the party newspapers of the Democratic Bloc, since these parties represented "the great majority of the German people." Adequate coverage would, Pieck promised, "legitimize for the future the proceedings and results of the trial for the German people."[75] To this request the Control Council agreed on December 21, 1945. The parties of the Democratic Bloc, including what was then Pieck's and Ulbricht's Communist Party of Germany (KPD), were allotted two seats each.[76] Coverage of the trials was indeed broad in the Communist press, and the expectation was that all defendants would be executed afterward.

Such explains the open bitterness of the Communist world after the verdicts of October 1, 1946, which spared the lives of nearly half the Nuremberg defendants. Yet bitterness alone would not add up to organized protests, and Moscow left little to chance. The Soviet authorities issued directives to the SED leadership to stage coordinated mass demonstrations against the Nuremberg verdicts throughout the Soviet occupation zone and to coordinate media efforts with Moscow.[77] For weeks after the trial, *Täglische Rundschau,* the newspaper of the Soviet military authorities in Germany, and *Neues Deutschland*, the SED organ there, carried hostile editorials aimed at the Tribunal's lenience. The greatest bitterness was reserved for the three men who had been acquitted, particularly Schacht, who represented the eternal crimes of finance capital, and von Papen, who represented what Ulbricht called the "elegant" elements who had brought the fascist criminals to power.[78] *Neues Deutschland* and *Täglische Rundschau* both reprinted Nikitschenko's dissent concerning Schacht and laid out the entire antifascist case against Hitler's one-time economics minister and Reichsbank director.[79]

Yet there was also a consistent, steady call for the hanging of those who had received jail time, not just from SED leaders but also, ostensibly, from the proletarian Everyman in the street. Surveys of working class opinion in the Communist press brought numerous comments such as: "The ones that we are not hanging remain a danger," "All of them deserved the same punishment – Death." Ulbricht himself published a call for the criminals now to be handed over to the German people for judgment. "Twelve criminals," he said, "were sentenced to death. Every right-thinking person regrets that all of the accused war criminals will not go to the gallows."[80] On October 3, 1946, a well-advertised rally of 50,000 such right-thinking working men and women at the August Bebel Platz in eastern Berlin focused on the prison sentences and likewise brought calls such as "Death to all the Nuremberg War Criminals" and "To the gallows with all of them." Resolutions from Soviet-licensed proletarian organizations such as the Free German Federation of Trade Unions of Greater Berlin (FDGB) expressed "no comprehension that people like Hess, Funk, Raeder, Schirach, Speer, Neurath, [and] Dönitz are not killed for all of the crimes they have committed and suffering they have caused."[81]

This SED campaign was not limited to Berlin. In a series of speeches throughout the Soviet zone, Pieck emphasized not the death sentences, which he found pleasing, but rather his profound disappointment over the prison sentences and acquittals. He demanded that at least, those not condemned to death be handed over to a German people's court that would give them a proper verdict. "We hear with . . . disappointment the judgment that has come down from the International Military Tribunal," he said on October 5, 1946, at an election rally in Königswusterhausen:

> If only 12 of the 22 active Nazis and war criminals have been sentenced to hang, then this is a half-measure which can only . . . encourage . . . reaction in Germany. The German people have demanded with justification the death sentence for all of the accused. And I am convinced that had a German people's court been set up it would have needed no time at all to establish guilt and decide on the death penalty. What has been established here? The proof of guilt are the millions of dead, the wreckage and destruction. . . . We raise the strongest protest against the fact that . . . three major criminals are acquitted. Also the remainder that received only prison sentences deserve the death penalty. For example this England flyer! But such is the case with the other men who have been sentenced to nothing more than prison. None are distinguished from the others in the degree of the crimes which they perpetrated on Germans and other peoples. And thus it is the demand of our people that these bandits be delivered up to the German people. . . . Our demand is: An eye for an eye, a tooth for a tooth.[82]

Such sentiments were echoed elsewhere. The Czech Communist newspaper *Rudo Pravno* called for von Neurath to be tried again in Prague, where he had served as Hitler's *Reichsprotektor*. Voices in Vienna called for a retrial of Baldur von Schirach for his activities as Gauleiter there; and Nikitschenko's case against Hess was printed by the Soviet authorities.[83]

The bloodthirstiness of the Communist world can be understood in several ways. First, such commentators truly believed that the accused deserved death, especially because, to the Communist mind, Nazism was viewed as a heightened form of class warfare against the proletariat. The association with specific crimes was not as important as the hostile principles represented by the Nazi elite. Second, and perhaps more importantly, the Communist world could not believe that Nazism had been killed. Minor Nazis and party members, who had obviously been duped by Nazism, were now welcome to join their true allies in the Communist fold. Yet Nazi leaders had to be eliminated publicly. Sparing them the noose let them get away with murder, but it also let them live to fight another day. Indicative of this problem was that following the acquittals of Schacht, von Papen, and Fritzsche, the Western members of the Quadripartite Commission for the Detention of Major War Criminals in Nuremberg had no easy time convincing their Soviet counterpart that the three acquitted men could indeed now indeed go free.[84] The argument between the Allies over the regulations at Spandau Prison, and the policies of the Soviets toward Spandau thereafter, must be seen within this context.

It is impossible to argue that disappointment over Hess alone determined Soviet policies concerning Spandau in 1947 (they certainly determined Soviet policies after 1966 when Hess was the only prisoner left at Spandau). Perhaps Soviet attitudes would have been as venomous had Hess been executed at Nuremberg. They certainly did not have quite the same feelings with regard to von Neurath, von Schirach, Funk, Speer, or the naval officers. Regardless, the fact that Hess was among the men to be imprisoned at Spandau, and the fact that the Soviets continued to see him as dangerous, did not help to mitigate Soviet policies on the type of prison Spandau would be.

There were several disputes with regard to the draft regulations even within the Kommandatura Legal Committee. The Soviets, for example, did not even wish to establish the principle of visitation by family members or mail correspondence, arguing instead that "visits and correspondence should, in the interests of security, be allowed only in exceptional cases."[85] But the chief question lay in whether the seven prisoners were to serve their sentences in absolute solitary confinement or whether they would be allowed to engage in common activities such as work and religious worship while in prison. The judgment of the International Military Tribunal gave not a bit of guidance on the issue, nor did Control Council Directive Number 35.

As the Legal Committee drafted the regulations for Spandau in January 1947, the Soviets insisted on solitary confinement so that the prisoners would be, in essence, entombed alive. Paragraph 9 of the original Spandau draft regulations in January 1947 thus included the ominous, bare provision that "Confinement shall be solitary."[86] No provisions were made for work, for exercise, or for worship, much less for any of these activities to be communal.

Such conditions would be onerous indeed. Speer noted that in Nuremberg the prisoners could no longer talk to one another or go for walks in the prison yard once the Tribunal had passed sentence. "The loneliness," he said only three days after the pronouncement of his sentence, "is growing unbearable." On October 11, after concentrating on the minutia of his cell for more than a week, he lamented: "I have to get out; the cell is beginning to feel unbearably oppressive." When in late November he heard the rumors of the Soviet demand for "strict solitary confinement and harsh conditions," Speer was duly terrified. "Worried about Spandau," he wrote on December 11, despite the fact that his cell in Nuremberg hovered around the freezing point for lack of coal.

Though they cared little for one another personally, Speer and his fellow inmates stretched menial jobs such as sweeping and mopping for as long a time as they could simply for the human contact.[87] Raeder, who four months after his sentence could still reprimand a Norwegian junior interrogation officer for not addressing him as a ranking superior, admitted to his own attorney that "I keep myself busy with light work of my own accord, for example sweeping the hall and raking away leaves.... I do it to be friendly with the others and because exercise is good for me."[88] The report in December by the new American governor of the prison at Nuremberg, Major Frederick C. Teich, that the "discipline [of the prisoners] is excellent" is probably indicative of the prisoners' hope that subservience would mean more time out of their cells.[89]

Yet the British authorities refused to acquiesce to the Soviet insistence on solitary confinement for the seven prisoners. The Kommandatura Legal Committee had originally been ordered on October 4, 1946, to draft the Spandau Prison regulations in accordance with Allied Control Council Directive Number 19. This directive, dated November 12, 1945, concerned the Allied supervision of German prisons for common criminals. Here, administration of prisons was aimed at the "rehabilitation and reformation of the offender." To this end there was to be a program of "useful physical work to the end that the prisoner will appreciate fully the consequences of his criminal acts." Directive 19 also provided for reasonable opportunities to maintain physical well-being of prisoners, reasonable opportunity for religious guidance, and regular correspondence and visitation with friends and relatives. In fact, it had been the Soviet Representative to the Control Council's Legal Committee, J. N. Karrasov, who had insisted on the religious provisions.[90]

For the British authorities, the moral issue was undoubtedly as important as the legal one. Since Spandau was located in their sector of Berlin, the British clearly understood that they more than any other power would be held responsible for what occurred there. They also understood the Soviets well enough to know that differences of opinion concerning the Spandau regulations had to be worked out *before* they went into effect, lest the Soviets insist on following the agreed regulations to the letter. Even when the Kommandatura Legal Committee submitted the original draft regulations to the commandants themselves, the British Legal Representative C. W. Harris noted his displeasure. The draft, he said, could be no more than a basis for discussion because, in his view, the regulations as they stood "did not conform to modern penal practice or to Directive No. 19 of the Allied Control Council. The absence of provisions for work and the provisions as to occupational pursuits in cells, visits, letters and religious observances in particular require alteration."[91] The French and American members of the Legal Committee agreed that amendments might have to be made.

But the driving force for more humane regulations was the British Foreign Office in London. There is a certain irony to this. It had been Winston Churchill who had steadfastly resisted the idea of war crimes trials in lieu of the summary execution of Nazi leaders. His government had accepted the notion of trials only with great reluctance in April 1945 – this at American and Soviet insistence. Once the trial was under way, however, the new Labour government in London expected guilty verdicts and death sentences down the line. "There can be no doubt," said British Treasury Solicitor Sir Thomas Barnes, "that these men will be executed." Even Clement Attlee, who took over as prime minister after the Labour Party's victory in July 1945, assumed that the military figures at the very least would be shot.[92] Now that prison sentences had been issued, however, the British would stick to what they viewed as the more enlightened aspects of the Western legal tradition. "The draft regulations as they stand," said one Foreign Office official,

> are not in accordance with the moral code of civilized nations in that [organized work and religious worship have long been recognized as] essential ingredients of penal administration.... It is a basic factor in the imposition of imprisonment as a penalty that the prisoner shall not, merely as a result of imprisonment, deteriorate in any way and organized work is essential to this end.

If the regulations were not changed to include communal work and worship, they would be "degrading to... the Allied Kommandatura and the countries represented thereon" while also running counter to "British policy and British public opinion."[93] In Berlin, the argument was carried out on the level of the deputy commandants, and specifically British Brigadier William R. Hinde, who insisted that the regulations be amended to include visits and letters in regular intervals, as well as communal work, exercise, and reasonable facilities for worship. Work geared toward the physical conditions of the individual prisoners, moreover, should amount in principle to ten hours a day.

Thus, while each prisoner would have his own cell, the Spandau regime would not be one of solitary confinement. "This," said Hinde, "was a question of principle, for solitary confinement would constitute a penalty over and above that envisioned by the Tribunal itself."[94] "My amendments," he said, "are based on the need to treat prisoners in an enlightened manner, and not treat them in the way that I should have expected the Nazis to treat them."[95] More importantly, the British added a clear threat to the rest of the Kommandatura. If their amendments were not accepted, they would refuse to accept the transfer of the prisoners to their sector of Berlin, even on a provisional basis.[96] The British were thus willing to cause a rift in the Four-Power control in Berlin over these issues of principle.

Colonel Alexei I. Yelizarov, the Soviet deputy commandant in Berlin, disagreed vehemently. Yelizarov was no typical Red Army officer. Described by U.S. deputy commandant Colonel Frank Howley as "a big, powerful bruiser, who had married a sister-in-law of Lenin and [then] become the father of an astonishing sixteen-pound baby," Yelizarov had previously served as chief of the political division in the Soviet sector of Berlin. Thus, he had been the political adviser to the Soviet commandant Kotikov, before becoming deputy commandant in October 1946, when he mysteriously replaced Colonel Danila S. Dalada, presumably because the latter was too friendly toward the Americans. It was surely no accident that Yelizarov assumed this post in the middle of the Berlin municipal election campaign in which the Soviets expected victory for the SED but were bitterly disappointed with the vote of October 20, 1946, despite their strong-arm tactics in their Berlin sector. Howley, an avid sportsman, remembered Yelizarov for hunting wild boar with a machine gun in the woods outside Berlin. And on the few occasions when Yelizarov smiled, Howley said, "it was like ice breaking up on the Yukon.... He and I always kept one hand on the trigger."[97]

With regard to the Spandau prisoners, Yelizarov argued from the start that "our efforts should be directed ... to make the Prison Regime for these criminals as strict as possible and as severe as possible."[98] Yelizarov and his legal advisers would make a number of tortured arguments: Life sentences *always* implied solitary confinement; since the Tribunal had not sentenced the prisoners to *hard* labor, there could be no labor of any kind; since the prisoners were Nazi pagans, "we cannot find priests for them"; since Spandau was an Allied rather than a German prison, Directive 19 did not apply. The British found such reasoning absurd. "Does Colonel Yelizarov believe," Hinde asked rhetorically, "that extremely harsh treatment of these people will make any contribution toward the future peace in Europe or any ameliorations of conditions in Russia?" Moscow's answer was yes. In the first place, the civilized world, as the Soviets saw it, had wanted them dead. "We saw and witnessed," Yelizarov argued, "all the mass demonstrations in Berlin and elsewhere in other countries which expressed their disapproval of the light sentences given to these prisoners ... and I am inclined to listen more to the sentiments expressed by the Mass of people."[99]

But there was also a practical argument that reflected real Soviet concerns. The Soviets knew as well as anyone that prison terms were often not the final act in political careers. Vladimir Ilyich Lenin, after all, had returned from exile to lead a Communist revolution; Stalin joined him after escaping from what was thought to be secure imprisonment. Hitler's own rise to power, as the Soviets well knew, had come after a very comfortable confinement in Landsberg Prison where he ate good food, relaxed in wicker furniture, received numerous sympathetic visitors, and planned the future with his Nazi comrades while dictating what would be the first part of *Mein Kampf* to Hess himself. Spandau would, of course, be different, but the men condemned to spend their prison terms there had already made comments to the effect that Spandau would not be the last chapter of their lives. Dönitz had made the comment under interrogation that he was Hitler's legal successor. And in Nuremberg Prison after the verdicts, Hess mused openly about a new Nazi government, put together with the help of the Western allies, with himself at the head and with Speer as his supply minister. Funk might have remarked that Hess's ruminations were nothing but "craziness." But American doctors believed that "in Hess's confused mind, he is actually sincere about the new Reich."[100]

The Soviets took it seriously, too. Yelizarov warned that the prisoners could form a "shadow of Hitler's cabinet meetings." "We all know," said the Soviet colonel, "that amongst the prisoners is the last Reichskanzler of the Third Reich [Dönitz] and several other ministers; therefore the Cabinet of Ministers is already there. We do not agree that these heads of the Nazi regime should guide the underground movement in Germany and prepare different plans."[101] Yelizarov thus "could not agree to allow that Hitler clique to consult together and to work out a general policy. Followers of Hitler should not be permitted to prepare a new war under the aegis of the Allied Prison in Spandau."[102]

At first, the American and French representatives in Berlin agreed with the British. In February, the Spandau Prison complex was not ready to receive the prisoners anyway, and theoretical arguments cost nothing. The U.S. representative to the Kommandatura Legal Committee, Wesley Pape, whom Howley later described as one of his "wise men," registered his agreement that the prisoners be allowed to do communal work while the French legal representative Pierre Blanchet at least agreed that they be allowed to work in their cells if not together.[103] Both Howley and the French deputy commandant Colonel Patricot agreed with their Legal Committee counterparts; Howley accepted all British amendments, and Patricot accepted all British amendments save communal work.[104]

But their tune changed by mid-February when the prison was declared ready to receive the prisoners, and the British refused to accept them. The Americans would have to hold the prisoners under their care in Nuremberg until some sort of compromise was struck, and the French had no sympathy at all for the prisoners. Howley argued that a deadlock that delayed the transfer of the prisoners was unacceptable whether they lived the rest of their lives in solitary confinement or not. "We Americans," he said on February 21, "are very anxious to get rid of these peoples [sic] and to get them to Berlin." "He could not agree," he continued,

> to the prisoners being left several months longer in Nuremberg awaiting the decision of the Allied Control Authority. He considered that the differences between the proposals of the British and Soviet representatives were inconsiderable and that the Soviet amendments could be accepted provisionally. He maintained that the prisoners should be transferred at the earliest possible moment to Berlin.

At this point, he added, he was willing to accept the Legal Committee Draft of the regulations "without change."[105]

American policy sprung from the way in which U.S. officials had held the major Nazi war criminals thus far. From the end of the war to August 1945, more than fifty top Nazi figures had been held for interrogation in the Palace Hotel in the Luxembourg spa town of Mondorf-les-Bains. Code-named "Ashcan," the hotel and surrounding area were stripped of all fineries, made secure with barred windows, stockades, and watchtowers, and placed under the stringent rule of Colonel Burton C. Andrus, a career Army prison officer. Though he had to protect the prisoners from angry townspeople,

Andrus also left no doubt in the minds of the Nazi leaders that they were in prison. Their rooms contained straw mattresses and no pillows and their diets contained no more than 1,550 calories per day. Andrus prevented suicide attempts by strip searching arriving inmates to seize poisons and sharp objects while confiscating shoelaces, belts, neckties, and the like. Complaints were common from the prisoners, who had grown accustomed to more lavish surroundings during the Nazi years. Field Marshal Albert Kesselring even warned that the Spartan conditions threatened the prospects of future peace. Solitary confinement was rejected at Ashcan mostly for practical reasons. Prisoner conversations were tape recorded without their knowledge for evidentiary and intelligence purposes.[106]

When the defendants of the Nuremberg trial were flown from Mondorf to Nuremberg in August 1945, Andrus came with them to assume control of the Nuremberg Prison, adjacent to the Palace of Justice where the trial would take place. In this wrecked Bavarian city, security conditions were more difficult. The damaged prison would hold not only those slated to stand trial before the Tribunal but also German witnesses, many of whom would later stand trial themselves. There were breaches in the outer wall, former SS members were charged with repairing the Palace itself when the prisoners arrived, the prison staff was undermanned, and once the trial started, an array of visitors from defense attorneys to U.S. congressmen would go through the prison.

The flaws in the system were revealed on the night of October 25, 1945, when Robert Ley, the indicted leader of the Nazi Party's German Labor Front (DAF), strangled himself with a towel. Tight security thus became tighter. Under constant observation by guards, the prisoners lived in bare cells under the rule of constant searches, solitary confinement, heavily censored mail, and procedures of silence that precluded speaking with one another except at lunch on court days. Foreign Minister Joachim von Ribbentrop complained of losing his mind, and as a result of concomitant concerns, psychiatrists evaluated the prisoners regularly, and clerics visited when requested.[107]

The security-conscious regime at Nuremberg helps to explain why in the early stages of the arguments over Spandau, the Soviets held the American regime at Nuremberg as a worthy model for the incarceration of convicted war criminals,[108] and why at least at first, the Americans had less sympathy for the British view on the Spandau regulations. C. W. Harris, meanwhile, could only say in the last week of February 1947 that he "understood very well that his U.S. colleague was anxious that the prisoners be brought to Berlin as soon as possible," while French deputy commandant Patricot lamented irritably that it might be best to inform the quadripartite authorities at Nuremberg that the prisoners, who were slated at that point to travel to Berlin on March 10, might have to wait longer.[109]

By March, however, the entire prison regime for Spandau was threatening to unravel. By the first of the month, Yelizarov, after insisting that the prisoners be allowed no more than one visitor every four months and one letter every four months (the latter in exceptional cases only), had agreed with a British amendment mandating a visit every two months and a letter sent and received every four weeks.[110] But on March 4, the Soviet colonel reiterated that the Soviets interpreted the Nuremberg sentences as calling for solitary confinement. He threatened to withdraw the concessions over letters and visits if the British did not provisionally accept the current state of the draft prison regulations and thus accept the transfer of the prisoners from Nuremberg to Spandau, with disagreements on solitary confinement to be ironed out by the Allied Control Authority later.

Howley actually agreed in principle with the Soviets, noting that Directive 35 "contained no provision which required the prisoners to remain at Nüremberg [sic] until the regulations had been approved. The facilities at Spandau Prison were satisfactory for the immediate acceptance of the prisoners." Patricot agreed that the prisoners should be transferred immediately with the details over the regulations to be worked out later by the Allied Control Authority. The Americans and the French also backed away from the U.S.-inspired Control Council Directive Number 19, with Howley arguing that the directive "should be a guide and not a rule." He proposed a compromise whereby confinement would be solitary except during periods of work and religious worship, but in these cases the prisoners would not be allowed to communicate with one another. Such would satisfy the British insistence on communal activity while assuaging Soviet concerns that the prisoners never be allowed to communicate. "In view of the enormity of their crimes," Howley said in agreement with Yelizarov, "the prisoners should never communicate with each other." In truth, as he had said in an earlier meeting, he was willing to accept "any compromise... that would result in bringing the prisoners from Nuremberg."[111] Patricot expressed satisfaction with this amendment so long as periods of work, worship, and exercise remained "strictly limited," and Hinde was willing to accept it as well. Yet here Yelizarov firmly refused, arguing that it would be impossible for the warders to keep the prisoners from talking.[112]

Patricot proposed yet another compromise. Communal activity would be limited to two hours a day, thus making practical a rule of silence. Hinde expressed willingness to accept this provision, but Yelizarov balked. "Members of the Nazi Council of Ministers [sic]," he said, "should not be permitted in the company of one another even for two hours a day." As of this point, all but the British were willing to accept the regulations in their current state as provisional pending consideration by the Allied Control Council. Hinde, however, reiterated that there would be a final agreement before the prisoners were moved to Spandau or none at all.[113] By the end of March, after six unsuccessful attempts to reconcile the issue in Kommandatura meetings, the Spandau regulations would be kicked upstairs to the Allied Control Council itself.[114]

But by then the Americans had swung to the British side. Noting on April 8 to General Clay, now the U.S. military governor, that "irreconcilable differences remain," Howley said that

> The U.S. representatives have heretofore indicated a willingness to compromise... between the British and Soviet views for the purpose of accomplishing a speedy transfer of the prisoners from Nuremberg to Berlin. It is felt, however, that as these efforts at compromise have failed, the U.S. deems it necessary to support the British position completely and considers it inadvisable to consent to the transfer of the prisoners... if some form of communal work, exercise, and religious worship is not provided.[115]

Clay did not disagree, but still wanted the issue settled within three weeks since in his view "immediate action is necessary... so that the prisoners may be moved from Nuremberg at the earliest possible date."[116]

On the eve of the Allied Control Council discussions regarding the regulations, the Americans attempted to embarrass the Soviets publicly over the issue. The U.S. Army newspaper *Stars and Stripes* reported that while the Americans, British, and French authorities were for humane treatment at Spandau, the Soviets were insisting on solitary confinement and harsh conditions. The reporting surely had an effect on the Nuremberg prisoners. "Confused images pass through my head," Speer wrote. "Dark cells, watery soups, ban on reading, beatings with clubs, harassment, sadistic guards.... Repeatedly I start into wakefulness, bathed in sweat." A "bout of fear," Speer called it. "My dreams are repeatedly haunted by images relating to Spandau and my fear of the Russians. For me that is a nightmare."[117]

But the public airing of the dispute, which included a misrepresentation of the French position in order to make it look as though the Soviets were alone in their harsh demands, had little effect on Moscow. On April 21 and 24, 1947, the Legal Directorate of the Allied Control Council reached impasse just as had the Kommandatura. The British representatives stated that solitary confinement was penalty over and above the simple imprisonment imposed by the International Military Tribunal. Moreover, they said, "solitary confinement could cause great mental distress. [In] meting out punishment to these men we should show that we were superior to them." The American delegate Alvin Rockwell, agreed. "[In] spite of the horrible crimes committed by these prisoners," he said, "it was below [Allied] standards to subject them to such cruel and unusual punishment as unqualified solitary confinement.... [Such] would go far beyond the judgment of the International Military Tribunal."

Soviet representative V. P. Kardasev maintained Moscow's position. In view of the "human misery and disaster" caused by the condemned men, they should remain in solitary confinement for the duration of their sentences, and the French delegate Lebegue, agreed in principle. The French continued to argue for a middle way, however. Since the main purpose of solitary confinement, as Lebegue understood it, was to prevent the prisoners from speaking to one another, perhaps they could work, worship, and exercise by themselves with no communication allowed. Neither the British nor the U.S. viewed the principle of absolute silence as desirable or practical. They favored instead language that would provide for "limited conversational privileges ... as may be prescribed by the Governorate." Neither the French nor the Soviets were willing to accept this wording. There was also disagreement over work itself. By now the British and U.S. representatives favored a normal work day of eight hours excepting Sundays and holidays, while their Soviet and French counterparts "considered this proposed addition unacceptable."[118]

The issue was not solved until May 16, 1947, within the Coordinating Committee of the Allied Control Council. By now it was clear that there would be no second international trial.[119] Spandau would not hold fifty or a hundred German war criminals, but only the seven convicted at Nuremberg. Should they be allowed to work and worship together, it would not be impossible to keep them from communicating with one another, or at least so it seemed. In addition, the British had shown no signs of budging. If their principles were not accepted, the prisoners would never arrive in the British sector. Major General Frank Keating, now Clay's deputy military governor, tried to smooth the waters by explaining that at Spandau, solitary confinement "connotes a sense of isolation ... rather than in the American prison sense in which solitary confinement is an additional punishment." Soviet General Pavel Kurochkin added that if such was to be the case, the Soviets could accept what he viewed as the French provisions on isolation, that "confinement shall be solitary ... however work, religious services and walks shall be in common and under the rule of silence subject to certain privileges which could be granted by [the Governorate] of the prison." "It does not satisfy me entirely," Kurochkin said, "but in principle I agree."

As for work hours, the Coordinating Committee reached agreement to the effect that the prisoners would work every day except for Sundays and holidays, and that work hours would be determined by the Governorate."[120] There was no hard and fast rule that the prisoners would be out of their cells for eight hours per day, but the Americans were willing to make this concession here for an agreement on the more crucial issue of work in principle.[121] These principles were sent back to the Kommandatura, which on June 10 approved the final set of regulations. All prisoners would "work to the best of their ability," the governors would "make reasonable provision for the prisoners to practice suitable religious rites," and the prisoners would "not talk or communicate with one another . . . without special permission."[122] Time would tell if such provisions were workable. The Americans, based on what they knew of federal prisons in the United States, were convinced that they were not.[123]

Why the Soviets accepted the principle of communal work at all is difficult to say. They had maintained stubbornly for nearly half a year that the major war criminals in their charge would serve every hour of their sentences in solitary confinement. It is doubtful that the Soviet authorities in Berlin were fully convinced by the legal argument made by the British and Americans, but it is also true that the Soviets could not counter the fact that neither the London Charter, which established the International Military Tribunal, nor Control Council Directive Number 35, which regulated punishment, mentioned anything beyond simple imprisonment.

In the end, they were outvoted three to one on the principle of communal work and worship, even though the French continued to insist on absolute silence during these activities. Having sent the issue from the Kommandatura to the Allied Control Authority, the Soviets realized that these were the harshest terms they were likely to get, and because the British authorities would not accept the prisoners without the minimal standards on which they had insisted, it was better to go along. In fact, such a system seemed to work in the prison at Nuremberg, so long as it was enforced. The condemned prisoners after mid-November 1946 were allowed to take a half-hour walk each day, but they were separated by ten meters. "We are forbidden to talk with one another," noted Speer, though a few words could be exchanged during work details under the eye of a sympathetic American guard.[124] The Soviet representative to the Quadripartite Commission for the Detention of Major War Criminals registered no complaints with this treatment, and the Soviet element to the Kommandatura praised the efforts of the U.S. jailers, whom they said held the prisoners in solitary confinement.[125] In fact, a major complaint by Yelizarov in February 1947 was that the prisoners could not arrive from the U.S. prison in Nuremberg to Four-Power prison in Spandau only to find their conditions softened.[126]

By May 1947, however, the U.S. regime at Nuremberg was softening for the seven condemned men. Unrestricted correspondence was allowed, the rule of silence had been lifted, and the food, according to Speer, had been "first rate."[127] A return to the earlier U.S. standard by this time, then, would represent harsher and more isolated treatment for the prisoners. And since the rule of silence had been made to work at one time in Nuremberg, it could be made to work at Spandau as well. Time would show that such was indeed the Soviet intent. The alternative to accepting the compromise, on the other hand was the complete erosion of Four-Power punishment of the major war criminals in the former capital of the Reich and the indefinite stay of the prisoners at Nuremberg, where the conditions of their imprisonment were growing increasingly lenient. Such did not seem impossible. Von Schirach, von Neurath, Raeder, and Funk all believed by the end of June based on the rumors they had heard that the whole idea of Spandau had been dropped.[128]

Yet the particular Four-Power principle of joint trial and punishment was a serious issue for the Soviets; it was so serious in fact that they had insisted in 1945 that if the Trial of the Major War Criminals were to be held in Nuremberg rather than in Berlin, then the administrative headquarters for the trial should remain in the Four-Power capital and that the trial should formally open there.[129] Moscow had also assumed that there would be a series of international trials – that the famous trial held at Nuremberg in 1945 and 1946 would be the first of many. They and the French both badly wanted a second international trial featuring German industrialists such as Alfried Krupp who, thanks to administrative mistakes, had avoided indictment in the first Nuremberg trial. The Soviets wanted to hold this second trial in Berlin, and the French, after the International Military Tribunal acquitted Hjalmar Schacht, even suggested an international trial in Paris.[130]

British officials, who had been lukewarm about the first trial, were never sanguine about a second, especially should it become an ideological trial of capitalists.[131] The United States, meanwhile, was now going it alone. In May 1946, while the Trial of the Major War Criminals was still underway in Nuremberg, U.S. counsel Telford Taylor supported a second international trial owing to his reluctance to terminate the London Charter, in which the United States had "an enormous moral investment."[132] Yet Justice Jackson, still Taylor's superior in Nuremberg, would make a contrary argument to Truman shortly after the Tribunal's verdicts in October. It was true, Jackson said, "that a very large number of Germans who have participated in the crimes remain unpunished. There are many industrialists, militarists, politicians, diplomats, and police officials whose guilt does not differ from those who have been convicted except that their parts were at lower levels."[133] The United States was already preparing in 1946 for subsequent war crimes trials that it would carry out on its own as per Truman's Executive Order of January 16, 1946. But it would be easier, Jackson now argued, for the United States to conduct these trials itself, within its own occupation zone, and for the other powers to do the same. "A four-power, four-language international trial," he told Truman, "is inevitably the slowest and most costly method." "There is neither moral nor legal obligation on the United States," Jackson continued, "to undertake another trial of this character.... The quickest and most satisfactory results will be obtained, in my opinion, from immediate commencement of our own cases."[134] Jackson left out of this letter his constant irritation at Nuremberg with his Soviet colleagues, which was

4. Nuremberg prosecutors Sir David Maxwell-Fyfe and Robert Jackson survey the courtroom, July 1945. Photograph courtesy of the Harry S. Truman Museum and Presidential Library.

well known at the time. But Truman and he both agreed that a Four-Power trial was a cumbersome business in any event. "I note what you say," the President wrote, "concerning the method through which these remaining criminals are to be brought to justice."[135]

By the middle of 1947, it had been clear for some time that there would be no more major international war criminal trials. As of May, U.S. military tribunals in Nuremberg had already completed the trial of former air minister Erhard Milch, had four more in progress (the Medical, Justice, Flick, and Pohl cases), and was in the process of preparing eleven others.[136] A Four-Power prison in Berlin might be the only physical remnant left of the international trial that the Soviets had wanted.

But the Soviets were clearly not happy, and their distrust of the British was augmented by the entire argument over the regulations. In the same deputy commandants' meeting in which the Spandau Prison regulations were accepted, Hinde suggested that the Kommandatura return to the idea broached in October 1946 that a new, permanent prison be constructed for the Nuremberg criminals. The use of Spandau, he said, was impractical in light of general prison overcrowding in the city, in which three men lived in single cells. Civil unrest in Berlin, which involved mass arrests, would cause a greater problem so long as Spandau was not usable for ordinary criminals. Yelizarov acidly noted that he "found it strange that the British delegation unexpectedly advanced new demands . . . after trying for many months to lighten the regime of the criminals in prison."[137]

Thus, on July 18, 1947, the Americans and British implemented Operation "Traffic," the transfer of the seven Nuremberg war criminals to Spandau Prison. Planned back in December 1946, the transfer called for an armed U.S. military guard to remove the prisoners from their cells in Nuremberg and to fly them to Gatow Air Base in the British sector of Berlin, where the British would take custody. A special military police truck fitted with a separate cubicle for each prisoner would drive them to their new place of confinement, preceded and followed by armored troop transports loaded with heavily armed British infantry drawn from the RAF regiment in Berlin. The date, time, and methods of transfer were to be kept highly secret.[138] At 4:00 A.M. Friday morning, July 18, the prisoners were suddenly awakened in their cells, while a platoon of American soldiers hurried them out with the few possessions that they were permitted to take. Each prisoner was handcuffed to an American soldier as the seven were led out of the jail where they had spent the past months. In two ambulances accompanied by a convoy of personnel trucks, they were quickly driven through the prison gate and to the American airfield through the wreckage of Nuremberg.

The flight to Berlin in an American Dakota passenger aircraft was brief, but pleasant according to Speer's recollection. "I was given a window seat," he said, "[with] my guard beside me. . . . After my long imprisonment this flight in glorious weather was a stirring experience." As the aircraft circled Berlin, Speer was able to make out the east–west axis of the city that he had laid out for Hitler's fiftieth birthday in 1939, the stadium that had hosted Hitler's Olympics in 1936, and the new yet badly damaged Reich Chancellery building he had designed. The heavy trees of the Tiergarten had been chopped down for firewood.[139]

As the Dakota descended toward Gatow, the guards slapped the handcuffs back on the prisoners, and Speer could see British military vehicles scrambling to meet the aircraft as it stopped. From the airplane, the prisoners were led with their escorts onto a bus, the windows painted black so that no resident of Berlin could see the infamous men inside. The journey from Gatow to Spandau was undertaken with speed, lasting but twenty minutes from the time the prisoners landed in Berlin to the time they entered what Speer called the "medieval sort of entrance" at the prison gates. Surrounded by Allied

5. A Soviet sentry in one of Spandau Prison's six guard towers in the first month of prison operations, July 1947. Photograph courtesy of the Associated Press.

military personnel, the prisoners had their handcuffs removed and entered the prison for their initial physical examination. The operation had gone smoothly. Major General P. M. Malkov, a former NKVD leader who doubled as the Soviet delegate to the Quadripartite Commission in Nuremberg, was impressed enough to congratulate his American and British counterparts on their efficiency following the transfer.[140] Yet for the criminals themselves and for the powers that would hold them in custody, a new, long, and difficult chapter had begun. As Major Walter Giese, the first American governor of Spandau, put it back in January 1947, "When Hess and Doenitz and the [others] get here, maybe in a year they will be forgotten men. But I rather think it will be the other way around."[141]

## CHAPTER TWO

# An Enduring Institution

"Even if the Spandau prisoners were hanged by the Russians, we couldn't do anything. We are not going to start a war on their account."

An unknown British general[1]

"I am back in Berlin, the city I love" wrote Albert Speer in late July 1947. "I imagined the return rather differently."[2] Indeed he might have. The regime waiting for the seven prisoners at Spandau was truly peculiar. Yet the imposing prison in which Speer would spend the next two decades of his life was, aside from the Berlin Air Safety Center, the single Four-Power institution in Berlin that would survive the breakdown of Four-Power cooperation in Germany, the Soviet blockade of Berlin in 1948 and 1949, and the onset of the Cold War in Central Europe that would last for the next forty years.[3]

Joint enterprises between East and West were improbable by 1948. The U.S.-Soviet argument over Central and Eastern Europe's postwar fate had already spiked in various spots thanks largely to Joseph Stalin's determination to enhance Soviet security on the Soviet Union's borders and his suspicions concerning Western aims. And no state's future was as contentious as Germany's. No one assumed in 1945 when the Four-Power occupation began that the result would be two separate German states for the next four and a half decades. But the character of the respective occupation zones helped to ensure this result. Resources were a key part of the dispute. The Soviets scoured their occupation zone for much-needed reparations in the form of machinery, locomotives, rolling stock, German engineers, and anything else of value. Thanks to agreements struck with Franklin D. Roosevelt and Winston Churchill at the Yalta meeting of February 1945, Stalin also expected deliveries from the western occupation zones to offset Soviet wartime damages, particularly coal and steel from the Ruhr valley in the industry-dominated British zone.[4] But the western occupation zones would never recover if normal production was not allowed to proceed, and the Allies did not wish to sustain their zones indefinitely. Indeed, the British and the French, battered by the war themselves, could not do so. Already before the Potsdam summit meeting in July 1945 between Stalin, new U.S. president Harry Truman, and Churchill (who was replaced by Attlee after the conference began), the Americans were speaking a different language concerning reparations, and in January 1947 Washington and London joined their zones economically into a unit known as "Bizonia," setting industrial targets for western German recovery. The French, who had hoped for a partitioned Germany and international control over the Ruhr region, joined their zone's economy to Bizonia in 1949.[5]

The occupation zones followed their own political paths as well. Stalin had hoped that the German Communist leaders flown into Berlin in April 1945 would form the basis of a new all-German government of a permanently subservient Germany. In April 1946, the Soviet authorities forced a union in their zone and in their Berlin sector between the Communist Party of Germany (KPD) and the more democratically minded Social Democratic Party (SPD) there, thus forming the Socialist Unity Party of Germany (SED). It was a merger of the political left in the Soviet zone in which the Communists held the whip hand. The western zonal military governments opposed extreme political movements of all stripes and encouraged instead the development of broad-based democratic parties on the grassroots level such as the SPD itself, which had led Germany's first democratic experiment in 1919 and which had bitterly opposed the Nazis. The Western Allies also licensed the new Christian Democratic Union (CDU), a traditional yet broad-based conservative party leaning toward liberal democracy and freer markets.[6] The preferences of Berliners was made clear in municipal elections there in October 1946 in which the SED received less than 20 percent of the more than two million votes cast. None of Greater Berlin's twenty district mayors were Communists, and the Allies and Soviets were unable afterward to agree on a permanent lord mayor for the city as a whole.

Deteriorating East-West relations over Germany and Berlin came to a head with the German currency reform essential for Germany's participation in the Marshall Plan, a massive infusion of American financial aid for European reconstruction announced by Secretary of State George C. Marshall in June 1947. American policymakers hoped that Marshall aid, aside from bringing European self-sufficiency and trading capability, would stem the appeal of communism in war-torn Western and Central Europe. But in Moscow's more jaundiced view, the Marshall Plan was an American maneuver aimed at undermining Soviet security through encirclement by hostile American client states.[7] Czechoslovakia's interest in Marshall aid resulted in a Soviet-sponsored Communist coup in Prague in February 1948. The determination of the Western powers to include Germany in Western Europe's recovery helped to trigger the country's partition. The new Deutschmark was introduced in the western zones on June 20, 1948, to eliminate black market trading and to jump-start the economy. Already on March 20, 1948, however, Marshal Sokolovsky and the Soviet delegation walked out of the Allied Control Council, claiming that the Western Allies had abandoned Four-Power governance. On June 16, the Soviet Commandant in Berlin, Major

General Alexander Kotikov, withdrew from the Kommandatura with his delegation. Soviet harassment of Allied road and rail traffic from their zones to the western sectors of Berlin began in April 1948 and hardened into a full-blown blockade on June 24. If Germany was to be divided, then Berlin – all of Berlin – would be the capital of the eastern state. The western sectors of the capital could not be allowed to serve as a western outpost for everything from free trade to espionage. In the meantime, the Cold War that had been brewing since 1947 had become a face-to-face military confrontation, and Berlin was on the front line.

Stalin miscalculated badly in his expectation that Western forces would quit Berlin.[8] For the next eleven months until the Soviets lifted the blockade in May 1949 Western forces airlifted food and medicines to sustain the two million inhabitants of their sectors as well as the Allied military position there. By this time, it was a foregone conclusion that there would be two German states, and the Federal Republic of Germany in the West and the German Democratic Republic in the East were formed with their own governments by the autumn of 1949. Divided Berlin formed rival municipal governments as well. But because the city's ultimate status could not be agreed upon thanks to its precarious location within the borders of the East German state, Berlin remained in the limbo of continued de jure Four-Power occupation without de facto Four-Power cooperation. Though the rump Kommandatura continued to meet, the Soviets never returned to it and would try, with East German insistence, to end the Four-Power occupation of western Berlin in the years ahead.

Yet despite the complete breakdown of Four-Power cooperation in Germany and in Berlin, despite the threat of war over Berlin in 1948 and 1949 complete with Soviet maneuvers and reinforcements and the stationing of additional U.S. bombers in England, and despite the formation of separate municipal governments for Berlin and the splitting of Germany into two states, Spandau Prison remained a functioning Four-Power institution – the sole remnant of the grand alliance that had defeated Nazism. It was surely not inevitable that Spandau would survive the split. But if the Spandau arrangement were to have disintegrated, then it was most likely that it would have done so in the shadow of the blockade and the division of Berlin. How this odd institution survived and cemented itself into the landscape of the Cold War is the subject of this chapter.

## HARD TIME: LIFE IN SPANDAU

Most public and official discussion concerning Spandau Prison and the possibility of ending the arrangement centered on the degree to which the harshness of day-to-day conditions there justified an end to Western cooperation with the Soviets in the punishment of the major war criminals. Indeed conditions in Spandau were austere. But the handwritten daily log of the chief duty warder, which is an hour-by-hour diary of the prison, shows that conditions (though more severe than at the Allied war crimes prisons in western Germany) were never as poor as they appeared to journalists or to advocates of the prisoners. If the Soviets pulled the Western Allies into directions that they did not wish to go concerning the punishment of the major war criminals, then the reverse is also true. At Spandau the Allies softened Soviet penal methods. Nazi enemies shipped to concentration or work camps between 1933 and 1945 would have been pleased to have had the privacy of their own cells and their own toilets, hot water for baths, thousands of books at their disposal, round-the-clock medical care including massages by orderlies and examinations by specialists when needed, private meals, and periods for exercise. The same is true of Germans condemned of war crimes and held in the U.S.S.R.[9]

And Albert Speer's published *Spandau Diaries* shows that though the prisoners' days were regimented as per typical prison life, the most onerous of the regulations were often not followed to the letter.[10] Each prisoner was allowed creature comforts in his cell. Speer enjoyed a daily pipe, photographs of his family, a slide rule, paper on which to sketch, tools with which to draft architectural projects, as well as the Bible. All received daily rations of tobacco. During the Soviet month of July 1947 – the initial month of the prison – the prisoners walked around a tree in the prison yard for a half-hour a day for exercise with their hands behind their backs.[11] But the following month with the United States in the chair, the prisoners began productive and reasonably satisfying work that defined their days thereafter. Each had specific cleaning chores in the cell bloc (four of the prisoners swept the corridor after each meal; Speer cleaned the cell bloc toilet area each day from 7:30 to 8:00 A.M.). On temperate days, the prisoners could work in the large (5,000 to 6,000 square meters) prison garden for roughly three hours in the morning and two and a half in the afternoon. Productive work was the condition for which the British had fought so hard, and Speer along with the others (save Hess who often just sat on the bench) was pleased to be able to work in the open air of the garden, planting vegetables and even pulling weeds.[12]

The prisoners could also request a variety of books from the forty thousand volumes available at the Spandau district public library and could receive books from family so long as the books were not of dangerous political content or post-1918 historical analysis. These volumes were kept in a prison library tended eventually by Erich Raeder.[13] Speer noted that he devoured Zola, Dostoyevsky, and volumes on the Italian Renaissance in his first months in the prison, commenting at one point that he read for five hours a day.[14] The other prisoners read too though the chief warder duty log only refers to books by their number and not by title.

Church services were conducted each Saturday after October 11, 1947, in a double cell converted into a chapel with music, sometimes recorded and sometimes provided by Walther Funk on an organ received by the prison in January 1948.[15] The French Reformed Pastor Georges Casalis accepted the initial position of prison pastor on the noble assumption that he could help the prisoners to become better men. This was of course no easy task because none of them, Speer's protestations notwithstanding, felt especially guilty in the first place. Casalis's first sermon on the lepers of Israel who were cut off from their community insulted Raeder, Dönitz, von Schirach, Funk, and von Neurath who understood that they might have been the figurative lepers to whom Casalis had referred. Raeder protested to Casalis the following week in the name of the others, but none of the prisoners – save Hess – missed the following services.[16] Casalis, for his own part, was undaunted. He insisted to the French commandant in Berlin, General Jean Ganeval, that the prison regulations be amended so that he could hear private confessions from the prisoners in their cells. Anything less, he said, was an "unbearable mutilation of [a cleric's] ministry."[17]

The Soviets repeatedly denied Casalis's request, but speaking by the prisoners was less tightly regulated than the public understood. Though Speer noted in July 1947 on arrival at Spandau that "We are not permitted to speak a word to one another," he also noted by the end of that year that the prisoners spoke often amongst themselves and even to the warders to the point where the prisoners had become familiar with the minutia of some warders' private lives. Such was possible only in the bizarre world of Spandau in which there were more guards than prisoners. Speer noted by December 1947 that many of the warders, even the younger Soviet ones, seemed sympathetic to the prisoners, though some Soviet warders were certainly intelligence officers placed in Spandau to try to learn the prisoners' future plans.[18] In any event, Dönitz's temperamental announcement in early 1949 that he would not speak to the warders for the rest of the year (this, evidently to punish the warders) illustrated that he had conversed with them quite a bit in the first place. So did the admonishment by Raeder and von Neurath to Speer and von Schirach that small talk with the warders amounted (nearly four years after the war) to fraternization with the enemy.[19]

A constant source of complaint for the Soviets early in the life of the Four-Power prison was their inability to stop the prisoners from speaking to each other and to the Allied warders whether in the garden or in the cell bloc itself. By the time the Soviets implemented the blockade in Berlin, the Soviet prison governor, Major Politov, was calling for the punishment of American, British, and French warders who had been allowing the prisoners to speak. At one point, Politov appeared in the prison garden personally and told the prisoners that they had to work and rest in silence – out of the ordinary for a governor since warders handled the prisoners.[20] But as Speer's *Diaries* and

6. A smuggled photo of Walther Funk playing the organ during Saturday chapel services. Published in the Munich illustrated weekly *Revue* series, "Hinter den Mauern von Spandau," by Jürgen Thorwald, 1951.

the continued Soviet complaints on the eve of the blockade show, the talking never stopped.

Nor were any of the prisoners corporally punished. Even had the Soviets prescribed such a thing – and they never did – the Allied governors would have vetoed it. Punishments, few and far between, usually consisted of brief suspension of reading privileges, the removal of mattresses from the cells during daylight hours, and, more rarely, a cutting of rations, but never below what all four medical officers would countenance, namely Berlin Ration Card 3. Had Spandau been a normal prison, Speer noted, and he surely meant the Nazi prisons with which he had become so familiar, "we would presumably long ago [have] gone off the rails."[21] And aside from Hess, who was a bit off the rails to begin with, the prisoners never did.

Medical care for the prisoners was also better than one might suppose. A medical board of one doctor from each of the Four Powers oversaw the health of the prisoners. And specialists in everything from urology to cardiology were available at the Allied and Soviet military hospitals in the four sectors of Berlin. A dispensary within the prison provided all of the medications the prisoners needed from nitroglycerin pills to eyewash to hot water bottles, and the orderlies, aside from filling prescriptions from the dispensary almost every night (dangerous pills were kept in a safe) also provided therapeutic massages to the prisoners on numerous occasions even in 1948 and 1949. Raeder received numerous back massages in his cell in February 1948, Speer had his leg massaged the following month, and Dönitz benefited from therapeutic massage as well.[22] It was the nature of the imprisonment at Spandau that made medical care so thorough. No doctor wanted a high-profile prisoner to die on his watch. This concern for the prisoners even affected the kitchen staff, which on the order of the medical board was examined twice monthly for venereal diseases, intestinal parasites, tuberculosis, and other bacteriological illnesses.[23]

To prevent suicide attempts cells were equipped with forty-watt light bulbs turned on every ten minutes at night to keep the prisoners from taking their own lives. Though some (even Soviet) warders allowed the prisoners to sleep without turning them on, the lights were enough of an irritant that Funk at one point convinced a warder to gum his switch (and was punished for it).[24] In addition, the prisoners could not shave themselves and were never allowed to hold a razor. This task was performed by a barber who would enter and leave the prison each day with his equipment bag inspected to make sure that he left with as many razors as he entered with.[25] The prisoners were allowed no forks or knives either – they ate their meals with spoons.[26]

Contacts with the outside world were tightly circumscribed for security purposes. Information about the prison, should it leak, could provide valuable information to anyone using the prison for propaganda or as unlikely as it seems, anyone plotting the escape of the prisoners. Rumors in 1953 that SS-Obersturmbannführer Otto Skorzeny, Hitler's famous commando leader, had planned a Spandau Prison break complete with helicopters and a hundred specially trained troops were taken seriously by all four powers.[27] Such rumors might explain why Soviet sentries in the guard towers were armed with fully automatic machine guns plus multiple clips and why a Soviet sharpshooter was always on duty.[28] Information leaking into the prison could also bring the prisoners dangerously up to date with current affairs to the point where they could plot political strategy with former Nazis on the outside.[29] Letters that revealed too much about the prison or that stated untruths were returned to the prisoner with threat of punishment. Funk and von Neurath had letters returned immediately – von Neurath claimed to his family to have lost twenty pounds in two weeks, and Funk claimed that he had been wrongly imprisoned on fabricated evidence.[30] The prisoners were allowed absolutely no newspapers. Rules covering letters and visits could be relaxed at times as per the governors' discretion. Speer was allowed to send his mother an elaborate picture that he had drawn for her birthday, an extra letter was allowed in 1948 at Christmas time, and visiting minutes were generally allowed to accrue should they not be used every period.[31] Such relaxations often depended on the Soviet mood, and again, the Soviet censors who read mail and observed visits were surely intelligence officers owing to Moscow's suspicion of the prisoners themselves.[32]

And Spandau was a prison with leaks despite the regulations. Prison employees sold information and even photographs to the German tabloid press from time to time regardless of their pledges not to do so. But the most famous leak was Albert Speer's secret channel through a Dutch prison orderly named Toni Proost (a.k.a. Anton Vlaer) who claimed to have been well treated during the war as a forced laborer in Germany. Through Proost, Speer could smuggle piecemeal – on strips of toilet paper, tobacco wrappers, and so forth – additional letters and notes that would after his release in 1966 amount to a volume of memoirs and an entire prison diary, though Speer constructed the latter partly from dated narrative letters to his family and not from a finished diary as such. Speer excitedly wrote when offered the channel that, "My life, or at least my sense of it, has assumed a totally new quality."[33] It was an ironic twist, especially since Speer's formal request to write his memoirs in prison was rejected by the Soviets on the (fully justified) fear that Speer would use the opportunity to sanitize his role in the Third Reich.[34] Amazingly Speer's extensive writings were never discovered throughout the nearly two decades he spent at Spandau. The chief warder logs show that each cell was searched twice daily and that the prisoners were also searched each day on their return from the garden. The searches were simply not that intrusive most of the time. "A few weeks ago," Speer noted, "I put a piece of folded toilet paper under my bed . . . to see whether it would be found; no one paid any attention to the paper. Such lack of distrust is really almost insulting."[35]

On balance though, Spandau remained a rough place, not as bad as a Soviet prison camp, but worse than the Allied prisons in western Germany for German war criminals at Landsberg (United States), Werl (Great Britain), and Wittlich (France), which allowed access to newspapers and radios, greater contacts with family (including food parcels), a greater variety of indoor work activities, and common rooms for eating, talking, playing cards, and so on.[36] Friction between the Western Allies and the Soviets often sprang from the fact that the Soviets meant to follow the regulations as written. To Moscow, the Nuremberg prisoners validated Soviet suffering during the war and the international success in bringing the major criminals to justice in what turned out to be the first and last international trial of leading Nazis. Because the seven men in Spandau had cheated the hangman's noose with the help of soft Allied judges, they would live a life of maximum difficulty in Spandau, and they would live it for every hour of their sentences. Such was clear from the moment they arrived. The former leaders of Hitler's Reich were assigned numbers in the order by which they entered the prison. The numbers would be their official names for the remainder of their sentences, and they would wear them on the backs of all clothing as follows:

| | |
|---|---|
| Prisoner No. 1 | Baldur von Schirach |
| Prisoner No. 2 | Karl Dönitz |
| Prisoner No. 3 | Konstantin von Neurath |
| Prisoner No. 4 | Erich Raeder |
| Prisoner No. 5 | Albert Speer |
| Prisoner No. 6 | Walther Funk |
| Prisoner No. 7 | Rudolf Hess |

Two issues that would strike anyone as harsh concerned the inability of prisoners to have surgery outside the prison (until 1956, nearly a decade after their arrival) and the utter inability of prisoners to challenge any aspect of their own sentences. Walther Funk, the former Reich economics minister and Reichsbank president, provides a case in point for each problem. Funk was a thoroughly unsympathetic figure who became even less sympathetic during his trial at Nuremberg. U.S. prosecutor Telford Taylor described him as a "pasty, pudgy... blubbering... pitiful wreck of a man who had fallen beneath respect and knew it."[37]

Born in 1890 in East Prussia, Funk began his career as a journalist during Germany's imperial period, focusing on financial news. By 1921, he had become editor of the *Berliner Börsenzeitung* and gained the reputation as an authority on economic questions, though much of his reputation was built on nationalist bromides such as the argument that reparations owed to France and Belgium after 1919 were wholly responsible for Weimar Germany's chronic economic problems.[38] In 1931, Funk met Hitler, and, deeply impressed, he quickly joined the Nazi Party and held a number of positions thereafter thanks to his background in economics and journalism. In May 1931, he was an editor of the party's political-economic press service while acting as a party liaison to major industrialists. In July, he became Hitler's personal economic adviser. Once the Nazis came to power in 1933, Funk worked as Hitler's government press chief, achieved the rank of state secretary in Joseph Goebbels's Propaganda Ministry owing to his organizational work there (Funk claimed at Nuremberg to admire the "absolute genius" with which Goebbels conducted his propaganda), and was deputy president in the Reich Chamber of Culture.[39] At Nuremberg in 1946, he accepted no responsibility for anything he did in these offices, since he was not a cabinet member. On the other hand, he defended the Reich Chamber of Culture by noting – during his defense – that "Jews had a particularly strong influence on cultural life, and their influence seemed to me particularly dangerous... because [of] tendencies which I felt to be... un-German."[40] He

7. Rudolf Hess with Walther Funk during Heroes Day, Munich, March 1935. Photograph courtesy of National Archives and Records Administration (Heinrich Hoffmann Collection).

also admitted to having made a speech justifying the Kristallnacht pogrom in November 1938 as a spontaneous "explosion of indignation" owing to "a criminal Jewish attack against the German people."[41]

Funk's true rise came after 1937 when Hitler decided that the time had come to relieve the minister of economics and Reichsbank president Hjalmar Schacht of his duties thanks to disagreements concerning the financing of rearmament and the German trade balance. Funk became minister of economics in February 1938 and Reichsbank president in January 1939. A less likely choice could hardly have been made. Funk was known less for his economic wizardry than for his ceaseless philandering, his touch on the piano, his card playing, and his love of a good party. Funk was chosen because he was willing as a faithful stooge to submit both of his new offices to Hermann Göring's Four Year Plan apparatus in preparing Germany for war.[42] It was this willingness to be a sop to others that led to his conviction at Nuremberg and perhaps, ironically, his escape of the noose as well, for as Telford Taylor explained, "Funk's greatest asset was that it was hard to think that anyone could be afraid of him."[43]

Funk's lowest moment (in a series of them) at his trial came when U.S. prosecutor Thomas Dodd confronted him with evidence that SS deposits of valuables taken from slaughtered Jews were placed in Reichsbank vaults from 1942 to 1944 with Funk's agreement. These shipments consisted of gold and jewels taken from Jews in the East but also rims of glasses, candlesticks, and dental work. Dodd's evidence came from a few quarters. One piece of evidence was a film made by the U.S. Army of some of the loot. Another consisted of two signed affidavits – one by Funk's own vice president in the Reichsbank, Emil Puhl, and the other from SS-Obergruppenführer Oswald Pohl, chief of the SS Economic Administration Main Office. Puhl said that in the summer of 1942,

> Funk told me that he had arranged with *Reichsführer* [Heinrich] Himmler to have the Reichsbank receive in safe custody, gold and jewels for the SS. Funk directed that I should work out the arrangements with Pohl, who... administered the economic side of the concentration camps.
>
> I asked Funk what was the source of the gold, jewels, banknotes and other articles to be delivered by the SS. Funk replied that it was confiscated property from the Eastern Occupied Territories and that I should ask no further questions.... Funk stated that we were to go ahead with the arrangements for handling the material, and that we were to keep the matter absolutely secret.
>
> ... deliveries were made from time to time, from August 1942, throughout the following years.... The material deposited by the SS included jewelry, watches, eye-glass frames, dental gold and other gold articles in large quantities, taken by the SS from Jews, concentration camp victims and other persons. This was brought to our knowledge by SS personnel who attempted to convert this material into cash, and who were helped in this by the Reichsbank personnel with Funk's approval and knowledge.
>
> From time to time, in the course of my duties, I visited the vaults of the Reichsbank and observed what was in storage. Funk also visited the vaults from time to time.[44]

Oswald Pohl's affidavit was worse. Pohl remembered two deals conducted at Himmler's insistence with Funk. "One deal," Pohl said, "concerned clothing from persons killed in concentration camps." "The other," said Pohl, "concerned... jewelry, rings, gold teeth, foreign exchange, and other articles of value from the possessions of people, particularly Jews, who had been killed in concentration camps." Himmler wanted these goods deposited in the Reichsbank, and Pohl claimed that he met personally with Funk on the clothing issue for about ten minutes and that the discussion was friendly, with Funk agreeing to SS demands. The issue of Jewish gold was handled in a discussion between Pohl and Emil Puhl. Oswald Pohl claimed that he himself saw a portion of the Jewish valuables "when... Funk and Vice-President Puhl invited us to an inspection of the Reichsbank vaults.... After we had inspected the various valuables in the vaults of the Reichsbank, we went upstairs... in order to have lunch with Reichsbank President Funk.... I sat beside Funk and we talked, among other things about the valuables which I had seen in his vaults."[45]

Neither Funk nor his attorney, Dr. Fritz Sauter, had been prepared for these affidavits when they were presented at Nuremberg. Sauter tried to have both of them excluded; Puhl's on the grounds that he had not seen a German-language copy before its presentation in court and Pohl's on the grounds that Pohl was a known murderer. Both affidavits were admitted anyway, and Funk's entire façade of knowing nothing about the Jewish gold fell apart with their presentation. He insisted that both Puhl (for whose honesty he had just vouched) and Pohl were slanderers and liars. "On no account," he said, "will I take this responsibility.... These things were news to me.... I personally had nothing to do with it all."[46] Fighting for his own life in his closing statement, Funk understood that the loot in his own vaults was the unbearable weight that would pull him to the bottom. But he could do little better in defending himself:

> Until the time of the trial, I did not know and did not suspect that among the assets delivered to the Reichsbank were enormous quantities of pearls, precious stones, jewelry, gold objects and even spectacle frames, and – horrible to say – gold teeth. This was never reported to me and I never noticed it.... I never saw these things.
>
> ...the grave would have been a better place for me than this tormented life, this life full of suspicions, slanders and vulgar accusations.[47]

*Hamlet* it was not. The point, however, was that Funk's entire case in his own eyes had come to depend on his counteraccusation that Puhl and Pohl were liars. Yet as U.S. prosecutor Robert Kempner said regarding the Pohl affidavit, "even murderers sometimes tell the truth." The judges agreed. They unanimously found Funk guilty on Counts II, III, and IV of the Nuremberg indictment. Funk received a life sentence, with Soviet judge Nikitschenko dissenting and voting for death.

The delay in moving the condemned men to Spandau meant that Funk was still in Nuremberg to follow the proceedings of subsequent trials carried out by the U.S. military authorities including the case against Oswald Pohl and his subordinates in the SS Economic Administration Main Office. Pohl's defense attorney was Alfred Seidl who had just had one client, Hans Frank, hanged and come within a hair of a having a second, Rudolf Hess, sharing the same fate. As part of his equally incompetent defense of Pohl, Seidl on June 2, 1947, placed before his client the same affidavit that had been used against Funk. Now that Pohl was the defendant and his own affidavit was used against him, Pohl swore that it was all untrue. He had been badly tortured by his British captors before his interrogation, he now said, and thus had not even known at the time what statements he was making.[48] There was more. Emil Puhl was one of the defendants in the U.S.-prosecuted "Ministries Case" at Nuremberg, in which government ministers were tried for their complicity in German war crimes. The film of Jewish loot used by Dodd against Funk was not admitted into evidence against Puhl, and for his part in his government's crimes, Puhl would eventually receive a comparatively easy sentence of five years. Much of this was related to Funk by Sauter while Funk was still in Nuremberg. And according to Funk, Kempner had said after the international trial that the Pohl affidavit was the key piece of evidence convicting him.

Funk was sure that these developments offered the chance of a new trial or even a dismissal of his case. From October 1948 to May 1953, he repeatedly petitioned the Spandau Prison governors, asking to see Sauter and then Rudolf Aschenauer, another attorney enlisted by Funk's wife Louise, perhaps best known for defending the infamous Otto Ohlendorf at Nuremberg during the U.S.-prosecuted case against officers of the Einsatzgruppen – the murder squads that carried out Hitler's racial war in the Soviet Union. In December 1953 and November 1955, Funk tried to write the Allied and Soviet governments themselves. Funk's arrogant and annoying tone never evoked compassion. He doggedly maintained his innocence of any wrongdoing: As he wrote to the prison governors on May 16, 1950, when requesting a visit from Aschenauer:

> The interview with my lawyer is necessary to discuss with him the steps which must be undertaken . . . with the Allied governments . . . to bring an annulment of the Nuremberg sentence which wrongly condemned me. . . . I make this request after having suffered imprisonment – even though innocent – for nearly four years.[49]

The prison directors never once allowed a lawyer to visit Funk, nor did they allow Funk to correspond with Sauter or Aschenauer by mail, nor did they allow him to sign a power of attorney so that they might somehow pursue his case. In fact, they never answered a single one of Funk's letters. A letter from Funk to his wife, in which he claimed to have been wrongly convicted "on the basis of perjury and false documents" was censored and returned with the offensive material removed and a warning that Funk "is not to write such things in the future."[50]

Whether or not subsequent statements by Pohl or others might have helped Funk, a man who deserved little empathy, is not the point here. It was Funk's misunderstanding of his own case that led him to believe that he was convicted solely on the basis of an affidavit or two. Crucial is the fact that the Soviets would allow nothing to occur in Spandau that might threaten the legitimacy of the verdicts including discussions with lawyers or petitions to higher authorities. Thus, in his ten years in Spandau, Funk was never allowed a word of spoken or written communication with his attorneys. When the issue was discussed in the governors' meetings beginning in October 1948, Soviet Governor Kartmasov brusquely stated that the decisions of the International Tribunal were final – there could be no petitions or appeal – and that the Allied Control Council had reviewed the sentences after the trial anyway. The three Allied prison governors did not question the Nuremberg verdicts either. But they wanted to send Funk's petition to the Allied Control Council because, as prison governors, they had no authority or expertise in dealing with such a petition, which was considered proper under U.S., British, and French law. Because there was no Allied Control Council that included the Soviets after 1948, the matter was shelved permanently.[51] Petitions by Aschenauer to interview Funk in 1952 and 1953 in connection with West German denazification proceedings were likewise denied on the grounds, enumerated by the Soviets, that "no German judicial authority has the right to revise or cast doubt on [the International Military Tribunal] decisions.[52] The episode was no credit to Allied justice's ability to handle posttrial petitions, especially since Louise Funk told anyone who would listen that her husband had been convicted on lies by Pohl.[53] Yet the Allies were never prepared to act on Funk's rather flimsy appeal. From 1948 forward, they had far larger worries.

Funk was also in the middle of the struggle regarding emergency surgery because, by any reasonable standard, he was the sickest man in Spandau. It was another surprising oversight in the drafting of the Spandau regulations that no one discussed hospital facilities when everyone knew that men who were already old at the time of their sentencing could only get older in the prison. On their committal in July 1947, von Neurath, aged 74, was noted to have hypertension and arteriosclerosis, and Raeder, aged 71, had a hernia condition controlled somewhat ineffectively by a truss. But Funk, aged 57, was a wreck. No attempt will be made here to explain Funk's 557-page handwritten medical file from the Spandau records. It would cause anyone besides an experienced urologist to wince.[54] Suffice it to say that as a result of gonorrhea and diabetes, Funk was a very sick man long before he arrived at Spandau. Chronic blockage of the urinary tract meant that during the Nuremberg trial itself Funk had to undergo a painful catheterization procedure once a week to drain his bladder. Even before he was moved to Berlin, American doctors recommended surgery as soon as possible to remove blockages.[55] Colonel Andrus apparently refused to make the arrangements, which led to a further memo by the U.S. doctors to the effect that "We will try and carry prisoner Funk without an operation until his transfer to Berlin."[56]

The delay did not help. By January 1948, Lieutenant Colonel F. T. Chamberlain, the U.S. medical officer in Spandau, noted that Raeder was a "surgical risk every hour of the day and every day of the week," and that Funk would at the very least need his bladder drained periodically through catheterization.[57] But where would such procedures occur? The Allies were aware of the political and even moral need to provide the prisoners with the best possible medical care. Immediately after the prisoners arrived at Spandau, General Jean Ganeval, the French commandant in Berlin, told his superiors that France's best army surgeons had to be made available in Berlin

8. Walther Funk during his trial at Nuremberg. Photograph courtesy of the National Archives and Records Administration.

during the French months in charge of the prison.[58] And the Allied doctors naturally wanted surgical procedures performed in the sterile environment of a military hospital in Berlin. The Soviet medical officer, Lieutenant Colonel Tyuryayev, insisted from the start that an operating theater be created in the prison itself with the nation in the chair providing sterile instruments as needed. Such would obviate the need to move prisoners outside the prison for surgery. The Soviets were already concerned that prisoners who left the prison on medical grounds might never return. But the idea of performing operations in a prison cell did not sit well with the other doctors, particularly since there were four military hospitals in Berlin, all of which had modern X-ray equipment, laboratories, trained specialists, nurses, and so forth. "It is foolish and dangerous," Chamberlain argued, "to carry out an operation in the prison when we have the hospitals of the four allied nations in Berlin."[59]

Warnings of foolishness and danger would of course not move Moscow one way or the other. Thus, upon inspection of every possible room in the prison cell bloc building (but not the hospital building in the complex), the medical officers chose the room best physically suited to conduct surgery. In a macabre twist, the new operating room would be the prison's execution chamber in which strangulations and beheadings had recently taken place. Though the medical officers thought that the chamber could be converted for surgery, the prospective patients themselves were far less sanguine about operations in a room from which no inmate had ever emerged alive. Funk, when told he would have to have an operation in the (still unconverted) execution chamber, refused surgery altogether. Tyuryayev suggested to the other doctors that Funk be forced to submit. Forcing patients to have surgery against their will, the Soviet doctor learned to his disappointment, was not a part of postwar Western medical ethics. But when the issue was referred to the Kommandatura Legal Committee, the authorities ruled that "under no circumstances would a prisoner be removed from the prison." The execution chamber, on which little work had been done by early 1948, was swiftly converted for use as an operating theater and recovery room.[60]

Even so the Soviets were suspicious of Allied medical advice, believing medical care to be something of a luxury for the inmates. By May 1948, Funk began hemorrhaging. With his blood pressure low and his white count high, he would need an emergency blood transfusion. Soviet doctors then questioned the amount of blood to be transfused, arguing that the 1,200 cc prescribed by the other three doctors was excessive and that Louise Funk, then living in Bavaria, need not be informed about her husband's serious medical condition.[61]

The transfusion was carried through (with complications that later resulted in partial blindness for Funk), but the other unresolved issue was who would perform surgery if needed. The British medical officer, Colonel William J. F. Craig, had suggested German surgeons with top reputations, reasoning that "if an operation were to go badly it would perhaps be better if the responsibility for this was placed on the Germans." The Soviets would not agree. Allied specialists would be called in if needed, and if the French, British, and Americans refused to provide sterile instruments in protest of the surgical conditions, then the surgeon could bring his own.[62] Indeed French and Soviet surgeons came to Spandau to examine Funk in May 1948.

Against an uncomfortable political backdrop, which is described later, Raeder was the first inmate to undergo surgery in the execution chamber on May 19, 1949, for his hernia condition after being warned of the risks caused by his age. Funk had bladder surgery there in October 1949, whereupon the Soviets complained that he should quickly return to his cell rather than convalesce in a hospital bed adjacent to the execution chamber.[63] And in fact his condition did not improve much. In the months ahead, Funk needed catheterization three times per month, antibiotics to fight terrible bladder infections, and strong pain killers such as morphine to make it all bearable. According to the chief warder's log book, Funk skipped work detail and remained in bed whenever he needed to do so. Even the Soviets by 1951 agreed that he should have twenty-four hour bed rest following his procedures and that the nightly bulb should not be switched on so often so that he could sleep. By this time, the French doctors were convinced that Funk's problems were due to an inflamed appendix, and they convinced Funk of the same.[64] In June 1952, Funk had his appendix removed, also in the execution chamber, but the urinary and bladder blockage and infections remained. It would not be until September 1954 – more than two years later and in conjunction with other agreements described in Chapter 3 in this book – that Funk could have a risky prostatectomy in the British military hospital. By then, none of the Allied medical officers would take responsibility for operations performed in the prison.[65]

The bitterest argument between the Allies and the Soviets in the earliest days of the prison concerned the amount of food the inmates would receive. In the Kommandatura, the argument until April 1948 centered on whether the prisoners should be fed in accordance with Berlin Ration Card Number 2 which was for physical laborers (1,167 grams at 2,202 Calories per day, favored by the Western Allies) or Ration Card Number 3 which was for nonlaborers (1,032 grams, 1,887 Calories per day, favored by the Soviets). In fact, 60 percent of the Berlin population at the time lived officially on Ration Card Number 3 with only heavy laborers receiving the rations prescribed by Card 2. Though Berliners had access to supplements through the black market or home-grown vegetables, even British officials noted that "It appears unreasonable that convicted war criminals should receive higher rations than a Berlin housewife, for example, who has to run a home." On the other hand, the prisoners' decline in weight and potential illness from malnutrition would be an Allied responsibility. The British prison staff worried that Dönitz resembled "one of the Belsen victims."[66] And Germans in other prisons were allowed to receive food parcels from their families. The Soviets were unmoved. The Spandau prisoners did not perform strenuous labor, and as the Soviet member of the Kommandatura Legal Committee put it, "it [is] inadmissible to create any privileges in the feeding of major war criminals in comparison to the working population of Berlin, since this would profane anti-fascists and all honorable citizens of Germany struggling to uproot fascism"[67] Because conditions within the prison were to remain secret, it is not clear how the number of Calories ingested by prisoners there would have become public knowledge, but this was the Soviet position from which they would not willingly budge.

The need to compromise meant that the prisoners would receive rations as per Card Number 2 on days they worked, so most worked every day with varying degrees of effort. Only Hess had his rations reduced to Card Number 3 at one point, this owing to his determination not to work at all.[68]

But even the 2,200 Calories provided by Card Number 2 was not much. Strict adherence to the current ration cards of occupied Berlin meant that the prisoners lost weight in their first months in Spandau – (six and a half to fifteen and a half pounds) each by December 1947. Speer noted in his *Diaries* that he bent over after meals to pick up his crumbs from the floor of his cell. "For the first time in my life," he said, "I am discovering what it means not to have enough to eat." Caught sneaking a raw cauliflower from the garden during a daily search after garden work, Speer received a week in the punishment cell without reading and writing privileges.[69] In September, a small fire in the garden lit to burn dead leaves was found to have potatoes in it by a British warder. Hess admitted that he had placed the potatoes there to roast on the expectation that he would – his self-described attacks of amnesia notwithstanding – remember to fetch the potatoes later.[70]

Among the Spandau medical officers, the argument over Calories was bitter because the doctors could see that the prisoners were dramatically losing weight. Von Neurath, for example, weighed 163 pounds in August 1947. By November 1948, he weighed 137 pounds.[71] Dönitz had sunk from 150 to 125 pounds over the same period.[72] Speer's diary notes that by April 1948 he had dropped to 146 pounds – forty pounds below his normal weight and his lowest weight to date. "I don't dare lose much more," he wrote, and yet he was in the habit of giving Dönitz, "who is eternally hungry," part of his bread.[73] By August Speer spoke of "constant hunger," slightly appeased by British warders who snuck food to the prisoners and the chance to quickly munch fallen nuts in the garden.[74] Hess, whose hypochondria prompted constant visits by doctors who could find nothing physically wrong with him, was noted in December 1948 to suffer from "no abnormal findings except definite malnutrition."[75] British medical officer G. W. B. Shaw had noted in January 1948 that German prisoners in Allied prisons in the Western zones were allowed to receive food parcels from relatives. Why could the Spandau prisoners not receive extra food?

In fact, the Soviets on the Kommandatura Food Committee wanted to reduce the daily intake at Spandau even more, to Ration Card No. 3, regardless of work performed by the prisoners, "as these were the same [rations] received by ordinary German prisoners doing the same amount of work." The Soviet contingent in Spandau argued, moreover, that the weight loss by the prisoners was due not to their low caloric intake but rather the moral burden of their guilt.[76] Silly as this argument seems, it might have been aimed at removing the issue of Calories from the purview of the medical board, since the Allied doctors agreed that if food were made a health issue then the prison governors should not be allowed to veto medical decisions concerning it. Yet Major M .C. Volkov, the new Soviet medical officer, pointed out that even a medical prescription of higher food rations would need unanimous approval of the medical board, which, he warned, would surely not come.[77]

In the meantime, the medical officers could only argue while the prisoners became slimmer. Lieutenant Colonel Chamberlain suggested that the lowest allowable weight for each prisoner be fixed and that the prisoners be maintained at that weight. He also had the prisoners weighed constantly. And when Volkov complained that the regulations only called for the prisoners to step on the scales twice per month, Chamberlain shot back that he and the other Allied doctors could "weigh the prisoners a hundred times if they wanted."[78] For the moment, rations remained where they were, and Raeder's prescription of ten grams (a third of an ounce) of extra butter per day in October 1948 only brought Soviet ire.[79] It was not a good sign headed toward the break between the Allies and Soviets in Berlin.

## BEHIND THE BLOCKADE

The Soviet blockade of Berlin in June 1948 complicated all matters at Spandau, none of which ran smoothly even before the breakdown of Four-Power control in Berlin. But in a strange way Spandau Prison continued to function as though it were an island of isolated stability oblivious to the crisis beyond its walls. The external prison guard continued to change each month and inside the cell bloc, warder teams of mixed nationality routinely changed every eight hours. Pastor Casalis came and went each week, and the barber came and went each day. One reading the daily warder log books sees little evidence that the first global crisis of the Cold War was raging beyond the prison walls. In fact, the prisoners themselves seem to have been unaware of the breakdown in Allied-Soviet relations until January 1949. "The conflict," Speer noted more than a half year after the blockade was in place, "has led to disputes over access routes to Berlin. Now Berlin is said to be blockaded."[80] On the other hand, the prison personnel surely wondered what the blockade would mean for the prison. Allied warders in their daily kitchen inspections in June 1948 began to count the loaves of bread while calculating how long the food there might last.[81] Later in June, a U.S. Army truck arrived to remove American property from the prison.[82] In July, the chief U.S. warder Harvey B. Fowler reported uncomfortably that the new Soviet doctor had arrived and that he and the new Soviet governor, Kartmasov, spoke to one another in hushed tones for a half hour in the prison dispensary.[83]

But if anything had become clear, it was that the Soviets had no plans to leave Spandau as they had left the other agencies of Four-Power governance in Berlin. And during the months of the blockade and airlift, the Soviets became grotesquely compulsive concerning the prison regulations. Possibly they saw any relaxations in the regulations as a precursor to the Allies freeing the Spandau prisoners altogether. War crimes issues in general were not running smoothly in 1948 and 1949. Most irritating to Moscow was the British stance on war crimes trials for notorious Field Marshals Gerd von

Rundstedt, Erich von Manstein, and Walther von Brauchitsch, all of whom were in British custody. The Soviets insisted beginning in March 1948 that the British hand over the three generals for trial for crimes against Soviet troops whereupon the British government refused. Bitter arguments followed in the Houses of Commons and Lords as to whether the Field Marshals should be tried at all, and though the Labour government felt it had no alternative but to try von Manstein before a British tribunal in Hamburg, opposition groups led by Churchill had helped with his defense, prompting complaints from the Soviet newspaper *Pravda* that the former Prime Minister was working for the release of the "Hitlerist Murderer Manstein."[84] During the Manstein trial in Hamburg in 1949, the Communist press in East Germany complained that von Manstein's attorneys blamed the German army's victims in the Soviet Union rather than the German army itself for the atrocities of the latter. "The course of the trial," it continued, "points to the tendency . . . toward a rehabilitation and glorification of Hitlerism. . . . These tendencies clearly [serve] the reactionary part of the German people which still harbors hopes of revenge."[85]

It is partly in this context that the feuds within Spandau should be understood. Developments in the prison had surely been followed with reasonable closeness by the Soviet commandant of Berlin, Major General Alexander Kotikov, just as it was by the other commandants. Kotikov had dramatically walked out of the Kommandatura in June with the imposition of the full Soviet blockade. But he was still stationed in the Soviet sector. In the Soviet month of July 1948 shortly after the beginning of the Soviet blockade, Kotikov removed Major Politov as the Soviet prison governor and replaced him with the higher ranking officer, Lieutenant Colonel Kartmasov. Little is known about Kartmasov beyond the fact that Kotikov installed him and that he went to unusual lengths to enforce the prison regime. Just as the Soviets had believed that the Western Allies would leave Berlin if threatened, they evidently hoped that they would leave the Spandau prisoners behind as well should life there become difficult enough.

It was a foolish strategy on a number of counts. Just as the Allies were determined to remain in Berlin, they remained determined not to abandon the seven prisoners, for whom they already felt some empathy, to what would clearly be Soviet mistreatment under a harsh regime that would include slow starvation, inadequate medical care, and solitary confinement. And just as the Allies would challenge the blockade with the airlift that began on June 26, 1948, they would challenge Soviet demands at Spandau with thoughts of removing the prisoners outright from Berlin. Moreover, the Soviets by their actions achieved what most would have thought impossible only three years earlier. They turned major Nazi war criminals into sympathetic victims before the eyes of the very Western public that they had tried to impress with war crimes trials in the first place.

On the first day of the next American month in the chair, August 1, 1948, Kartmasov appeared at the serving of the prisoners' breakfast and then visited the kitchen. He made it a habit to visit the kitchen thereafter, ordering that the food served the prisoners be weighed by grams. It was odd, even at Spandau, for a governor to act this way. The warders inspected the kitchen each day, and food in August was the responsibility of the Americans. Kartmasov's actions meant that at various meals the American governor Major Maxwell Miller, the French governor René Darbois, and the British governor Colonel R. B. Burke-Murphy began to show up to ensure that the prisoners were getting their rations.[86]

In governors' meetings in August, Kartmasov complained repeatedly that meals served by the U.S. authorities on various days had exceeded prescribed rations. Arguments between the governors raged for hours in weekly meetings well into November 1948 on the relationship between food weight and food calories, whether cooks should be fired for providing too many grams, whether the Berlin *Magistrat* or the Four Powers themselves should supply the food to the cooks, whether the weight of vegetables should be the precooked weight (without water) or postcooked weight (with water), and whether the Allied doctors could prescribe higher rations without the threat of the Soviet governor's veto. And in November, the next Soviet month in the chair, the food served to the prisoners was noticeably poor and sparse.[87]

The absurdity of a senior Red Army officer arguing with local cooks while bending over a scale each day to weigh dried broccoli as the threat of World War III loomed above his head should not obscure the bitterness of the episode. On the contrary, it reveals the implicit Soviet belief that they could make Four-Power trusteeship over the prison unbearable for the Allies as well as the Soviet concern that if the line were crossed on something as basic as food portions, then the entire Spandau regime could fall apart, and seven dangerous men could return to the political fold in Germany. Such would, at the very least, cause a rethinking of the legitimacy of Nuremberg itself. But it also showed that the Soviets were at Spandau to stay.

It all had its effect on the prisoners, too. In October 1948, von Neurath complained to the governors that he had stopped digging in the garden because he was "weakened by insufficient nourishment" whereupon a young Russian warder "in a rude tone," commanded "No. 3 Work On!"[88] It is characteristic of the aristocratic von Neurath that the rudeness of a commoner bothered him more than the prospect of his own starvation. Regardless, the Legal Committee of the rump Kommandatura noted that at the end of November 1948, the seven prisoners were "in a very reduced physical and mental state due to the harsh manner in which the Soviet authorities interpreted the prison regulations and to the poor quality of the food provided during that month."[89] In the middle of the month the U.S. prison governor Maxwell Miller complained to Colonel Frank Howley, now the U.S.

commandant in Berlin, that "imposing an unbearably harsh routine upon the prisoners . . . will inevitably lead to early physical and mental breakdown for some of them, and in all probability all of them if continued for a much longer period of time."[90]

The question of what to do about Spandau in 1948 was complicated by pressures from western Germany itself. In the wretched immediate postwar world in which cigarettes and chocolates were currency, few Germans cared about the seven prisoners in Spandau much less about what they were eating. And there was no German government to press for better treatment or for their release. The only major concerns came from the families of the prisoners, and most of these families were of no political or social importance. One family, on the other hand, had the means and connections necessary to channel complaints about Spandau – von Neurath's.

More will be said on von Neurath in the next chapter, but for now it can be noted that his aristocratic background and his estate in Württemberg still provided a certain amount of stature in western Germany. Baroness Marie von Neurath (his wife) and Winifred von Mackensen (his daughter) would spark the early West German campaign against the Four-Power prison.[91] The family never pressed for the betterment of conditions or the release of all the prisoners. Neither Funk nor Raeder ever earned a line in the family's numerous letters to German and British personalities (though to be fair it is doubtful whether the von Neurath women knew much about the other prisoners). Only the Baron himself interested them. This is understandable – wives and children of prisoners cared primarily about their own husbands and fathers. Yet there seems to have been an implicit understanding that von Neurath was not quite like the other prisoners thanks to his noble stature, and that improved treatment or even release for von Neurath would confirm that neither he nor his family had been so tainted with Nazism as the rabble who now made up his next door neighbors. But in raising the issue of von Neurath, the family also raised the issue of conditions at Spandau, especially since they exaggerated the harshness of these conditions on von Neurath himself while consciously attempting to turn his case into a humanitarian rather than a legal issue. In the shadow of the Berlin blockade, it all had an impact.

Von Neurath's career as a diplomat, particularly as ambassador to London from 1930 to 1932 and foreign minister until 1938 still provided connections abroad, particularly in Great Britain. These contacts ranged from anti-Communists who had clumsily advocated appeasement of Germany before the war and a close relationship afterward at nearly any price; to clerics who opposed Nazism and Communism in equal measure as evil regimes ruling over good people and who now called for a generous spirit of Christian forgiveness toward Germans in the postwar world; to moral relativists unbothered by much the Germans had done under the Nazis. The von Neurath family's initial contact was Lady Nancy Astor, the Virginia-born expatriate who, after marrying into the wealthy and connected British family, became Britain's first female Member of Parliament (MP) in 1919. Lady Astor was famous for her advocacy of women's suffrage and temperance laws; her legendary social gatherings at the Astor family estate at Cliveden; and a few mildly clever quotations (e.g., "I married beneath me. All women do.") A staunch anti-Communist and polite antisemite, Lady Astor had been a vocal advocate of peaceful relations with Hitler's Germany before the war. She commented to the *New York Times* in 1937 that "if the Jews are behind [anti-German feeling in the United States] they are going too far, and they need to take heed." She remained one of Neville Chamberlain's staunchest backers after the October 1938 Munich agreement that triggered Czechoslovakia's dismemberment, repeatedly interrupting Churchill during the latter's famous critique of Chamberlain's policy in the House of Commons.[92] After the war, Lady Astor traveled to America and speedily insulted the black population with her fond reminiscences about her family's black servants. She then commented that there were too many Jews in New York and that frankly, "I don't care how many Jews are killed in Palestine," since the entire British debacle there was controlled by Jews in the United States.[93]

Thus it was that Baroness Marie quickly wrote Lady Astor on learning of the latter's tour of Germany in November 1947. Marie emphasized her husband's status as a "political prisoner" while complaining that the treatment "is that of common, not of political prisoners." Marie then complained that he had not enjoyed a church service in three months; that he was awoken every five to ten minutes at night; that his children were not allowed to write him; that he had not had a decent meal since arriving in Berlin; that he was "dreadfully neglected" despite impending deafness and blindness. "A pity Sir Neville Henderson is dead," wrote Marie, referring to the last peacetime British ambassador to Berlin who had empathized with German territorial aims before his death in 1942. "He was a good friend of ours and could tell a lot about my husband's work for your country as Foreign Minister in Berlin."[94] Nancy quickly intervened with her contacts in the Foreign Office on her return from Germany. Shortly afterward, Marie wrote Lord Halifax, Britain's foreign secretary under Chamberlain, complaining about her husband's poor health and bad treatment and raising the possibility of moving him to U.S. custody in Stuttgart. Adding what was supposed to be a heart-tugging note, Marie pointed to their home "full of dogs, [which] all miss their imprisoned master." Halifax responded. "I have always thought," he wrote to the Foreign Office, "that the old man had a rather rough deal."[95]

Winifred von Mackensen was even more distressed. Her marriage into the prominent Prussian aristocratic von Mackensen family had once seemed a fine coup. Later it seemed less so. Her father-in-law, the aged Field Marshal August von Mackensen, Germany's only field marshal after President Paul von Hindenburg's death in 1934, was uneasy with the Nazis' violent methods but allowed himself to be used as a stage prop at public functions to give Hitler legitimacy among the aristocracy and the army. Hitler had bought the old man's loyalty with a Prussian landed estate in 1935.[96] Winifred's husband, Hans-Georg von Mackensen, served as Hitler's ambassador to Italy from 1937 to 1943. His job in Rome included the demand that the Italian government hand over those Jews seeking refuge in the Italian-administered areas in southern France in March 1943. The Italians, von Mackensen had complained to Berlin at the time, were governed by "sentimental humanitarianism, which is not in accord with our harsh epoch."[97] With Germany's defeat, Winifred's father-in-law was dead; the new von Mackensen estate was gone; and Hans-Georg was quickly arrested by the French and held in Überlingen, where he died in 1947.[98] In her letter to Lord Halifax, Baroness Marie played up the fact that Winifred was now a lonely widow. Winifred seems to have known better than to mention her husband. But she used a variety of channels toward London to have her father released.

Winifred's main channel ran through the Evangelical bishop of Württemberg Theophil Wurm, one of the most important German figures in the U.S. occupation zone. Wurm was not a Nazi. He had been placed under house arrest by the Nazi government in 1934 because he opposed the creeping Nazi dominance of German Protestantism. Wurm had also opposed the Nazi program of murdering the handicapped. On the other hand, Wurm was, like many other German Evangelical leaders, fiercely nationalist, staunchly anti-Communist, and antisemitic to the point where he had welcomed Hitler's rise to power while defending – even in the wake of the Kristallnacht pogrom – the state's right to act against alien Jewish influences. Wurm did not intervene for Germany's Jews until 1943, after he understood that mass murder was well underway. Even here, Wurm's efforts focused on Jews who had been baptized, and these quiet efforts stopped once the government threatened him.[99] And after the war, Wurm immediately and regularly intervened for German war criminals convicted at the U.S. trials at Nuremberg and Dachau – even for such wretched men as Oswald Pohl who had borne responsibility for mass murder. Wurm spoke for many Germans who believed that war crimes trials were fundamentally unjust in that they were seemingly based on ex post facto law, in that they represented victor's justice, in that they implied collective German guilt, in that they ignored Germany's own suffering in the war, and in that they overshadowed the need for Western nations to close ranks against Communism. Wurm based his efforts on extensive reading of defense statements, but tellingly, he never took up U.S. offers to examine prosecution evidence for himself. And when quiet efforts did not work, Wurm used the press to attack U.S. prosecutors, judges, and occupation officials.[100]

Von Neurath and his family received Wurm's special attention. Both Wurm and von Neurath himself were leading Württemberg conservatives, they were long-standing friends, and Wurm owed von Neurath a personal debt. It was von Neurath who had Wurm freed from Nazi arrest in 1934. Wurm became increasingly convinced that von Neurath's sentence was illegal thanks to Soviet participation at the trial and the Tribunal's misreading of the evidence and that von Neurath's prison sentence was inhumane.[101] Wurm wrote a number of people on von Neurath's behalf over the years from Pope Pius XII to West German Chancellor Konrad Adenauer. But at the center of Wurm's lobbying efforts for von Neurath was the Anglican Lord Bishop of Chichester in England, George Kennedy Allen Bell. Well-connected in the prewar and war years with anti-Nazi German Protestant leaders, Bell tried to distinguish (not always successfully) between a handful of Nazi tyrants on the one hand and a mass of decent Christian Germans on the other. During the war, Bell had been the German conservative resistance's chief voice in London. He tried to move the British government to open lines of communication to conservative resistance circles while opposing Allied policies, such as heavy bombing and the insistence on Germany's unconditional surrender, that could harm the resistance's chances to keep Germany geographically intact as a bulwark against the Soviets.[102] After the war, Bell, in frequent touch with Wurm, quickly became the primary voice in the House of Lords against harsh treatment of Germany and against what he viewed as one-sided and legally dubious war crimes trials. Bell emphasized Christian brotherhood, mercy, and anti-Communism between the English and German people for the future.[103] Spandau's location in the British sector of Berlin and Bell's access to the Foreign Office meant that Bell would be Wurm's primary contact concerning von Neurath's case in the late 1940s. And Wurm was never above bending the truth with Bell. In June 1947, before Hans-Georg von Mackensen's death in captivity, he thanked the Bishop of Chichester for the latter's efforts on behalf of "this brave man."[104]

All information on Konstantin von Neurath that circulated in this group filtered through the eyes of Winifred, who, along with Marie was the only person not affiliated with the prison who had actually seen him. By February 1948, Winifred had visited her father twice, and her reports formed the basis of Bishop Wurm's complaints to Bell, echoing Marie's complaints, that von Neurath's "treatment has been that of a convict and not a political prisoner." Aside from mentioning his poor health, lack of good food, and inability to write more than a letter per month while receiving brief and infrequent visits, Wurm further complained that von Neurath had to dig in the garden and glue bags together. Some of these complaints were accurate, some were not. Speer's *Diaries* show that von Neurath rather liked working in the garden, perhaps because the prison governors placed him in charge of the layout, planting, and harvesting. Unlike the other prisoners, von Neurath also

9. A smuggled photo of Dönitz and von Neurath working in the Spandau Prison garden. Published in the Munich illustrated weekly *Revue* series, "Hinter den Mauern von Spandau," by Jürgen Thorwald, 1951.

refrained from constant complaints. "Neurath," Speer noted, "remains even in this environment a nobleman of the old school, always amiable, helpful [and] modest. He never complains. That gives him a certain dignity and an authority which, however, he never exploits."[105] Nor was his health especially poor, at least in 1948. The medical board was aware of von Neurath's high blood pressure and arteriosclerosis. But discussions from the arrival of the prisoners in late 1947 to late 1951 show that Funk and Raeder were the main concerns of the doctors there. Von Neurath, despite his age, occasioned very few comments from the doctors.

And the British Foreign Office was not sympathetic to the stream of complaints from Württemberg, from Lady Astor, from Lord Halifax, from the Bishop of Chichester, or from anyone else before the Soviet blockade of Berlin. London was far more concerned with how the victims of Nazism in the Low Countries, Scandinavia, and Eastern Europe might react to an easing of prison conditions in Spandau. The Spandau regulations, added Lorna Newton, a Foreign Office clerk, did not compare unfavorably with those in

British prisons anyway. And recalling the 1947 argument with the Soviets and with the French over communal work and religious services in Spandau, Newton noted that no easing of conditions could be expected there. The Soviets and French would both use their veto to prevent any liberalization[106]

Only with the blockade did Spandau become a more urgent political issue. More letters from Württemberg in the summer of 1948 triggered parliamentary discussion and public questions why von Neurath was not receiving food packages that had been sent to him and why he and the other prisoners still had such restricted visitation and letter-writing privileges.[107] And during the blockade, Labour Party MP Richard R. Stokes of Ipswitch would become one of the major advocates of the Spandau prisoners. Stokes, who had won his seat in a by-election in 1938, ought to inspire a study of his own. Before the war, he had been a behind-the-scenes advocate of efforts to strike a deal with Hitler's Germany. On the outbreak of war in September 1939, Stokes created the Parliamentary Peace Aims Group, and in October, with Poland completely overrun, he distributed a memorandum in Commons entitled *What are we fighting for?* In March 1943, he questioned the methods and aims of British bombing in Germany to the point where some dubbed him the "MP from Hamburg."[108] Following the war, Stokes protested the Czech expulsion of Germans from the Sudetenland and the drawing of Germany's eastern border with Poland. But his chief cause during the blockade crisis in 1948 and 1949 concerned the trials of German war criminals.

His motives are mysterious. Stokes was pro-German, antisemitic, and a moral sophist to say the very least. He was the first to comfort Charlotte von Brauchitsch at the deathbed of her husband, Hitler's faithful army commander-in-chief Field Marshal Walther von Brauchitsch, in October 1948. A few months later he openly protested against the cruelty of Jewish kosher slaughter in England.[109] In 1947, he had come out against the extraditions of all German war crimes suspects to states in either Eastern or Western Europe on the basis that they could not receive a fair trial, but when pressed, he admitted that he did not think that even Nuremberg was a fair trial and that "I find the greatest difficulty in deciding who is a war criminal.... Is the man who lets off an atomic bomb a war criminal or not?" Among those who Stokes would not have extradited included Dr. Wladyslaw Dering, a Polish doctor wanted for trial in his home country for his numerous sadistic medical experiments in Auschwitz.[110] The Spandau prisoners were one of his pet causes as well, and though he was wise enough not to ask for their releases immediately, he could conflate his sympathy for them with the larger issue of human rights. "Isn't it about time," he wrote to Foreign Secretary Ernest Bevin personally in late October 1949, "that we tore up this particular quadripartite regulation and removed the prisoners to our Zone where they could be properly looked after? In the name of Humanity this ought to be done whatever the past deeds of the prisoners may have been."[111]

The increased pressure from Wurm, Bell, and voices in the House of Commons combined with the general revulsion at the blockade itself brought a slew of internal comments within the British Foreign Office to the effect that "The conditions at Spandau are no credit at all to a civilized nation," and "we may expect to hear more about this prison."[112] The question was what to do. Bevin had no sympathy with the convicted war criminals or their advocates. Against heavy opposition from Parliament, Bevin had been resolved that Field Marshal von Manstein be tried as a war criminal as late as 1949. He seems to have had no desire to break up Spandau Prison either. But he hoped for political reasons that perhaps conditions could be brought quietly into line with those at the British military prison for German war criminals at Werl. He ordered General Brian Robertson, the British military governor in Germany, to raise the issue of Spandau's regulations with the Soviets. The Soviets had already left the Control Council and Kommandatura, but Robertson was skeptical anyway after talking with the British governor at Spandau, Lieutenant Colonel R. B. Burke-Murphy. "Indeed," wrote Robertson:

> the Soviet representative [Kartmasov] wishes to make conditions still more harsh and has put forward proposals to re-impose solitary confinement, to limit the hours of sleep and rest, and to impose further restrictions in regard to library books, family visits and incoming letters.[113]

Sir Ivone Kirkpatrick, the Permanent Undersecretary for German Affairs in the Foreign Office, suggested something bolder. Negotiation, which he expected to fail, would be followed by a declaration that Four-Power administration of the prison was at an end, whereupon the prisoners would be airlifted to the British zone. But such a step carried heavy political and perhaps even military risks. "I fear, wrote one Foreign Office official

> that such a move would cause not only a vigorous row with the Russians, out of which they would make much propaganda, but would scarcely be acceptable to the United States and French Military Governors. We might possibly modify it to the extent of removing the prisoners and dividing them between prisons in the three Western Zones but even this seems a violent step which it would be difficult to defend abroad in the face of Russian propaganda.[114]

Bevin understood these concerns. He asked Robertson if negotiations stood any chance, but Robertson remained doubtful, believing that perhaps a public offensive begun in the House of Commons might do a better job of pressuring the Soviets. "The only chance of getting any alleviation," he said, "is to expose by full publicity the state of affairs and the failure of our attempts to rectify them."[115] Yet parliamentary questions and debate would only increase the pressure in London for the outright removal of the prisoners by the likes of Bell and Stokes, which Bevin wished to avoid.

As instructed by Bevin, Robertson raised the Spandau issue in early November 1948 (the Soviet month) with the other two military governors in the rump Allied Control Council. His suggestion that the Soviets be approached on improving conditions brought a daring suggestion from General Lucius D. Clay, the U.S. military governor, which mirrored Kirkpatrick's suggestion in London. It had been Clay who in June 1948 advocated an armed challenge to the Soviet blockade of Berlin by running it with armored columns. Regarding Spandau, Clay wanted to tell the Soviets during the U.S. month of December that because Moscow had abandoned the Allied Control Council "the Western Powers would in the future assume the guarding of the [Spandau] prisoners." The prisoners would then be moved to the western zones with or without Soviet consent. Clay's argument made legal sense. By leaving the Kommandatura, the Soviets had left the Four-Power prison without its legally constructed Four-Power authority. General Pierre Koenig, the French military governor in Germany, added that were Spandau in the Soviet sector of Berlin, the Soviets would have kicked the Allies out long ago.

But legal or not, Clay's scheme carried big risks for little reward. Koenig's personal comments notwithstanding, the French government did not wish to challenge the Red Army over Spandau, especially because there was no sympathy in France for any of the inmates. Any move on their behalf, said Koenig, would be interpreted as coddling the prisoners.[116] Washington was cautious for fear of military consequences. What if the Soviets began shooting? State Department officials noted that Gatow Air Base in the British sector of Berlin was only fifteen to twenty minutes away from the prison and that "it would probably take at least twenty minutes for any reinforcement from the Russian sector to arrive at the prison" should the prisoners be stolen away. Yet even in the best scenario, this was cutting matters close for the sake of seven convicted war criminals. The State Department ultimately feared that moving the prisoners to the West without Soviet consent "would have political implications... felt to be... prohibitive."[117]

Robertson next raised the possibility of a high-level approach to General Vasily Chuikov, the new Soviet military governor in Germany. An approach could alleviate political pressure in London. But Clay and Koenig argued against negotiation, ironically, because they feared the possibility of Soviet *agreement*. Soviet willingness to accept lighter prison regulations would remove the pretext for a bold Allied move later, which Clay still hoped to engineer. In the end, the three military governors accepted a compromise fashioned by Clay. During the American, British, and French months in the Spandau chair, conditions for the prisoners would be improved to some degree. In the Soviet month, they could stay the same. Such improvements could not be kept secret because Soviet warders were always on duty. But Soviet protests, Clay suggested, should be disregarded. If the Soviets wished to quit the prison they could do so – Clay hoped that they would – but the onus for leaving would be on Moscow and any propaganda benefit would belong to the Allies because they would not have broken a Four-Power arrangement over the treatment of convicted war criminals.[118] Back in London, Richard Stokes was warned not to raise the question of Spandau in Parliament before the changes took place because the need to give him an answer would give the Soviets time to take countermeasures. After the changes were implemented, however, Parliament could be told the truth – that "the Western Military Governors have decided that the prisoners in Spandau will be treated during their months of control according to civilized prison methods. This will not apply to one month in four when the U.S.S.R. Prison Governor is in the Chair."[119] It was the best that could be done.

## THE SOVIETS STAY

At Clay's direction Colonel Frank Howley informed Maxwell Miller, the U.S. prison governor, of the steps to be taken. The prisoners would receive additional Calories each day to arrest weight loss. They would be allowed to lie on their beds when they wished at any time of day regardless of Soviet objections. They would be able to receive food parcels twice per month of two kilos each. And if a prisoner were to fall critically ill, he would be moved to an Allied or German hospital so that a German surgeon could operate "under circumstances which will protect us against any . . . guilt as having . . . through intent or negligence, causing the death of a prisoner." "I will not permit," Howley continued, "this order to be vetoed by Russian obstruction or Russian delay."[120] Howley expected trouble though, and he provided Miller with "three able bodied additional wardens" while ordering Miller to call on the armed U.S. Army exterior prison guard if he felt the need. "If physical force is used by the Soviets to prevent [the improved conditions]," Howley warned, "then appropriate force will be expended to prevent interference."[121]

In fact, Howley's sweeping command could not be implemented unilaterally, and it was quickly diluted, possibly after discussion with Miller. The only truly urgent issue for the Americans was that the prisoners receive better rations to stop what was becoming dangerous weight loss. Beyond this and the provisions for prisoners to talk under supervision and rest on their beds when they wished, little could be done without violence. The Soviets would fight over two-kilo packages of food every two weeks for security reasons alone, and if rations were improved then there was no need for outside food anyway. Movement of sick prisoners to hospitals beyond the prison walls meant the possibility of transporting them past Soviet warders and possibly soldiers at gunpoint. And so the American changes, while bold enough for the moment, were sanitized of especially high risk before they were presented to the Soviets.

At the first governors' meeting of the month – December 2, 1948 – Miller announced the changes with the help of an English-Russian interpreter so that no misunderstanding could occur. Rations for the prisoners, Miller said, would be increased by 700 Calories per day. Prisoners would be able to lie down in their cells regardless of the hour. They would be allowed to speak to one another under supervision. They could receive a thirty-minute visit each month if it were to appear psychologically desirable. They would always be given indoor work during inclement weather. Finally, Miller announced a blanket statement whereby "to provide more humane treatment, other reasonable measures will be instituted if they are considered necessary to maintain the physical and mental health and wellbeing of the prisoners." The new British governor R. B. Le Cornu and French governor René Darbois announced immediately that they supported these measures.[122]

Kartmasov was caught fully off guard by Miller's announcement, thus revealing that the Soviets did not expect this particular step. The Soviet governor said nothing and immediately reported to his superior, Major General Kotikov, who sent a letter of protest to Clay. But Soviet options were few.[123] On the basis of this provocation, the Soviets could have left the prison administration as they had already left the Kommandatura and Allied Control Council with protests of American perfidy. But quitting the prison could have resulted in the removal of the prisoners or even their freedom – a possibility that the Soviets would not accept because it could vitiate the Nuremberg verdicts. At the end of the month, Kartmasov responded that the U.S.S.R. did not accept the "unilateral" U.S. changes. During their own months in the chair, he said, the Soviets would enforce previous agreements concerning the prison. U.S. actions, Kartmasov added bitterly, "were breaking down the basis of the rules in the Allied Prison."[124]

For the moment though, the Soviets were shrewder than Kartmasov showed. As the next Soviet month (March 1949) approached, the Americans expected an array of Soviet actions such as refusal to remove their external guard at the end of the month (thus preventing a changeover to the Americans), the attempted removal of the prisoners to the Soviet zone of Germany, or possibly a staged escape of the prisoners whereby Soviet sentries would shoot them in the back. At the very least, the Soviets could revert to their interpretation of the regulations, since Kartmasov remained openly opposed to the Allied treatment of the prisoners. Clay expected that "during their month of chairmanship in March the Soviets will insist upon reverting to their former inhumane treatment of these prisoners," including poor food, little exercise, and no bed rest from six in the morning to ten at night.[125] The rump Kommandatura Legal Committee discussed options for the coming Soviet month ranging from Allied warders sneaking the prisoners food to compensate for reduced Soviet rations to moving the prisoners to the West before the Soviet guard appeared.[126] Clay argued in early February and then again on March 1 that because the level of care for the prisoners was below American standards and because the problem could not be remedied in Berlin, the transfer of the prisoners to the United States [!] was "a U.S. obligation." The Four-Power administration of Spandau should be discontinued because the Soviets would refuse "to agree to revisions... which are required by the generally accepted rules of humanity."[127]

The seven prisoners themselves knew little of this argument. All they understood for the moment was that following a medical examination in December 1948 they began receiving more food including creamed soups.[128] There seems to have been a higher degree of comfort overall. By February 1949, Raeder was confident enough in the prison doctors to ask for a hernia operation despite the clear risks brought by his old age. Funk agreed to his bladder surgery later in the year.[129] As for the fate of the prison as such, the seven prisoners were dependent on the rumors circulated by the warders themselves in the atmosphere of the blockade. The warders all thought that, one way or another, Four-Power control of the prison would be dissolved.

The prisoners came round to the prediction that each prisoner would be remanded to the custody of the country that captured them. Von Schirach was surely pleased at the prospect – he had been captured by the Americans. Dönitz, Hess, Funk, and Speer would revert to British custody. Von Neurath would have gone to the French. Raeder was undoubtedly terrified because, among the seven prisoners, he alone had been captured by the Soviets – perhaps this explains his speedy request for surgery before the Soviet month of March 1949.[130]

But there was no danger of such a solution. If the prisoners could think of it then the Soviets could think of it too, and Moscow would not accept a solution whereby six of the major war criminals, especially Hess, would pass to Allied custody. The Soviets would have to live with the new arrangements as best they could. Thus, as the blockade continued into 1949, the Soviets actually softened at Spandau, apparently in fear that the Western nations might terminate the prison if they did not. Gritting their teeth, they accepted the American changes. Speer complained in his *Diaries* that though he had gained fifteen pounds by mid-January 1949 the Soviet months would surely constitute an "ascetic phase" whereby the prisoners would lose an average of six pounds each.[131] But the Soviets surprised everyone by mitigating conditions during their month. By mid-March General Clay noted, surely with disappointment, that the Soviets "have continued our improvements of the past months." "It is quite clear," he added, "that they guessed what was coming and put themselves in a position where it was very difficult to attack them." They had, Clay concluded, "stolen our thunder." Koenig, whatever his past comments, was visibly relieved: "The essential [issue] was that the lives of the prisoners be easier," he said. "I think we have nothing more to do now."[132] Koenig and Robertson both deliberately stonewalled Clay's March 2,1949, proposal that Spandau become a tripartite prison with the Soviets receiving nothing more than inspection rights.[133]

Indeed Kartmasov, surely with Kotikov's reluctant approval, agreed to some uncharacteristic kindnesses. Von Neurath was allowed to sign a power of attorney for his denazification hearing in the west to try to save the family estate even though the Soviets characteristically feared that West German denazification hearings could challenge the Nuremberg verdicts. Speer was allowed to send a letter of 1,800 words to his children. Kartmasov agreed to additional rations for Raeder, von Neurath, and Speer as per orders of the Soviet medical officer, who was usually sticky on health-related dispensations. Long visits were also allowed – an hour for Winifred von Mackensen, an hour for Louise Funk, an hour for Speer's wife Margret, and two hours for Raeder's wife Erika in connection with her husband's operation. It is true that during the blockade visiting minutes had accrued, but the Soviets still could have vetoed longer visits had they wished. And Soviet indulgence had its limits. Von Schirach was not allowed to sign a power of attorney, and Speer was not allowed to make sketches during his rest period in 1949. In sum though, the prison governors' minutes from 1949 contain some surprising Soviet agreements.[134] American visitors in November 1949, a year after serious worries about the prisoners had circulated, noted that "the prisoners all looked well-fed" and that they had "no particular complaints."[135]

By now, however, there were West German authorities who could complain on their own to the new civilian-run Three-Power Allied High Commission, which replaced the military government in 1949 and which oversaw the new West German state until full West German sovereignty in 1955. One was the new municipal government of West Berlin, formed by January 1949 as a result of the blockade, which consisted of the west's own *Magistrat* (city council) and a lord mayor, the Social Democrat Ernst Reuter. The other was the West German government in Bonn under its first Chancellor Konrad Adenauer. West Berlin's municipal authorities first protested the sheer cost of the Allied prison – a cost that they now had to bear. In October 1949, the *Magistrat*'s legal department pointed out that in 1949 alone the budget for the prison was DM 450,000 with a substantial part of that sum paying twenty-one salaried employees (including eight cooks, two waiters, and three stewards) and fifty-one hourly wage earners (including six waitresses, fourteen kitchen helpers, and ten craftsmen). The pay for these workers was up to 33 percent more than workers in the same jobs made elsewhere in the city. The high costs were also due to the housing facilities and meals provided for the warders and external guard troops who remained at Spandau each night rather than returning to their barracks. Constant repairs and maintenance were also the responsibility of the Berlin city government. Because seven regular prisoners only cost the city DM 8,000 per year, the city government at the very least wanted the wages of the prison workers cut to normal levels. Preferably the prison should be closed altogether or handed over to the *Magistrat* for its own needs, which with a shortage of prison space in West Berlin were acute.[136]

French commandant Jean Ganeval himself noted soon after the blockade the "ridiculous costs of this immense apparatus supplied by the Allies and the Germans for the imprisonment of seven war criminals." Major General Geoffrey Bourne, the British commandant, spoke of moving the prisoners to the West, but as Ganeval was quick to point out, it was dangerous to break a Four-Power agreement with the Soviets, and the movement of the inmates could only be by force.[137] The Allied impulse was thus to try to cut costs, and indeed it was only now that civilian officials closely studied the history and procedures of the Allied Prison at Spandau. On taking a detailed tour of the prison in May 1950 Edgar M. Gerlach, the head of the Prisons Division of the American High Commission under John J. McCloy, was aghast at the waste of manpower. It was Gerlach, a man with considerable prison administrative experience, who pointed out that the ratio of personnel to prisoners in Spandau was many times higher than it was at the famously secure American prison at Alcatraz. And the skewed ratio of personnel to prisoners seemed normal compared to the fact that one needed Four-Power agreement for even the tiniest deviation from the regulations or medical prescriptions. "If one had started out to establish the most unwieldy, inefficient and the most expensive prison," Gerlach concluded, "he could not possibly have done better than has been accomplished at Spandau. There are so many things wrong with this institution that it would take a memorandum of many, many pages to list them all."[138]

The Four Powers had actually tried to find a newer, less expensive facility before the blockade. The four prison governors visited a number of sites though the Soviets would not allow them to look in their own sector, possibly fearing the possibility of an Allied listening post there. In February 1948, the governors unanimously approved moving the prisoners to a facility in the French sector, but the Kommandatura was unable to agree on the move before the blockade.[139] Another possibility discussed was the reconditioning and use of the infirmary building in the Spandau complex, which in keeping with the ironic history of the prison, was not being used for hospitalization. The smaller building would demand less space while freeing up the remainder of the complex for the West Berlin government. After the blockade was lifted in May 1949, the Allies and Soviets agreed to reduce the German and United Nations prison staff from seventy-five to twenty-nine staff members. This saved the city DM 11,000 per month. Moving the prisoners to the old infirmary building would save far more money, not counting the economic benefit to the city once it could use the main building. But when Reuter heard of the estimated renovation cost of DM 170,000 in January 1950, he balked. He might not have had he prorated the cost over the next thirty-seven years.[140]

The *Magistrat*'s complaints also prompted the Kommandatura to revisit the old idea of moving the prisoners from West Berlin altogether. Though the prisoners were "men of unusual importance," the financial costs of the prison were "out of all proportion to the number of prisoners," and the political and public relations burdens were too much to bear.[141] The U.S. element of the Kommandatura in October 1949 proposed moving the six men captured by the Americans, British, and French to the west. Such would save money while guaranteeing better treatment for six of the seven prisoners.[142] General Robertson argued that all seven be moved west "on the score of humanity." Perhaps they could be moved under the pretext of necessary prison repairs, never to be returned to West Berlin. Yet the political risks remained. Ganeval argued that stealing the prisoners could not be defended legally and that in any event conditions were improving.[143] U.S. Secretary of State Dean Acheson, meanwhile, remained unwilling to consider overtly provoking the Soviets over this issue. And though Erich Raeder would never know or appreciate it, Acheson flatly rejected the plan (supported by French high commissioner André François-Poncet) of dividing the prisoners for concern of what might happen to Raeder in Soviet custody.[144]

Because the city would not pay renovation costs and because no one wished an open breach with the Soviets in which the Allies would be legally in the wrong, the best solution was again to keep the prisoners at Spandau under more improved conditions, informally implemented. Between October and December1950, small improvements included the following. The search light–style lamps on the cell door grilles were replaced with small light bulbs on the cell ceilings; part of the grille in the visitors' room was removed; books were now obtainable from any library in Berlin; hot water for daily wash-up was provided as well as a foot bath; a new hot-water heater for showers and baths was installed as was hot-air heat for the cell bloc in lieu of the old coke-burning furnace; censorship of incoming letters was speeded to three days rather than one to two weeks, and the inmates received new mattresses, pillows, and better clothing.[145] Though the Soviets held in theory to the practice of illuminating the cells four times per hour at night, the Allies sometimes lit them but once an hour. Prisoners were sometimes allowed by the Allied warders to see letters before censorship and sometimes they learned what had been censored so long as it did not compromise security. And when the chief Russian warder was on break the prisoners were allowed to visit one another in their cells. The prison's own library by the end of 1950 included four hundred books all but forty of which had been sent by family members.[146]

Spandau was still not especially pleasant. The Soviets remained stubborn more often than not, as when the four hundred words in Raeder's extra letter to his daughter in August 1950 were charged against the twelve hundred words allowed for September.[147] Raeder was also not allowed a thirty-minute visit from his wife on his seventy-fifth birthday in April 1951 despite two hours of argument by the Western governors, probably because of Erika Raeder's constant harangues to the right wing press in West Germany.[148] But conditions had surely improved to the point where the Allies considered a formal approach to the Soviets suggesting more frequent letters and visits, common dining and relaxation facilities, and more imaginative indoor work tasks such as carpentry, despite the fact that the prisoners themselves in comments to the Allied governors wanted neither additional work nor common facilities, preferring to eat alone in their cells rather than with each other.[149] As Darbois noted to the Berlin commandants, the Soviet governor that followed Kartmasov in July 1950, Major Potyomin, was the first since Darbois's arrival in 1947 to have shown any interest in the prisoners. The three Western governors had invited Potyomin for drinks, snuck him bottles of French wine, and had Russian meals prepared for him. "This guy," noted the U.S. prison governor Major Roger F. Smith, "once in a while will agree to something." Now might be the time to make Spandau into a more normal prison.[150]

The hope evaporated in 1951. In the summer of that year, the popular Munich weekly illustrated magazine *Revue* began publishing a series of eleven articles entitled "Behind the Walls of Spandau" by journalist Jürgen Thorwald (whose real name was Heinz Bongartz). The series contained detailed descriptions of the prisoners' cells, photographs of the prisoners and the prison grounds, exaggerations regarding conditions, and a highly anti-Soviet tone. To Moscow, this was a serious affair. Thorwald's work often aimed at the rehabilitation of German officers who had served Hitler, many of whom were now a part of rearmament discussions in West Germany that had intensified owing to the Communist adventure in Korea that had begun the previous year. More alarming was the fact, surely known to the Soviets, that Thorwald was closely connected with West Germany's foreign intelligence service, the Gehlen Organization, which was riddled with former German army and SS officers and which was sponsored, though never effectively controlled, by the Central Intelligence Agency.[151] The entire business prompted the Soviet installation in October 1951 of a new team of warders at Spandau commanded by a new governor, the exceptionally difficult Major Viktor Alabjev.

Relations within the prison entered a whole new phase of difficulty. Acrimony at weekly governors' meetings over the *Revue* series ran from June into November with Alabjev finally cross-examining the new U.S. governor Major Joseph L. Rice with the following question: "Do you consider the

10. The changing of the external guard at Spandau Prison, December 1951, from the Soviets to the Americans. The courteous changeover belied difficult relations inside the prison. Note that the Soviet guard is armed with machine guns. Photograph courtesy of the National Archives and Records Administration.

publication of articles on the Interallied Prison by the magazine *Revue* as an offence against the prison regulations?" Rice said that he did not. The West Germans, Rice said, had a free press.[152] Though the governors could agree that leakage of news and photos from the prison violated prison rules, the Soviets were convinced that the Americans had planted the series in *Revue* as an anti-Soviet propaganda maneuver aimed at discrediting the Nuremberg verdicts while rehabilitating Nazism at a time when West German rearmament talks were underway. Propaganda was part of the Soviets' own repertoire. Why would the Allies not do the same?

Alabjev and his staff thus became more difficult on all security-related issues. In January 1952, Alabjev demanded that the formal rule against prisoners speaking with one another again be enforced. Citing numerous recent violations, he demanded that prisoners who broke speaking regulations receive stiff punishment and that the warders who allowed and encouraged speaking also be punished. Le Cornu, Darbois, and Rice insisted that speaking had long been a custom at Spandau and that it would be "quite impossible to change the interpretation of Prison Regulations or customs which have been in existence for years."[153] The Soviet staff responded by limiting the prisoners' outdoor exercise time whenever they could do so in an effort to keep them from speaking. "Recently," Le Cornu complained, "it has been the regular practice of the Soviet Team to keep the prisoners locked up without work or exercise."[154] At the end of March 1952, an argument broke out between Soviet and French warders when the Soviet warders demanded that von Schirach, Dönitz, and Raeder stop speaking in the garden and the French warders, while swearing at the Soviets, actually ordered the German prisoners to keep talking. Alabjev demanded that chief French warder Alphonse Gerthoffer be punished, but Darbois refused commenting coolly that "the French warders had instructions to allow the prisoners to talk, to walk together, and they will fulfill these instructions in the future."[155] In February 1953, the Soviet warder Mogilnikov actually locked an American warder in von Schirach's cell while the latter two were speaking.[156]

Alabjev attacked from other directions as well. In January 1952, he complained that the American warders' help to von Neurath in going up and down stairs must stop because the prison regulations did not permit it.[157] Raeder was prevented from doing cardiovascular exercises in his cell because the regulations did not mention them. Alabjev also rejected Funk's request to have his cell light off from 10 P.M. to 6 A.M. as per the French medical officer's prescription that he have undisturbed sleep for the benefit of his health. On Darbois's ironic comment, "I presume that we should not be afraid that the prisoner [Funk] will escape from his cell at night," Alabjev became apoplectic. The governors, he said,

> were charged to keep in prison the main war criminals who are capable of committing any offense and that is why they should be under constant and severe surveillance day and night. If we leave the prisoner without surveillance for eight hours we will violate thereby the prison regulations and will create the conditions for the escape of the prisoner from jail.[158]

Arguments between British and French warders on the one hand and the Soviet warders on the other thus took place outside Funk's cell at night over the issue of lighting until October 1952. The noise bothered Funk more than the lights ever had. The French and British accused the Soviets of harassing the prisoners by switching on their lights. Alabjev countered that the offending French warder Gerthoffer was out of uniform, "looking like a cowboy or partisan."[159]

The fall and winter of 1952 brought perhaps the most ridiculous argument in the history of the prison. The British replaced Le Cornu with a new governor, Lieutenant Colonel Roy Johnson Meech, who arrived breathing the defiance of a man loath to tolerate Soviet difficulties. In the U.S. month of December 1952, Meech allowed the prisoners to fetch their dinner trays in the cell bloc simultaneously rather than by the traditional method of one by one. On the night of December 15, Alabjev entered the cell bloc as the prisoners were being served, and he abruptly ordered them all back to their cells. An argument erupted between Meech and Alabjev in front of the warders and prisoners. At the next governors' meeting, Alabjev argued that the new British procedure violated the principle of solitary confinement and was a security risk since together, the prisoners could overpower the warders, take the keys, and organize an escape from the prison. At the very least, he said, the warders should be issued truncheons to deter such thoughts. Meech argued that the prisoners should have their food while it was still hot; Alabjev refused to bend, arguing that the food was hot enough and that the British warders should be punished.[160] Prison governance had been reduced to finger pointing between Alabjev, who claimed to be the only official enforcing the regulations, and the other three governors, who accused Alabjev of violating a body of custom and practice that were in essence a part of the regulations as well.[161]

It was not an auspicious time for improvements. Yet it was at this particular time that the Allies would have to press for them since the pressure from West Germany and from the advocates of the prisoners began to reach a new intensity. On the other hand, the pattern of the prison had been set despite the split in the alliance that had once been united against Nazism. If there had ever been a time for the West to pull out of the Spandau arrangement and to take the prisoners with them, it was in the months of the Soviet blockade from mid-1948 to mid-1949. The Western Allies chose not to end the arrangement to which they themselves had agreed. In the first place, the Spandau prisoners were hardly sympathetic martyrs despite the ways in which the Soviets aimed to treat them. Paris could not be expected to lift a finger for the men that had helped occupy and exploit France. Washington, in spite of its distaste for the Soviets, was not willing to assume the political consequences of ending the Spandau arrangement. London was the only capital outside of Germany in which the seven prisoners evoked much sympathy, but it was never with the cabinet ministers such as Bevin, with whom power lay.

By not taking an alternative route, the Western Allies established a pattern whereby Spandau would remain open for the next four decades. Clay's risky proposal aside, however, the British, French, and Americans were stuck with the arrangements they had made in the days after Nuremberg. The Soviets had no intention of leaving the prison. For reasons clearly understood only to them, the remnants of the Nuremberg verdicts would be enforced to the last day regardless of the Berlin crisis, the war by proxy in Korea, the formation of NATO and two German states in 1949, and the rearmament of West Germany and the formation of the Warsaw Pact in 1955. Even the Berlin crisis of 1958 to 1961, which culminated in the building of the Berlin Wall and the Cuban Missile Crisis of 1962 would not upset the orderly changeover of duties month by month at Spandau Prison. The Western powers were never willing to test this Soviet determination, either by stealing the prisoners to the West or by attempting to force the Soviets to leave. As Albert Speer heard secondhand from a British officer, the Spandau prisoners were never worth the risk of a war.

## CHAPTER THREE

# Von Neurath's Ashes: The Battle over Memory

> "They won't release me even after my death! What good is an old man's corpse to them?"
>
> Konstantin Freiherr von Neurath, 1954

The most macabre discussion of the Cold War was surely that regarding the remains of prisoners who might die at Spandau. It was no small issue. Everyone understood how the Nazis had turned funerals into political events that celebrated martyrdom to the Nazi movement and to the nation. It was why the major war criminals sentenced to death at Nuremberg had had no funerals and why, at first, the Spandau prisoners were to have none either.

But the changing political circumstances after the Berlin blockade in which many began to view the Spandau inmates as political prisoners rather than bona fide criminals brought fear that the secret disposal of their remains would never be forgiven, particularly in West Germany. The Allies had to change the policy, if possible, so that the next of kin could receive the body. But would the Soviets go along?

Adding to the urgency of the question was the fact that Konstantin Freiherr von Neurath was expected to die first owing to his advanced age and to his declining health. Among the Spandau prisoners, von Neurath was the inmate who many in West Germany viewed most sympathetically. Even the simple fact of von Neurath's imprisonment was a political problem for the Allies by 1950. The secret disposal of his ashes should he die in Spandau could be a disaster of the first magnitude.

### THE PROBLEM OF VON NEURATH

Upright and correct, the aged Konstantin Freiherr von Neurath was the one Spandau prisoner with whom most West Germans felt sympathy. His biographer John Heineman charitably concludes that "Neurath's story is one of a man trying to tame a whirlwind which he never quite understood."[1] Von Neurath's aristocratic Swabian background and lifetime as a gentleman hunter and diplomat hearkened to old romantic notions of nobility as well as the respectable German conservatism that, thanks to its own delusions, was hijacked by the Nazis. Like many of his social order, including his one-time friend Field Marshal Paul von Hindenburg, von Neurath was no intellectual, despite serving (or perhaps because he had served) in the German diplomatic corps since 1901. Despite arranging for the abdication of the King of Württemberg during the revolutionary upheavals of 1918 in which crowns rolled in European gutters, he was no democrat either.

But as a part of the educated and ruling class, von Neurath felt a calling to serve his country regardless of the republicanism that he detested. As the Ambassador to Rome after 1922, von Neurath had formed a friendly relationship with the new fascist dictator Benito Mussolini despite his suspicions of the black-shirted rabble that had helped bring *Il Duce* to power. Serving as the German Ambassador to Great Britain from 1930 to 1932, he made the German Embassy one of the centers of London society, though he remained skeptical that the British would ever allow a rearmed Germany. In May 1932, at von Hindenburg's request, he accepted the foreign minister's portfolio in Franz von Papen's conservative "Cabinet of Barons," which he hoped would bring stability to German society while increasing its stature abroad.

But national stature to von Neurath always meant a preponderance of military power. Like most Germans, he viewed the 1919 Treaty of Versailles as a national humiliation. The borders prescribed for Germany together with the treaty's reparations and disarmament clauses were to be rejected and overthrown. Yet von Neurath also rejected the Locarno Accords of 1925, which only acknowledged Germany's western borders and the permanent demilitarization of the Rhineland while conspicuously leaving unmentioned the much-resented German borders with Poland and Czechoslovakia. Von Neurath was also openly skeptical of the League of Nations, which Germany had joined in 1926, as well as the League-sponsored disarmament talks that were underway when he became foreign minister. A small act illustrated his outlook. On assuming the post of foreign minister, he removed from his new office a framed memento placed on the wall by the former foreign minister and Nobel Prize winner Gustav Stresemann. It was the telegram from Geneva that confirmed Germany's seat in the League Council. Von Neurath replaced it with a portrait of Otto von Bismarck.

Von Neurath's relationship with Hitler and Nazism was marked by the brackish concoction gargled by many German aristocrats. On one hand, von Neurath was in agreement with the outlines of the Nazi program such as the restoration of German power, the elimination of Communism, and the ending of Jewish influence in Germany. On the other had he was uncomfortable with Nazi methods while maintaining the naïve hope that the regime would outgrow its tendency toward wanton violence. Lacking from the mixture was any moral initiative on von Neurath's part as a senior official to see that it did so or to cease all contact with the regime in time to save his own soul.

Von Neurath remained foreign minister at von Hindenburg's request after Hitler became chancellor in January 1933 to help keep a rein on Hitler.

But the repulsive tenor of the new regime was obvious early, and still von Neurath remained. He remained despite the creation of concentration camps (February 1933); despite the Enabling Act which established the Nazi dictatorship (March 1933); despite the regime's anti-Jewish boycott (April 1, 1933); and despite the bloody Night of the Long Knives (June 30, 1934) in which a former chancellor and nobleman (General Kurt von Schleicher) was murdered along with his wife. Heineman remarks that "during the first eighteen months [of Hitler's chancellorship] Neurath's resignation would have triggered a presidential crisis which Hitler might not have survived" thanks to von Neurath's close relationship with President von Hindenburg.[2]

And von Neurath did more than remain. The day after the anti-Jewish boycott, von Neurath thanked the Italian government for Rome's public statement that international press accounts of the treatment of German Jews were simply propaganda. Later that week, Hitler was von Neurath's dinner guest. Even in his own defense at Nuremberg years later, von Neurath would comment that Jews had enjoyed too much influence in Germany before 1933 and that the treatment of Jews in that year represented a "necessary cleaning up of public life." "That is still my view today," von Neurath said during cross-examination by Sir David Maxwell-Fyfe on June 25, 1946, "only it should have been carried out by different methods."[3] As to the question, "Why did you continue in a government that was using murder as an instrument of political action?" Von Neurath could only answer that "such mishaps cannot be avoided, most unfortunately."[4]

Insofar as Nazi Germany's early foreign policy was concerned, von Neurath and Hitler were in accord. Germany's exit from the League of Nations and the League's disarmament talks in October 1933 suited both men as did the announcements in March 1935 that Germany would go forward with conscription and with the building of an air force. In the west, von Neurath fully favored the German remilitarization of the Rhineland, and he earned Hitler's gratitude for his iron nerves during the reoccupation crisis of March 1936.[5] In the south, he favored an *Anschluss* with Austria and advocated Berlin's support for Austrian Nazis to that end. Even after the murder of Austria's Chancellor Engelbert Dolfuss by Austrian Nazis in July 1934 and the international revulsion that followed it, von Neurath argued that time was on Germany's side insofar as Austria was concerned. In the east, he created funds in the foreign ministry to help Sudeten Germans in Czechoslovakia as early as 1933, hoping to use that disgruntled population as a counterweight to Soviet influence in Prague. And like most Germans, he never accepted the border with Poland, claiming at one point that "an understanding with Poland is neither possible nor desirable."[6] Resplendent at the Berlin Olympics in the summer of 1936, von Neurath preened that "The whole world has come to pay respects to the new power of Germany."[7]

11. Konstantin von Neurath stands in his honorary SS uniform next to Propaganda Minister Joseph Goebbels at Hitler's birthday celebration, April 1938. Marie von Neurath stands at the far right. Photograph courtesy of Corbis.

As for the German drive toward war after 1937, von Neurath could claim disagreements with Hitler, but again they were over method rather than principle. He was present on November 5, 1937, when Hitler revealed at the famous Hossbach meeting that Austria would be annexed, Czechoslovakia destroyed, France and Britain defeated, and Germany's Living Space conquered by 1946 at the latest. Von Neurath had confided months earlier to a friend that Czechoslovakia would have to be destroyed.[8] His disagreement with Hitler – and indeed that of War Minister Werner von Blomberg and Army Commander-in-Chief Werner von Fritsch with Hitler as well – was with Hitler's belief that Britain and France would stand aside while Germany conquered Central Europe. It was this concern that brought von Neurath's replacement as foreign minister by the less cautious Joachim von Ribbentrop. And even after his removal, von Neurath remained in Berlin on Hitler's request as president of Hitler's so-called Secret Cabinet Council to lend an air of respectability to the events that would follow. In this position, he enjoyed a generous expense account while moving into a rich home in Dahlem provided by the government after it was purchased at substantial discount from a mixed German-Jewish couple.[9]

The most damning evidence against von Neurath at Nuremberg concerned his service in Prague from 1939 to 1941 as *Reichsprotektor* of Bohemia and Moravia after the full dismemberment of Czechoslovakia. Though he claimed to have opposed the German takeover of the Czech region in March 1939 because it subverted the Munich agreement that Hitler had just signed the previous October, von Neurath accepted the post when Hitler offered it. Perhaps he truly hoped he could engineer the peaceful assimilation of the bitter Czech population there. He surely was at odds at times with his zealous state secretary in Prague, SS-Gruppenführer Karl Hermann Frank. Yet in accepting the position of *Reichsprotektor* and in holding it as long as he did, von Neurath accepted a devil's bargain wherein Heinrich Himmler would increasingly control police functions in Bohemia and Moravia. Waves of arrests by the SS under von Neurath's purview occurred soon after he assumed office, and under von Neurath's authority, Germany's anti-Jewish laws were extended to Bohemia and Moravia. Von Neurath remained after November 1939 when the SS arrested nearly 1,900 Czech university students, executing nine of them at random and confining the remainder to concentration camps. He remained through September 1940 when Hitler spoke of assimilating the "racially useful" population in the Protectorate while eliminating the rest.[10] And though von Neurath lodged protests against SS excesses from time to time, he also found plenty of time to hunt stags in the Moravian forest.[11]

And that for which von Neurath accepted full responsibility was never benign. When confronted by his own defense attorney in 1946 with Frank's proclamation of August 1939, which threatened to meet acts of sabotage with "unrelenting harshness" against "the entire Czech population" – a proclamation issued under von Neurath's signature – von Neurath could only say, "I cannot imagine from what point of view . . . this public warning against sabotage can be used as the basis of an accusation against me."[12] When confronted by the prosecution with memoranda from himself and Frank dated in August 1940 and then presented to Heydrich and Hitler which spoke of the need to expel Czech leaders and intellectuals from Bohemia and Moravia, von Neurath could only say that "the intelligentsia . . . was the greatest obstacle to co-operation between Germans and Czechs. . . . The intelligentsia had to be reduced in some way . . . their influence had to be diminished."[13]

He did not leave the position of *Reichsprotektor* until September 1941 when Hitler dispatched Himmler's second-in-command Reinhard Heydrich to Prague in order to instill a full-blown terror (von Neurath was not officially dismissed from the post until August 1943). But though Joseph Goebbels had once complained of von Neurath that "he does not belong to our era," he wrote the following after von Neurath visited him in mid-April 1942 looking for a new job. "He feels," said Goebbels, "shoved to the side and finds himself in the best of health. His attitude toward the Führer is most positive.

Overall Herr von Neurath is a gentleman who has never shown incorrectness or disloyalty toward the Führer."[14] Von Neurath spent much of the war's remainder at his Württemberg estate of Leinfelderhof in Kleinglattbach. He accepted a tax-free gift of RM 250,000 from Hitler on the occasion of his seventieth birthday in February 1943. This gratuity was standard fare for the Third Reich's leading diplomats and military figures, and though von Neurath noted his discomfort, he kept the check.[15] And despite his concern for Germany's situation in 1944 von Neurath had labor details from a nearby concentration camp work on his estate.[16]

It did not make a pretty picture at the trial. Yet von Neurath has benefited from charitable readings of his role under Hitler. His stature, bearing, and age of 74 years when seated amongst the likes of Göring, Streicher, Kaltenbrunner, and Ribbentrop made it impossible not to notice that he was somehow removed from the others. He also seemed weary on the witness stand, possibly owing to a prostate operation four months before the trial. And his defense by East Prussian attorney Otto Freiherr von Lüdinghausen was uninspired. It was a droning, almost lazy strategy based largely on character testimonies (one of them by fellow defendant von Papen), none of which provided defense against specific charges. The rest was based on the argument that von Neurath's aggressive foreign policy until 1938 and indeed the war itself had been caused by the injustices of the Treaty of Versailles – a defense that the Tribunal had warned von Lüdinghausen would not be admitted.[17] In fairness to von Lüdinghausen, he never had much of a case. But Bishop Theophil Wurm in Stuttgart argued later that "Freiherr von Neurath had nothing whatever to do with the preparation of the war in 1939," that Lüdinghausen "was unequal to the task in Nürnberg," and that because of this "a misjudgment was pronounced."[18]

Lost in Wurm's selective assessment is that the Tribunal found von Neurath guilty on all four counts because he facilitated Nazi criminality from various positions of great responsibility. It would never have been much of a defense to say that von Neurath had not been so wanton a foreign minister as von Ribbentrop or so iron-hearted a man as Heydrich. Von Neurath was not the worst that Nazi Germany produced. Yet he was nothing to be proud of either. And because every other defendant found guilty on all four counts of the indictment (Göring, Ribbentrop, Rosenberg, Keitel) was dead two weeks after the verdicts, von Neurath was perhaps fortunate to receive a prison sentence of fifteen years.

## VON NEURATH AND THE WEST GERMAN STATE

Von Neurath's postwar advocates never saw it that way. Instead, his age and stature combined with his family's connections in Stuttgart, Bonn, and London made von Neurath a cause célèbre particularly after the formation of

12. Konstantin von Neurath and Hermann Göring confer during their trial at Nuremberg. Photograph courtesy of the Harry S. Truman Museum and Presidential Library.

a West German state in 1949. And with each passing month, von Neurath's family and friends pointed to his advanced age (77 as of February 1950) and declining health within the context of what they saw as the abominable conditions of Spandau. To a degree, they had a point. Relations between the West and the Soviets had completely broken down, and it was not easy to explain to West Germans, whose very country was founded on Soviet noncooperation with currency reform, U.S. financial aid, liberal democracy, and human rights, how the Allies and the Soviets could jointly administer a prison in West Berlin.

This was surely the position of Konrad Adenauer, the leader of the Christian Democratic Union and as of September 1949 at age 73, the first chancellor of the Federal Republic of Germany. Adenauer, the former lord mayor of Cologne, had never been on the Nazis' good side. The Gestapo arrested him in 1934 and again in 1944 despite his efforts to keep a low profile.[19]

But after the war he had his own ideas concerning war crimes trials and the punishment of convicted war criminals. Having never advocated the Trial of the Major War Criminals itself – in May 1946 he argued that it had gone on too long – Adenauer had stated on many occasions during the occupation that only the "*wirklicher Schwerverbrecher*" (truly worst criminals) should be punished, and by West German courts. Nazi followers and fellow travelers, Adenauer said, should be allowed to move on with their lives. With this argument Adenauer represented broad swaths of West German public opinion, from the conservative Catholic and Evangelical Churches, to millions of war veterans, to the leadership of the Social Democratic opposition.

On becoming chancellor on September 21, 1949, however, Adenauer still confronted Allied supervision and limited sovereignty. Because West Berlin's security depended on theoretical continuation of Four-Power rule in Berlin as a whole, West Berlin remained distinct from the new Federal Republic of Germany. Its western sectors were under the military rule of the rump Kommandatura despite the Soviet exit from that organization the year before. After 1950, the West Berlin "governing mayor," together with a new city council, now called the *Senat*, oversaw city business (the new titles were consistent with those in German free cities; the old designations of lord mayor and *Magistrat* remained in East Berlin). In the Federal Republic itself, military government gave way in September 1949 to an Occupation Statute, which ensured Allied civilian authority over West German foreign policy, security, trade, and other issues including the control of German prisoners sentenced by Allied courts through a Three-Power Allied High Commission seated in Petersberg, literally overlooking the new West German capital in Bonn. The first Allied high commissioners were old hands familiar with Germany. U.S. high commissioner John J. McCloy (1949–1952) had been the undersecretary of war during World War II and had been one of the architects of the Nuremberg trial. Sir Brian Robertson of Great Britain (1949–1950) had been the British military governor for the past two years, and his successor, Sir Ivone Kirkpatrick (1950–1953), had been a British Embassy official in Berlin before the war who interrogated Hess after his flight to Britain in 1941. After the war, Kirkpatrick advised the British military government and then returned to the Foreign Office as assistant undersecretary for Western Europe.[20] French high commissioner André François-Poncet (1944–1955) had been the French ambassador in Berlin from 1931 to 1940, was interned by the Germans for the last two years of the war, and had served as General Pierre Koenig's political adviser afterward. He was the only high commissioner to serve throughout the period of the Statute and worked hard for a new Franco-German relationship that would enhance French power and security while remaining vigilant of right-wing apologists. The Soviets responded with the foundation of the German Democratic

Republic in October 1949, the formal dissolution of their own military government, and its replacement with a Soviet Control Commission.[21]

Many aspects of Allied policy rankled in Bonn. One was the Occupation Statute itself, which limited German sovereignty in everything from foreign policy to coal and steel production. Adenauer's gesture at the Petersberg ceremony that inaugurated the Occupation Statute, where the chancellor deliberately stood on the same carpet as the high commissioners themselves, implied this restlessness.[22] Specific irritations included the continued incarceration of Germans convicted of war crimes and held in the Allied prisons of Landsberg, Wittlich, and Werl as well as in other European states. From the moment he was in power, Adenauer pressed for fuller national sovereignty partially embodied by a West German military contribution to Western European defense and far-reaching clemency for Germans convicted of war crimes, including the commutation of death sentences even for the worst offenders. Bonn gained greater leverage after the North Korean attack on South Korea in June 1950 because the attack seemed to portend a similar Communist adventure in Central Europe. A West German defense contribution was now essential. But new soldiers, it was said, would not march past the cell windows of their old commanders.[23]

It was always understood in Bonn that Spandau was different than the other prisons. The difference was not so much the fact that inmates there bore the label "Major War Criminals" and thus represented the centerpiece of the first large-scale experiment with postwar justice. Rather it was the fact of Soviet participation. Moscow's agreement was needed for any change in the regulations there to say nothing of clemency and release for the seven inmates. Here was a complicated matter because West Germany and the U.S.S.R. did not recognize one another diplomatically before 1955. Thus, in an October 1950 memorandum concerning the conditions of German rearmament, Adenauer's foreign policy adviser Herbert Blankenhorn argued that the Western Allies would have to grant full sovereignty to the Federal Republic and to free in stages those whom the Allies had condemned as "war criminals." For the Spandau prisoners, however, Blankenhorn said that the Allies would simply have to negotiate with the Soviets.[24]

In fact, reviews of sentences for Germans imprisoned by the Allies had already begun in 1949. By June 1951, Germans held at Landsberg Prison had decreased from 663 the previous year to 464, and the number of British-held prisoners in Werl decreased to 231 from 379 in April 1950.[25] It would remain a West German point of contention that these reviews would have to move more swiftly, particularly with the French, who had the most stringent review process and who held far more Germans on war crimes charges than any other state in Western Europe.[26]

But thanks to Konstantin von Neurath's many advocates, Bonn could not place Spandau on indefinite hold. Following her visit to Spandau in April

1950, von Neurath's daughter, Winifred von Mackensen, sent Adenauer a long list of grievances, which exaggerated her father's condition. The prison, Winifred said, had become worse rather than better since the prisoners were moved from Nuremberg. Cell lights were deliberately illuminated nightly in the faces of the prisoners two to three times per hour to deprive them of sleep. Prisoners could neither sit nor lie on their beds from 6 A.M. to 10 P.M., and they had nothing to sit on in their cells but a backless stool. Prisoners were never allowed to speak, and all reading materials were forbidden. Exercise consisted of walking in circles around a tree twice a day for thirty minutes. Wretched prison food during all months led to dangerous weight loss. And, Winifred added as a *coup de grâce*, the pastor was French.[27]

On October 15, 1950, Winifred sent a similar memorandum to a list of British contacts. Recipients included the Bishop of Chichester (the aforementioned George Bell), who had been in steady contact with Bishop Wurm and who made a long speech in the House of Lords on May 5, 1949, against what he viewed as one-sided trials against Germans.[28] They included military theorist Basil Liddell Hart, who was sympathetic to the imprisoned German generals who had granted him interviews so that he could write an unusually stupid book sanitizing the German side of the war.[29] They included Churchill's former cabinet secretary Lord Maurice Hankey who had opposed Nuremberg and other postwar trials because they created bitterness between the victors and the vanquished and because all countries, according to Hankey, were guilty of aggressive war at one time or another.[30] Also included was MP Richard Stokes who was more disturbed by Jewish kosher slaughter of animals than with the Nazi slaughter of Jews. And in a remarkably weird choice, Winifred's correspondents included Dr. Eduard Hempel, Hitler's former minister to Ireland who had received the Irish government's official condolences on Hitler's death in April 1945.

Winifred's new appeal stated that the Russians did not let the prisoners into the open air, that the fare consisted of potato peel soup, and that all of von Neurath's teeth had been pulled in August. All copies of her letter were forwarded to the Foreign Office in London with the request that von Neurath be released on parole, granted clemency, or, at the very least, moved to a sanitarium in West Germany. Lord Chichester made additional moral arguments to the Foreign Office on Bishop Wurm's urging. "One does not like to think," he warned, "what the judgment of history will be on Spandau, as an example of the justice of those nations which have been victorious over Nazism."[31] Chichester, Hankey, and Liddell Hart all tied von Neurath to the more general problem of German officers in the British military prison in Werl since the West Germans, they argued, would be hard put to contribute to Western European defense if former officers were in Allied jails.[32]

Sentimental issues were thrown in. Von Neurath's golden wedding anniversary was approaching in May 1951. Raeder's thirtieth wedding anniversary had come and gone in August 1950 without a public debate, but von Neurath's fiftieth would not. At the behest of the von Neurath family and of his superiors in London, British prison governor R. B. Le Cornu called a special governors' meeting at Spandau to propose a visit by five of von Neurath's family members for forty-five minutes as well as a special religious service performed by Otto Dibelius, the Bishop of Berlin–Brandenburg, as requested by von Neurath's family. Dibelius himself was not an uncontroversial figure. Like many Protestant clerics during the Third Reich, he had protested Nazi abuses against the Evangelical Church but defended the state's persecution of its Jews. Regardless, he would write the prison governors on May 19 asking to perform a religious service for von Neurath in Spandau. It would be, Dibelius said, an act of humanity.[33]

U.S. prison governor Maxwell Miller and French prison governor René Darbois agreed with Le Cornu's proposal, with Miller noting the "exceptional occasion" of a golden wedding anniversary and Darbois adding that von Neurath did not have much time left. But the Soviet medical officer, Major Pusankov, would hear none of it. "None of [the] governors," Pusankov countered, "can tell the possible duration of life of the prisoner." And age could not be used as an excuse to circumvent the rules. The most Pusankov would advocate was a fifteen-minute visit by Baroness Marie with either Winifred or von Neurath's son Constantine. A religious service could be performed by Pastor Casalis but with the other prisoners in attendance, not von Neurath's family.[34] Von Neurath seemed "bitter and completely hopeless" after a gloomy visit by his wife and daughter in late April. Winifred, sure that her parents would never be reunited, claimed to wish privately for an early death for both.[35] Filled with ire, Bishop Wurm complained to Adenauer and the Baden-Württemberg state assembly (*Landtag*) in Stuttgart passed a June 20, 1951, resolution calling for von Neurath's release on humanitarian grounds.[36]

As the pressure on Adenauer grew, so did Adenauer's complaints to the Allies. Responding to Winifred's letter of June 1950, Adenauer wrote the high commissioners on June 20, listing her complaints and adding the modest request that "for humanitarian reasons" Spandau should operate like prisons "in civilized countries."[37] In June 1951, he wrote McCloy that "it truly seems to me a demand of Humanity that Herr von Neurath ... be moved to a hospital," and in October 1951 that "Of late ... I am being constantly urged by people from different quarters to make further efforts in favor of Herr von Neurath."[38]

The British government understood that Winifred's complaints were exaggerated but realized the political problem that the prison caused. London hoped as early as 1950 that the Spandau problem could be obscured by the early release of the elderly von Neurath and understood too that the argument could only be made on health grounds. A British medical examination of von Neurath from May 1950 helped their case. "This man's expectation of life," it said, "may be measured in months. The recurring attacks of acute bronchitis is likely to produce heart failure. The possibility of sudden heart failure due to coronary thrombosis is ever present. He may be regarded as an exceptional case among the prisoners at Spandau."[39]

From this point on, it would be the accepted wisdom in London that von Neurath's near-death state warranted immediate action. General Robertson had already raised the possibility of a medical parole for von Neurath twice in March 1950 after having heard of von Neurath's poor health from the family attorney. In May the British high commissioner Sir Ivone Kirkpatrick planned to ask his counterparts McCloy and François-Poncet to make a three-way approach to the Soviets concerning von Neurath's removal to a hospital in the British zone where he would remain in custody. Von Neurath was, in the Foreign Office's view, "clearly an exceptional case whose removal would not be followed by other similar proposals based on medical grounds."[40]

But the Americans were unwilling. Secretary of State Dean Acheson pointed out that medical parole for von Neurath (and presumably Funk, who despite the British nonmention was the sickest man in Spandau) would lead to the establishment of a Soviet guard presence in West Germany. Acheson thus warned McCloy that if a medical parole were to be proposed, then the two prisoners had better be extremely sick.[41] And von Neurath, at that point, was not. It was true that he suffered from chronic hypertension and angina pectoris. But the minutes of Spandau's medical board show that his was never an urgent medical case in 1950 or even 1951. If anyone was in chronic misery, it was Funk, who on top of his other problems now suffered from impending blindness in one eye thanks to his earlier blood transfusion, as well as severe disorientation at night when his cell lights were illuminated owing to his heavy medications. The French commandant in Berlin, General Jean Ganeval, and his British counterpart, Brigadier General Edward Benson, pointed out that Funk was in far worse health.[42] But whether deserving of anyone's sympathy or not, Funk was never the beneficiary of any government's official efforts. His support network in West Germany included no one besides his wife Louise – a woman of few financial means, poor health, and her own delusions that her husband had been framed at Nuremberg by Oswald Pohl and that she could somehow communicate with him telepathically.[43]

The Americans had their own evaluation of both men conducted as per the orders of the U.S. commandant in Berlin, General Maxwell Taylor. Funk, the report said, was a mess. But his problems "would probably be present [even] if [he] were living under different conditions."[44] Von Neurath's examination revealed moderate emphysema and slight heart enlargement. But von Neurath made no health complaints and revealed no symptoms attributable to his cardiovascular problems. His physical exam "revealed a well developed, well nourished white male ... who did not appear acutely or chronically ill and in no distress." Mild sedation and a low salt diet was the extent of the U.S. medical recommendation.[45] All in all, U.S. officials had the impression that "these examinations do not support the contention of the British high commissioner that the physical condition of von Neurath and Funk is critical and warrants medical parole."[46] McCloy had already told Brian Robertson that though the United States did not oppose a medical parole in principle, the medical results did not warrant it in either the case of von Neurath or Funk.[47] And when the high commissioners met on May 31, 1950, Kirkpatrick did not even raise the idea. "[McCloy's] demeanor," Kirkpatrick said, "indicated that he would be reluctant to involve himself in the consequential difficulties."[48]

The Americans were not even that sure how inhumane Spandau was. After Adenauer's letter of June 20, 1950, the high commissioners ordered a study of the prison by the Kommandatura. Robertson had been outspoken about conditions at Spandau, but Ganeval shrugged that the regulations would be impossible to change and that conditions had slowly improved anyway, while Maxwell Taylor did not feel that conditions at Spandau were particularly unsatisfactory. Though the British thought certain aspects of Spandau inhumane from the standpoint of outside and family contacts, Taylor argued that materially, the conditions in Spandau were not substantially different from those at the U.S. war crimes prison at Landsberg in Bavaria. And it was clear that "the Chancellor has been misinformed" with regard to many of his assertions.[49] "Spandau conditions," added McCloy, "were on the whole good and ... except for Funk [the] health and spirits of all prisoners were reasonably good."[50] Even the Soviets had made considerable improvements in their months, and the food, though monotonous, was, according to Kirkpatrick, "adequate and wholesome."[51]

Using the West Berlin commandants' report, the high commissioners disabused Adenauer of the notions he had received from Winifred von Mackensen. The prisoners were allowed to lie on their beds when they wished, to speak with one another, and to read books of their choice after screening to the point where each cell had a bookshelf and the prison had a library. Nighttime illumination of cells was for security reasons and steps were being taken to shade the bulbs. The food, they continued, was "quite adequate" during the Western months, and even in the Soviet month, the prisoners ate the same food as the Soviet guards. Though a German cleric had not been allowed for security reasons, no one had seriously complained about Pastor Casalis, and chapel services even included music. As for the health of the prisoners, it had improved over the past months rather than deteriorated, and the prisoners had excellent medical care. In all, Adenauer was told that "the prisoners sentenced by the International Military Tribunal, serve their terms... in accordance with the principles adhered to in all democratic countries."[52]

At this point, the British and the Americans operated briefly at cross purposes. On July 4, 1950, without informing the Americans or the French, Kirkpatrick sent a letter to General Vasily I. Chuikov (the commander of Soviet occupation troops and chairman of the Soviet Control Commission) calling for better conditions including more letters and a greater number of visits. Kirkpatrick also mentioned von Neurath's health (though again not Funk's) perhaps as an opening salvo in an attempt to have him removed from Spandau.[53] Kirkpatrick noted to London that the Americans and French "fear that representations on a higher level [than the prison governors] might cause the Russians to notice what had in fact been done to improve the prisoners' lot and so lead to aggravation of the regime during the Russian month."[54] But he went forward anyway. No Soviet reply came until October, and this came from deputy high commissioner Ivan Fedorovich Semichastnov, who claimed as the Americans had that a recent Soviet medical exam showed no deterioration in von Neurath's condition.[55]

McCloy, meanwhile, visited Spandau in January 1951 "to acquaint myself first hand with the conditions... and to learn first hand the complaints, if any, which the prisoners had to make." Part of the tour included a personal visit to von Neurath in his cell. McCloy surely wished that Spandau Prison had not existed. He noted to the other high commissioners that the regulations concerning family contacts were too harsh, proposed the creation of a Four-Power working party to study improvements, and even suggested that the time had come to review the sentences themselves.[56] The French, perhaps fearing repercussions in Paris, refused a formal approach even to Chuikov and preferred instead to work quietly for small ameliorations on the prison governors' level concerning longer and more frequent visits, more correspondence, and packages.[57] McCloy was thus more circumspect with Adenauer, noting that though improvement remained to be made to bring the place fully up to Western standards he was also "satisfied" at the number of "creature comforts" ranging from the garden to the library.[58] The West German government privately noted McCloy's inherent contradiction that Spandau was at once humane but needed improvements to align with Western standards.[59] And Bonn remained under heavy pressure to get von Neurath moved or freed. In January 1951, the minister president of Baden-Württemberg, Dr. Reinhold Maier, asked Adenauer to contact McCloy so that von Neurath could be moved to a hospital. Adenauer forwarded the request with the comment that it showed "how much the fate of [von Neurath] moved the German *Volk* and the people close to him in his state [seine engeres Landesleute]."[60]

Their irritation increased when McCloy informed the chancellor's office in July 1951 that von Neurath's health problems, such as they were, resulted from his age rather than his imprisonment.[61] No one was angrier than Bishop Wurm. "I must confess," he wrote to Adenauer:

> that I am incensed over Mr. McCloy's answer to the Federal Chancellor. It is really irrelevant whether Herr von Neurath's level of sickness is due to his age or his imprisonment.... What matters is the question whether it contradicts the demands of humanity to keep an old sick man locked up until the end of his life as dictated by ... a negligent and pointless sentence of fifteen years.[62]

Adenauer passed along the comment to McCloy that "the execution of a sentence on a man as advanced in age as 78 years makes it impossible to avoid certain hardships which were not necessarily the object of the sentence."[63] But McCloy's most detailed response, of July 30, 1952, simply stated that von Neurath's health had not changed to the point where a move to a hospital was justified. "It can be assumed from this," noted Heinz von Trützschler, the head of the Foreign Ministry's section on prisoners and war criminals "that the three western Allies think that the conditions in Spandau prison are unsatisfactory, but that they do not see themselves in the situation to increase the level of conflict with Soviet Russia over this issue."[64]

## THE DEATH PROCEDURE

Martyrdom was a pillar of the Nazi regime. Historian Jay Baird's example of the sixteen Nazi "immortals" killed in Hitler's failed Munich putsch of November 9, 1923, is a case in point. In the 1920s, the Munich authorities forbade the Nazis from burying the "martyrs" in a common grave or holding memorial ceremonies. Once in power, Hitler built a monument to the martyrs next to the nineteenth-century *Feldherrnhalle* (Hall of the Commanders) in Munich, where the martyrs had fallen. The reinterment ceremony – a three-day affair in November 1935, was as elaborate a display as any the Nazis orchestrated. It included sixteen bronze sarcophagi; horse-drawn cassions; a midnight transfer of the remains to the *Feldherrnhalle* where the bodies temporarily lay in state guarded by Hitler Youth; two neoclassical *Ehrentempel* (Temples of Honor) as the new burial sites, each with eight tombs facing each other astride the Königsplatz; sixteen wreaths laid at the *Ehrentempel* by Hitler himself; as well as torchlight processions, oaths, speeches, flags, and the like. All typified the ways in which the regime celebrated death in order to identify its eternal friends and its eternal enemies.[65]

The states that destroyed Nazism understood. When U.S. forces arrived in Munich, they removed the monument to the sixteen Immortals from the *Feldherrnhalle*, and in 1947 they dynamited the *Ehrentempel* while reinterring the sixteen sets of remains in separate cemeteries throughout Munich.[66] When the Nuremberg war criminals sentenced to death by hanging were executed on October 16, 1946, the Allied Control Council took pains to ensure that they would never become martyrs to the population that they had once ruled. The bodies were moved by truck to Dachau and cremated, their ashes dumped into the river Isar, a tributary of the Danube.[67] Though the bodies had been photographed to preserve a record of the execution, the negatives were to be guarded so that they would "in no case . . . be reproduced in the German press."[68]

It is surprising that the Four Powers did not think at the time of the mortal remains of the seven condemned men who were given prison sentences. Control Council Directive No. 35 said nothing as to what must be done on the event of a prisoner dying.[69] The Spandau Prison regulations were also silent on the issue – quite an oversight since common sense dictated that four of the condemned men (von Neurath, Raeder, Funk, and Hess) could die in prison thanks to their age, their health, or the length of their sentences.

The Kommandatura did not agree on a procedure until December 1947, and it was to be kept strictly secret.[70] On the passing of a prisoner, the four medical officers would determine the cause of death. There would be no funeral service. The prison employees would receive orders to keep silent, and the prison joiner would construct a coffin. The body would be moved to a German crematorium in the British sector of Berlin at night in a procession of two covered military trucks bearing the corpse, an armed military guard of twenty men coming from the nation holding the chair, the four medical officers, and all four prison governors. The crematorium staff would have been contacted beforehand as to the exact hour of the cremation, but the identity of the body would be kept secret until its arrival. After the cremation, the deceased's ashes, on the insistence of the Soviets, would not go to the family. They would be scattered by the four governors at a mutually agreed spot, also to be kept strictly secret, away from the immediate vicinity of the prison. (The Soviet prison governor Politov originally made the ghoulish suggestion that they be dumped in the prison garden, where they would be ploughed under by the other prisoners.) The box used for dumping the ashes would then be burned in the presence of the four governors. Only then would the family of the deceased learn that their relative had passed on, but the manner of the body's disposal would not be revealed.

The British authorities in Berlin had never been pleased with the idea of a secret cremation, arguing from the very start that the family of the deceased prisoner should receive the body. They pointed out that a Spandau inmate who had served his sentence and been released would receive a regular funeral. Why should a prisoner who died within Spandau's walls have anything less? The French, thanks to their cultural aversion to cremation, agreed. The Soviet authorities were adamant, however. The shortest sentence, they reasoned, was ten years. No one could say what would transpire in Germany in that time. The British proposal, said the Soviets, "hides within it a great danger [that] militarist elements could use the tombs of these criminals for all sorts of Nazi demonstrations." The condemned men should thus be treated as the others sentenced at Nuremberg, and the Kommandatura did not have the right to change this procedure. The Americans found themselves on the side of the Soviets, insisting that regular burial could easily create "a cult of martyrs." Faced with united Soviet and American insistence, the British and French elements to the Kommandatura reluctantly agreed, with French prison governor René Darbois complaining almost immediately that it would be impossible to implement the procedure in secret. After all, prison regulations stated that a prisoner's family was to be kept informed of any dangerous illness a prisoner may have. Surely the world would know when a prisoner was dying.[71]

Dr. Wesley F. Pape had been the American legal adviser in Berlin in 1947 who had advocated cremation. Now in 1950, he defended the decision to General Taylor. "Although the procedure agreed upon may seem rather harsh at first blush," he wrote,

> it must be considered that the prisoners were convicted as war criminals by the International Military Tribunal. If the body were released to the relatives, there is some reason for believing that a big event might be made of the funeral services, and, in fact, it is feared . . . that they may be considered as martyrs of a noble cause. The burial place might well in later years become a national shrine. Hence, the decision after mature reflection that the bodies will be cremated and the ashes disposed of secretly without any publicity to the relatives or to anyone else concerned.[72]

Yet the change in mutual perception between the Allies and the West Germans in 1948 and 1949 had brought the fear that such a gruesome procedure concerning the remains of a deceased prisoner, particularly one for whom many West Germans felt sympathy, could have a dire political and diplomatic impact on the new West German state.[73] As the blockade came to an end in May 1949, the three Western prison governors made attempts to get the procedure changed informally so that the suggestion would not be noted in the minutes of governors' meetings. A formal attempt to change the procedure could have opened the West to the Soviet charge that they had gone soft on Nazism – a trump card that Allied capitals never wished to give. Yet the Soviets refused to consider changes in the cremation procedure. The best that the governors could hammer out was a minimal agreement on October 14, 1949, that if they could not agree on a suitable spot for releasing the ashes, the remains would be kept in a safe in the main prison office, to be guarded by a representative from each of the Four Powers until an agreement was finally reached.[74]

When the Allied high commissioners began to consider the "disposal" issue, they were unsure of how to balance it against the more general aim of improving day-to-day conditions at Spandau. An approach to the Soviets would have to be made, but could one issue be allowed to harm the other?[75] In a high commissioners' meeting on April 26, 1951, it was agreed at McCloy's urging that the disposal issue was the priority. Letters, visitation, and so forth could be worked out with the Soviets over the long haul. If the Soviets refused to budge on disposal, then at least the Western governments could say that they had tried, thus avoiding maximum political fallout in West Germany when the inevitable occurred.[76] But what of public reaction elsewhere to improvements in conditions for the major war criminals just six years after the war? Though British commandant Major General Geoffrey Bourne pointed out in February 1951 that secret cremation was not a part of the 1943 German prison regulations and argued that the bodies of deceased prisoners be returned to their families, Bevin in June 1951 worried about "the climate of public opinion in this country" and the "possibility of considerable public reaction . . . in cases like this where the action proposed may be falsely construed as leniency."[77] In mid-July, François-Poncet relayed Paris's policy that secret cremation might not be a bad idea after all in light of potential nationalist demonstrations. He pointed to German demonstrations that had followed the executions of Otto Ohlendorf, Oswald Pohl, and five other notorious SS officers hanged at Landsberg earlier that month despite the fact that the bodies were returned to the families for burial.[78]

McCloy countered that he "deplore[d] the French government's attitude." By late July the three Western governments agreed to approach the Berlin representative of the Soviet Control Commission, Sergei Alexeivich Dengin.[79] The next of kin should receive their loved ones' remains for humanitarian reasons, so went the approach by Lemuel Mathewson, the U.S. commandant in Berlin on July 20, 1951, though a big public funeral would not be allowed. Dengin, who two months earlier had personally refused that Baroness Marie attend the religious ceremony allowed for von Neurath's golden wedding anniversary, was not impressed. He "displayed no interest in the issue and said that it was a very small matter which he regarded of no importance." Out of courtesy, Dengin said he would study the issue. Dengin gave the same answer to the British commandant in Berlin who followed Bourne, Major General Cyril F. C. Coleman, on July 30. But a Soviet reply did not come until Coleman reminded the Soviets in October 1951. Dengin did not even provide the answer himself. His deputy, M. A. Susin, brusquely referred Coleman to the agreement of 1947.[80]

The failed approach in the summer of 1951 got Dean Acheson's attention. Acheson, as has been seen, did not advocate trying to free von Neurath or even move him to better conditions in West Germany. But he recognized the death procedure as a major potential problem within the context of West German rearmament discussions then underway, particularly since Adenauer had mentioned von Neurath specifically when Acheson visited Bonn in November 1951.[81] In December, Acheson decided that a more formal tripartite approach should be made in Moscow to Soviet Foreign Minister V. M. Molotov. The argument would be based on legal grounds – provisions regarding the disposal of remains were not part of the actual Spandau regulations. Moreover, the German prison regulations of 1943, on which the Spandau regulations were consciously based, called for the handing of remains to the next of kin. A diplomatic justification was added, namely, that "the old procedure can be expected to give rise to emotional feeling and disturbances in the German population," thus causing demonstrations of the type that the secret cremation was designed to avoid. As the high commissioners worked out the approach to Molotov, the Kommandatura in Berlin drafted a press release to meet public outcry in case the approach was unsuccessful. The Allies, the statement said, had tried since 1949 to have the cremation procedure changed "out of consideration for . . . close relatives," but the Soviets had refused.[82]

It was at this point that von Neurath's health actually became alarming. A U.S. medical report of December 1951 after an angina attack on the seventeenth described his condition as "serious" to the point where the French doctor did not want him working in the cold weather and the British and American doctors wanted him to have assistance going up and down staircases. U.S. warders began providing him with such help in December 1951. Allied authorities talked of his "imminent death," and the French medical officer in Spandau confirmed that his condition was indeed "grave" after an EKG.[83] Three angina attacks followed in February 1952, and von Neurath was given nitroglycerin pills to take as needed when attacks occurred. From Leinfelderhof, Baroness Marie wrote Lady Churchill personally to appeal for her husband's release "before it is too late."[84]

Now that it seemed von Neurath was actually dying, Allied policy unanimously worked toward two ends. First, von Neurath should be moved to the British Military Hospital in Berlin, with Soviet guards if necessary; second, his remains should be returned to his family should he die there. Toward this end, the Allied High Commission through its diplomatic officers in Berlin would approach General Chuikov himself, bypassing for now Acheson's suggestion that the issue be raised in Moscow with Molotov.[85] The Americans sought a quick meeting with Chuikov, who claimed unavailability. Instead, Cecil B. Lyon, the Director of the U.S. high commission's Berlin element met with Chuikov's deputy Semichastnov on January 26, 1952, in the latter's office. Pointing to von Neurath's ascending age and descending health, Lyon spoke of the desire that he be moved to a hospital and that, should he die there, the family be allowed to indicate their wishes concerning the remains. Semichastnov suspiciously asked why the Allies had a "sudden interest" in von Neurath and said that it was all "a very serious question" that could upset existing quadripartite arrangements. He would reply soon after consulting with the Soviet doctors and his advisers.[86] He did not. The Allies began drafting press releases to explain von Neurath's death and cremation.[87]

Meanwhile, the Soviet staff at Spandau became tougher in their interpretation of regulations. The medical meeting of February 12 in which von Neurath's EKG was discussed brought the argument from Soviet medical officer Major Pusankov that von Neurath's health had not changed. Although von Neurath could be excused from work detail, guards should not help him to get up and down steps. "We should not lose sight of the fact," said Pusankov, "that we are dealing, not with patients of hospitals, but with prisoners who must conform their lives to the regulations of the prison." The warders were not the prisoners' servants. An argument over the meaning of the term "grave condition" followed. The only agreement was that von Neurath would not work and that he would not be allowed to walk in the cold.[88]

It was in fact at this time that Soviet governor Major Alabjev sought to enforce the daily regulations more stringently, arguing against such informal relaxations as had occurred, such as the practice of allowing prisoners to speak with one another during work and exercise. As mentioned in the previous chapter, such was probably due to the recent 1951 series on Spandau which had appeared in the Munich periodical *Revue*.[89] To McCloy, Soviet behavior confirmed the correctness of focusing more broadly on the issue of prisoners' remains rather than regulations.[90]

On the night of March 31, 1952, von Neurath had his most serious heart attack to date, made worse by the fact that no doctor was available for two hours because it was the last day of the month before the changeover of the guard.[91] Such, combined with the difficulties brought by Alabjev and Semichastnov, increased the pressure on the Allies to take unilateral action. Lyon went as far as to propose that if von Neurath died during the U.S. month in the chair (April 1952), then the U.S. governor should announce that the body was being handed to the next of kin, albeit with the understanding that the funeral would have no fanfare. If the Soviets objected meekly, then such a plan would be carried out. If the objection were stronger with an indication that the Soviets would use force, then the plan would be abandoned.[92]

Acheson was not willing to go this far. Instead, he continued to insist that there be a tripartite approach to Molotov in Moscow that would go through official diplomatic channels (with all three Western ambassadors visiting Molotov the same day) so that the Soviets would understand that the proposal had the backing of the three Western governments and was not just an issue of local interest in Bonn or Berlin. The issues of visitation and correspondence would be raised, too.[93]

But the approach on von Neurath's behalf would not be made in 1952 thanks to the demands of international and domestic politics. The impending Contractual Agreements on German sovereignty [Convention on Relations between the Three Powers and the Federal Republic of

Germany – also known as the "General Treaty" or *Deutschlandvertrag*] – had to come first, as did the European Defense Community (EDC) Treaty, which provided the continental alliance framework around West German rearmament. The treaties would create a largely sovereign West German state, which would contribute to an integrated Western European defense.[94] On May 15 with the signing of the agreements in Bonn less than two weeks away (the Convention was signed on May 26 and the EDC Treaty on May 27), Acheson commented that he did not want to burden the U.S. High Commission's Law Committee with a proposal concerning von Neurath. Despite the urgency of von Neurath's "precarious position," he suggested that the approach to Moscow be delayed until the Convention was signed.[95]

But Adenauer, despite the fact that the treaties constituted a tremendous step in bringing the Occupation Statute to an end, would not let his new Western Allies forget Spandau. As it was, the Convention provided for a mixed clemency commission with German participation to review the remaining cases at Landsberg, Werl, and Wittlich.[96] But in a meeting of the foreign ministers the day before the Contractual Agreements were signed in Bonn, the Chancellor reminded Acheson, British Foreign Secretary Anthony Eden, and French Foreign Minister Robert Schuman that he still hoped that something could be done to improve conditions at Spandau, particularly for von Neurath.[97] The French and British were hesitant. A démarche in Moscow on behalf of major war criminals, which the Soviets might publicize, could smell of an Allied quid pro quo with Bonn, which could in turn wreck the ratification of the Convention in London and of both treaties in Paris (Bonn would ratify both in March 1953). Schuman was already worried that the French National Assembly would reject the European Defense Community Treaty (they in fact rejected it in August 1954), and he understood that French public opinion was especially sensitive on the issue of German war criminals whose crimes had affected France. He had told his Allied counterparts for some time that the French would not change their view of the Germans so easily.[98] At the meeting on May 25, 1952, he and Eden both reminded Adenauer that lesser-known war criminals in Werl and Wittlich were already receiving generous clemency provisions, so that each held but about 100 German inmates.[99]

On May 26 and 28, the French Embassies in Washington and London argued that an approach in Moscow regarding Spandau was "inopportune." The complex of issues at Spandau, said the French note, should be left on the level of the High Commission and General Chuikov, where, as the French well knew, no headway had been made. Mostly, Paris feared the domestic political repercussions of a splashy démarche in Moscow on behalf of a major war criminal.[100] Perhaps Paris was also alarmed at the recent trajectory the United States seemed to be taking. McCloy had suggested on April 3 that should von Neurath have another heart attack, the Allies should move him to a hospital with or without Soviet agreement. On April 15, the American Berlin element suggested that should von Neurath die during this U.S. month, the United States should unilaterally take control of the body. The British refused to consider such a dangerous step for fear of Soviet retaliation, and Acheson himself might never have gone this far either.[101] But the secretary of state's acerbic reply to the French reminded them of the unsuccessful approach to Dengin in 1951, which provided the reasoning for the approach in Moscow. "The humanitarian questions involved," Acheson said, "would seem to make the question important enough to be pursued further."[102] The Foreign Office in London agreed that "now that we and the Americans have agreed to a démarche in Moscow, it is rather tiresome of the French to have second thoughts."[103]

Paris refused to budge. Schuman had after all been resistant to the idea of releasing all Germans held at Landsberg, Wittlich, and Werl, as well as the notion of turning them over to German authorities, for fear of rehabilitating those convicted and angering the French public.[104] He was even more cautious about Spandau. "In spite of the interest which this matter has from the point of view of German opinion," said the French *aide-mémoire* of June 10, 1952, "a démarche at the governmental level might have a very unfortunate effect on French opinion, by which time it could be interpreted as a result of a secret agreement concluded at the time of the contractual arrangements concerning the problem of war criminals." In Bonn, François-Poncet was even more adamant, pointing out that any approach to Moscow for the benefit of convicted war criminals "would not be understood by French public opinion." Anyway, he continued, von Neurath's most recent medical examination showed that he was in no imminent danger. This was true. By late April, von Neurath was herding rabbits, walking in the garden, and discussing the past with Speer.[105] Irritated by Paris's stance, the State Department pointed out to the French that it still backed the Moscow approach because it was the only one likely to work. Acheson asked McCloy's staff how they thought that a Moscow approach might work despite the French attitude.[106]

The British in the end developed cold feet, too. Eden was part of the Conservative cabinet of Winston Churchill that had returned to power in October 1951. Both men had been ambivalent about Nuremberg in the first place, and both believed London had to solve quietly the problem of the Germans still interned at Werl, especially after Adenauer pressed the issue with Churchill in London in December 1951.[107] Yet on July 16, 1952, Eden's Foreign Office echoed the *Quai d'Orsay*'s concerns regarding Spandau with the comment that the approach in Moscow would not work and that the backlash in British public opinion brought by "adverse publicity" could have an "unfortunate effect on ratification" of the contractual agreements. The démarche in Moscow was "a risk not worth taking." As late as August 14, the British had not changed this position. Ivone Kirkpatrick, who had once advocated removing the Spandau prisoners from Berlin altogether, now announced in a High Commission meeting that he had received instructions from his government to back the French in rejecting the approach in Moscow. Walter Donnelly, the new American high commissioner, could only register the facts that the U.S. position had not changed and that both the British and the French were reneging on the spirits of their policies thus far.[108]

And the West German government had only become testier since the signing of the treaties in May. A long internal memorandum prepared in the Foreign Ministry in June by Heinz von Trützschler was the strongest statement yet. Trützschler's own Nazi background was not entirely clean. He had served in von Ribbentrop's Foreign Ministry as a propagandist, justifying German aggression in published documentary "White Books." Now he was angry about von Neurath.[109] Aside from mentioning that at age 79 von Neurath was not fit to be in prison and that Hitler's one-time foreign minister had the sympathy of numerous dignitaries (which now included Pope Pius XII), von Trützschler also questioned the very validity of von Neurath's conviction. Von Neurath's opposition to Hitler at the Hossbach Meeting of November 7, 1937, made him noncomplicit on the charge of Crimes against Peace and the fact that von Neurath quit the post of *Reichsprotektor* absolved him of Crimes against Humanity and War Crimes charges, too (von Trützschler ignored the fact that these had been mitigating factors at Nuremberg that might have spared von Neurath's life). The West German government, von Trützschler said, should emphasize the "de facto illegality" of the cases against the prisoners and "demand redress." "From the standpoint of law and humanity," he concluded, "[it is] unsustainable that the fate of the Spandau prisoners, and especially that of Herr von Neurath, should be sacrificed to high politics." Trützschler toned down the rhetoric when approaching the Americans, emphasizing only von Neurath's age and the (still exaggerated) conditions of his imprisonment.[110] Adenauer followed up with a milder letter to Kirkpatrick of July 9, 1952. The chancellor did not raise Spandau in his next trips to London (December 1952) and Washington (February 1953). But he did demand of Kirkpatrick that the conditions at Spandau, whatever they were, be eased, since, in his words, "it appears to me hardly compatible with the conception of human dignity, as prevailing in the Western democracies, to expose those seven men to such methods of penal enforcement."[111]

Though the high commissioners drafted a response correcting von Trützschler's exaggerations, the hint was taken.[112] A démarche in Moscow remained out of the question, but all three high commissioners wrote General Chuikov on September 1, 1952, for whatever small favors they could get. The letters called for the Spandau prisoners being allowed visits each month for thirty minutes instead of every other month for fifteen minutes, and that they be allowed to receive and send a letter a week and not every fourth week. Along with these small alleviations the high commissioners also asked that the death procedure be changed so that the bodies would go to the next of kin with the four wartime allies controlling all news of the death. The Americans, without consulting their allies, leaked the news of the démarche, though not its actual contents, to the U.S. organ *Neue Zeitung*, which gave Adenauer credit for the Allied approach to Chuikov. If Chuikov agreed to changes, Adenauer and the Allies would enjoy what political rewards there were. If he did not, then the public record would show that the effort had been made and that the Soviets had refused.[113]

Perhaps as part of the Communist "peace offensive" aimed at disrupting West German rearmament – an offensive highlighted by public East German and Soviet offers in 1951 and 1952 for a united, neutral Germany – the Soviets surprisingly granted the Allied proposals for more frequent visits and letters.[114] In fact, they responded to the September 1 letter in a little more than a month. Such minor concessions cost the security-minded Soviets nothing, since the rules of censorship on letters and discussions would still apply. But the reply from Semichastnov flatly rejected any change regarding what he referred to as the quadripartite agreement concerning the death and disposal procedures. This, he said, must remain in force.[115] The Americans, who had once objected to the tying of the death and disposal procedure to smaller concessions for the very reason that the Soviets could accept the latter while rejecting the more important former, immediately pressed for more. On October 23, the three high commissioners thanked Chuikov for the concessions while mentioning that they hoped for more changes at some point in the future, particularly concerning the prisoners' remains.[116]

In the meantime the Western Allies had made a critical blunder. Having informed the West German government of the September 1 letter to Chuikov complete with the letter's warning that the death procedure as it was could provoke a "vehement reaction in public opinion," the Allies had forgotten that the West Germans had never asked nor even known what the secret procedure concerning the disposal of prisoners' remains was. The Americans also printed in the *Neue Zeitung* Semichastnov's letter that approved more frequent visits and letters but that rejected the changes in the death procedure. Bonn tried to find out the death procedure afterward, but this was not easy. Ministry of Justice efforts came up short as did the efforts of the German attorneys who had defended the Spandau prisoners at Nuremberg.[117]

The Foreign Ministry in Bonn suggested that the chancellor go right to the Allied High Commission, and Adenauer did, asking directly in a letter of November 11, 1952.[118] Now the Allies were in another quandary. The U.S. element of the High Commission pointed out that nothing regarding the disposal procedure had ever been revealed to the West Germans and that to do so now would surely "furnish a foundation for the Soviet charge of violation of confidence." In addition, "the consequences of such a disclosure are unpredictable in nature and scope." It could "open the floodgates of German public criticism against each Element of the Allied High Commission." It would perhaps be best to disclose the procedure and the discussions with the Soviets so that the Allied High Commission could dissociate itself from the procedure before its implementation. But Bonn would have to keep the procedure secret, which the Americans saw as "a highly improbable event." On the other hand, nondisclosure combined with the procedure's implementation should von Neurath die would cast the United States in the same savage light as the Soviet Union in spite of recent American efforts to get the procedure changed. "To disclose or not to disclose," U.S. officials pointed out, "involves an evaluation of the political consequences and a weighing of political advantages and disadvantages." In any event, the decision over what to tell the West German government should be a tripartite one, since the West German perceptions of all three Western Allies would surely be affected.[119]

The decision was that Adenauer's letter of November 11 would be answered, but the Allies would also take the chancellor into their confidence. In January 1953, during his month in the chair of the Allied High Commission, François-Poncet met with Adenauer and told him what the procedure was in an oral statement. Adenauer was given nothing in writing and was told that the Allies would not provide him with a written answer to his letter. Whatever Adenauer's personal revulsion at the fate that awaited the Spandau prisoners, he kept the secret, though he did request of the high commissioners that von Neurath's remains be handed over to the family.[120]

In the meantime, despite the recent magnanimity shown by the Soviets concerning letters and visits, there was little sign that the Soviets would ever make greater allowances for the prisoners' families or the prisoners themselves. Requests for a special family visitation on von Neurath's eightieth birthday were rejected, and the West German government's efforts to arrange a furlough for Raeder so that he could visit his dying 31-year-old son Hans, or at least attend the funeral once Hans died of a brain tumor in January 1953, fell on deaf Soviet ears.[121] All von Neurath received was the old armchair from the infirmary for his cell, ironically a chair designed by Speer in 1938. And the Soviets complained bitterly about that, too.[122] "This," wrote Churchill to Eden after reading a general summary of conditions in Spandau, "is a shocking tale. Can nothing be done?"[123]

## PREPARING FOR THE WORST

Josef Stalin's death on March 5, 1953, and the minor thaw in Soviet foreign policy that followed encouraged the Allies to make another attempt with the U.S.S.R. Soon after Stalin's death, Soviet police chief Lavrenty Beria allowed a sweeping amnesty for roughly a million Soviet GULAG prisoners. Richard C. Hagen, the chief of the U.S. High Commission's Prisons Division, thought that a new démarche concerning the remains of Spandau prisoners might be opportune. Moscow, he said, "appears to be embarked on a maneuver ostensibly aimed at settling problems with the western world. How far and how deep this attitude runs cannot be ascertained without testing in specific fields."[124] In Washington, Adenauer suggested the same to the new secretary of state under President Eisenhower, John Foster Dulles. If Soviet policy was truly relaxing, said Adenauer, then it was his own "moral duty" to raise the problem again, particularly regarding the old and sick at Spandau.[125]

The Allied High Commission's Law Committee immediately discussed an approach to the Soviets. The British and French members of the committee wanted to request more changes in the daily prison regulations as well, but the American argument was that "no procedure of the Four Powers has merited the concern of the Western High Commissioners more than the disposal of remains," and that the Allies should not allow discussions with the Soviets to bog down over mundane matters like the lighting of cells and the availability of reading materials. U.S. officials prepared a draft letter to send to Chuikov that concluded,

> I am sure that you will agree with me that it is desirable to make this substitution in the interest of conforming more closely with established procedures for the disposition of remains of a prisoner not only within Germany but also in the civilized world. Preservation of the existing procedure can afford none of the Four Powers interested in the administration of the prison any particular satisfaction or find any real justification either in security or political background.[126]

The French, for the same reasons as before, hoped to stall. In May 1953, they commented that Spandau should not be discussed for the moment because talks over air corridors to Berlin were underway. But Hagen insisted that the two issues had no connection and that there was no time to lose. "It is believed," he said in a brief to his superiors

> that the Allied High Commission would be remiss in its duty to attempt to conform the existing arrangement for disposition of remains to a more modern procedure with all the political benefits of the latter if it were not to test the proposal by actual negotiation at this time. In view of the Moscow "line" on the Three-Power Conference in Bermuda scheduled for June, the "honeymoon" tactics of the Soviet maneuver may fast be approaching an end. Now is the time to test this issue.[127]

Such was indeed the case given the health of von Neurath and Funk but also given West German law. So far as anyone could tell, the controlling legal authority for cremations was still the German Cremation Law of 1934 [*Gesetz über die Feuerbestattung*], which allowed next of kin the choice over burial or cremation while ordering that no cremation take place without the approval of the local police. To cremate one of the Spandau prisoners, the Allies would have to requisition a German crematorium in West Berlin on military authority. Should the staff of the German crematorium refuse to cooperate, the West German public would surely be on the staff's side. Should a prisoner suddenly die with no new agreement in place, and such could occur at any time, "it would probably be impossible to hand over the remains to the next of kin without provoking an incident, the consequences of which cannot be foreseen.... It is therefore a matter of great urgency that a decision should be made now about the course to be adopted on such an event, and that the necessary instructions be given to the Allied Kommandatura."[128]

This was enough to concern James P. Conant, the new American high commissioner under the Eisenhower administration, especially in the wake of the bloody Soviet repression of a spontaneous East German revolt in June 1953. Kirkpatrick and François-Poncet agreed on July 28 that a new, stronger approach would be made. The occasion was to be Kirkpatrick's upcoming farewell reception because the new Soviet high commissioner in East Germany, Vladimir Semeonov, was expected to attend.[129] Semeonov would be told that if a new, more humane procedure could not be adopted; then the Soviets would have to assume responsibility for the remains themselves. If the Soviets did not wish to assume the responsibility, then the Allies would hand the remains over to the next of kin if the death in question were to occur during a month in which a Western governor was in the chair. The burial, however, would take place in Berlin and an explicitly political funeral would not be allowed.[130]

Yet time continued to move forward, especially for von Neurath. On the morning of July 29, 1953, he suffered another severe heart attack, and though he seemed in no immediate danger afterward, the episode emphasized the need to come to a new agreement with the Soviets quickly. Since August was the U.S. month in the chairmanship of the prison, Cecil Lyon proposed in West Berlin that should von Neurath die that month, the body should be handed over to the next of kin – despite Soviet objections – "by means short of shooting." It was a step too far for Dulles, who back in Washington rejected Lyon's proposal due to the "unpredictable and possibly adverse results."[131] Conant agreed. By this time, Kirkpatrick had spoken with Semeonov and had come away with the impression that the Soviets would not change their minds. The "sensational news" (as Speer called it) that the Western high commissioners were trying to help von Neurath reached the prisoners in Spandau. But as a former diplomat himself, von Neurath clearly understood that his fate depended on nonexistent Soviet goodwill, which forbade him even from telling his wife and daughter that he was ill. "Next," he told the American governor dryly, "you will forbid me to think about my illness."[132]

Indeed two days after von Neurath's heart attack, Dengin would not even agree that he be moved to a hospital for observation when asked by

British Berlin commandant Cyril Coleman. "If his health had deteriorated," Dengin dryly noted, "it was because of his age." The prison had adequate medical facilities, and as Dengin ominously noted, "dying could happen to anybody."[133] Alabjev, who had been promoted to the rank of lieutenant colonel in 1953 for his stringency at Spandau, refused throughout August even to consider the installation of a hospital bed in von Neurath's cell, instead complaining that the food provided the prisoners during the American month was too plentiful and too tasty.[134] Thus, all three Western high commissioners agreed that to hand the body over to the next of kin without a Soviet agreement "might prompt Russian retaliation in other fields of quadripartite agreement (e.g., communications) with serious consequences for Berlin."[135] The high commissioners drafted a new letter to Semeonov, this one emphasizing legal rather than political arguments, namely that the "enforcement of a prisoner's sentence of confinement is terminated by his death. Disposal of the body of a prisoner who dies while serving his sentence cannot, therefore, be treated as part of the enforcement of the sentence." A response was not expected.[136]

At the same time, the Western Allies prepared for the worst. On August 12, 1953, General Thomas Tiberman, the U.S. commandant in Berlin, visited Ernst Reuter, the Social Democratic governing mayor of West Berlin, to discuss von Neurath's possible cremation. Reuter was "extremely negative" toward the entire prospect, especially given what he called the deep antipathy with which Germans regarded cremation. At the same time, Reuter expressed some sympathy with the Allied predicament. He promised to go along with the procedure so long as he was ordered to do so by the Allied authorities and said he would do everything to ensure that the cremation and aftermath proceeded with "a minimum of friction and publicity."[137] Reuter's successor, Walther Schreiber, reacted no better when the British commandant Coleman briefed him in October 1953. "He was clearly unhappy," Coleman reported. "He said it was punishing the relatives after the prisoner was dead and would shed discredit on the Allies." But as Coleman explained, there was nothing that could be done, and Schreiber closed by asking that the ashes at least be preserved until they could be handed back to the relatives one day.[138] For the rest, a prewritten Kommandatura order for the cremation in the British sector, drafted for the occasion of von Neurath's death, sat at the ready. "You are hereby ordered," it told the governing mayor, "to cooperate."[139]

Elaborate plans for von Neurath's cremation in the Wilmersdorf district of West Berlin's British sector were drawn up. There would be a dummy procession of Army trucks from the prison before the genuine procession to the crematorium in order to fool any crowds that may form outside the prison. Von Neurath's ashes would be stored in the Spandau Prison safe until their disposition could be decided.[140] The high commissioners drafted a new letter dated January 11, 1954, to Semeonov regarding conditions in Spandau

Prison, not so much on the expectation that the Soviets would accept Allied arguments, but so that the Allies could meet the predictable West German outcry with the answer that they had tried to change the Soviets' minds in each of the years from 1951 to 1954.[141] There was little else to do. As one British Foreign Office official noted, "Having let ourselves in for this macabre business, there seems little to be gained by prolonging the uncertainty."[142]

## THE SPANDAU PRISON CEMETERY

The issue entered a new phase toward the beginning of 1954 for three reasons. First, von Neurath's heart attack of late July 1953 at age 81, though serious, did not result in death, and his health stabilized thereafter. Thus, Allied negotiations over the death procedure gained a new lease on life as well. Second, a Four-Power foreign ministers' conference was scheduled for January and February 1954 to discuss the possibility of a general peace treaty with a unified Germany. Churchill had called for a Four-Power conference on Germany since Stalin's death, and in fact it would be the first such meeting of foreign ministers since 1947.[143] Finally, Adenauer himself became more involved, thanks partly to his personal feeling that several of the Spandau prisoners were being punished too harshly; partly because of pressures from the West German population to do something about Spandau; and partly because of the momentum caused by recent Allied releases of Germans convicted of war crimes from their military prisons in West Germany. Indeed, the British noticed that the West German public was becoming "increasing interested in the matter" of Spandau, and the Evangelical Press Service itself had even begun asking questions concerning burial procedures.[144]

Adenauer sent a lengthy appeal for the Spandau prisoners to Kirkpatrick's successor as British high commissioner, Frederick Hoyer Millar, on January 6, 1954, during the latter's month as chair of the Allied High Commission. The chancellor asked that Spandau Prison be on the agenda of the upcoming foreign ministers' conference while making sweeping proposals aimed at eliminating Spandau as a public issue as soon as possible. Adenauer was highly skeptical of the conference itself, which he viewed as a pointless impediment to the long-delayed French ratification of the EDC Treaty and thus West German sovereignty. Thus, the conference might as well be used for the Spandau prisoners. Adenauer suggested first that all prisoners older than 75 years of age should be released immediately, which would have meant immediate freedom for von Neurath and Raeder. Second, a good conduct remission equal to one third of the sentences should be granted with pretrial custody counted toward the total length of the sentences. This provision would result in the immediate release of Dönitz and the release of von Schirach and Speer within five years. With the exception of Walther Funk and Rudolf Hess, then, who had received life sentences, and for whom there was no public pressure in West Germany, the Spandau prisoners would be released with relative speed.[145] To add pressure, the chancellor's office leaked the fact of the note, though not its contents, to the West German press.[146]

In Washington, Dulles was also skeptical of the foreign ministers' conference, believing that the Soviets would again use the chimera of German reunification to slow the progress of West German integration into the Atlantic community. But raising the Spandau prisoners there could complicate issues all the more because the authority to alter the sentences handed down by the International Military Tribunal, according to Article 29 of the London Charter itself, was held by the Allied Control Council. Thus, a change in sentences would mean that the Control Council itself would have to be reconvened with Soviet participation. Such could cause endless complications over the future of Germany and Western European security.[147]

Adenauer's démarche was discussed at greater length in the British Foreign Office, where H. W. Evans of the German Political Department argued that "it seems to me that at the age of 75, and after all these years these old and now harmless men have served such punishment as we need give them. Dr. Adenauer's proposal offers an opportunity of magnanimity. We ought not to take the responsibility of rejecting it." On the other hand, Adenauer's older-than-75 proposal had no precedent in Western criminal law, and the Spandau prisoners were viewed as *the* major war criminals in the West. Advocating for them while getting some released immediately would likely not be understood in the court of public opinion.

Sir Ivone Kirkpatrick, in any event, took issue with the notion that all the Spandau inmates were harmless. Now the permanent undersecretary for Eden in the Foreign Office, the former high commissioner was determined to keep Dönitz and Speer behind bars as long as legally possible for reasons to be discussed in Chapter Four in this book. The consensus reached in London was that even though the issue of Spandau could indeed be raised at the foreign ministers' conference, the most that ought to be attempted should be betterment in living conditions within the prison, because, as Deputy Undersecretary Sir Frank Roberts put matters, "the prisoners in Spandau are in no sense ordinary criminals." An improvement in conditions, meanwhile, would perhaps find Soviet agreement while appeasing Bonn and not offending public opinion.[148]

Most importantly, such an attempt had the backing of Prime Minister Winston Churchill himself, who had long advocated releasing the Germans held at Werl and who especially deplored the Spandau arrangement. Most recently, the former German diplomat and chancellor Franz von Papen, who had been among the three acquitted at Nuremberg, had written Churchill on von Neurath's behalf in January 1954. "Is there no means," Churchill implored Foreign Minister Anthony Eden on January 21, "of raising this or indeed the whole question of the Spandau prisoners during your informal discussions with Molotov in Berlin?"[149]

Spandau was not on the agenda of the foreign ministers' conference in Berlin, but with the approval of Dulles and French Foreign Minister Georges Bidault, Eden approached Molotov at a private lunch on February 17.[150] "I was not going to suggest their releases," Eden reported back to Churchill. But he did ask Molotov to instruct Semeonov to hold discussions with the three Western commissioners on the treatment of ill prisoners and on the handling of the remains of deceased ones. The Western governments, he continued, believed that the conditions as they stood were simply too harsh from a humanitarian point of view.

It is a measure of Molotov's bigger concerns about impending West German rearmament under a West German government that he viewed as hostile, revanchist, and militarist that he seemed fully unfamiliar with the issues surrounding Spandau Prison.[151] The Soviet foreign minister was the same acidic and suspicious character that Eden had known from the war years – he even complained to Eden one night about the music provided by the band of the Royal Irish Fusiliers, since Irish musicians in the British army smacked of imperialism.[152] But Molotov promised to raise Spandau with high commissioner Semeonov. The Soviets were in no special hurry. Having decided long before that all the defendants at Nuremberg should be hanged – and having tried at one point to create a prison regime that included nothing but gruel and solitary confinement – the comfort of prisoners and the disposition of their remains was not high on Moscow's agenda. Churchill's note to Eden of March 3 that "surely we should press Molotov" revealed a level of impatience in the West that did not exist in the U.S.S.R.[153]

The next day, the Allied high commissioners decided that the most recent appeal to Semeonov on hospitalization and remains (dated January 11, 1954) should be published in the event of a death in Spandau. Adenauer understood as well, especially after a conversation with Dulles after the foreign ministers' conference, that it was best to say nothing in public to avoid jeopardizing whatever concessions the Soviets might have been considering.[154] In any event, Semeonov received instructions from Molotov by the end of March, and Semeonov informed the Allied high commissioners that the matter of ill prisoners and the disposal of bodies could be discussed by a commission of experts on a quadripartite basis.[155] The Spandau prisoners, who heard about Molotov's order but not its limited content, were briefly euphoric. "Some kind of movement," noted Speer, "is apparently beginning." "I'll not believe it," deadpanned von Neurath, "until I stand on the other side of the gate."[156]

The Soviets were careful that discussions would never reach the point where releases of the Spandau prisoners would be considered. On the same day that London was informed of Molotov's instructions to Semeonov, a vocal backbencher Labour MP named Arthur Lewis began to raise repeated questions in the House of Commons as to whether the British government was attempting to secure the release of the most notorious Nazi war criminals. It is not known if there was any connection between the Soviets and Lewis himself. Still, Lewis's later meetings with East German Communist leaders, together with the nature of his comments, which accused the British government of attempting to secure the release of Spandau prisoners so that they could assume command positions within the EDC, prompt speculation that his parliamentary hectoring was not coincidental.[157]

In any event, the Allied high commissioners scrambled to secure a meeting with the Soviets as soon as possible. The first round of talks were on April 6, 1954, in the former Allied Control Council building in West Berlin. Leaks in the West German press to the effect that the Four Powers would discuss the releases of the Spandau prisoners were countered with official statements that better conditions within the prison was the only item on the agenda.[158] The Western high commissioners were represented by members of their own legal committees, while Semeonov was represented by his political adviser, G. P. Zimin and a delegation of six others. The idea from the Western perspective was to secure a betterment of day-to-day conditions within the prison, which included a number of rather mundane changes in the prison regulations. It was also to enable seriously ill prisoners to spend time in a real hospital. The most important issue, however, was the remains of deceased prisoners.

The Allied proposal was to turn the remains over to the next of kin for a quiet burial within Berlin. The proximity of the burial would prevent a long trip for the body and the attendant risk that segments of the public would turn out to view the train. It would also allow the Western Allies to prevent a large public gathering at the funeral itself. From the start, the Soviets were apprehensive. At first Zimin refused even to discuss the issue and refused to set a date for future rounds of talks, revealing that the Soviet government was primarily interested in what the Allied proposals were. Yet the Soviets also feared West German revanchism, which was closely tied to funerals. Was it not true, Zimin asked, that militarist organizations existed on a greater scale in 1954 than they did in 1947, when the cremation agreement was struck? The Western delegations said no, arguing that though they would ensure steps to prevent public funerals, they also felt, in the words of British legal representative Maurice Bathurst, that the present cremation agreement carried the seeds of greater disasters.

> In the first place, we believe that it is hopeless that the procedure can be kept secret. Secondly, we believe that there is far more danger that the prisoners be made martyrs if a procedure of this kind is carried out in 1954 or subsequent years. Finally, we believe that those of us . . . responsible for carrying out [the] procedure which was subsequently elaborated in all its ghoulish details would be held in scorn and ridicule in world opinion.[159]

Three more rounds of discussions followed in the final week of April 1954, each almost completely consumed with the issue of burial. The Soviets made one major concession. On April 26, Zimin announced that instead of cremation, the bodies of deceased prisoners could receive burial within the walls of Spandau Prison itself.[160] By April 30, the Soviets agreed that the immediate family could be present for the burial and that the ground in which burials would take place could be consecrated as such. Why the Soviets made the concession remains a mystery. Perhaps they agreed that the cremation of bodies at this point would fuel rather than defuse what they viewed as militant West German revanchism. In any event, they still refused to release the bodies to the next of kin – the deceased would remain under Four-Power control within the prison walls.

Bathurst on orders from the Foreign Office struggled mightily to convince the Soviets that a burial site within the prison walls could create precisely the type of Nazi shrine that the Soviets wanted to avoid.[161] Worse, London could imagine a scenario wherein, once all the condemned men had been either released or buried, the bodies would be reinterred by the relatives anyway, possibly with a certain amount of political fanfare. The British had some unfortunate experience in this regard. After the war, the British authorities buried some one hundred condemned and executed German war criminals in unmarked graves within the walls of Hamelin Prison in Westphalia. The dead included concentration camp officials from the Bergen-Belsen and Auschwitz-Birkenau camps. German resentment at the time was high, and the West German government was now in the process of exhuming the bodies for burial elsewhere. It would be better, Bathurst said, to allow normal burial for the Spandau prisoners somewhere else in Berlin. The Allies could control the funeral services, the graves would one day be forgotten, and Spandau Prison itself would remain a prison, not a Nazi shrine. "I think undoubtedly," Bathurst argued to Zimin,

> [that] the average German when he thinks of war criminals thinks of Spandau prison. Now if one of those prisoners dies and he is buried outside the prison my belief is that he will soon be forgotten. If, however, he dies and is buried in the prison it will be long remembered by the Germans that Spandau prison contains war criminals who have died there and have been buried there, and that way it will live in the minds of the Germans. When all the prisoners have died and have been buried outside the prison or have served their terms and have been released, I believe that Spandau prison will be forgotten by the German public and no such encouragement will be given to disruptive elements.

The French representative, Michel Bourély, agreed. The current arrangement, he said, was "shocking," while the Soviet suggestion for "the concentration of bodies at Spandau would create a legend for future consciousness." Zimin was unmoved. "Fascist and militaristic elements," he argued, "are now going with heads high," and burial outside the prison walls would only "stimulate the activity of the militaristic elements . . . now underway in West Germany."

When asked directly, Zimin conceded that the Soviets were determined to control the funeral service itself. Burial within Spandau together with the ability to choose the attendees would allow them to do so. Bathurst could only report to his superiors that "I did my best" to convince the Soviets otherwise. The half-loaf the Soviets had offered was better than none at all, and the three Western high commissioners recommended that their governments take the offer before it vanished. "The Russians," wrote Hoyer Millar to the Foreign Office, "have been more forthcoming than we expected, and it would be a mistake to press them too hard to make further concessions lest we lose what we have already gained."[162]

Thus, the fourth and final round of negotiations concerned the smaller details of an agreement. The prison regulations would be eased to a certain degree. Cell lights could be turned off earlier in the evening (6:45 P.M.); prisoners would be allowed to correspond with their attorneys on personal legal matters (subject to governors' approval on a case-by-case basis); attorneys could use a scheduled visit by a relative if the prisoner requested; prisoners would be allowed to speak amongst themselves at exercise or work; the metal grilles in the visitors' area would be removed and prisoners would be allowed to discuss health matters with their loved ones; prisoners would receive an extra visit at Christmastime; there would be four daily newspapers, each chosen by one of the Four Powers; and there would be classical music recordings played in the prison chapel twice a month and on holidays. Hospitalization of seriously ill patients at the nearby British Military Hospital was at least a theoretical possibility now, so long as the four governors agreed, and so long as the prisoner was guarded while in the hospital.[163]

But the major provision concerned burial. The deceased would be buried at Spandau Prison in accordance with his faith with the immediate family (spouse, children, siblings, parents) present. The relatives would be allowed "reasonable opportunities" to visit the site. Soviet paranoia concerning the funeral remained. At Soviet insistence, the funeral could not exceed fifty minutes, and the ceremony at the grave site could not exceed ten, with no photographs allowed at any point. But at least there would be a funeral.[164] Adenauer and Foreign Ministry State Secretary Walter Hallstein had the same reaction. Both were worried that Spandau could become a Nazi Valhalla, but both were pleased that here would at least be a burial.[165] Von Neurath's family was less impressed. His son Constantine called the changes in the prison regime "inconsequential," and he told Blankenhorn, now the head of the Foreign Ministry's Political Division, that the family did not see the change in burial procedure as a great favor.[166] Neither did von Neurath the elder. "They won't release me even after my death," he confided to Speer. "What good is an old man's corpse to them?"[167]

## VON NEURATH'S RELEASE

Despite the agreements of April 1954, the prisoners were treated terribly in July, the Soviet month in the chair. Censorship of letters became more strict, with mentions of garden work and musical recordings heard in chapel services stricken from prisoners' letters home. Alabjev would not even discuss the procedures by which a critically ill prisoner might be sent to the British Military Hospital for surgery, a serious problem because Funk was in urgent need of a prostatectomy. And the food during July, according to the Kommandatura "is always disgustingly bad," to the point where the seven prisoners lost about thirty-three pounds among them by the end of the month.[168]

Von Neurath got the worst of it. On the night of July 7, 1954, the Soviet warder Mogilnikov inspected von Neurath's cell and found a piece of chocolate that another warder had slipped him to compensate for the food during the Soviet month. The Soviets were determined to harass von Neurath rather than find the guilty warder on their own. Darbois called the Soviet insistence "ridiculous" because "the prison was not a house of miracles and the Prisoner No. 3 was no conjurer" who whipped up the chocolate on his own. Alabjev countered that von Neurath was the guilty party and that "[von Neurath] should be punished severely for illegal possession of chocolate."[169] Three searches of the cells were carried out the evening of July 7, the last near midnight, and on the nights of the July 11, July 12, July 13, July 20, and July 23, the Soviet warders carried out midnight and postmidnight searches of each cell. In such searches, the prisoners had to stand for twenty minutes outside the cells and then take another thirty minutes to clean the cells before they could return to sleep.[170] Alabjev was determined that von Neurath say where the chocolate had come from, but von Neurath would not budge. "Tell who gave it to you," insisted Alabjev, "We already know anyhow." "Then you know more than I," said a tired, but stubborn von Neurath.[171] To twist the screws, Alabjev disallowed a joint visit by von Neurath's wife and daughter. Joint visits, though never within regulations, had been allowed for some time.[172]

Why would Alabjev have caused such difficulties after the April agreements? The Kommandatura theorized that it had to do with the replacement of Dengin with General Pavel Dibrova, who during his first visit to the prison in mid-July noted that the prisoners were "enemies of the people" to be "treated with special strictness."[173] The British government theorized that the hard Soviet attitude had something to do with the appearance in Britain of a book-length account of life within Spandau called *The Seven*

*Men of Spandau* by the journalist Jack Fishman. Based on interviews and containing unauthorized photographs of the prisoners, the book infuriated the Soviets, who argued that security had become especially lax during the Allied months in the chair.[174]

But the effect of the searches on von Neurath, who by the summer of 1954 could barely dress himself each morning, was distressing. The American prison physician Major Wright reported that the night searches, if they were to continue, could easily kill him, and at the prison governors' meetings of July 15 and July 23, the three Western governors complained that Soviet actions were inhuman, beyond all proportion to security concerns, and that they endangered the life of von Neurath and possibly Funk as well. The British in West Berlin called a commandants' meeting to discuss options.[175]

Von Neurath's condition did not improve. At the start of August, the American month in the chair, Major Wright posted a note on von Neurath's cell door that the prisoner was not to be disturbed at night. Mogilnikov ignored the note and conducted a 1:00 A.M. search, despite protests by the Allied warders on duty.[176] In the early hours of September 1, von Neurath nearly died in his cell and the next morning looked "helpless and broken," according to Speer.[177] He was, according to Wright, "more seriously ill than I had ever seen before."[178] Von Neurath was moved to an oxygen tent and the prison authorities summoned his family to West Berlin to stand by for his possible death. On their visit, which Alabjev restricted to the allowed thirty minutes, neither Marie nor Winifred were allowed to take his hand; they could only sit at the end of von Neurath's bed.[179] Furious, Marie complained to the governors, and Winifred von Mackensen wrote a long article for *Die Welt* describing once again the conditions of the prison and the state of her father.[180] Fully five decades later, one Soviet warder still remembered the seething anger in the two women's faces.[181] Adenauer now called privately for von Neurath's complete release from Spandau Prison. In the past, he said, he had asked the Allied High Commission that von Neurath simply be moved to a hospital. Now, however, he was convinced that von Neurath was incapable of remaining under guard, and that in the name of humanity he should be allowed to spend his final days at home, where he could receive proper medical treatment and where his family could have unlimited access.[182] The Kommandatura and the High Commission drafted a strong protest to Semeonov, since, as François-Poncet put it, the Soviets respected "neither the spirit nor the letter" of the April 1954 agreement while "recently applying inhumane treatment to the prisoners."[183]

But before the protest was sent, the Soviets softened. Alabjev agreed in late August that Funk could have his prostatectomy in the British Military Hospital rather than in the prison, where complications during surgery would surely have killed him.[184] In November, the Soviets replaced Alabjev after more than three years as Moscow's Spandau Prison governor. Most startling,

13. Konstantin von Neurath prepares to leave West Berlin following his release from Spandau Prison in November 1954. He is flanked by a flight attendant and his daughter Winifred von Mackensen. Photograph courtesy of Corbis.

however, was this: Konstantin von Neurath would be released as the first inmate to leave Spandau since the takeover of the prison by the Four Powers. On November 3, 1954, the Soviet ambassador to East Germany, Georgy M. Pushkin (the German Democratic Republic became officially sovereign in March 1954) unilaterally proposed to François-Poncet von Neurath's release, after having checked with the Communist government in Prague, which had a special interest in von Neurath's case.[185] Allied agreement came quickly. On November 7, without a chance to say good-bye to his fellow inmates, von Neurath was given a change of clothes and led to a waiting room where his daughter Winifred awaited him. A car in the prison yard drove them away from Spandau. The shock on the other inmates was profound. So was the shock on von Neurath. On the day of his release, he revealed how small his world had become when he worriedly asked a reporter, "What will become of my garden without me?"[186]

Why did the Soviets allowed von Neurath to walk free? The press saw the answer in terms of Cold War politics, and particularly in terms of a Soviet "peace offensive" aimed at pleasing West German sentiment to some degree, thus disrupting the adhesion of the Federal Republic to the West. Career military officers in East Germany who belonged to the National

Democratic Party there could also be won through this concession.[187] It is true that the Soviets decided in July 1955 to release nearly 10,000 German prisoners from Soviet soil, many of whom had been convicted of war crimes or violations of Soviet law. It is also true that Nikita Khrushchev, the new general secretary of the Soviet Communist Party, made this move to normalize relations with Bonn inasmuch as possible while fostering some level of trade between the two states. He explained as much to SED general secretary Walter Ulbricht.[188] But it is clear from all Soviet comments concerning Spandau that the prisoners there were considered different than the army rank and file or even the Nazi police officials in the U.S.S.R. These were the major war criminals, convicted before the entire world. It is also clear from the records that the Soviets had not cared in principle if the prisoners in Spandau died there. Provisions had existed for the case of their deaths since 1947, and the Soviets changed these provisions only reluctantly.

It is more likely that, with Funk and von Neurath on the edge of death, the Soviets realized that the British had been right during the Four-Power negotiations in April. A common gravesite in Spandau for the prisoners would become the very shrine that the Soviets hoped to prevent. In attempting to retain control over the funeral service, they had outsmarted themselves. The best of the available alternatives now was to allow von Neurath to go home, die quietly, and hopefully be buried quietly. If political gains could be had, so much the better. Such explains why Pushkin made the suggestion for von Neurath's release as a démarche to the Allied powers. As Maurice Bathurst would later theorize, the Soviets probably proposed von Neurath's release to avoid the dangers of memorialization that Bathurst himself had mentioned to them earlier in the year.

For the rest, the world press greeted the release of a very ill 81-year-old man from what was becoming the world's most famous prison. He was a "pathetic sight" as he emerged, barely able to walk, leaning on his daughter and wearing the frayed jacket and pants that comprised his prison wardrobe, and unable to answer the questions of journalists who had assembled outside the prison gates.[189] Even the Israelis and Western European socialists saw the release itself as a welcome act of humanity.[190] The release dominated the West German press for several days. Every detail of von Neurath's last days in Spandau was recounted as was his return home. More controversial were comments, such as those in *Frankfurter Allgemeine Zeitung*, that von Neurath's release should now occasion the revision of all the Nuremberg judgments.[191] For some, it represented a "delayed revision of a judicial mistake."[192]

Von Neurath received a festive welcome on his return to his Württemberg estate of Leinfelderhof in Kleinglattbach complete with flowers and ringing church bells. A published telegram from Adenauer awaited him. "The news that freedom has been restored to you after long, hard years," it said, "has sincerely gladdened me. I express to you, your wife and your children my heartiest congratulations and couple them with my best wishes for the restoration of your health." More explicit was the open letter von Neurath received from the Federal president and fellow Württemberger Theodor Heuss. Though Heuss's place as a responsible and sober proponent of memory in the early years of the West German state cannot be doubted today, his remarks were ill considered:

> With pleased satisfaction . . . I read the report this morning that . . . the martyrdom [*Martyrium*] of these years has come to an end for you. I am happy that you are now restored to your family and to your Württemberg home, with which you always remain linked, and that our cares and thoughts must no longer be troubled by bitter imagination. I can only wish that your naturally strong disposition will soon recover from the consequences of these harsh years, and that, restored to your familiar surroundings, you will find peace of mind too.[193]

Heuss's choice of the word "martyrdom" triggered an international outcry, for the world had not forgotten what the Trial of the Major War Criminals had meant. The criticism took many forms – that the West German government and press had insulted the memories of the millions who had died at the hands of the Nazis, that they had unjustly questioned fair verdicts, that they were making a provocative comment concerning German war criminals still held in custody in various Western European states, that they were playing to the West German right by adopting the argument that punishment and martyrdom were one and the same, and that perhaps the new West Germany could not be trusted as a member of the new Europe after all. The French Press – from the liberal center to the Communist left – universally condemned Heuss's comments.[194] The leading socialist newspaper of the Netherlands called Heuss's and Adenauer's remarks part of a "characterless policy of opportunism," aimed at winning support among West Germans who denied Nazi criminality. A "war criminal receiving clemency," it continued, should not be treated like a "hero." A cocktail party in the West German Embassy at The Hague was filled with negative comments concerning Heuss's choice of words.[195]

The reaction in Britain was not much better, even from the *Yorkshire Post*, which stood closely to Anthony Eden. It acidly commented that Heuss had done no service to the remaining Spandau prisoners. *The Times* commented that regardless of Heuss's intent, the affair would remain in the British memory for a long time. The *Daily Mirror*, meanwhile, contained a cartoon in which Hitler, Goebbels, and Göring complained from Valhalla that they had committed suicide too early.[196] The liberal Belgian paper *La Lanterne*, meanwhile, commented on the affair on three separate occasions, even linking the deaths of Belgian citizens with what it called the German reaction to von Neurath's release.[197] It would have been better, said the Swiss *Nationalzeitung*, if von Neurath had left Spandau as would a thief in the night. The latent mistrust of Germany would not be alleviated by the display of faux pas at the highest levels.[198] As U.S. observers pointed out, "If the Soviet intention in acceding to the release of Konstantin von Neurath from Spandau Prison was to stir up comments and reactions in Germany of a nature to alarm French public and political opinion at this critical time, the Soviet move achieved its purpose."[199] To top it off, Heuss's letter was debated after an inquiry in the Bundestag, West Germany's federal parliament.[200]

The damage control launched by Bonn centered on the word *Martyrium* itself, which the president and Bonn insisted was misunderstood by translators. It referred to the fact that von Neurath had undergone terrible suffering in Spandau owing to the conditions there – it did not mean that the suffering was for a noble or just cause.[201] In his circular to all West German representatives abroad, Herbert Blankenhorn commented that "non-judgmental circles" in other states would understand this.[202] Heuss was angrier. In a letter to a German writers' union in London, he stated that he was "a bit astonished" that in certain agencies abroad and even in Germany so many people had such a weak understanding of the difference between "an expression of humanity and a political judgment." Without addressing whether von Neurath was guilty of anything, the president then compared Spandau with Nazi concentration camps, adding that the Western Allies and the Germans were disturbed by each, and that anyone would be pleased that such tortures would no longer be applied to an old, sick man. Those who insisted on reading his heartfelt words to von Neurath differently were themselves guilty of a "willful misunderstanding." In any event, he would not explain himself publicly on the issue, having made his sentiments toward Nazism known on previous occasions.[203] Such would have to be enough.

For the rest, the release of von Neurath set a pattern. Men dying in Spandau would be allowed to die at home with the family burying the remains as they saw fit. In September 1955, Erich Raeder was released from Spandau thanks to severe illness. Moscow's concern that Walther Funk might die in prison even prompted them to agree to surgery in the British Military Hospital for obstructive jaundice in August 1956. In May 1957, however, after medical evaluations proved pessimistic, Funk hobbled free from Spandau as well. In each of these to cases, the Western ambassadors proposed the release of the prisoner to the Soviets so that the Soviets could gain no propaganda advantage. But in each case, the Soviets agreed, thus revealing that a Nazi graveyard at Spandau was what bothered them the most, regardless of which country made the suggestion.[204]

Von Neurath died at Leinfelderhof on August 14, 1956. He was buried quietly in the family plot at Kleinglattbach where fellow Nuremberg defendant

Franz von Papen delivered the eulogy.[205] But few can say today, and indeed few care, where von Neurath's remains lie. The struggle over martyrdom was ultimately won by the Western Allies and, in spite of themselves, by the Soviets. And it was won, ironically, by doing nothing. Such can be viewed as evidence of Germany's transformation after World War II. Still, before von Neurath's release, the Four Powers had come uncomfortably close to creating martyrs through their own elaborate efforts to avoid the same.

CHAPTER FOUR

# Hitler's Successor: A Tale of Two Admirals

"I am still and will remain the legal chief of state.... Until I die!"

Karl Dönitz, 1953

Spandau's inmates included Hitler's two naval commanders-in-chief, Grand Admirals Erich Raeder and Karl Dönitz. Dönitz carried the additional distinction of having been named Hitler's successor shortly before the latter's suicide on April 30, 1945, and until the German surrender on May 8 he presided over the Third Reich's denouement. The two admirals, like von Neurath, demonstrated that there were differences among Spandau's prisoners. If von Neurath had a support network that included notables from Württemberg, then the two admirals, like German military commanders in the Allied prisons in West Germany, had a network that included German veterans' organizations who did not see their former officers as criminals.

The captivity of Raeder and Dönitz is of interest for other reasons, too. The public nature of the Raeder-and-Dönitz issue led to as vocal a soul-searching as the West German public had regarding any individual war criminal, complete with a lengthy debate in the Bundestag on what it meant to be a senior officer in the new West German armed forces (the *Bundeswehr*). In addition, Dönitz was a political figure by default – as Hitler's successor he was of special concern to the Allied powers, particularly the British Foreign Office. Hoping to keep him in jail as long as possible, London sabotaged every attempt to allow his eighteen months of pretrial custody to count against his sentence. As the Americans would point out to their British friends, the holding of a man for what he might do as opposed to holding him for what he had actually done changed the nature of the inmate from criminal to political prisoner. Regardless, Dönitz's case showed that the Soviet government was not the only one that feared the future actions of Hitler's closest associates.

## OFFICERS OR PIRATES?

When Hitler became chancellor in 1933, Erich Raeder had already been the commander of the German Navy for five years. Of the service chiefs in office in January 1933, Raeder was the only one still in power when Germany went to war in 1939. To a strong degree, Hitler and this veteran seaman were in accord on German continental and global aims.

Born near Hamburg in 1876, Raeder was a product of the Imperial Navy that had been constructed under Alfred von Tirpitz to strive for Germany's "place in the sun" against Great Britain. His most colorful assignment was to serve for two years as the navigation officer on Kaiser Wilhelm II's royal yacht *Hohenzollern*. Like other naval officers who came of age under the Kaiser (and thus under the influence of the theories of Alfred Thayer Mahan), Raeder believed firmly in the navy as an instrument of German global power. Like most naval officers, he chafed under the restrictions of the Treaty of Versailles, which limited German tonnage to coastal defense capabilities while outlawing submarines and heavy battleships entirely so that Germany could present no oceangoing threat to the war's victors.

Raeder rose quickly in the 1920s. After writing a two-volume history of German cruiser operations in World War I he became a rear admiral responsible for naval training (1922), for naval forces in the North Sea (1924), and for German sea power in the Baltic (1925). Once he became chief of the German Navy in 1928, Raeder commissioned the so-called pocket battleships – armored cruisers technically illegal under the Versailles restrictions in that they slightly exceeded the prescribed limit of 10,000 tons and could outgun enemy cruisers then in existence while outrunning the battleships of the time. The first of these, *Deutschland*, was completed in 1933. *Admiral Scheer* was finished in 1934.

The advent of Hitler, who challenged the Versailles restrictions more openly, was appealing to Raeder even though Hitler was a naval amateur. It was under Raeder that the navy took the oath of allegiance to Hitler after President Paul von Hindenburg's death on August 2, 1934, and under Raeder that the swastika was incorporated into the flag under which the fleet sailed. It was also under Raeder that the Germans signed the Anglo-German Naval Accord of 1935, limiting German overall tonnage, and then immediately broke it by contracting the 48,000 ton battleships *Bismarck* and *Tirpitz*. (The internationally accepted battleship displacement limit was 35,000 tons.) By December 1937, the German Navy approved a plan for the building of six more battleships of 56,000 tons each. At the time the expectation was that these mammoth ships would be completed by 1944.[1]

This date was not coincidental. It was on November 5, 1937, in the famous Hossbach meeting that Hitler informed his service chiefs that Germany's living space on the continent would be won between 1943 and 1945. Raeder had not only been at the meeting, but he was the only service chief to raise no objections whatever to Hitler's timetable – a point not lost on the prosecution at Nuremberg nine years later.[2] The surface fleet, as discussed in 1937, was surely intended to protect German global interests after the conquest of

14. Adolf Hitler and Erich Raeder during a naval inspection in Kiel, 1933. Photograph courtesy of the National Archives and Records Administration (Heinrich Hoffmann Collection).

Europe – possibly against residual British resentment, possibly against the United States. The contracts for the 56,000 ton battleships were awarded in April and May 1939, and because it was expected that they would take at least five years to build, they could not have been intended solely for the coming European war.

Raeder hoped that the German war against Poland could be localized. He did not think that the German fleet as it then stood, with fewer than fifty operational submarines, twenty-two of which were ocean-going, was up to a long war with Britain and France. But once Britain and France declared war, Raeder thought strategically even with regard to neutrals. Convinced that Britain could not survive without U.S. supplies, Raeder urged Hitler to launch a war against the United States in October 1939 while the United States was still unprepared. Hitler rejected this idea as premature.[3] Raeder instead called for and planned the German occupation of Denmark and Norway in order to protect the flow of German iron ore imports from Sweden along the Scandinavian coast, and the operation was carried out the following April.[4] A month later, with the Scandinavian ports occupied, the French defeated, and the British gasping for breath, Raeder and his naval staff thought more broadly in terms of global power. Bases in the east Atlantic had been a desire even before the war, but in May 1940 Raeder ordered studies as to what

15. Reichsführer-SS Heinrich Himmler and Erich Raeder hear Hitler speak on the occasion of the launching of the battleship *Tirpitz* at Wilhelmshaven, April 1939. Photograph courtesy of Corbis.

bases Germany would need for future operations against the United States. Trondheim, Iceland, Casablanca, the Canary Islands, the Azores, and Dakar were among the many areas that Raeder suggested to Hitler.[5]

Hitler and Raeder had their disagreements. Before the war, Raeder called for a more balanced building program that would give Germany at least 240 submarines by 1948. Hitler emphasized battleship construction with submarines to be added later. Raeder was so strongly against the plan to attack the U.S.S.R. while the war with Great Britain was still in progress that Hitler waited for Raeder to leave the room before announcing his intentions to his other service chiefs on July 31, 1940. But this is the point. Raeder always made his differences with Hitler known – when he had them. And on the larger issues of violating treaties and aggressive war against Germany's neighbors, Raeder had none. To ensure that he did not, Hitler gave him a tax free gift of RM 250,000 on his sixty-fifth birthday in April 1941.[6] When

Hitler replaced Raeder with Dönitz as naval commander-in-chief in January 1943, Raeder had served Hitler for a decade. And he continued to enjoy illicit gratuities from Hitler including a monthly tax free gift of RM 4,000 in addition to his regular salary.

And though not directly involved in the Holocaust, Raeder never disapproved of the German treatment toward Jews. On March 12, 1939, on the occasion of the first Heroes' Day after the Kristallnacht pogrom of November 1938, Raeder gave a speech in which he praised Hitler for "the clear and unmerciful declaration of war against bolshevism and international Jewry, whose drive for the destruction of peoples we have felt quite enough in our own racial body." When confronted with his own words more than seven years later at Nuremberg, Raeder said, in his own *defense*, that from 1917 to 1919 "international Jewry had destroyed the resistance of the German people . . . and had gained an excessively large and oppressive influence in German affairs."[7]

Despite his propensity to cite defense needs to justify treaty violations and wartime needs to justify legal violations, Raeder's guilt was not difficult to prove. Sir David Maxwell-Fyfe exposed most violations of the Versailles and Anglo-German Naval Treaties. "For 20 years, from 1918 to 1938," he charged, "you and the German Navy had been involved in a course of complete, cold and deliberate deception of your treaty obligations. . . . Do you deny that this is so?" Raeder could only counter that "It was not a cold blooded affair."[8] Maxwell-Fyfe made hay of Raeder's defense assertions that one could not take seriously Hitler's comments concerning war planning at the Hossbach meeting or at later talks in May and November 1939 with high ranking officers. But the invasion of Norway was the most salient issue. In November 1945, the prosecution had pointed out that "the Norwegian invasion is . . . not a typical Nazi aggression in that Hitler had to be persuaded to embark upon it. The chief instruments of persuasion were Raeder and [Alfred] Rosenberg; Raeder because he thought Norway strategically important and because he coveted glory for the Navy." U.S. prosecutor Telford Taylor added that, in cases against Raeder and other senior officers, following orders as technicians of policy was no defense anyway. "It is an innocent and respectable business to be a locksmith," Taylor noted, "but it is nonetheless a crime if the locksmith turns his talents to picking the locks of neighbors and looting their homes."[9]

Raeder did not help his own case. He admitted to having favored the Norwegian invasion though he couched it in terms of German intelligence reports that pointed to an imminent British occupation.[10] Yet Raeder's own statement to Hitler on March 26, 1940, read by Maxwell-Fyfe, noted that a "British landing in Norway [is] not considered imminent – [Raeder] suggests action by us at the next new moon – to which Hitler agrees."[11] Raeder also admitted that on September 3 and again on October 15, 1939, he argued for unrestricted submarine warfare against Britain wherein British and neutral merchant ships could be sunk without warning. "Measures which are considered necessary from a military point of view," Raeder noted on the latter date, "will have to be carried out, even if they are not covered by existing international law.... Every protest from neutral powers must be turned down.... The more ruthlessly economic warfare is waged... the sooner the war will come to an end."[12] For Raeder, the onus would thus be on neutrals for running the risk. As he let slip at his trial: "Neutrals are acting for egotistical reasons and they must pay the bill if they die."[13] He also admitted that he had distributed Hitler's Commando Order of October 18, 1942 (whereby captured enemy shock troops would be summarily shot), to naval troops and that he thought the order justified. Thus, he could be held responsible for the execution by naval troops of two British commandos in Bordeaux in December 1942.[14] Raeder was speedily convicted on Counts I, II, and III. The judges compromised on his punishment between the low suggestion of twenty years (Donnedieu de Vabres) and the high suggestion of death (Nikitschenko). He received life imprisonment.

If Raeder was a lifelong naval professional who had made a Faustian bargain with Hitler over more ships and bases, then Dönitz was the closest thing the German Navy had to a Nazi admiral.[15] Born in 1891 near Berlin, Dönitz, the son of an engineer, joined the navy in 1910. In 1916, after having served in the Black Sea on the cruiser *Breslau*, Dönitz was promoted to the rank of top lieutenant and transferred to the submarine fleet, which was then wreaking havoc on British commercial shipping. As a submarine commander, he was taken prisoner by the British. He never forgot the value of commercial raiding, which had nearly brought the British to ruin before the United States entered World War I. After the war, Dönitz became a naval staff officer.

Dönitz was a believer in Nazism from the moment Hitler took power, and his speedy ascent began with Hitler's desire to ignore the 1935 naval agreement with London, which allowed Germany to have submarines amounting to 45 percent of British submarine tonnage. Dönitz, now charged with the development of German submarine forces, ignored the agreement though the emphasis on surface craft made for a smaller submarine force than Dönitz had hoped. In 1939, Dönitz was promoted to the rank of rear admiral and given the title Commander of Submarines (*Führer der U-Boote*) within the naval command. His "wolf pack" tactics, wherein groups of submarines attacked British convoys, maximized the small number of German submarines available in 1939. His ruthless prosecution of the commercial war together with his devotion to Nazism and to Hitler helped to ensure that he would replace Raeder as naval commander-in-chief in January 1943.

Dönitz remained devoted to Hitler through the worst of times. In August 1943, he praised Hitler's prophecy that the anti-German alliance between the Western Allies and the Soviets would split, noting "what very poor little

16. Heinrich Himmler and Karl Dönitz at Hitler's East Prussian Headquarters on the occasion of Hitler's birthday, April 1944. Photograph courtesy of the National Archives and Records Administration (Heinrich Hoffmann Collection).

sausages we are in comparison with the Führer."[16] In a speech to his senior officers on December 17, he argued that soldiers must be motivated by ideology as well as duty. The traditional notion that soldiers should be apolitical, he said, was nonsense.[17] In February 1944, the month he broke this tradition by joining the Nazi Party, Dönitz elaborated that "the whole officer corps must be so indoctrinated that it feels itself co-responsible for the National Socialist state in its entirety." On July 21, 1944 – the day after the failed plot by German army staff officers to assassinate and replace Hitler – Dönitz made a speech, described in more detail later in this chapter, praising "our beloved Führer" who had been "spared by Providence."[18] In August, he commented to subordinates: "I would rather eat dirt than see my grandchildren grow up in the filthy, poisonous atmosphere of Jewry."[19] Naval officers and seamen, meanwhile, were occasionally tried and executed simply for saying bad things about the Führer – Dönitz confirmed one such execution order of a lowly machinist four days after Hitler's death.[20] Small wonder why Hitler named Dönitz as his successor in his final testament. While Hitler's other paladins such as Himmler and Kaltenbrunner were trying to save their own skins through secret peace deals with the Allies, Dönitz would fight until the last bullet was fired.[21]

The decision whether to try Dönitz as a major war criminal was not easy. He did not command the navy until 1943; regarding the conspiracy count, he was not present at key prewar conferences such as the Hossbach meeting. The Soviets correctly pointed out that as Hitler's successor Dönitz had deliberately prolonged the war after all hope of victory had vanished, but since Dönitz's responsibilities for most of the conflict pertained to the high seas, he, like Raeder, was not indicted for crimes against humanity. Yet the savage nature of the Battle of the Atlantic and the tens of thousands of merchant seamen lost in submarine attacks could surely be attributed to the ways in which Dönitz prosecuted the commercial war against the Allies.[22]

The chief evidence against Dönitz thus fell under the aggressive war and war crimes sections of the indictment. International maritime prize law – reaffirmed by the 1930 London Naval Treaty and the Submarine Protocol of 1936 – held that submarines could not sink merchant vessels without warning and without the movement of the target ship's passengers and crews to safety.[23] Germany had signed both agreements, but from the start of the war Dönitz's submarines torpedoed Allied and neutral commercial shipping in violation. Aside from thousands of wrecks at the bottom of the Atlantic, there was plenty of documentation to tie the practice to Dönitz beginning with the deliberate falsification of official records relating to the German sinking of the British passenger liner *Athenia* on the first day of the war with Great Britain.[24] A subsequent Naval Command memorandum of September 22, 1939, noted that Dönitz intended to permit the sinking without warning of any ship running without lights and that submarine captains in logging such attacks were to attribute their actions to confusion as to whether the merchant vessels were warships.[25] Press releases were to say that ships torpedoed near coastal areas had struck mines.[26]

And survivors were not to be helped. Dönitz's signed order Number 154 from late in 1939 proclaimed: "Do not save anyone... regardless of weather conditions and distance from land.... We must be hard in this war. The enemy began the war in order to destroy us... therefore nothing else matters."[27] The principle of killing as many merchant seamen as possible was augmented after the United States entered the war. Hitler and his naval officers understood that though the United States could replace lost ships quickly, it could not so easily replace trained seamen. "Once it gets around that most of the seamen are lost," said Hitler to the Japanese ambassador Hiroshi Oshima on January 3, 1942, "the Americans would soon have difficulties in enlisting new people. The training of maritime personnel takes a long time. We are fighting for our existence and can therefore tolerate no humanitarian viewpoints."[28]

Dönitz agreed. It is here that the so-called "*Laconia* Order" came into play. The *Laconia* was a British steamer carrying a crew of eight hundred seamen and eighteen hundred Italian prisoners. Off the West African coast the German submarine U-156 sank the *Laconia* and then helped to save all the crew and about 450 of the Italian prisoners. During the rescue operation, however, two American bombers attacked and damaged the submarine. The next day, September 17, 1942, Dönitz issued the following order via radio:

> No attempt of any kind must be made at rescuing members of ships sunk and this includes picking up persons in the water and putting them in lifeboats, righting capsized lifeboats, and handing over food and water. Rescue runs counter to the most primitive demands of warfare for the destruction of enemy ships and crews.[29]

Did this order mean that crews were to be left since the risk to the submarines would be too great? Or did it mean that shipwrecked crews were to be murdered after the engagement? At Nuremberg, Lieutenant Peter-Joseph Heisig and Captain Karl-Heinz Möhle signed affidavits and testified that they understood from Dönitz's subsequent speeches to U-Boat trainees that though the United States could build more ships than the Germans could sink, the bottleneck would lie with trained seamen. Thus, no crewman of a torpedoed ship was to return home.[30] Dönitz was careful enough never to issue official criminal orders. When Hitler mused about openly renouncing the Geneva Convention in February 1945, Dönitz warned him that it would be best to act without openly renouncing international law. It would, the grand admiral said, keep up appearances.[31]

Dönitz had the most able defense attorney of all the Nuremberg defendants. Tall, fit, and clean-cut, Otto Kranzbühler was a veteran German Navy judge who understood – as most of the German defense attorneys did not – that he had to attack the indictment and the evidence directly. His legalism here and in the years ahead was not without irony. After the attempt to assassinate Hitler in July 1944, Kranzbühler publicly endorsed the Nazi kangaroo courts that did away with the plotters.[32] At Nuremberg, he argued that the German submarine war did not violate international law because enemy merchantmen were de facto combat vessels. If armed, they could attack surfaced submarines; if not armed, they could report a submarine's position. This is why, Kranzbühler and Dönitz argued, they were considered legitimate targets less than a month into the war. "Germany," Dönitz said, "considered the crews of merchantmen as combatants because they fought with weapons."[33] Neutral merchantmen, meanwhile, were given fair warning not to enter German-blockaded areas.

As for orders not to rescue shipwrecked crews, Kranzbühler distinguished between the nonrescue of shipwrecked crews and their murder. Rescue was out of the question owing to the danger surfaced submarines engaged in rescue operations faced from the air. Dönitz's priority had to be his boats and their crews. If a couple of subordinates mistook the orders to mean that shipwrecked crews were to be murdered, the fault lay with them. Dönitz maintained further that there was but one documented case of bullets fired at a shipwrecked crew, namely the attack on the Greek steamer *Peleus* in

March 1944 by Captain Heinz Eck's boat, U-852. By the time Dönitz testified at Nuremberg, Eck had been sentenced to death for war crimes by a British tribunal in Hamburg. Dönitz argued that Eck was trying to sink the debris of the *Peleus* so that his position would not be spotted. "After the war," he said coolly, "one views events differently."[34]

But ultimately Kranzbühler's defense was that "no evidence has been found that a written or oral order for the shooting of shipwrecked prisoners was issued."[35] Comments such as these were not helpful. Nor was Dönitz's icy reasoning behind his appeal to Hitler in May 1942 for a magnetic detonator on torpedoes. Such detonators, he explained to Hitler, would sink ships more quickly, preventing countermeasures while also having "the great advantage that the crew will not be able to save themselves on account of the quick sinking.... This greater loss of men will no doubt cause difficulties in the assignment of crews." Dönitz's argument in court, in other words, was that killing merchant crews *during* engagement was entirely legal if done right. Maxwell-Fyfe brought out his cold logic during cross examination. Sir David also pointed out that the wording of the *Laconia* order contained a deliberate ambiguity in the words, "the elementary demands of warfare for the destruction of ships and crews are contrary to rescuing." Why, he asked Dönitz, could the order not have said, "you are forbidden to rescue because in view of the Allied air cover it is a matter of too great danger for the safety of yourself and your boat," especially when Dönitz's own staff officers warned against misinterpretation of the wording that was chosen?

Dönitz had no good defense for evidence of other war crimes. In response to proof that in late 1944 he demanded twelve thousand foreign slave laborers from concentration camps to step up shipyard production, Dönitz argued that he did the slave laborers a favor; they received better rations by working in shipyards. "At any rate," he added, "I did not worry about... [concentration camp] methods... it was none of my business."[36] In response to the charge that he had known that his subordinate Admiral Otto von Schrader handed over ten uniformed torpedo boat prisoners to the notorious *Sicherheitsdienst* (SD) for shooting in May 1943 as per Hitler's Commando Order, Dönitz claimed ignorance.[37] As for his glowing speeches about the Führer from 1943 to 1945, which included praise for the defense against bolshevism and Jewry, Dönitz's defense was that, "it shows that I was of the opinion that the endurance... of the people... could be better preserved than if there were Jewish elements in the nation."[38]

Dönitz's case was theoretically bolstered by the later arrival of an affidavit from the commander of the wartime U.S. fleet in the Pacific, Admiral Chester W. Nimitz. Kranzbühler had requested Nimitz's written answers to a number of pointed questions in order to make the argument that all states engaged in commerce raiding had interpreted the London Agreements as had Germany. He read Nimitz's comments into evidence on July 2, 1946. Nimitz made

17. Karl Dönitz's final statement at Nuremberg, September 1946. Erich Raeder sits to his left. Hermann Göring sits in the foreground. Photograph courtesy of the National Archives and Records Administration.

clear that in the war against Japan, the Americans practiced unrestricted submarine warfare from the beginning and that "on general principles, U.S. submarines did not rescue enemy survivors if undue additional hazard to the submarine resulted."[39] Of course, Nimitz mentioned no gray areas whereby American sailors should murder Japanese survivors; the U.S. Navy did not use concentration camp inmates in American shipyards; and Nimitz's officers did not hand prisoners over to the FBI for summary execution. But Dönitz's final statement demonstrated the hubris caused by an adequate defense. "I would," he said, "do exactly the same all over again." He returned to await judgment, convinced that he would be acquitted.

And he came closer than he deserved. U.S. Judge Francis Biddle voted for Dönitz's acquittal based on Kranzbühler's interpretation of maritime law and the Nimitz affidavit. But Donnedieu de Vabres saw the Nimitz parallel unwarranted; the Russians voted for conviction on all three counts as a matter of course; and Lawrence thought that Dönitz should be found guilty on Count II at the very least. In the end, the Tribunal convicted Dönitz on Counts II and III in a muddled judgment that tried to balance the vagaries of naval warfare against Dönitz's more doubtful actions and statements. Dönitz was found in violation of the Submarine Protocol of 1936 and censured for the ambiguity of the *Laconia* order, but convicted on the basis of neither (a point lost on his later advocates). On the other hand, the Tribunal found Dönitz guilty of crimes against peace, and his acceptance of the Commando Order and use of concentration camp labor were clearly war crimes. Because Dönitz was Raeder's subordinate until 1943, the judges all agreed that his penalty should be less than Raeder's. Thus, in an odd case where Nikitschenko did not vote for death, Dönitz received a penalty of ten years.[40] In a pair of judgments that would bring no end of controversy and bitterness, Germany's two top naval officers from World War II were going to jail.

## THE VETERANS' LOBBY

Germany was allowed no veterans' organizations immediately after the war. Yet there were fifteen million veterans in the western zones alone, and once the Federal Republic of Germany was born in 1949, veterans' organizations began to come together. Veterans' leaders were concerned with various issues from the reinstatement of pensions, to the elimination of the postwar military stigma, to the infusion of the soldierly ethic of loyalty and sacrifice into the new West German state. But in the shadow of the Korean War and the decision to rearm West Germany, veterans' groups also pressed hard for the release from captivity of former military officers. New German soldiers could never march, so the argument went, past the cell windows of their former commanders.

The Western Allies never accepted this reasoning in full. But they did understand that Germans, particularly former officers, in Allied prisons were an increasing political burden for themselves and for the new Adenauer government in Bonn. Bundestag delegates, journalists, and veterans groups pushed incessantly for the freedom of Allied-held prisoners with the argument that the convicts were prisoners of war rather than criminals and that as new citizens of the Federal Republic they were entitled to its protection. As seen in the last chapter, judicial reviews moved steadily forward after 1949. The most famous senior officers to benefit were Field Marshal Albert Kesselring, who was released from Werl in October 1952 after commutation of his life sentence, and Field Marshal von Manstein, who left Werl in May 1953 after serving less than four years of a twelve-year sentence.

In Spandau, Raeder and Dönitz kept a certain professional distance from one another. Raeder saw Dönitz as an overambitious subordinate and treated him, as Speer noted, "with the condescension of a superior officer." Dönitz angrily blamed Raeder for losing World War II by not building more submarines. "It had been Raeder's fault," he excitedly told von Neurath one day in the Spandau garden, "that until the middle of 1940 only two U-Boats a month slid down the ways."[41] But both Raeder and Dönitz flatly rejected their legal guilt and moral responsibility. They could agree in their dislike of Speer for his betrayal of Hitler at Nuremberg.[42] And they hoped that the West German veterans' lobby would somehow overcome Soviet vetoes at Spandau. By December 1951, Dönitz expected that he would be freed soon, for as he told Speer, "a German army cannot be organized as long as our new allies are holding high ranking military officers in Spandau."[43] Of course, the Soviets were not among the new West German allies, and Dönitz was no common officer. But the flood of appeals on behalf of the two grand admirals from veterans' groups began as early as did the appeals for senior officers in Landsberg, Wittlich, and Werl.

The appeals followed two lines of argument. One, as with von Neurath's case, was humanitarian. Raeder was 75 by 1950. He had already had a hernia operation in the prison, and he now suffered from various bladder ailments. He was not fit, so went the argument, to remain. Erika Raeder, his exaggeration-prone and increasingly embittered wife, claimed publicly that she could barely recognize her husband's decrepit form during visits and said that he was subjected to "hard labor" in Spandau. Raeder's job was to tend to the library.

The retired Admiral Gottfried Hansen, chairman of the 100,000 strong *Verband deutscher Soldaten* (VdS) – the closest thing West Germany had to an umbrella veterans' organization – went even further in his correspondence with the three Allied high commissioners. "As a friend of many years' standing," Hansen said,

> and certain that all ex-members of the Navy will agree with me, I venture to say that no military leader could have educated and influenced his subordinates from a higher moral and Christian level than did Raeder . . . both as a man and a Christian. . . . How can genuine peace and real understanding among the nations of the occident be brought about . . . if true right and true justice are not applied to the Germans that are still being kept prisoners?[44]

Other naval officers agreed. Raeder indeed suffered tragedy in prison when his 31-year-old son Hans died of a brain tumor in January 1953. Attempts by the Western high commissioners to allow Raeder a brief furlough to visit his son in Münster one last time and then to attend the funeral met Soviet refusals. In his stead, nine German admirals attended Hans's burial.[45] To make matters worse, painful bladder surgery similar to Funk's was carried out in the prison later in the year after the Soviet authorities refused to allow Raeder's temporary movement to the nearby British Military Hospital.[46]

The second line of argumentation was a quasi-legal argument mixed with moral equivalency and willful ignorance. Both grand admirals, so went the argument, were victims of ex post facto law for having been on the losing side, since Britain and the United States had engaged in the same sorts of aggressive warfare for which the two admirals had been convicted. A number of aforementioned British figures who had never approved of Nuremberg used the argument repeatedly. With West German rearmament seemingly in the balance, the continued imprisonment of Raeder and Dönitz was a liability. Oft cited in Raeder's case were Winston Churchill's first volume of war memoirs, *The Gathering Storm*, which appeared in 1948. The volume reproduced verbatim Churchill's December 1939 argument as first lord of the admiralty in Neville Chamberlain's war cabinet that British forces occupy Norwegian ports. The statement was cited repeatedly in a 1949 House of Lords debate by Lord Hankey, while Liddell Hart raised the point with the West German press.[47]

Raeder's German advocates cited the Churchill memorandum on Norway as though it had come down from Mount Sinai. Erika Raeder mentioned it in letters to the Four Powers, Bundestag deputies, the West German Foreign Ministry, British and German newspapers, Adenauer's daughter, and whomever else she could think of.[48] Her lack of perspective was conspicuous. "The treatment we Germans have had to endure," she commented once, "is worse than anything that happened to the Jews."[49] Regardless, a sympathetic West German press portrayed her as another victim of Allied injustice, while asking, "where does [Raeder's] guilt lie?"[50]

In fact, the Norway comparison was rotten with moral equivalency and historical misreading. Churchill's 1939 memorandum proposed a British occupation of Narvik and Bergen only in response to a German strike on Norway. His considerations accounted for the legitimate Norwegian government, Norwegian neutrality, the protection of small nations' integrity, and the fact that a British violation of Norway's neutrality would be "unaccompanied by inhumanity of any kind." Churchill also wrestled with an occupation as a violation of international law, concluding that it was morally permissible in this case because Britain took up arms "in order to aid the victims of German aggression" and because "we are fighting to reestablish the reign of law." There were no such considerations in Berlin. And in any event, Chamberlain's cabinet rejected the idea. Raeder's advocates ignored Churchill's report of April 10, 1940, made on the heels of the German occupation of Norway and also printed in *The Gathering Storm*: "Norwegian neutrality and our respect for it have made it impossible for us to prevent this ruthless *coup*."[51]

And not everyone swallowed such comparisons. Gottfried Hansen, considered a moderate by U.S observers, made the same arguments on Norway and added in November 1950 that U.S. forces in Korea would be found guilty of aggressive war too if the same criteria of guilt were ever to be applied.[52] French high commissioner André François-Poncet, who could still remember after four months that Kim Il Sung attacked the thirty-eighth parallel first, tartly replied that Hansen's definition of war crimes did not correspond with his own, and that, in any event, Raeder was found guilty by four powers, not one.[53]

West German veterans also believed that Dönitz's case contained legal grounds for argumentation. Retired General Admiral Hermann Boehm (who had commanded German units during the invasion of Norway) took his point to the Secretary General of the United Nations that both admirals were political prisoners. That Dönitz's submarines were ready for deployment from the start of the war was proof that he kept his forces ready – no crime according to Boehm, who ignored that Dönitz had been convicted for other crimes entirely.[54] A meeting of more than two thousand former U-boat officers and crew in the spring of 1954 – at which Dönitz's wife Ingeborg spoke, reached similar conclusions while pointing to the heavy casualty rates among German submarine crews.[55] Veterans' groups repeatedly mentioned the Nimitz affidavit from Nuremberg to argue that unrestricted submarine warfare was the norm, while ignoring that Nimitz only answered broad questions while never speaking to the bulk of Dönitz's conduct.[56] "In any State," read a petition from the Members of the Former German Navy (*Angehörigen der ehemaligen Kriegsmarine*),

> officers are forbidden, during their active military service, to interfere in matters politic. It is for this reason that we believe the good faith in which the two admirals discharged their duties should be taken for granted.... There is an ancient tradition by which amnesty used to be declared when the war was ended regarding penal cases that had arisen as a consequence of the war. Now that more than five years have elapsed since the end of hostilities, we submit the request to consider whether the time has not arrived when these men should be set free.[57]

The other appeal was political, building on Dönitz's actions as Hitler's successor. In a petition to President Theodor Heuss, the premier lobbying group for East Prussian refugees in West Germany (*Landsmannschaft Ostpreußen*) argued that, in the final weeks of the war, Dönitz kept forces deployed in the East so that thousands of eastern Germans could escape the "infernal and bestial Soviet Russian scourge." Heuss should thus work for Dönitz's amnesty.[58] It was a pernicious argument. Dönitz had used it at Nuremberg to explain his continuation of the war after Hitler's death when in fact he had intended until May 4, 1945, to fight the Allies from Norway after Germany was lost.[59] And while the navy evacuated some forty-three thousand Germans to the West between May 5 and May 9, the twilight of the Nazi regime under Dönitz saw some ten thousand Germans die each day. Yet the West German far right, which still viewed Hitler's war as a defense against bolshevism, took the argument seriously (and still does so) because it legitimized so much of the Nazi past.[60] In fact the neo-Nazi Socialist Reich Party (SRP) still viewed Dönitz as the sole legitimate successor to Hitler since Hitler had legally passed the torch of government to him in the waning days of the war. Small wonder Heuss never made the appeal.

A certain official sympathy still existed for the fate of the two admirals simply because they had commanded so many men. Herbert Blankenhorn's long memorandum of 1950 to Adenauer on the conditions of German rearmament included the proviso that the Allies work toward the release of the Spandau prisoners, but made special mention of Raeder and Dönitz.[61] Adenauer worked for the senior officers in Landsberg, Werl, and Wittlich. Regarding Spandau, Adenauer focused on von Neurath from 1950 to 1954. But his long proposal regarding Spandau for the Berlin foreign ministers' conference of January 1954, discussed in the previous chapter, demonstrated the importance that Bonn placed on the admirals as well. The call for all prisoners older than the age of 75 to be released immediately affected not only von Neurath, but Raeder. And the inclusion of pretrial custody into all sentences and the remission of the final one third of all sentences would have meant Dönitz's immediate release. Had Adenauer's proposals been accepted by all four powers in 1954 no other Spandau prisoner would have been released in that year. Bonn's arithmetic was not random.[62]

## THE ISSUE OF PRESENTENCING CONFINEMENT

An unusually negligent oversight at Nuremberg was the court's omission of any statement regarding pretrial custody. The prisoners arrived at Spandau in July 1947 without commitment papers, standard at any prison, which said when the inmates' sentences officially began and when their release dates would be.[63] Adenauer's 1954 proposal brought the Dönitz case into focus because even without a good conduct remission, the inclusion of pretrial custody meant that Dönitz would be released in May 1955.

Dönitz's release carried a potential problem. Since his arrest in May 1945, he had been convinced that as Hitler's legitimate successor, he could not be legally removed from power. He continued in Spandau to view himself as the legitimate German head of state and would not be convinced otherwise. Theodor Heuss, Dönitz told Speer in February 1953, was illegitimate because he had been "installed under pressure from the occupying powers." "I am still and will remain the legal chief of state," Dönitz insisted, "until I die!" The radical right viewed matters the same way. The hoax by which Otto Skorzeny was going to rescue the Spandau prisoners mentioned Dönitz as the next head of state as did the SRP.[64] A March 1953 letter smuggled from Dönitz to his wife Ingeborg by U.S. warder Robert Owens and intercepted by the British instructed her to make inquiries as to his political standing in West Germany. And when warders snuck Dönitz contraband newspapers, he reveled in polls that that showed most Germans held him in high regard. "Because the German people cherish me in their hearts," he said in April 1953, "I shall soon be getting out." Surely he overestimated himself, as his confusion with the poor electoral showings of the SRP demonstrated. But even newspapers said in early 1954 that he expected to be chief of state again after his release.[65]

The British were well informed as to Dönitz's notions of legitimacy.[66] In the Foreign Office no one was more concerned than Sir Ivone Kirkpatrick, once the British high commissioner and now permanent undersecretary in the Foreign Office. As it was, Kirkpatrick had an uncompromising streak – "over-quick to dismiss men as no good."[67] In considering release for Germans held at Werl, London routinely counted pretrial custody and granted good conduct remissions.[68] But Kirkpatrick was sure that Dönitz, thanks to his relative youth, his closeness to Hitler, and his evident ambitions would be a political threat once released. Thus, when Adenauer's 1954 proposal for the foreign ministers' conference in Berlin concerning remission and pretrial custody found some sympathy in the Foreign Office, Kirkpatrick single-handedly quashed it: "[We] should make a great mistake if we were to intervene . . . with the result that Admiral Dönitz come out at once. I am not so sure either that I wish to accelerate Speer's release. In the remaining five prisoners we have, of course, no particular interest."[69] It was wiser, Kirkpatrick thought, to work at the Berlin conference for better medical treatment and release on grounds of poor health. Such would cover von Neurath and Raeder.[70] And as shown previously, Molotov was amenable to discussions on prison conditions only with the result that a committee of experts met in April in Berlin and agreed on the Spandau graveyard and minor improvements in conditions.

The Americans wanted the 1954 discussions to address pretrial custody, too. After the first round of talks in West Berlin on April 6, the chief U.S. negotiator, Frederick Schwarz, insisted that the Allies issue vague press releases that did not exclude the possibility of early releases. On April 12, the British negotiator Maurice Bathurst warned Hoyer Millar that there might be trouble: "I had a tiresome time – about an hour's argument – with Mr. Schwarz when it came to authorizing the Press Officers in Berlin to answer press enquiries by saying that the subjects of release of prisoners or reductions of sentences were not subjects for discussion for which the Conference had been called . . . there is no doubt that the Americans are anxious to pursue at some time the granting of pre-trial custody and remission for good conduct."[71] Two days later, Hoyer Millar cabled London that according to one account he had heard from Spandau, "Doenitz was the only one of the prisoners who looked at all vindictive or potentially dangerous. I am afraid, however," he continued, "that the Americans . . . are inclined to take a different line, and it may not be easy for us to prevent them from bringing the matter up at some stage."[72]

London was furious. "The Americans," fumed H. W. Evans of the Foreign Office's German Political Department "are being tiresome and stupid."

> We must hope that they do not again raise the question of releases or reduction of sentences.... I do not think we can compromise on this. Ministers have assured Parliament that there is no question of discussing premature releases. This has been reiterated in press statements and correspondence. We are thus fully committed. In any case, we do not want to see their premature release.[73]

The argument between Bathurst and Schwarz may explain why Schwarz was replaced with Knox Lamb as the head of the U.S. delegation for the next three rounds of talks. London succeeded in keeping pretrial custody off the table.

The Spandau prisoners themselves, whose hopes for release were raised by the Berlin talks, understood that Dönitz was part of their problem. Aside from the annoying fact that Dönitz was openly bitter that the old and sick might be released before him (he had the shortest sentence), he would not be quiet about his imagined political status. "The idea has become an obsession with him," shrugged von Neurath. Von Schirach was less forgiving: "He is ruining everything for us with his playing [the role of] president. He [is] like a cork in front of a premature release for two of us."[74] Dönitz was clearly stunned rather than pleased for von Neurath when the latter hobbled free later in the year.[75]

Nor would Dönitz have been pleased, had he known, that von Neurath's release, which had been based on health, raised hopes among Raeder's advocates that the 78-year-old grand admiral was next. Petitions for Raeder poured into Bonn. As if to prove that there is truly no honor among thieves, even geriatric ones, Dr. Freiherr Viktor von der Lippe, who helped to defend Raeder at Nuremberg, argued that Raeder should be released because the crimes of which he had been accused (but of which he was, of course, not guilty) were far less serious than those leveled at von Neurath. If the Soviets had been willing to free von Neurath in spite of the hatred that the Czechs must have borne for him, then why would they continue to hold Raeder for alleged crimes against Norway? "The moment," proclaimed von der Lippe, "is favorable."[76]

The press got into the act, too. *Frankfurter Allgemeine Zeitung* decried the fact that as the government was about to screen prospective officers for the new *Bundeswehr*, Raeder and Dönitz were still in prison thanks to the need by the victors to show that the entire Wehrmacht was a criminal organization. Would there be no crisis of conscience for the new naval officers?[77] Some even hoped that Adenauer would raise the question of the Spandau prisoners during his July 1955 trip to Moscow, at which time he would press for the release of the thousands of prisoners still living in Soviet captivity.[78]

In the meantime, Otto Kranzbühler, still Dönitz's attorney, tried every possible contact to secure his client's release. In a private letter of January 1955 to Sir David Maxwell-Fyfe (now Lord Kilmuir and the lord chancellor in the British government), Kranzbühler pointed out that the International Military Tribunal had made no decisions and issued no statements regarding pretrial custody. He added that Anglo-American law left the issue to the discretion of the courts and that French and Soviet law mandated the counting of pretrial custody. Thus, Dönitz should be released on May 23, 1955 – the ten-year anniversary of his actual arrest. "It would be far from justice and a wanton hardship," Kranzbühler said to Sir David, "to detain Dönitz not 10, but 11½ years just because there is no authority to apply the general rule to his case."[79]

On January 28, Kranzbühler met with Bathurst who claimed to have received no instructions from London.[80] Kranzbühler then filed a formal petition on May 5, 1955, to the four ambassadors (full West German sovereignty on the same date eliminated the High Commission). For Soviet Ambassador Georgy Pushkin in East Berlin, Kranzbühler cited the Soviet Code of Criminal Law with amendments to prove that Dönitz should be released on May 23. Keeping Dönitz in prison beyond that date, Kranzbühler said, "would obviously violate international principles of justice."[81]

Still stinging from the public fiasco of von Neurath's release, Bonn worked behind the scenes. Regarding Raeder, Adenauer's new foreign minister Heinrich von Brentano, State Secretary Walter Hallstein, and other Foreign Ministry officials wrote and met the Western ambassadors to convey that Adenauer was "very disturbed" over Raeder's health. His death in prison would have a terrible effect on the veterans' organizations and naval circles whose support was needed for the German military contribution to NATO. Raeder should be released on humanitarian grounds and for the "strong psychological impression" such an act of mercy would make.[82]

Regarding Dönitz, Bonn was at once irritated with Kranzbühler for conducting private diplomacy with the Allies and with the Allies for not counting Dönitz's pretrial custody.[83] The Foreign Ministry contacted Bathurst on January 25, March 27, and April 4 but received no answer until Hoyer Millar informed Adenauer in late April that the Three Powers did not think it possible to take up Dönitz's release with the Soviets.[84] On May 20, Hallstein testily told all three ambassadors that they should do so anyway.[85] Hallstein at least smoked out the truth. The U.S. Embassy noted confidentially that it had been London that was completely negative toward the May 1955 release of Dönitz.[86]

Bonn issued bland press releases the week of May 23 – when many expected Dönitz to walk free – that the West German government had raised the pretrial custody issue, but that the Allies were unable to work for Dönitz's release.[87] The Allies insisted publicly that allowance for pretrial custody would entail a revision of the Nuremberg judgments because it was understood in 1946 that pretrial confinement did not count.[88] Bonn tried to damp down public disappointment. A June 1955 speech by Defense Minister Theodor Blank in the naval city of Kiel conspicuously omitted the two admirals. The omission sparked open frustration from naval veterans and a formal inquiry from Kai-Uwe von Hassel, the minister-president of Schleswig-Hollstein, of which Kiel is the capital.[89] Dönitz had predicted that the Spandau prisoners would be home by the spring of 1955 owing to such pressures. Should NATO insist on West German rearmament without releasing him, he smugly noted, "My naval officers wouldn't go along with it."[90]

After Kranzbühler's contacts with Lord Kilmuir in January 1955, Kirkpatrick confessed that the law was on Dönitz's side. There had been no ruling on pretrial confinement at Nuremberg, and it was within the competence of the three Western powers at least to raise the issue with the Soviets. But, Kirkpatrick added,

> We have . . . never been willing to raise the issue with the other Three Powers. The fact is that we do not wish to take any action which could lead to the premature releases of either Doenitz or Speer. It is true that most of the prisoners at Spandau are old and have received such long sentences that remissions of this kind would have little practical significance. But Doenitz is still a dangerous man, and our view is that we would resolutely oppose any move to put him at large before we are compelled to. This view is shared by the French and by the United States High Commissioner in Germany.[91]

Kirkpatrick chose his words carefully, for Washington did not agree even if Conant did. The State Department recognized the "potential trouble" that Dönitz represented, but argued that refusal to release Dönitz for political reasons would be "such a conspicuous departure from established U.S. and French practice that it might be interpreted by some as confinement without trial for what Dönitz might do in the future, rather than confinement after trial for what he actually did in the past."[92]

A compromise lay in crediting Dönitz's pretrial confinement on the condition that he refrain from any political activity after release. Such could perhaps be worked out with the West Germans. But London and Paris would have none of it. London's representatives in Bonn told the Americans there that they were under strongly worded instructions to resist "resolutely" any effort to release Dönitz before September 30, 1956, and the French representation in Bonn answered the Americans with the same firmness, despite Washington's concern that "refusal [to] give Dönitz such credit could constitute discrimination against him for political reasons having no connection with his conviction and sentence" and that it would provide a bad precedent for the other Spandau cases.[93]

Kirkpatrick iced down Dönitz's advocates in London, too. Lord Hankey planned to raise Dönitz's presentencing confinement in the House of Lords in the hope that the issue could be discussed at the Four-Power Geneva Summit in July 1955 – the first such meeting since the Potsdam conference a decade earlier. But on June 23, Hankey was summoned to the Foreign Office and told to "go slow on Dönitz" because Dönitz was "relatively young, very aggressive and very Nazi [and thus] quite likely to make trouble when he came out of prison." Kirkpatrick continued that "any sensible Government might wish to reflect before taking on itself the onus of sponsoring a proposal for the release of Dönitz."[94]

## RAEDER WALKS FREE

Most cynical was London's tying of Raeder's release to Washington's agreement not to insist on counting Dönitz's presentencing confinement. By 1955, Raeder was 79, with a considerably enlarged heart together with blood pressure and circulatory problems that might have decreased the flow of blood to the heart and brain. Angina attacks, slurred speech, dizziness, and trouble with small tasks became routine. "Death," said the specialists in the British Military Hospital, "might occur without warning" though Raeder had good days and bad.[95] Erika, who claimed that her husband could not move following a visit on July 8, fanned the fires. Even Kranzbühler understood that right-wing demonstrations against the Allies and the Adenauer government would erupt should Raeder die in prison.[96] The Americans had already proposed in May 1955 that the western powers work for Raeder's release.[97] London balked, citing impending parliamentary elections.[98]

The true reason was more complicated. On July 20, when Foreign Ministry official Wolfgang Freiherr von Welck visited Hoyer Millar on Brentano's orders to relay Adenauer's personal concerns regarding Raeder, Sir Frederick agreed that Raeder should be released. But he warned von Welck that any linkage of Raeder's case with that of Dönitz would have a bad effect on the former.[99] The British also became very dilatory with Bonn concerning the details of Raeder's health.[100] After all three Western ambassadors received an official petition for Raeder's release from Brentano, François-Poncet reported to Paris that he was willing to sound Pushkin out on obtaining Raeder's freedom, though he remained concerned about a public backlash in Paris should France intervene for a major war criminal. It would have to look like a quadripartite initiative. But the British, said the French ambassador, seemed even more reserved, perhaps because Raeder was an admiral.[101] The British Embassy in Bonn revealed to their allies on July 26 that London was reluctant to release Raeder out of the concern that such would lead to increased calls for Dönitz's release. If the Americans and French would stand firm against the release of Dönitz, *even if the Soviets suggested Dönitz's release*, then London would agree to release Raeder on health grounds. As for the previous American suggestion that Dönitz could be released on the condition that the West German government would muzzle him, the Foreign Office had little confidence that Bonn would be able or willing to undertake the task. In any event, Kirkpatrick himself and then the cabinet would have to agree. Conant responded with Washington's view that "Dönitz should be released," as a matter of law, and John Foster Dulles concurred that London's conditioning of Raeder's release on American nonsupport for Dönitz's release was unacceptable. François-Poncet indicated that Paris would not oppose Dönitz's release either.[102] In the end, Washington's refusal to stand firm on Dönitz's incarceration did not matter because each of the Four Powers held a veto anyway.

The West German government, meanwhile, clearly understood that the release of Raeder was conditional upon a lack of support (or at least tepid support) for Dönitz's release, and given the choice, it was paramount to remove a sick 79-year-old former admiral from Spandau. Two days after Hoyer Millar's warning to von Welck, Adenauer personally wrote Raeder's only daughter, Anita Diestel, who lived in Hamburg and who had induced the city council there to represent her father's case in Bonn. He gently advised her "to handle the entire affair very confidentially."[103]

Bonn was less gentle with Kranzbühler. Dönitz's lawyer had already complained to the German press in mid-June that Bonn had done nothing for his client.[104] On July 11, he had the gall to inform Adenauer not only that he had submitted another petition on Dönitz's behalf, but that he was also single-handedly holding back an increased and even violent radicalization of younger army and naval officers over the Dönitz case. Adenauer, Kranzbühler warned, had better take the issue up with the Western foreign ministers.[105] With barely concealed impatience, Brentano informed Kranzbühler that Bonn had indeed petitioned the ambassadors regarding Dönitz in May, that the government was now working on getting Raeder released from Spandau before he died there, and that "I do not need to emphasize that a very confidential handling of this news is indispensable in the interest of those affected."[106]

In the meantime, key figures in West Germany warned Washington not to dawdle. In early August, the American Consul General in Bremen, Andrew G. Lynch, met with former Admiral Gerhard Wagner, who during the war had served as a staff officer in the naval command under Raeder and then Dönitz. Wagner had testified at Nuremberg in the case of the latter. While discussing the selection of the first six thousand officers for the new German Navy, Wagner said that former officers eligible were of two types. One held that West Germany must rearm and align with NATO lest it be overrun by Communists within a few years. The second, as a matter of personal loyalty, refused to associate itself with the new naval force so long as their former grand admirals sat in prison. Wagner commented that most officers were aware that the United States supported the grand admirals' release and that most blamed tepid efforts by Adenauer's government for their continued incarceration. Wagner was evidently unaware of the steps that Adenauer's government had taken, but in his report to the State Department, Lynch emphasized that with regard to Raeder and Dönitz, "the feeling does exist and . . . until some way can be found to overcome it, a future German Navy will not have the support of its former officers." Wagner, Lynch said, was not the only former naval officer to make the point.[107]

If nothing could be done about Dönitz, then something could perhaps be done about Raeder. Thanks to the comparative ambivalence coming from London and Paris, Raeder's eventual release was pushed harder by Washington than anyone else. By the final week of August, the American Embassy in Bonn had drafted a tripartite letter to be sent to Ambassador Pushkin in Berlin, which mentioned Raeder's age and his "seriously deteriorated" health of the past few months while proposing that he be released as von Neurath had been.[108] Nearly a month passed with no Soviet reply, all the more disturbing following a medical report from Spandau that warned Raeder's health was indeed becoming worse. Yet just before a follow-up note was drafted, Pushkin conveyed the agreement of the Soviet Union that Raeder could be released. No doubt the medical report played a role in the Soviet decision as did the hope that Raeder's quiet death and burial could take place somewhere other than in Spandau Prison.

The Allies this time would reap whatever propaganda rewards there were, and since Raeder's case had been watched closely by the new military establishment, the rewards were considerable. François-Poncet, whose country had done little to get Raeder released, made a point to emphasize to the West German Foreign Ministry that though the Soviets might try to exploit the propaganda value of the release for themselves, the initiative for this particular release originated with the Western powers, with Pushkin taking a month to answer the Western proposal.[109]

Raeder was released from Spandau Prison at 11:37 A.M. on September 26 without incident, despite the large number of journalists and photographers awaiting him outside the gates.[110] In the afternoon Raeder and his wife, who had come to Berlin to meet him on his release, were flown to Hanover, where a private car drove them to Lippstadt and the hospital there. The West German government, stung by its own effusiveness on the release of von Neurath, kept the entire affair low key. There were no public letters or telegrams from Bonn. A bland press statement, which welcomed on humanitarian grounds the decision of the Four Powers, was drafted, and Raeder was publicly referred to as "Herr" Raeder rather than "*Großadmiral*." Kranzbühler was also asked to keep his comments bland.[111] This must have been difficult. Kranzbühler's own client had legal grounds to

18. Erich Raeder with his wife Erika on his release from Spandau Prison, September 1955. Photograph courtesy of the Associated Press.

have been released more than three months before, and Raeder had received a life sentence. After Raeder's release, veterans' groups themselves pointed this problem out to Bonn along with the well-worn proviso that linked the enthusiasm of West Germany's new naval officers with the fate of the former grand admirals. Hallstein answered such groups privately, explaining that the Allied resistance to releasing Dönitz was psychological and political.[112]

Most noise regarding Dönitz after the Raeder release actually came from Dönitz's British advocates, though they too were prodded at times by his German friends. Lord Hankey went on record by stating that Spandau Prison was a manifestation of hypocrisy in light of Churchill's statements in *The Gathering Storm* and in light of the inability of the Western Allies and the Soviets to agree on any other policy aim in Germany.[113] Toward the end of 1955, Hankey lobbied heavily in the Foreign Office for Dönitz's benefit, approaching Prime Minister Anthony Eden in December and Foreign Secretary Selwyn Lloyd in January. Hankey also met with NATO Secretary General Lord Harold Ismay. Eden commented confidentially that the entire issue of Spandau was under review, Lloyd promised to make the Dönitz case a priority, and Ismay stated baldly that the release of Dönitz would "greatly facilitate things at NATO."[114]

Kranzbühler was busy, too. On December 8,1955, he wrote to a sympathetic British contact at the NATO staff, Colonel R. H. Stevens, who had recently retired, that

> The apprehension, which apparently exists in the Foreign Office, that Doenitz might become the 'Fuehrer' of some sort of nationalist circle is, in my opinion, without foundation.... Indeed, I am sure that his early release would constitute the surest way of scotching any public radical agitation which might be brewing. Admiral Raeder, who had long political discussions with Doenitz in Spandau, asserted recently to me that he regarded as 'quite absurd' the idea that Doenitz form some sort of 'right-radical' group. Doenitz, he said, was neither a fool nor an adventurer.[115]

Kranzbühler continued that in West Germany there were rumors that the Soviets, deprived of any propaganda value from Raeder's release, would soon propose the release of Dönitz, Speer, and Funk. "I cannot believe," he taunted, "that the Western Powers will allow the initiative to come from the Russians."

In fact, a new wind was blowing in the Foreign Office. It just did not affect Dönitz. On January 3, the cabinet approved a Foreign Office memorandum that recommended the setup of a Four-Power judicial board to review the sentences of the five remaining Spandau criminals. The impetus apparently came from the fact that in Japan, the sentences of all Class A war criminals had been reduced to the effect that all were being released, while clemency measures in the British zone of Germany meant that there were but fourteen Germans remaining at Werl. London also did not want to leave the initiative on Spandau to the Soviets. Such may have been the cause for Selwyn Lloyd's sympathetic words to Hankey later in the month.

But none of this, substantial though it would have been, meant that Dönitz would be released immediately. In Bonn, Hoyer Millar told the Americans that "Dönitz [is] the most dangerous criminal in Spandau. His release [is] due [on] October 1, 1956."[116] Back in London, the Foreign Office had come to realize that "everything which is written to Lord Hankey appears to go straight...to Doenitz's lawyer – who also appears aware of the fact that the [Foreign Office's] objections to Doenitz's release are based on political rather than legal grounds."[117] Obviously, Kirkpatrick's confidential request to Hankey of the previous June that he "go slow about Dönitz" was no longer having its effect. After Hankey wrote yet another letter to Selwyn Lloyd on Dönitz's behalf on January 24, however, there was some discussion of how to reply. No one wished to insult Hankey, and no one wished for him to raise the Dönitz case in the House of Lords. "Let us say and do nothing," commented Sir Ivone by way of a solution. "We only have to play out time for 6 months and three weeks. Lord Hankey will doubtless return to the charge when the [Foreign Secretary] returns and we can then devise [a reply] – Or I could see him. By, say, June it will not be worth doing anything."[118]

The British were unmoved even with an apparent threat to Dönitz's health. On February 13, 1956, the former admiral experienced a sharp jump in his blood pressure that brought the risk of a cerebral hemorrhage.[119] Paris and Washington showed due concern that Dönitz could become a martyr, especially because his detention at this point was so controversial (Funk remained the most urgent medical case).[120] Yet far from the cases of von Neurath and Raeder, it would take far more than risk of death for the British to agree to move Dönitz even to their own military hospital "There appears to be . . . a certain risk to Doenitz's life," reported Hoyer Millar in a classic British understatement, "and it would . . . be unfortunate if he died in prison. The French and Americans feel this very strongly. On the other hand, I feel bound to say that if Doenitz is transferred to a hospital, it may well be awkward to return him to prison before the expiration of his sentence next September."[121] The most the British would agree to at the moment was a Four-Power medical consultation because "Doenitz is the one of the remaining prisoners whose case has aroused [the] most interest in Germany . . . and we should probably be criticized if he were to die in prison and it was thought that he had not been accorded adequate medical treatment."[122] Though clear to both Paris and Washington that London would not agree to a full release for Dönitz, it was also unclear whether the British government would even follow the advice of a quadripartite medical consultation, even if such a consultation recommended that Dönitz be moved to a hospital.[123] Fortunately for all concerned, Dönitz could be treated with injections for the time being, and his blood pressure returned to approximately normal by the end of February.[124]

## THE EMBARRASSING ADMIRALS

In the meantime, Bonn suffered its own embarrassments thanks to the grand admirals and their supporters in the first half of 1956. In the case of Raeder, the embarrassment was not Bonn's fault. The government had said practically nothing on Raeder's release and did not answer – even privately – Raeder's note of thanks to Adenauer, a note that also called for the release of his fellow Spandau prisoners, especially "my comrade Dönitz, whose ten year captivity has indeed expired even according to international law and who was only sentenced because he carried out my orders during the war."[125]

This time, the culprit was the lord mayor of Kiel, Dr. Hans Müthling, who on March 2, 1956, issued a resolution to the Kiel city council that restored Raeder's honorary citizenship to the naval port city. Raeder had received the honor from the Nazis only to have it stripped after the war on December 27, 1945. The stripping of the honorary citizenship may have been technically illegal as Müthling claimed, but the mayor's 1956 resolution was still issued against the will of the socialist majority on the city council, which announced that it would stand by the decision of 1945 on political rather than strictly legal grounds.[126]

The state government of Schleswig-Hollstein and the federal government in Bonn saw the potential for discomfiture. President Heuss, ironically Kiel's only other honorary citizen, had warned the Kiel municipal government against taking such a symbolically charged step two years before, but his warnings seemed to pale in comparison with the incessant harangues of Erika Raeder, who not only took the initiative with regard to her husband's honorary citizenship, but also planned for a big reception for her husband at the annual Kiel Week regatta festivities, which take place each year in June.[127] The West German Foreign Ministry understood clearly that "there [would] be no understanding for this abroad," and that at the very least the entire business should have been delayed for a year.[128]

Indeed, complaints concerning the March 2 resolution came quickly from Denmark and Norway, each of which saw itself as a victim of Raeder's aggressive wartime strategy, that had resulted in more than four years of German occupation. The Danish press from left to right labeled the resolution as "an especially unfriendly act," and called for boycotts of Kiel Week. At the very least, said one newspaper, Bonn should make clear that unlike Kiel, the new federal capital had made some strides since the Nazi period. Heuss should decline to share the honorary citizenship in Kiel with Raeder.[129] At the same time, a number of well-known Scandinavian academics wrote the rector of the Kiel University to say that they would no longer participate in programs sponsored there. In fact, Raeder also held an honorary doctorate from that university, whose senate had pressed for Raeder's release for years.[130]

Bonn launched various efforts at damage control, which included asking the Schleswig-Holstein state government and its minister-president Kai-Uwe von Hassel to intervene with Müthling. But since Müthling was uncooperative, the only option was to influence Raeder himself. On April 16, 1956, Raeder with obvious reluctance wrote to Müthling and rejected the honorary citizenship with the backhanded comment that though he still felt a bond with the people of Kiel, misunderstanding at home and abroad of his service for the Fatherland demanded that he not accept the honor.[131]

The urgency with which Hallstein handled this issue was due to a far larger problem concerning the navy that arose in the winter and spring of 1956 – the so-called Zenker affair. The issue was a January 1956 speech in Wilhelmshaven by Captain Karl-Adolf Zenker, the chief of the Naval Division in the then-developing Ministry of Defense, to the first company of naval officer recruits for the new West German Navy.[132] As it was, the Wilhelmshaven city council had lobbied in 1954 for the release of both admirals, "whose lives" it pleaded, "are closely bound with Wilhelmshaven's history."[133] Now Zenker focused on the grand admirals. He argued that Raeder and Dönitz had commanded the *Kriegsmarine* honorably, that

neither had committed any legal or moral wrongs, that their Nuremberg convictions were political in nature, and that neither man would have been convicted in 1956 because they "had done nothing more than fulfill their duty" in a war thrust upon them. Worse yet, Zenker rhetorically asked "whether we may take up our work, as long as our former commanders-in-chief... are still in prison." He answered affirmatively only thanks to "the danger threatening from the East," then dropped the bomb that he had discussed the issue with Raeder himself. Zenker's speech was an unusually clumsy attempt – in front of new recruits yet – to forge a new tradition from the navy's past, especially since the denazification court in West Berlin confirmed the confiscation of DM 100,000 worth of Dönitz's assets there later that same day![134]

Though the West German press quickly described the speech as unfortunate, it was noted abroad, as was the fact that Zenker delivered it in the presence of Defense Minister Blank himself, even though Blank quickly issued orders that officers' speeches to recruits would be brief and would avoid politics.[135] In any event, the Social Democratic opposition in the Federal Parliament, which at that point had yet to lose the constitutional argument in Bonn for parliamentary control of the military, did not let the occasion pass.[136] At the instigation of SPD Vice President Fritz Erler, the Bundestag Defense Committee discussed the speech three days after it was given.[137] On February 10, the SPD announced a grand inquiry, which contained the following questions: Was the cabinet aware of the contents of the Zenker speech? Did they approve that new recruits were being told that Raeder's and Dönitz's records were without blemish and that both men were role models even though both were among Hitler's closest associates and even though both had made antisemitic speeches? Did the cabinet approve of the fact that Zenker held up Raeder and Dönitz as examples of duty even though duty ought to include humanity and righteousness as well as the ability to lead?[138]

Before the parliamentary debate on the questions even occurred in April, more embarrassments surfaced. The Ministry of the Interior announced that the chief of the Federal Border Patrol (the twenty thousand–man precursor to the West German Army), former Wehrmacht general Gerhard Matzky, displayed an autographed portrait of Dönitz on his office wall. In the meantime, influential veterans were pressing as hard as ever for Dönitz's release. In early March, Gottfried Hansen was proposing that Kiel Week would be a good time to raise the issue of Dönitz's release with the representatives of other navies.[139] Later in the month former Vice Admiral Helmuth Heye, now a parliamentary deputy who had been conducting his own foreign policy with London on Dönitz's behalf, informed Hallstein that Lord Hankey and the Bishop of Chichester would soon make another attempt with the British Foreign Office for the release of Dönitz. Yet Hankey and Chichester, Heye said, expected the German Foreign Ministry to take corresponding steps as well so that they would not have to act alone![140]

Meanwhile in an effort to stir up more popular sympathy, Kranzbühler leaked to the press information concerning Dönitz's health, which he had received from Dönitz's wife Ingeborg. The information by this time was dated. Dönitz's blood pressure had returned to normal. "I have the impression," said Karl-Hans Born of the Foreign Ministry's war prisoner/war criminal section, "that [Kranzbühler] is preparing a new press campaign regarding Dönitz."[141] Heye asked the Foreign Ministry whether Dönitz's hypertension might not provide a good lever to secure his release. Karl Carstens, deputy head of the Foreign Ministry's Political Department, believed that Adenauer should raise the issue with the American embassy because the hypertension could again become acute. Moreover, if the Soviets were to suggest Dönitz's early release, the propaganda benefits – as with the von Neurath release – would belong to them and not the Western capitals.[142] Although Dr. Wilhelm Grewe, the head of the Political Department, believed it desirable on domestic political grounds to have Dönitz released at least a month before October 1, 1956, Grewe also noted that the public pressure did not make the task any easier.[143] In any event, it did not make sense to act before learning the results of the parliamentary debate.

The parliamentary debate on the grand inquiry, which occurred on April 18, 1956, was a disaster for Dönitz's advocates. It began with a blistering attack on the Defense Ministry by SPD leader Carlo Schmid. Schmid prefaced his remarks with the critique of Nuremberg, generally accepted in West Germany, that the trial represented victor's justice and ex post facto law, and that generally "Nuremberg was the wrong route." Schmid further noted that he approved of the release of Raeder on humanitarian grounds and that he would also approve of Dönitz's release now that his health too was in question. These issues, however, were separate from whether Raeder and Dönitz were proper models for the new West German navy and armed forces, and the definition of military leadership in a democracy that had to value humanity and human rights. It was "political schizophrenia," Schmid argued, to say that such men were good officers in the technical sense while ignoring that they were Hitler's aides who helped implement the Nazi vision while writing humanity off as an inconvenience.

Schmid then pointed to the pro-Nazi speeches both men had given during their careers. These speeches had been published when originally given and then read into evidence at Nuremberg, but they had been forgotten or ignored by the advocates of both men. Raeder, Schmid pointed out, gave a speech in 1939 in which he warned not only of the dangers of bolshevism, but also of the dangers of "international Jewry." It was a phrase right out of Julius Streicher's antisemitic newspaper *Der Stürmer* and it precluded Raeder from ever being a military role model in a democratic state. Such speeches, Schmid added, helped create the climate for Auschwitz.

Schmid saved his most damning comments for Dönitz, whose speeches revealed an even greater devotion to Hitler. On March 12, 1944 (Heroes' Day), when according to Schmid even corporals knew what was happening in the death camps, Dönitz asked his naval officers, "What would become of our *Heimat* today if the Führer had not united us in National Socialism?!" The answer, he said, was that Germany would be torn into parties, infiltrated by the "poison of *Judentum*," and at the mercy of its enemies. On July 21, 1944, the day following the failed attempt to assassinate Hitler, Dönitz again made it clear where he stood in a statement to his subordinates. "We are filled," he said, "with holy fury and limitless courage" thanks to the "criminal attack" that was intended to take the life of "our beloved Führer." "Providence had other intentions: It protected and defended the Führer" and thus "did not desert our German Fatherland in its fateful battle." The plot, he continued, was the work of a dishonorable clique of idiotic generals, but "the Navy stands true to its oath, in proven loyalty to the Führer, unconditional in readiness for battle.... You will destroy ruthlessly anyone who reveals himself as a traitor. Long live our Führer Adolf Hitler!"

Nor was Dönitz covering his own back for the good of his career. A speech of April 7, 1945, demonstrated that he supported the hanging of deserters. Dönitz's speech of May 1, 1945, after Hitler's suicide stated that the Führer, who had identified the great struggle with bolshevism sooner than anyone else, had charged him with maintaining the fight, and that Dönitz would continue to fight not only against the Soviets but also against the United States and Britain who were themselves fighting for world bolshevism.

Here then, said Schmid, was a clear choice for the new armed forces. Either they could embrace the spirit of July 20 or they could embrace the spirit of an officer who identified with Nazi ideals from antisemitism to the killing of fellow servicemen. "So long as officers believe," Schmid continued, "that they need to justify their service to the Federal Republic to Dönitz, then so long are they not living in the spirit that must animate our *Bundeswehr* if they are to serve honorably."

Attempts to apologize for the Zenker speech were not successful. Theodor Blank said that Zenker had attempted to assure recruits that the German Navy had a good and honorable tradition. Zenker's reference to the two grand admirals might have been clumsy but it only sought to tell new officers that they should not be ashamed of their service arm. It was not intended, Blank said, to raise doubts as to whether one should enter the naval service in present conditions. Zenker, who was cleared to serve the new navy by the personnel committee charged with screening the political reliability of officers, surely did not identify with the Nazi spirit, and the federal government was against any surviving remnant thereof. In any event, said Blank, the government had removed Zenker from his post in the Ministry of Defense.

The longest apology for the Zenker speech, however, came from Heye, who represented not only the traditions of the *Kriegsmarine*, but who was also working behind the scenes for Dönitz's release from Spandau. Heye pleaded ignorance on Zenker's behalf. The captain surely did not know about the speeches that Schmid had cited – no one, Heye said, could read everything. Zenker's motives, Heye continued, were honorable. They reflected the camaraderie of the naval forces even in defeat and the bond between officers and enlisted men, which was especially tight in the navy. Collective thought was essential aboard ship, especially since the navy had faced a numerically superior enemy in both world wars from start to finish with a far higher casualty rate than was suffered by Allied crews. Without mentioning Dönitz specifically, Heye said that there was a question of sovereignty that officers of the new navy would have to confront as well. "We do not recognize foreign judgments," he said, "even if a German court were to come to the same verdict. . . . The federal government has indeed represented this standpoint in the extradition treaty and the western powers have recognized it. Why should an officer not be allowed to hold this opinion?" The *Bundeswehr*, he said, would have a far better beginning if the Federal Republic, as a sovereign entity, were to assume sovereignty over the Spandau prisoners. If Zenker were to have displayed any civil courage at all, then he had to raise this problem.

Heye then turned to the speeches raised by Schmid in a lengthy and somewhat bizarre effort to clear the names of the grand admirals. Despite the extensive efforts of the International Military Tribunal to convict these officers, he said, these speeches were the only [public] statements that anyone could find that the grand admirals had made against Jews – and despite the speeches, neither was convicted of crimes against humanity (Heye ignored the other counts). Both made little effort, he said, to enforce Aryan laws against naval officers who were either partial Jews or who were married to partial Jews (he did not mention full Jews). But in the final analysis, he continued, both Raeder and Dönitz were military men, and in a dictatorship, neither had any choice but to limit their activities to purely military issues of battle on the high seas.

Heye explained the sentences against both officers as an episode of "postwar psychosis" which created an "absurd situation" wherein both officers were condemned for activities that fell outside their area of competence. "Even the hangman," taunted Heye in an unwittingly Janus-faced reference to Nuremberg, "bears no political responsibility." Neither Raeder nor Dönitz could influence their government – each was tragically entangled in an overwhelming political system with duty the only frame of reference. They would thus live in military history as "militarily clean leaders in an epoch dominated by National Socialism." And Dönitz, Heye continued, as if to point to the greatest injustice of all, remained in Spandau despite the expiration of his sentence. He and Raeder both were victims of tragic judgment rather than true guilt. It was a shame, he added in an effort at negative integration that rivaled Otto von Bismarck himself, that the SPD had even raised this inquiry. It was even worse, he said, that Schmid, as a formal sailor, himself would have been its chief advocate. Heye's long speech was not only an extraordinary effort at selective memory and political advocacy in the guise of apolitical military language but also an indictment of the Social Democrats for their lack of proper patriotism and recognition of the needs of the military. It was his lowest moment.

And Heye discovered, once he finally sat down, that the large number of subsequent speakers, none of whom came from the SPD, disagreed. Paul Bausch, a member of Adenauer's CDU and a member of the Bundestag Defense Committee, noted that the committee had been unanimous in its assessment of the speech. Though they had generously attributed honorable motives to Zenker himself, they were disturbed by the references to Dönitz because one could not speak of the navy's military accomplishments while ignoring the fact that Dönitz was a confidante of Hitler who shared his political beliefs. Hitler would not have chosen him as a successor otherwise. The committee simply could not get around the fact that Dönitz enjoyed the full confidence of history's greatest criminal. Zenker had a decade to inform himself. He could have given a speech that mentioned tradition as well as the tough fate of Raeder and Dönitz and that also emphasized the responsibility of the new armed forces to protect free institutions. Yet he did neither.

Dr. Franz Böhm, also of the CDU, granted that Zenker had honorable motives but noted that his speech amounted to false legend building that groomed collective historical excuses. Dr. Ferdinand Friedensburg, also of the CDU, made reference to Adenaeur's own condemnation of the speech and then noted that though German society would always have a place for former naval officers, Raeder and Dönitz bore special responsibility. Those, he said, who found themselves in an atmosphere of stench and did not remove themselves – and here Friedensburg could have been speaking of von Neurath as well – would be covered with the smell until the end of their days. If such men wished to endure their shame in silence, then they should be left alone. But they should never be made into models. If the new German state had any service to offer the world, then it had to recognize the criminal nature of the Nazi past, particularly for the benefit of new officers.

Representatives of other parties were no more forgiving. Dr. Erich Mende of the Free Democratic Party (FDP) noted that the myth of a clean, apolitical officer corps was just that. Many officers were stained indelibly with national socialism when they accepted Hitler's monetary gifts.[144] The real issue, he said, was whether the Ministry of Defense knew the text of Zenker's speech before it was given. "I am... of the conviction," Mende challenged, that [Captain] Zenker did not compose this speech himself. I am further of the conviction, that... other decisive members of the Federal Ministry of Defense knew word for word the speech... in advance." "Here," Mende challenged, "stands indeed the question of political responsibility." Dr. Johannes-Helmut Strosche of the All-German Bloc (representing Germans driven from their homes in the East) warned that those in command positions bore a different responsibility and indeed guilt in their darker political side. To make idols of such men at the critical historical juncture of the *Bundeswehr's* birth would be "imprudent and stupid... it is dangerous... very dangerous."

Schmid closed the debate with the comment that Blank's answers to the inquiry were laconic at best and evasive at worst. Zenker was not just a subaltern but an officer charged with the setup of the naval arm of the new *Bundeswehr*.

> If you say that you did not know about the speech, then well enough. But after you heard of the speech it was your duty in my opinion to ask Captain Zenker's superiors if they knew of the speech and then to take the appropriate measures. I believe that such falls under the obligations of your office. That you did not do this allows censure of you by this house.

Turning then to Heye, Schmid argued that the separation of military competence from political outlook was artificial, deceptive, and dangerous – Hitler himself had been a decorated soldier. Schmid then commented on Dönitz himself: "What I see as deserving of condemnation in Dönitz is not only his low level of political understanding, but also the fact that in his function as supreme commander of the navy, he failed morally. [SPD applause] It is for this that I reproach him!" Closing the debate, Schmid then commented on the responsibility that all peoples bear for their uncomfortable histories:

> Anyone who knows me knows that I do not subscribe to those who believe that one must go with sackcloth and ashes, as is wished abroad. I am of the view that even a beaten and conquered people are still a people on whose shoulders great responsibilities have been laid, who have a right to self-respect and [who] must show such self-respect to themselves and to others.... But [such] is only permitted if one has the courage to speak the truth even when this truth is bitter as bile.

Despite the discomforts of Spandau Prison, Karl Dönitz may well have preferred the confines of his cell to the floor of the Federal Parliament on April 18, 1956.

## THE AWKWARD RELEASE OF HITLER'S SUCCESSOR

Following this debate, Bonn could not press for Dönitz's release. He and Raeder had become embarrassments and the cabinet's first steps following the Bundestag debate was to prevent them from becoming worse. The first problem concerned Raeder, who had agreed not to accept the restoration of his honorary Kiel citizenship. Shortly after the Bundestag debate, it was revealed that he was slated to receive an honorary membership in the *Deutsche Marinebund* (German Naval Federation) at the annual meeting of the *Marinekameradenschaft* (Naval Comradeship Society) which took place during Kiel Week. Senior officers now serving the *Bundesmarine* who had once served under Raeder added their voices to the chorus of those urging Raeder not to make the trip. These included Admiral Friedrich Ruge of the Defense Ministry, who contacted Raeder personally, though without success. No lesser a figure than Hallstein himself thus asked Defense Minister Theodor Blank to intervene with the chairman of the *Marinebund* to have Raeder abstain from the trip. "The presence of Herr Raeder at the meeting in Kiel," warned Hallstein, "would give this event an explicitly political character." Blank, Hallstein continued, should mention that Raeder's presence would make it all but impossible to have Dönitz released from Spandau early, and that Raeder's health could be blamed for his failure to make the trip.[145]

At the same time, there were concerns that public demonstrations would erupt on behalf of Dönitz. Pointing to Dönitz's high blood pressure as a humanitarian pretext, retired Captain Heinz Bonatz of the *Marine-Offizier-Hilfe* (Naval Officers' Mutual Aid Society) – a veteran's organization numbering roughly four thousand – threatened a public demonstration in the first week of April. To avoid this spectacle, the German Foreign Ministry decided to provide Bonatz with a polite yet general answer from Foreign Minister Brentano stating that the chancellor had raised the possibility of Dönitz's release on health grounds with the Allies and that the government was watching his health very closely. Brentano also warned Bonatz in no uncertain terms that "You will understand that the mention of this case in public does not make easier any remonstrance which promises success. [A] demonstration . . . would only likewise damage the efforts for a solution to the question of men convicted from the war."[146]

In truth Adenauer wanted nothing to do with the Dönitz case after the public debate on the Zenker speech. In late March 1956 when the danger to Dönitz's health had subsided, Hallstein had asked Adenauer to decide whether the admiral's blood pressure should be linked with another attempt to have him released before October 1. Adenauer made no decision throughout the spring and well into the summer. Officials in the Foreign Ministry understood why. The former admiral's speeches concerning Hitler, Jews, and deserters had not made the task of asking for his release a pleasant proposition.[147]

In the meantime, Dönitz's well-placed advocates did what they could on their own. Ruge, now Zenker's replacement as the head of the Naval Department at the Ministry of Defense, told the American naval and air attaché on June 4 that it would be to everyone's advantage if Dönitz could be released even a few days before September 30. Ruge spoke of Dönitz's popularity with refugee organizations that viewed him as something of a savior and noted that, according to his own discussions with Dönitz's son-in-law, the former admiral had no political ambitions. Dönitz could change his mind, though, if embittered by the fact that he remained in prison eighteen months past his sentence.[148]

Dönitz engaged in his own theater. When visited by Kranzbühler at Spandau on July 31, Dönitz insisted, with interpreters listening closely, that he wanted only a quiet retirement. Yet he also revealed his true colors. When asking Kranzbühler to help with the recovery of his former possessions confiscated at the Dönitz denazification proceeding, he mentioned but two items from his lost home in West Berlin. The first was his family coat of arms. The second was "a painting which was given to him by the government on his birthday." The painting was, of course, no ordinary governmental gift. It was likely one of the many paintings presented to favored subordinates on birthdays by Hitler himself. More than a dozen years after the collapse of the Third Reich, Dönitz revealed that his most prized possession had come from Hitler.[149] The comment by Bausch in the Bundestag debate that Hitler chose his successor purposefully thus received quiet confirmation within the walls of Spandau.

The final efforts from Bonn were conspicuously halfhearted. A flurry of correspondence from Kranzbühler, Heye, and other retired admirals in the spring and summer of 1956 brought Adenauer to the reluctant decision that one more try would be made on Dönitz's behalf, simply because a step had to be made for the record. Protests would result if it were ever learned that nothing had been done.[150] But this final attempt could not have been less enthusiastic. Discussions with the Western Allies were not held until August – four months after von Brentano's vague assurances to Bonatz – and these steps were low-level. Contrary to the discussions over von Neurath's release, Adenauer did not get personally involved, nor was anyone of the ambassadorial rank ever contacted. In fact, the British embassy was deliberately not contacted at all, even though it was clear in Bonn that London had been the main impediment to granting Dönitz credit for his presentencing custody.[151]

The key discussion took place on August 3 between Dr. Wilhelm Grewe, the chief of the Foreign Ministry's Political Division, and the American counselor of embassy, Elim O'Shaughnessy. Grewe stated briefly that the West German government would consider it desirable if Dönitz could be released before the end of his term so that his supporters could not turn him into a martyr and thus use the situation to Bonn's detriment. O'Shaughnessy replied that such was impossible in an American election year and in light of expected protests from Jewish groups. Besides, he said, the British would never agree. Grewe did not argue. He filed his report, met the French counselor the following day, received the same reply, and left for his summer vacation two days later.[152] The embarrassment of Dönitz remaining in Spandau past his term was greater than the embarrassment of making a real effort to get him released, despite the legal argument.

The remaining obstacle was that Dönitz would indeed be released on October 1, 1956. Given the fact that many already viewed him as a political prisoner, the release itself could trigger demonstrations. Discussion concerning the nature of the release began as early as August 1956 when Kranzbühler, on the occasion of his visit to Dönitz in Spandau, tried to learn from the prison personnel the procedures that would be followed. Though both Dönitz and his lawyer stated for all the interpreters to hear that neither craved publicity on the day of the release, the prison authorities themselves felt that "the lawyer was seeking to gain information rather than to put forward proposals."[153]

Within a week, the British Foreign Office began discussing the big day, for ironically the British would also be in the Spandau chair throughout the month of September, and Spandau was in their sector of Berlin. The Foreign Office noted the fact that "the press will congregate at Spandau" but wondered whether a deliberate evasion of the press would be prudent. "We must not give the impression that we are anxious to stop him talking," said one official, because "this would do more harm than good."[154]

The official release plan was worked out by Colonel E. R. Vickers – the British governor at Spandau – in the first week of September. It called for moderate sleight-of-hand. Press inquiries concerning the time of the release would be handled vaguely; Vickers would not decide the exact time of the release until September 30. Ingeborg Dönitz would be told as late as possible when to show up with a car to pick up her husband. As for Dönitz himself and the possibility that he would convene a press conference, the Foreign Office stated on the record that the former admiral would be a "free agent" after his release, and that "there is nothing we can or should do to prevent interviews with the press."[155] "This seems to be the best we can manage," commented one Foreign Office official. "There will inevitably be a gaggle of Press around, which no arrangements will ever drive away."[156]

By mid-September, there had been a number of inquiries by the press and thus attendant concern by the Americans and French that an embarrassing scene would indeed take place. The French mentioned the possibility of a throng of naval officers and the Americans were concerned about Ingeborg, who according to their sources, was in a vindictive mood. The British authorities in Berlin and Bonn decided that the exact timing of the release would not even be given to the West Germans but that Bonn would be asked what its plans were for "damping down" the excitement. Frau Dönitz herself would be told nothing until the final moments because if she did wish to exploit the situation, "then surely we are handing her the opportunity on a plate."[157]

Colonel Vickers, General Francis David Rome, the British commandant in Berlin, and the Foreign Office itself played with the idea of letting Dönitz out a day or two early in order to avoid as much press as possible, preferably at 5:00 A.M. on September 30, which was a Sunday. The American and French prison governors approved of the idea and plans were created to move Dönitz to the sick bay adjacent to the British chief warder's room on the twenty-eighth to receive his effects and await his wife's arrival on the thirtieth. Vickers would decide the time of the release at the last possible moment, and Frau Dönitz, who would be standing by in West Berlin with Kranzbühler, would then be telephoned and instructed to pick up her husband immediately. All powers at Spandau agreed that there would be no publicity other than a brief official statement that the prisoner had served his sentence and was thereby released.[158]

But this scheme ran aground. The Soviet prison governor, Lieutenant Colonel Makaritshev, was away during the first part of the last week of September, and no deal could be struck until his return, though Makaritshev's deputies at one point seemed sympathetic to the idea of an early release. Makaritshev however, informed his fellow governors on September 29 that the stroke of midnight on October 1 was the earliest possible time that he was authorized to allow for the release (Dönitz would not even receive his civilian clothes until 11:55 P.M.). As an aside, Makaritshev warned Vickers personally that should the British argue, the Soviet representation would insist that Dönitz not be released until 4:00 P.M. on that day. It was at 4:00 P.M. a decade earlier that the Nuremberg sentences were pronounced. Vickers, despite the fact that a vigil was already forming outside the prison on the morning of the twenty-eighth, was obliged to accept that the prisoner would not be released until the first, and on the twenty-ninth, the timing was set for midnight on that date – an essential agreement for the British because the Soviet guard would assume the direction of Spandau prison at noon the next day.[159]

As the day and hour drew nigh, General Rome advised the Foreign Office in London that

> in the interests of normalcy we should accept a flurry of photographing, though my police would move the Doenitz car on with a minimum of delay. Any deep laid plan to use decoys, etc., would provoke the press and probably add to the excitement which might surround Doenitz in Berlin before he leaves the city.

Dönitz, it was learned from Kranzbühler, hoped to fly to Hamburg as soon as possible after his release, so the British authorities in Berlin would inform the governing mayor of Berlin Otto Suhr and the police president there of the release time twelve hours in advance so that they could take whatever precautions at Tempelhof airport that might be necessary. The British military authorities in Berlin would also issue general directions to the West Berlin police for the maintenance of order outside the prison – orders that included that they ensure Dönitz's speedy exit from the area.[160]

In fact, the West German government did not want a major scene at Spandau either. On learning (falsely) from the Americans that Dönitz would be released a day early, September 30, the Foreign Ministry booked flight tickets for Dönitz and his wife from West Berlin under phony names while informing the West Berlin police themselves of the possible need to keep order. When the West German Foreign Ministry learned from the British later that the release date would be October 1 after all, they planned to send Heye to Berlin to meet Dönitz and to "advise him to behave quietly" on the assumption that Heye was one of the few people to whom the former grand admiral would listen.[161] As it was, no one in Bonn intended to allow Dönitz to hold a press conference in West Berlin either. The Foreign Ministry's office there received explicit instructions to move Dönitz from the divided city the quickest way possible while avoiding all contact with the press, and the West Berlin city government agreed with the intent.[162]

Yet the press – both German and international – had begun to assemble outside of Spandau on September 28, and on the thirtieth the Berlin police reported that the journalists were planning to hold up Dönitz's car, open the doors, and question him. In fact, photographers would arrange their cars blocking the Wilhelmsstraße intersections in front of the prison so that indeed Dönitz's driver would have to stop. On the thirtieth, the crowd had grown to about four hundred reporters, photographers, and navy veterans, and at 11:30 P.M. the West Berlin police were deployed outside the Spandau gates complete with trucks that blocked the Wilhelmsstraße directly in front of the prison as well as the view of the prison's front gate, from which Dönitz was to emerge.

Contrary to what the British had originally wished to do, Vickers decided on a ruse. Near midnight, the British stationed more troop trucks on Wilhelmsstraße to further block the view of the front gate from the street. Vickers, meanwhile, asked the U.S. and French prison governors to remain in their quarters and to make no telephone calls. Dönitz was taken from his cell at five minutes to midnight – his effects would be mailed to him later – and hustled to a side exit. The former admiral's car met him there and pulled away from Spandau Prison three minutes after midnight. He was secretly taken to the home of a former U-boat captain in the West Berlin district of Zehlendorf where he was to await quietly his flight to West Germany, which was to leave West Berlin in the afternoon. Because the troop and police trucks blocked the view from the front, most of the crowd did not even see Dönitz's car leave, and because photographers too were stationed at the wrong end of the prison building, none managed to get photographs. The real problems began, however, when the press made a dash to follow the car. The West Berlin police trucks were themselves blocking the Wilhelmsstraße and were deliberately slow to unblock it, and in the rush, fighting – some of it rather rough – ensued between the press on the one hand and the West Berlin police on the other.[163]

Though no one was seriously injured, the press – foreign and West German alike – made immediate protests about the roughness and unconstitutionality of the incident to the three Western powers and to the West Berlin authorities as well. American journalists were especially furious that they had missed their scoop, and the Berlin Press Union complained that the Basic Law itself had been breached. The guilty parties, they insisted, should be called to account. Berlin police president Dr. Stumm blamed the British military authorities, which had ordered the screening of the prison.[164] Nevertheless, the West German government was faced with an unanticipated embarrassment – the accusation that it had hindered a free press. It was also faced with the possibility of another press vigil at Tempelhof airport, which could become far uglier than the pushing and shoving at Spandau.

To alleviate the vocal protests, the Foreign Ministry quickly decided at the explicit requests of the American embassy in Bonn and by Dr. Stumm himself to stage the one event that everyone had hoped to avoid – a press conference in West Berlin featuring Hitler's successor, Karl Dönitz. The Foreign Ministry's office in West Berlin hastily arranged the conference for the afternoon of October 1 from Dönitz's temporary quarters at Zehlendorf before his flight. But precautions were taken to muzzle the former admiral as much as possible. Shortly before he left Spandau, Vickers – perhaps at the behest of Kirkpatrick – had already threatened Dönitz that his future actions could have an adverse effect on the four prisoners still left in Spandau.[165] Now, as the press conference was being arranged, German Foreign Ministry officials warned Dönitz that "it would be better for him" if he did not make hastily considered statements. According to a government memo, Dönitz "loyally followed the advice... although he originally had other intentions."[166]

Such explains the bizarre silence from the last ruler of the Third Reich on his first day of freedom. In a brief statement that struck everyone as "obviously prepared," he said, "My task now is to maintain silence. I would like to remain silent today and will remain silent in the future." He continued that as a man isolated for the past eleven and a half years, he was in no position to offer any comments or render any judgments.[167] As his fellow inmates would have attested if only they could have, this was indeed a first. "He had little to say," said John Robey, the political adviser to General Rome, "but the photographers were allowed to take all the pictures they wanted.... The press have been somewhat assuaged."[168]

Only the memoirs remained. Despite the fear that he would die in Spandau in 1955, Raeder did not die until November 6, 1960, at age 84 in Kiel. He was thus able, with considerable help, to publish his memoirs by 1957. Raeder pointed to "the deadly effect of the terms of the Versailles treaty,"

19. Karl Dönitz in West Berlin the afternoon following his midnight release from Spandau, October 1, 1956. Photographers could take pictures but Dönitz had been warned not to make speeches. Photograph courtesy of the Deutsches historisches Museum.

in justifying rearmament, and explained Germany's "sacrifice" of accepting the Anglo-German Naval Treaty, which he helped to break before the ink was dry.[169] He claimed to have been bamboozled by Hitler's lies. "It was the tragedy of my life," he said, "that our future took a completely different path." He claimed uneasiness with Hitler's statements at the November 1937 Hossbach meeting while at the same time misunderstanding them.[170] He omitted his call in October 1939 for war with the United States, stating instead that "we had to consider the neutrals [to] avoid any possible unfortunate incidents."[171] He misrepresented the planning for the German invasion of Norway as necessary to preserve Norwegian neutrality against an identical British operation (pointing again to Churchill's memoirs).[172] Raeder also forgot to mention his acceptance of the Commando Order and his cash gifts from Hitler. Nuremberg, he concluded, was a political trial against which he

20. Karl Dönitz stands before the coffin of Erich Raeder, Kiel, November 1960. Photograph courtesy of the Associated Press.

and Dönitz were determined to preserve the German Navy's honor. And the Tribunal, Raeder argued, "completely vindicated the German Navy and its methods."[173] In fact, the Tribunal vindicated neither.[174] Raeder's graveside eulogy at Kiel's *Nordfriedhof* in 1960 was delivered by Karl Dönitz at the request of Friedrich Ruge, now the general inspector of the West German Navy. Hitler's two grand admirals, who disliked each other personally, thus entered a partnership even in death wherein their reputations were bound to one another.

Dönitz's first volume of memoirs, *Ten Years and Twenty Days,* which appeared less than two years after his release, were more imaginative than Raeder's. He painted his wartime role in technical terms, distanced himself from Hitler, and blamed the Allies and Soviets for Germany's current woes. Great Britain, bent on "the destruction of [the] political and economic power of Germany," was the true aggressor in 1939.[175] Roosevelt connived the United States into London's "war on the German people and their industrial power" and Roosevelt's insistence on Germany's unconditional surrender forced the Germans to fight until the bitter end.[176] Nazism was correct in its call for national freedom, an end to class war, and full employment. As for the atrocities, Dönitz knew nothing until after the war.[177] "I...regarded," he wrote, "the command of the Navy as my sole duty. To bother myself about the...political direction of the country was quite impossible."[178] As chief of state, Dönitz claimed to have worked exclusively from the start to rescue eastern Germans from the Soviet onslaught.[179] He omitted his high regard for Hitler, he miscast the *Laconia* order by pretending that his submarines would have rescued merchant ship survivors if not for callous Allied attacks, and he concluded that Nuremberg displayed a "complete lack of any moral foundation."[180] It was the book one might have expected. So was Dönitz's next effort, *My Changing Life* (1968), which concluded that the Nuremberg verdict against him was entirely political in nature.[181] It was the story Dönitz stuck with until his death in 1980.

Back in Spandau, Albert Speer understood the irony after warders smuggled him a copy of *Ten Years and Twenty Days*. "The longer I read these *Memoirs*," he wrote, "the more incomprehensible it is to me that Dönitz should systematically obscure his personal relation to Hitler.... Why has he concealed his cordial relationship to Hitler?...Nothing of all that. Even on trivial matters Dönitz pretties up the picture."[182] It was a lesson Speer would recall when considering the public presentation of his own past.

CHAPTER FIVE

# The Foiled Escape: Albert Speer's Twenty Years

"To what extent was I required to trouble myself with questions of human rights?"

Albert Speer, 1952

In August 1960 at the beginning of his thirteenth year in Spandau Prison, Albert Speer received a rare, nonfamily letter, which the prison governors allowed him to see. It was from the Property Administration for the former German National Railroad in West Berlin. The letter revealed that on October 4, 1938, Speer bought a valuable lakefront estate in the wealthy Schwanenwerder island-district of Berlin from Marie-Anne von Goldschmidt-Rothschild, a prominent woman from a Jewish banking family, for the bargain price of RM 150,000. Other Third Reich dignitaries including Joseph Goebbels had already bought waterfront homes in Schwanenwerder at low prices from wealthy Jews.[1] But in 1943 Speer sold his new Schwanenwerder property to the German National Railroad for RM 389,506, a profit of nearly a quarter million marks, a fortune in those days.

Marie-Anne had fled in 1938 to New York, but in 1959 she returned to West Berlin to reclaim her property. The restitution court there in August 1959 returned the estate to her in return for payment of DM 15,000, the new West German currency, the ratio of which against the old currency was 1:10. The money went to the Railroad Property Administration, which quickly discovered that they had paid Speer far more than they received from Marie-Anne. They wrote Speer asking for nearly DM 24,000 in compensation. The proof of what Speer had done lay in the real estate transfer books from 1938 and 1943. Now he acted in character. He ordered his lawyer to handle it. Speer owned no real assets in his own name. After the death of his mother in 1952, the substantial properties he stood to inherit were put in his children's names to protect the property from confiscation in West German denazification proceedings. The debt was never paid.[2]

In the years after his release from Spandau, Speer repeatedly insisted that he had been too occupied with architectural projects to have noticed that his government in 1938 had raised anti-Jewish policy to its most violent level to date or that it had begun a systematic Aryanization campaign in that year in which Jewish property was purchased far below its real value.[3] Thus, Speer's real estate windfall of the same year, the postwar exchange over which has been buried in the Spandau Prison archive, signifies a few points to be elaborated in this chapter. First – and this is neither the first nor the last place such will be read – Speer was a liar. He lied at Nuremberg, he lied repeatedly to his children, and he lied in his post-Spandau writings about his role in the Nazi state and his consciousness of its anti-Jewish policies. Second, he never accepted, despite his famous faux penitence, that his sentence was just. He spent the better part of his twenty-year sentence attempting to escape it. Some attempts involved bribery, arm twisting, and influence peddling. Some involved the callous use of friends and family. But all attempts involved lobbying government officials with the idea that Speer's guilt was very limited. This web of lies, much of which Speer wove in Spandau, had the original aim of getting him out of prison rather than simply out of posterity's dark side.

Speer's problem was not that no one believed him. The Allied and West German governments accepted his story to a degree. But no one who mattered was willing to prioritize his case above cases more pressing or more possible to resolve. German POWs in the U.S.S.R. were a higher priority for the West German government in the mid-1950s as were the more "possible" cases of the Germans convicted of war crimes held in Allied prisons in West Germany. Even in Spandau, the old and sick came first, and as has been seen, Bonn prioritized von Neurath and Raeder. After 1957 when Speer was one of three prisoners left in Spandau and one of the few war criminals still imprisoned anywhere, the ship bearing his case sailed between the Scylla and Charibdis of postwar West Germany – the razors' edge fate of West Berlin on one hand and the public reacquaintance, after more than a decade of amnesia, with the horrors of the Nazi past on the other. In such a storm, Speer had no safe port. But when Speer emerged from Spandau in 1966, he was wearing a life vest, stuffed with cash from friends and notes for his books, which would allow him to float above the waves of guilt for years.

## THE SPEER MYTH

Following the war, during his trial, during his two decades in Spandau, and in his three best-selling books written after 1966, Speer built a reputation as a different kind of Nazi.[4] The argument was this. In the 1930s, Speer was a young apolitical architect who, like many of his generation, latched on to the national renaissance that Nazism provided. He lacked understanding of Nazism's terrible implications. His service as Hitler's minister of armaments after 1942 was based on Hitler's eccentric whim, and Speer's aim after 1942 was simply to provide his county with the best chance of surviving the war. He thought little and knew less of Germany's treatment of Jews. In the first draft of his memoirs, *Inside the Third Reich*, Speer did not even mention Kristallnacht but then added a single passage on the urging of his collaborator, journalist Joachim Fest. This mention came with the caveat that as Hitler's chief architect, he was "sheltered from [the] harsh reality" of Hitler's antisemitism, which he never saw for its murderous reality. As Hitler's armaments minister, Speer knew little of German heavy industry's use of slave labor either.

On trial at Nuremberg and in Spandau, Speer became the "duly national penitent" not for what he knew or did but for that of which he allowed himself to remain ignorant.[5] It was a popular story. If Speer had been bewitched by Hitler while millions of Jews and others mysteriously vanished, then was this not an alibi for all Germans struggling to master the past? As Fest has written in the most recent and apologetic Speer biography, "Speer personified a type in which many saw themselves" – namely a type that could support the Nazi regime for its national power and its steadfastness against the scourge of the interwar and postwar periods, Communism. It was also a type that could compartmentalize the horrible deeds of others while maintaining a distinction between the nightmarish public and the sheltered private spheres – a characteristic that Fest says "has deep roots in the German national character."[6]

Speer bolstered the story in the 1970s with the publication of the aforementioned memoirs and his *Spandau Diaries*, allegedly a day-by-day reckoning with his past blindness in which Speer humbly accepts the purgatory of Spandau with no complaint despite the argument by many others as the years passed (also recorded in the *Diaries*) that he should be freed. In fact, even the *Diaries* are a post-Spandau creation. Speer cobbled large chunks of the daily entries together verbatim from detailed letters he had written to his children on the daily minutiae of prison life. While the *Diaries* are cleverly accurate on day-to-day events in prison (they can be checked against the Chief Warder's log), the passages in which Speer introspectively wrestles with his past are pure invention – and he does not mention at all his numerous frenetic attempts to have himself released. Speer engineered the *Diaries* to show himself suffering for Germany's sins.[7] As his lifelong friend Rudolf Wolters cracked after their estrangement in 1975, Speer "would have stolen the show from Jesus of Nazareth."[8]

Fest's recent account is a response to a series of European journalists and historians who meticulously stripped away Speer's veneer of lies beginning in the early 1980s, partially with official Nazi records but also with the records of Rudolf Wolters himself.[9] The key document was Wolters's "Chronicle," a set of unofficial annals kept after January 1941 of Speer's official duties, hidden after the war during Speer's trial, sanitized of passages concerning Jews, then handed over in original form to the German Federal Archives following Wolters's rift with Speer.[10] Had the Chronicle together with the rest of Speer's story been available at Nuremberg, there would surely have been thirteen death sentences instead of twelve.

Speer was born in Mannheim to the well-to-do-family of architect Albert Speer Senior in 1905, though the family moved to Schloss-Wolfsbrunnenweg in Heidelberg in 1918. As an architectural student in Berlin in the dying days of the Weimar Republic, Speer joined the Nazi Party in January 1931 after having been mesmerized by a Hitler speech to students and professors in Berlin the previous month.[11] His first architectural jobs for the Nazi Party were small ones, but having caught Hitler's eye, Speer began working on projects of top importance in 1933 at the young age of 28. He remodeled Goebbels's Ministry of Propaganda and Enlightenment as well as the new residence of the Reich chancellor and also designed the gargantuan stone installation at the zeppelin field at the Nazi Party's rally grounds at Nuremberg.

Hitler's enthusiasm for grandiose architecture together with Speer's penchant for getting big jobs done quickly meant that the two became personally close and remained so until the final days of the regime. This closeness, even "a kind of love" was noted by Traudl Junge, one of Hitler's secretaries in the Führer's bunker in the last weeks of the war.[12] Hitler rewarded Speer by charging him with the complete remodeling of Berlin in January 1937 with the title *Generalbauinspektor* (inspector general for construction) – a position responsible not to the city authorities but rather to Hitler alone. Speer would claim at Nuremberg and in his books that this position was based on art, not politics. Art and architecture though, have been political expressions since the Pharaohs, and they were surely political in the Third Reich.[13] And Speer was no lone architect sitting at a drafting table. By January 1942 Speer's *Generalbauinspektorat* (GBI) employed some 65,000 workers.[14]

The "apolitical" Speer could play politics with the best, using his place in Hitler's inner circle to reap maximum advantage. He claimed a generous salary and an even more generous expense account through which he began amassing a private fortune. He had his enemies removed from office.[15] Through it all, Speer worked diligently on the reconstruction of Berlin, creating a garish new Reich Chancellery in nine months in 1938 and 1939 and further redesigning the future city, to be known as *Germania*, with wide boulevards, a massive domed hall, and man-made lakes. For the sake of the new capital, Speer also sought and received the cooperation of SS-owned quarries worked by slave laborers from late 1937.[16] And the new Berlin would have no Jews. Wolters's Chronicle shows how tens of thousands of Berlin Jews were evicted from their homes from 1939 to 1941 to make room for Aryans who lost their homes to urban renewal planning or, later, to British bombs.[17] Documents found more recently by historian Susanne Willems show that Speer proposed the eviction of Berlin Jews into camps

21. Albert Speer with Hitler at the Berghof, Hitler's Alpine retreat, 1937. Photograph courtesy of the National Archives and Records Administration (Heinrich Hoffmann Collection).

outside the city as early as September 1938 (the month before he purchased the Goldschmidt-Rothschild estate). Moreover, Speer's office collaborated with the Gestapo in the deportation of more than 50,000 Berlin Jews to the East after October 1941, where they were subsequently murdered.[18]

Speer's rise to the status of a major war criminal insofar as the Allies were concerned came with his appointment as minister of armaments and munitions in February 1942 on the accidental death of Fritz Todt, the previous armaments minister.[19] At 36, Speer was the youngest minister of state, but he was ruthless beyond his years. To consolidate war production, he speedily used his relationship with Hitler to shove aside rivals in the economic sphere, namely Göring as chief of the Four-Year Plan and Funk as the Reich minister of economics. Speer enlisted Himmler's police organs to locate materials hoarded for civilian uses by small and large companies. From the beginning, Speer's ministry also pursued a mutually beneficial relationship with SS leaders for concentration camp labor in expanded camp armament factories.[20] As the war progressed, Speer prescribed the severest penalties for malingering and sabotage while his ministry pressed the SS to expand the concentration camp labor supply while disposing of those who had been worked to death.[21] The relationship with Himmler also acquainted Speer with the terrible fate of Europe's Jews in Poland despite Speer's postwar claims to the contrary.[22] Very recent findings show that Speer not only knew of the camp at Auschwitz-Birkenau but was included in discussions with the SS on the camp's expansion to a giant work and extermination facility in 1942.[23] And to the end, Speer never wavered in his devotion for Hitler or his faith in victory despite his later claims to the contrary. He remained loyal in the wake of the July 1944 assassination attempt, even offering advice to Goebbels for crushing the coup. Speer was convinced that German V-1 and V-2 rockets would turn the war around. Wolters remembered later that Speer entertained fantasies of millions of ordinary Germans holding off Allied tanks with hand weapons.[24] Speer's loyalty to the Nazi regime was recognized after Hitler's suicide when he continued in a ministerial role in the twenty-three-day Dönitz government. By now, however, Speer expected an important role in postwar Germany, perhaps heading reconstruction. His arrest by British authorities at Glücksberg Castle near Flensburg in northern Germany on May 23, 1945; his removal to the Allied interrogation centers "Ashcan" at Mondorf and "Dustbin" at Kranzberg Castle; and his indictment as a major war criminal were true surprises to him.

Yet he did not go to trial unprepared. Just as Speer maneuvered against rivals while in power, he maneuvered against them when he had none. His defense, as he informed his skeptical defense attorney Hans Fläschner, would be to claim responsibility while the other defendants did not. This did not mean that Speer would grasp the nettle of true individual responsibility where he would admit his role in the ghastly crimes of the regime. His would be a vague "collective responsibility" in which he would admit serving the regime while denying direct involvement or even knowledge of its worst atrocities. It would be the guilt not of a criminal, but of a man who had allowed himself to be shielded from the worst. "This trial is necessary," Speer properly noted to U.S. Army Captain Gustav M. Gilbert, who provided psychiatric evaluations of the Nuremberg defendants and who later wrote that Speer's conception of Nazi guilt was "more sincere," but "less demonstrative" than that of the other defendants.[25] It was a charitable assessment. Speer testified that

> This war has brought an inconceivable catastrophe upon the German people and indeed started a world catastrophe. Therefore it is my unquestionable duty to assume my share of responsibility for this disaster before the German people. This is all the more my obligation . . . since the head of the Government has avoided responsibility before the German people and before the world.[26]

It was a backhanded contrition from the start – a panacea to an absent apology from Hitler made mostly toward the German nation and not to the rest of Europe.

Speer separated himself from the other defendants, whom Göring had expected would form a united front against the Tribunal. Speer testified that he was accepted into Hitler's inner circle because like Hitler he was an artist. His appointment as minister of armaments was nonpolitical, to last only for the duration of the war, and was to be followed by a return to architectural practice.[27] The increase in the number of workers under his authority, from 2.6 million in February 1942 to 14 million in the summer of 1944 was in part coincidental, since more tasks were assigned to him thanks to his organizational skills. He admitted asking for laborers and even knowing that foreigners were included in the labor pool. But the recruitment of foreign workers was the responsibility of Fritz Sauckel, the former Reich plenipotentiary for labor. If foreign workers were brought to work in Germany, then they were obliged to do so by German laws. "Whether such laws were justified or not," he said, "was no concern of mine."[28] The health of such workers was the responsibility of others, too, such as the Interior Ministry, the Supreme Command, or even factory managers. Workers, he said, were generally treated well in any case – exceptions to this rule were beyond his control. The proximity of concentration camps to factories, in Speer's retelling, permitted "the workers to arrive fresh and ready for work."[29] Fläschner admitted in his closing statement that Speer used foreign labor, but that given the heavy bombing of German industry, he had little choice. Total war on such a scale was new and not envisioned by the Hague Conventions, which had prohibited slave labor. Anyway, Fläschner concluded, it was Sauckel who had been responsible for the roundup of foreign workers, the details of which Speer's ministry could not influence. This was nonsense. Sauckel's decrees concerning the use of foreign labor were well known to Speer's ministry, and Speer representatives accompanied Sauckel's press gangs as they combed occupied areas for men and women fit enough to work.[30]

The other crucial point of Speer's defense was not even relevant to the charges against him. These concern his "awakening" and alleged opposition to Hitler as the war ground to a close. Speer claimed to have subverted Hitler's orders in late 1944 and 1945 for "scorched earth" during the German retreat whereby nothing of industrial value was to fall into enemy hands, and the Germans themselves, as a penalty for losing the war, were to be left with nothing either. Speer thus claimed to have saved industrial plants in Germany, France, the Low Countries, Austria, Italy, Yugoslavia, Finland, Hungary, Poland, and Czechoslovakia.[31] Speer had a point, particularly with regard to Hitler's "Nero Order" of March 19, 1945, which would have destroyed German coal and steel production in the Ruhr had it been implemented.[32]

22. Albert Speer's testimony at Nuremberg, June 1946. Photograph courtesy of the National Archives and Records Administration.

But the preservation of German heavy industry was fully in the interest of Speer and his industrialist friends. The latter owned the Ruhr mines and steel mills that Hitler wanted destroyed. In helping Speer to sabotage the order German industrialists were saving their own property.[33] As for the preservation of foreign industry, there are many instances in which the failure of scorched earth had little to do with Speer. The destruction of mines and power stations in the area in the northern French Lille region, for example, was planned in great detail in September 1944 with maps and diagrams of what the army was to destroy. Destruction was stymied by the speed of the German retreat, which precluded setting the charges properly, and to the opposition of local German army commanders.[34] Speer's most dramatic claim was that he had plotted to kill Hitler in March by poisoning the air supply in the Führer bunker. This story was so silly that Fläschner soft-pedaled it in his closing, and it was never employed in subsequent clemency arguments.[35]

Speer's cross-examination was botched. Maxwell-Fyfe, the devastating British cross-examiner, did not examine Speer because Speer was not guilty on the count – crimes against peace – for which the British were responsible.

It was thus left to Jackson, who was badly prepared. Jackson had no clear line of argumentation, bounced from issue to issue, and asked open-ended questions on which Speer could pontificate but not provide clear answers. Speer refuted or denied many of the clear points Jackson made. He dismissed a Krupp employee's affidavit on how foreign workers were treated as a lie designed to "drag the German people through the dirt." Poor conditions in factories and camps were mostly caused by Allied air raids – anyway they were not in his spheres of knowledge or responsibility.[36] He admitted the transfer of 100,000 Hungarian Jews for work in underground airplane factories (he had mentioned it in an earlier interrogation) but claimed it justified "in view of the whole war situation."[37] He dismissed the Geneva Prisoner of War Convention as an outdated "old conception."[38] At the end, Jackson asked but a single open-ended question on what Speer meant by the "common responsibility" that he accepted for the Nazi state, and then failed to probe the answer.[39]

It was a fine performance in light of the sorry testimonies and blanket denials from the other defendants. Telford Taylor recollected years later that "I remember many comments favorable to Speer," and U.S. Judge Francis Biddle called him "the most humane and decent of the defendants." Maxwell-Fyfe regarded him as "by far the most attractive personality among the defendants." Given Speer's company, this impression was not hard to make. But Taylor, who later prosecuted the German industrialists Friedrich Flick and Alfred Krupp, recollected that despite it all, Speer was "loaded with crime."[40]

And the entire act came within an ace of failure. Speer was acquitted on the two counts of Conspiracy and Crimes against Peace because he was not a minister until 1942. He was found guilty on the counts of War Crimes and Crimes against Humanity thanks to his use of slave labor. Nikitschenko demanded hanging, and at first Biddle agreed. But the American judge eventually voted with Lawrence and Donnedieu de Vabres that Speer should receive a prison term instead, fixed at twenty years, thanks to the combination of guilt and poised contrition.[41] Speer quickly noted for the record that his sentence was a just one and maintained this stance. After the sentence, he did not even petition for clemency. It was enough for now not to face the gallows. But a petition for clemency would have run counter to the entire argument constructed for the trial – that Speer was willing to accept a share of responsibility, generally speaking, for the Nazi period. Clemency, when it came, would have to come under circumstances that would preserve the honor of Hitler's favorite minister. As Wolters sardonically put it in 1975, "on the one hand was the 20 year prison sentence which [Speer in his public statements] saw as proper, while on the other side were the intensive efforts to be released from custody, indeed from the first day forward."[42]

## EARLY ATTEMPTS AT RELEASE

If clemency came it would be with the help of an outside support network that was already working on Speer's behalf after his arrest. It was headed by Rudolf Wolters of Coesfeld, Speer's devoted friend from their student days in Munich and Berlin in 1924 and 1925 who had kept the hidden-and-then-sanitized Chronicle.[43] Working closely with Wolters was Annemarie Kempf, who in 1938 as a young woman became Speer's private secretary at the *Generalbauinspektorat*. Like Wolters, she remained absolutely loyal to Speer, smuggling documents from Speer's hidden trove to Fläschner as she worked for the Allies there as a transcriber of interrogations.[44] Both Wolters and Kempf also served as clearinghouses for Speer's massive secret correspondence illegally smuggled out of Spandau by the prison orderly Toni Proost and later by fellow Dutch orderly Jan Boon. Wolters's secretary Marion Reisser typed thousands of pages from 25,000 scraps of Speer's scrawl smuggled out of Spandau, including letters to family, orders and strategies for attempting his release, management of assets, and material eventually used in his memoirs and to create his *Spandau Diaries*.[45]

Wolters also helped build and manage from the summer of 1948 a secret bank account in Coesfeld known as the *Schulgeldkonto*, or school money account. The account was to help Speer's wife Margret and the six Speer children, the oldest of whom (Albert Jr.) was 14 in 1948, with their educational and household needs. Margret drew monthly on the account based on what Wolters said the account could bear. But the largest outlays would finance clemency attempts overseen by Wolters and insisted on by Speer. Contributors to the account included a variety of architects and industrialists who had worked under Speer during the Third Reich, who became richer under Speer, who pursued successful postwar careers, and who sensed that Speer's redemption meant their own as well. The industrialists had been the backbone of Speer's so-called *Kindergarten* – a group of young men whom Speer had given key positions in the Ministry of Armaments and Munitions in 1942 in order to raise production and press to final victory. Owing to Speer's conviction that private industrial and state interests were one and the same and that the future belonged to big industry rather than smaller firms, Speer became their patron, and they became his independent power base essential for the struggle against other state and party agencies with a stake in the war economy.[46]

Foremost among them was Walter Rohland who could easily have been prosecuted for war crimes. A superior organizational talent, Rohland was a senior director at *Deutsche Edelstahlwerke* during the 1930s before his fortieth birthday. In 1941 he became a board member and in 1943 board chairman of United Steel Works (*Vereinigte Stahlwerke, AG*). Government contracts for armored vehicles were Rohland's bread and butter to the point where he earned the nickname "Panzer Rohland" in 1943. He began producing armored trucks in 1935, and by the mid-1940s he was Fritz Todt's chief private consultant for increasing tank production. Speer and Rohland formed a close working relationship after Todt's death. Rohland became a chief subordinate as head of the ministry's Main Tank Committee, and the key deputy chief of the ministry's Iron Manufacturing Ring and the Reich Union of Iron, two cartels aimed at channeling that resource. Rohland was thus deeply complicit in the requisitioning and use of slave labor. His name is on numerous documents assembled for the eventual U.S. Military Tribunal trials of German industrialists regarding labor allocation and workers' punishment.[47] In a U.S. army interrogation of February 1947 Rohland admitted that United Steel Works used 59,000 civilian foreign laborers and 28,000 prisoners of war in 1943 alone.[48] Rohland joined the Nazi Party in April 1933 out of what he called the duty of Germans to influence the party in a positive way. He also claimed later to have helped a few Jews during the war.[49] But an OSS report of 1945, aside from labeling him the "leading personality of the steel firms of the Northwest," also noted that Rohland was "an ardent Nazi before 1933," and that he hindered Allied investigations of the steel industry since lower level employees "seemed afraid to cooperate with Allied investigators because of their greater fear of such top Nazi executives as Rohland."[50]

The Americans considered Rohland a war crimes defendant after arresting him in July 1946 and sending him to the "Dustbin" interrogation facility.[51] But he remained a defense witness for older industrialists such as Friedrich Flick and Alfred Krupp, who could be charged more easily with complicity in starting the war as well as with war crimes and crimes against humanity.[52] After his release by the U.S. authorities in September 1947 and a very sympathetic denazification hearing in Düsseldorf in January 1948 in which Rohland paid no fines, he rebuilt his fortune as well as his reputation as an apolitical iron and steel man. Indeed, the reconstruction of reputation as plain businessmen was an aim of many Nazi industrialists, particularly as they regained their places at the head of West German industry.[53] But Rohland's true colors were never far below the surface. The destruction of his family estate by Allied bombs, he said in a 1953 interview over too much wine, meant for him that "the account with the Jews is settled."[54]

Other advocates from the old *Kindergarten* included Willy Schlieker, born in Hamburg in 1914 and destined to become one of the great West German shipping magnates until his empire fell to ruin in 1962 for lack of diversification. In 1940, Schlieker began work for *Vereinigte Stahlwerke*, and, like Rohland, he became the chief of one of the twenty-one main committees in Speer's Ministry of Armaments. He briefly worked for the British occupation authorities helping to allocate steel and iron in their zone but was forced out of this position as a result of denazification court findings in

January 1947. Because Schlieker had worked for the Flick concern at one point during the war, U.S. authorities wanted him as a witness, but the British never complied.[55] Speer's friends in heavy industry also included Ernst Wolf Mommsen, another steel executive and senior wartime Speer subordinate who resumed a successful postwar career in the Ruhr pipe-producing industry after working with the British during the occupation. Mommsen would conduct trade negotiations with the Soviets as early as 1952 and would also serve as state secretary to Helmut Schmidt after the latter became defense minister in the 1969 cabinet of Willy Brandt. When Speer emerged from Spandau in 1966, it was Mommsen's car that met him.[56]

Many of Speer's former architects from the *Generalbauinspektorat* contributed and helped with clemency planning as well. Friedrich Tamms, who served under Speer in the GBI, is indicative of the architectural circle, perversely dubbed "the twelve disciples" by Wolters. Tamms's designs include a series of massive bridges including the Niebelungen Bridge leading across the Danube into Hitler's hometown of Linz, begun in 1939 but destroyed by the Allies. Tamms also conceptualized and drafted a series of massive atheistic battle monuments, reminiscent of those left by the ancient Romans, to stand, as Tamms explained in 1943, "from Narvik to Africa, from the Atlantic to the Russian plain." They would memorialize fallen German heroes, but at the same time, Tamms said, they would form an aesthetic "rampart . . . against the hostile flood of enemy feelings and desires."[57]

Speer's family's efforts were more limited thanks to their smaller influence and also per Speer's orders. Speer's wife Margret, for whom he used the pet name Gretel, was informed of all steps but initiated none herself. In part, Speer lacked confidence in her. His constant drafting and redrafting of letters from Spandau for her to send as well as his self-evident instructions might have insulted anyone else. But Speer was also convinced that noisy press campaigns carried on by the Spandau wives in the right-wing press and based on exaggeration were counterproductive. He could follow them since newspapers and magazines were smuggled to his cell by sympathetic warders. Speer was especially critical of Erika Raeder's efforts and the Jürgen Thorwald series in *Revue* in 1951, which was loaded with easily refuted hyperbole. "Anything we can do," he told Margret referring to the two of them, "plays absolutely no role." Speer ordered her not to seek out the press like the other wives. When asked by reporters, she was to point simply to the hard situation for their six children. Margret herself wrote Winifred von Mackensen that exaggerated press accounts were not helpful.[58]

On the other hand, Speer worked himself to breach Spandau's walls. In her thoroughly researched study of Speer, Gitta Sereny argues that he accepted his sentence for the first few years.[59] Maybe. But in the first few years, Speer expected that he would never serve his full sentence anyway thanks to the growing rift between the Four Powers. His talents as an armaments czar, he thought, like those of German scientists and engineers, would be in demand by the Soviets. Thus, the West would spirit him away. It occurred to him during the Berlin Blockade that a shooting war between Germany's former enemies would obliterate what was left of the country, and he noted to Margret that "I would not like to be a beneficiary of a war."[60] It was a strange statement from one whose entire career was built on history's most terrible conflict. Even without shooting, he believed the prison scuttlebutt that Spandau would break up.[61] He was already planning his memoirs, instructing Margret what to say to prospective publishers, and hoping that British historian Hugh Trevor-Roper, whose *Last Days of Hitler* was serialized in the American press, might arrange a book deal.[62]

When Spandau did not dissolve, even as a result of the war in Korea, Speer began his own efforts with the help of the *Schulgeldkonto* and various lawyers. Despite his comments in the published *Spandau Diaries* that the old and sick should be removed first (he seems to have had some sympathy for von Neurath), Speer tried to separate himself from the other inmates. The argument used for the next decade and a half would focus on what Speer and his friends understood to be his mitigating circumstances. These centered on his sabotage of Hitler's scorched earth orders. Speer wrote Margret in 1950 that scorched earth could not be mentioned too many times and ordered her to assemble everything she could on the scorched earth policy and send it to Trevor-Roper, whose work had been moderately sympathetic to Speer. "I think," said Speer, "that he will make something of it."[63] He also hoped to use his contrition act from Nuremberg. "My guilt," he wrote in 1952 to Werner Schütz, an attorney friend of Wolters, "is in my opinion limited by my voluntary and conscious statements [at Nuremberg] that I demanded workers that came to Germany against their will." This, Speer said, had scored points with Jackson. Anyway, he added, the Foreign Ministry and the High Command were the ones responsible for the laws of war. "To what degree was I required," Speer asked rhetorically, "to trouble myself over questions of human rights?"[64]

Mostly Speer depended on lobbying. He had lost confidence in Fläschner during the Nuremberg trial, and though Fläschner remained officially responsible for the case, Speer used other, better connected lawyers for politics. The first was Otto Kranzbühler, Dönitz's defense attorney who had impressed everyone at Nuremberg and who, as a defense attorney in the U.S. cases against Flick and Krupp, knew Speer's friends like Rohland, whom he used as defense witnesses. On February 10, 1951, there was a Saturday afternoon meeting in Düsseldorf that included Wolters, Kempf, Tamms, and two other sympathetic attorneys, Schütz and Gerhard Fränk. The group decided to have Kranzbühler move key West German politicians on Speer's behalf.[65] Kranzbühler, who still represented Dönitz, would not come cheap – DM 10,000 would have to be raised from the *Schulgeldkonto*, which in turn meant that the fund itself would need more money. Rohland assured Wolters that he could raise it. Speer had already sent a long list of suggestions for additional contributors to the *Schulgeldkonto*, all of whom owed him favors from the Hitler years. The list shows that Speer could still twist arms. It also shows that he knew during the war that Jews were in lethal danger. Dr. Wilhelm Haspel, the general director of Daimler Benz, Speer remembered, had been married to a Jew. Speer claimed to have removed many "substantial" difficulties for him. The same was true of Otto Meyer, the general director of M.A.N. (*Machinenfabrik Augsburg-Nürnberg*), whose Jewish wife had fled to Switzerland and of whom Speer said, "I protected him from the same difficulties." It was normal, Speer said, for such men to have been removed from their positions, with "unforeseeable consequences."[66] Now he expected them to contribute. In the summer of 1951 Rohland solicited large contributions from companies on Speer's list including Haspel's Daimler Benz (DM 2,000). The largest outlays of the *Schulgeldkonto* to date were paid to Kranzbühler that year. At the same time, Margret begged local banks to let her withdraw far smaller sums from the various accounts in her husband's name to pay for clothes, food, heat, doctors' and dentists' visits – and ironically school expenses – for Speer's children.[67]

Juggling his responsibilities to Dönitz, his desire to bring an end to Spandau, and his new obligations to Speer was not easy for Kranzbühler. In July 1951, he told U.S. high commissioner McCloy that the time had come for the Nuremberg judgments to receive legal review. McCloy was sympathetic but said the Soviets would never agree. Kranzbühler decided to create a clemency petition for Speer accompanied by lobbying of West German leaders.[68] Wolters was hopeful. "I think," he counseled Margret when explaining the first DM 2,500 payment to Kranzbühler, "that we should trust him and let him do what he thinks is right."[69] By February 1952, Kranzbühler had met with both Adenauer and Theodor Blank, raising to them the Dönitz and Speer cases specifically. But Adenauer, who by this time had already written the high commissioners complaining about what he understood to be Spandau's inhumane conditions and about von Neurath's health, pointed to the risk of raising Spandau when a better chance existed for review of the Landsberg, Werl, and Wittlich cases. Adenauer also surely felt that any public move on behalf of Dönitz and Speer would endanger steps that might be taken for von Neurath. Kranzbühler took the point. Afterward, he noted to Wolters that "unfortunately, there is no cause for optimism yet."[70]

Speer was bitter. Though he approved of Kranzbühler's hiring after discussions with Dönitz (Speer's code for Kranzbühler in his secret correspondence was "Herr Zweig"), he was depressed by Kranzbühler's letter to Dönitz in late 1952 cautioning him that he may have to serve his entire sentence. "The idea that we could be free . . . is completely gone to the winds (*abgestrahiert*)."[71] Speer was also suspicious that Kranzbühler was

23. Prisoner Number 5 Albert Speer walks near the garden at Spandau Prison with the prison wall in the background. Published in the Munich illustrated weekly *Revue* series, "Hinter den Mauer von Spandau," by Jürgen Thorwald, 1951.

not earning his money from the *Schulgeldkonto*. In April 1953, Speer wrote Margret that though Kranzbühler had spoken to Adenauer, "I assume [he spoke] only for Dönitz. I do not believe [that] he is troubling himself over me – but he is taking the money."[72] Given Adenauer's broader concerns, Kranzbühler had done as much as he could. But he had also received his final payment from Speer's secret account.

Speer had other hopes by now, namely his eldest daughter Hilde, who turned 17 in April 1953. She was clearly Speer's favorite child – charming, intelligent, and in possession, apparently from her mother's side, of a powerful moral compass.[73] Her pointed letter to her father of that month, which questions why "educated people did not turn against [Hitler] when he began persecuting the Jews," is a justifiably famous appeal for truth from the generation born under Hitler to their parents. "What I do not understand," Hilde asked, "is why you did not break with him in 1940." Speer's equally famous reply to Hilde of May 14 should be taken seriously only to the degree that Speer was determined to maintain his story (he made a special point of showing the letter to later biographers) and the degree to which he needed his daughter to believe it for practical and emotional reasons. "There is no excuse," he said. "There are things for which one has to carry the blame." He woke up to Hitler's evil too late, but he repeated his refusal of the scorched earth orders. And, he told his teenage daughter, "I knew nothing of all the horrors" concerning the Jews. Like all children Hilde wanted to believe the best about her father.[74]

The timing of the exchange is interesting. It occurred at the same time that Kranzbühler's efforts had failed and reflects Hilde's assigned role as a back channel spokesperson for the Speer myth and for his release from Spandau. The idea began with Hilde's trip to the United States for the 1952–1953 school year as a visiting American Field Service (AFS) high school student. When in the summer of 1951 it looked as though the trip would be prevented by the State Department's denial of Hilde's visa, Speer commented to Margret that it was for the best. "This trip at her age," he said, "worried me somewhat because she would perhaps become too 'Americanized.'"[75] Once the trip had been facilitated by the intervention of McCloy (who returned to the United States from Germany in 1952), Speer's view changed. He now told Hilde that "you are a good 'ambassador' for me."[76] Speer's letters to Hilde became longer, his letters to Margret became shorter, and in December 1952 he told Margret that he was saving his paper supplies so that he could write more to Hilde.[77] His letters reveal a father's pride, but it was also clear who could help him the most.

Speer coached Hilde extensively. Worried in 1951 that Hilde would become too Americanized, he now urged her to read popular novels in order to learn American English. She was to make no political comments concerning her father's case when asked by the press, referring to her age. Yet Speer gave her (the short) list of books sympathetic to him including Gustav M. Gilbert's *Nuremberg Diary*, Trevor-Roper's *The Last Days of Hitler*, and the Nuremberg judgment itself.[78] The news in October 1952 that Hilde was invited to visit McCloy and his wife caused a "sensation" in the Spandau cell bloc. After consultations with von Neurath (as professional diplomat), Speer spent two and a half hours writing Hilde to prepare her for the visit. Robert Jackson, he told her, had told Fläschner at Nuremberg that Speer was the only defendant who earned his "complete respect." Hilde should remind McCloy of the comment.[79] Yet this was a game to be played carefully by the rules Speer had always used. Loud press statements were to be avoided. Release would be won "by quiet means."[80] Though Hilde could have no success in these years, Speer would employ her later in the same capacity.

In the subsequent years, it was Annemarie Kempf's turn. It may be, as Gitta Sereny writes, that Kempf was a likable woman who faced a host of dreadful family problems after Nuremberg. Her husband had been killed in the East; her mother had cancer; her sister had multiple sclerosis, and her brother emphysema. After Nuremberg she was the means of family support.[81] Yet it only makes the time and manner with which she represented Speer's interests more curious. The failure of the foreign ministers' conference in Berlin in early 1954 to mention anything of Spandau beyond its regulations rankled Kempf as did Bonn's apparent timidity. Hans Fläschner had met resistance when he spoke with Wilhelm Grewe in the Foreign Ministry in February to discuss the agenda. It was best, Grewe warned Fläschner, not to raise the issue of release because the Soviets viewed the prisoners as harbingers of renewed German militarism. The disappointing results of this meeting, Kempf angrily wrote Wolters, "speak for themselves."[82] She ordered Fläschner to press everyone he could find in Bonn with the arguments that Speer was not guilty on an individual basis; that a third of his sentence had already been served; that he was not a politician; and that he had six children whereas the other prisoners, even the aged and sick von Neurath, did not.[83]

Following von Neurath's release in November 1954, Kempf met with Heinz von Trützschler at the Foreign Ministry. She argued that Speer's ministry used but did not control slave labor; that Speer sabotaged Hitler's scorched earth orders; and that he had six children to care for. Von Trützschler, despite his own role in the Nazi state, was unmoved. The public embarrassment over von Neurath's release made it inadvisable to raise other cases.[84] Anyway, a public discussion over the next release from Spandau would, thanks to the veterans' lobby, focus on Raeder and Dönitz, not on Speer – these were the cases on which the Foreign Ministry focused into 1955 and the 79-year-old Raeder was the only Spandau case Adenauer considered raising in Moscow when he traveled there that year in the context of the larger POW discussion.[85]

Kempf discovered somehow to her surprise that with nearly 200 German war criminals still locked up in prisons from West Germany to Brazil, and with about ten thousand German prisoners still in the Soviet Union, no one in Bonn would prioritize Speer.[86] Wolters scotched Kempf's hope that she could move Speer to the front of the line by collecting testimonials from prominent architects and industrialists. "The whole bunch," Wolters warned, "[are] former Nazi architects."[87] Kempf's desperation even extended to the East German state-controlled labor unions, which she contacted with the argument that Speer's sabotage of scorched earth had preserved workers' jobs in the last months of the war![88]

Speer and Wolters meanwhile had concluded that the best strategy in light of von Neurath's release and the return of German POWs from the U.S.S.R. in 1955 was a petition from Margret. Despite his ostensible sympathy recounted in the published *Spandau Diaries* for the old and sick to be released first, Speer had Margret send an appeal to Adenauer in January 1954 on the eve of the foreign minister's conference before von Neurath's release. It emphasized Speer's children, who, "after eight years of hopelessness," might hope now to "soon see their father again."[89] Now, days before Raeder's release on September 26, 1955, he arranged for Margret to send her first formal petition to the three Western ambassadors (dated September 22). The petition

again pointed to the children, now aged 11 to 21, but it also emphasized Speer's Christ-like sacrifice at Nuremberg. "It is sometimes very hard for me to understand the views expressed by my husband," said Margret, "when he believed that a high ethical concept ... placed on him the obligation to assume responsibility even where there could be no question of personal responsibility. We respected his attitude, and for ten years have accepted in silence his course of action."[90] Maurice Bathurst, the British legal adviser in West Berlin, who had negotiated the improvements in the Spandau regime the previous year, wryly noted that Margret's petition was something new, written not in support of a sick old man, "but on the ground that Speer was not really guilty of the offense with which he was charged." Margret's petition was given little thought, especially in London, where it was understood that Speer could not be released before Dönitz and that Dönitz would remain in Spandau as long as possible.[91]

## "NOW THERE ARE ONLY THREE OF US"

Walhter Funk was released from Spandau in 1957 having served twelve years of his life sentence. The reasons were health related. Thanks to the onset of jaundice in 1956, Funk underwent surgery in the British Military Hospital in August amidst concerns that his would be the first Spandau funeral.[92] Even the Soviet governor Lieutenant Colonel Makaritshev raised the possibility before the surgery that Funk might be released. In March of the following year, the Soviets had become worried enough about Funk dying in prison that they had a specialist examine him even though some Soviet officials still registered their theory that Funk was faking.[93]

Funk remained in the hospital for more than three weeks after his operation and never fully recovered on his return to Spandau in late September 1956. He was an encyclopedia of illness. He staggered when he walked, needed constant medical attention, and was barely conscious of people entering his cell even when lucid. "His entire energy," said one American report, "is devoted to existing."[94] Even Speer noticed that Funk had lost his old jocularity, resembling more a sarcophagus frieze, staring blankly at the ceiling from his bunk.[95] After an Allied petition in late March 1957 Moscow agreed to Funk's release on May 11. He hobbled out of Spandau where his wife Louise met him on May 15.[96] He would die in 1960 in Düsseldorf.

"Now," Speer noted two days later, "there are only three of us."[97] Indeed, the entire war criminal question seemed to be moving toward a close. Most German POWs held in the U.S.S.R., war criminals or not, returned to the two German states by the end of 1955. By the summer of 1957, the final German war criminals had been released from the British army prison at Werl and the French prison at Wittlich, though war criminals in custody in France itself would remain a sore point into the 1960s. By the end of 1957, there were four prisoners left in the U.S. prison in Landsberg, all to be freed by May 1958.[98] There seemed no political risk for Bonn to work for the closing of Spandau.

In April 1957, West German Foreign Minister Heinrich von Brentano, having learned that there had been an Allied proposal to the Soviets for the release of Funk, made an appeal to the three Western ambassadors, David Bruce (United States), Sir Christopher Steel (United Kingdom), and Maurice Couve de Murville (France) to close Spandau. Brentano's note, dated April 23, 1957, showed that Speer's supporters had had an effect. The proposal prioritized Speer by noting the 1955 appeal from Margret and "the sad fate of Herr Speer's family." Rudolf Hess, Brentano said, should be removed to a sanitarium owing to his mental state and Baldur von Schirach should receive a pardon "in due course."[99] An Allied reply was delayed to the point where the Foreign Ministry's legal officials drafted a similar text for Adenauer to use in Washington in May 1957, and in October Brentano's subordinates urged him to approach the three Western Ambassadors again "above all for a speedy decision concerning a clemency attempt for Herr Speer . . . because this case is not comparable with the two others."[100] In November, Brentano sent another appeal to the three ambassadors calling for a general solution to Spandau and for special attention to Speer's case.[101]

The Allies had discussed a solution to Spandau since early 1956 in the form of a mixed clemency commission comparable to those reviewing the cases of the Landsberg, Werl, and Wittlich prisoners.[102] London became very interested once Dönitz was released and in fact hoped to delay Funk's release until a general plan for closing Spandau could be worked out.[103] In January 1957, a delay was fine with Secretary of State John Foster Dulles owing to the outcry in the United States that accompanied the parole of SS-Obersturmbannführer Joachim Peiper the previous month from Landsberg. Peiper, for American veterans, was the most hated of Nazi officers, having commanded the battle group in the Ardennes that in December 1944 committed the Malmédy Massacre in which more than eighty U.S. Army prisoners were murdered. Sentenced to death by a U.S. Army tribunal at Dachau in July 1946, Peiper would go free after ten years. The outrage, Dulles feared, "would be intensified with the release of the Spandau prisoners."[104] It was in fact the French government that noted that Funk's death in prison would be a greater political problem than his release.[105]

Funk's uneventful freedom triggered a new Allied strategy on Spandau, but it was at odds with Bonn's prioritization of Speer. The plan was this. Allied psychiatrists, after a full examination of Hess, were to declare him insane. With Soviet agreement, Hess would be moved to an asylum, after which, it was believed in the Allied capitals, the absurdity of maintaining two men in Spandau would become obvious even in Moscow. But when three Allied psychiatrists examined Hess in July and August 1957, none believed he was clinically insane, and none recommended his transfer to a mental hospital. "We are dealing," said the American psychiatric report on Hess, "with a paranoid-schizophrenic ... [but] he is not at the present time in such a state of insanity or mental disease as to require a mental institution."[106] The French report added that "Prisoner No. 7 is not dangerous to others [or] dangerous to himself." Politics might have seeped in. Though the French Embassy in Bonn favored the step-by-step liquidation of Spandau, French officials in West Berlin griped in the summer of 1957 that "it is a great mistake to be taking people out of Spandau. We should be putting more people in."[107] U.S. officials in West Berlin meanwhile wanted to alter the report to make Hess look as crazy as possible.[108] Whether this approach would have worked with the Soviets, who had always argued that Hess's mental state was an act, was debatable anyway. Even Speer and von Schirach understood that Hess's mental examinations were ultimately aimed at closing the prison.[109]

The British in October 1957 considered asking Moscow for a general release of the three prisoners, but the French would not support such an appeal. As Couve de Murville had noted to Foreign Minister Christian Pineau, Brentano's earlier idea of individual releases over time was "relatively discreet [and] preferable to a general liberation which would risk evoking unfavorable reactions in French opinion."[110] He repeated this concern to Steel. Thus, the prisoners were reprioritized. The Allies settled on Bonn's argument that Speer was "the most deserving case," based on his admissions at Nuremberg and that with six children there was also a humanitarian element. Von Schirach and Hess could perhaps be released a few months after Speer. The overall reasoning given to Moscow would be that the costs of maintaining "these three discredited war criminals" was out of proportion to their present importance, and the fact that "some Germans persist in regarding them as martyrs."[111]

There was actually reason to think the Soviets might agree. On gaining decisive power in the Soviet Union in 1955, Nikita Khrushchev followed a policy of peaceful coexistence with the West, including West Germany. The early climax of this policy was the September 1955 trip by Adenauer to Moscow. The meetings were not easy, but they yielded mutual recognition, formal trade contacts that were especially helpful to the Soviets, and the return home of roughly 10,000 German POWs still held in Soviet camps. There were hints that this thaw might extend to Spandau after Funk's release. In July 1957, the Soviet deputy commandant in Berlin, Ivan Kotsiuba, suggested to the U.S. Spandau governor Ralph George during a visit to the prison that a solution to the Spandau problem might take place the next year. Already by May 1957 a large percentage of Spandau's civilian staff (stokers, electricians, kitchen workers) had been laid off. In November, it was formally agreed on Kotsiuba's surprising suggestion that the number of warders also be reduced on any shift from five to three so that warders from all Four Powers would now not even work the same shifts. Whereas Spandau cost the Berlin Magistrat DM 450,000 in 1949, the cost for the West Berlin *Senat* was now about DM 260,000 ($62,000).[112] The overall costs could and did increase from year to year, however, owing to the constant need for repairs to the increasingly decaying cell bloc building and guard towers.

U.S. officials in West Berlin and Bonn were convinced that "it seems best to lay our cards quite candidly on the table and say that we think it as much in [the Soviet] interest as ours to liquidate this expensive and anachronistic commitment. We want to avoid any of the prisoners dying on our hands, and there seems no point in trying to make arrangements for their incarceration at less cost elsewhere."[113] Kotsiuba was to be approached with the idea of closure. If he showed any enthusiasm at all, Speer would be labeled as the most deserving of the three prisoners for immediate release.[114] The West Germans were informed of the approach in January 1958 and were warned that any mention of Spandau in the press would complicate matters.[115]

It would seem from the available records that the Soviets seriously considered Allied proposals. A story in *Frankfurter Allgemeine Zeitung* dated January 8, 1958, based on Soviet Embassy sources from East Berlin, reported that Moscow was tiring of the Spandau arrangement.[116] In a meeting on January 22, 1958, with the British political adviser Bernard Ledwidge in the Soviet compound in Karlshorst, Kotsiuba responded to Ledwidge's initial inquiry "with a broad smile," noting that he had not given much thought to Spandau but that preliminary talks were desirable.[117] He promised to study it seriously while warning that there must be no leaks to the press. British Foreign Office sources said later that month that "We are quite happy about the way things are going."[118]

The problem came from the East German leadership under Walter Ulbricht, who had led the SED since its foundation in 1946 and who was one of the few men on the planet who still missed Joseph Stalin. On February 5, 1958, the East German Politburo discussed Spandau – the only time in its four-decade history that it did so. SED leaders noted that they had "no objections to the dissolution of the prison," but there was also agreement that though von Schirach and Hess could go to the West, Speer must remain imprisoned in East Germany.[119]

Why the East German agreement that Spandau be closed down? The SED leadership had been wary of Khrushchev's policies toward West Germany. The legitimacy of the West German state necessarily impugned that of East Germany, but the main concern was the continued Allied presence in West Berlin, through which hundreds of thousands were leaving East Germany each year for the West. Ulbricht's preference was never to seal the sector border with a wall but rather to end the Four-Power control of Berlin so that the entire city could serve as the East German capital. Ending Four-Power control at Spandau was part of this question, and though the

East Germans loathed the prospect of the major Nazi war criminals going free, it was a small price to pay for the larger prize of a whole Berlin. Though the end of Four-Power control in Berlin would not be Khrushchev's policy until November, the feverish nature with which Ulbricht pressed the Soviets earlier in the year shows that his preferences on Berlin were now helping to drive the question of the Nuremberg punishments.[120]

Yet why must Speer remain in East German custody? Ulbricht had been concerned since 1949 with what he saw as Bonn's Nazi-inspired revanchism. In an angry letter to the Soviet Ambassador Georgy Pushkin in May 1956, Ulbricht expounded on ex-Hitler servants in senior positions in Bonn. He mentioned Hans Globke (senior Nazi Interior Ministry official and enforcer of the 1935 Nuremberg Laws, now Adenauer's state secretary); retired General Hasso von Manteuffel (who as a Bundestag deputy in 1953 demanded the release of all officers held as war criminals but who would be tried himself by West German authorities in 1959); Robert Pferdmenges (who as director of electrical concern Allgemeine Elekricitäts-Gesellschaft [AEG] had belonged to Himmler's "Circle of Friends" and was now an economic adviser to Adenauer); and Hermann Josef Abs (IG Farben official and Deutsche Bank director who in 1942 helped Aryanize foreign property and who also became a financial adviser to Adenauer). "They suffer," Ulbricht argued, "from the same sickness as Hitler and Göring."[121]

But it was West German rearmament, possibly with nuclear weapons, that worried Ulbricht the most. Adenauer, Ulbricht warned Pushkin, hoped to intimidate East Germany by obtaining nuclear weapons that Bonn would control.[122] The advent of arch-conservative Bavarian Franz Josef Strauss as West German Defense Minister in 1956 only increased Ulbricht's distemper. Strauss had been Adenauer's minister for nuclear questions in 1955 and 1956 and had argued publicly along with former Hitler General Adolf Heusinger (now head of the West German Defense Ministry's Military Office) that NATO needed an integrated forward nuclear strategy in order to deter an attack. It would become standard East German propaganda to argue that the rotund and outspoken Strauss was the "Göring of Bonn."[123]

West German nuclear strategy actually came from an argument within NATO. With the United States after 1954 committed to Dulles's "New Look," which depended primarily on nuclear deterrence rather than conventional forces; with Great Britain, a nuclear power since 1952, thinking along the same lines; and with French troops committed to Indochina and then Algeria, a West German nuclear capability seemed the only guarantee of real deterrence so that the *Bundeswehr* would be more than a shield protecting a NATO retreat to the Rhine.[124] But the origins of the argument mattered little in East Berlin, which only saw continuity with the past and revanchism. Field Marshal Erwin Rommel's wartime subordinate Lieutenant General Hans Speidel, now chief of the weapons division in the West German

Defense Ministry, argued in 1956 for the immediate first use of nuclear missiles in the event of conflict and the integration of tactical missiles in forward divisions.[125] Heusinger's comments in the spring and summer of 1956 on how a limited nuclear exchange might be "won" by using the London Blitz as an negative example of the need for combined air and land operations did not help, nor did Adenauer's remark in October 1956 to U.S. journalists that tactical nuclear missiles could be used more or less as conventional artillery and that all armies should be so outfitted.[126] Ulbricht likened Adenauer's Bundestag comments of March 23, 1958, which argued for nuclear weapons on West German soil, to Joseph Goebbels's raving *Sportpalast* speech of 1943, while noting that they came on the twenty-fifth anniversary of Hitler's Enabling Act.[127]

Given East German convictions that former Nazi generals and businessmen were driving West German rearmament policies, it is no wonder that, when asked, they refused to let Speer, Hitler's former minister of armaments, go free. When Ledwidge met a second time with Kotsiuba on February 7, 1958, at Soviet headquarters at Karlshorst, days after the aforementioned East German Politburo meeting, Kotsiuba's attitude had changed palpably. When Ledwidge answered Kotsiuba's question as to who would be released from Spandau first by noting Speer as the most deserving owing to the mitigating circumstances of the Nuremberg trial, Kotsiuba argued that mitigating circumstances had already been considered when Speer was not hanged. Ledwidge drearily reported to his superiors in classic British understatement that Kotsiuba was "not particularly forthcoming."[128] He sensed that it was the Speer idea that had left Kotsiuba cold. "Speer," Ledwidge now understood, "is the only one of the three who could still be useful to the West." He continued:

> It would not surprise us if Kotsiuba's point of view were shared at higher levels, and if Speer seemed to the Russians to be the only prisoner whose release involved any practical risk. He is the only one who has remained mentally active and abreast of events, and the only one capable of playing a significant part in industrial or public life. We cannot help thinking, therefore that any approach to the Russians that singles Speer out for more favorable treatment than his companions is apt to provoke suspicion.[129]

And the Soviets would not budge. On April 26, 1958, David Bruce approached the Soviet ambassador in East Berlin, Mikhail Pervukhin, on Speer's release. Despite a few cocktails beforehand, Bruce received the "completely negative" answer that the fate of the prisoners had been settled long ago by the International Military Tribunal, and that because the three prisoners were in good health, there was no question of releasing them. Bruce recommended that no more approaches be made to the Soviets for at least six months. "I have the impression," Bruce reported to Dulles, "that Speer is the one the Soviets are most reluctant to release since he is probably still capable of resuming an active life and could undoubtedly be of use in the Federal Republic."[130]

Ledwidge and Bruce were more right than they knew. Unbeknownst to the Allied diplomatic establishments, Speer and his supporters had again taken up the case privately, surely harming whatever slim chance he had for release. This intense private effort is unmentioned in Speer's published *Spandau Diaries*, which paints the gloomy picture of a man resigned to his sentence, who refuses even to put forward an amnesty petition, and who chafed at the public comments regarding his deserved release for the fact that "This will not make the Russians any kindlier."[131] But on Funk's release in May 1957, Speer and Wolters were sure that Spandau's days were numbered. As Wolters told Margret, "At this point it cannot last much longer for you."[132] The question was how to proceed. Typically, Speer rejected any possibility of working for the closure of Spandau as a whole. As at Nuremberg, it was every man for himself. The key was to separate his case from those of von Schirach and Hess. "My good points," Speer wrote, "are only sufficient to pull me out. As long as I am saddled with the other two, I do not foresee any great prospects."[133] Speer's advocates followed these orders oblivious to the fact that in the current political climate an effort for Speer alone was bound to increase suspicion from the Soviets and their East German allies.

The first major attempt after Funk's release was spearheaded in the summer of 1957 by Walter Rohland (who was to approach the British); Willy Schlieker (who was to approach the United States), and Ernst Wolf Mommsen (who was to approach the Soviets). All had high-level political and business contacts in the countries that they were to approach. Wolters assured Annemarie Kempf that "these men indeed have a good nose for this sort of thing and they tackle something only if there is some prospect of success."[134] Rohland's appointment books do not reveal who he met. Schlieker met with Carmel Offie, who had been a chief figure in the Office of Policy Coordination (OPC) – a covert CIA-funded agency that used former SS officers and Nazi collaborators for underground anti-Communist operations in Europe. For Schlieker's sake Offie seems to have posed as a regular State Department official. In any event, he was very sympathetic to Speer's release. Both Rohland and Schlieker returned to Düsseldorf convinced that the British and the Americans would help.[135]

Mommsen's efforts with the Soviets were the most crucial. Mommsen had numerous business contacts in Eastern Europe and had dealt with Anastas Mikoyan – Khrushchev's key ally in the Soviet Politburo – on trade issues. In November 1955 after Adenauer's return from Moscow, Mommsen had written to then-Ambassador Pushkin in East Berlin on Margret's behest, arguing that Speer's freedom would help normalize relations, adding rather amazingly that Speer's subversion of Hitler's scorched earth orders had enabled the Poles and East Germans to benefit from former German factories and mines (some of which had been appropriated from the Poles by the Nazis in the first place) in Silesia and on the Oder.[136]

In May 1957, Mommsen would try with Alexander Smirnov, the Soviet ambassador in Bonn, whom he had known from trade talks. Smirnov granted him a surprisingly long meeting on Speer's case which suggested that he had recently discussed Speer with Soviet authorities in East Berlin. Mommsen greased the wheels by presenting Smirnov with a long list of West German industrialists who would be well disposed toward the U.S.S.R. should Speer go free. He was sure that the question would be kicked up the Soviet chain of command. Afterward, Mommsen told Margret that the Soviets had "an extremely high respect for the abilities of your husband; a respect which surely shows that the Russians are most occupied with his case." This was not necessarily good. Smirnov had expressed concerns about German rearmament and various recent statements by Franz Josef Strauss. "The main worry on the Russian side," Mommsen wrote Margret, "plainly concerns your husband's age and the possibility of new activity in the armaments area." The Soviets, he continued, "are . . . worried that your husband would become newly active at least as an adviser to Strauss or even for the Americans." Mommsen thus repeated the pledge to Smirnov that Moscow's magnanimity for Speer would enhance trade relations with West Germany, and he told Margret to stand by for possible meetings with Smirnov or Pushkin, but as Wolters said, the outlook was not "absolutely rosy."[137]

This private diplomacy of Speer's old *Kindergarten* was conducted without any consultation in Bonn. Neither the West German government nor their interlocutors in the Western embassies were aware of these private efforts when the diplomats made what they thought was a well-thought-out and careful attempt through Kotsiuba in early 1958. Yet Mommsen's earlier effort with Smirnov was no secret in Moscow or in East Berlin. Already concerned that a vengeful, militarist West Germany held the whip hand in NATO, the East Germans and Soviets were surely suspicious that top West German industrialists who had once served the Nazi regime would call for Speer's release and that the Allied diplomatic establishments would follow on their heels. They would only become more convinced with the passage of years.

For the moment, Schlieker, Wolters, and Speer had decided that the failure of their private efforts by the end of 1957 was due not to Speer's actual guilt, the possible connection of Speer with West German rearmament, or even their own ham-fisted statements. They blamed everything on the timid nature of the Bonn government, which none of them consulted but which had twice in 1957 formally pressed the Western Allies to solve the Spandau problem. Schlieker vented his bile at Adenauer specifically, who, he said in mid-December, could have brought the entire problems of Landsberg and Spandau to a close "had he seriously troubled himself over it."[138] This false assessment came from Schlieker's CIA contact in Washington, Carmel Offie, who had just written Schlieker that "the German government has shown absolutely no interest whatsoever [in Speer] since the September elections."[139]

It was because Speer and his advocates believed this assessment that Wolters, on Speer's request, enlisted a new attorney, Werner Schütz in early 1958, precisely when the Allies were in contact with Kotsiuba. Wolters had retained Schütz, a gregarious old friend, in the early 1950s to help Speer and his family with a number of legal and financial issues.[140] Now Schütz would be used for his political connections. He had been the deputy chairman of the CDU in Düsseldorf during the British occupation and enjoyed good connections within Adenauer's party. From 1954 to 1956, he served as the state minister of culture in North-Rhine Westphalia – a step Wolters characterized as "a great success for us" thanks to what he saw as Schütz's "direct connection to Adenauer."[141] After stepping down as state minister, Schütz became a member of the state parliament. Now with their efforts of 1957 stalled supposedly thanks to Bonn, Wolters, Schlieker, and Mommsen met in Düsseldorf with Schütz, who confirmed that the key to Speer's freedom lay with Adenauer, who could raise the issue with the powers. The key, Schütz said, was to get to Adenauer through his "prelates" in the Foreign Ministry, especially Foreign Minister Heinrich von Brentano. The arguments for Speer's freedom would be the same as always – that he had subverted Hitler's scorched earth orders, and that owing to improved relations with Moscow now was the time to act.[142]

On Speer's absolute insistence Schütz was to receive a generous "honorarium" for his work amounting to more than DM 10,000, the highest installment of DM 3,000 to be paid once Schütz met Adenauer. Speer was certain, thanks to his years under Hitler, that financial incentives inspired greater activity. But the *Schulgeldkonto* was down to DM 600 at the end of 1957, and by now, twelve years after the Nuremberg verdicts, Wolters had difficulty trying, in Speer's words, "to pump up the sum." Of the twelve former Speer associates that Wolters wrote for contributions, only half answered immediately (one asking if the donation was tax-deductible), results described by Wolters as "pretty catastrophic."[143]

Herbert Rimpl, one of the regular contributors to the *Schulgeldkonto*, represented those wary of the new request. In the Nazi years, Rimpl was best known for his design of the massive Heinkel Aircraft Works at Oranienburg complete with living communities for Heinkel employees. In building the complex, Heinkel was the first German company to contract with the SS for slave labor.[144] Afterward, Rimpl became director of the construction department for the *Reichswerke Hermann Göring*, enthusiastically designing in the late 1930s plans for the modern *Göring Werke* city in Salzgitter, which was to house a quarter-million people and on which work continued into 1944.[145] After 1944, Rimpl served directly under Speer working on reconstruction of damaged towns. After the war, he remained in business, receiving private and state jobs ranging from new steel works to the modern *Bundeskriminalamt* (Federal Criminal Office) all in the early to mid-1950s.[146]

Rimpl thus shied from new associations with Speer. "You know yourself," he complained to Wolters,

> how hard we architects who received big contracts during the Third Reich... must still struggle against the odium of having criminally supported the Nazi regime through our activity.... I would not like to experience under any circumstances [the newspaper headline] "Speer architects attempt to bribe politicians."

Rimpl contributed DM 500 after a testy exchange with Wolters, but it was the first time that Wolters had had trouble soliciting money, raising less than half what he had hoped.[147]

Speer remained upbeat, writing about the Schütz effort extensively in his secret letters, though none of these considerations are in his published *Spandau Diaries*. "The main point," he said to his family when suggesting that Hilde be part of Schütz's efforts,

> is to win over Adele [Speer's secret code for Adenauer]. Only when he gives the nod will there be a green light for Brenner [Speer's code for Brentano] and we will then find a whole new [level of] preparedness. Until this has happened, Brenner will always be hesitant. I consider it *the absolute most important thing* that [Rudi's] friend... be brought into this to push forward with Hilde to Adele.

Speer continued that "Money is no object," while suggesting that Hilde meet with Winifred von Mackensen, von Neurath's daughter, for pointers on how to conduct herself during such a campaign. "Everything depends on this operation," he continued. "If it succeeds, then perhaps the inhibitions and the apathy as well as the contrary interests of others can be overcome."[148]

Schütz's attempts in 1958 to scale the official ladder in Bonn are hard to gauge. His contacts in Bonn were never as good as he thought they were, but beyond that, the Adenauer cabinet was not going to make Albert Speer the center of its policy. Globke made this clear in a telephone conversation with Schütz, noting that a solution wherein Speer would go to West Germany would be unacceptable if the other Spandau prisoners were to fall to East German control.[149] Globke then delayed a face-to-face meeting with Schütz, while Schütz tried to remind Globke that the last prisoners had left Landsberg and that they were "inordinately much more guilty than Albert Speer."[150] With Speer's blessing, Schütz enlisted Hilde to make the rounds amongst lower level officials in the Foreign Ministry's Legal Division and church leaders.[151]

Perhaps it all had some effect. In May 1958, Brentano met with U.S. ambassador David Bruce, who updated him on the Ledwidge-Kotsiuba talks in Berlin as well as Bruce's own failed effort with Pervukhin. Brentano wanted to press the issue of closing Spandau entirely with Moscow through Hans Kroll, the West German ambassador there. Bruce was equivocal to the idea. The French feared that direct West German success with the Soviets might trigger decreased German confidence in NATO while conjuring the poisonous spirit of the Treaty of Rapallo, which fostered Soviet-German cooperation against French strategic interests in the 1920s. But London noted that an approach by Kroll "might induce the Russians to look at the question again from the angle of their relations with the Federal Republic." By late July the Western Allies agreed with Brentano's idea that the approach be for all three prisoners because it was clear that the Soviets had no sympathy for Speer. "Herr von Brentano," the British Embassy in Bonn noted at the end of July, "was delighted and agreed in toto."[152]

In a whirlwind set of meetings in August, Schütz was finally able to sit with Globke. He had brought Hilde along for what Schütz called a sentimental effect, though by now Hilde was every bit the player in the drama of her father's release. Schütz reported to Wolters as follows:

> He [Globke] promised me to report to the Chancellor on the urgency of clemency and release and he hopes that in one of the next discussions the Chancellor will be able to point out to a new Russian interlocutor the necessity of preparing . . . serious discussions on at least "playing down" Spandau.
>
> It is encouraging that . . . Globke in taking leave spoke also with Hilde Speer, who was waiting in the anteroom, and heartily expressed his former acquaintance with Albert Speer.[153]

But Globke had said nothing about a formal démarche to be made in Moscow through Kroll. In an ironic twist, Ernst Wolf Mommsen contacted Kroll on his own in August, since he had recently met Kroll at the West German Embassy in Moscow and since Kroll had a friendly relationship with Mikoyan. The release of "my old boss," Mommsen advised Kroll, had broad international support, but it had hit snags. One, Mommsen said, was that Speer was only 53 and could resume a career in armaments. Speer, Mommsen said, would gladly pledge not to do so. The other problem was that Bonn was not moving quickly enough to free Speer, despite Globke's recent promises to Schütz and Hilde. "I believe to have understood from Mr. Smirnov," Mommsen said, "that the affair is being handled in the Soviet Union at the very top. It would likely need only a push from a man who can speak openly with Mikoyan. Without knowing one way or another if you need authorization from Bonn for this, I would like to make you aware of the problem."[154] Kroll wrote Mommsen back that once Mikoyan returned from vacation, he would indeed "happily try my best" to bring his attention to Speer's imprisonment.[155] Hilde was hopeful. By late September, she reported to her father that Kroll would soon speak to Mikoyan in Moscow on Spandau.[156] But Wolters was skeptical. "The letter from Mommsen to Kroll," he said, "is not worth much so long as Kroll does not have orders from Bonn."[157] In fact, Kroll seems to have received no orders as of September.[158]

And just as suddenly Bonn dropped the attempt along with the entire issue of Spandau in mid-October 1958. The reason was a press leak to the Springer newspaper *Die Welt*, which reported on October 13 on its front page that the Foreign Ministry was "negotiating" with the Western powers, that it would soon negotiate with Moscow over the closure of Spandau, that Pervukhin had indicated Moscow's flexibility on the issue, and that at the very least Bonn was working for the release of Speer who was, according to the report, "seriously ill."[159] The East Germans surely took notice, and the immediate public response of the Soviet Embassy in East Berlin, published in numerous Western papers, was that there was no chance of early release for any of the Spandau prisoners because there were no legal or moral grounds and because closing the prison would only encourage the many war criminals now serving the West German military, government, and business communities. There was no question either of moving the prisoners to a smaller facility (something Pervukhin had been willing to discuss with Bruce back in April). "Spandau," said the Soviet statement, "has for the entire world a symbolic significance which also speaks to future war criminals."[160]

It was a big embarrassment for Bonn. When asked in a press conference about Spandau later on October 13, an irritated Adenauer noted that though his government followed the problem "with interest" Spandau was a Four-Power responsibility and thus out of Bonn's hands. The British government, which had been very hopeful regarding a West German approach in Moscow, was disappointed by this performance, especially since the foreign secretary himself, Selwyn Lloyd, was personally interested. As the British Embassy in Bonn reported, "our plans have rather gone off the rails as a result of German ham-handedness, which . . . will cause the [Foreign Ministry] to put the whole question into cold storage for the time being." For its own part, Bonn searched for the press leak within the Foreign Ministry that had proven so embarrassing, and Brentano stated that further work on the Spandau issue was "undesirable at present."[161]

Indeed the leak had come at the worst possible time, since the East Germans, who could not have cared less about increased West German-Soviet trade, were helping to fuel more aggressive Soviet policies. A Soviet note to Bonn on September 18, 1958, had demanded Bonn's recognition of the East German state and a general German peace treaty while censuring Bonn's adherence to the NATO alliance.[162] Now in the wake of the Spandau humiliation, West German diplomats endured miserable meetings with their Soviet counterparts wherein the Soviets repeated their demands while specifically impugning Bonn's desire for nuclear armaments as well as a recent speech by Heusinger on West German army maneuvers, which harkened back to the Army's capabilities in the last war. Speer's moment, if it had existed at all, had surely passed.[163] As Hilde would report the following April after a visit to the Foreign Ministry, "I learned that last fall the endeavor . . . had already progressed quite far . . . when in October the press learned of it and . . . the action had to be broken off."[164]

It is likely that the press leak never came from Bonn at all but from one of Speer's own supporters. From Wolters to Mommsen to Hilde herself, all of them seem to have expected that Kroll was to raise the question of her father's freedom with Mikoyan and that all that was needed was an instruction from Bonn. Schlieker had long boasted about his connections with Axel Springer, the right-wing press magnate who owned *Die Welt*, the paper that carried the leak. Back in December 1957, Carmel Offie had asked Schlieker whether he could arrange a story in the West German press that might induce the West German government to speed up Speer's case. "I think," Offie suggested, "that the German press ought to carry something which can be used as an excuse by the foreign embassies in Bonn to generate a further push."[165] Schlieker immediately argued to Wolters's circle that the media could force the government into action.[166] Schlieker was thus a leading candidate for having leaked the story in *Die Welt*, triggering the sharp Soviet reaction. If Schlieker had been the guilty party, then it would surely have been ironic that one of Speer's most devoted friends was responsible for stopping a possible West German initiative in its tracks. But then again, the efforts of Speer's industrialist friends, coming as they did amidst more careful efforts by the Allied governments, only piqued Communist suspicions. "The sad fact is," Offie wrote Schlieker in mid-October, "that the Soviet government has decided definitely and flatly against closing Spandau prison."[167] In November, Schütz was still trying unsuccessfully to win an appointment with Adenauer while continuing to blow smoke about the chancellor raising Speer's case in his next meeting with Smirnov.[168] And within days the world would have far more urgent problems to consider in Berlin.

## COMEDY AMIDST CRISIS

Nikita Khrushchev's ultimatum to the three Western Allies on West Berlin of November 27, 1958, marked the decisive shift from his policy of peaceful coexistence. The Western powers, Khrushchev said, had broken all previous Four-Power agreements on German disarmament from the Potsdam conference, but they had kept the Four-Power arrangement in Berlin. West Berlin had meanwhile become a surgical tube in the heart of East Germany – a separate subversive and aggressive state within East Germany, occupied and exploited in full by foreign troops. Khrushchev called for the definitive end of Four-Power administration in Berlin and the handover of the entire Berlin administration to the East German government within six months. If the Allies remained in West Berlin past the deadline, the Soviets would conclude a peace treaty with East Germany and hand over questions of Western access to their faithful ally.[169]

The Allies would not sacrifice West Berlin, but they agreed to hold a foreign ministers' conference in Geneva in May 1959 to discuss it. The Geneva meetings lasted from May 11 to August 5 of that year, and the six-month deadline mentioned by Khrushchev the previous November was thereby suspended. The question of Spandau was tiny compared to the fate of West Berlin and Germany as a whole, to say nothing of the prospect of war and the NATO allies' possible willingness to make concessions, such as the recognition of the German Democratic Republic, to avoid conflict. Bonn and its Western Allies thus placed Spandau on ice. As Brentano put it, the fall of West Berlin would mean the loss of the city itself, the end of the freedom-route used by East German refugees, and a defeat for the entire free world.[170] Khrushchev's note to the West Germans (also on November 27) mentioned, in a frenzied attempt to prove the obsolescence of Four-Power control in Berlin, "that aside from the technical contacts concerning air connections from Berlin to the BRD [Federal Republic of Germany], the only remaining and functioning organ in which representatives of the four powers cooperate is the Allied Prison at Spandau . . . where major war criminals are held."[171] The significance of the statement was duly noted. "Khrushchev ironically pointed out," noted Heinrich Northe, head of the Foreign Ministry's Eastern Department, "that Spandau Prison represents the one remaining remnant of four-power responsibility for Germany."[172] Now was not the time to discuss its closure.

Speer's published *Spandau Diaries* also notes with a certain irony that Spandau had become "a kind of juridical Rock of Gibraltar," on which Allied access to West Berlin could be based. It also notes von Schirach's wry comment that "Maybe the citizens of Berlin will actually make us honorary citizens."[173] But the *Diaries* leave out Speer's efforts to place his case above West Berlin's fate. Speer noted to Annemarie Kempf in April 1959 that Spandau provided a legal and even necessary justification for Four-Power supervision in Berlin. Since the Four-Power governance of Berlin would surely be reworked as a result of the Soviet ultimatum, Spandau was bound to come up at Geneva. The prison, he thought, would remain as a face-saving measure to denote Allied rights in West Berlin, which Speer thought would be reduced to a token level. But if the prison had to remain, all three prisoners did not have to. One of the "guests," he said, could be freed, and Speer felt that it ought to be him. He thus urged Kempf and the others to continue to raise his case with the churches, the Red Cross, and anyone else who could press his name forward at Geneva, making the well-worn arguments concerning his limited guilt.[174] The timing seemed all the more precipitous thanks to a Soviet Embassy statement carried in *Der Spiegel* in May 1959 to the effect that Moscow was now "disinterested" in Spandau and that the prison was a matter for the Red Cross to handle.[175] The comment was surely made in the broad context of the Berlin crisis and Soviet confidence that the West would concede its position there.[176] Yet for Speer and his advocates, the latest Berlin controversy was thus the ideal time to press their case.[177]

The German Red Cross and its director, Dr. Heinrich Weitz, had been contacted by Speer's friends in Düsseldorf back in 1957.[178] Now Weitz, who had no background in diplomacy or the Berlin question, became deeply involved in the effort to free Speer. In May 1959, he wrote to the Foreign Ministry in Bonn arguing that Speer was punished too harshly, that Hess belonged in a sanitarium, and that von Schirach after fourteen years in Spandau simply deserved clemency.[179] Contacts with the Soviet Red Cross/Red Crescent further convinced Weitz that the Soviets were willing to release the three prisoners if only the Western Allies would raise the issue, although Weitz did not understand that this willingness carried the expectation of an Allied exit from West Berlin.[180] Weitz also misread London's policy thanks to a misinterpretation of a boilerplate comment by Ambassador Steel that Soviet agreement would be needed before anything could be done at Spandau. Weitz reported to the West German Foreign Ministry and to Speer's friends in November 1959 that though the French and the Americans were willing to see Spandau closed, the British were "completely negative."[181] Annemarie Kempf repeated these misperceptions to the effect that the Soviets wanted to close Spandau, and that "The main difficulty lies . . . with the English."[182]

London of course had wanted to close Spandau nearly since its inception. But the misunderstanding of the issue by Weitz and by Speer's backers prompted a new campaign by Hilde Speer, starting with a trip to London in November 1959, for her father's release. Hilde was now a 23-year-old university student, wise beyond her years. Her efforts in 1959 were hardly the way Speer described them in the published *Spandau Diaries* – as the pitiable, lonely visit of a desperate yet naïve daughter who "with all the ardor of her twenty years [sic!] writes letters and appeals . . . to free her father" while Speer sat in prison "gratefully, but indifferently," believing in light of Adolf Eichmann's pending trial in Israel that "the desire for release [is] almost absurd."[183] Hilde was now the spearhead, having withdrawn more money from the *Schulgeldkonto* for her efforts than Kranzbühler or Schütz had earned combined. Hilde also went to London with quiet support from Bonn lined up over the course of the previous year. Before leaving for London, Hilde visited the U.S. and French Embassies in Bonn once and the British Embassy twice and had met with members of the British Red Cross. She also kept the West German ambassador in London informed of her efforts.[184]

Hilde's first meeting on December 4 in London was with Geoffrey "Khaki" Roberts, one of the former members of the British prosecutorial team at

Nuremberg and now a member of Parliament. In the fall of 1958, Roberts had written a series of letters to the British press calling for the release of all three Spandau prisoners on humanitarian grounds.[185] Roberts was impressed by Hilde but worried by her impression that the British government was stopping the release of her father. He quickly secured meetings for her in the Foreign Office and lord chancellor's office. Hilde, Roberts reported, was a "charming young woman and I am anxious to do all I can for her, as you will understand."[186] The lord chancellor was Lord Kilmuir, the chief British cross-examiner at Nuremberg, David Maxwell-Fyfe. Though in New Zealand during Hilde's visit, he too believed it time to end the three remaining Nuremberg sentences on humanitarian grounds. "If David could use his powerful influence," said Roberts, "he would . . . be doing a service toward justice and mankind."[187] For the moment, Hilde received noncommittal answers and warnings that statements to the press would not help her father.[188] She knew as much. But she continued to press British officials with the statement that "now is the time to act."[189]

Back in Spandau, Speer placed his hopes entirely on Roberts, whom he now hoped to hire in the same lobbying capacity as Schütz, who had never managed to arrange the meeting with Adenauer. In February 1960, Speer wrote that since Fläschner was too weak, Roberts should be hired "if it costs 2000 pounds a month or even more."

> We must take new *energetic* new steps . . . which once and for all distinguish my case from the other two. Roberts is . . . a respectable man [and] as Hilde's visit shows, [he] has more influence, as he confesses with typical British understatement. We should like once and for all that my case . . . is not handled as a collective case but as a *single one*; exactly as if I were in [Spandau] with 500 others.[190]

"I must say," Wolters had just written Hilde about her father, "how repeatedly astonished I am at how clearly he sees all the connections even though he sits completely isolated in Spandau."[191]

It was now the eve of the much-anticipated Paris summit, scheduled for May 1960, which would include the Four Powers' heads of state and focus on the problem of Berlin. Despite the high stakes of the summit for all Germans and indeed all Europeans, Speer worried that an amicable Four-Power agreement there on the Berlin issue could delay his own freedom. In February, he thus ordered his family and friends as he had once ordered his wartime subordinates: "*No rest [but] rather activity!*"[192] And indeed this attitude was reflected by Speer's friends and family. In a letter of March 11, 1960, Hans Reuter a former Speer *Kindergartner*, who now ran the Duisburg heavy machinery firm Demag, argued to Brentano that "the Speer question [must not be] dependent on high policy" and "[should] not be coupled to the question of the release of the other two prisoners."[193] Hilde, meanwhile, spent the second half of March in Paris in meetings with French officials while trying to reach the ear of Charles de Gaulle himself. The papal nuncio in Paris, Monseigneur Benelli, promised Hilde he would raise Speer's case with the French president.[194]

In fact, the British were hoping to include the Spandau problem in the Paris summit, having believed the comments from Hilde and the German Red Cross that the Soviets would be amenable. The willingness to discuss three convicted war criminals whom the Soviets had badly wanted to hang at a meeting of immense global security significance shows that either the British were tremendously irresponsible or that London thought it could end the Spandau arrangement relatively easily. In December 1959, British representatives had hinted to Mikhail Pervukhin, the Soviet ambassador in East Berlin, that Spandau could come up in Paris and the West German Embassy in London reported to Bonn that the British government believed "that the time had come to bring a solution to the [Spandau] question in the context of a four power discussion." At one point, London considered handing Khrushchev a note on Spandau.[195] Christopher Steel was ordered to see if there were any objections from Bonn.[196] Heinrich Weitz traveled to Berlin with Bonn's blessing to meet Allied and Soviet authorities and gauge if the Soviets might be convinced to close the prison – if there were any positive answer at all, then Spandau could be raised at the summit conference.[197]

But over the next weeks and months Bonn cooled to the idea. When asked by Steel about Spandau in late December 1959, the West German Foreign Ministry liaison Herbert Northe "did not seem particularly enthusiastic." On the contrary he argued that Spandau should be *preserved* since it was "one of the few remaining quadripartite institutions." Northe then made the even stranger argument that of the three prisoners, Hess had the best claim to clemency. "This," said the British Foreign Office, "is a rather odd performance on the part of Germany."[198] In the months ahead, it became even clearer that Bonn was stalling.[199] What had happened?

Adenauer's heart was never in the Speer case. He never mentioned it in public and never wrote anyone on Speer's behalf. Even when furnished with a memorandum on Spandau before his three-day trip to London in mid-November 1959, he did not raise the issue there even though the British Foreign Office hoped to prepare the Spandau question for the Paris summit meeting.[200] By the end of the year, whatever Adenauer's personal feelings, the case had become potentially dangerous to Bonn's interests. The chief problem was West Berlin. Globke told Hilde earlier in the year that it would be irresponsible to raise her father's case with the Soviets in light of this far more urgent question.[201] This point had been made originally by the West German Foreign Ministry's experts on the Soviet Union. "The aim of Soviet policy in Berlin," they argued, "is to replace the current occupation arrangement for Berlin with one determined by treaty." Four-Power discussions over the closing of the prison, especially at the Paris summit, would only fuel Khrushchev's argument for "the need to liquidate the occupation regime" as a whole. Should Spandau close, the Soviets would gain propaganda success in that the last immediate postwar remnant of Four-Power responsibility for Berlin was finished. Raising the matter in Paris would mean "negative repercussions ... for the entire western position in the Berlin question."[202]

When the Paris summit was wrecked by the famous U-2 spy-plane incident, this argument was only strengthened. "There should be no mistake," said an internal West German October 1960 report, "that the [Spandau] affair has a humanitarian aspect.... But it is difficult [to argue against measures] that shall lead to the later release of the prisoners, who are not in Spandau without reason [should there be] a weakening of the freedom of 2 million people."[203] Adenauer surely did not change his mind when Khrushchev, as late as December 1962, harangued the chancellor about fascist provocateurs in West Germany while arguing that the only way to peace lay in the signing of a German peace treaty and the normalization of West Berlin, which meant, in Khrushchev's words, "the liquidation of the obsolete occupation regime which hides the reality of a NATO base." The flags of the NATO powers, he warned, had to be removed from West Berlin.[204]

Adenauer and his cabinet were also sensitive in 1960 to what Bonn called the "defamation campaign" by the East Bloc on the war criminal issue.[205] The flashpoint was the intense wave of antisemitic activity at the turn of the decade culminating in the vandalizing of the main synagogue in Cologne in December 1959. The comparison of the Federal Republic with Nazi Germany obliged Bonn to undertake a global campaign of damage control that included Adenauer's televised speech of January 16, 1960, in which he mentioned kindnesses given his family by Jews in the early Hitler years. The chancellor also made his first (overdue) visit to a concentration camp, laying a wreath at Bergen-Belsen in the raw January cold.[206] Adenauer was sure, and there is evidence to support him, that some of the antisemitic acts were carried out by East German agents in the hope that Bonn might be isolated from its allies.[207] Ulbricht was desperate to move the Western powers out of West Berlin before East Germany's citizens had all left the country via that portal, and his own allies were adamantly against sealing the sector border in Berlin.[208] East German speeches and publications against senior political figures in Bonn with Nazi pasts, especially Globke, as well as constant mention of the large numbers of Nazi judges on West German benches, were not without their effect.[209] By February 1960, West German embassies reported anti–West German statements in London, New York, Tel Aviv, and elsewhere.

If this were not enough, the sensational Israeli capture of Adolf Eichmann in Argentina in May 1960 and the beginning of his trial in Jerusalem in April

1961 focused the attention of the world on the most important war crimes trial since 1945. Bonn was extremely conscious that its behavior in Eichmann's shadow would reflect back on the West German state. A month after Eichmann's capture, Bonn pressed Argentina to locate and extradite the infamous SS doctor Joseph Mengele, presumably for a trial in West Germany. And after stalling throughout 1959, the Foreign Ministry in May 1960 quickly announced a restitution arrangement of DM 400 million with ninety French women who had been victims of Nazi medical experiments. More intensive restitution discussions with other states followed in the months and years ahead, even for Jews whose families were shipped to Auschwitz from the Greek island of Rhodes. With Western solidarity on West Berlin seemingly in the balance, the confrontation with the past meant something more than what Selwyn Lloyd called the "psychopathic hysteria" of the Germans confronting for the first time the shock of their own past.[210]

Brentano thus understood in January 1960 that a step on behalf of the Spandau prisoners would "in the highest likelihood be exploited by the Soviet Union," that positive work on Spandau had been "wrecked by the press campaign that began at the start of this year against the Federal Republic," and that the world saw Spandau "as a political . . . not a humanitarian question."[211] By the summer, Bonn worried that any initiative on Spandau would be greeted with the headline "Federal Government Campaigns for War Criminals"[212] The letter received by Heinrich Weitz from the Soviet Red Cross, in which the latter organization now professed surprise at the "heightened interest" for the release of war criminals who caused the suffering of millions, only confirmed that silence was the right course.[213]

The irony in 1960 and 1961 was thus that London, Washington, and even Paris pressed Bonn rather than vice versa. Officials in Paris had professed to Hilde in March 1960 that the Paris summit would be "a real chance" to raise the question of her father's release. But the West German government itself, they said, had never asked for such a step. If Adenauer would just write a few lines about Spandau to de Gaulle, the government would have cover from adverse public opinion in France.[214] London, meanwhile, had asked Bonn for a position on Spandau every week until the very eve of the Paris summit. It never came, and London decided that the heads of state should refrain at Paris from mentioning Spandau because inaction "is what the Germans seem to want."[215] Indeed, when Hilde Speer appeared at the British Embassy on April 29, 1960, to press the British to raise Spandau at the summit, officials there told her to press her own government. Hilde then revealed to the British that Globke himself had been unwilling to press her father's case. "Since Globke is presumably reflecting Dr. Adenauer's own opinion," said R. F. Stretton of the British Embassy, "it is doubtful how far this proposal will get."[216] Fläschner's connections in Bonn confirmed the same.[217] "I now know for certain," Hilde wrote at the end of the year, "that the English and the Americans want to undertake another such attempt, but they lack the necessary official suggestion from the German government."[218]

After the failed Paris summit, London continued to nudge Bonn each week and U.S. ambassador Walter Dowling told Albert van Scherpenburg, the state secretary in the West German Foreign Ministry, that Washington expected the Germans to become more involved in the Spandau problem soon. Brentano's legal department recommended in late October the safest political route. Brentano should ask the Allies to propose to the Soviets that the three inmates continue to serve their sentences in the custody of the power that arrested them. In such a scenario, Britain would be responsible for Hess and Speer, and von Schirach would fall to the United States. "To avoid political repercussions," legal director Hans Gawlick cautioned Brentano, "this step should be based only on the unreasonably high [Spandau] prison costs." Assurance would also be "expressly given that the prisoners will not be freed, but that they will serve their sentences."[219] Brentano could not accept Gawlick's idea, wherein Bonn would ask for the dissolution of Spandau, but the prisoners would remain jailed so that Bonn could avoid Communist propaganda. Brentano made it clear that he would not press for the continued imprisonment after the dissolution of Spandau but rather for clemency for the three prisoners.[220]

But the answer to the question how and when did not bode well for Speer. Responding to British pressure in January 1961 the Foreign Ministry told the Western ambassadors that Adenauer would raise the issue of clemency for Speer on humanitarian grounds when he received Ambassador Smirnov that month. Though he met Smirnov on January 12, he did not raise Spandau. Instead, contact was made on a lower level between Karl Carstens, now state secretary in the Foreign Ministry, and Andrei Timoschenko, the chargé d'affaires in the Soviet Embassy, on January 17. Timoschenko blandly said he would raise the issue with Moscow but never provided an answer to Carstens. And Carstens never asked for one. Throughout 1961, the British Embassy asked what had come of Carstens's inquiry, and they received the same answer week after week – it was in his pending tray. In answering a letter from Ernst Wolf Mommsen, in which Mommsen said that he was now prepared to support Bonn's steps for Speer, Carstens said politely that "I will happily inform you, as soon as we believe the moment has arrived for a new intervention by you or your friends." By September, it was clear to the Allies that the West Germans, having done due diligence with a request to the Soviets, had no interest in pressing the matter. Spandau would be dropped until the West Germans themselves raised it again.[221] And with the construction of the Berlin Wall in August 1961, this would not be anytime soon.

## SPEER'S DÉNOUEMENT

The construction of the Berlin Wall in August 1961 represented a defeat for the Communist policy of driving the Western powers out of Berlin. As John F. Kennedy understood, the wall sealed East German citizens into East Germany while avoiding the provocation of war through a forced end to Four-Power control. And because the Allies remained in West Berlin, military liaison missions across sector borders did as well. For various reasons, not the least of which was intelligence, the Allies expected to maintain their liaison missions in East German territory.[222] The maintenance of the Berlin Air Safety Center was also essential. Only if the Soviets were to withdraw from these Four-Power arrangements would the Allies be legally justified in violating another Four-Power arrangement by denying Soviet access to Spandau Prison.[223]

Otherwise the Soviets could not be denied access to Spandau because, as the U.S. Berlin Command put it, denial "would be interpreted as Western recognition of the Soviet withdrawal from Four Power functions in East Berlin, and would be a severe blow to the position that Berlin continues to be a place where Four Power institutions are preserved by the West, since Spandau is one of the very few visible and active Four Power institutions." The Americans had come to the West German understanding of Spandau's importance for the legal status of West Berlin. Soviet insistence on its continuation as a Four-Power institution was a *good* sign.[224]

And despite huffing and puffing, the Soviets would not give up their rights at Spandau. The armed Soviet detachment that guarded the prison continued its routine of crossing the sector boundary at the U.S. checkpoint at the start of each Soviet month despite the occasional complaints that the Soviet troops had to keep their weapons out of sight during the drive to the prison. The Soviets also continued the tradition of routine inspection of the prison during their month by a senior officer. Up until 1961, this had been done by the Soviet sector commandant Colonel Andrei Solovyov. Solovyov had been denied access to the U.S. sector in December 1961 as a response to an incident when East German border guards had stopped the passage of U.S. sector commandant Major General Albert Watson to the Soviet military headquarters at Karlshorst.[225] The Soviets abolished their sector commandant position in August 1962 in response to the East German desire to rid Berlin of the Kommandatura altogether. But on November 19, 1962, the inspection was carried out by a less conspicuous staff officer from the GSFG (Group Soviet Forces Germany), who complained that the prisoners' bath area was "too luxurious."[226] If the Western powers were to stay in West Berlin, then the Soviets would remain at Spandau. Besides, as the British put it, "it has suited the Russians to have a few Nazis still under lock and key [as] evidence that German revanchism was a menace to the rest of the world."[227]

This was not entirely so. The Soviets throughout the Cold War used Spandau so that they could claim moral high ground. But they also played the war criminal issue differently when practical. In January 1955, Field Marshal Ferdinand Schörner, whom Hitler in his Last Testament had designated army commander-in-chief, appeared in West Germany after the Soviets cut short the twenty-five-year sentence he was serving in the U.S.S.R. Schörner was best known in the West for his fanatical devotion to Hitler and for having troops under his command shot for desertion in the latter stages of the war. Thus, his release at a climactic point in the West German rearmament debate was likely designed to throw a monkey wrench into German rearmament (U.S. and West German intelligence officers agreed on this point). Schörner only helped the Soviet cause by demanding his pension on his return to the West. Even noisy veterans' organizations like Gottfried Hansen's *VdS* kept their distance while former soldiers vilified the field marshal.[228] In January 1956, Friedrich Panzinger returned to West Germany from Soviet captivity. Panzinger, a former Gestapo counterintelligence chief, was set free so that he could help in the KGB penetration of West Germany's intelligence service, the Gehlen Organization, through his old Gestapo contacts who had taken intelligence jobs there. In return, the Soviets promised to protect him from war crimes charges resulting from his command of *Einsatzgruppe A* from September 1943 to May 1944. When Panzinger was arrested by the West German authorities, he took his own life rather than trust Soviet assurances.[229]

There is some evidence that the Soviets considered something similar with Speer in 1962. On June 18, Carstens raised the issue of Speer with Ambassador Smirnov. It had now been more than a year since Bonn had mentioned Spandau to Timoschenko. Smirnov launched into a righteous dissertation on Speer's character and his crimes and said he would have to consult Moscow. But Smirnov then obliquely suggested that perhaps Speer's freedom could be bought for the release of a Soviet spy – Valentin Pripolzev. The West German authorities had arrested Pripolzev, a member of the Soviet trade office in Cologne, on August 25, 1961, as he tried (without success) to swallow incriminating evidence. The arrest of a high-level KGB operative was surely a major shock to the Soviets, who generally received advanced warning of such steps thanks to their thorough penetration of West German counterintelligence.[230] A month later, the KGB responded by arresting two Heidelberg university students, Walter Naumann and Peter Sonntag, for photographing Soviet installations. Each was sentenced to three years' imprisonment and nine years in a work camp. Yet Bonn reasoned that trading a known Soviet spy (Pripolzev was tried in February 1962 and sentenced to four years imprisonment) for Speer would only encourage the Soviets to make future arrests of West Germans, and the Americans agreed that Speer's freedom was not worth such an arrangement.[231] In fact, Bonn just preferred to trade Pripolzev for the two students rather than for Speer. As the first step in a "gentleman's arrangement" struck between Carstens and Smirnov on June 27, 1962, Bonn released Pripolzev on July 3. Carstens expected the students to return immediately, but to his great frustration they remained in Soviet prison until 1969.[232]

In May 1963, surely feeling that he had been had in the Pripolzev affair, Carstens raised the Speer case with Smirnov more energetically than Bonn had ever done. It was Bonn's first official approach to the Soviets on behalf of one of the Spandau prisoners. The exchange was acrimonious. Carstens noted that the Western Allies had long advocated clemency for Speer and pledged repeatedly that Speer would not resume his old duties. Smirnov became belligerent. "The Soviet Union," he said, "sees no reason to make it possible [for] Speer to resume his old activities under new conditions." Just as former Hitler generals had resumed their old professions, so Speer "would build missile bases in the Federal Republic which would have the same aim of extending Europe to the Urals."[233] In response to Carstens's protest that no one in Bonn contemplated an attack on the U.S.S.R., Smirnov answered that Moscow had once heard the same from Hitler.

In the meantime, 1963 was also the first year that anyone in official circles expressed concern for Baldur von Schirach, the former Hitler Youth leader who had received the same twenty-year sentence as Speer. Schirach had had few advocates since 1945. Unlike the conservative lobby in Baden-Württemberg that pressed for von Neurath, the veterans' lobby that pressed for the freedom of Raeder and Dönitz, and the former Nazi business lobby that worked behind the scenes for Speer, there was no lobby of former Hitler Youth members who saw in von Schirach a justification of their time in Nazi youth organizations. Von Schirach's estranged wife Henriette, who divorced Baldur in 1950 while he was in prison, traveled to London in March 1958 to press publicly for his release, but the trip was a press stunt arranged and financed by *The Daily Mail*, which reported Henriette's trip as front page news and probably paid her. Henriette's heart was never in the trip. She spoke to the press but did not contact any West German or British government officials. (It was partly thanks to Henriette's behavior that Hilde Speer made such a fine impression in London later the same year.)[234] Thus, von Schirach, who did little at Spandau besides complain and do crossword puzzles in his cell, could depend on no one but his children, particularly his eldest son Klaus, now an attorney, who told exaggerated stories to the German Red Cross and to the press about Spandau, which he said included forced labor.[235]

Throughout 1963, von Schirach suffered from a blood clot in his femoral artery. In December 1963, he was moved to the British Military Hospital for two weeks to treat the condition.[236] In his published *Spandau Diaries*, Speer professes concern for von Schirach (the two generally never got along in Spandau), but in fact Speer was furious especially when the Soviet prison director hinted to him that von Schirach might be released. Speer burned with indignation that von Schirach had apparently leapfrogged him by virtue of nothing more than a blood clot in a major artery. In a series of letters to Hilde that complained about von Schirach and his entire family, Speer proclaimed, "We fight only for me."[237] London thought more broadly. With the fourteen-year Adenauer era having just ended earlier in 1963, London hoped that von Schirach's case could be used to take another crack at Moscow for the humanitarian release of all three prisoners, especially since the Kremlin seemed to be looking, in the wake of the October 1962 Cuban Missile Crisis, for areas where peaceful coexistence with the West might work.[238]

It was not an auspicious time for such a gesture. The Soviet prison governance had recently disallowed extra Christmas parcels for 1963 as well as an extra half hour of visiting time for the holidays.[239] Nor was the American government overly enthused. Public appeals for von Schirach from the German Red Cross and from Klaus von Schirach, said Undersecretary of State George Ball, "have stirred considerable public opinion here against [the] release of these men. Any indication or willingness of the U.S. government to grant clemency to these prisoners would undoubtedly arouse [an] outburst of protest and criticism of [the] Department reminiscent of [the] Sepp Dietrich and [Joachim] Peiper cases." Secretary of State Dean Rusk did not want to discuss von Schirach without the other two prisoners because he wished to end what he called "this complicated, burdensome, and expensive arrangement." Von Schirach was returned to prison from the British Military Hospital on December 13, 1963, and the Soviet governor Lieutenant Colonel Lazarev commented a few days later that Spandau would not close a day before October 1, 1966.[240] The West German Foreign Ministry was not disappointed. In January 1964, Carstens spread the rumor that von Schirach had become a Communist and planned to live in East Germany and also worried aloud that because of Hess's black past, "no one in Germany would be especially keen on seeing him released."[241]

Impatient with West German stalling, the British Embassy convinced the U.S. and French representations in Bonn to proceed with a note, delivered to Moscow on April 25, 1964. The text called for the release of the three prisoners by May 25 for humanitarian reasons and because "the three criminals are no longer a possible source of danger to the nations who overthrew Nazi Germany."[242] The Soviet response to the three embassies, which the French called "extremely disagreeable," did not come until June. It catalogued a whole series of old Soviet complaints on the war criminal issue in West Germany including the recent acquittal of former SS-Sturmbannführer Erich Deppner who was on trial for the shooting of Soviet prisoners in the Netherlands "on the monstrous pretext that reprisals against prisoners of war were justified." "In such conditions, the early release of leading military criminals could only stimulate the authorities of the FRG in their unjustified intention to stop the judicial prosecution of crimes committed by the Nazis, which, it is stated, is in prospect for 1965." Moreover, "the liberation of the chief war criminals would only encourage adventuristic moves in the revanchist circles in the Federal Republic." The West Germans angrily wished to counter these charges in a formal response. The British Embassy simply noted that the "tone of the [Soviet] note seems stronger than justified."[243]

There was one last try to get Speer out of prison early, this undertaken by Speer's family and supporters in 1964 and spearheaded by Fabian von Schlabrendorff, the former resistor who had been involved in the plot to kill Hitler in July 1944 and was now a successful partner in a Wiesbaden law firm. The details are murky since Schlabrendorff's papers are not publicly available. The money to finance Schlabrendorff's efforts was raised by Ernst Wolf Mommsen, and the efforts themselves, which involved the ransoming of Speer through increased West German-Soviet trade, surely bore Mommsen's stamp.[244]

In November 1963, Hilde had written her father that Schlabrendorff was going to Washington in the expectation of getting President Kennedy's ear. Speer never mentioned it in the published *Spandau Diaries*, but he detested von Schlabrendorf, possibly for the latter's role in a *real* plot to kill Hitler, and sardonically said, in a classic case of pots calling kettles black, that von Schlabrendorff was only interested in his image. But when Speer learned that Schlabrendorff's mission was to purchase his freedom, Speer became more optimistic.[245] Kennedy did not survive the month. But Hilde's connection to John McCloy still remained. McCloy had never stopped following Speer's case, commenting to Dulles in June 1958 that Speer's continued imprisonment in light of the releases from Landsberg "galls me whenever I think about it" especially because "Speer helped us greatly in gathering material after the close of the war." Thanks largely to McCloy, Schlabrendorff was received in March 1964 by William R. Tyler, the assistant secretary of state for European affairs.[246]

It was not the White House, but as Ball and Rusk had mentioned, the U.S. government did not want to be too closely associated with efforts concerning the Spandau prisoners. Less than a year earlier on Rusk's behalf, Tyler had publicly assured the Jewish War Veterans of the USA that the State Department had taken no action on the release of the major war criminals. Schlabrendorff now revealed that he had just met with the Soviet ambassador in Washington Anatoly Dobrynin about Speer and that Dobrynin had suggested "that [Speer's] release may be possible under certain circumstances." Speer, Schlabrendorff had told Dobrynin, had protected a number of industrialists during the war who "would be ready to help if the Soviets would agree . . . by making cash available or by making certain trade arrangements." For example, said Schlabrendorff, "the Soviets might want more of some goods from Krupp than Krupp is able to deliver. It might be possible . . . for Krupp to increase the percentage of key products that Krupp can now only deliver in limited quantities." The entire idea, Schlabrendorff now told Tyler, could be floated in Moscow if the United States were to agree.[247]

The ransom idea had some traction in Washington. It was a private initiative with no official fingerprints, and it could work. Schlabrendorff wrote back to the Speer family on a high note. Speer was ebullient. "If I had not followed how the U-2 pilot Gary Powers was released," Speer wrote,

> I would have considered the report from Schlabrendorff to have been fantastic [Powers was released on February 10, 1962, in a spy exchange]. I had to rub my eyes when I read that the release was the work of an unknown U.S. attorney. Only months before Khrushchev said no. . . . And then the whole thing gets taken care of through political channels! Naturally everyone knew that the entire affair was directed from above.

Speer was sure that the ransom idea had a toehold in Moscow or Dobrynin would not have acted as he had. In any event, he said, "Bonn would never have the courage to undertake anything like this."[248] Schlabrendorff then traveled to Moscow and met with Khrushchev's son-in-law. Speer and Hilde agreed not to discuss the efforts through their secret channel for fear that it might get intercepted and wreck the delicate negotiations. Instead, Speer received on June 7 a Larousse French dictionary and a U.S. Webster's dictionary, which was a signal that "Schlabrendorff has not fashioned a bad atmosphere in Moscow."[249]

How far the attempt might have gone is hard to say. The stinging rejection from Moscow of the 1964 official appeal for all the prisoners, which had mentioned the Deppner case, was dated June 15, 1964, while Schlabrendorff's negotiations were still in progress. Khrushchev's fall from power in October surely closed the door on the effort. Speer hoped that the new Soviet leadership under the technocratic Leonid Brezhnev might understand that "my offenses were conditioned by the war." But he could not hide his "long face" over Khrushchev's fall. Perhaps, Speer said, Schlabrendorff could now try just to get him credit for pretrial confinement so that he could be out of Spandau the following May.[250]

When this did not happen, Speer turned to the dénouement of his twenty years. Having smuggled thousands of pages of rough memoir material out of Spandau, he now ruminated about the size of the contract he would sign for his memoirs, the high-paid interviews he would give to popular magazines (among which would be *Playboy* in 1971), and how all of the money would have been earned anyway had he not been in prison.[251] Wolters and Rohland in Speer's final month raised money for the depleted *Schulgeldkonto* in order to present their friend with a sizable sum as a gift on his release. The possibility of a denazification hearing loomed over the family, Wolters

24. Albert Speer poses with his *Spandau Diaries*, 1975. Photograph courtesy of Corbis.

wrote all his contacts, and the money might well be needed. Wolters and Rohland raised nearly DM 25,000. Speer avoided denazification hearings thanks to then-vice chancellor Willy Brandt, who had been sympathetic to Hilde's pleas years earlier and who viewed Speer as the only Nuremberg defendant who had admitted his guilt. Thus, on receiving the money, Speer bought a sports car.[252] Bonn had prepared for Speer's and von Schirach's freedom with a bland press statement that simply acknowledged the releases while pointing out that neither man had claim to a state pension.[253]

The rest is recounted elsewhere – the noisy release from Spandau in which von Schirach was, charitably, ignored; the sad reunion between Speer and his six children and their empty relationship with their utterly self-absorbed father; Speer's bitter break with Wolters, who by 1971 had grown weary of the discrepancy between Speer's comfortable lifestyle and the "sackcloth and ashes" story that had made it possible; and Speer's own bitter struggle with the truth, which he ultimately lost. In September 1981 at age 76, Speer told his story one final time in London for a BBC documentary. Afterward in his hotel room, he suffered a fatal stroke while in the company of a woman about half his age. The two had begun an affair in 1980, and it was she who called Margret with the news of the stroke. A German expatriate in England, the woman had first written Speer some two years earlier to praise the honesty and decency of his *Spandau Diaries*. It was, she told him, the most wonderful book she had ever read.[254]

For Speer, Spandau meant little beyond addition to the mystique and marketability of his life story. Despite the supposed twenty-year self-introspection recounted in the published *Spandau Diaries*, Speer's penance in Spandau was served with little penitence. Much of his energy and most of the *Schulgeldkonto* were spent on trying to escape punishment. To his many friends who contributed to the account while trying to free him, Spandau meant nothing either. Their repeated arguments on his behalf were aimed at their own historical vindication as much as they were aimed at Speer's. Today one can only be satisfied that they wasted so much of their time and money, in effect serving part of Speer's sentence with him. For the West German government, Speer's meaning was entirely political. Though many in Bonn viewed him as unjustifiably punished, Spandau in certain moments served their purposes as well. Bonn's decision not to press for his release from 1958 to 1961 provided some additional shelter to Berlin's Four-Power status, while sheltering Bonn, a little, from the first consciously absorbed hammer blows of the Nazi past.

But for the notion of international justice as a whole, Spandau had an ironic meaning from the mid-1950s to the mid-1960s. Though many of the worst German and Japanese war criminals were freed prematurely in those years, the Spandau prisoners served their entire sentences. As luck would have it, this was due not to the Allies, who accepted Speer's Nuremberg story, but to the Soviets and the East Germans, who never did. The Communist world shamelessly used the Nazi past and German war criminals for their own political ends. But it ultimately had the decisive voice in keeping Speer in prison. The justifiable irritation expressed at the early release of those war criminals held by one country or another in return for quick political gain is thus at odds with the fact that Speer served his entire sentence only because two blood-soaked regimes insisted that he do so, and because his sentence became conflated with the problem of Berlin, which should have borne no relationship whatever to postwar justice. And yet the fact that he served his entire sentence was in spite of it all, as Speer falsely pretended to have understood afterward, a very rare case of justice served.

CHAPTER SIX

# "I Regret Nothing": The Problem of Rudolf Hess

"I am happy to know that I have done my duty... as a loyal follower of my Führer."

Rudolf Hess, 1946

It is fitting that Rudolf Hess served his full life sentence. Aside from Hermann Göring, he was the closest associate of Hitler tried at Nuremberg, and his name was on a variety of laws synonymous with Nazi crimes. The verdict on Hess – conviction on two counts and acquittal on two counts – was generous. And of the Spandau prisoners, Hess stood alone in his refusal to distance himself from Hitler. He remained a National Socialist until the day he died.

Nor was Hess the only Nazi criminal serving a life sentence. Erich Koch, the infamous Gauleiter of East Prussia, died in a Polish prison in 1986. The Netherlands enforced several life sentences in the Siegburg military prison at Breda. Josef Kotälla, the notoriously cruel deputy Kommandant of Amersfoort transit camp, died there in 1979. SS-Hauptsturmführer Ferdinand Hugo aus der Fünten and SS-Sturmbannführer Franz Fischer, notorious for the deportation of Dutch Jews, were not released until 1989, two years after Hess's death. The Italian government meant to hold former SS-Obersturmbannführer Herbert Kappler, infamous for the Ardeatine Caves massacre of 335 Italian and Jewish civilians in 1944, for his full life sentence despite his terminal colon cancer. After his comic escape to West Germany in August 1977 (his wife snuck him from an Italian military hospital in a trunk after leaving a dummy in his bed), relations between Bonn and Rome visibly cooled. The Italians held SS-Sturmbannführer Walter Reder, who was responsible for the murder of more than 1,800 Italian civilians, in their military prison in Gaeta until 1985. Broad insistence in these states that full sentences be served was partly disingenuous. It reflected selective memory whereby Germans were the only war criminals and no local collaboration existed. As one West German observer noted, "a large part of the Dutch population considers the last convicted Germans still sitting in Breda as a living memorial to the spirit of the Dutch resistance," even though the "Dutch had very much cooperated in the persecution of Jews."[1]

But if Hess was not the only imprisoned war criminal in the 1970s and 1980s, why was his sentence so bitterly controversial? There was a lot of bad luck. The Allies and the Soviets had both hoped to move Hess to a less conspicuous facility, but no one wanted to pay the bill. Thus, Hess remained, absurdly, the sole inmate in a prison with six watchtowers and a rotating military guard disproportionate to his safekeeping. This combined with Spandau's secrecy, the fact that the Soviets held the veto, the popular idea that Hess was clinically insane, and the shrillness of Hess's advocates led to the notion that Hess was a martyr. "Hess," Winston Churchill had argued privately back in 1952, "is a dreadful case of cruelty."[2] The perception became only stronger with time.

In fact, Hess was not held in solitary confinement as was often argued. He ate a lot, read a lot, wrote a lot, watched a lot of television, and took lots of walks. He received more family visits and had closer medical attention than many elderly people who are *not* major war criminals. His decent treatment meant that he lived too long – past his ninetieth birthday – becoming a more pitiable figure as he aged. The circumstances triggered efforts to free Hess as an act of mercy even from political leaders who recognized the horrors of the movement that Hess helped lead.

Part of the problem might have been foreseen. Hess embodied rival national official and popular memories of World War II, the chasms between which were less understood because of the Cold War. He was a pillar of official Soviet memory, which emphasized the suffering of millions at the hands of fascism. In October 1946 Soviet judge Ion Nikitschenko protested Hess's partial acquittal, and Nikitschenko's dissent was Moscow's official verdict. Hess's life sentence legally allowed the Soviets to keep him in prison consistent with Soviet practice, which did not distinguish between mercy and pardon and which routinely assigned political significance to imprisonment. The U.S.S.R. was not the only state unwilling to see Hess freed. In July 1973 Israeli Foreign Minister Abba Eban publicly stated that Hess should serve his full sentence.[3] But as *The Times* noted in 1979 Hess was the U.S.S.R.'s "surrogate to Hitler . . . the living symbol of the enemy they still need and perhaps still genuinely fear."[4]

And it was the repressive Soviet system, notorious under Stalin for mass murder and under his successors for repressing dissidents, that made the sentence odious to many in the West. How could liberal democratic governments cooperate with Moscow in operating a prison for a single man? The question was raised most in Great Britain where the memory of the war and Hess's role in it was quite different from that in the U.S.S.R. The answer, provided repeatedly by the Americans, was that the security of West Berlin hinged on Four-Power agreements, all of which had to be honored, even those concerning Spandau. And the late 1970s and early 1980s saw the deepest freeze in the Cold War since the Cuban Missile Crisis. It was not the time to break Four-Power agreements. Hitler's deputy thus sat at the intersection created by the very Nazi movement he had helped lead – that crossroads where the memory of wartime suffering met Cold War security. He would never leave the Spandau regime alive.

## A TWISTED ROAD TO SPANDAU

Hess was born in Alexandria, Egypt, in 1894, but his merchant family originally hailed from Wunsiedel in Bavaria, and Hess returned to Germany in 1908. He fought in World War I, first as an infantryman on the western and Romanian fronts, then as a flyer toward the end of the war. Like many Bavarian veterans who insisted Germany had been stabbed in the back at home rather than defeated at the front, Hess drifted to the radical right in Munich. He joined the Nazi Party in July 1920 and became a devoted follower of Adolf Hitler. In the early years, he spoke with Hitler almost every day, wrote articles for the Nazi Party newspaper *Völkischer Beobachter*, helped to create the paramilitary Sturmabteilung (SA), recruited university students to Nazism, and made party contacts in conservative circles. A player in Hitler's failed Beer Hall Putsch in November 1923, Hess escaped but turned himself in to the Bavarian authorities in May 1924 to serve time with Hitler at Landsberg prison.[5]

At Landsberg, Hess became more devoted. He took much of Hitler's dictation for what would become the first volume of Hitler's book *Mein Kampf* – the signpost of the Nazi movement. Perhaps Hess even influenced Hitler with the ideas of Professor Karl Haushofer, a Munich history professor whom Hess had known since 1920 and who propagated the idea of increased "Living Space" for dynamic populations.[6] Hess wrote Haushofer from prison that Hitler had also reached thoughtful conclusions on the "Jewish question," doubtless referring to the coagulation in Hitler's mind of world Jewry as the all-pervasive alien enemy, destroying the world's Nordic peoples from within through a combination of finance capitalism (which promoted chaos in national economies and antiwar pacifism through the Jewish-controlled media); class strife within the Nordic race (through bolshevism and its spread into Europe through class-oriented political groups); and blood poisoning (through arguments for human equality, assimilation, and interbreeding). Hess wrote his fiancée Ilse that he had come to love Hitler while praising Hitler's masterpiece, the frenetic and millennial tones of which blended an all-knowing, uncompromising stance toward the removal of Jewry with the obdurate demand for war and the conquest of Living Space in the East.[7]

After leaving Landsberg in January 1925, Hess became Hitler's private secretary. He received Hitler's guests, handled Hitler's correspondence, and made innumerable routine decisions.[8] Hess sat beside Hitler at party rallies and backed him against party opponents. Hess was the first to use the expressions "Mein Führer" and "Heil Hitler," which he thought embodied "Germanic democracy" as opposed to the "western-Jewish" kind.[9] On the

25. Adolf Hitler, Albert Speer, and Rudolf Hess inspect construction at the Nuremberg Party Grounds, 1936. Photograph courtesy of the National Archives and Records Administration (Heinrich Hoffmann Collection).

night of January 30, 1933, it was Hess (along with Göring and Goebbels) who stood beside Hitler as he waved to the crowd from the window of the Reich Chancellery in Berlin. Yet as Hess wrote to Ilse, the chancellorship was but a step – "the second tough period of struggle has begun."[10]

Hess assembled new responsibilities. In April 1933 Hitler named him deputy of the Führer (*Stellvertreter des Führers*) in all party affairs; in June he began attending cabinet meetings at Hitler's side; in December he became a minister without portfolio; and in July 1934 Hitler decreed that drafts of all new laws would go through Hess for approval.[11] Hess was conscious of his place, insisting to all ministers in October 1934 that he receive drafts of legislation with time to comment lest he withhold consent. "Only by proceeding in this manner," he said, "can I do justice to the wish of the Führer."[12] Though Hess never sank into the corruption and womanizing that characterized Göring and Goebbels, he understood that certain trappings were desirable. He was assigned a portrait painter in 1937; he insisted in 1939 that he be alerted to the presence of media so as to avoid portrayal in poor light; Ilse received attendants and a private chauffeur. Public statements and official lexicons emphasized his discipleship to Hitler. "I took part in his suffering," Hess proclaimed on the radio in 1934, "and I took part in his hopes and beliefs."[13]

More than anyone besides Goebbels, Hess was responsible for the creation of the Führer myth of divine mission. There is hardly a Hess speech that does not point to it.[14] Days before the Night of the Long Knives on June 30, 1934, wherein Hitler had the disobedient leadership of the SA (and a few other political enemies) murdered, Hess foreshadowed the bloody events. "He has always been right," Hess said of Hitler, "and he will always be right . . . woe to those who break their allegiance."[15] At the subsequent Nuremberg rally of 1934, immortalized in Leni Riefenstahl's film *Triumph of the Will*, Hess proclaimed to Hitler that "You are Germany. When you act, so acts the nation. When you judge, so judges the Volk. Our thanks is the solemn vow to stand with you in good times and bad, come what may." On the edge of war over Czechoslovakia at the September 1938 rally, Hess maintained: "Führer, whatever path you take, we shall follow. . . . Our faith in this world is for you."[16] And on Christmas Eve 1940 with much of Europe at Germany's feet, Hess proclaimed "Lord God, you have given us the Führer!"[17]

Hess was deeply involved in Germany's anti-Jewish policies. At the party rally of 1935, which promulgated the infamous Nuremberg Laws, Hess emphasized their millennial significance. He signed the Law for the Protection of German Blood and Honor, which prohibited intermarriage and intimate relations between Germans and Jews. And the Reich Citizenship Law, which defined Jews racially while denying them citizenship, contained a provision for Hess as party deputy to issue necessary decrees for the law's implementation.[18] All anti-Jewish laws passed through Hess's chancellery for authorization, and his signature is on decrees from 1933 to 1939 denying Jews the right to vote, to hold office, or to work as dentists, doctors, or lawyers.[19] In May 1938, he signed the decree extending the Nuremberg Laws to Austria and then personally named the party Gauleiter there who would enforce them.[20] Hess criticized the adverse foreign reaction after the Kristallnacht pogrom over what he called a few broken windows, and the following day he and Ilse hosted Hitler for the naming of their son, Wolf Rüdiger. Afterward a stream of orders and decrees went from Hess to the party membership on everything from the plunder of Jewish property to the exclusion of Jews from German swimming facilities.[21]

Hess was no military planner, but he helped to start the war nonetheless. He signed – along with Göring, von Neurath, Frick, Schacht, and Frank – the conscription law of March 16, 1935; propagated the call for "guns before butter" in 1936; signed the Austrian annexation decree in March 1938; and helped prepare Czechoslovakia's destruction through discussions with the Sudeten German leadership.[22] Because he agreed with Hitler that the war was a defensive one against international Jewry, he did everything he could to promote it as such. As early as 1927, he wrote that

> Upon the solution of the Jewish question we shall take a great step forward on the path of understanding among peoples, and especially among related peoples. World peace is certainly an ideal worth striving for; in Hitler's opinion

> it will be realizable when one power, racially the best one, has attained complete and uncontested supremacy.... Today's League of Nations is really only a farce which functions primarily as the basis for the Jews to reach their own aims. You need only note how many Jews sit in the League.[23]

In 1937 he blamed international Jewry for the civil war in Spain, referred to Soviet Foreign Minister Maxim Litvinov as "a dirty Jew," and claimed that without Hitler and Mussolini, "Jewish Asiatic Bolshevism would dominate European culture."[24]

The outbreak of war in 1939 accelerated Hess's efforts. He had Alfred Rosenberg assemble pamphlet materials that showed Jewish responsibility, and his wartime speeches referred to the Jews' instigation of the conflict.[25] In an especially well-publicized speech of April 1940 (given on the occasion of Hitler's birthday), Hess stated that the defeat of 1918 had been the work of "Jews and their fellow travelers," and that an occupation by "niggers" followed. "How the Jewish hounds will howl when Adolf Hitler stands before them."[26] After German forces overran Poland, Hess and his staff busily helped reorder the Polish areas joined to the Reich. He signed, along with Hitler and Göring, the annexation decree of October 8, 1939; appointed some of the most ruthless Gauleiter Germany had to offer; expressly forbade the rebuilding of Warsaw or any industry in the General Government; enacted, along with Himmler, a racial registry of annexed Poland to determine which elements of that population were of Germanic descent; and worked on draconian penal laws for Poles and Jews, since in his words, "the Pole is less susceptible to the infliction of ordinary imprisonment."[27] Even though Hess was physically not in Germany during the implementation of the Final Solution, he had done more than his share to create German support or indifference to the horrors to come.

And despite the argument that Hess's influence waned during the war, Hess was as important as any other nonmilitary or nonpolice figure. Hitler placed Hess second in line for the succession (after Göring) when the war began – no small issue given Hitler's obsession with his own death. In Hitler's "victory speech" on July 19, 1940, Hess was the first nonmilitary figure named – before Himmler, Goebbels, Ley, or Ribbentrop.[28] On May 4, 1941, days before his fateful flight to England, Hess sat beside Hitler at Kroll Opera House for Hitler's speech decrying Churchill and his Jewish backers for continuing the war.[29] It may have been Hess's perceived seniority within the Nazi hierarchy that led him to believe that personal negotiations with the British would bear success.

Hess's solo flight to Britain on the night of May 10, 1941, is the great curiosity of his life.[30] Hitler had spoken in the 1920s both in *Mein Kampf* and in his unpublished "Second Book" of winning British agreement with German continental dominance. Now Hess – a very accomplished pilot – flew

26. Konstantin Von Neurath, Joachim von Ribbentrop, Rudolf Hess, and Adolf Hitler before Hitler's Reichstag speech of May 4, 1941. Hess made his famous flight to Scotland six days later. Photograph courtesy of the National Archives and Records Administration (Heinrich Hoffmann Collection).

a Messerschmitt 110 from Augsburg to Scotland, expecting to meet the Duke of Hamilton at his home near Glasgow. Hess imagined that Hamilton, now an RAF officer, was at the head of a "peace party," which might intervene with King George VI to remove Churchill and make peace with Germany.[31] Such would end a fratricidal struggle between Nordic peoples while clearing the German flank for the impending attack on the U.S.S.R. – the grand drive for *Lebensraum* in the East.

The mission was a fiasco. After parachuting to earth, Hess was "captured" by a ploughman and handed to the authorities. The Duke of Hamilton, who was stationed in Edinburgh and as surprised to hear of Hess's presence as anyone, spoke with him the next morning but knew nothing of Hess's scheme. Official interrogations followed, three in May by Ivone Kirkpatrick, who had known Hess from his prewar work as a British Embassy secretary in Berlin; one in June by Lord Chancellor John Simon; one in September by Lord Beaverbrook.[32] Hess confirmed repeatedly that Hitler had not sent him but that he was speaking on the Führer's behalf. His statements hearkened back to those in *Mein Kampf* and Hitler's Second Book regarding Berlin's need to gain London's acquiescence for German continental dominance. The peace offer was the sort of fare Hitler had long offered whereby Great Britain would accept German conquests while returning the German colonies lost in 1919. In return, Britain could keep (some of) its overseas interests. By now Hitler was just as pleased to destroy Great Britain. The night of Hess's flight was one of heavy air raids on London, and Hitler flew into a rage when learning of Hess's mission.[33]

Hess's behavior became increasingly unusual as he realized his failure and once the war in the U.S.S.R. turned against the Germans.[34] Though kept comfortable in South Wales for most of his British captivity (he spent less than a week in the Tower of London), he became convinced in June 1941 that his English captors, "under the hypnotic influence of Jews" were trying to poison him.[35] He also began a series of pathetic suicide attempts – jumping over a banister in June 1941 (he broke his leg), stabbing himself with a bread knife in February 1945 (he needed stitches), and trying to starve himself (until he got hungry). In late 1943 Hess had his first feigned amnesia episode, and on news of the German defeat at Stalingrad, he began having imaginary stomach cramps that returned periodically throughout his life. British army psychiatrists described him as a paranoid hypochondriac – others marveled at his sheer weirdness. What to do with him became a difficult question.[36]

Joseph Stalin had an answer. Hess, Stalin was convinced, was part of a scheme by the Nazi state and British intelligence in 1941 to unite Berlin and London against the U.S.S.R. The Soviets were also convinced that the British held Hess in reserve after 1941 for a possible separate peace with Germany. These beliefs stemmed partly from British disinformation aimed at Soviet intelligence to ensure Moscow's continued cooperation with London. It was perhaps too-clever-by-half. It fed pathological suspicions by Stalin of British intentions.[37] And London's handling of the Hess flight threw a long shadow. Irrespective of Moscow's long-held suspicion that the British had been in cahoots with Hess all along (voiced personally by Stalin to Churchill in October 1944 and repeated by Russian intelligence officers as late as 1991), the Soviets understood Hess's flight not as some curiosity but as the core of Hess's direct responsibility for the millions of deaths the Germans caused in the U.S.S.R. Soviet official studies of the war included this point for decades.[38] The supposed connection between British intelligence and Hess led to wild conspiracy theories in future years including one yarn whereby the British had killed the "real Hess" and then a "Hess double" on trial in 1945. British intelligence, according to this imaginative theory, murdered the Hess double in Spandau in 1987 supposedly because he was about to be released against London's wishes and would thus spill the beans of the entire affair.[39] Spandau's secrecy only provided more grist for these mills.

Stalin personally insisted from 1942 forward that Hess be tried by an international body and reminded Churchill at the July 1945 Potsdam summit that

27. Rudolf Hess feigns amnesia during his interrogation by U.S. Colonel John Amen, October 1946. Photograph courtesy of the National Archives and Records Administration.

Hess was on the Soviet list of major war criminals.[40] The British delivered Hess to Nuremberg on October 8, 1945, where U.S. interrogations tried repeatedly to crack his "amnesia," which had disappeared in June 1944 but returned in February. They confronted Hess with an irritated Göring and with Hildegard Fath, Hess's faithful former secretary [he nicknamed her Freiburg], who became hysterical at Hess's "inability" to remember her.[41] But numerous psychiatric reports concluded that Hess, though paranoid and a hypochondriac, was "not insane in the strict sense of the word." His amnesia was "a conscious exaggeration . . . to protect himself against examination" rather than "the result of some kind of mental disease."[42] U.S. prosecutor Robert Jackson added that since Hess had refused medication to recover his memory (an unusual refusal for amnesiacs), he was "in the volunteer class with his amnesia."[43]

Hess was indeed faking. On the trial's third day, Hess and Göring, seated next to each other in the dock, shared a laugh when a prosecution statement transposed the places of Hess and Göring in the succession order behind Hitler. Though Hess could not remember who Göring was earlier, he caught the mistake now.[44] Then came Hess's statement to the court of November 29:

> Henceforth my memory will again respond to the outside world. The reasons for my simulating loss of memory were of a tactical nature. . . . I emphasize that I bear full responsibility for everything that I did, signed or co-signed. My fundamental attitude [is] that the Tribunal is not competent.

His "amnesia" returned intermittently, and he behaved oddly during the trial by reading novels, feigning apathy, and not testifying in his own behalf. Yet his behavior, as he explained in a letter to Ilse, was to manifest his nonrecognition of the court.[45] After the sentences were pronounced, Hess told Speer that the amnesia was an act. "The psychiatrists all tried to rattle me," he said. "I came close to giving up when [Fath] was brought in. I had to pretend not to recognize her, and she burst into tears. It was a great effort for me to remain expressionless. No doubt she thinks I am heartless."[46] More than four decades later, as he was planning his suicide, Hess still felt remorse for this episode (though nothing else) as reflected in the suicide note to his family found in his pants pocket: "Tell Freiburg [Fath] that I was extremely sorry that I had to behave ever since the Nuremberg Trials as if I did not know her. There was nothing else I could do, since otherwise all attempts to free me would have been useless."[47] Though Hess feigned amnesia from time to time in Spandau, Speer noted that "Hess has amazingly detailed memories when he wants to. . . . I sometimes think [his] amnesia is the most convenient way to turn a deaf ear to the world."[48]

Hess's defense attorney at Nuremberg, Dr. Alfred Seidl, did not help his client. Seidl, then a 35-year-old Bavarian attorney with a thick accent and high voice also defended the German general governor in Poland Hans Frank and would defend Oswald Pohl, the chief of the SS Economic Administration Main Office, both of whom were hanged. He was a model of insouciance. His only interesting step was the attempted introduction of the then-leaked Secret Protocol to the Nazi Soviet Pact of August 1939 to show that the Soviets were complicit in the war his client had helped start.[49] The rest of his defense seemed contrived to get Hess hanged. Seidl's opening statement of July 5, 1946, argued that Hess acted justifiably given the illegality of the Versailles Treaty and "its most unbearable terms." Lord Lawrence cut Seidl off and told him to try again later.[50] Seidl did no better, stating that Hitler and Hess had worked for "the rebirth of the German people," who had been shackled with "the reparations policy of the victor states in 1919."[51] He challenged the legality of the Tribunal. He argued that Hess's role in the annexation of Austria, the Sudeten crisis of 1938, and the outbreak of war with Poland in 1939 was in keeping with Woodrow Wilson's principle of national self-determination. He insisted the war was triggered by Poland's refusal of reasonable German demands and that it would have been localized

28. Alfred Seidl, the attorney for Rudolf Hess, addresses the International Military Tribunal at Nuremberg. Photograph courtesy of the National Archives and Records Administration.

if not for French and British aggression.[52] Seidl argued for the legitimacy of Living Space, the demand for which, he said, "appeared to be all the more justified for the German people as the relation between area and the number of inhabitants is very unfavorable compared to other countries."[53] Finally, he argued that Hess's flight obviated him from guilt. It was, Seidl said, "a mission of humanity."[54]

Hess approved of this defense as reflected by his final statement of August 31, 1946. Expecting the death penalty, he impugned witnesses for their "shameless utterances about the Führer"; he spoke of strange conspiracies, glassy-eyed British guards, and hidden poisons; and he again rejected the Tribunal's authority to meddle in German affairs. Owing to the length of Hess's statement (each defendant was allowed twenty minutes), Lord Lawrence cut Hess off. Hess jumped to his final passage: "I do not defend myself against accusers to whom I deny the right to bring charges against me and my fellow countrymen.... I was permitted to work for many years of my life under the greatest son whom my people has brought forth in its thousand year history.... I regret nothing."[55] He had worked on the statement for days and was angry that Lawrence had not allowed him to read it all.

Returning to his cell, he began work on a typed version, which he intended to send to Ilse for posterity following his expected death sentence.[56]

But Hess's life was spared. Nikitschenko and Lord Lawrence voted for guilt on all four counts but Francis Biddle and Donnedieu de Vabres, ignoring Hess's actions from 1939 to 1941 and taking into account his absence from Germany after May 1941, thought Hess guilty only of conspiracy and crimes against peace. Nikitschenko voted for death, Donnedieu de Vabres for twenty years' imprisonment, and Biddle and Lawrence for life imprisonment, which carried the day. Telford Taylor later wrote that "after watching the crazy behavior of a man clearly unable to defend himself, it would take an ice-cold judge to send him to the gallows."[57] But Hess's addled behavior *was* his defense. More poignant was Taylor's observation that the trial of Hess stole from the dignity of the trial. Maybe so. But since most evidence of Hess's fakery would not emerge until after the trial, it is hard to imagine an alternative. In the meantime, Hess's escape of the rope helped no one. He was the only defendant found guilty who Nikitschenko discussed in his dissent and Soviet ire might have contributed to Moscow's insistence on the harshest of regimes for all of the Nuremberg prisoners.

## ALONE

Hess's strangest behavior in prison took place in the earlier years. "Like Hitler when things started to go badly," Speer wrote in April 1947, "[Hess] has built up an escapist world.... at last he can play the martyr and the buffoon, thus fulfilling the two sides of his personality."[58] He spent most of his time complaining. He claimed to have excruciating stomach cramps from the moment he arrived at Spandau, as well as other ailments from heart trouble to cold feet. He complained of draftiness, insufficient reading light, gnats in his cell, and disrespectful warders.[59] He never went to Saturday chapel services in the early years (this he was allowed to refuse), but from time to time he also refused work in the cell bloc or garden or sometimes even to get out of bed. To defy the warders, he once carried his blanket to the garden and lay under a tree.[60] He moaned incessantly at night from his stomach cramps, which he told Speer was his form of resistance.[61] The moaning, Speer once wrote, "sounds ghastly in the empty hall."[62] "In all my years of experience with prisoners," said career British warder Wally Chisholm, "nothing like this has ever happened."[63] In 1952 and again in 1953, the governors considered moving Hess to a more isolated part of the cell bloc for the other prisoners' mental health.[64]

Hess won attention but not sympathy. The orderlies provided extra blankets, hot water bottles, mild medications, and placebo injections of distilled water. The doctors visited him promptly whenever he wished, though medical exams revealed nothing.[65] He was interviewed at length by psychiatrists, who diagnosed paranoia but found Hess clinically sane with a detailed memory and affable personality.[66] The prison governors tried to alter Hess's behavior with mild punishments, but there was little they could take away. Hess did not even receive his first visitor (Seidl) until November 1964, and he refused all family visits until 1969 because he did not want to be seen in prison. In November 1947 the governors temporarily reduced Hess's meals to Ration Card Number 3 when he refused work. Sometimes he lost his library privileges. Sometimes his bedding was removed from his cell to make him go to the garden even if to sit and munch nuts.[67] Sometimes he was placed during work hours in a "punishment cell" which had no bed – just a chair and table with no reading materials.[68] But despite Hess's mouthy behavior toward warders, he was never manhandled or mistreated. Even when the Soviet governor unilaterally assigned Hess to the punishment cell in July 1956, the other governors abrogated the order.[69] Sometimes they quietly gave in, allowing Hess to remain in bed until 9:30 A.M. on days when he claimed pain and having his breakfast delivered to his cell.[70] Hess's fellow inmates thought the governors too mild. Raeder complained constantly about Hess's episodes and prescribed, along with Dönitz, stiff physical military-style discipline.[71] Alas, neither was in command anymore.

By 1959 the doctors and governors were concerned that Hess's occasional refusal to eat or leave his cell even for washing or fresh air could affect his health. In November, he lost twenty-two pounds in three weeks, dropping to ninety-nine pounds, which one doctor thought "dangerously low." Late that month, he made what might have been a half-hearted suicide attempt, this with broken spectacles.[72] Later the same day though, he began to eat like a horse, gaining nearly thirty-one pounds in two weeks by mid-December. He also began brisk walking the following year.[73] He read voraciously, taking extensive notes while bewailing social ills such as American consumerism.[74] The stomach cramps returned periodically, and, at the end of 1963, Speer complained that Hess "wails and moans just like years ago." But Hess announced to the governors in February 1965 that henceforth he would have no more cramps.[75] With Speer and von Schirach nearing the ends of their sentences, Hess was readying himself for release, too. In January 1966 Hess expressed no complaints to British Ambassador Frank Roberts during the latter's visit to Spandau, and in September 1966 he expressed his expectation to Ilse that he would soon walk free.[76]

The Hess family expected his freedom, too.[77] Their efforts were spearheaded even before Funk's release in 1957 by Seidl, who since Nuremberg had grown a decade older though certainly none wiser. Seidl's avalanche of petitions to the prison governors; to the West German, Allied, and Soviet governments; to the United Nations; to the European Commission on Human Rights; to the Red Cross; to assorted federal German administrative courts; and to whomever else Seidl could think of, was ham-fisted. Each petition obnoxiously began with reference to his client as "the former Reich Minister Rudolf Hess." Each finished with the conclusion that Hess had been illegally tried and imprisoned (since there was no law against aggressive war before the Nuremberg trial); that he had been acquitted on the war crimes and crimes against humanity counts (even though an acquittal from an illegal tribunal should have meant little); and that Hess was thus a victim of various human rights violations. Each petition also used the *tu quoque* argument on aggressive war by pointing to the secret protocol of the Nazi-Soviet pact and further post-1945 conflicts ranging from the Korean War to the Suez Crisis to the Vietnam War to the Soviet invasion of Afghanistan as these events occurred.

From 1945 to his death in 1993, Seidl never understood that these arguments, which debased Nuremberg while placing the Allies in the same legal boat with the Nazis, would not persuade. They did not even show understanding of key international statutes. Seidl's petition on Hess's behalf to UN Secretary-General Kurt Waldheim in 1979 (before Waldheim himself was discovered to have been a Nazi) ignored that the UN's own founding charter and subsequent resolutions had enshrined the legal principles of Nuremberg, which Seidl now expected the UN to declare illegal.[78] His lawsuit against the state government of West Berlin the same year for illegally financing Spandau missed the fact that West Berlin did not pay for Spandau by its own law but by Kommandatura order.[79]

Seidl's grandstanding for the West German press, which already exaggerated the severity of the prison, did not help either.[80] Seidl's first visit to Hess in November 1964 – five years before Hess received his wife and son – was followed by a public pronouncement that the Nuremberg sentence was legally invalid. Speer wrote that "this bars all efforts to obtain a release for Hess. The Russians in particular will regard the statement as an affront."[81] Indeed they did. Though the 1954 agreements over Spandau allowed inmates to consult with attorneys, and though Seidl visited each year from 1964 to 1969, the Soviets became increasingly angry. With Allied agreement, they banned him from Spandau in 1970, telling Hess he should hire someone else.[82] Seidl would not visit Hess again until 1979. Even then in 1979, Walter Stoessel, the U.S. ambassador to Bonn, reported that "Seidl [is] a major liability to Hess' cause . . . irritating the Soviets unnecessarily."[83]

If the prison governors could ignore Seidl, the West German government could not, at least in the mid-1960s, when Hess's release seemed possible. A leading member of the Christian Social Union (the Bavarian sister party to the ruling CDU), Seidl was a member of the Bavarian State Parliament from 1958 to 1986 and the Chairman of the CSU contingent there from 1972 to 1974. In 1974 he was state secretary of the Bavarian Ministry of Justice, and from 1977 to 1978 he was the Bavarian interior minister. How the chief advocate of Hitler's deputy could rise so high in Bavarian politics is a subject that

29. Rudolf Hess's indefatigable attorney Alfred Seidl rings the doorbell at the Spandau gatehouse to visit his client, April 1967. Photograph courtesy of the Associated Press.

could stand investigation as is the collection of state and federal decorations Seidl won while doing so.[84] Yet Seidl's connections with Bavarian political giant and CSU boss Franz Josef Strauss, who served as Adenauer's defense minister from 1956 to 1961 and Chancellor Kurt Georg Kiesinger's finance minister from 1966 to 1969, meant that the Foreign Ministry had to take Seidl seriously.[85] By the mid-1960s, Seidl was in regular contact with Hans Gawlick, the Foreign Ministry's expert on Germans imprisoned abroad. The two men had known each other for at least twenty years. At Nuremberg, Gawlick defended the *Sicherheitsdienst* (the SS intelligence arm) as an organization as well as two defendants in the subsequent U.S. case against the SS Economic Administration Main Office (where Seidl had defended Oswald Pohl) and two defendants in the U.S. case against twenty-two Einsatzgruppen officers. Gawlick kept Seidl informed of what Bonn knew concerning Allied efforts to close Spandau, provided Seidl with translation services, and provided some standard financial support for Seidl's travel.[86]

Bonn understood the hazards in Seidl's arguments. When in May 1966 Seidl drafted a blistering petition to Charles de Gaulle and the other three heads of state listing the international transgressions of their own countries while concluding that "From all of this it follows that Rudolf Hess is not guilty.... For twenty years he has been illegally deprived of his liberty," there was a lively discussion over how involved with the Hess case the

West German Foreign Ministry should be.[87] "In the present form," Gawlick commented on Seidl's petition, "it would likely . . . cause additional political problems."

> Whatever the present French government might think about the Suez campaign or the Vietnam war, [the French] will in no case be told by the Germans that it is a matter of a war of aggression which can be placed on the same level with Hitler's war of aggression in 1939.
>
> The . . . statement that Hess is without guilt and has been robbed of his freedom illegally for the past twenty years may not correspond with the interpretation of the [West German] government. In any event the French will surely see it as a slap in the face.[88]

Seidl refused to change a word, admonishing Gawlick that "he is an independent attorney and will have no directions given to him."[89] The government continued to provide some quiet support, but in 1966 when Speer and von Schirach were released, neither Chancellor Ludwig Erhard nor Foreign Minister Heinrich von Brentano would go near the Hess case.[90] Even de Gaulle, who took an interest in Hess as part of his policy in cementing ties between Paris and Bonn independent of London and Washington, found Seidl's May 1966 petition too obnoxious to answer.[91]

Efforts by the Hess family were no more helpful. First, there was Hess himself, who saw himself as a prisoner of conscience.[92] During Seidl's visit to Spandau in August 1965, Hess argued in front of the Soviet interpreter that he was in Spandau "for no juridical reasons [and] no reason at all."[93] In November 1966 he wrote to his family, through the prison censors, that "My honor is worth more to me than freedom."[94] Ilse Hess's efforts were equally dim-witted. In 1952 she had published Hess's prison letters in book form with a forward arguing that Hess had risked his life for peace and was now a political prisoner.[95] The volume included various letters in which Hess explained his contempt for the International Tribunal and his pride in fooling the British into believing he had amnesia.[96] Ilse's petition of 1958 that her husband be released as an act of humanity was surely compared with these statements.[97]

Hess's lone child Wolf Rüdiger Hess, who had not seen his father since he was 3 years old, became fully involved in his father's case when his father became Spandau's sole inmate. By 1966 Wolf Rüdiger was a 28-year-old civil engineer. He combined a son's normal concern for his father's well-being with a growing bitterness toward the victors and a conviction that his father was a noble martyr. The Hess family statement of October 1, 1966 (the date Speer and von Schirach left Spandau without Hess), embodied Wolf Rüdiger's arguments. Sent to the Four Powers, Pope Paul VI, the European Human Rights Commission, and other groups, it argued, as had Seidl, that Hess had been acquitted on Counts III and IV and that "even those who recognize" the conviction on Counts I and II knew that Hess tried to end the war with his flight to England." It finished with the call: "We appeal to all believers in humanity to oppose this martyrdom before it ends on its own."[98]

In 1967 Wolf Rüdiger founded the *Hilfsgemeinschaft Freiheit für Rudolf Hess* (HFRH – the Freedom for Rudolf Hess Aid Society), a public lobbying group that by September had collected more than seven hundred signatures for Hess's release from "absolute solitude." The names included former French Ambassador André François-Poncet, West German historian Golo Mann, British historian A. J. P. Taylor, and other leading political and literary personalities of the day who had axes to grind over Nuremberg. Statements for Hess's freedom also came from two of the Nuremberg judges, Lord Lawrence (who had voted Hess guilty on all counts) and Biddle, as well as chief British prosecutor Hartley Shawcross, who was convinced that Hess was mad.[99] In future years, the HFRH would hold press conferences and demonstrations, publish brochures, and purchase full-page advertisements in respectable newspapers like the *Frankfurter Allgemeine Zeitung*, which if nothing else angered the Soviets, especially when Hess himself saw the ads.[100] By Hess's eightieth birthday in 1974, the HFRH had collected more than 350,000 signatures.[101] The entire effort intentionally blurred the line between Hess's guilt and Hess's punishment. Wolf Rüdiger became even more shrill as time moved forward, publishing apologetic books that offended even advocates of a humanitarian release for his father.[102] In the years following Hess's death, Wolf Rüdiger became an attraction at Holocaust denier conventions.[103]

The West German government understood early that even a quiet association with Wolf Rüdiger's efforts, as opposed to those of Winifred von Mackensen years before, was not in its interests. As the first anniversary of Hess's sole incarceration approached in October 1967, Wolf Rüdiger attempted to convince Chancellor Kurt Georg Kiesinger to sign a petition for the release of his father. It was clear that Kiesinger should not sign lest he open himself and the West German government to Soviet attacks. Kiesinger had skeletons in his own closet. He was a former Nazi Party member and a midlevel propaganda official in Ribbentrop's foreign ministry.[104] And there was little popular support for Hess in the mid-1960s anyway. Though West German chancellors would become involved in Hess's case after Hess turned 80, it was purely on the basis of humanitarianism, without coordination with the Hess family, and generally with no suggestion that Hess was anything but guilty.

In the mid-1960s Hess's advocates only made more remote the Allied hope to close the prison. With the attempts of the 1950s to close Spandau having failed, the Allies returned to the problem with the impending release of Speer and von Schirach with a démarche to Piotr Abrassimov, the Soviet ambassador to East Germany, on April 13, 1966.[105] There was some reason for optimism. The Soviets had agreed to the release of von Neurath, Raeder, and Funk based on health and Hess was now 72. Soviet prison governor Lieutenant Colonel Lazarev had also privately commented to French governor Max Farion in February 1965 that in view of the large Four-Power commitment at Spandau, Hess could perhaps be moved to a German prison (he did not say whether it would be in East or West Germany) or to a neutral country such as Switzerland. Spandau Prison in Lazarev's view, would likely be liquidated with the releases of Speer and von Schirach.[106] Understanding that Hess could not be sent to East Germany, that no West German government would accept the problem of holding him, and that no neutral country would accept the burden, the Allies proposed in early 1966 that Hess be released on October 1 or shortly thereafter.[107] They based the proposal on Hess's age and the large commitment in personnel that the maintenance of a single prisoner would now demand.

Abrassimov's response to the Allied démarche, delivered in June 1966, iced these hopes. It also became the template for Soviet responses for the next two decades. "The position of the Soviet side on the given question," Abrassimov said,

> is unalterably laid down by the obligations assumed by the Soviet Union, as well as the United States, Great Britain, and France on the prosecution and punishment of Nazi criminals who committed the most serious crimes against peace and humanity. As is known, Rudolf Hess, formerly the closest confidante of Hitler and occupying a special position in the leadership of the Nazi party and state, was condemned by the International Tribunal in Nuremberg to life imprisonment. Any kind of leniency toward such criminals cannot be justified to peoples and history. Therefore the Soviet side does not consider it possible to agree with the proposal for the release of Hess ahead of time. Such a step would, moreover, encourage those forces in West Germany which again threaten the security of the peace-loving peoples of Europe.

Abrassimov's statement (and those subsequent) thus incorporated Nikitschenko's 1946 dissent. Hess, he inferred, was guilty of crimes against humanity regardless of the actual Nuremberg verdict.[108] Subsequent appeals in February 1968 and May 1969 and February 1970 (when Hess was hospitalized) brought similar Soviet refusals, which also pointed to recent successes of the neo-Nazi National Democratic Party (NPD) in West Germany, which the Allied Kommandatura had considered banning in West Berlin.[109]

The Soviet refusals especially rankled the British government, which in the years ahead would make more official appeals for Hess's release than any other government.[110] Questions in the House of Commons were repeatedly raised by conservative MP John Biggs Davidson to the effect that the expense of Spandau was out of all proportion to the task and that Hess should be released.[111] The British press took an interest in the case too, with the sensationalist *Daily Express* bringing Wolf Rüdiger to Britain in June

1967 for a "pilgrimage" to the spot in Scotland where his father had landed twenty-six years earlier. Wolf Rüdiger received relics (a cable said to be Hess's rip chord), made public statements ("I am proud of my father"), and met with sympathetic members of Parliament, though Foreign Office officials (for the time being) avoided him.[112] Regardless, the Foreign Office was irked that Great Britain was serving Soviet aims in the British sector of Berlin. "We are," complained Permanent Undersecretary Sir Paul H. Gore-Booth to Foreign Secretary Michael Stewart, "going through the farcical gavotte of discussing with three other major powers how to guard this feeble-minded, elderly Nazi, who can do no possible harm. At the end of it all, if Hess survives for a few more years and the Russians cannot be made to relent, we shall have spent several tens of thousands of pounds to earn the undesirable entry in the international dictionary: "'Hess, R: died in captivity.'"[113]

But what to do? The Foreign Office in late 1966 considered a unilateral pullout from Spandau on the hope that the Four-Power arrangement there might collapse without British participation. The British command in West Berlin quickly pointed out the risk. The Soviets would try to keep Hess at Spandau with or without Western participation, which would bring West German pressure on the British to cut off the prison's water and electricity. If the Soviets tried to move Hess to East Berlin, there would be a military standoff that could escalate into crisis. Frank Roberts, Britain's ambassador to Bonn at that time, explained:

> there *is* rather strong Russian feeling on this question and it runs completely counter to our own feelings.... The Russians feel very strongly indeed that the Nazi leaders who were responsible for destruction of their country should fully purge their offenses. We may make some allowances for Hess because he flew to England, but in Russian eyes this only aggravates his crime because his object in flying to England was to unite the "superior" Western nations against the Communist menace.

The Russians, Roberts warned, had always been suspicious of London's intentions regarding Hess. "This," he said, "like chess, is the kind of game they can play much better than we can." Besides, Roberts said, there was no groundswell of support for Hess in West Germany anyway – he would never become the martyr Wolf Rüdiger predicted.[114]

There was a partial way out. The Soviets too were concerned with the illogic of holding one man in a prison meant for hundreds. Abrassimov had suggested in April 1966 to the French Ambassador François Seydoux that Hess might go to another facility in West Berlin. The Allied Kommandatura began considering alternative sites despite the conundrum that a more proportional arrangement might impede Hess's future release. Spandau's absurdity, in other words, had been the best argument for ending the entire arrangement. Yet Spandau cost the Berlin *Senat* more than DM 427,000 in 1965. The six watchtowers there meant that the exterior guard could not be reduced and it was clear that "Western public opinion questions the sense of keeping [Hess] on the present scale of Spandau." The best alternative lay in using the old, dilapidated infirmary building within the prison walls toward the southeast corner of the complex. The Allies would have to renovate it completely and wall it off so that the Berlin *Senat* might use the main building – as it wished – as a women's prison to offset the shortage of prison space in West Berlin. Hess's smaller structure would demand but two watchtowers so a guard detachment could consist of twelve men rather than twenty-five. Fewer warders and domestic staff would be needed as well.[115]

The Soviets were agreeable because Hess would remain in Spandau proper. As Soviet Embassy officials told French representatives in Berlin, "Spandau was to remain the symbol of Germany's defeat and the judgment of the war criminals."[116] By British estimates, the renovation would cost the *Senat* up to DM 1 million while saving DM 180,000 per year and providing needed prison space.[117] Yet the issue was political too. As governing mayor of West Berlin in 1966, Willy Brandt understood that the memories associated with Spandau made its use for any other purpose politically difficult.[118] And though the *Senat* continued to favor the renovation (making a favorable public statement in June 1968 and continuing private discussions with the Allied authorities well into 1969), discussions in Bonn produced the following consensus.

> The German interest in principle is that the entire "Spandau" business be concluded through closing the prison and the release of all inmates including Hess.
>
> If now through the transfer of Hess a "humanizing" of the imprisonment occurs, and we cooperate in this transfer coming about, [then] the chance that the entire complex will be made to disappear is diminished considerably, (and with our cooperation).[119]

On the orders of Karl Carstens, since 1960 the state secretary in the Foreign Ministry, Bonn stalled on this question. Bonn gave final refusal in 1968 on the reasoning that movement to the new building would not improve Hess's conditions of confinement. If the Allies wanted to pay for the renovations or force payment from the Berlin occupation budget they could do so.[120] The Allies hoped that Bonn might change its mind. Discussions with the Soviets and with the *Senat* resumed in 1969, especially after June when Abrassimov rejected another appeal for Hess's release. Yet by now the Soviets had had second thoughts about the infirmary scheme since Hess's new exercise yard would be visible from the windows of surrounding buildings, and they refused access to *Senat* representatives who wished to inspect the site.[121] The Allies concluded that they would be stuck with Spandau for the foreseeable future. Hess would thus not be released thanks to the Soviets; he would not be moved thanks to the West Germans; and so in Spandau would he remain.

## THE DANCE OF DEATH

In late 1969 Rudolf Hess became seriously ill. From November 24, 1969, to March 13, 1970, he was in the British Military Hospital to treat blockage owing to an ulcer that, upon spontaneous healing, had narrowed his large intestine, thus causing peritonitis, of which Hess nearly died. Conspiracy theorists holding to the bedtime story that the British had Hess (or his double) murdered should check the Spandau Prison records for the years of Hess's dotage, substantial portions of which concern arguments with Hess that medical tests and hospitalization were for his own good. With even the Soviet medical officer agreeing that his condition was urgent, Hess refused for more than a week to be moved. The Allies were ready to transfer him to the hospital anyway and considered the legal implications of surgery against the patient's wishes to avoid a preventable death and a political storm. The Soviets, ever suspicious of Hess's ailments, were willing to prolong Hess's life through unwanted surgery.[122] After Hess was treated at the British Military Hospital and his condition improved, he expressed tremendous confidence in the British specialists, even refusing his family's insistence that a German specialist be flown in.[123]

By 1969 the new spirit of détente began to characterize Soviet-West German politics. Willy Brandt, who became West Germany's first Social Democratic chancellor in October 1969, pushed agreements regularizing Bonn's relationship with the U.S.S.R. and the East Bloc states, including East Germany, while recognizing current borders. Falling to his knees at the Warsaw ghetto memorial in December 1970, Brandt, though an anti-Nazi resistor, also accepted German responsibility for the German past. The Soviets, who had always feared West German territorial revanchism, took up Brandt's signals under Leonid Brezhnev, general secretary since 1964, and his utterly humorless Foreign Minister Andrei Gromyko, a veteran diplomat who as Molotov's protégé had served Stalin at the Teheran and Yalta conferences.

New arrangements concerning West Berlin were also in the offing. The bitter quarrel over West Berlin's existence by no means vanished with the construction of the Berlin Wall, and a minicrisis in 1968 and 1969 regarding Bundestag sittings and CDU/CSU meetings in West Berlin, East German harassment of civilian access, and Warsaw Pact maneuvers in the area prompted new talks culminating in the landmark Quadripartite Agreement on Berlin, signed in September 1971, in which the Four Powers reaffirmed and strengthened quadripartite rule for the city, defined the city's legal status, and for the first time guaranteed West German civilian access to West Berlin as well as secure road and rail routes.[124]

But the Soviet understanding of the Nuremberg legacy remained firm, despite the British public's increased interest in Hess triggered by his illness and despite West German official hopes that, combined with Brandt's *Ostpolitik*, Hess's illness might trigger his release.[125] When Hess was moved to the British Military Hospital in late November 1969 the Soviets maintained their exterior guard in the six prison watchtowers (with their full compliment of Kalashnikov machine guns, multiple ammunition clips, and a trained sharpshooter) despite what U.S. minister in Berlin Brewster Morris called "the silliness" of "guards in towers surrounding a prison known to be empty."[126] When U.S. troops took control at the beginning of December, U.S. governor Lieutenant Colonel Eugene Bird suggested the towers remain unmanned, especially since the German and British news media had noted the absurdity.[127] U.S. sentries, some of whom believed the guard towers were haunted at night, were no doubt pleased. Yet Soviet governor Lieutenant Colonel P. P. Tarutta, acting on orders from the Group Soviet Forces Germany at Karlshorst, insisted that U.S. troops man the towers. "The Soviet side," he insisted at an angry meetings of December 2 and 3,

> cannot tolerate any weakening regarding the guard of Spandau Allied Prison, as well as any changes of the quadripartite agreements to assure the security of Spandau Allied Prison and will protest against all attempts to violate the quadripartite decision....
>
> From my side I have to note that for us it is absolutely incomprehensible to understand the reasons which oblige the American side to seek...in a persistent way...a weakening of the Guard...and also to violate quadripartite agreements.[128]

Subsequent Allied arguments had no effect.[129] As the British command in West Berlin noted, "the Russians may very well see Allied efforts...as the start of a manoeuvre to achieve Hess's release and the closing of the prison," especially since the Allies had made another request for Hess's release the previous May.[130] U.S., then British, then French troops guarded a prison with no prisoner until Hess's return in the Soviet month of March 1970. It was the only deployment of Allied troops during the Cold War on which the Soviets insisted, and in a city where the Soviets preferred the Allies not to be.

The Allies went along because of a more urgent issue – the disposition of Hess's remains should he die. Even Hess thought in December 1969 that the end was near. Imagining that his heart had stopped beating at one point, he asked to see his wife and son for the first time in twenty-three years.[131] He survived, and the visits from Ilse and especially Wolf Rüdiger became regular events. But the drama reminded the Allies that the 1954 agreement on prisoners' remains called for burial at Spandau. Hess would be the only man buried there. In a ghoulish twist, his coffin (built originally for Funk) was already prepared. Worse, the Soviets might insist on guarding the tomb. "Burial at Spandau," Morris warned the State Department, "gives [the] Soviets [the] possibility of insisting upon four-power custody of [the] grave site and, thereby [to] continue this element of Soviet presence in

West Berlin." Morris suggested a return to the 1947 cremation arrangement whereby Hess's ashes would be scattered. President Richard Nixon's secretary of state William Rogers was even willing to have the Soviets bury Hess in East Berlin.[132]

The Soviets were worried about the burial arrangements too, understanding that Four-Power governance at Spandau expired on Hess's death and that his gravesite could become a shrine should the prison be turned over to the West Berlin *Senat*. After the changing of the guard on December 1, 1969, the Soviets suggested that Hess be cremated with the urn given to the family.[133] Discussions between the governors began on December 4 when Bird, joined by British governor Ralph F. Banfield and French governor Max Farion, proposed to Tarutta that Hess's family should receive Hess's body for burial outside of Berlin. Tarutta held firm. The body had to be cremated first.[134] Washington was willing to accept the cremation offer because it brought a sure end to the Soviet presence at Spandau. Paris and London loathed it and held out as long as they could, but the Soviet response was unyielding.[135] "[We] have no right to allow the relatives to decide as to what should be done with the prisoner's remains," said Tarutta. "Cremation of the prisoner's remains is most closely in [the] spirit [of] the sentence of the Nuremberg Tribunal." The conveyance of the urn was, Tarutta said, "a big concession," and he insisted that there be immediate agreement.[136]

Talks were deadlocked for three months during which time London complicated matters by delaying Hess's return to prison. British Foreign Secretary Michael Stewart tried to appease Hess's vocal advocates in London (175 MPs had signed a petition for Hess's release by February 6 and 190 by March 14) by keeping Hess hospitalized as long as possible. British doctors emphasized Hess's old ailments and made up new ones, such as stress, which even struck the Americans as a "particularly suspect... entering wedge for... indefinite hospitalization." Stewart even considered a proposal to allow a new Soviet trade mission in an old Soviet-owned property on the Lietzenburgerstrasse in the British sector as a quid pro quo for Hess's release. The Soviets, who had thought Hess fit to return to Spandau in late January, were livid. Washington and Paris refused to anger the Soviets over Hess, especially with more general negotiations over West Berlin's status in progress, and the United States would not consider a new Soviet trade mission in West Berlin, which would surely be used for espionage. They urged London to accept the Soviet offer on cremation and to agree to return Hess to prison.[137]

The British understood that the stability of Four-Power relations in Berlin came before the domestic pressure to free Hess. As Deputy Foreign Minister George Thomson who was well versed with the Hess case noted, "We shall be in total breach of Four Power agreements if we take unilateral action to release Hess or to keep him in the British Military Hospital without the agreement of at least the three Allied doctors."[138] London thus agreed to return

Hess to prison but only if Hess, now 76 years old, received a host of new permanent conditions. He would be allowed to sleep until 7 A.M. rather than 6. Lights out would be anytime he wished; he would receive a roomier double-sized cell (in the cell bloc's old infirmary) with the door open; he would have a hospital bed; "work" would be nothing more strenuous than making his bed and caring for plants; he would have two one-hour exercise periods per day; and his diet would be prescribed by the prison medical board. Determined to secure the cremation agreement, the Soviets agreed to the new rules after trying to make them temporary. The governors signed the new cremation agreement on March 12, and Hess returned to Spandau the following day.[139] Thanks to the delay, the Soviets never allowed hospital tests again without arguing first that the necessary medical equipment, such as X-ray machines, could be moved to Spandau.[140]

In the next weeks, months, and years, Hess received additional amenities. These included the keeping of snacks and coffee in his cell; a knife and fork for his meals; a new wall radiator that he could adjust; new windows that he could open and close; free movement in the cell bloc; freedom to arise from bed and go to bed when he wished; and choice of his own menus.[141] "He has an abundance of food," reported the French governor Michel Planet in 1977, "even in the months of Soviet presidency."[142] As of 1972, Hess was allowed to speak with the prison pastor in the privacy of his cell or in the garden for an hour a week. In 1975, the Soviets agreed that Hess could take his exercise in a shady courtyard after dinner on hot days and that he could sleep in a cooler cell during the summertime. As of June 1977 he could take up to four hours exercise daily and watch color TV in the afternoons and evenings in a special double-sized viewing cell.[143] As Planet reported in 1977, "This is a man of eighty-three years, in good physical condition and intellectually in possession of all of his faculties."[144]

Yet as Abrassimov had noted in 1970, the main Soviet consideration concerning amenities was Hess's health. Moscow held the line on non-health-related amenities. Hess would not receive more than thirty minutes visiting per month with but one visitor at a time. And though he received 230 visits before his suicide from his wife, son, daughter-in-law, sister, and nephews, he would never be allowed to visit with his grandchildren. Repeated requests for more liberal visitation rules met absolute Soviet refusals. "Prisoner Number 7," said Soviet Major W. G. Dejev in December 1974, "is a war criminal."[145] The Soviets were also worried that Hess would rehabilitate himself as had Raeder, Dönitz, and Speer. Arguing that Hess was writing on the Nazi period, they refused to allow him extra notebooks and insisted that the five notebooks compiled since 1967 be destroyed.[146] The Soviets also became incensed when British or American officials, including visiting Berlin commandants, conversed with Hess in English.[147] Moscow had good reasons for this concern. During his tenure as U.S. prison governor,

Lieutenant Colonel Eugene Bird prepared a book on Hess by taping long interviews with Hitler's one-time deputy in the cell bloc and garden; by taking "dignified" photographs of Hess; and by stealing 5,000 unclassified and 440 classified documents from the prison.[148] Bird was quietly placed on permanent leave in March 1972 when his superiors learned of his numerous violations of Four-Power prison agreements. He nonetheless published his book in 1974 calling for Hess's release, and then launched a dubious second career as a Hess advocate.[149]

But the main issue in the 1970s and early 1980s concerned the cremation agreement. Would it be honored? Paris never intended to do so. French diplomats argued before the ink dried that the agreement was illegal. U.S. officials groused that "the source of the French flip flop is at the very top of the government," and British officials theorized that French prison governor Max Farion had mistakenly signed the agreement without Paris's approval. Indeed Foreign Minister Maurice Schumann's personal objections to cremation without familial consent were unyielding.[150] Paris refused to budge for more than a decade, creating potential crisis for the moment Hess died. "The French," reported the U.S. embassy in Paris,

> realize that a lack of precise planning for the scenario following Hess's death risks a confused situation.... They are counting on being able to place the blame for this confusion on the Soviets' attitude, which they assume will arouse strong feelings of moral indignation in Berlin and Germany. They are hoping the situation at the time will force the Soviets to drop their insistence on cremation.

This hope was mighty optimistic.[151] Yet as late as February 1979, the French, on President Valerie Giscard d'Estaing's insistence, were trying to get Hess moved permanently to a hospital. This rare French initiative was another attempt to avoid the cremation agreement, but as the Americans reported, "The phantom French proposal [is] a step below stillborn."[152]

London was never thrilled with the March 1970 agreement but accepted it as preferable to a Hess grave in West Berlin guarded by the Four Powers.[153] A press leak revealing the procedure in 1976 made the British more reluctant. Wolf Rüdiger publicly demanded that his father's remains be given to the family and asked the Western ambassadors in June that they prevent Moscow from "taking revenge against the body of my father." The West German Foreign Ministry, which had kept its distance from the Hess family, now suggested that the embassies receive Wolf Rüdiger, predicting a public outcry if they did not. "Cremation," said Bonn's representatives, "would be rather hard to understand now over 30 years after the end of the war."[154] But London could not change Moscow's mind. British Ambassador Sir Oliver Wright raised the issue with Abrassimov in East Berlin in January 1977. Abrassimov dismissed the request as "on par with [London's] wish to free the prisoner."[155] The Allies, shrugged West Berlin's Governing Mayor

Dietrich Stobbe in February and March 1979, would have to "face their responsibilities" on the matter, adding that no German crematorium would incinerate the body without family consent, even with an order from the Kommandatura.[156] Stobbe's successor, Hans-Jochen Vogel, was more direct in April 1981. Whatever Hess's crimes might have been, said Vogel, it was contrary to Western principles to hold a man his age in prison and most inhumane not to take the family's wishes into account. The present plan, he predicted, could speedily devolve into a macabre "discussion around a cadaver."[157]

London's policy had by then descended into confusion. In January 1979 British officials suggested moving Hess's body to Gatow Air Base, where a U.S. military helicopter (they hoped) might fly the coffin to Bavaria. Maybe the Soviet response would be limited to words.[158] The following month, British officials studied the possibility of sending to West Berlin a special unit from their chemical and biological weapons research facility in Porton Down, the function of which was to incinerate infected animals.[159] By the end of the year, Julian Bullard, the deputy undersecretary in the Foreign Office, hoped the Americans might carry out the cremation in their sector, thus offering the government political cover against what he called the "Hess lobby" in Parliament.[160]

This lobby was not inconsiderable nor was it led by nobodies. It had grown throughout the 1970s. For the first half of the decade, it was led by Airey Neave, the British army officer (and former German prisoner) who had personally served the defendants with their indictments back at Nuremberg and who as head of the "Neave Commission" had assembled massive amounts of evidence on the Nazi organizations on trial there.[161] As the MP from Abingdon in Northern Ireland, Neave remained a defender of the Nuremberg trial and its verdicts. "I have never defended Hess as a Nazi," he said. But Neave led the effort in London for Hess's release on humanitarian grounds when Hess entered the British Military Hospital in 1969 and would continue to see Hess's punishment as "a blot on the record of the trial and a lasting disgrace to international justice."[162] Despite the fact that the HFRH could muster no more than twenty of their number for a demonstration in front of Spandau in April 1969, Neave arranged for Wolf Rüdiger to visit the Foreign Office in January and February 1970 while Rudolf Hess was hospitalized and then quietly advised Wolf Rüdiger to take his case to the State Department in Washington (the *Daily Express* paid for the trip).[163] Should Hess return to Spandau, Neave warned the Foreign Office in January 1970, the House of Commons would erupt in unanimous condemnation. And Neave did his best to cause such an eruption. "For how long will this pointless and cruel detention be allowed to continue?" Neave asked in the House of Commons in April 1971. "A man who is quite unfit for solitary confinement

30. Wolf Rüdiger Hess with Member of Parliament Airey Neave in London, January 1970. Photograph courtesy of Corbis.

has been in detention for more than 30 years. Will [the government] not tell the Russians that we do not intend to behave like Nazis and intend to take action ourselves to release Rudolf Hess?"[164]

Neave's pressure triggered official British solo attempts to free Hess with Soviet Ambassador Mikhail Smirnowski in May 1971 by Foreign Secretary Alec Douglas-Home and in June by his deputy foreign secretary Geoffrey Rippon, despite the fact that negotiations over the Quadripartite Agreement on Berlin were at a very critical point and that Moscow would surely not free Hess on the thirtieth anniversary of his flight and the German attack on the U.S.S.R. Bonn, Paris, Washington, and even some in London could not believe the bad timing.[165] Nonetheless, Rippon suggested to Smirnovski on June 17 that "if the Russians were looking for some symbol of détente why did they not release Hess? Hess was old, ill, half mad, and could do no harm to anyone. It would make a great difference if the Russians could be generous and release him. He could think of no gesture which would cost the Russians so little which would make so much difference." The ambassador, reported Rippon, was visibly "non-plussed by this argument. He said there were many reasons against releasing Hess. For his country, which had lost 20 million dead in the last war, it was hard to imagine releasing such a criminal."[166] Douglas-Home did no better with Gromyko in Helsinki in July 1973 during security talks there. "If in asking the question," Gromyko said brusquely,

"Sir Alec was proceeding on the assumption of a negative reply he was quite right. If he was proceeding on the assumption of a positive reply he was quite wrong."[167]

Neave and other advocates of Hess's release were advised of the realities. But by 1979 the calls in Parliament had become longer and more frequent, led by James Douglas-Hamilton (the late Duke of Hamilton's son) and Cyril Townsend (the chairman of the "All Party Freedom for Rudolf Hess Campaign"). These statements never questioned the Nuremberg verdict. They emphasized Hess's age (he turned 85 in 1979), his decades in prison and his current harmlessness; his "solitary confinement"; the absurdity of the Spandau arrangement; and the danger of Hess becoming a martyr. "Three books of letters [Hess] has written to his wife," argued Douglas-Hamilton, "have sold better than any of the works on the German resistance to Hitler." "No country that calls itself civilized," added Townsend, "can continue endlessly with the Spandau charade.... Britain has a special responsibility in this matter, and the rest of the world recognizes that."[168]

Perhaps they all meant well. But the effort in Britain was tainted by its long association with Wolf Rüdiger, who played the humanitarian role in London but who openly questioned the verdict back in West Germany. To appease Neave, Foreign Office officials received Wolf Rüdiger in October 1973. The same month an article by Wolf Rüdiger appeared in *Der Freiwillige*, a vile SS veterans magazine, in which the younger Hess rejected the Nuremberg verdict.[169] Many of the MPs in question had also signed the HFRH petition.[170] Worse yet petitions for Hess's freedom were also assembled in 1970 and 1971 in such dubious places as Juan Perón's Argentina and Francisco Franco's Spain, both of which had been allied to Nazi Germany and the latter of which had sent a division to fight on the eastern front. The two thousand signatures on the Spanish petition included Ramón Serrano Suñer (Franco's wartime foreign minister who had called for Spanish volunteers to fight the Soviets) and former SS-Obersturmbannführer Otto Skorzeny, who had been evading prosecution in Spain since the 1950s.[171]

It obviously played poorly in Moscow where the official Soviet press called the parliamentary effort a wolfish racist campaign dressed as sheepish humanitarianism. *Pravda*'s comments likened Hess's British sympathizers to the pro-Nazi element Hess tried to contact in 1941.[172] The Soviet press fulminated about neo-Nazis and their British sympathizers, mentioning Neave and Douglas-Home by name.[173] Even former Nuremberg participants who had by now come out for Hess's freedom, including judges Geoffrey Lawrence and Francis Biddle and prosecutor Telford Taylor, were not spared Soviet wrath.[174] And the British lobbying became more unfortunate given Wolf Rüdiger's later publication of *Mein Vater Rudolf Hess* in 1984. Hess's son now argued that the world should not pity but rather honor his virtuous father. The Allies, he said, were cooperating with the

Soviets in Hess's imprisonment to hide Britain's guilt for rejecting the peace mission of 1941 and thus prolonging World War II, causing the deaths of millions. In *The Times* of London, Bernard Levin, who had called repeatedly for Hess's release on humanitarian grounds, now called Wolf Rüdiger's effort a "shameless and disgusting book."[175] The issues of Hess's guilt and his punishment had indeed been blurred. But would it not all become worse should Hess be forcibly cremated?

The Americans never liked the cremation agreement either. As the U.S. mission in West Berlin recalled, "We all considered that... using supreme Allied authority for a purpose not specifically envisaged in the Nuremberg judgment... was morally repugnant." But breaking a Four-Power agreement would entail consequences for West Berlin, whose Four-Power status was now stable for the first time since World War II. "It would be very dicey indeed," warned Scott George, the U.S. minister in West Berlin in 1974,

> if we were to insist on taking control of the body in violation of four power agreements and under the noses of Soviet troops... we would have to face the possible consequences of our unilateral abrogation of a four power agreement. We have for many years considered the Spandau agreement to be out of date and inappropriate. We would like to parole Hess and close the prison for both humanitarian and practical reasons. We have not attempted to do this without prior Soviet agreement because we have felt that we would lose more in the general Berlin situation than we would gain. . . .
>
> There are a great many four power agreements about Berlin which are far more favorable to us than to the Soviets. We do not wish to lend credence to the idea that when one side feels that a particular agreement is out of date or offensive, it is free to abrogate that agreement.... The Soviets would be far more sympathetic to the suggestion that, for example, our unimpeded access [to] Berlin is an anachronism offensive to the GDR, than they would be to the suggestion that we show great concern for the feelings of the family of Hitler's deputy or even the feelings of the FRG populace.[176]

The U.S. mission in Berlin tried to develop a procedural timetable for Hess's death, but the French and British refused. Secretaries of state from Henry Kissinger to George Shultz feared a disastrous international tussle over Hess's body.[177] The issue only became more urgent with the freeze in the Cold War in the late 1970s. The deployment of Soviet SS-20 intermediate range missiles in 1978; NATO's decision to respond with its own new deployment of Pershing IIs and cruise missiles; the Soviet repression of dissidents like Anatoly Sharansky in 1978; the Soviet invasion of Afghanistan in December 1979; and the fear that the Soviets might invade Poland in 1980 to crush the Solidarity movement led to the tensest moments since the early 1960s. A blowup in Berlin over Hess was not at all desirable.

The moment of truth seemed to arrive in late 1979. Tests in the British Military Hospital in September 1979 revealed that Hess had a prostate condition, which, if not treated surgically while he was in relatively good health, could, in the words of the British specialist, trigger "a fatal outcome."[178] But Hess refused surgery. In a letter to the four governments (not to the prison governors) on September 8, he proclaimed, "I will not permit the operation unless I am released from prison." He continued:

> Since the German Federal Government has ascertained that I was falsely convicted, it strikes me as self evident that the four powers responsible for my imprisonment should immediately release a man who for more than 30 years has found himself innocently in prison. The sooner this happens, the less will increase the related danger of the postponement of the operation....
>
> I place therefore to the governments of the four custodial powers the request to release me immediately from illegal imprisonment.

Thus, Hitler's deputy believed the threat of his own death was the key to redemption.[179] He was returned from the hospital to Spandau on September 10 in good spirits while the Allies fretted over what would happen if he died.[180] President Jimmy Carter's secretary of state Cyrus Vance saw the letter for what it was. "Far from representing the beginning of irrationality," Vance mused, it reflected "Hess' well-considered attempt to use the medical situation to try to 'force' his release."[181] Vance was surely correct. When Hess turned eighty back in 1974 he had fully expected his release thanks to the milestone birthday.[182] Now he would obtain it any way he could.

The Allies proceeded on a number of tracks. First, Hess should have the surgery if for no other reason than to delay his death and a possible fight over the body. In response to Hess's September 8 letter, the prison governors jointly wrote Hess "to draw your attention to the medical risks you are running if you do not have surgical treatment."[183] The British minister in Berlin Francis MacGinnis visited Hess in his cell on September 20, assuring him that the West German government did *not* believe him innocent while urging him to have the surgery.[184] The Allied embassies asked Wolf Rüdiger to persuade his father to have the operation, partly because Hess's son might have some effect and partly because, as the Americans put it, "our public position would be more comfortable" should Hess die after his son refused to cooperate with the Allies. Wolf Rüdiger and Seidl did not disappoint on this score. Neither pressed Hess to have the operation, and Hess would in fact never undergo the surgery.[185]

London and Paris tried meanwhile to dodge the cremation procedure by convincing the Soviets to release Hess before his health deteriorated. The chances that the Soviets would agree after Gromyko's stinging rejection of Douglas-Home in Helsinki were not even remotely promising. Bonn had made low-level efforts with Soviet ambassador Valentin Falin from 1971 to 1973, and in April 1974 (Hess turned 80 that month) Federal President Gustav Heinemann wrote the four heads of state. While Nixon's personal reply was sympathetic, Moscow's reply, delivered through the Soviet Embassy, was not.

> A pardon for the Nazi war criminal Rudolf Hess who represents a symbol for the grisly acts and crimes of Nazism and Fascism throughout the world, and who during his long imprisonment has shown no remorse, would be misunderstood by the entire democratic world. Like it or not, an amnesty for Rudolf Hess would signify an amnesty for Nazism and Fascism.

Hess's well-documented lack of remorse had become another reason to keep him imprisoned.[186]

In April 1977 Vance had raised in Moscow with Gromyko the lesser possibility of moving Hess permanently to a hospital where he could be treated by German doctors. This step was spurred by a suicide attempt on the night of February 22 in which Hess tried to cut himself with a table knife left in his cell by a warder (Hess received plastic utensils thereafter).[187] The Spandau governors viewed the suicide attempt as tentative, had resolved to keep it secret, and tried to make Hess more comfortable. (It was now that he received his color television.)[188] But news of the attempt leaked to the West German press anyway. Wolf Rüdiger held a bustling press conference at the Hilton in West Berlin on February 28 wherein he blasted the prison's attempted cover-up of the suicide and Allied cooperation with the Soviets in what he now (rather inappropriately) called a "systematic extermination campaign."[189] Press coverage obliged Bonn to act. Karl Carstens, now Bundestag president, called in writing on March 2 for Hess's permanent movement to a hospital, and Hans-Dietrich Genscher, the foreign minister in Chancellor Helmut Schmidt's cabinet, urged Vance on March 14 to do something. Yet Vance's démarche in Moscow that April was stopped cold. According to Vance himself, "Gromyko replied with a flat, emphatic 'NO.'" The incident was so embarrassing that Vance asked that it not be mentioned in the Bundestag that month.[190]

Though tempers had cooled in the following year, the West Germans fared no better with the Soviets. German Federal President Walter Scheel, who as Brandt's foreign minister had spearheaded *Ostpolitik* earlier in the decade, at least received a polite response from Brezhnev when the latter visited Bonn in May 1978. Brezhnev said "the case was a domestic political issue for him which would not allow him to make any concessions." Brezhnev added that it was customary in the U.S.S.R. for life sentences to be served.[191] The Allies also failed in June 1978 when they raised Hess with the Soviet ambassadors in London, Paris, and Washington. Anatoly Dobrynin, the veteran Soviet ambassador in Washington, tried to take the edge off Moscow's refusal. "Memories were long in the Soviet Union," Dobrynin said, "and [Hess's] imprisonment should not be seen as an act of cruelty."[192]

Thus, whatever efforts the Allies could make after September 1979 were certain to fail. The new British prime minister Margaret Thatcher was clearly irritated at Seidl's continuous efforts to question the validity of Hess's sentence and told Seidl as much.[193] But Thatcher's foreign secretary Lord Peter Carrington was determined that a high-level ministerial approach be made for Hess's release again with the uncompromising Gromyko. This time Gromyko did not even reply himself. Instead he had oral messages delivered in October stating that Hess was responsible for the deaths of millions, that he had not shown "even a shadow of repentance," and that in his own most recent statement he claimed to be in prison illegally.[194] Another three-way démarche was made in Moscow in February 1980, and Moscow did not convey a formal rejection until mid-June.[195] The French tried their own approach in East Berlin on January 8, 1980, through Ambassador Jean-Pierre Brunet. Abrassimov now expressed irritation that the Allies had proposed Hess's release so often and even claimed (wrongly) that von Neurath and Raeder had served their full sentences.[196] Irked U.S. diplomats saw these efforts from Paris and London as cynically geared for public consumption should the worst happen. And they brought no consensus on what to do should Hess die in the meantime.[197] The French even refused to raise the issue of changing the 1970 agreement formally with the Soviets, for fear that a Soviet refusal would add to its legality.[198] "There remains no commonality of view among capitals on what should be done in the event of the prisoner's death," reported the U.S. mission in West Berlin. "If this disparity . . . is not resolved well before the event, chaos will reign on the appointed day."[199] U.S. officials thought that the continued requests for Hess's release would only make the Soviets more obstinate on the burial arrangements.

Ronald Reagan's inauguration in 1981 brought a new energy to Allied discussions under Secretary of State Alexander Haig and Lawrence Eagleburger, the assistant secretary for European affairs. At the Rome NATO meeting of May 1981 (shortly after Hess had been in the British Military Hospital with pneumonia), Eagleburger suggested the following: The Allies would propose changes in the 1970 arrangement to Moscow but that the cremation would occur without complaint should Moscow refuse. Such, said Eagleburger, "would promote our greater interests in Berlin by avoiding the precedent of breaking a Quadripartite Agreement with the USSR." Breaking such an agreement, he warned, would set a "dangerous precedent" that could include a Soviet resort to force.[200] Yet the French and British were unconvinced. Paris just stalled.[201] And by May 1981 Lord Carrington decided, against the advice of his own Foreign Office, that London would not implement the 1970 agreement under any circumstances. He feared a "world spectacle" if the West Germans refused to cremate the body and the British had to do it themselves. According to Julian Bullard, the foreign secretary thought the "moral and political consequences of such a situation [were] too great."[202]

Haig wrote Carrington personally, attempting to convince him that in the current climate, a crisis in Berlin had to be avoided. "While there are disadvantages attached to [the 1970 agreement]," Haig argued,

> I strongly believe that, of the available options, it best serves our larger security interests as well as the greatest moral good in the area, namely the security of Berlin, its distancing from the complex of East-West tensions, and the continuation of the peace. . . . It is my very real concern that yielding to the wishes of the family . . . and preempting a possible public outburst over the cremation of Hess' body, i.e., by deliberately breaking a Quadripartite Agreement, we will weaken the whole framework of custom and legality which has served as a basis for our position in Berlin.
>
> It would be difficult for the Soviets to resist the temptation to threaten us with their own changes in agreements, whether affecting the air corridor regime, Berlin-FRG ties or the visits of West Berliners to the East.[203]

Carrington was unmoved. "I am afraid," he wrote Haig, that

> I still see great difficulty in going ahead as agreed in 1970, involving as this would the possibility of having to use British troops to occupy and operate a crematorium in the British sector of Berlin in the face of opposition from the Hess family and criticism from many quarters both inside and outside Germany.

Though Carrington agreed that the Soviets could be sounded out on altering the 1970 agreement, he refused to commit to anything should they refuse.[204] For the remainder of the year, the three capitals struggled over the wording of the proposals to the Soviets. It is hard to say what might have happened should Hess have actually died in these years. It is truly one of the oddest legacies of Nuremberg, however, that the fate of his remains had become so potentially explosive.

On April 2, 1982, in a low-level approach, the political advisers of the Allied missions in West Berlin personally delivered to the Soviet Embassy in East Berlin a proposal to allow the Hess family to have his remains for burial outside of Berlin. Avoiding any phrase that could appear apologetic to Hess or Nazism, the proposal said that the 1970 arrangement might focus the sort of attention on Hess that everyone hoped to avoid. The new Soviet Embassy councilor, who went by the name Dmitri Kosobrodov, replied that "of course we are surprised by this subject." But he was visibly intrigued. The Soviets had come by now to realize that the cremation agreement provided no safeguard against a political funeral or a shrine to Hess in Bavaria.[205]

Moscow's realization came with Karl Dönitz's funeral in January 1981 in Aumuhle near Hamburg following his death at age 89 on Christmas Eve. Thousands of World War II veterans and serving officers (the former in uniform, the latter not as per government orders) stood in the bitter cold to watch ten holders of the Knight's Cross carry the coffin of Hitler's successor.

Funeral wreaths piled up in the snow as naval veterans praised Dönitz's heroism while cursing the Nuremberg verdicts and the West German government. Moscow angrily protested the event.[206] The Soviet Foreign Ministry in August 1981 also made an official protest to the West German ambassador in Moscow against the production and sale by a Munich firm of silver and gold souvenir medallions (for nearly DM 200 and DM 400 each) commemorating Hess's fortieth year in prison. The Soviets demanded that Bonn halt the distribution of the medallions and punish the sellers for their popularization of the Hitler regime.[207] "Neo-Nazis," Kosobrodov told the Allied political advisers in the April 1982 meeting, "are more numerous today than yesterday." He asked if there might be assurances from the Hess family and the West German authorities that Hess's funeral remain small and quiet. It was a more positive response than anyone could have imagined. On April 16, Abrassimov registered Moscow's sense of urgency by telling U.S. ambassador Arthur Burns over lunch that talks should start immediately. Moscow, Burns reported, "attached considerable importance . . . to guaranteeing that neo-Fascist groups did not exploit the occasion of the prisoner's death."[208]

From May to October 1982, amidst some of the harshest public rhetoric of the Cold War, a new "Spandau Protocol" was hammered out in unusually friendly Four-Power meetings at Moscow's embassy in East Berlin.[209] Nothing, it seemed, could spoil these talks. The British made another attempt for Hess's freedom in July with the Soviet ambassador in London Viktor Popov despite Haig's warning that the attempt bore no chance of success and could derail the negotiations in East Berlin. Arthur Burns angrily reported that

> The British apparently contend that the domestic pressure to make the approach to the Soviets on Hess outweighed the arguments we advanced both in Washington and Bonn that such an appeal now may adversely effect the negotiations on the disposal of Hess' remains. We can only hope that the British appeal does not jeopardize our progress to date.[210]

In the fall came more petitions for Hess's release, from Hess himself (giving his word of honor that he would remain silent if freed), from Wolf Rüdiger, and even from West German chancellor Helmut Schmidt.[211] Hess meanwhile mused about his death to Ilse:

> Scattering the ashes of our bodily remains after death from a boat into the sea or from an aircraft into the air seems to you to be the most beautiful in that it is a rapid and direct return to the eternal cycle. However, in burning to ashes, gases probably escape into space and do not return to the eternal cycle, at least not to our planet. Burial is the most natural return to the cycle, even if it is not the quickest. By this method, nothing is lost.[212]

But Moscow was too concerned about the funeral arrangements to be indignant. Hess had two mild heart attacks in June and July 1982, and the Soviets had even brought in a heart specialist. As U.S. legal adviser John Byerly noted after the first episode of June 29, "[Hess's] high pulse rate does underscore the fact that the man, at 88 years, could die at any time, with no prior warning."[213] Hess was in the hospital with pleurisy the last two weeks of September 1982.[214] At a lunch with British Ambassador Jock Taylor, Abrassimov complained bitterly about Thatcher's recent condemnation of the Soviet presence in Afghanistan; the failure of NATO to scale back its conventional forces in Central Europe; and Allied encouragement of Solidarity in Poland. Yet he insisted the new agreement over Hess's remains be signed immediately.[215]

It was signed within days, on October 1, by Four-Power representatives in Berlin. The new Spandau Protocol provided for the immediate notification of the Hess family; a speedy autopsy in the British Military Hospital, the transport of the body to the family in Bavaria; a brief, innocuous official statement for the press of Hess's death; a ban on press coverage inside the prison or in the British Military Hospital; Allied steps with the West German government aimed at the minimization of public demonstrations; and the timely demolition of the prison after Hess's death.[216] The protocol hinged on a statement that Wolf Rüdiger was to sign, promising that "I am authorized, after the death of my father, Rudolf Hess, to take care of his funeral. The funeral is to take place privately in the immediate family circle in Bavaria, Federal Republic of Germany. I promise that my obligation remains confidential." He signed the statement on October 4 (but never felt bound by the agreement since he did not receive a copy of the Protocol itself).[217] Three days later, West German authorities promised within the limits of the law to ensure a quiet burial, and in mid-October the Bavarian state government (which had called for Hess's freedom earlier in the year) received warnings from Bonn that a noisy Hess funeral would be viewed with great dismay.[218] Everything was in place for a peaceful liquidation of the last remnant of the Nuremberg trial. Only a freak accident could spoil these carefully laid plans.

## THE BITTER END

On the eve of Hess's ninety-first birthday in April 1985, Julian Bullard asked the Soviet chargé d'affaires in London, Vyacheslav I. Dolgov, why the Soviets had agreed in the mid-1950s to release von Neurath, Raeder, and Funk from Spandau but would not release Hess, who was now older than the others had been.[219] Bullard could have answered the question himself. Moscow released these men because of its uneasiness with the funeral arrangement it had struck in 1954. But after 1982 the Soviets had an agreement for Hess's death that served their purpose and thus could comfortably hold Hess in prison until the end. And Hess's life – thanks to twice daily walks, thorough weekly medical exams, daily vital sign readings, and his own eccentric insistence on a diet of fruits and leafy vegetables – continued for nearly five years after the 1982 agreement. Hess was alert and in good condition for his age. His health did not begin serious deterioration until the final year of his life with heart, prostate, and vision problems.[220] He also worried in his last year about a descent into senility.[221] Yet Hess's deteriorating condition only meant the streamlining of the emergency procedure, codenamed PARADOX, by which Hess would be moved immediately to the British Military Hospital without the time-consuming consultation of all four governors.[222] Even if Moscow had wished to release him, the increasingly shrill statements of Wolf Rüdiger and Alfred Seidl, who both published argumentative books in 1984, made release improbable even after Mikhail Gorbachev came to power in March 1985. On the other hand, the imprisonment of a man in his nineties drained more public meaning from the punishment itself. Despite Hess's guilt and despite the increasingly offensive nature of Wolf Rüdiger and Seidl's appeals, responsible West German leaders viewed Hess as an increasingly urgent humanitarian issue.

The Soviet fear of an extreme-right-wing resurgence should Hess be released was always overblown in the 1970s and 1980s. Wolf Rüdiger's HFRH held numerous demonstrations after 1973 for Hess's freedom but never mustered more than a few thousand people. On Hess's eighty-fifth birthday, they gathered no more than sixty members at the gates of Spandau.[223] The mid-1980s saw the advent of new far-right groups, but their efforts on Hess's behalf were limited.[224] The greatest spectacle came from a Hamburg youth group *Konservativer Aktion* which saw in Hess's case fuel for a broad agenda which included a positive reading of Nazism together with hostility to the Soviets and to Turkish immigrants. In November 1985 the group held a "Freedom for Rudolf Hess Congress" in West Berlin which featured Wolf Rüdiger and Seidl as speakers. Hess, said the U.S. mission there, offered rightist youth "a politically respectable opportunity" to enunciate German nationalism unburdened by the Nazi genocidal past.[225] On May 10, 1986, the forty-fifth anniversary of Hess's flight, *Konservative Aktion* held another meeting in West Berlin as right-wing and left-wing groups squared off in front of the prison.[226]

But Hess's imprisonment brought few acts of violence. At 2:00 A.M. on October 23, 1986, a Molotov cocktail exploded in Building 21, Spandau's administrative structure and mess hall, situated outside the prison walls, destroying the building's interior. It was the most violent act against the prison, accompanied by a note and a telephone call from the *Befreiungskommando Rudolf Hess* threatening that if Hess were not released by the twenty-fourth, they would blow the entire prison "sky high" (which would seem to defeat the purpose of freeing Hess). The group also promised further attacks on the Allies while threatening Governing Mayor Eberhard Diepgen and his children.[227] Hess's later birthdays brought lots of flowers and cards (none of which reached Hess) but German police in West Berlin expected far worse than the anemic demonstration of twenty neo-Nazis from Hamburg on his ninety-second birthday in April 1986. On Hess's death in August 1987, neo-Nazi skinheads could muster no more than twenty-five of their number for a pathetic vigil outside the prison.[228]

More prevalent as Hess grew older were the official West German efforts to have Hess freed for reasons of mercy. The Bundestag did not discuss Hess nearly as often as did the British Parliament, though questions were raised more often after Hess's seventy-fifth birthday in April 1969. In May of that year, Bundestag representatives questioned Hess's continued incarceration and Spandau's costs. Officials in the Federal Chancellor's office hoped that Willy Brandt, on becoming chancellor that October, might make the first official West German approach to the Soviet Embassy on Hess's behalf at the earliest opportunity. Brandt, it was argued within government circles, carried the "personal authority" as an enemy of the Nazi regime and enjoyed a currency in Moscow that previous chancellors had not. Brandt himself was positive toward the idea. Perhaps Brandt hoped that the release of Germany's last war criminals might inoculate his larger policies against the West German right. From 1971 to 1973, thanks to repeated Bundestag inquiries, Brandt tried in several personal discussions with Italian leaders to win Herbert Kappler's freedom. Bonn also worked at high levels to free the three Germans held at Breda since, as Brandt's foreign minister Walter Scheel put it, it was unfair that the three prisoners there bore practically the entire burden for Nazi crimes in the Netherlands.[229] Yet the new chancellor refrained on Hess. In 1969 and 1970 Hess's long stay in the hospital; the absolute Soviet insistence that Hess return to prison; and the Soviet argument that anyone who wanted Hess's freedom was a neo-Nazi, surely convinced Brandt that the step was not worth the risk to an agenda of global importance.[230] Scheel issued a statement in April 1971 for a story on Hess in the West German magazine *Stern* that Hess should be released for humanitarian reasons but he noted that Spandau remained a Four-Power prerogative. In light of the larger polices Bonn pursued with Moscow, Scheel was very reluctant to raise Hess personally with the Soviet ambassador to Bonn Valentin Falin.[231] Brandt later considered raising Hess on the occasion of Brezhnev's visit to Bonn in May 1973 but again refrained.[232]

Greater efforts were made by Brandt's Social Democratic successor Helmut Schmidt (1974–1982) after a Bundestag question of March 14, 1979. Schmidt was the first chancellor to visit Auschwitz, where he wrestled with the Nazi past in a speech discounting the collective guilt of all Germans while stating that all Germans still must bear Nazism's legacy. He was also the first to participate in a commemoration of the anniversary of Kristallnacht (1978).[233] Yet on July 29, 1980, he surprised Brezhnev by asking him directly during a trip to Moscow if it was really in Moscow's interest for a sick 86-year-old man to die in prison when the entire world knew it had been the Soviets who had kept him there. Gromyko was not there to provide Moscow's stock answer, and Brezhnev, though he had refused a similar request from Walter Scheel two years earlier, seemed impressed by Schmidt's argument. He agreed to discuss it with Politburo members.[234] Schmidt was hopeful, but before Brezhnev's return visit to Bonn in December 1981, the Soviet Embassy warned the West Germans not to raise Hess again. For the sake of larger strategic issues, Bonn did not.[235] But as a parting shot on leaving office in September 1982, Schmidt wrote the four heads of state asking for Hess's release so that Hess could spend his final days with his family, and he revealed his petition to the press.[236]

By the end of the year, the Bundestag unanimously called for the new CDU-led government of Helmut Kohl to seek the release of Hess and of the remaining Germans convicted of war crimes and imprisoned since the war. The resolution showed that Hess's punishment rankled on the right as well as the left.[237] Kohl's early efforts with Brezhnev and his successor Yuri Andropov failed, and the chancellor's legendary rhetorical missteps concerning the official memory of the Nazi past helped to torpedo future attempts.[238] Kohl clouded his January 1984 visit to Israel with his statement that the "grace of late birth" would strike a new tone for him and other Germans. The new generation, he said, "refuses to admit collective guilt for the deeds of its fathers."[239] Kohl's disastrous visit to Waffen SS graves at Bitburg with President Reagan in May 1985 was a more palpable failure. His efforts to have Hess released were thus doomed when Bonn renewed its efforts near Hess's ninetieth birthday. In a letter to the four heads of state dated March 14, 1984, Kohl stated that Hess's imprisonment "does not truly meet the purpose of punishment anymore" and that releasing him "would not diminish the memory of the untold harm which National Socialism inflicted on Europe and the world." The chancellor foolishly added Seidl's and Wolf Rüdiger's old line that Hess had been acquitted on Counts III and IV of the Nuremberg indictment.[240]

Moscow's rejection prompted the Bonn government to make a public statement on April 25, 1984, the eve of Hess's ninetieth birthday, with the same arguments.[241] And by now interest by the West German and even the world press was substantial, complete with various factual errors. *Stern*'s story "A Day in the Life of Number 7" reported that Hess would be cremated after his death and even the French newspaper *Le Monde* and the U.S. magazine *Newsweek* came out for Hess's freedom. Angry statements from the Bundestag and, most predictably, from British and American movie actors became part of the record. But if Hess's advocates were willing to fight in public, so was Moscow. Already on April 14, the Soviet newspaper *Izvestia* stated that Hess had never repented his faith in Hitler, and that "the West German movement to release Hess is directed . . . at denigrating the Nuremberg Tribunal, whitewashing Hitler's cohorts, and in general rehabilitating the leaders of the Third Reich." The strong language suggested official imprimatur. But a new medallion struck in Munich for Hess's ninetieth birthday in 1984 gave Moscow all the ammunition it needed.[242]

And it did not bode well for the three-way Allied démarche for the 90-year-old Hess to be released. The personal reply delivered by Dobrynin to Reagan's secretary of state George Schultz on May 10, 1984, carried daggers. "The Soviet side," said Dobrynin, "continues to see no reason whatsoever for his release."

> His name, along with the names of other Nazi criminals, is directly associated in the minds of our people with the death of 20 million . . . Soviet people during the Second World War.
>
> The pardoning of this criminal and inveterate advocate of [the] misanthropic ideology of Nazism would have been interpreted as some kind of encouragement to those who today, too, ignore the grim lessons of history. The release of Hess who is a symbol of the atrocities committed by Nazism would not be understood either by the Soviet people, or by the peoples of other countries who suffered from the Hitlerite aggression.

The statement, also given in London and Paris, showed that Moscow made no distinction between mercy and pardon. In addition, Hess had become a living symbol of the past. And with major commemorations planned in Moscow for the approaching fortieth anniversary of Germany's surrender, the Soviets were in no mood to change their minds.[243]

The lack of mercy and the use of Hess as a symbol angered no one more than Federal President Richard von Weizsäcker, a CDU moderate, the Bonn Republic's most revered head of state and, unlike Kohl, a careful and eloquent speaker on the Nazi past. On the fortieth anniversary of the German surrender on May 8, 1985, von Weizsäcker gave a globally famous speech calling on all Germans to "look truth straight in the eye – without embellishment or distortion" and accept unconditionally the inhumanity of the Third Reich. He listed all of Nazi Germany's victims from Jews, whose genocide was "unparalleled in history," to members of local resistance movements to workers and Communists. Rather than view Nazism through the bitter prism of the Soviet advance and a divided Germany – thus emphasizing German victimization since 1945 – von Weizsäcker accepted Germany's responsibility for its fate while cutting across Cold War boundaries. And while von Weizsäcker rejected the idea of collective guilt, he acknowledged that all Germans bore a collective responsibility to remember and to reconcile with Nazism's former enemies. In future years, von Weizsäcker would also reject attempts by right-wing West German academics to diminish the Holocaust by comparing it to the crimes of other regimes. "Auschwitz," he said, "remains unique. . . . This truth is immutable."[244]

But the continued incarceration of Hess irked von Weizsäcker as unnecessarily cruel. In June 1982 while still the governing mayor of West Berlin, von Weizsäcker received Francis MacGinnis, the chief of the British mission there. Hess was now 88, and MacGinnis wished to discuss the handling of what was thought to be his imminent death. Von Weizsäcker, who had no sympathy with Hess the man, spoke frankly, directly, and even emotionally. "One thing," MacGinnis reported from his discussion with von Weizsäcker, "was crystal clear . . . the death of Hess would release a wave of pent-up emotion publicly. Speaking courteously but with some passion, [von Weizsäcker] said that never in the twentieth century had victors behaved so harshly as they had toward Hess."[245]

Von Weizsäcker did not change his mind as president. When delivering his presidential Christmas message in December 1985, he called for the releases from imprisonment of Nelson Mandela in South Africa, Andrei Sakharov in the U.S.S.R., and Rudolf Hess in West Berlin. It was an unfortunate grouping, but one von Weizsäcker made regardless in an attempt to tie a responsibility to the past with a call for mercy. "Hess," he said,

> was truly no fighter for human rights and freedom. As Hitler's Deputy he was sentenced to lifelong imprisonment. This corresponds with our legal perceptions. But now he has served his sentence for 44 years. He is a 92 year-old man. He has no more earthly hopes. For what sensibility [and] for what human value is such a punishment to serve? In the Hitler period there was no such thing as clemency. And today? Mercy would not lift the judgment regarding the outrages committed, but would only now strengthen it. 'Mercy is the basis of justice,' according to a profound and generous Russian proverb. It should be granted in the year of peace, 1986.

Hess should thus have mercy, the definition of which took into account that mercy might not be deserved. Weizsäcker repeated the request six months before Hess's death.[246] But by this time the elements of Hess's confinement were so conflated by the length of the sentence, the various misstatements, and the confusion between moderate and unapologetic positions that even von Weizsäcker could not slice through what had become the Gordian knot of Nuremberg's legacy. He only made it tighter. "Coming from a man as respected, perhaps as revered as von Weizsäcker," reported the U.S. mission in Berlin, "such a call for Hess' release cannot help but give momentum and added respectability to the Free Hess movement in the FRG."[247] It is a sad lesson perhaps inherent in the nature of international justice.

Hess's own efforts did not help. In November 1980 and September 1984, he asked the prison governors to release him based on a variety of health problems, many of which he exaggerated. In May 1986, at age 92, he asked for a furlough so that he could see his grandchildren, giving his "word of honor" that he would return to Spandau and that he would give no public statements or interviews.[248] On March 25, 1987, a few months before his suicide and in badly deteriorating health, he noted that he had but a year to live and asked to spend it with his son and grandchildren, and on June 24 he demanded to see a copy of the Nuremberg judgment so that he could be sure he was properly sentenced to life imprisonment.[249]

But to the very, very end, Hess remained a faithful follower of Hitler. Among the more bizarre legacies from Spandau is a sheaf of loose handwritten papers discovered by Soviet prison governor Lieutenant Colonel Gennady Chernykh in Hess's cell on June 25, 1986 (shortly after Hess promised to make no public statements if released).[250] A cover note showed that Hess had been smuggling information to the outside through the French pastor, Charles Gabel. Gabel, who had worked at Spandau since 1977 and who had been secretly helping the Hess family in their liberation campaign, was supposed to take the current batch of papers and drop it in a mailbox to an unknown recipient to whom Hess referred as "Der Meister" and as "Mr. U." The Soviets had suspected earlier that Gabel was a security threat. They had suggested in 1985 that the pastor's visits take place in the visiting room only and that he be subject to the same rules as Hess's other visitors. Now, they argued that Gabel was helping Hess to smuggle memoirs out of Spandau. After some stalling by the French, Gabel was fired and the last papers Hess tried to smuggle were sealed, placed in the prison archives, and are thus preserved on microfilm.[251]

Hess had instructed Gabel: "Send the enclosed to the Master [der Meister] and be sure to drop the letter in a post box *when you are out of town*, by no means in Berlin." Enclosed were a number of handwritten pages with another cover note:

> Dear Mr. U.
> Thank you very much for your declaration of readiness. Be so kind as to insert the enclosed additions.

Another instruction read as follows:

> In the present conclusion of my report I thank those who have worked for my liberation, above all the Pastor. If I have forgotten to mention my son, then at the proper point, something like this should be said: Above all I thank Pastor Gabel and my son Wolf Rüdiger who have outdone each other in activities carried out.

The "enclosed additions" to which Hess referred amounted to seventeen messy, hurried, unfinished, handwritten pages that were to have been part of a larger statement. The pages discussed Hitler's reaction to the outbreak of war in 1939 and the attack on the U.S.S.R. in 1941. Hess insisted that Hitler had not wanted war in 1939, especially with Great Britain. It had been the British guarantee to Poland that had ruined what would surely have been a peaceful solution over the German-Polish border. "I can say one thing with absolute certainty," Hess wrote, "Hitler did not want the war." On the other hand Hess claimed to remember a discussion with Hitler in the winter

31. Rudolf Hess, Spandau's lone prisoner, eerily walks along the Spandau garden path.

of 1940–1941 wherein both agreed that the Soviets were bent on world revolution and that Moscow saw Germany as the key to the bolshevization of Europe, particularly since Germany was still at war with the British. "In recognition of this danger from the East," Hess continued, "there was for us but one conclusion: To anticipate the Soviet attack and to attack ourselves. Attack as soon as possible."

Thus, Hess made the decision, which he kept secret from Hitler, to fly to England to broker an understanding between the Nordic peoples. Despite the complications that had arisen since 1939, Hess said, all would have gone well had Hitler, other Germans, the British, and even the Americans not been influenced by a "secret force" that could control men's words and actions. Hess deduced the existence of this secret force while reading everything he could during his captivity in Britain. This secret force caused the British leadership to fight Germany and caused Hitler to make poor political and strategic decisions that brought the destruction of the Third Reich. It was even responsible for SS atrocities in concentration camps and also for Hitler's "order" to murder the Jews. "It is certain," he said, "that there is a secret force through which people can be forced not only to speak but also to act as they are commanded." But what was this secret force and who was behind it?

The seventeen pages that Hess tried to smuggle through Pastor Gabel in 1986 were scribblings from memory of the older, much longer final statement that Hess had wanted to make at Nuremberg on August 31, 1946. On rising after Göring's statement on that day forty years before, Hess pulled from his pocket several sheets of paper, on which he had made a long outline of his intended speech.[252] Upon opening with a roundabout discussion of his glassy-eyed British guards under the influence of the "secret force," Hess was cut off by Lord Lawrence, the president of the Tribunal. Hess thus jumped to the very end of the statement praising the Führer, read it, and sat down. Later, over lunch he had a heated argument with Raeder as to whether a man could be hypnotized into performing criminal acts. He then returned to his Nuremberg cell and began typing.[253]

By October 16, 1946, Hess had completed a typewritten version of the entire statement which he signed, along with a cover sheet asking that it be sent to British fascist leader Oswald Mosley for translation. Mosley, he added, would be well paid for his work. This statement (nearly fifty single-spaced typed pages with Hess's signature) was intercepted by the U.S. authorities and subsequently stolen, along with other documents, by the Nuremberg Prison governor, Frederick C. Teich. It was recovered by the U.S. National Archives in the early 1990s. It has not been used by Hess's biographers or the many authors who have written on Nuremberg.[254] It provides no new historical information – just more detail on Hess's delusions. But it shows that Hess paid close attention to the proceedings at Nuremberg and that he had his own rather involved theory as to why the German leaders were in the dock. The war, the atrocities, the destruction, the chaos, and even his own chronic stomach pains were all the work of the Jews, who controlled the secret force that Hess had supposedly discovered in Britain.

The war, Hess had wanted to say at Nuremberg, was a tragic alignment of unintended actions. It was not wanted by the Nordic leaders of Britain and Germany, yet they went to war with each other and remained at war for six years. It was not wanted by American leaders, yet the United States entered the war as well and fought until the end. Thus, Gemany's justified struggle for needed Living Space and its defense against aggressive Communism became a general conflict that destroyed Europe's best racial elements, while leaving Jewish bolshevism victorious. There was more. German atrocities in concentration camps (camps Hess said were quite humane before the war) were engineered from behind the scenes by the Jews so that the bodies would be discovered by the victors, who would then publicize the atrocities, put Germans on trial, and execute them while ensuring that Germany would never rise from the ashes. As for the slaughter of millions of Europe's Jews, Hess posited the following:

> The Jews, with the help of the [secret] force, caused the Germans and Russians in occupied Poland to decimate the anti-Semitic Poles, who the Jews so hated. Thanks to the mood of the Germans against the Jews, this action then transformed itself gradually into an extermination campaign against the Polish Jews and then against the Jews in general – quite contrary to the Jews' intent. After the Jews lost control, they endeavored at least to bring about a great propaganda campaign against Germany.

Thus it was the Jews, who had the most to gain from the destruction of Germany and the advance of bolshevism, who had been behind it all even to the point of benefiting from the slaughter of millions of their own. Hess then built to a crescendo:

> I accuse the criminals [and their] conspiracy against the peace of the world. I accuse them furthermore of crimes against humanity . . . I accuse the background-criminals in the name of the 20 million [sic!] dead of the two world wars . . . I accuse them in the name of widows . . . and in the name of the mothers who lost their children. . . . I accuse them in the name of those whose homes and possessions were destroyed or taken [and in] the name of the refugees who have been driven from their *Heimat*. . . .
>
> I accuse the Jews in the name of all humanity. . . . Only when they are judged can true and long lasting peace come to a tortured world.

No wonder Hess expected in 1946 to be hanged. While the other defendants distanced themselves from the truth in their final statements, Hess aimed to embrace it and then stand it on its head. Had Lord Lawrence not interrupted him, Hess would surely have been the first to climb the gallows. The Führer had understood everything and was to blame for nothing. The Jewish conspiracy extended even to the Holocaust. And now, four decades later, Hess wanted the same delusions published as his final statement to the world.[255] He had not changed his mind since the 1920s, and had his final statement ever become known, his advocates might have been limited to his galling son, his churlish attorney, and a small collection of bigoted cranks. But for bad luck he became a political problem nearly without end. It is to that macabre end that we can now turn.

# Burials: An Epilogue

"On the death of the last prisoner, the prison ceases to exist."
British Government Talking Point, 1982

At 2:30 P.M. on August 17, 1987, Rudolf Hess entered a small garden cottage during his afternoon walk within the Spandau Prison walls. Here he had grown accustomed to reading newspapers or napping on temperate afternoons. Prison regulations prohibited the one warder on escort duty from ever allowing Hess to leave his sight. Soviet warders on escort duty thus watched Hess through the windows of the garden cottage. But Allied warders had routinely allowed the 93-year-old inmate some privacy. And on the afternoon of August 17, the escort warder was Anthony Jordan an African-American who Hess had repeatedly tried to get fired for racial reasons and who had been ordered by his superiors to allow the cantankerous Hess a bit of latitude.[1] Jordan had in recent exercise periods allowed Hess a few minutes in the cottage without observation.

Understanding his opportunity Hess acted. In the cottage was a plastic-coated electrical extension cord, which Hess had used with the reading lamps there. The input end of the chord was tied, as usual, to the window handle, roughly four feet above the floor. Hess looped the other end around his neck and slumped toward the ground, hanging himself. Jordan found Hess a few minutes afterward. He removed the cord, laid Hess on the floor with a pillow, and called for medical assistance. But attempts by the orderlies to revive Hess failed. By 3:12 P.M. the ambulance arrived to take Hess to the British Military Hospital, where he was pronounced dead at 4:10 P.M. A hand-scrawled suicide note written on the back side of a letter from his daughter-in-law Andrea was found in Hess's pants pocket with the heading, "To the Directors to send home please, written a few minutes before my death."[2]

Two days later on August 19, 1987, British pathologist J. Malcolm Cameron of London Hospital Medical College performed a full autopsy at the British Military Hospital in the presence of medical officers from each of the Four Powers. Toxicology samples were taken and sent to London for lab analysis. Hess's death was caused by asphyxiation, compression of the neck and suspension. Marks on the body, aside from that left by the lamp cord, were consistent with resuscitation efforts.[3] At 8:00 A.M. the next morning, the four governors followed the closed military truck with Hess's coffin to Gatow Air Base. The body was flown in a Hercules transport aircraft to a U.S. Army airstrip at Grafenwöhr near Nuremberg. Here the governors officially handed the coffin over to Wolf Rüdiger, Hess's nephew Wieland Hess, and Alfred Seidl. "Well," said U.S. governor Darold Keane to Wolf Rüdiger, "I think that concludes our business." Back at Spandau, the British Special Investigations Branch (SIB) opened a full investigation of Hess's death. The report was completed by September 11, 1987. The cause of death was heart failure due to asphyxiation, the suicide note was genuine, and Anthony Jordan was judged to have performed his duties correctly and in keeping with prison practice. Back in 1985 the Allies had flatly rejected a Soviet proposal for a closed-circuit surveillance system and the division of the prison into sealed security zones. Thus, the world's most heavily guarded prisoner had not been that heavily guarded in his final years, and Hess used the more relaxed atmosphere to kill himself.[4]

The Hess family never accepted that Hess's death was a suicide. On August 19, 1987, Darold Keane read the contents of Hess's suicide note to Wolf Rüdiger over the phone. But on receiving the body on the twentieth, Wolf Rüdiger and Seidl argued that Hess's death was the result of foul play.[5] On August 21 the family commissioned a second autopsy performed by German pathologist Dr. Wolfgang Spann at the Institute of Forensic Medicine in Munich. Spann, who had yet to see the SIB report and whose knowledge of the facts surrounding the case were nil, concluded that the marks Hess's neck were consistent with strangulation, not suspension.[6] It was all the now completely embittered Wolf Rüdiger, Seidl, and various other conspiracy theorists needed. Using the West German tabloid *Bild* as their mouthpiece, Wolf Rüdiger and Seidl argued that the entire affair had something to do with secrets the British hoped to keep regarding Hess's flight forty-six years earlier. Wolf Rüdiger and Wieland also posed in a ghoulish photo beside the open Hess casket, which appeared in *Bild*.[7] As the U.S. mission in West Berlin sardonically reported, "The Hess family has been busy since taking custody of Hess' body at Grafenwoehr."[8]

In part, the Allies had asked for it. They botched the original announcement of Hess's death. Soviet prison governor Lieutenant Colonel Gennady Chernykh was on leave in Siberia when Hess killed himself, and the acting Soviet governor on August 17, the chief warder Kolodnikov, had no authorization to issue any statement other than the preplanned press release written back in 1982, which was based on the assumption that Hess would die of natural causes. Kolodnikov threatened a formal protest should the agreement of October 1982 be breached.[9] Thus, despite Allied irritation that they would look foolish, the press was told on the day of Hess's death that Hess had "died" with no further comment despite the rumors of suicide already leaking from the prison.[10] Not until the evening of the eighteenth did the British military government announce, with Soviet agreement, that Hess had been discovered with a cord around his neck.

But official news of the suicide note was held back on Soviet insistence.[11] The Soviets were furious that Keane had read the contents of the note to Wolf Rüdiger the next day. Acting on orders, Kolodnikov formally protested to the other governors later on August 19 that Keane had acted unilaterally and in breach of Four-Power agreements. "All this," Kolodnikov said, "is leading to totally unnecessary agitation and rumors surrounding the death of Rudolf Hess.... This is our firm position."[12] Though willing to have a handwriting expert authenticate the note (this was done on August 25), the Soviets would have preferred that all evidence of the suicide be suppressed in lieu of what Hess's incarceration had meant all along for official Soviet memory of the war. As the French Embassy in Moscow reported, the Soviet press emphasized Hess's responsibility for bringing the Nazis to power, for the war against the U.S.S.R., and even for the death camps. "His name," said the official Soviet Communist Party statement, "has become synonymous with genocide."[13] Moscow wanted the world to remember Hess for the Nazi regime's crimes, not for the Allies' punishment. Yet this hope had been lost years before. In London, Moscow's inflexible policies had made Hess into front page tabloid fodder – a lone prisoner under a regime described by the *Daily Express* "as close to prolonged mental torture as any system has been able to devise."[14]

And if SS veterans could conjure statements such as, "It is a disgrace that this honorable decent man was allowed to waste away,"[15] more reasonable Germans came in the next few days to see a capstone of Allied incompetence in dealing with the legacy of Nuremberg. The Allies, the West German press argued, had contributed to the Hess family's claims to martyrdom by not freeing Hess as he became a geriatric. The warders, they said, allowed Hess – who had attempted suicide several times before – out of their sight. Finally, the Allies let Hess's death become grist for right-wing conspiracy theorists through their initial untruthfulness. "It is absolutely incomprehensible," claimed the *Berliner Morgenpost*, "why the public has not been accurately informed regarding the death of Rudolf Hess after 24 hours.... It is not to be excluded that Nazis young and old, however small their number may be, will spread rumors and legends that shall make [Hess] into a martyr or even a hero."[16]

The Allies did what they could to minimize the damage without getting into a shouting match with the Hess family. On August 18 Keane had insisted that the family receive a copy of the suicide note because it had been Hess's final request and because it was the most important piece of evidence that Hess intended to take his own life. On August 20 and 21, British governor Tony Le Tissier and French governor Michel Planet insisted that the family receive a copy of the letter "to remove doubts about the authenticity of the intentions of the prisoner to commit suicide." Because the suicide note was not written on authorized, stamped letter paper, and had not gone through censorship as had normal family letters, the Soviets had insisted on the eighteenth that it be destroyed and on the twenty-first they reiterated this position.[17] The British did not discover until August 28 that the "Freiburg" to whom Hess conveyed his final regrets in the suicide note was Hess's former secretary Hildegard Fath, but even the possibility of embarrassing the Hess family did not worry the Americans at this point.[18]

> By breaching its agreement with the four powers to bury Hess quietly after the transfer of his body, leaking an inaccurate text of the suicide note, making accusations of murder and malfeasance, and tasteless exploitation of the affair via the Springer Press, the Hess family has shown that there is no need for the Allies to be solicitous of its feelings in taking future steps.[19]

Chernykh did not agree to provide the family with the letter until September 15, nearly a month after the suicide, and then only because Keane had already let the cat out of the bag. But even the actual note would not convince Wolf Rüdiger that his father's death had been a suicide.[20]

The bubbling controversy over Hess's death made a normal funeral impossible despite the agreement of 1982. On the evening Hess died, only three hundred people (including some skinheads with flowers) appeared outside the prison to sing old German nationalist songs by torchlight.[21] But the increased attention over the next week brought more incidents. Anthony Jordan received death threats in West Berlin. Neo-Nazis attacked U.S. army trucks in Frankfurt. Eighty-four people were arrested at the Hess family burial plot in the small Bavarian town of Wunsiedel. Memorial marches commemorating Hess's "murder" were planned.[22] The city authorities in Wunsiedel feared that neo-Nazis would overwhelm their town, which would now become known in spite of everyone's best efforts as Hess's final resting place. On top of it all, Wolf Rüdiger suffered a heart attack on August 23. The burial would have to be elsewhere. Thus, on the night of the twenty-third, West German federal authorities played the same shell game with Hess's body that the Allies had planned for von Neurath in the early 1950s. Several hearses left the Institute for Forensic Medicine to fool the press, then a normal minibus moved Hess's coffin to a secret location. The burial took place at midnight in the presence of Hess's daughter-in-law Andrea. Nearly eight months later, the body was moved under police escort and reinterred in a quiet ceremony at the family plot in Wunsiedel.[23] Hess's tombstone bears the inscription "Ich hab's erwagt" (I dared). It was an expression of the Protestant reformer-knight Ulrich von Hutten in 1521 now chosen to ennoble Hess's 1941 mission to Great Britain and thus his supposed role as a crusader for European peace.[24]

Wolf Rüdiger devoted the remainder of his life (he died in 2001) to canonizing his father through increasingly odd books. In 1987 he published a collection of his father's letters from 1908 to 1933.[25] In 1989 he published a book on the "murder" of his father by British intelligence.[26] Bernard Levin of *The Times*, who had argued that Hess should have been released for humanitarian reasons, could only shake his head that "the apple doesn't fall far from the tree."[27] Wolf Rüdiger's legacy is now the annual convocation of neo-Nazis in Wunsiedel each August, which in 2004 reached a high of 3,800. But if the annual march is an embarrassment to the town's residents (they managed to ban it in 2005), they can take some solace in this: It was not the result that the Allies and Soviets had hoped for either.

Hess's burial was not the only one to take place in 1987. Spandau Prison itself was also put underground. The fate of the prison buildings had been discussed since the early 1960s, when it was thought that Hess would be released along with Speer and von Schirach. At that time, the West Berlin authorities were to get the prison grounds for their own use. But by the late 1970s, with Hess having been alone in the prison for a number of years, the character of the place had changed. Physically it had been falling apart for years. As a British position paper put it, "the main building is in poor repair, while the outbuildings are practically in ruins." More importantly the prison could become a shrine to Nazism. West Berlin's governing mayors in the late 1970s and 1980s all shared this concern. Dietrich Stobbe, "anxious to avoid the prison becoming either a museum or a tourist attraction" had mentioned informally to the Allied authorities in West Berlin that he wanted the entire complex razed. In April 1981 Stobbe's successor Hans-Jochen Vogel reiterated that Spandau should be destroyed as quickly as possible after Hess's death. As the U.S. mission reported, the mayor "saw nothing good, and indeed only bad, resulting from any lengthy argument over the future of Spandau Prison."[28] The Allies agreed: "Although the prison might serve as a permanent reminder of the Nuremberg Tribunal and thus of Nazism in general," read one position paper, "it could also create a focus for resurgence of Neo-Nazi sentiment."[29]

There was some concern before 1982 that the Soviets would want the prison preserved as a monument of sorts under Four-Power watch, thanks to several offhand Soviet comments. A Soviet colonel named Grishel commented to the British authorities during a meeting in Potsdam in 1970 that Spandau could be used for war criminals yet to be punished or, failing that, as a memorial and warning to future would-be war criminals.[30] In April 1978 Abrassimov said to the Western press that the fate of the prison would be decided by the Four Powers after Hess's death. The French took this to mean that "the Soviets . . . will wish to preserve Spandau indefinitely as a quadripartite institution."[31] The Allies had to be sensitive to Soviet wishes while trying to change the cremation arrangement of 1970 because that agreement was what had obviated the need for an indefinite Soviet presence at Spandau to guard a Hess tomb.[32] But the British had noted that "there will probably be an argument with the Russians about the disposal of the Prison building and site.... they value their existing presence in the Western Sectors of Berlin, of which the regular guard they provide at Spandau Prison is an important and conspicuous element."[33] In fact, the Soviets had no legal claim to remain at Spandau Prison. As closely as anyone could tell, the British military government in Berlin could legally dispose of the prison as it liked and could thus return it to the local West Berlin authorities.[34] Control Council Directive Number 35 gave the Soviets no rights at the prison after the last prisoner had died or left. The most the Allies would allow was a small plaque noting where the prison had been, but as the Americans put it, "there could be no question of a permanent or semi-permanent quadripartite presence at Spandau."[35] The prison, agreed all three Western Allies, should be destroyed, and it would be best if the British demolished it under their military prerogatives in West Berlin in order to save the West Berlin government any embarrassment.[36]

The Soviets on considering the issue in 1982 in connection with what became the Spandau Protocol evidently understood that they had no perpetual rights at Spandau either. When the issue of the prison came up in the Soviet Embassy, Kosobrodov noted that "the Soviet desire... was that Spandau Prison not become a memorial, a pilgrimage site, or in any other way a remnant of Nazi Germany." Moscow made no claim to continuing rights there after Hess's death, but noted its preference that the place be leveled before the land went back to the West Berlin authorities.[37] Allied negotiators were pleased. Before signing the protocol though, they discussed the fate of the prison with Richard von Weizsäcker, then the governing mayor. Already angry that Hess was still imprisoned, von Weizsäcker nonetheless agreed that it would be best for the British to destroy the prison as quickly as possible and replace it with something more mundane. It was, he told Francis MacGinnis, "the least bad choice among evils." Von Weizsäcker added the barb that the demolition was "a commentary upon the Four Powers' past actions, as a sign of a guilty conscience."[38] With von Weizsäcker's agreement in hand, the Allies included provisions for the destruction of Spandau in the October 1982 protocol via a local German contractor. Though this provision was to remain a secret, it too leaked to the press within a brief time.[39] In 1984 Moscow hoped to preserve something of Spandau through a Soviet-made documentary film, but the Allies rejected this request, fearing a Soviet propaganda job on West German revanchism. Besides, the Soviets had not allowed Western camera crews earlier.[40]

After Hess's suicide, Spandau's demolition became awkward. The British had been unable throughout the 1980s to have West German demolition specialists reconnoiter the site before Hess's death thanks to the security-minded Soviets.[41] After the suicide, the British assumed control of the prison from the Americans (formally on August 24) but now the garden house and much of the Spandau complex were subjects of the SIB investigation into Hess's death. Seidl himself insisted on investigating the cottage and wanted it preserved. Mail poured in to the British and local German authorities arguing that the complex should not be destroyed. Many of the calls for preservation came from cranks, but some too came from local preservationists who saw in Spandau a surviving example of Prussian military architecture and argued (on that dubious basis) that the building should be saved.[42] Even the *Senat* requested to photograph the inside of the prison for historical purposes (the British allowed this) and requested the altar, pulpit, and organ from the prison chapel (this was denied).[43]

The West Berlin *Senat* stated publicly that the fate of the prison was a matter for the Allies to decide, and that "the *Senat* believes that controversy over the demolition of Spandau prison would damage the image of the city at home and abroad."[44] Privately, Governing Mayor Eberhard Diepgen complained to the Allied authorities that he was under increasing pressure to work for the prison's preservation and that the Allies had best destroy the complex as soon as possible despite the investigation. He told U.S. minister Harry Gilmore on August 24 that it was important to move quickly lest a public debate break out.[45] And by September 1, the British complained that "We are under strong and continuing pressure from the *Senat* to begin demolition without delay.... The longer we wait, the more difficult the situation will become," since pressure on Diepgen and the *Senat* to work for preservation was increasing daily.[46]

The garden cottage where Hess had hanged himself was the most immediate issue. It was placed under guard after Hess's suicide to prevent souvenir-stealing by the prison staff; then, it was demolished and burned along with the suicide cord and Hess's walking stick on September 18. Extensive photographs of the cottage were taken beforehand. The British were not entirely comfortable with the decision but noted that "Anyone who refuses to believe the SIB account... would be equally capable of believing, even if we showed him a Portacabin, that we had it constructed specially to fit our version of the facts."[47] From 11:00 P.M. on August 23 to 6:00 A.M. on August 24 the British Royal Engineers secured the Spandau complex with a two-meter tall fence. Everything was cleared from the main building by the end of August.[48] Even British Governor Le Tissier put on jeans and enjoyed tossing old furniture down the steps of the main building. The church organ and the pews were thrown through the broken windows of the makeshift chapel cell, smashing to pieces on the ground below.[49] Trucks hauled scrap wood and metal to Gatow Air Base where it was mixed with other scrap so as to "lose its identification with the prison before eventually going to the civilian sector."[50]

Hess's immediate possessions from the Nazi period, most notably the leather flight suit and fur-lined boots in which he flew to Scotland (but not the jacket and helmet), were similarly destroyed. Fifteen boxes of his more mundane possessions (thousands of letters, books, and family photographs) were delivered to the family after the warders, on Chernykh's insistence, wiped off, with toilet bowl cleaner, the inked Spandau prison stamps from the back of each document, photo and book.[51] On September 25 Le Tissier personally handed Andrea Hess and Seidl the original copy of Hess's suicide note.[52]

After studying bids, the British hired the German construction firm Hafermeister to perform the demolition. Part of the contract demanded that the firm make its best efforts to keep workers from stealing souvenirs. Before the contract was even announced, the firm received threats, and thanks to the need to clear the prison while conducting the SIB investigation, demolition was delayed. To accommodate Diepgen's calls for a demonstration that the prison would be destroyed, Le Tissier arranged as early as September 2 for one hundred British royal military engineers (disguised in the blue overalls of German workers) to start destroying the roof of the main building with axes. They did so, amidst taking souvenir photos of each other on the roof.[53] The full demolition began on September 21 with a wrecking ball smashing into what had once been the cell bloc of the Spandau prisoners. Truck after truck after truck then hauled the pulverized Spandau rubble to Gatow Air Base. Here the remains of the prison were poured into a great hole which was then filled in and planted with grass and trees.[54] The 110-year-old prison thus followed its inmates into the earth. The final meeting of the prison governors, the 2,102nd, took place on January 5, 1988, forty-one years and four months after the pronouncement of sentence at Nuremberg. On January 11, the original records of the prison – having been microfilmed – were burned in a bonfire in front of the prison governors. And on Friday, January 15 at 4:00 P.M., nearly five months after Hess's suicide, the prison governorship was officially dissolved.[55] The aftermath of Nuremberg had ended, more than forty-one years after the sentences were pronounced.

Within a year of the demolition, the British began construction on a shopping and recreation center for their troops at the site of Spandau Prison. It was christened Britannia Center, opened in September 1990, and the British used it for three and a half years. In November 1995 after German reunification and the end of Four-Power control in Berlin, the property reverted to the locals, who turned the complex into a general shopping area with a parking lot.[56] So it remains today.

What had it all meant? Did the imprisonment of the men sentenced at Nuremberg add to the meaning of their trial and sentencing? Or did the cumbersome nature of the prison, its location on the great Cold War divide, the long sentences served by prominent individuals, and the increasing political discourse on the prisoners themselves somehow detract from Nuremberg?

Because the Soviets were wrong on just about everything between 1917 and 1991 it is hard to imagine that they might have been right about anything. But maybe Andrei Vishinsky had a point in November 1945 when he raised his vodka glass to the Nuremberg judges and prosecutors and toasted the executions of the men yet to be tried. Perhaps all the men convicted at Nuremberg should have been executed. Gitta Sereny wrote that when Speer died in 1981 "I thought that his death was right and, in a terrible way, overdue; fate had given him thirty-five years after the Nuremberg trials, at which he should probably have been sentenced to death, as were others perhaps less guilty than he."[57] It is possible that before his death Speer admitted the truth of his enormous guilt to himself – it is also possible that he never really did. He certainly never admitted the worst in his best-selling books written after his release. His long avoidance of the truth is of great academic interest to historians, but at the same time it obscured the issue more than was ever desirable.

And Speer was the most subtle of the Nuremberg defendants. Raeder and Dönitz aimed to rehabilitate themselves, and each succeeded in doing so among their followers through their own exculpatory memoirs. Raeder had to turn down honors after his release from prison in Kiel and elsewhere. Dönitz received a hero's funeral when he died the year before Speer. Church bells greeted von Neurath's return to his home in Baden-Württemberg. And though no statues were erected in Hermann Göring's honor as the *Reichsmarschall* had predicted at Nuremberg, the memory of the man who sat beside him at Nuremberg, Rudolf Hess, is commemorated with an annual pilgrimage to the town of his burial, which attracts more people – and nauseates more people – with each passing year. The major war criminals hanged at Nuremberg, whose ashes were dumped into an obscure Bavarian river, received no such honors.

On the other hand the execution of each guilty defendant would have detracted from the meaning of the landmark trial. As a judicial proceeding, Nuremberg already had a great deal to criticize. The Communist insistence after October 1, 1946, that all the defendants should have hanged, came from a political culture with history's poorest track record for honest judicial proceedings. A blanket punishment of death would have left a more bitter legacy of victors' justice while suggesting, as did the Soviet war crimes trials, that Nuremberg was more about vengeance than justice and truth. Though the ways in which the Nuremberg justices arrived at their sentences was badly flawed, sentences, like guilt itself, were best varied. And the prison sentences, having been pronounced in October 1946, had to be served.

But it is hard to imagine a more difficult arrangement than Spandau. Though criminals convicted by the Four Powers had to remain in the custody of all four, the location of the prison was hastily thought out with no sense that the Four Powers could be stuck with their decisions for the next four decades. The breakdown of Four-Power control in Germany and the Allied insistence that Spandau's finances were a responsibility of Berliners meant that the prison venue would be impossible to change. The prison regulations of 1947 – a compromise between Soviet bitterness and British recognition that punishment reflected back onto the punisher – were a constant source of friction even after the death of the final prisoner. Security measures regarding visits, letters, food preparation, overall secrecy, and so forth, though valid enough in a prison holding men of such high profile, added to the mystique of Spandau as a house of horrors rather than a mundane place with increasingly mundane men living terribly mundane lives.

Spandau's tight security regulations were intended to make the inmates forgotten men. But prominent Nazis from one of history's most important trials could never be forgotten. The public thirst for news about them triggered security breaches. In a particularly comic case discovered in August 1986, two slow-witted British warders broke into the prison's "secure locker" and the prison safe one day and stole Hess's flight jacket and helmet, as well as his dentures, his cigarette case, pocket watch, and signet ring. They were apprehended in 1988 when they tried to sell the items to Wolf Rüdiger for DM 500,000. These items, which were to have been destroyed with the rest of Hess's flight clothing, went to the Hess family.[58] Other breaches were more serious. Warders, orderlies, and even tower guards made extra cash by snapping unauthorized photos and selling them to periodicals such as *Revue*, *Quick*, *Stern*, *Bunte*, and *Berliner Zeitung*.[59] U.S. prison governor Eugene Bird stole a trove of documents, tape recordings, and photographs from the prison, wrote a book based on them, and then became a public advocate for Hess. Some prisoners had secret channels via warders, orderlies, or pastors running to their sympathizers on the outside. Speer's were the most extensive – using them he concocted strategies for his exit from prison and for his rehabilitation. Funk and Dönitz had lines to their wives; von Neurath used Speer's lines of communication when he wished. Even Hess smuggled information in and out of the prison through Pastor Gabel. There was never enough security to seal the prisoners hermetically. Small wonder Chernykh complained to Planet in 1985 that it was really "too bad that the establishment had not been situated in East Berlin."[60]

Yet there was always too much security to convince the prisoners' advocates that their punishments were anything but politically inspired. As Winifred von Mackensen showed as early as 1950 when complaining about her father's treatment, even a forty-watt light bulb could trigger outrage if lit in a certain way. All families were angry that they could not see the prisoners as much as they wanted; that they could not write and receive more letters of greater length; that they could not speak freely during visits; that they could not bring food; that they could not have privacy during visits; and that they could not touch hands through the prison grate. These sorts of restrictions, furiously described by wives such as Erika Raeder, created fodder for the tabloid West German press. The prisoners became sympathetic figures to many Germans, thus growing political problems for the Western Allies.

Nothing illustrated the problem better than the argument over the deaths of prisoners. The Allies and Soviets feared that such men would become martyrs in death. On the other hand, the Four-Power arrangements of 1947 and 1954 designed to prevent the creation of shrines only increased the risk. Had the bodies of von Neurath and Raeder been cremated as per the Four-Power arrangement of 1947, the West Germans might never have forgiven their new allies. Had there really been a grotesque Spandau Prison graveyard, the bodies would have been ceremoniously reinterred one day. Luckily the Allies and the Soviets recognized the potential problem to the point where von Neurath, Raeder, and Funk were released before the ends of their sentences so that they could all hopefully die in obscurity. The Soviets would not repeat this generosity with Hess, who they argued was not worthy of an early release. They may have been right. But it may be the supreme irony of the prison that the most negotiated and most detailed death arrangement, designed to prevent the martyrdom of Hitler's deputy, blew up in the faces of all four powers.

Located at the fault line of the Cold War on the one hand and of bitter wartime memories on the other, Spandau was also poisoned throughout with East-West politics. The Allies tired of the Spandau arrangement almost before it began. But because the security of West Berlin depended on the sanctity of Four-Power agreements, the Allies could not risk moving the inmates to another facility in the West without Soviet agreement. And the Soviets, whose dominance of Eastern Europe depended on the legitimacy provided in part by Nuremberg, would never agree to have the prisoners beyond their purview, lest they be released or celebrated as heroes. In a sense, Soviet intransigence was not for the worst. Under pressure from Bonn after 1949, the Western powers emptied their own prisons in West Germany within the next several years. Most prisoners in the West never came close to serving their full sentences, and many such as Field Marshals Erich von Manstein and Albert Kesselring, lived to repair their battered reputations. At the very least, Soviet obstinacy meant that the Spandau prisoners would serve the sentences they received.

Yet the Soviets should never have truly expected that their sentences in war crimes trials would be taken seriously in the West. In the first place,

32. Members of the Soviet 6th Independent Motorized Rifle Brigade during the last guard change at Spandau Prison, August 1, 1987, seventeen days before Rudolf Hess's suicide. Photograph courtesy of United States Army.

the Soviets were not and could never be on the moral high ground. They foolishly included crimes in the Nuremberg indictment that they themselves committed. They held nearly ten thousand Germans prisoners ten years after the war after brief and questionable judicial proceedings. They released bona fide criminals such as Gestapo officer Friedrich Panzinger and Hitler's last army commander-in-chief Ferdinand Schörner to serve as spies and agents provocateurs in West Germany when it suited them. They were willing to trade Spandau's inmates to the West for a united Berlin under East German rule if such an arrangement could be managed. And beyond all of this, the U.S.S.R. was a regime built on terror with its own bloody history; its guns, tanks, and missiles were aimed at West Germany, and it threatened the security of more than two million Germans in West Berlin. Moscow's insistence that Germany's major war criminals serve out their entire sentences could never ring anything but hollow, whether the prisoners in question deserved to serve their full sentences or not. And over time the ring became more hollow still. Though Konrad Adenauer would do nothing for Speer in the shadow of the 1958 crisis in Berlin and the 1961 trial of Adolf Eichmann in Jerusalem, even Richard von Weizsäcker was calling for Hess's release by the end. Sadly the Allies failed to immunize themselves from this same problem. Perhaps Karl Dönitz deserved to be in jail for more than ten years.

But ten years was his sentence, and London's refusal to count his eighteen month pretrial custody toward the total smacked badly of political rather than judicial punishment. Those who carried Dönitz's coffin in January 1981 surely remembered it.

What then does Spandau mean? It means that high-profile national leaders, no matter how guilty they may be and regardless of the best efforts of their international judges and captors to try them appropriately, are political figures by their very nature. If they are not to be executed, then the political problem lasts the length of their punishment and perhaps even beyond. Trials are short. Prison sentences are long. Time will tell if the kinder prison regime received by contemporary war criminals will alleviate the problems encountered at Spandau. In viewing the bombastic funeral procession held for Slobodan Milosević in 2006, there is reason to think that it will not. In accepting the responsibility to punish notorious international criminals, the international community accepts a task of unknown proportions and unknown length especially since evidence against the accused becomes minimized over time by political advocates. It is best that this responsibility be accepted with open eyes and with thick skin. Hannah Arendt, in any event, was correct when she noted at Nuremberg that the crimes of history's worst men make impossible a proper punishment. If execution is insufficient, then prison is certainly so. The bar of international justice, strong though it may be, can never be strong enough to punish men whose crimes are of historic proportions. For in the end, it is before the bar of history that they all must stand.

APPENDIX

# Prison Regulations for Spandau Allied Prison

*Berlin-Spandau*, GERMANY

## PART I. AUTHORITIES

### 1. SUPREME EXECUTIVE AUTHORITY

In implementation of Directive 35 of the Allied Control Council, supreme executive authority over Spandau Allied Prison for the confinement of War Criminals sentenced to imprisonment by the International Military Tribunal is vested in the Allied Kommandatura Berlin.

### 2. HIGHER EXECUTIVE AUTHORITY

(i) The Legal Committee of the Allied Kommandatura Berlin is the Higher Executive Authority for the Spandau Allied Prison.

(ii) It is the responsibility of the Higher Executive Authority to direct the execution of sentences, and to supervise the carrying out of punishments and the administration of the Penal Institution, to recommend the appointment of the prison staff, and to inspect the Institution frequently enough to keep itself informed of all matters of importance including any that could give rise to a revision of these Prison Regulations.

### 3. EXECUTIVE AUTHORITY

(i) The Executive Authority shall be the Governorate of four officers acting by unanimous decision, each of the officers being appointed by the Supreme Executive Authority on the recommendation of the Higher Executive Authority, in such a manner that each Member of the Governorate is the delegate and representative of one of the Four Allied Powers. A member of the Governorate must be represented by a deputy during periods of absence from the Prison.

(ii) The Prison Governorate in deciding questions at their meetings will be guided by the rules of procedure of the Allied Kommandatura.

(iii) Any Governor may raise any question pertaining to the administration of the Prison, and may demand an immediate meeting of the Governorate to consider it.

(iv) In case of disagreement between the Governors, the Governorate will submit to the Legal Committee of the Allied Kommandatura a report setting out the divergent opinions.

(v) The Chairmanship of the Governorate shall change among its members in the same order and at the same time as the Chairmanship of the Kommandatura changes.

(vi) The Governorate is responsible for the direction and supervision of the entire service routine, and its members are superior to prison staff, employees and workers engaged in duties or work connected with the institution. The Governorate will jointly give necessary instructions to the External Military guard through the Guard Commander.[1]

(vii) The Governorate is responsible for the safe custody of all prisoners within the institution, and it is invested with powers, within the framework of these Regulations, to make supplementary rules for the control and management of the institution.

(viii) The Governorate shall conform to the orders and instructions issued from time to time by the Higher Executive Authority, and will report to the Chairman of that Authority without delay any extraordinary incidents occurring within the institution.

(ix) The Governorate may demand information and make suggestions in matters of medical service and religious welfare. Where any measure ordered by a medical officer, instructor or clergyman constitutes, in the opinion of the Governorate, a danger to the security of the institution, to the orderly administration thereof, or to the proper treatment of the prisoners therein, it shall have the power to revoke such measure.

## PART II. STAFF

### 4. MEDICAL OFFICERS

(i) A Medical Officer shall be appointed by each of the Four Allied Powers, and the Chairmanship among the Medical Officers shall follow the rules for that of the Governorate as given in paragraph 3 (v).

[1] As per agreement of February 12, 1947, each external military detachment guarding the prison was to consist of two officers, two sergeants, six corporals, and forty-four sentries. The detachment would work in two rotating twenty-four-hour shifts with the main tasks guarding the front gate and the six guard towers.

(ii) The Medical Officers shall be under the direct control of the Governorate for prison administrative purposes.

### 5. RELIGIOUS WELFARE

For religious welfare the Higher Executive Authority shall appoint suitable clergymen of the Allied or United Nations.

### 6. DISCIPLINARY STAFF

(i) Disciplinary staff shall consist of civilian warders belonging to the Four Allied Powers and their numbers shall be fixed on a numerical quadripartite basis.

(ii) Each nation will not necessarily be represented by an equal number of warders on each shift, but a quadripartite representation shall be maintained at all times.[2]

### 7. OFFICE AND DOMESTIC PRISON STAFF

Office and domestic staff employed inside the institution shall consist of male persons of the United Nations, whose past has been specially checked up for this purpose and warrants confidence.

### 8. GERMAN STAFF AND EMPLOYERS

While no German persons may be employed within the exterior walls of the prison, they will normally be engaged to perform domestic and other duties in the offices and officers' and staff billets and canteens which are outside the walls.

## PART III. ADMINISTRATIVE AND PENAL REGULATIONS

### 9. GENERAL

(i) WAR CRIMINALS shall be confined under guard in accordance with the sentence of the International Military Tribunal.

[2]The first warder rules of 1947 called for four teams of seven warders by day and five warders by night rotating on eight-hour shifts. By day and night, teams would consist of a chief warder and a deputy chief warder, both of the same nationality, plus two warders in the cell section and one warder at the main gate coming from the other three powers. By day, teams would also have two warders with escort duties. As of March 14, 1974 shifts were made up of three warders. These consisted of a duty chief warder, a warder in the cell bloc who was to observe the prisoner at all times, and a warder at the main gate. The duty descriptions from both periods are in AAPS, roll 1.

(ii) Prisoners will be called by their convict numbers and will never be addressed by name.

(iii) The prisoners will be kept in solitary confinement (separate, isolated cells) though work, religious services and walks shall be communally conducted. Prisoners shall neither talk with one another nor communicate with each other or others unless specifically authorized by the Governorate. The Governorate will establish a daily work timetable but in principle there shall be work every day except Sundays and general German holidays.[3]

## 10. DISCIPLINE

(i) All kinds of non-official intercourse between prison staff or employees on the one hand and prisoners on the other is strictly forbidden.

(ii) The greatest reserve shall be shown towards relatives and friends of prisoners as well as to released prisoners and their relatives and friends. To have any business transaction with them is a serious offense, and will be punished as a violation of a Military Government Order.

(iii) Staff or employees may not derive advantage in any way either from their official position or from their connection with the institution. They will not employ the services of prisoners for their own private purposes.

(iv) Personal circumstances and matters concerning prisoners coming to the knowledge of the staff or employees in the course of their official duties may not be divulged to any person other than the Executive Authority. Only the Executive Authority may, on well-founded application, impart information about prisoners to a third party.

(v) In the treatment of prisoners, institution staff will show firmness, calmness and determination.

## 11. SECURITY

(i) The Executive Authority will arrange duties in such a manner that security, discipline and order in the prison are at all times assured.

(ii) It is the duty of any employee of the institution detecting an apparent danger to the security of the institution, to report this immediately to the Executive Authority.

[3] As per Four-Power agreement of April 29, 1954. "The prisoners will be allowed to converse among themselves during work and during exercise." Revised regulations of 1954, AAPS, roll 1.

(iii) Entrance to courts, buildings and cells as well as to other rooms in the institution shall always be kept locked except as may be permitted by supplementary rules and regulations.

(iv) Keys, weapons and service clothing when not in use, will be kept under safe lock and key. Keys and weapons will be registered and signed for on each occasion they are issued. Losses will be reported immediately, and a full report in writing to the Directorate of the circumstances under which a loss occurred must be rendered within twenty-four hours.

(v) Articles which might facilitate escape will not be permitted to come under the control of prisoners when not under direct supervision.

(vi) No prisoner will enter the courts unless under adequate guard by warders. Vision must be unhindered and no articles will be left so near to walls as to facilitate escape.

(vii) Spectacles, etc., will be taken from prisoners before lights-out at night.

(viii) All foodstuffs for inmates will be provided from Allied Military sources, and will be inspected daily by a medical officer. The kitchen will be inspected frequently by the chief warder on duty, and all meals will be served in cells under the supervision of warders. The use of a spoon only is permitted; knives and forks will not be allowed.

(ix) Only members of the Supreme Executive Authority, the Higher Executive Authority, and the Governorate, and the medical officers, warders and other permanent institution staff and employees will be permitted to enter and leave the prison freely, for which purpose they will be issued with a permanent pass.

(x) Special permits for official visitors may be issued by the Governorate upon orders of the Commandants, the Deputy Commandants, or the Legal Committee of the Allied Kommandatura or they may be issued by the Governorate upon the written request of a Commandant of a Sector, his Deputy in the Allied Kommandatura or a member of the Legal Committee of the Allied Kommandatura. All such permits will be registered and retained after use by the Governorate, and the visitor will conform to all orders issued by the member of the Governorate on duty at the time of the visit.

(xi) By night no person shall enter the institution except members of the Governorate or permanent prison staff specifically authorized by the Governorate.

(xii) No vehicles except those bringing or fetching loads of materials will enter the prison gate. Other vehicles will park outside.

(xiii) Adequate fire fighting appliances will be maintained in good condition.

(xiv) Prisoners, their belongings and their cells may be searched at any time. Cells will be thoroughly searched at least twice daily and window bars will be tested by tapping each morning and evening. Chief warders will maintain a log of all examinations and searches carried out.

(xv) Prisoners will be under the close supervision of warders at all times by day and they will be observed through the trap door at frequent intervals throughout the night.

## 12. EXECUTION OF SENTENCE

(i) *Admission.* On admission a prisoner will strip naked and his body will be carefully searched. Four warders will carry out the search which will be in the presence of the Governorate but will not be in the sight of other prisoners. All parts of the body including the anus will be covered in the search for articles which might be smuggled into the institution. After the search the prisoner will bath[e] himself and cleanse his body thoroughly and dress in regulation prison clothes.

(ii) *Medical Examination.* Prisoners will be medically examined in the course of admission formalities or immediately afterwards, and the Medical Officer will see each prisoner daily thereafter. If and when dental treatment is found necessary, the Medical Officer will arrange to call in a Dental Officer of one of the Four Allied Powers.

(iii) *Personal Records.* The personal records of each prisoner will be entered up in German, and will begin with the documents relating to his commitment. They will contain all records, remarks, reports, orders and other documents referring to the prisoner. They will be open to inspection by the Supreme Executive Authority and by the Higher Executive Authority. True copies will be maintained in the English, French and Russian languages.

(iv) *Conduct of Prisoners.*

(1) The prisoner will subject himself unconditionally to the discipline of the institute, and will observe all regulations and rules of conduct as may from time to time be laid down. A copy of the rules of conduct will be exhibited in each cell.

(2) Prisoners will show respect to officers and to warders of the institution as well as to members of superior Authorities. They will obey all orders and instructions without question, even if they consider them unjustified. They will truthfully answer all questions put to them. A prisoner will speak to an officer or warder only if required to do so or if he wishes to bring forward a request.

(3) Discipline in the institution includes upright posture of the prisoner. The prisoner will salute an officer, official or warder by standing at

attention, or by passing him in a straight posture. The prisoner will remove his cap at the same time.

(v) *Daily Programme.*

(1) Prisoners will rigidly adhere to the daily programme.[4]

(2) At Reveille the prisoner will rise at once, dress himself and put his bed in order. He will then strip to the waist and wash himself thoroughly, clean his teeth and rinse his mouth.

(3) Clothes, shoes or boots, as well as his cell and its furniture, will be cleaned by him at prescribed times and in the prescribed manner.

(4) A prisoner will not show himself at the window.

(vi) *Silence Regulations.*

(1) Noise, such as yelling, shouting, whistling, singing and music-making is prohibited.

(2) Prisoners will not talk or communicate with one another or with others without special permission from the Governorate.

[4] In 1947, the program was as follows as amended slightly in 1954, 1956, 1957, 1959, 1960, 1961 (schedules in AAPS, roll 1):

| | |
|---|---|
| 1. Rising | 6:00 |
| 2. Washing, making up of beds, cleaning of cells, issue of eyeglasses | 6:00–6:45 |
| 3. Breakfast | 6:45–7:30 |
| 4. Cleaning of cells and cell bloc | 7:30–8:00 |
| 5. Work | 8:00–11:45 |
| 6. Body search, washing of hands | 11:45–12:00 |
| 7. Mid-day meal, shaving | 12:00–12:45 |
| 8. Rest, read, write, smoke (Barber Monday, Wednesday, Friday) | 12:45–14:00 |
| 9. Work | 14:00–16:45 |
| 10. Body search, washing of hands | 16:45–17:00 |
| 11. Evening meal, exchange library books | 17:00–17:45 |
| 11. Rest, read, write, smoke | 17:45–22:00 |
| 12. Preparation for sleep, removal of eyeglasses | 21:45–22:00 |
| 13. Lights out | 22:00 |

(as per agreement of April 29, 1954 prisoners could have cell light extinguished any time after 18:45)

| | |
|---|---|
| Saturdays and Sundays: No work, walk in prison garden | 15:30–16:00 |
| Saturday: Thorough cleaning of cells and cell bloc | 8:00–10:30 |
| Saturday: Bath, shave, haircut | 10:30–11:45 |
| Saturday: Church service, rest, read, write, smoke | 14:00–16:45 |
| Sunday: Exercise, rest, read, write, smoke | 8:00–16:45 |

In the February 1968 revision, Hess was allowed to rest in his cell or work in the garden from 9:30 to 10:00, then take exercise from 10:00 to 11:00; exercise from 14:30 to 15:00, then rest in his cell or work in the garden from 15:00 to 16:30. In the revision of March 1970, his cell bloc work consisted of tidying his cell from 8:30 to 9:30, rest or light work in the garden from 9:30 to 10:30, then exercise in the garden from 10:30 to 11:30. Weekday afternoons consisted of exercise in the garden from 14:30 to 15:30, and rest or light work in the garden from 15:30 to 16:30. The revision of April 1978 included reveille (officially) at 7:00; exercise in the garden from 9:15 to 11:15; rest, reading, writing, or television from 12:30 to 14:15; and exercise in the garden from 14:15 to 16:15. In this revision, he was thus permitted four hours exercise per day.

(vii) *Unauthorized Possessions.*
A prisoner may not have in his possession any article other than those the rules permit him to retain. If he finds anything he must immediately hand it to the warder.

(viii) *Care of Equipment, Clothing, etc.*
(1) Equipment, clothing, materials and any institution property will be carefully treated and handled by the prisoner and may only be used for their proper purpose. He may not pass on any article in his possession to other prisoners. Unauthorized handling of fire or light is forbidden.
(2) The prisoner is liable for any damage caused by him deliberately or by neglect.

(ix) *Compulsory Reporting.*
The prisoner will immediately report to a warder any serious illness, injury, skin eruption or vermin. Any knowledge of intended self-inflicted injury or suicide, of aggression, escape, or conspiracy connected with disobedience or mutiny, will be immediately reported to a warder.

(x) *Interviews with the Governorate.*
A prisoner may apply for an interview with the Governorate at fixed times or, in urgent cases, outside such times. Such permission will be granted unless the Governorate has special reasons to the contrary.

(xi) *Personal Belongings.*
(1) The Prisoner's personal belongings will be withheld from him for the time of his detention.
(2) Subject to approval of the Governorate, certain articles of his belongings may be left with the prisoner, including the picture of one or more of his family or relatives.

(xii) *Prison Diet.*
Prisoners will receive food of the same calorific value as normal German prison fare. Extra food may be granted only when prescribed by the Medical Officer on account of illness or poor physical condition.[5]

(xiii) *Work.*
(1) All prisoners will work to the best of their ability and complete within the prescribed time all tasks allotted to them. When allotting work,

[5]By tentative agreement by the prison governors of December 9, 1947, the prisoners were to be fed according to Berlin Ration Card No. 2 (1167 grams, 2202 Calories of food) when they did physical work in the prison garden and according to Berlin Ration Card No. 3 (1032 grams, 1887 Calories) when they did not in conformity with Berlin Kommandatura Order (47) 7 of January 14, 1947. See Henry Frank, U.S. governor Spandau Prison, to Legal Committee, Allied Kommandatura, December 9, 1947, AAPS, roll 1.

consideration will be given to the prisoner's physical strength and condition, abilities and age.
(2) There will be no work on Sundays or on Holidays authorized by the Allied Kommandatura, except necessary domestic duties or work which cannot be postponed.

## 13. HYGIENE

A high standard of hygiene will be maintained throughout the institution. Prisoners will be required to take a hot bath once weekly. They will be shaved by the institution barber and their hair and beards will be cut as often as necessary.

## 14. SPIRITUAL AND MORAL MATTERS

(i) *Prison Library*. The institution will be provided with a suitable library, and in the distribution of books the character and aims of the prisoner, and his reasonable preferences and wishes will be taken into consideration.[6]

Books used by prisoners suffering from contagious diseases will not be issued to other prisoners.

(ii) Other occupations may be allowed to prisoners with the approval of the Governorate on each particular occasion.

(iii) *Religion*. Religious books will be made available for the use of prisoners, and a prisoner may, if he wishes, receive the administration of a priest of his faith. The Governorate will make reasonable provision for the prisoners to practice suitable religious rites within the prison.[7]

## 15. MEDICAL CARE

(i) Medical Officers will pay constant attention to incidents and conditions which may affect the general state of health in the institution, and they will report to the Governorate any apparent danger to the hygiene of the institution.

(ii) The bodily and mental condition of the prisoners during confinement is to be kept constantly under observation.

[6] As per Four-Power agreement of April 29, 1954 the prison library was supplemented by four daily newspapers, each governor selecting one. Revised regulations of 1954, AAPS, roll 1.

[7] As per Four-Power agreement of April 29, 1954 the Governors were to allow more frequent recorded classical music in the prison chapel. Revised regulations of 1954, AAPS, roll 1.

(iii) On the advice of a Medical Officer the Governorate may deviate from the Regulations in carrying out the sentence in order to preserve a prisoner's health.

(iv) Prisoners will be weighed every two weeks and their weights recorded.

(v) Medical orders will be strictly obeyed, and all medicines will be taken by a prisoner under the supervision of the Medical Officer or his Medical Orderly when so directed.

(vi) Poison and dangerous drugs will be kept permanently under lock and key when not in use. This is the responsibility of the Medical Officer on duty at the time.

(vii) A specialist may be called in if the Medical Officers of the institution consider the case warrants such course.

(viii) Cases of serious physical or mental sickness, attempts to commit suicide or suspicion of serious sickness will be reported forthwith to the Governorate.

(ix) In cases of dangerous illness the Governorate should inform the clergyman of the prisoner's faith. The prisoner's next-of-kin shall also be informed, and if necessary, by telegram. The request of a prisoner that other persons should be informed shall be granted as far as the Governorate may consider proper.[8]

## 16. INTERCOURSE WITH THE OUTSIDE WORLD

(i) *Private Visits.*

(1) A prisoner will be permitted to receive one visitor in each period of two calendar months unless the Governorate withdraws this privilege for sufficient reason. The Governorate shall determine the day and time of each visit.

(2) The Governorate shall determine which persons shall be permitted to visit a prisoner.

(3) Not more than one visitor or one visitor accompanied by one child under the age of 16 years will be permitted to visit a prisoner at one time. It is forbidden to visit several prisoners at the same time.

[8] As per Four-Power agreement of April 29, 1954. "In cases where the health of the prisoner requires complicated treatment which cannot be carried out satisfactorily in the prison itself, the patient may be transferred for a specific period of time to the hospital which is nearest to the prison and which is under the jurisdiction of one of the Occupying Powers of Germany. This may be done by agreement of the four Governors of the prison.... The four Governors of the prison will continue to carry the responsibility for guarding the prisoner while in transit to and from the hospital and during his stay in the hospital and should take all necessary measures to this end." Revised regulations of 1954, AAPS, roll 1.

(4) Children of the prisoner under the age of 16 years shall be admitted only when accompanied by an adult who shall be responsible for seeing that the child complies with all the regulations as to behavior of visitors. Other persons under 16 years will not be admitted.
(5) Additional private visits in connection with urgent family affairs may be authorized by the Governorate without observing the fixed interval.[9]
(6) If a person applies for permission to visit a prisoner the latter shall be asked whether he wishes to see such person.
(7) If the prisoner is ill the opinion of the Medical Officer will be sought before a visit is permitted.
(8) The duration of each visit shall be fifteen minutes or such longer time as the Governorate may allow.[10]
(9) Special rooms and waiting rooms will be prepared for visitors and suitably furnished. The erection of separation devices in the case of a particular prisoner, lies in the discretion of the Governorate.[11]
(10) Visitors shall be admitted to the prisoner's cell only in case of serious illness.
(11) Conversations between visitors and prisoners shall be at all times in the presence of a warder or warders and a representative of each of the four Governors.[12]
(12) Visitors will be instructed how to behave during visits and be warned that conversations with prisoners will be in the German language unless there are valid reasons to the contrary. If another language is used it must be one known by the representative of the Governors. A suitable interpreter may be called in with the approval of the Governorate.
(13) Communications by signs, gestures and other means which cannot be interpreted are forbidden.
(14) All visitors will be subject to search of the outside garments, and handbags or other containers will be left in the waiting rooms.

[9] As per Four-Power agreement of April 29, 1954. "[In] addition to the visits by relatives now permitted, visits [are allowed by] . . . a lawyer whose name the prisoner has notified to the Governorate, at the prisoner's own request and with the concurrence of the Governorate [and] any other person . . . if the prisoner makes a request for the visit in place of a normal visit by a relative [and] if the Governorate does not object to the visit on grounds of security." Revised regulations of 1954, AAPS, roll 1.

[10] As per Allied-Soviet agreement in October 1952: Prisoners were allowed to receive one visit each month for a duration of thirty minutes. Semichastnov to Kirkpatrick, October 4, 1952, AAPS, roll 1.

[11] As per Four-Power agreement of April 29, 1954: "The grilles in the visitor's room which hinder vision between the prisoner and visitor shall not be used." Revised regulations of 1954, AAPS, roll 1.

[12] As per Four-Power agreement of April 29, 1954: "[C]ensorship during visits [will] take into account that the prisoner and his visitor may discuss matters relating to his family and his own health." Revised regulations of 1954, AAPS, roll 1.

(15) Prisoners shall not be permitted to receive anything from or to hand anything to a visitor without the approval of the Governorate.

(16) Rules as to the conduct of visitors during visits, written in block letters in German shall be posted up in the Visitors' Room and visitors' attention shall be specifically directed to these rules on the occasion of each visit. If the visitor is unable to read the rules they shall be read to him or her in a language which he or she understands. These rules shall contain a provision that any person violating any rule will be prosecuted for violation of a Military Government Order and may in consequence be placed under arrest for this purpose on the order of the Governorate. If the rules for visitors are violated in any way the visit will be broken off immediately.

(17) Each visitor will record his or her name in the Visitors' book, and the visit will be recorded in the prisoner's personal file.[13]

(ii) *Mail.*

(1) A prisoner will be permitted to write and receive not more than one letter every four weeks, unless the Governorate, for sufficient reason, withdraws this privilege. In exceptional cases the Governorate may allow the writing of one additional letter.[14]

(2) All letters shall be written in German. Exceptions are allowed only with permission of the Governorate. Letters must be legible and not in cipher or shorthand. Letters shall not consist of more than one official sheet of note paper of four pages.

(3) Letters shall be handed over by the prisoner for despatch in an open envelope.

(4) The prisoner may at the discretion of the Governorate be allowed to receive letters at the same intervals at which he may write them.

(5) The Governorate will supervise all correspondence of prisoners. Copies of all correspondence to and from prisoners will be kept in their personal files.

(6) Marginal notes should not be made on letters nor should any parts of them be deleted. All incoming correspondence shall be submitted to the Governorate unopened.[15]

[13] As per Four-Power agreement of April 29, 1954: "[Prisoners are] allowed an extra visit from his relatives at Christmas time." Revised regulations of 1954, AAPS, roll 1.

[14] As per Allied-Soviet agreement in October 1952: Prisoners were allowed to write and receive one letter per week. Semichastnov to Kirkpatrick, October 4, 1952, AAPS, roll 1. The Soviets agreed in June 1986 to allow two letters sent and received per week, but never agreed to telephone calls. See Minutes of the Governors' Meeting, May 23, 1986, AAPS, roll 9.

[15] As per Four-Power agreement of April 29, 1954: "[Prisoners may] in accordance with the agreement of the four Governors of the prison ... correspond on legal matters with the lawyer whose name he shall have notified to the Governorate." Also: "Censorship [will] take into account that the prisoner is permitted to write concerning his health, legal matters, and matters concerning his family." Revised regulations of 1954, AAPS, roll 1.

(7) The Governorate may withhold a letter even though the conditions governing correspondence are otherwise fulfilled if it considers there has been an abuse of the letter-writing privilege. Any such action of the Institution shall be made known to the prisoner, and the Governorate may permit the prisoner to write another letter in place of the one impounded. The Governorate may make known or hand to the prisoner unobjectionable parts of an in-coming letter that has been withheld.

(8) Whether and to what extent mentally deranged prisoners may be allowed to correspond or to receive correspondence will be decided by the Governorate in consultation with the Medical Officers.

## 17. HOUSE PUNISHMENTS

(i) The Governorate may inflict house punishment upon prisoners who willfully violate the institution rules or regulations. This may take the form of a warning in the cases of less serious offenses. Permissible house punishments are: –

(1) Withdrawal of privileges, including those of reading or writing or both for a period to be decided by the Governorate.

(2) Cutting off lighting in the cell for a period of not more than four weeks.

(3) Exclusion from open air exercise for not longer than two weeks.

(4) Reduction of food for not longer than two weeks.

(5) The prisoner may be deprived of furniture and/or clothing.

(6) The light may be kept on continuously in his cell and the prisoner may be fettered if this is considered necessary. At open air exercise a fettered prisoner shall be kept apart from the other prisoners, with whom he may not communicate in any way. Fetters may be attached to the hands or feet, but a different kind of fettering may be ordered in agreement with Medical Officers in special cases.

(ii) The Medical Officer shall visit a prisoner placed in fetters forthwith and thereafter each day. His visits and remarks shall be recorded in a report.

(iii) Several kinds of punishment may be combined into one.

(iv) Reduction of food consists either in depriving the prisoner of one of the three meals in turn or in restricting his food to bread and water.

(v) When punishment combines a hard bed and bread and water diet this punishment shall be lifted on the fourth and eighth day and thereafter every day.

(vi) When punishments are for a limited period, at least one week should intervene before the same punishment is repeated.

(vii) Punishment shall not be imposed if all four medical officers consider the health of the prisoner to be endangered thereby.

(viii) The imposition of a punishment will be entered in a special Punishment Book and recorded in the file of the prisoner. Every entry will be initialed by all four Governors.

## PART IV. ESCAPES AND ATTEMPTS TO ESCAPE

### 18. ACTION

(i) The escaped prisoner shall be pursued energetically and without delay.

(ii) The Governorate will immediately notify the German Police Headquarters and the local Police Station by telephone. Each Governor will immediately notify his Commandant and his Public Safety and Legal Branches. Written reports to the Supreme Executive Authority will follow forthwith with full personal description of the escaped prisoner.

(iii) An inquiry into the escape shall be opened immediately by the Governorate who will submit a full written report together with its findings to the Higher Executive Authority.

## PART V. USE OF FORCE AND THE CARRYING AND USE OF FIREARMS BY WARDERS AND MILITARY GUARDS

### 19. USE OF FORCE

Warders and Military Guards will not strike or lay hands on a prisoner unless it be in self-defense, necessary to prevent escape, or serious injury to person or property be threatened. Only the amount of force necessary to overpower the prisoner should then be used.

### 20. CARRYING OF TRUNCHEONS AND FIREARMS

(i) The carrying of firearms by warders within the prison is forbidden, but truncheons only will be carried at all times when on duty.

(ii) Only with the special approval of the Governorate will firearms be carried when escorting prisoners at exercise.

(iii) Military guards when on duty will always carry firearms.

### 21. USE OF FIREARMS

(i) The use of firearms will only be resorted to when absolutely necessary in self-defense or where serious injury to the person is threatened, or when the escape of a prisoner cannot be prevented by other means. When firing, the object will be to disable the prisoner to prevent his escape.

(ii) *Reporting.*

(1) Any case of force being used will be immediately reported to the Chairman of the Governorate.

(2) Every case of firearms being used will be immediately reported to the Chairman of the Governorate, who will at once report the incident to the Chairman of the Higher Executive Authority. The Governorate will thereupon carry out an Enquiry, and on completion will submit all papers together with the findings to the Higher Executive Authority.

22. Anything forbidden by these rules shall be allowed by the Governorate only with the previous written permission of the Higher Executive Authority.[16]

[16] As per Four-Power agreement of April 29, 1954: "In case of the death of one of the major war criminals, the body of the deceased must be buried in the territory of Spandau prison. The burial shall take place in accordance with the normal religious procedures of the deceased prisoner's faith and in the presence of his near relatives if they wish to be present. Thereafter his near relatives will be allowed by the Governorate reasonable opportunities to visit the grave in accordance with the procedure which will be agreed upon by the four Governors of the prison." Revised regulations of 1954, AAPS, roll 1.

# Notes

## INTRODUCTION

1. Darold Keane (U.S. governor, Spandau Prison) to Donald Koblitz (U.S. legal adviser, U.S. Mission Berlin), April 11, 1989, National Archives and Records Administration, College Park, Maryland [hereafter NARA], Record Group [hereafter RG] 84, Entry 1006-A, Box 1, Folder: Hess/Spandau – Theft/Archives/Death.
2. Memorandum by Koblitz and attachment, August 11, 1986, NARA, RG 84, Entry 1006-A, Box 2, Folder: 1986.
3. Spandau Allied Prison, June 29, 1983, unnumbered memorandum, NARA, RG 84, Germany, Berlin Mission, Records Relating to Spandau Prison, 1947–1987 (Archives of the Allied Prison Spandau) [hereafter AAPS], Microfilm Publication Number A3352, roll 1.
4. Agreement signed by Wolf Rüdiger Hess for his family on October 4, 1982, and the four governors on the 8th, AAPS, roll 1. Explained in Chapter 6 in this book.
5. Protocol, October 1, 1982, meeting between Nelson C. Ledsky (U.S. minister Berlin), Francis R. MacGinnis (British minister Berlin), P. H. Gaschignard (French minister Berlin), V. A. Kopteltsev (U.S.S.R. Embassy, East Berlin), AAPS, roll 1.
6. U.S. Mission Berlin (James Williams, political adviser) to secretary of state, No. 2861, August 18, 1987, NARA, RG 84, Entry 1006, Box 7, Folder: Spandau General, 1987.
7. Michael Burton (British minister Berlin) to Jean-Marc Voelckel (French minister Berlin) and Harry Gilmore (U.S. minister Berlin), No. 391, September 1, 1987, NARA, RG 84, Entry 1006, Box 3, Folder: Hess and Spandau 1987.
8. U.S. Mission Berlin (Gilmore) to secretary of state, No. 3046, September 4, 1987; U.S. Mission Berlin (Williams) to secretary of state, No. 2909, August 21, 1987, both in NARA, RG 84, Entry 1006, Box 7, Folder: Spandau: General, 1987; U.S. Mission Berlin (Gilmore) to secretary of state, No. 2944, August 25, 1987, NARA, RG 84, Entry 1006, Box 6, Folder: Hess and Spandau 1987, Suicide.
9. 2076th Meeting of the Directors of Allied Prison Spandau, August 20, 1987, AAPS, roll 9.
10. 2079th Meeting of the Directors of Allied Prison Spandau, August 25, 1987, AAPS, roll 9.
11. U.S. Mission Berlin (Gilmore) to secretary of state, No. 3160, September 16, 1987, NARA, RG 84, Entry 1006, Box 7, Folder: Rudolf Hess, Suicide 8-17-87; U.S. Mission Berlin (Gilmore) to secretary of state, No. 3578, October 26, 1987, NARA, RG 84, Entry 1006-A, Box 1, Folder: Hess/Spandau – Theft/Archives/Death.
12. The best journalistic account is Jack Fishman, *Long Knives and Short Memories: Lives and Crimes of the 7 Nazi Leaders Sentenced at Nuremberg* (New York: Richardson and Steirman, 1987 [1986]). The best memoir account is Tony Le Tissier, *Farewell to Spandau* (Leatherhead: Ashford, Buchnan and Enright, 1994).
13. Bundesarchiv Koblenz [hereafter BA-K], NL 1340.

14. Albert Speer, *Spandauer Tagebücher* (Frankfurt am Main: Ullstein, 1975). English-language version is *Spandau: The Secret Diaries*, trans. Richard Winston and Clara Winston (New York: Macmillan, 1976) [hereafter *SSD*].
15. Cited throughout as AAPS. NARA, RG 84, Germany, Berlin Mission, Records Relating to Spandau Prison, 1947–1987 (Archives of the Allied Prison Spandau), Microfilm Publication Number A3352.
16. Specifically these records are in NARA, RG 84, Entry 1006, Germany, Berlin Mission, Political Section, Hess Files (Group 50) and NARA, RG 84, Entry 1006-A, Germany, Berlin Mission, Political Section, Hess Files (Group 18).
17. See especially the pioneering work by Norbert Frei, *Vergangenheitspolitik: Die Anfänge der Bundesrepublik und die NS-Vergangenheit* (Munich: Beck, 1996) and Jeffrey Herf, *Divided Memory: The Nazi Past in the Two Germanys* (Cambridge, MA: Harvard University Press, 1996).
18. The most recent survey is Mary Nolan, "Germans as Victims During the Second World War: Air Wars, Memory Wars," *Central European History* 38, No. 1 (2005): 7–40. See also Robert Moeller, *War Stories: The Search for a Usable Past in the Federal Republic of Germany* (Berkeley: University of California Press, 2001); Peter Reichel, *Vergangenheitsbewältigung in Deutschland: Die Auseinandersetzung mit der NS-Diktatur von 1945 bis heute* (Munich: Beck, 2001); Bill Niven, *Facing the Nazi Past: United Germany and the Legacy of the Third Reich* (London: Routledge, 2002).
19. For the broader aims of the prosecution see Donald Bloxham, *Genocide on Trial: War Crimes Trials and the Formation of Holocaust History and Memory* (New York: Oxford University Press, 2001).
20. The British Channel Islands notwithstanding. See Madeleine Bunting, *The Model Occupation: The Channel Islands under German Rule, 1940–1945* (London: Harper Collins, 1996); Asa Briggs, *The Channel Islands: Occupation and Liberation* (London: B. T. Batsford, Ltd., 1995).
21. Mark Connelly, *We Can Take It!: Britain and the Memory of the Second World War* (New York: Longman, 2004).
22. See, for example, Sarah Farmer, *Martyred Village: Commemorating the 1944 Massacre at Oradour-Sur-Glane* (Berkeley: University of California Press, 1999); Claudia Moisel, *Frankreich und die deutschen Kriegsverbrecher: Politik und Praxis der Strafverfolgung nach dem zweiten Weltkrieg* (Göttingen: Wallstein, 2004).
23. George Ginsburgs, *Moscow's Road to Nuremberg: The Soviet Background of the Trial* (The Hague: Martinus Nijhoff, 1996), pp. 37–41.
24. Arieh J. Kochavi, "The Moscow Declaration, the Kharkov Trial and the Question of Policy towards War Criminals in the Second World War," *History* 76, No. 3 (1991): 401–17; Alexander Victor Prusin, "'Fascist Criminals to the Gallows!': The Holocaust and Soviet War Crimes Trials, December 1945–February 1946," *Holocaust and Genocide Studies* 17, No. 1 (2003): 1–30.
25. See the Russian essays from 1985 in George Ginsburgs and V. N. Kudriavtsev, eds. *The Nuremberg Trial and International Law* (Boston: Martinus Nijhoff, 1990).
26. For discussions on truth commissions as opposed to trials, see A. James McAdams, ed., *Transitional Justice and the Rule of Law in New Democracies* (Notre Dame, IN: University of Notre Dame Press, 1997).
27. Hannah Arendt, *Eichmann in Jerusalem: A Report on the Banality of Evil* (New York: Viking, 1963). For elaboration on these points see Mark Osiel, *Mass Atrocity, Collective Memory, and the Law* (New Brunswick, NJ: Transaction, 1997).
28. Lawrence Douglas, *The Memory of Judgment: Making Law and History in the Trials of the Holocaust* (New Haven, CT: Yale University Press, 2001).
29. Bloxham, *Genocide on Trial*, passim.
30. For these British considerations see Arieh J. Kochavi, *Prelude to Nuremberg: Allied War Crimes Policy and the Question of Punishment* (Chapel Hill: University of North Carolina Press, 1998), pp. 73–80.
31. Quoted in Osiel, *Mass Atrocity*, p. 39. Priebke was extradited to Italy in 1995, found guilty without punishment in 1996, received a fifteen-year sentence reduced to five years in a subsequent trial in 1997, and then received a life sentence in 1998 after his appeal.

32. Quoted in Gary Jonathan Bass, *Stay the Hand of Vengeance: The Politics of War Crimes Tribunals* (Princeton, NJ: Princeton University Press, 2000), p. 13.
33. G. M. Gilbert, *Nuremberg Diary* (New York: Farrar, Strauss & Co., 1947), p. 70.
34. An introduction to the larger problems is Bass, *Vengeance*.
35. See Ian Buruma, *The Wages of Guilt: Memories of War in Germany and Japan* (New York: Farrar, Strauss, and Giraux, 1994).
36. Francis O. Wilcox to Acting Secretary of State Christian Herter, June 17, 1960, NARA, RG 59, Entry 1494-I, Lot File 62 D 205, Box 88.
37. Bass, *Vengeance*, pp. 271 ff.
38. On Bormann, see Richard Overy, *Interrogations: The Nazi Elite in Allied Hands, 1945* (New York: Viking, 2001), pp. 93–114. On Müller, see Timothy Naftali, Norman J. W. Goda, Richard Breitman, and Robert Wolfe, "The Mystery of Heinrich Müller: New Evidence from the CIA," *Holocaust and Genocide Studies* 15, No. 3 (2001): 453–67.
39. For legal background see Bradley F. Smith, *The Road to Nuremberg* (New York: Basic Books, 1981). For diplomatic background, see Kochavi, *Prelude to Nuremberg*. For earlier failed efforts at justice, see Bass, *Vengeance*, pp. 3–146.
40. For the Charter of the International Military Tribunal, see International Military Tribunal, *Trial of the Major War Criminals before the International Military Tribunal, Nuremberg, 14 November 1945–1 October 1946*, 42 vols. (Nuremberg: International Military Tribunal, 1949) [hereafter *TMWC*], v. 1, pp. 10–16. For the indictment, see *TMWC*, v. 1, pp. 27ff.
41. For considerations of the Tribunal on Count IV see Bloxham, *Genocide on Trial*, pp. 18–20, 63–64; Michael Marrus, "The Holocaust at Nuremberg," *Yad Vashem Studies* 26 (1998): 5–41; Bradley F. Smith, *Reaching Judgment at Nuremberg* (New York: Basic Books, 1977), pp. 50–51, 132–39, 233 ff, 258 ff; Telford Taylor, *Anatomy of the Nuremberg Trials: A Personal Memoir* (New York: Knopf, 1992), pp. 549–53, 582–83. A bevy of articles in contemporary legal journals dealing with the ex post facto argument are cited in Norman Tuturow, ed., *War Crimes, War Criminals, and War Crimes Trials: An Annotated Bibliography and Source Book* (New York: Greenwood, 1986).
42. Drexel Sprecher, *Inside the Nuremberg Trial: A Prosecutor's Comprehensive Account*, 2 vols. (Lanham, MD: University Press of America, 1999), v. 1, p. 102; v. 2, pp. 1113–23.
43. Jochen P. Laufer and Georgij P. Kynin, *Die UdSSR und die deutsche Frage, 1941–1948: Dokumente aus dem Archive für Außenpolitik der Russischen Föderation*, v. 2 (Berlin: Duncker und Humblot, 2004), p. 679, n. 151 [hereafter *UdSSR* with document number].
44. Sprecher, *Inside the Nuremberg Trial*, v. 1, p. 44.
45. Considerations of both trials in this sense are in Douglas, *The Memory of Judgment*.
46. This was the task of the four military governors in Germany, discussed in Chapter 1 in this book.
47. Frank M. Buscher, *The U.S. War Crimes Trial Program in Germany, 1946–1955* (Westport, CT: Greenwood Press, 1989), pp. 31ff.
48. Adalbert Rückerl, *The Investigation of Nazi Crimes, 1945–1978: A Documentation*, trans. Derek Rutter (Hamden, CT: Archon Books, 1980), pp. 29–30; Yveline Pendaries, *Les procès de Rastatt (1946–1954): Le jugement des crimes de guerre en Zone française d'occupation en Allemagne* (Berne: Lang, 1995). French trial figures do not include trials conducted in France or in North Africa.
49. On veterans' groups, see Jay Lockenour, *Soldiers as Citizens: Former Wehrmacht Officers in the Federal Republic of Germany, 1945–1955* (Lincoln: University of Nebraska Press, 2001).
50. Thomas Alan Schwartz, "John J. McCloy and the Landsberg Cases," in *American Policy and the Reconstruction of West Germany, 1945–1955*, Jeffry Diefendorf, Axel Frohn, and Hermann-Josef Rupieper, eds. (New York: Cambridge University Press, 1993), pp. 433–53.
51. Figures printed in Buscher, *The U.S. War Crimes Trial Program*, Appendix B.
52. Andreas Hilger, Ute Schmidt, and Günther Wagenleher, eds., *Sowjetische Militärtribunale*, Bd. 1, *Die Verteilung deutscher Kriegsgefangener 1941–1953* (Cologne: Böhlau Verlag, 2001), p. 239.
53. Christina Morina, "Instructed Silence, Constructed Memory: The SED and the Return of German Prisoners of War as 'War Criminals' from the Soviet Union to East Germany, 1950–1956," *Contemporary European History* 13, No. 3 (2004): 323–43.

## CHAPTER ONE. "TO THE GALLOWS WITH ALL OF THEM"

1. G. M. Gilbert, *Nuremberg Diary*, pp. 431–2.
2. For organizational breakdown, see Christoph Weisz, *OMGUS Handbuch: Die amerikanische Militärregierung in Deutschland 1945–1949*, 2nd ed. (Munich: Oldenbourg, 1995), pp. 681ff.
3. For the Charter see *TMWC*, v. 1, pp. 10–16.
4. Copy of Control Council Directive Number 35 can be found in AAPS, roll 1.
5. Prusin, "Fascist Criminals to the Gallows!"
6. Legal Committee discussions DLEG/P(46) February 21 and 24, 1946; DLEG/P(46)24 (Revise), March 30, 1946; DLEG/M(46)14, April 9–10, 1946; DLEG/SEC(46)64, April 11, 1946; Coordinating Committee Discussion CORC/P(46)144, April 18, 1946; Fahy to Clay, April 23, 1946, all in NARA, RG 260, Entry 1790, Box 63.
7. ACA Control Council Meeting of September 20, 1946, CONL/M(46)25, NARA, RG 260, Entry 1792, Box 94. On Douglas, see Taylor, *Anatomy*, pp. 603–4; Sholto Douglas (Lord Douglas of Kirtleside), *Combat and Command: The Story of an Airman in Two World Wars* (New York: Simon and Schuster, 1963), pp. 736–55.
8. Fahy to Clay, April 23, 1946, NARA, RG 260, Entry 1790, Box 63.
9. ACA Control Council Meeting of September 30, 1946, CONL/M(46)26, NARA, RG 260, Entry 1792, Box 92.
10. Taylor, *Anatomy*, pp. 605–6.
11. Seidl to Allied Control Council, October 2, 1946 (and marginalia), The National Archives (Kew) [hereafter TNA], Foreign Office [hereafter FO] 1060/1381.
12. ACA Control Council Extraordinary Meeting, October 10, 1946, NARA, RG 260, Entry 1792, Box 92.
13. Chapter 6 in this book.
14. On these issues, see NARA, RG 260, Entry 1790, Box 63; RG 260, Entry 1792, Box 94.
15. The Göring investigation is in NARA, RG 260, Entry 1790, Box 2. For assessment, see Taylor, *Anatomy*, pp. 618–24. For the arguments over the clemency rejection notification, see NARA, RG 260, Entry 1790, Box 63.
16. For Control Council discussions on the issue through October 23, 1946, see NARA, RG 260, Entry 1790, Box 63.
17. ACA Control Council Extraordinary Meeting, October 10, 1946, NARA, RG 260, Entry 1792, Box 92.
18. Six Months' Report, January 4–July 3, 1946, Office of Military Government, U.S. Berlin District, p. 62; Historical Report, Office of Military Government, Berlin District, October 1, 1946–December 31, 1946, p. 131, both in NARA, RG 260, Entry 139, Box 550.
19. Allied Kommandatura Berlin, Legal Committee, LEG/R(46)40, September 21, 1946, NARA, RG 84, Entry 1016, Box 12.
20. Allied Kommandatura Berlin, Public Safety and Legal Committee, PUSA/LEG/R(46) October 3, 1946, NARA, RG 84, Entry 1016, Box 12.
21. Allied Kommandatura, Appendix A to BKC/M(46)25, September 24, 1946, Minutes of the Commandants' Discussion on Directive 35, NARA, RG 84, Entry 1016, Box 12. On Thälmann, see Nikolaus Wachsmann, *Hitler's Prisons: Legal Terror in Nazi Germany* (New Haven, CT: Yale University Press), p. 370.
22. Allied Kommandatura, Appendix A to BKC/M(46)25, September 24, 1946, Minutes of the Commandants' Discussion on Directive 35, NARA, RG 84, Entry 1016, Box 12.
23. Le Tissier, *Farewell to Spandau*, pp. 14–15. See also "Die Planierraupe sollte die Erinnerung haben," *Frankfurter Allgemeine Zeitung* [hereafter *FAZ*], July 17, 1997.
24. Allied Kommandatura Berlin, Public Safety and Legal Committee, PUSA/LEG/R(46), October 3, 1946, NARA, RG 84, Entry 1016, Box 12.
25. For the order placing prisons in Berlin under the responsibility of the *Generalstaatsanwalt*, see Allied Kommandatura Berlin, BK/R(46)303, August 22, 1946, NARA, RG 466, Entry 49, Box 27.
26. Abschrift, May 3, 1945, Landesarchiv Berlin [herafter LAB], B Rep 59, Bd. 32.
27. On the general state of the grounds in late 1946 and early 1947 see LAB, B Rep 59, Bd. 32.
28. Allied Kommandatura Berlin, BK/R(46)303, August 22, 1946, NARA, RG 466, Entry 49, Box 27.

29. Stephen Henry (Chief Legal Officer, Legal Division Kommandatura) to Manpower Branch, 15/1200 K14/30, January 20, 1950, TNA, FO 1012/515. The closest definition came in British Military Government Sector Ordinance 202 of December 30, 1949, which stated that former Reich and Prussian state property located in the British sector was transferred to the City of Berlin as trustee for any future German state recognized by the British occupation authorities as being appropriate for final ownership. Article 2(b) of that ordinance excluded from the ordinance any property temporarily used or occupied by the occupation authorities in the British sector of Berlin. The final disposition of this property "will be dealt with in accordance with the decisions of the Occupation Authorities in the British Sector of Berlin." For explanation, see David H. Small to Charles N. Brower, March 10, 1970, NARA, RG 84, Entry 1006-A, Box 1.
30. U.S. Army, Military Government Report, October 14–20, 1946, p. 5, NARA, RG 260, Entry 139, Box 558. The prisoners were moved to Tegel Prison in the French sector.
31. Details in LAB, B Rep 62, Bd. 20. Spandau was completely evacuated by mid-November 1946. See U.S. Army, Military Government Report, November 11–17, 1946, NARA, RG 260, Entry 139, Box 558.
32. U.S. Army, Military Government Report, December 23–29, 1946, NARA, RG 260, Entry 139, Box 558.
33. Allied Kommandatura Berlin, Building and Housing Committee, Inspection Report on State Prison, Spandau, October 15, 1946, in Annex B to the Historical Report, October 1, 1946–December 31, 1946, both in NARA, RG 260, Entry 139, Box 551.
34. Allied Kommandatura Berlin to Oberbürgermeister of Berlin, BKO(46)426, November 25, 1946, TNA, FO 1012/515, and in NARA, RG 84, Entry 1015, Box 44.
35. Contracts are in LAB, B Rep 059, Bd. 32. On costs, see LAB, B Rep 059, Bd. 31.
36. U.S. Military Government Report, October 14–20, 1946, p. 5, NARA, RG 260, Entry 139, Box 548.
37. Memorandum on Implementation of Control Council Directive Number 35, AAPS, roll 1.
38. Allied Kommandatura Berlin, Minutes of the Deputy Commandants' 53rd Meeting, December 13, 1946, BKD/M(46)54, NARA, RG 260, Entry 139, Box 546. On arguments concerning supplies in general, see Frank Howley, *Berlin Command* (New York: Putnam, 1950).
39. On these security issues, see René Darbois (French governor, Spandau Prison) to Legal Committee, FO/I-1/47/14, February 20, 1947; Allied Kommandatura, Legal Committee, LEG/R(47)13, March 22, 1947; Allied Kommandatura, Legal Committee, LEG/R(47)23, April 24, 1947, all in NARA, RG 260, Entry 139, Box 571. See also Governors' Memorandum of April 9, 1947; Darbois to deputy director of Military Government, British Sector, June 9, 1947; Spandau Allied Prison, Regulations for the Electric Fence, December 16, 1954, AAPS, roll 1; Minutes of Special Meeting of the Directors of Allied Spandau Prison, April 9, 1947, AAPS, roll 2; Verbatim of the 21st Meeting, May 6, 1947, and Verbatim of the Deputies' 27th Meeting, Alliierten Museum Berlin, Sammlung Dokumenten [hereafter AMB/SlgD], AK 133/2; Commandement des Transmissions de Berlin/Service du Materiel, No. 478/12/D, January 4, 1947, Ministère des Affaires étrangères, Bureau des Archives de l'occupation française en Allemagne et Autriche (Colmar) [hereafter MAE-AOFAA], GMFB 15/1, Folder: Prison de Spandau.
40. Magistrat of Greater Berlin, 4402-I/A.1.49 (Legal Dept.), October 7, 1949 to Lieutenant Colonel G. M. Oborn, chief of staff, Allied Kommandatura Berlin, RG 84, Entry 1016, Box 12.
41. *SSD*, November 30, 1946.
42. The finished fifteen-page "Prison Regulations for Spandau Allied Prison" are in AAPS, roll 1. They are printed in the Appendix in this book with amendments noted.
43. The aggregate numbers of official personnel and staff tend to vary from document to document. The aggregate number of warders and exterior military guards recounted here come from Délégation du Ministère de la Justice, JUS/CG/JJS/AS/N. 141, January 10, 1947, MAE-AOFAA, GMFB 15/1, Folder: Prison de Spandau. See also Memorandum [undated] on Implementation of Control Council Directive No. 35, AAPS, roll 1.
44. Spandau Allied Prison Minutes, January 27, 1947, NARA, RG 260, Entry 139, Box 571.
45. Allied Kommandatura Berlin, Legal Committee, LEG/R(46)55, November 30, 1946, in Annex B to the Historical Report, October 1, 1946–December 31, 1946, NARA, RG 260, Entry 139, Box 551.

46. Explained in Exposé de Michel Planet (French governor, Spandau Prison, 1973–1987) to Jean-Pierre Brunet (French ambassador, Bonn), September/October 1977, MAE-AOFAA, GMFB 239/1, Folder: Divers. Germans were allowed to work in the Spandau buildings outside the wall such as the governors' mess. There would be twenty non-Allied staff personnel in 1977.
47. Darbois to Kommandatura Legal Committee, FO/I-1/47/14, February 20, 1947 and Allied Kommandatura, Legal Committee, LEG/R(47)13, undated, NARA, RG 260, Entry 139, Box 571.
48. Allied Kommandatura Berlin, Legal Committee, LEG/R(46)58, December 4, 1946, in Annex B to the Historical Report, October 1, 1946–December 31, 1946, NARA, RG 260, Entry 139, Box 551.
49. Darbois to Legal Committee, BO/I/1/47, February 12, 1947, NARA, RG 260, Entry 139, Box 571.
50. McLain to S. H. Souter (chief, Prisons Branch, HICOG), November 21, 1949, NARA, RG 466, Entry 48, Box 14.
51. AHQ/10102/Sec. G, March 25, 1947, TNA, FO 1032/2217.
52. Minutes of the Governors' Meeting, January 10, 1947, AAPS, roll 1.
53. Spandau Allied Prison to Allied Kommandatura, Legal Committee, A/I-1/47/153, December 9, 1947, AAPS, roll 1. Memorandum by Maxwell Miller to all directors, undated [December 1948], AAPS, roll 2.
54. Allied Kommandatura Berlin, BK(AHC)(51)58, July 16, 1951, NARA, RG 466, Entry 48, Box 14.
55. U.S. Army, Military Government Report, October 27, 1946, NARA, RG 260, Entry 139, Box 558.
56. OSS, Research and Analysis Branch, "Soviet Intentions to Punish War Criminals," April 30, 1945, NARA, RG 238, Entry 69, Box 39.
57. OSS pointed specifically to Major General Erich von Bogen (commander, 302nd infantry division), Major General Günther Klammt (commander, 260th infantry division), and Major General Hans Traut (commander, 78th infantry division), all of whom were named as guilty of war crimes by the Soviets' investigative body, the Extraordinary State Commission.
58. Prusin, "Fascist Criminals to the Gallows!," pp. 1–30.
59. V. N. Kudriavtsev, "The Nuremberg Trial and the Strengthening of the International Legal Order," in Ginsburgs and Kudriavtsev, *The Nuremberg Trial and International Law*, pp. 1–8.
60. Molotov's note read as follows: "The Soviet Government considers it imperative that any one of the ringleaders of fascist Germany who during the course of the war has already fallen into the hands of the authorities of the states fighting against Hitlerite Germany be brought to trial without delay before a special international tribunal and punished with all the severity of criminal law." This could only have referred to Hess. See Kochavi, *Prelude to Nuremberg*, pp. 36–7. See also the Stalin's aide-mémoire of November 1942, which mentions Hess prominently in *UdSSR*, v. 1, d. 34.
61. Quoted in Kochavi, *Prelude to Nuremberg*, pp. 224–5. The announcement of conviction insofar as Nikitchenko was concerned came with the Moscow Declaration by Stalin, Churchill, and Franklin D. Roosevelt of November 1, 1943, which warned that the perpetrators of atrocities would be tried and punished, and with the brief discussions at Yalta on war crimes trials in February 1945.
62. Overy, *Interrogations*, p. 16. On Vishinski, see Taylor, *Anatomy*, p. 211. See also Robert G. Storey, *The Final Judgment? Pearl Harbor to Nuremberg* (San Francisco: Naylor, 1966), pp. 107–8.
63. *TMWC*, v. 2, pp. 98–155. Consideration in Sprecher, *Inside the Nuremberg Trial*, v. 1, Chapter 14.
64. *TMWC*, v. 3, pp. 91–145.
65. Sprecher, *Inside the Nuremberg Trial*, v. 2, pp. 1113–23.
66. *TMWC*, v. 7, p. 169.
67. *TMWC*, v. 7, pp. 457–8. The Soviets in future years ignored that most victims at Babi Yar were Jews. See Judith Miller, *One by One by One*: *Facing the Holocaust* (New York: Simon and Schuster, 1990), pp. 187–90. On Auschwitz see *TMWC*, v. 8, pp. 317ff.

68. See the comments to this effect in Rudenko's opening statement in *TMWC*, v. 7, pp. 146–93.
69. See Nikitschenko's directive from Moscow, approved by Stalin, of September 17, 1946, in *UdSSR*, v. 2, d. 164.
70. For the dissent, see *TMWC*, v. 1, pp. 342–64. For subsequent Soviet opinion, see A. M. Larin, "The Verdict of the International Tribunal," in Ginsburgs and Kudriavtsev, *The Nuremberg Trial and International Law*, pp. 76–87.
71. *UdSSR*, v. 1, d. 34, 35.
72. On the latter, see Gilbert, *Nuremberg Diary*, pp. 136–7.
73. Taylor, *Anatomy*, p. 560.
74. Polls in the American zone of Germany showed that as the trial progressed, fewer Germans followed its daily progress in the newspapers. In March 1946 only 52 percent of those surveyed in the U.S. zone thought that all the defendants were guilty. Only 55 percent thought the sentences just in October 1946, with 9 percent seeing the sentences as too harsh and 21 percent, as too mild. See Anna J. Merritt and Richard L. Merritt, *Public Opinion in Occupied Germany: The OMGUS Surveys, 1945–1949* (Urbana: University of Illinois Press, 1970), pp. 33–5, 93–4.
75. Einheitsfront der antifasistisch-demokratischen Parteien Deutschlands to the Allied Control Council, Berlin, December 5, 1945 (Pieck signed for the Communist Party of Germany [KPD]). Stiftung Archiv der Parteien und Massenorganisationen der DDR im Bundesarchiv [hereafter SAPMO] (Berlin), DY 3, Bd. 4. The letter complained that of the 250 journalists allowed at the Nuremberg trial, only five were German and none were from the Communist or Socialist Party newspapers. The parties represented in the Democratic Bloc were the KPD (Communist Party of Germany), SPD (Social Democratic Party of Germany), CDU (Christian Democratic Union, Eastern Branch), and LPD (Liberal Democratic Party of Germany).
76. *Der Morgen*, December 22, 1945; *Neue Zeit*, December 22, 1945.
77. *UdSSR*, v. 2, d. 168.
78. Walter Ulbricht, "Jetzt soll das Volk urteilen," *Neues Deutschland*, October 3, 1946. See also *Täglische Rundschau*, October 4, 1946, for Communist opinion throughout Europe and the world.
79. *Neues Deutschland*, October 6, 1946, October 8, 1946; *Täglische Rundschau*, October 8, 1946.
80. Walter Ulbricht, "Jetzt soll das Volk urteilen," *Neues Deutschland*, October 3, 1946.
81. "Volksstimmen zum Nürnberger Urteil," *Neues Deutschland*, October 3, 1946.
82. The lengthy speech, as well as others along the same line, is in SAPMO, NY 4036, Bd. 429. See also Pieck's comments in Thuringia on October 3, 1946 in *Neues Deutschland*, October 4, 1946.
83. *Täglische Rundschau*, October 5, 1946, October 9, 1946.
84. Minutes of the Second Meeting of the Quadripartite Commission for the Detention of Major War Criminals, October 1, 1946, Com/Det/M(46)2, TNA, FO 1060/1385.
85. The comment came from the Soviet representative to the Legal Committee, Paskevitch. See Allied Kommandatura/Legal Committee LEG/R(47)3, January 30, 1947, NARA, RG 84, Entry 1016, Box 12.
86. The draft regulations of January 30, 1947 are enclosed in Allied Kommandatura, Legal Committee LEG/R(47)3, January 30, 1947, NARA, RG 84, Entry 1016, Box 12.
87. *SSD*, October 4, 1946, October 11, 1946, November 30, 1946, December 11, 1946, January 6, 1947.
88. Interrogation of Erich Raeder by Lieutenant Colonel Follestad, February 26, 1947, NARA, RG 238, Entry 20, Box 4; Conference between Kraus (deputy defense counsel) and Raeder, December 19, 1946, NARA, RG 238, Entry 20, Box 5.
89. Report by Teich, December 4, 1946, NARA, RG 238, Entry 22, Box 16.
90. For Directive 19, "Concerning Principles for Administration of German Prisons," see NARA, RG 260, Entry 31, Box 645. For the American memorandum of September 28, 1945, see Allied Control Authority, Legal Directorate, DLEG/P(28), NARA, RG 260, Entry 1790, Box 53. On Karrasov, see Extract from the minutes of October 10, 1945, DLEG/M(10)627, NARA, RG 260, Entry 1790, Box 53. On the October 4, 1946, directive to draft the Spandau regulations in accordance with Directive 19, see Excerpt from the

Deputy Commandants' 11th Meeting, March 4, 1947, NARA, RG 260, Entry 139, Box 571.

91. See Allied Kommandatura/Legal Committee LEG/R(47)3, January 30, 1947, NARA, RG 84, Entry 1016, Box 12.
92. For Churchill's policy, see Kochavi, *Prelude to Nuremberg*, pp. 73–80. For the Barnes and Attlee comments, see Overy, *Interrogations*, pp. 16, 30.
93. Johnston to Harris (Legal Committee, Allied Kommandatura), G/324, February 7, 1947, TNA, FO 945/336.
94. Allied Kommandatura Berlin, Appendix A to BKD/M(47)10, March 1, 1947, NARA, RG 84, Entry 1016, Box 12.
95. Verbatim of BKO/(47)8, February 14, 1947, AMB/SlgD, AK 133/2.
96. Appendix A to BKD/M(47)8, February 17, 1947, NARA, RG 84, Entry 1016, Box 12.
97. Howley, *Berlin Command*, pp. 125–6.
98. Verbatim of BKO/(47)8, February 14, 1947, AMB/SlgD, AK 133/2; Allied Kommandatura Berlin, Appendix A to BKD/M(47)8, February 17, 1947, NARA, RG 84, Entry 1016, Box 12.
99. Verbatim of BKO/(47)8, February 14, 1947, AMB/SlgD, AK 133/2.
100. On Hess, see *SSD*, 16 February 1947; Second Lieutenant Charles Backstrom to Colonel Andrus, October 12, 1947, NARA, RG 238, Entry 20, Box 5, p. 766. Hess intended to prohibit the genteel kissing of ladies' hands for all but the most important people.
101. Verbatim meeting of the Deputy Kommandants, February 28, 1947, AMB/SlgD, AK 133/2.
102. Allied Kommandatura Berlin, Appendix A to BKD/M(47)10, March 1, 1947, NARA, RG 84, Entry 1016, Box 12.
103. Allied Kommandatura/Legal Committee, LEG/R(47)11, February 19, 1947, NARA, RG 84, Entry 1016, Box 12.
104. Appendix A to BKD/M(47)8, February 17, 1947, NARA, RG 84, Entry 1016, Box 12.
105. Verbatim of Deputies' Meeting, February 21, 1947, AMB/SlgD, AK 133/2; Allied Kommandatura Berlin, Annex A to BKD/M(47)9, February 24, 1947, NARA, RG 84, Entry 1016, Box 12.
106. Burton C. Andrus, *The Infamous of Nuremberg* (London: Leslie Frewin, 1969), pp. 25–61.
107. Andrus, *Infamous of Nuremberg*, pp. 62–91; Overy, *Interrogations*, pp. 60–73.
108. Allied Kommandatura Berlin, Appendix A to BKD/M(47)8, February 17, 1947, NARA, RG 84, Entry 1016, Box 12.
109. Allied Kommandatura Berlin, Appendix A to BKC/M(47)5, February 25, 1947, NARA, RG 260, Entry 1790, Box 53.
110. Allied Kommandatura Berlin, Annex A to BKD/M(47)9, February 24, 1947; Allied Kommandatura Berlin, Appendix A to BKD/M(47)10, March 1, 1947, both in NARA, RG 84, Entry 1016, Box 12.
111. Allied Kommandatura Berlin, Appendix A to BKD/M(47)10, March 1, 1947, NARA, RG 84, Entry 1016, Box 12. Also, Excerpt from the Deputy Commandants' 11th Meeting, March 4, 1947, NARA, RG 260, Entry 139, Box 571.
112. Allied Kommandatura Berlin, Minutes of the Deputy Commandants' 11th Meeting, March 4, 1947, BKD/M(47)11, NARA, RG 84, Entry 1016, Box 12.
113. Allied Kommandatura Berlin, Appendix A to BKD/M(47)10, March 1, 1947; Allied Kommandatura Berlin, Appendix A to BKC/M(47)6, March 9, 1947, both in NARA, RG 84, Entry 1016, Box 12.
114. Allied Kommandatura Berlin, BK/ACC(47)8, March 31, 1947, NARA, RG 260, Entry 1790, Box 53.
115. Howley to Clay, Office of Military Government, Berlin Sector, Leg. Br. AAB, APO 742-A, U.S. Army, April 8, 1947, NARA, RG 84, Entry 1016, Box 12, Folder: Prison Regulations.
116. Extract from minutes of ACA Coordinating Committee, April 14, 1947, NARA, RG 260, Entry 1790, Box 53.
117. *SSD*, April 18–19, 1947, May 15, 1947. See also *SSD*, March 14, 1947.
118. Allied Control Authority, Legal Directorate, Minutes of April 21 and 24, 1947, DLEG/M(47)18, April 25, 1947, NARA, RG 260, Entry 1806, Box 189; Allied Control Authority, Coordinating Committee, CORC/P(47)116, May 7, 1947, NARA, RG 260, Entry 1797, Box 146.
119. Bloxham, *Genocide on Trial*, pp. 28–32.

120. Transcript of the Coordinating Committee Meeting of May 16, 1947, CORC/M(47)26, NARA, RG 260, Entry 1796, Box 137.
121. Brief on CORC/P(47)116, May 16, 1947, NARA, RG 260, Entry 1790, Box 53.
122. Text of complete Prison Regulations in AAPS, roll 1 and printed in the Appendix of this book. For acceptance, see Report No. 47–11, Office of Military Government Berlin Sector, June 1 to June 15, 1947, NARA, RG 260, Entry 139, Box 558; Kommandatura Interalliée, Bureau du Chef d'État Major Président, BI/Memo(47)29, June 16, 1947, NARA, RG 84, Entry 1016, Box 12.
123. Brief on CORC/P(47)116, May 16, 1947, NARA, RG 260, Entry 1790, Box 53.
124. *SSD*, November 11, 1946, December 1, 1946.
125. Allied Kommandatura Berlin, Appendix A to BKD/M(47)8, February 17, 1947, NARA, RG 84, Entry 1016, Box 12.
126. Allied Kommandatura Berlin, Annex A to BKD/M(47)9, February 24, 1947, NARA, RG 84, Entry 1016, Box 12.
127. *SSD*, May 15, 1947.
128. *SSD*, June 30, 1947.
129. Overy, *Interrogations*, p. 20; *UdSSR*, v. 2, d. 20, 44.
130. France, Ministère des Affaires étrangères. *Documents diplomatiques français, 1946*, v. 1 (Paris: Imprimerie Nationale, 2003), d. 256, 379; v. 2 (Paris: Imprimerie Nationale, 2004), d. 228.
131. Bloxham, *Genocide on Trial*, pp. 28ff.
132. Memorandum by Telford Taylor to the secretary of war, July 29, 1946, NARA, RG 260, Entry 22, Box 22.
133. Robert H. Jackson to President Harry Truman, October 7, 1946, NARA, RG 238, Entry 69, Box 46.
134. Ibid.
135. Truman to Jackson, October 17, 1946, NARA, RG 238, Entry 69, Box 46.
136. Telford Taylor (Chief Counsel for War Crimes) to Keating, May 20, 1947, NARA, RG 260, Entry 23, Box 26.
137. Allied Kommandatura Berlin, Appendix to BKD/M(47)26, June 10, 1947, Section 281, NARA, RG 260, Entry 1790, Box 53.
138. On the planning see TNA, FO 1012/786 (Operation Traffic). On secrecy and procedures, see the records of the Commandants' Meetings of June 25, 1947, and July 11, 1947, as well as C. W. Harris, 15/3040, March 29, 1947, AMB/SlgD AK 133/2.
139. *SSD*, July 19, 1947.
140. See the Ninth and Tenth Meetings of the Quadripartite Commission for the Detention of Major War Criminals, June 25 and August 19, 1947, TNA, FO 1060/1385.
141. Associated Press Report of January 16, 1947, NARA, RG 260, Entry 139, Box 571.

## CHAPTER TWO. AN ENDURING INSTITUTION

1. Quote attributed by Albert Speer in *SSD*, July 28, 1950.
2. *SSD*, July 24, 1947.
3. On November 30, 1945, the Four Powers agreed to the air corridors to Berlin and established the Berlin Air Safety Center (BASC), which began operation in February 1946. See I. D. Hendry and M. C. Wood, *The Legal Status of Berlin* (Cambridge: Grotius Publications Ltd., 1987), pp. 110–14.
4. *UdSSR*, v. 1, d. 144.
5. On Potsdam and its aftermath, see Carolyn Woods Eisenberg, *Drawing the Line: The American Decision to Divide Germany* (New York: Cambridge University Press, 1996), pp. 80ff.
6. The reality among the Western zones was in fact more complicated. The British in Hanover encouraged the CDU at the expense of the SPD's postwar development, and the French authorities encouraged regionalism in the parties of the French zone. See Barbara Marshall, *The Origins of Postwar German Politics* (London: Croom and Helm, 1988); Daniel E. Rogers, *Politics after Hitler: The Western Allies and the German Party System* (New York: New York University Press, 1995); Edgar Wolfrum, *Französische Besatzungspolitik*

*und deutsche Sozialdemokratie: Politische Neuansätze in der "vergessenen Zone" bis zur Bildung des Südweststaates 1945–1952* (Düsseldorf: Droste, 1991).

7. Scott D. Parish and Mikhail M. Narinsky, "New Evidence on the Soviet Rejection of the Marshall Plan, 1947: Two Reports," Cold War International History Project Working Paper No. 9 (Washington, DC: Woodrow Wilson Center, 1994).
8. Vojtech Mastny, *The Cold War and Soviet Insecurity: The Stalin Years* (New York: Oxford University Press, 1996), pp. 47ff.
9. See essays in Stefan Karner, ed., *Gefangenen in Russland: Die Beiträge des Symposions auf der Schalleburg, 1995* (Graz: Ludwig Boltzmann-Institut für Kriegsfolgen-Forschung, 1995); Klaus-Dieter Müller, Konstantin Nikischkin, and Günther Wagenlehner, eds., *Die Tragödie der Gefangenschaft in Deutschland und in der Sowjetunion 1941–1956* (Cologne: Bohlau, 1998).
10. This is also confirmed by the inspection report of Lionel Fox, chairman of the Prison Commission for England and Wales, April 23, 1951, TNA, FO 1060/544.
11. *SSD*, July 27, 1947.
12. *SSD*, August 2–4, 1947, February 8, 1948.
13. *SSD*, August 29, 1948.
14. *SSD*, April 10, 1948, October 24, 1948, November 3, 1948, January 3, 1949.
15. Chief Warder's Log Book, entry of January 29, 1948, AAPS, roll 22.
16. *SSD*, October 11, 18, 1947.
17. Casalis to Ganeval, October 2, 1947, MAE-AOFAA, GMFB 15/1, Folder: Prison de Spandau.
18. *SSD*, December 12, 1947, February 12, 1948. Soviet records relating to Spandau are closed, but former Spandau warder Georgy Morev, who had served in Soviet counterintelligence (SMERSH) from 1942 to 1945, was recruited from his home in Briansk to serve as a Spandau warder from 1953 to 1955. His recollections are in the Russian online magazine *Trud*, No. 074, April 22, 2004, http://www.trud.ru [accessed January 2006]. I am grateful to Arsen Djatej for this reference and translation.
19. *SSD*, February 3, 4, 1949.
20. See Minutes of the Governors' Meetings from April 19, 1948, April 29, 1948, May 18, 1948, July 5, 1948, July 12, 1948, July 21, 1948, AAPS, roll 2; *SSD*, May 5, 1948.
21. *SSD*, February 8, 1948.
22. Chief Warder's Log Book, entries in February and March 1948, AAPS, roll 22.
23. Minutes of Medical Board Meeting, August 6, 1947, AAPS, roll 10.
24. *SSD*, December 12, 1947; Minutes of the Governors' Meeting, December 7, 1950, AAPS, roll 2; Note from Warder Francis David, November 21, 1950, AAPS, roll 21.
25. Chief Warder Log Book, January 19, 1948, AAPS, roll 22.
26. *SSD*, December 18, 1947.
27. *SSD*, January 23, 1953.
28. See Nikolai Sysoev's account of the Soviet external guard armament in 1970 in "Victors: Guarding the Number 2 Nazi," *Bratishka* (*Brotherhood: Journal for Members of Special Forces*) October 2004, http://www.bratishka.ru [accessed January 2006]. I am grateful to Arsen Djatej for this reference and translation.
29. Minutes of the Governors' Meeting, August 2, 1947, AAPS, roll 2; Office of Military Government, Berlin Sector, Semi-Monthly Progress Report, August 1–15, 1947, NARA, RG 260, Entry 139, Box 571.
30. Minutes of the Governors' Meeting, November 4, 1947, AAPS, roll 2.
31. *SSD*, April 25, 1948; Minutes of the Governors' Meeting, May 4, 1948, AAPS, roll 2.
32. See the recollection of the censor Margarita Nerucheva in "Vozmezdie [Retribution]," *Sibirskie Ogni [Siberian Lights]*, No. 2 (2000), http://sibogni.ru/archive/2/215 [accessed January 2006]. Nerucheva served as a Soviet censor at Spandau after 1957. Aside from German, she also knew French and English. I am grateful to Arsen Djatej for this reference and translation.
33. *SSD*, October 14, 1947, December 5, 1947, December 7, 1947.
34. Minutes of the Governors' Meetings, August 18, 1949, September 8, 1949, AAPS, roll 2.
35. *SSD*, December 5, 1947.
36. See BK/AHC(50)37, July 21, 1950; Report by Lionel Fox, chairman of the Prison Commission for England and Wales, April 23, 1951, TNA, FO 1060/544.

37. Taylor, *Anatomy*, p. 392.
38. At Nuremberg in 1946, Funk still argued that Germany's weak economy in the early 1920s and early 1930s was "caused chiefly by reparations" and the resulting transfer of German marks abroad following the First World War. In fact, Germany's reparations burden was not nearly as severe as the public understood, and Berlin avoided payments whenever possible and by whatever means necessary, including the deliberate wrecking of the German currency in 1923. Funk himself had argued against the 1924 Dawes Plan – an international arrangement aimed at lightening an already-limited German reparations burden – for political rather than financial reasons. The damages in France and Belgium that German reparations payments were supposed to fix were mostly repaired at the expense of the taxpayers of those countries. Funk's comment of May 4, 1946, is in *TMWC*, v. 13, p. 79. On the myth of reparations that Funk furthered here, see Sally Marks, "The Myth of Reparations," *Central European History* 18, No. 3 (1978): 231–55.
39. On Goebbels, *TMWC*, May 4, 1946, v. 13, p. 108.
40. *TMWC*, May 4, 1946, v. 13, p. 109.
41. *TMWC*, May 6, 1946, v. 13, p. 143.
42. Gerhard L. Weinberg, *The Foreign Policy of Hitler's Germany*, v. 2: *Starting World War II 1937–1939*, reprint ed. (Atlantic Highlands, N.J.: Humanities Press, 1994), p. 26.
43. Taylor, *Anatomy*, p. 392.
44. Document 3944-PS, *TMWC*, v. 13, pp. 159–60.
45. Document 4045-PS, *TMWC*, v. 20, pp. 266–8.
46. *TMWC*, v. 12, pp. 160, 162.
47. *TMWC*, v. 22, pp. 394–5.
48. NARA, RG 238, Entry 33, Box 6, pp. 1824–5, 1931–5, 1992–3.
49. Funk to Spandau directors, May 16, 1950, Funk Personal File, AAPS, roll 13.
50. Funk's complaint about this is in Funk to directors, June 26, 1949, AAPS, roll 13. For their response, see Minutes of the Governors' Meeting, June 16, 1949, AAPS, roll 2.
51. Minutes of the Governors' Meetings, October 14, 1948, October 21, 1948, October 29, 1948, AAPS, roll 2. In November 1949, the rump Kommandatura forwarded Funk's petition to the Allied High Commission, which had replaced the Control Council in West Germany, but no action was taken. See BK/AHC(49)2, November 18, 1949, NARA, RG 466, Entry 59, Box 2.
52. Minutes of the Governors' Meeting, January 15, 1953, AAPS, roll 3. See also Minutes of the Governors' Meeting, May 28, 1953, and Funk to Allied high commissioners, December 12, 1953, AAPS, roll 3.
53. Fishman, *Long Knives*, pp. 159–63.
54. See the section of Funk's Personal File in AAPS, roll 14.
55. Memorandum by medical officers Lieutenant Charles Roska and Lieutenant Roy Martin, October 19, 1946, 6850th Internal Security Detachment, Funk Personal File, AAPS, roll 10.
56. Memorandum by Roska and Martin to the Quadripartite Commission, Oct 25, 1946, with a handwritten note to Andrus at bottom, Funk Personal File, AAPS, roll 10.
57. Minutes of Extraordinary Meeting of the Medical Board, January 6, 1948, AAPS, roll 10.
58. Ganeval to Koenig, September 2, 1947, MAE-AOFAA, GMFB 15/1, Folder: Prison de Spandau.
59. Minutes of Medical Board Meeting, July 28, 1947, AAPS, roll 10.
60. Minutes of Medical Board Meeting, January 29, 1948, AAPS, roll 10.
61. Minutes of Special Meeting of the Allied Prison Doctors, May 5, 1948, AAPS, roll 10.
62. Minutes of Medical Board Meeting, September 3, 1947, AAPS, roll 10.
63. Minutes of Medical Board Meeting, February 8, 1949, May 31, 1949, November 30, 1949 and Berlin Command, Medical Service, AAN Louis Pasteur, October 28, 1949, AAPS, roll 10.
64. Minutes of Medical Board Meeting, January 31, 1951, AAPS, roll 10.
65. Minutes of the Governors' Meetings, August 19, 1954, August 26, 1954, and special meeting of September 13, 1954, AAPS, roll 3.
66. Memorandum by K. D. Treasure (British Legal Representative, Allied Kommandatura) to Secretariat, April 1948, AMB/SlgD AK 135/7.

67. Allied Kommandatura Berlin, Legal Committee, LEG/R(48)6, March 31, 1948, NARA, RG 260, Entry 139, Box 571.
68. Minutes of the Governors' Meeting, November 6, 1947, AAPS, roll 2.
69. *SSD*, August 4, 16, 24, 25, 1947; Chief Warder Log Book, October 22, 1948, AAPS, roll 22.
70. Chief Warder's Log Book, September 22, 1948, AAPS, roll 22.
71. Von Neurath Medical File, AAPS, roll 12.
72. From August 1947 to December 1948, Dönitz Medical File, AAPS, roll 12.
73. *SSD*, March 26, 1948.
74. *SSD*, August 24–25 1948, September 28, 1948.
75. Hess Medical File, December 4, 1948, AAPS, roll 15.
76. Minutes of Medical Board Meeting, January 29, 1948, AAPS, roll 10.
77. Minutes of Medical Board Meeting, February 26, 1948, AAPS, roll 10.
78. Minutes of Medical Board Meeting, April 28, 1948, AAPS, roll 10.
79. Minutes of Medical Board Meeting, October 29, 1948, AAPS, roll 10.
80. *SSD*, January 3, 1949.
81. For example Chief Warder's Log Book, June 8, 1948, AAPS, roll 22.
82. Chief Warder's Log Book, June 10, 1948, AAPS, roll 22.
83. Chief Warder's Log Book, July 4, 1948, AAPS, roll 22.
84. For the longest debate in the House of Commons, see Great Britain, Parliament, House of Commons, *Parliamentary Debates (Hansard): Official Report* [hereafter *Hansard* (Commons)], 5th Series, v. 457, c. 57ff, October 26, 1948. On Churchill's role, see Ulrich Brochhagen, *Nach Nürnberg: Vergangenheitsbewältigung und Westintegration in der Ära Adenauer* (Hamburg: Junius, 1994), pp. 29–30.
85. *Neues Deutschland*, November 11, 1949, p. 1. On the political problems of the Manstein trial, see J. H. Hoffman, "German Field Marshals as War Criminals? A British Embarrassment," *Journal of Contemporary History* 23, No. 1 (1988): 17–35; Donald Bloxham, "Punishing German Soldiers during the Cold War: The Case of Erich von Manstein," *Patterns of Prejudice* 33, No. 4 (1999): 25–45.
86. Chief Warder's Log Book, August 1, 9, 14, 21, 23, 26, 1948, AAPS, roll 10.
87. Minutes of the Governors' Meeting, August 5, 1948 and subsequent in August, Minutes of the Governors' Meetings, September 9, 1948, October 21, 1948, October 25, 1948, November 12, 1948, AAPS, roll 2.
88. Von Neurath letter to directorate, October 17, 1948, Von Neurath Personal File, AAPS, roll 12.
89. Excerpt from Legal Committee Memorandum to chairman, chief of staff, Allied Kommandatura, January 1, 1949, NARA, RG 466, Entry 48, Box 14.
90. Miller to director OMGBS, Excerpt from Report of November 18, 1948, NARA, RG 466, Entry 48, Box 14.
91. Fishman, *Long Knives*, pp. 163–4, 257.
92. Quoted in Christopher Sykes, *Nancy: The Life of Lady Astor* (London: Collins, 1972), pp. 382, 386, 396–7.
93. Sykes, *Nancy*, pp. 487, 494.
94. Baroness von Neurath's two letters of November 14, 1947, are in TNA, FO 371/64710. See also Fishman, *Long Knives*, pp. 167–9, for printed versions. On Astor's trip to Germany, Sykes, *Nancy*, pp. 494–5. On Henderson, see Weinberg, *Foreign Policy*, v. 2, p. 60.
95. Quoted in Fishman, *Long Knives*, pp. 170–1.
96. See Theo Schwarzmüller, *Zwischen Kaiser und "Führer": Generalfeldmarschall August von Mackensen. Eine politische Biographie* (Paderborn: Schöningh, 1999), pp. 299–306; Norman J. W. Goda, "Black Marks: Hitler's Bribery of His Senior Officers during World War II," *Journal of Modern History* 72, No. 2 (2000): 430–1.
97. Susan Zucotti, *Under His Very Windows: The Vatican and the Holocaust in Italy* (New Haven, CT: Yale University Press, 2000), p. 128. See also Meier Michaelis, *Mussolini and the Jews: German-Italian Relations and the Jewish Question in Italy, 1922–1945* (London: Clarendon Press, 1978), pp. 307ff.
98. NARA, RG 549, Entry 2223, Box 21.
99. Wolfgang Gerlach, *And the Witnesses Were Silent: The Confessing Church and the Persecution of the Jews* (Lincoln: University of Nebraska Press, 2000), pp. 147–9, 198–205.

100. Jon David K. Wynecken, "Memory as Diplomatic Leverage: Bishop Theophil Wurm and War Crimes Trials, 1948–1952," Paper presented at German Studies Association, Annual Meeting, September 30, 2004; see also Frei, *Vergangenheitspolitik*, pp. 144–8.
101. Wurm to King George VI, January 7, 1947; Wurm to Sir Ivone Kirkpatrick, January 22, 1951; Wurm to Lord Chichester, February 7, 1951, Landeskirchliches Archiv (Stuttgart) [hereafter LKA-S], D 1 [Nachlaß Wurm], Bd. 304.
102. Covered in Klemens von Klemperer, *German Resistance against Hitler: The Search for Allies Abroad 1938–1945* (Oxford: Clarendon Press, 1992).
103. Wurm to Chichester, August 21, 1946; Wurm to Chichester, July 30,1948; Chichester to Wurm, September 11, 1948; Wurm to Chichester, September 29, 1951; LKA-S, D 1, Bd. 235. On this general problem in the Anglican Church, see Tom Lawson, "Constructing a Christian History of Nazism: Anglicanism and the Memory of the Holocaust, 1945–49," *History and Memory* 16, No. 21 (2004): 146–76.
104. Wurm to Chichester, June 17, 1947, LKA-S, D 1, Bd. 235.
105. Von Mackensen's statement on her visit of February 2, 1948, and Wurm's reply are in TNA, FO 371/70853. On von Neurath, see *SSD*, February 3, 1949; Governors' Memorandum of March 16, 1948, AAPS, roll 1.
106. Minute by Newton, January 30, 1948, TNA, FO 371/70853.
107. Question from Thomas C. Skeffington-Lodge, September 20, 1948, *Hansard* (Commons), v. 456, c. 489.
108. Tom Bower, *Blind Eye to Murder: Britain, America and the Purging of Nazi Germany – A Pledge Betrayed* (London: Granada, 1983), p. 285.
109. On Brauchitsch, see *Hansard* (Commons) v. 457, c. 62, October 26, 1948; on slaughter, see *Hansard* (Commons) v. 460, c. 85, January 24, 1949.
110. *Hansard* (Commons), v. 445, c. 673ff, December 4, 1947.
111. Stokes to Bevin, October 27, 1948, TNA, FO 371/70853.
112. Minute by Basil Marsden-Smedley, August 30, 1948; Minute by W. R. Cox, August 30, 1948, TNA, FO 371/70853.
113. General Sir Brian Robertson (HQ Control Commission for Germany), British Element, Berlin, HQ/10102/Sec G No. 19, October 26, 1948 to Ernest Bevin, in response to a dispatch from Bevin on September 25, 1948, in TNA, FO 371/70853.
114. Minute by M. H. O'Grady, November 3, 1948, TNA, FO 371/70853.
115. Robertson to Bevin, HQ/10102/Sec G No. 19, October 26, 1948, TNA, FO 371/70853.
116. Memorandum of Discussion at Meeting of U.S., U.K., and French Military Governors, November 4, 1948, NARA, RG 260, Entry 1954, Box 1. Clay's proposal is also referenced in Minute by M. H. O'Grady, December 4, 1948, TNA, FO 371/70853. For Koenig, see Jean Edward Smith, ed., *The Papers of General Lucius D. Clay: Germany, 1945–1949*, 2 vols. (Bloomington: Indiana University Press, 1974) [hereafter *Clay Papers*], v. 2, d. 593.
117. Unsigned Memorandum Regarding Prisoners Convicted by the International Military Tribunal and Confined in Spandau Prison, October 26, 1949, NARA, RG 59, Entry 1368, LF 61 D 33, Box 1.
118. Clay to Department of the Army, CC-6781, November 18, 1948; Robert Murphy to Charles Saltzman, assistant secretary of state, December 3, 1948, NARA, RG 260, Entry 1954, Box 1; U.S. Minutes of the Fifth Meeting of the U.K., French, and U.S. Military Governors, November 30, 1948, NARA, RG 260, Entry 1955, Box 4; Minute by M. H. O'Grady, December 4, 1948, TNA, FO 371/70853.
119. Minute by M. H. O'Grady, December 4, 1948; Robertson to Foreign Office, German Section, No. 2551, December 2, 1948, TNA, FO 371/70853.
120. Memorandum, Director OMGBS to U.S. director, Spandau Prison, December 2, 1948, NARA, RG 466, Entry 48, Box 14.
121. Colonel Frank Howley to Major General G. P. Hays, deputy military governor, December 2, 1948, NARA, RG 466, Entry 10-A, Box 29.
122. Minutes of the Governors' Meetings, December 3, 1948, December 7, 1948, AAPS, roll 2.
123. *Clay Papers*, v. 2, d. 651.
124. Minutes of the Governors' Meeting, December 27, 1948, AAPS, roll 2.

125. *Clay Papers*, v. 2, d. 651.
126. Excerpt from Legal Committee memorandum to Chairman, Chief of Staff, Allied Kommandatura, January 1, 1949, NARA, RG 466, Entry 48, Box 14; LEG/R(49)2, January 29, 1949, AMB/SlgD, AK 135/6.
127. *Clay Papers*, v. 2, d. 651. Verbatim of the Ninth Meeting of the United Kingdom, French and United States Military Governors, March 1, 1949; Verbatim of the Eleventh Meeting of the French, United States, and United Kingdom Military Governors, March 16, 1949; James Riddleberger to Murphy, March 18, 1949, all in NARA, RG 260, Entry 1954, Box 1.
128. *SSD*, December 7, 1948.
129. Minutes of Medical Board Meeting, February 28, 1949, AAPS, roll 10.
130. *SSD*, January 3, 1949, March 12, 1949. Kommandatura discussions in 1949 mistakenly classified Speer as an American arrest. Speer was handed back and forth between the British and Americans before his trial at Nuremberg, but it was British troops that first arrested Speer at Flensburg in May 1945. See Overy, *Interrogations*, p. 135.
131. *SSD*, January 10, 1949, August 1, 1949.
132. Verbatim of the Ninth Meeting of the United Kingdom, French, and United States Military Governors, March 1, 1949; Verbatim of the Eleventh Meeting of the French, United States, and United Kingdom Military Governors, March 16, 1949; James Riddleberger to Murphy, March 18, 1949, NARA, RG 260, Entry 1954, Box 1.
133. Seydoux to Quai d'Orsay, No. 1086, March 2, 1949, MAE-AOFAA, GMFB 15/1, Folder: Prison de Spandau.
134. Minutes of the Governors' Meetings, December 30, 1948, January 13, 1949, March 3, 1949, March 12, 1949, March 25, 1949, May 19, 1949, August 4, 1949, AAPS, roll 2.
135. Unsigned Memorandum of November 22, 1949, (describing Spandau visit by Chauncey Parker of the International Bank), NARA, RG 59, Entry 1368, LF 61 D 33, Box 1.
136. Magistrat of Greater Berlin 4402/ I /A.1.49 (Legal Department) to Lieutenant Colonel G. M. Oborn, chief of staff, Allied Kommandatura Berlin, October 7, 1949, NARA, RG 84, Entry 1016, Box 12; Gerlach to Souter, October 31, 1949, NARA, RG 466, Entry 49, Box 27. For Reuter's personal involvement, see HICOG Berlin to HICOG Frankfurt (for McCloy), CN-12506, October 22, 1949, NARA, RG 466, Entry 48, Box 14. Correspondence between the prison directorate and the Berlin city government on issues of repairs and pay scales are in the Spandau governors' official correspondence file, AAPS, roll 21. Monthly reports of financial expenditures are in AAPS, roll 9.
137. Ganeval to French High Commission, November 12, 1949, MAE-AOFAA, GMFB 363 (XA/1/3).
138. Gerlach to Souter, May 1950, NARA, RG 466, Entry 48, Box 14.
139. Prison Interalliée de Spandau a Monsieur Président du Comité Légal, FO/IV-1/48/29, February 10, 1948, AAPS, roll 2.
140. Allied Kommandatura, Office of the Chairman Chief of Staff, BH/AHC(50)5, January 15, 1950, NARA, RG 466, Entry 48, Box 14.
141. HICOG Berlin to HICOG Frankfurt, CN-15475, November 15, 1949 – 40th Meeting of the Kommandatura, held November 10, 1949, NARA, RG 466, Entry 48, Box 14; Allied Kommandatura Berlin/Office of the Chairman Chief of Staff, BK/AHC(49)1 (signed Evan Taylor), November 16, 1949, TNA, FO 371/85897.
142. Excerpt from Deputy Commandants' 38th Meeting, October 21, 1949, NARA, RG 466, Entry 48, Box 14.
143. Extracts from Meeting of the Allied Kommandatura, November 18, 1949, NARA, RG 466, Entry 48, Box 14.
144. HICOG Berlin to HICOG Frankfurt, CN-17130, December 1, 1949, NARA, RG 466, Entry 48, Box 14. On the French, see François-Poncet to Quai d'Orsay, No. 1008-10, December 15, 1949, MAE-AOFAA, GMFB 363 (XA/1/3).
145. Bourne to legal adviser, British High Commission, GOC/30, January 30, 1951, TNA, FO 1060/544. See also the list of informal improvements in MAE-AOFAA, GMFB 363 (XA/1/3).
146. See the list of improvements at the end of the Index of Basic and Reference Material for Study and Analysis of the Interallied Prison Spandau, January 7, 1951, in NARA, RG 466, Entry 48, Box 14.

147. Minutes of the Governors' Meeting, August 3, 1950, AAPS, roll 2.
148. Verbatim Report of the Commandants' Meeting, April 13, 1951, AMB/SlgD, AK135/5.
149. Discussions in TNA, FO 1060/544, 545. The prisoners' desire to eat alone and not perform new tasks such as carpentry are noted in Appendix B to BK/LEG(51)32, AMB/SlgD, AK 135/5.
150. Extract from Minutes of Commandants' Meeting, April 13, 1951, and Verbatim Report of the Commandants' Meeting, April 13, 1951, AMB/SlgD AK 135/5.
151. On Thorwald's connections see Memorandum from [redacted] to Richard Helms, November 10, 1950, NARA, RG 263, Entry ZZ-18, Box 23, Name File Reinhard Gehlen, vol. 1, Folder 2. See the Gehlen Name File more generally for the CIA relationship. On Soviet penetration of the Gehlen Organization, see Felfe, Heinz: Damage Assessment Report; and Felfe, Heinz: KGB Exploitation in NARA, RG 263, Entry ZZ-19, Box 1.
152. Minutes of the Governors' Meeting, November 12, 1951, AAPS, roll 2.
153. Minutes of the Governors' Meeting, January 31, 1952, AAPS, roll 2.
154. Minutes of the Governors' Meeting, February 28, 1952, AAPS, roll 2. See also Minutes of the Governors' Meeting, March 19, 1953, AAPS, roll 3.
155. Minutes of the Governors' Meeting, March 24, 1952, AAPS, roll 3.
156. Minutes of the Governors' Meeting, February 26, 1953, AAPS, roll 3.
157. Minutes of the Governors' Meeting, January 10, 1952, AAPS, roll 2.
158. Minutes of the Governors' Meeting, March 10, 1952, AAPS, roll 2.
159. Minutes of the Governors' Meetings, October 2, 1952, October 16, 1952, October 24, 1952, December 22, 1952, AAPS, roll 3.
160. Minutes of the Governors' Meetings, December 18, 1952, January 8, 1953, AAPS, roll 3.
161. Minutes of the Governors' Meeting, March 20, 1952, AAPS, roll 2.

## CHAPTER THREE. VON NEURATH'S ASHES: THE BATTLE OVER MEMORY

1. John L. Heineman, *Hitler's First Foreign Minister: Constantin Freiherr von Neurath, Diplomat and Statesman* (Berkeley: University of California Press, 1979), p. 2.
2. Heineman, *von Neurath*, p. 75.
3. *TMWC*, v. 17, p. 166, referencing von Neurath's comments in *Völkischer Beobachter*, September 17, 1933.
4. *TMWC*, v. 17, p. 168.
5. Heineman, *von Neurath*, p. 115.
6. Heineman, *von Neurath*, p. 98.
7. Heineman, *von Neurath*, p. 148.
8. Weinberg, *Foreign Policy*, v. 2, pp. 39–40.
9. *TMWC*, v. 17, pp. 184 ff, June 25, 1946.
10. The consideration is in Heineman, *von Neurath*, pp. 190–208.
11. Fishman, *Long Knives*, p. 165.
12. *TMWC*, v. 17, p. 141, June 24, 1946.
13. *TMWC*, v. 17, pp. 187–9, June 25, 1946. Document in *TMWC*, v. 33, pp. 252–9. See also Heineman, *von Neurath*, pp. 206–7.
14. Elke Fröhlich, ed., *Die Tagebücher von Joseph Goebbels,* Teil I: *Sämtliche Fragmente*, Bd. 4 (Munich: Sauer, 1987), April 15, 1942, April 20, 1942.
15. Details in Bundesarchiv (Berlin) [hereafter BA-B], R 43 II, Bd. 985c; Heineman, *von Neurath*, p. 214.
16. KZ-Gedenkstätte Vaihingen/Enz, *Das Konzentrationslager "Wiesengrund": Vom Arbeitslager zum Sterbelager*, 4th ed. (Vaihingen/Enz: IPA Verlag, 2002). The Vaihingen camp in Württemberg was part of the Natzweiler–Struthof complex in Alsace. Given the brutal quarry work performed by most camp inmates, those sent to the von Neurath estate considered themselves lucky.
17. Heineman, *von Neurath*, pp. 220ff.
18. Wurm to Chichester, December 30, 1949, LKA-S, D 1, Bd. 235.
19. Hans-Peter Schwartz, *Konrad Adenauer: A German Politician in the Age of War*, v. 1: *Revolution and Reconstruction,* trans. Louise Wilmot (Providence, RI: Berghahn Books, 1995), pp. 231–87.

20. Ivone Kirkpatrick, *The Inner Circle: The Memoirs of Ivone Kirkpatrick* (London: Macmillan, 1959).
21. Elke Scherstjanoi, ed., *Das SKK-Statut: Zur Geschichte der sowjetischen Kontrollkommission in Deutschland 1949 bis 1953 – Eine Dokumentation* (Munich: K. G. Saur, 1998).
22. In general see Ronald Granieri, *The Ambivalent Alliance: Konrad Adenauer, the CDU/CSU, and the West 1949–1966* (New York: Berghahn Books, 2002), pp. 32–3.
23. See for example the comments by retired General Hans Speidel to U.S. General Alfred Gruenther on April 9, 1952, Germany (West) *Akten zur auswärtigen Politik der Bundesrepublik Deutschland* [hereafter *AAP-BRD* with volume-year and document number] *1952*, (Munich: Oldenbourg, 2000), d. 100. On the war criminal question in general, see Brochhagen, *Nach Nürnberg*, pp. 32ff; Frei, *Vergangenheitspolitik*, pp. 133ff.
24. Germany, Bundesministerium des Innern, *Dokumente zur Deutschlandpolitik*, Series II, Bd. 3 (Munich: Oldenbourg, 1997) [hereafter *DzD* with series, volume, and document numbers], d. 402. The gratuitous quotation marks around the words "war criminals" are Blankenhorn's. The Federal Republic had no Foreign Ministry until the following year at which time Adenauer served as his own foreign minister with Blankenhorn as chief of the Political Division.
25. For 1950 figures, see Buscher, *The U.S. War Crimes Trial Program*, Appendix B. For July 1951 figures, see Memorandum by Herbert Dittmann (deputy chief Political Division), July 10, 1951, *AAP-BRD*, *1951*, d. 126.
26. Memorandum by Dittmann, July 10, 1951, *AAP-BRD 1951*, d. 126. As of that date, Bonn counted 227 Germans imprisoned in Wittlich and another 479 imprisoned in France. In April 1950, the French had 273 in Wittlich and another 864 in France.
27. Unsigned Memorandum for Herbert Blankenhorn, undated [1950], Politisches Archiv des auswärtigen Amtes (Berlin) [hereafter PA-AA], B[estand] 10, Bd. 2100.
28. Great Britain, Parliament, House of Lords, *The Parliamentary Debates (Hansard)*, 5th Series (London: H. M. Stationery Office, 1949) [hereafter *Hansard* (Lords)], May 5, 1949, v. 162, c. 376ff.
29. Alaric Searle, "A Very Special Relationship: Basil Liddell Hart, Wehrmacht Generals, and the Debate on West German Rearmament," *War in History* 5, No. 3 (1998): 327–57. The Liddell Hart book referred to here is *The Other Side of the Hill: Germany's Generals, Their Rise and Fall, With Their Own Account of Military Events* (London: Cassell, 1948).
30. See Lord Maurice Hankey, *Politics, Trials and Errors* (Chicago: Henry Regnery Co., 1950).
31. Chichester's letters are in TNA, FO 371/85897.
32. See the correspondence along with Winifred's memorandum in TNA, FO 371/85898.
33. Dibelius to President of the Directorate (Le Cornu), May 19, 1951, Von Neurath Personal File, AAPS, roll 12.
34. Minutes of the Governors' Meeting, May 28, 1951, AAPS, roll 2; Mathewson (Berlin) to McCloy, CN-54065, May 28, 1951, NARA, RG 466, Entry 10-A, Box 29. Two days later, the British commandant in Berlin, Major General Geoffrey Bourne, with the approval of the French and U.S. commandants, approached the Berlin representative of the Soviet Control Commission, Sergei Alexievich Dengin, to no avail. See Bourne to British High Commission Legal Branch, GOC/30, May 30, 1951, TNA, FO 1060/545. In fact, von Neurath's son Constantine was the only family member allowed to visit (for fifteen minutes) on the golden anniversary because Marie was ill and the Soviets would not allow the two children to visit together. McCloy to Adenauer, July 30, 1951, BA-K, B 305, Bd. 158.
35. *SSD*, April 25, 1951. Quote in Winifred von Mackensen to Margret Speer, May 1, 1951, BA-K, NL 1340/Sig. 107.
36. *Die Welt*, June 21, 1951; Helmuth Fischinger (von Neurath's attorney) to Wurm, June 26, 1951, LKA-S, D 1, Bd. 304.
37. See for example Adenauer to François-Poncet, June 20, 1950, PA-AA, B 10, Bd. 2100.
38. Adenauer to McCloy (including Wurm correspondence), June 13, 1951, zu 515-01 E II/6110/51, BA-K, B 305, Bd. 158; Adenauer to McCloy, 515-01 11539/51, October 21, 1951, NARA, RG 466, Entry 59, Box 21.
39. Stephen Henry, Legal Branch, British Military Government Berlin to N. H. Moller, Office of the Legal Adviser, British High Commission, May 6, 1950 (forwarded to FO as No. 708, May 8, 1950), TNA, FO 1060/449.
40. Kirkpatrick to Robertson, CG 1745/14/184, May 24, 1950, and Robertson to Kirkpatrick, HC/1544, March 18, 1950, both in TNA, FO 371/85897.

41. Acheson to HICOG Frankfurt, CN-35590, March 23, 1950, NARA, RG 466, Entry 10-A, Box 29.
42. Kirkpatrick to FO, No. 362, July 22, 1950, TNA, FO 1060/429.
43. Fishman, *Long Knives*, pp. 161–3.
44. Neuropsychiatric Report on Prisoner 6, April 22, 1950, Maxwell McKnight to Joseph Slater, May 3, 1950, with attached medical evaluations, NARA, RG 466, Entry 59, Box 5.
45. Office, Chief of Medical Service, 279th Station Hospital, Berlin Military Post, U.S. Army, April 12, 1950, NARA, RG 466, Entry 59, Box 4. Hess's evaluation pointed to a "memory disorder that fits no known ... picture ... in a probably very intelligent man of great will power."
46. Maxwell McKnight to Joseph Slater, May 11, 1950, NARA, RG 466, Entry 59, Box 5. See also Foreign Office Memorandum PC 2931/33/188, December 20, 1950, TNA, FO 1060/544.
47. McCloy to Robertson, May 2, 1950, NARA, RG 466, Entry 48, Box 14.
48. Tab 15b Other Business, May 31, 1950, NARA, RG 466, Entry 59, Box 5; Allied High Commission for Germany/Allied General Secretariat/AGSEC(50)1155, June 2, 1950, TNA, FO 371/85897. On McCloy's comment, see Kirkpatrick to FO, No. 1027, July 11, 1950, and Kirkpatrick to FO, No. 362, July 21, 1950, both in TNA, FO 371/85897.
49. On the British, see reports in TNA, FO 1042/544, especially Law Committee, Memorandum by the U.K. Member, Spandau Prison Regulations, Paper A (January 1950) and Ref L15/8/105, December 9, 1950. On the French, see Ganeval's reports to François-Poncet of June 22, 1950, and July 1, 1950, MAE-AOFAA, GMFB 363 (XA/1/3); on the United States, see Draft Allied Kommandatura Berlin, Legal Committee, LEG/R(50), July 13, 1950, NARA, RG 466, Entry 10-A, Box 29; Kirkpatrick to FO, No. 362, July 21, 1950, TNA, FO 1060/429.
50. Bonn (McCloy) to secretary of state, CN-31506, July 20, 1950, NARA, RG 466, Entry 59, Box 6.
51. Kirkpatrick to FO, No. 362, July 21, 1950, TNA, FO 371/85897.
52. George P. Hays, deputy U.S. high commissioner for Germany (for McCloy) to Adenauer, AGSEC(50)1691, August 9, 1950, PA-AA, B 10, Bd. 2100.
53. The letter is referenced in Kirkpatrick to Foreign Office, No. 391, August 9, 1950; Memorandum by Newton, October 3, 1950, both in TNA, FO 371/85898.
54. Kirkpatrick to Foreign Office, No. 362, July 21, 1950, TNA, FO 371/85898.
55. Memorandum by Newton, October 3, 1950, TNA, FO 371/85898.
56. Memorandum by Sir Alfred Brown (British High Commission, legal adviser), January 12, 1951, and Brown to chief legal officer, British Military Government Berlin, January 22, 1951, both in TNA, FO 1060/544.
57. See the letter from the chief of legal affairs of the French High Commission, February 23, 1951, MAE-AOFAA, GMFB 363 (XA/1/3).
58. McCloy to Adenauer, February 22, 1951, BA-K, B 305, Bd. 158.
59. Memorandum 515-01 E II/Neurath/51, unsigned and undated, BA-K, B 305, Bd. 158.
60. Adenauer to McCloy, October 21, 1951, 515-01 11539/51, NARA, RG 466, Entry 59, Box 21.
61. McCloy to Adenauer, July 30, 1951, BA-K, B 305, Bd. 158.
62. Wurm to Blankenhorn, August 16, 1951, BA-K, B 305, Bd. 158.
63. Adenauer to McCloy, October 21, 1951, 515-01 11539/51, NARA, RG 466, Entry 59, Box 21.
64. Memorandum by Dr. Heinz von Trützschler, May 6, 1952, PA-AA, B 10, Bd. 2106.
65. Jay Baird, *To Die for Germany: Heroes in the Nazi Pantheon* (Bloomington: Indiana University Press, 1990), pp. 41–72.
66. Baird, *To Die for Germany*, pp. 71–2.
67. Sprecher, *Inside the Nuremberg Trial*, v. 2, p. 1435.
68. Allied Control Authority, Allied Secretariat, ASEC(46)942, October 23, 1946, TNA, FO 1012/607.
69. W. Wallace Kirkpatrick, Chief, Legal Affairs Division, Allied Kommandatura, to Colonel W. H. Peters, HQ European Command, Judge Advocate's Division, War Crimes Branch, U.S. Army, APO 742, October 25, 1951, NARA, RG 466, Entry 16-B, Box 8.

70. The prison governors and medical officers agreed on a Four-Power autopsy, statement on cause of death, and cremation in August 1947 without further details. The Kommandatura Legal Committee approved the basic recommendation in October, and the commandants approved it in December. The procedural details described below were worked out by the Spandau governors and the Kommandatura Legal Committee in January and February 1948. See Henry H. Frank (U.S. governor Spandau) to Legal Committee, AO/I-3/47/91, August 11, 1947, MAE-AOFAA, GMFB 363 (XA/1/3); Kommandatura Interalliée de Berlin, Comité Legal, LEG/R(47)35, October 10, 1947; Kommandatura Interalliée de Berlin, Comité Legal, LEG/I(48)45, January 28, 1948 and enclosures SP/BGC/2, 16/1948, and the confidential unsigned note from Spandau Prison (probably from Darbois), January 13, 1948, all in MAE-AOFAA, GMFB 15/1.
71. On the deputy commandants' discussion, see Annexe à BKD/M(41)51, December 9, 1947, appended to Peter C. Bullard to Wesley Pape, December 17, 1947, and the "Note [from French High Commission Legal Group] pour le Général [Ganeval], February 24, 1951, both in MAE-AOFAA, GMFB 363 (XA/1/3). On the problem of secrecy, see Kommandatura Interalliée de Berlin, Comité Legal, LEG/I(48)45 and annexes, MAE-AOFAA, GMFB 363 (XA/1/3), and Darbois's protest, appended to SP/BGC/2 16–1948 in MAE-AOFAA, GMFB 15/1.
72. Office of the U.S. Commander, Berlin, APO 742, June 12, 1950, Memorandum to Dr. Pape from J. J. Ewell, Lieutenant Colonel GSC, executive officer (and all supporting documents therein), NARA, RG 466, Entry 16-B, Box 8.
73. On the political connections between the United States and West German authorities, see Eisenberg, *Drawing the Line*.
74. "Accord concernant la disposition a prendre pour les restes d'un détenus décede," October 14, 1949, MAE-AOFAA, GMFB 15/1; explained in Fredrick A. O. Schwarz, general council, to Department of State, Desp. 608, August 14, 1953, NARA, RG 59, Entry 1311, LF 59 D 609, Box 17.
75. Confidential Brief Tab N. 3 on HICOM/P(51)22, March 15, 1951; Secret Office Memorandum, AHCO Parker to McCloy, March 16, 1951, both in NARA, RG 466, Entry 48, Box 14.
76. Mathewson to McCloy, CN-50257, April 7, 1951; McCloy to Department of State, CN-51742, April 26, 1951, both in NARA, RG 466, Entry 48, Box 14. Further considerations in TNA, FO 1060/545.
77. On Bourne, see his Ref. 191/21/51 in MAE-AOFAA, GMFB 363 (XA/1/3). On Bevin, see Foreign Office No. 242 to Sir Gordon Macready, June 25, 1951, TNA, FO 1060/545.
78. Kirkpatrick to FO, No. 670, July 15, 1951, TNA, FO 1060/545.
79. McCloy to Department of State, CN-54411, June 1, 1951; McCloy to Department of State, CN-31233, July 19, 1951, both in NARA, RG 466, Entry 48, Box 14; Kirkpatrick to Foreign Office, No. 725, July 23, 1951, AMB/SlgD, AK 135/5.
80. Allied Kommandatura Berlin (Office of the Chairman Secretary), BK/AHC(52)16, February 18, 1952, NARA, RG 466, Entry 48, Box 14; Kirkpatrick to FO, No. 1252, November 30, 1951 and Susin's reply of November 6, 1951, both in TNA, FO 1060/545. On the golden anniversary, Bourne to Carolet, May 30, 1951, MAE-AOFAA, GMFB 363 (XA/1/3).
81. Adenauer–Acheson Discussion, November 21, 1951, *AAP-BRD-Adenauer und die Hohen Kommissare*, v. 1, pp. 526–28.
82. Acheson telegram CN-40478, December 21, 1951; Allied Kommandatura Berlin, BK/AHC(52)1, January 5, 1952; Brief for the U.S. member, January 18, 1952, all in NARA, RG 466, Entry 48, Box 14.
83. Neate (Secretary General) to chairman secretary, Allied Kommandatura AGSEC/SP(52)4, January 29, 1952, NARA, RG 466, Entry 48, Box 14; Lyon to USCOB, Colonel Legere, February 19, 1952, NARA, RG 466, Entry 16-B, Box 8.
84. Undated translation in TNA, FO 1060/545.
85. See Frank Roberts to Kirkpatrick, January 4, 1952, and Kirkpatrick to Roberts, L 15/6/411, January 25, 1952, both in TNA, FO 1060/545; See also Secret Memorandum, HICOM/SP/M(52)1, January 24, 1952, and Hagen (Chief, Prisons Division) to McDonald (Law Committee), January 30, 1952, NARA, RG 466, Entry 48, Box 14; Memorandum from McCloy to Mathewson, January 25, 1952, NARA, RG 466, Entry 16-B, Box 8.

86. Lyon to Department of State, Memorandum of Conversation with respect to Spandau prisoner von Neurath, January 31, 1952, NARA, RG 466, Entry 16-B, Box 8; Maurice Bathurst to W. D. Allen, FO, No. 437, February 22, 1952, TNA, FO 1060/545.
87. FO to British High Commission, No. 126, January 30, 1952, TNA, FO 1060/545.
88. Lyon to USCOB, Colonel Legere, February 19, 1952, NARA, RG 466, Entry 16-B, Box 8; Minutes of the Medical Board Meeting, February 12, 1952, AAPS, roll 10.
89. Lyon to Bonn, CN-43475, February 20, 1952, NARA, RG 466, Entry 48, Box 14.
90. McCloy to Department of State, CN-6/22, February 22, 1952, NARA, RG 466, Entry 48, Box 14.
91. McCloy to Department of State, CN-9976, April 3, 1952, NARA, RG 466, Entry 48, Box 14; Minutes of the Governors' Meeting, April 3, 1952, AAPS, roll 3. The seriousness is confirmed in part by the fact that it is the first attack that the self-absorbed Speer mentions in his diary. *SSD*, April 1, 1952.
92. Lyon memorandum of April 11, 1952, NARA, RG 466, Entry 16-B, Box 8.
93. Acheson to U.S. Embassy Moscow, CN-47100, May 2, 1952, NARA, RG 466, Entry 48, Box 14.
94. For the convention itself and the negotiations leading to the contractuals, see United States, Department of State, *Foreign Relations of the United States* [hereafter *FRUS*], *1952–1954*, v. 7 (Washington, DC: U.S. Government Printing Office, 1986), pp. 1–168. For summary, Hans-Peter Schwartz, *Geschichte der Bundesrepublik Deutschland*, Bd. 2: *Die Ära Adenauer 1949–1957* (Stuttgart: Deutsche Verlags-Anstalt, 1981), pp. 149–66.
95. Acheson circular CN-47869, May 15, 1952, NARA, RG 466, Entry 48, Box 14.
96. Buscher, *The U.S. War Crimes Trial Program*, pp. 76–7.
97. See the Memorandum of the Foreign Ministers' Meeting, May 25, 1952, in *FRUS, 1952–1954*, v. 7, d. 48.
98. See the comments of François-Poncet of February 5, 1952, in *FRUS, 1952–1954*, v. 7, d. 7. On the war criminals question, Adenauer and François-Poncet had already had an ugly exchange in November 1950 in which the French High Commissioner warned that regardless of how touchy German public opinion was on the issue, French public opinion was no less touchy, especially since Germans imprisoned in France had committed their crimes there. See Adenauer's discussion with the High Commissioners, November 16, 1950, *AAP-BRD-Adenauer und die Hohen Kommissare 1949–1950*, v. 1, d. 19. In fact, on the eve of the Contractual Agreements, the French held, aside from 152 Germans in Wittlich, another 311 in France itself: Schuman countered Adenauer's desire to include provisions for the release of the latter group in the Contractual Agreements with the answer that these prisoners were for bilateral Franco-German discussions only and that the number was quite fair given the length of the German occupation. See the protocol of the Foreign Ministers' Meeting (London), February 18, 1952, *AAP-BRD*, *Adenauer und die Hohen Kommissare 1949–1950*, v. 2, Anlage 23, also printed in *AAP-BRD 1952*, d. 52.
99. *FRUS, 1952–1954*, v. 7, d. 48; *AAP-BRD-Adenauer und die Hohen Kommissare 1949–1950*, v. 2, Anlage 26. Schuman also accepted Adenauer's proposal that there would be Franco-German discussions concerning German war criminals incarcerated in France.
100. Patricia F. Hancock, German Political Department, FO to M. F. P. Herschenroder (legal adviser, British High Commission), May 30, 1952, and Herschenroder to Hancock, No. 339, June 5, 1952, both in TNA, FO 1060/546.
101. McCloy's suggestion of April 3 resulted in a less drastic personal démarche from Major General Cyril F. Coleman to Dengin on April 10 to the effect that should von Neurath suffer another heart attack "he should be moved to a hospital outside Spandau Prison under quadripartite control." Dengin promised to study this proposal, but there was no reply until May 23, whereupon Dengin argued that Spandau's own medical facilities were adequate and that von Neurath's health was improving anyway. Churchill proposed that the Soviet refusal to agree to the British proposal of April 10 might be publicized. "Surely," he said, "it would have a good effect on German opinion if this became public." Eden cautioned that a demonstration of Allied impotence concerning von Neurath would not have a desirable effect, and publicity would also hurt any further démarche with the Soviets over prison conditions. On McCloy's April 3 proposal, see Kirkpatrick to FO, No. 433, April 4, 1952, TNA, FO 1060/546. On the April 15 U.S. suggestion and the British refusal, see Herschenroder to Robert McCheyne Andrew, German Political Department, FO, April

23, 1952, TNA, FO 1060/546. On Churchill's proposal, see his minute of June 8, 1952, Serial M. 321/52 and Eden's reply of June 12, 1952, PM/52/61 both in TNA, PREM 11/793.
102. Acheson to HICOG Berlin, CN-70117, June 4, 1952, NARA, RG 466, Entry 48, Box 14.
103. Hancock to Herschenroder, May 30, 1952, TNA, FO 1060/546.
104. Brochhagen, *Nach Nürnberg*, pp. 64, 71.
105. *SSD*, April 22, 23, 1952.
106. The French *aide-mémoire* of June 10 is included in Acheson to HICOG Bonn, a-1991, June 16, 1952, and also Samuel Reber to Department of State, CN-49365, June 12, 1952, in NARA, RG 466, Entry 48, Box 14.
107. Adenauer discussion with Churchill, December 4, 1951, *AAP-BRD 1951*, d. 196. At that moment, there were roughly two hundred Germans at Werl. Churchill told Adenauer he was quietly working on the release of Erich von Manstein, who had been sentenced to twelve years on December 19, 1949, and who, according to Churchill, had been able to play golf while in prison. Eden assured Adenauer that all prisoners in Werl would have their cases reviewed so that a handful would be released immediately. Adenauer called for these releases to occur by Christmas.
108. Gifford to U.S. Embassy Paris and HICOG Bonn, CN-30861, July 16, 1952; Dunn to HICOG Bonn and U.S. Embassy London, CN-30915, July 17, 1952; Donnelly to Department of State, CN-1975, August 14, 1952, all in NARA, RG 466, Entry 48, Box 14.
109. Hans-Jürgen Döscher, *Verschworene Gesellschaft: Das Auswärtige Amt unter Adenauer zwischen Neubeginn und Kontinuität* (Berlin: Akademie Verlag, 1995), pp. 231–3.
110. See the original draft of von Trützschler to John F. Golay (U.S. secretary, Allied General Secretariat, U.S. High Commission), June 4, 1952, appended to Memorandum by Moppe to Blankenhorn and Hallstein, June 30, 1952, PA-AA, B 10, Bd. 2106, and von Trützschler to Golay, 515-01 E II 7375/52, June 4, 1952, TNA, FO 1060/546. Trützschler said that, according to his information, the cells were illuminated day and night, the prisoners were prohibited from speaking with one another, they could correspond with one relative only, and they could receive but two or three visits per year. These mistakes were pointed out in Donnelly to Adenauer, AGSEC(52)839, August 29, 1952, TNA, FO 1060/546.
111. Adenauer to Kirkpatrick, 515-01-d II 8773/52, July 9, 1952, PA-AA, B 10, Bd. 2106 and TNA, FO 1060/546.
112. On the drafting, HICOM/P(52)40, August 1, 1952, MAE-AOFAA, HC 281/17.
113. Kirkpatrick's letter to Chuikov of September 1, 1952, is in PA-AA, B 10, Bd. 2106 and TNA, FO 1060/546. On the public announcement, see *Neue Zeitung*, September 11, 1952; Memorandum by J. G. Ward, September 11, 1952; and Minute by M. A. Robb, October 8, 1952, TNA, FO 1060/546.
114. On the nature of the Soviet offer, see Rolf Steininger, *The German Question: The Stalin Note of 1952 and the Problem of Reunification*, trans. Jane T. Hedges, ed., Marc Cioc (New York: Columbia University Press, 1990); Jürgen Zarusky, ed., *Die Stalin-Note vom 10. März 1952: Neue Quellen und Analysen* (Munich: Oldenbourg, 2002). See also the summary in Granieri, *Ambivalent Alliance*, pp. 49–54.
115. Semichastnov to François-Poncet, October 5, 1952, printed in *Neue Zeitung*, October 9, 1952.
116. Donnelly to Chuikov, October 23, 1952, NARA, RG 466, Entry 48, Box 14; François-Poncet to Chuikov, October 23, 1952, MAE-AOFAA, GMFB 15/1, Folder: Modifications.
117. Memorandum by Dr. Born, 515-01 d II 13714/52, November 4, 1952, PA-AA, B 10, Bd. 2106.
118. Adenauer to Donnelly, zu 515-01 d II 13714/52, November 11, 1952, PA-AA, B 10, Bd. 2106.
119. Brief for the U.S. Member of the Law Committee, Agenda of November 28, 1952, NARA, RG 466, Entry 48, Box 14.
120. Memorandum of January 13, 1953, zu 515-01 d II 13714/53, PA-AA, B 10, Bd. 2106; Adenauer to François-Poncet, 515-01 d E II 20851/53, September 24, 1953, AMB/SlgD, AK 135/4.
121. Lyon to Department of State, CN-40536, January 22, 1953, NARA, RG 466, Entry 48, Box 14; Memorandum by von Trützschler, 515-01 E II Raeder/53, January 21, 1953; Samuel Reber to Adenauer, AGSEC(53)95, February 6, 1953, BA-K, B 305, Bd. 159.

122. *SSD*, February 26, 1953; Minutes of the Governors' Meeting, February 19, 1953, AAPS, roll 3.
123. Churchill minute to Eden, December 5, 1952, Ser. M 561/52, TNA, PREM 11/793. Churchill's comments are based on a summary of an inspection report of Lionel Fox, chairman of the Prison Commission for England and Wales, April 23, 1951, in this folder. The full version is in TNA, FO 1060/544. Fox thought the conditions especially inhumane, pointing to the lack of productive work beside gardening, the lack of newspapers or a radio for contact with the outside world, and a lack of regular conversation between the prisoners in a common room or at mealtimes. The summary of the Fox report noted the improvements in visits and letters. Churchill commented that publicity might ease the lot of the prisoners but again Eden cautioned in his reply of December 17, 1952, that "Publicity would not, I fear, serve a useful part. If we whipped up an agitation, we should only lose face when it failed to achieve its object.... Publicity does not influence the Russians.... Such small success as we have had in getting the prison rules mitigated have come by private representations. Even here, if we push the Russians too hard, we are likely to lose what ground we have gained." Churchill replied, "I see your difficulty."
124. Brief for the U.S. member of the Law Committee, Agenda of April 1, 1953, NARA, RG 466, Entry 48, Box 14.
125. Adenauer–Dulles discussion, April 7, 1953, *AAP-BRD 1953*, v. 1, d. 114.
126. Brief for the U.S. member of the Law Committee, Agenda of April 20, 1953, NARA, RG 466, Entry 48, Box 14.
127. Brief for the U.S. Member of the Law Committee, Agenda of May 27, 1953, NARA, RG 466, Entry 48, Box 14. The reference is to the Bermuda Conference of December 4–8, 1953, between Eisenhower, Churchill, French Premier Joseph Laniel and their foreign ministers, which discussed the EDC, Korea, issues of atomic energy, and a Four-Power summit. See Klaus Larres, *Churchill's Cold War: The Politics of Personal Diplomacy* (New Haven, CT: Yale University Press, 2002), pp. 309ff; Martin Gilbert, *Winston Churchill*, v. 7: *Never Despair* (Boston: Houghton Mifflin, 1988), pp. 916–42.
128. Allied High Commission for Germany/The Council HICOM/P(53)13, July 25, 1953, NARA, RG 466, Entry 48, Box 14.
129. The Soviets in June 1953 dissolved the Soviet Control Commission and replaced it with an office of the Soviet High Commission in Germany with its headquarters in Berlin. Semeonov took up his duties on June 5, 1953, and Chuikov was relieved of duties in Germany on June 10. See Scherstjanoi, *Das SKK-Statut*, pp. 97–9.
130. Conant to S. Houston Ley, assistant to the general counsel, May 26, 1953, NARA, RG 466, Entry 48, Box 14; Conant to John Foster Dulles, No. 436, July 28, 1953, NARA, RG 59, Entry 1311, LF 59 D 609, Box 17.
131. On von Neurath's heart attack and the scheme to move the body, see Lyon to Dulles, No. 133, July 29, 1953; Lyon to Dulles, No. 143, July 30, 1953; Dulles to HICOG Berlin and Bonn, No. 391, July 30, 1953, all in NARA, RG 59, Entry 1311, LF 59 D 609, Box 17.
132. *SSD*, August 5, 1953, November 9, 1953. On the censorship for health information from von Neurath's letters and visits, see Minutes of the Governors' Meetings, April 2, 1953, September 9, 1953, AAPS, roll 3.
133. Record of discussion between Dengin and Coleman, July 31, 1953, AMB/SlgD, AK 135/4.
134. On Dengin and Alabjev, see HICOG Berlin to Department of State, No. 133, August 26, 1953, NARA, RG 466, Entry 48, Box 14; Minutes of the Governors' Meeting, August 1953, AAPS, roll 3. Other amenities requested for von Neurath included an extra letter and visit per month, reassignment to the more comfortable cell used for chapel services, a bedside light, and night checks with a flashlight instead of the internal 40-watt bulb. Von Neurath eventually did receive, with Soviet agreement, a hospital bed, a small rug beside the bed, an armchair, an adjustable light, and flashlight night checks. See W. Wallace Kirkpatrick, Chief, Legal Affairs Division, HICOG Berlin, to Department of State, No. 153, August 4, 1953, NARA, RG 59, Entry 1311, LF 59 D 609, Box 17; Minutes of the Governors' Meeting, September 3, 1953, AAPS, roll 3. On the food, Minutes of the Governors' Meetings, September 9, 1953, September 23, 1953, AAPS, roll 3.
135. On the High Commissioners, see Conant to Department of State, No. 605, August 1, 1953, NARA, RG 59, Entry 1311, LF 59 D 609, Box 17.

136. Draft letter to Semeonov, undated, NARA, RG 466, Entry 48, Box 14; François-Poncet to Semeonov, August 1, 1953; Haute Commission en Allemagne, Secrétariat Général Alliée, AGSEC(53)698, August 11, 1953, both in MAE-AOFAA, GMFB 15/1, Folder: Modifications. In fact, Semeonov did respond on August 29, 1953, refusing the request by referring to previous quadripartite agreements and Semichastnov's refusal of October 4, 1952. Semeonov to François-Poncet, August 29, 1953, MAE-AOFAA, GMFB 15/1, Folder: Modifications.
137. Kommandatura Interalliée de Berlin, Bureau de Secrétaire Président, BK/AHC(53)71, August 13, 1953, MAE-AOFAA, GMFB 15/1, Folder: Modifications; Lyon to HICOG Bonn, CN-31621, August 12, 1953, NARA, RG 466, Entry 48, Box 14.
138. Report of a meeting between the chairman commandant (U.K.) and the governing mayor, held on October 23, 1953, MAE-AOFAA, GMFB 15/1, Folder: Modifications. See also W. Wallace Kirkpatrick to Frederick O. Schwarz, October 29, 1953, NARA, RG 466, Entry 16-B, Box 8.
139. Draft BK/O(53), MAE-AOFAA, GMFB 15/1, Folder: Modifications.
140. Report by the Legal Advisers Concerning the Disposal of Remains of Spandau Prisoners in the Event of Death, Second French Draft, February 24, 1954, TNA, FO 371/109331.
141. On the draft note, see Memorandum by H. W. Evans, January 7, 1954; Draft letter to Semeonov enclosed in Hoyer Millar to Berlin, No. 14, January 9, 1954; Herschenroder to Evans, L/15/8/105, January 20, 1954, all in TNA, FO 371/109330; François-Poncet to Semeonov, January 11, 1954 (delivered by French Liaison Mission to Karlshorst), MAE-AOFAA, GMFB 15/1, Folder: Modifications.
142. Minute by Evans, April 1, 1954, TNA, FO 371/109331.
143. The British and French governments called the conference to get a sense of the intentions of the Soviet government after Stalin's death. For background, see Anthony Eden, *Full Circle* (Boston: Houghton Mifflin, 1960), pp. 59ff.
144. Memorandum from Sir Frank Roberts to Anthony Eden, February 4, 1954, TNA, FO 371/109331. See also the numerous German press clippings in this folder and in FO 371/109330. On the Evangelical Press Service, see High Commission for Germany/Allied General Secretariat, AGSE (54)11, January 11, 1954, TNA, FO 371/109330.
145. Drafts of the proposal from December 1953 are in BA-K, B 305, Bd. 154. The original proposal was for the release of the prisoners over 70 years old, but since von Neurath and Raeder were both older than 75 anyway, the number was raised to seventy-five to make a greater humanitarian impact. The Adenauer letter is described in Hoyer Millar to Foreign Office, No. 23, January 9, 1954, TNA, FO 371/109330. Adenauer also proposed a special Four-Power commission charged with dealing with Spandau Prison exclusively.
146. For press accounts of Adenauer's note, see *Die Welt*, January 11, 1954; *Bonner Rundschau*, January 11, 1954; *General Anzeiger*, January 11, 1954. See also Herschenroder to Evans, L 15/8/05, March 19, 1954, TNA, FO 371/109331.
147. Dulles to HICOG Bonn, No. 2139, January 20, 1954, NARA, RG 59, Entry 1311, LF 59 D 609, Box 17. On Dulles and the Berlin Conference see Eden, *Full Circle*, pp. 61–3.
148. Minute from Sarner, January 12, 1954; Minute from Hancock, January 18, 1954; Memorandum by Hancock, January 20, 1954; Memorandum by Sir Frank Roberts, January 21, 1954; Kirkpatrick to Sir Frank Roberts, January 22, 1954, all in TNA, FO 371/109330; Memorandum from Roberts to Eden, February 4, 1954, TNA, FO 371/109331.
149. Von Papen to Churchill, January 8, 1954, and Churchill minute to Eden, January 21, 1954, Ser. M. 18/54, both in TNA, PREM 11/793 and also TNA, FO 371/109330.
150. Dulles (from West Berlin) to Dowling, CN-37885, February 12, 1954, NARA, RG 466, Entry 10-A, Box 166.
151. Eden to Foreign Office, No. 202, February 17, 1954, TNA, 371/109331; Eden to Churchill, P.M./54/38, March 1, 1954, TNA, PREM 11/793.
152. Eden, *Full Circle*, pp. 76–7.
153. Comment on bottom of Eden to Churchill, PM/54/38, March 1, 1954, TNA, FO 371/109331.
154. Bathurst to Evans, L 5/8/105, March 5, 1954, TNA, 371/109331. The letter, to which Semeonov had not replied, is in Hoyer Millar to FO, No. 22, January 11, 1954, TNA, PREM 11/793.

155. Foreign Office to British Embassy in Moscow, No. 390, March 24, 1954; Hoyer Millar to FO, No. 253, March 26, 1954, both in TNA, FO 371/199331; Parkman to U.S. High Commission, CN-39187, March 24, 1954, NARA, RG 466, Entry 10-A, Box 166.
156. *SSD*, March 27, 1954, March 31, 1954.
157. On Lewis's questions in the House of Commons beginning March 24, 1954, and running into April, see TNA, FO 371/109331, FO 371/109332. On SED contacts with Lewis in 1960, SAPMO, DY 30 [Büro Norden], Bd. 5.
158. Hoyer Millar to FO, No. 189, March 27, 1954; François-Poncet to Adenauer, AGSEC(54)206, March 30, 1954, TNA, FO 371/109330.
159. For the first round of talks, see Lieutenant General Sir William Oliver (commandant British sector Berlin) to British Embassy Bonn, Telegram No. 133, April 6, 1954; Summary Record of the Meeting of the Representatives of the Four Powers on Spandau Prison held at the ACA building on April 6, 1954; Minutes of the Meeting of the Representatives of the Four Powers on Spandau Prison held at the ACA building on April 6, 1954 at 11:00 A.M., all in NARA, RG 466, Entry 48, Box 15; General Oliver to FO, No. 38, April 9, 1954, TNA, FO 371/109332.
160. The second round of discussions is covered in Oliver to British Embassy in Bonn, No. 156, April 26, 1954; Summary Record of the Second Meeting of the Representatives of the Four Powers on Spandau Prison held at the ACA Building on April 26, 1954; Berlin Telegram No. 157 from Bathurst to Bonn, April 26, 1954, all in NARA, RG 466, Entry 48, Box 15; Oliver to FO, No. 169, April 26, 1954, TNA, FO 371/109333.
161. On the third round, see Berlin Telegram No. 160 to Bonn, April 27, 1954; Summary Record of the Third Meeting of the Representatives of the Four Powers on Spandau Prison held at the ACA Building on April 27, 1954; Verbatim Minutes of the Third Meeting of the Representatives of the Four Powers on Spandau Prison held at the ACA Building, Berlin, on April 27, 1954, all in NARA, RG 466, Entry 48, Box 15; Bathurst to Hoyer Millar, L 15/8/21, April 29, 1954, TNA, FO 371/109333.
162. Hoyer Millar to Berlin, No. 96, April 29, 1954, NARA, RG 466, Entry 48, Box 15.
163. The British chose *Die Welt*, the Americans chose *Frankfurter Allgemeine Zeitung*, the French chose *Der Kurier*, and the Soviets surprised their counterparts by choosing the Western *Berliner Zeitung* rather than one of the Communist organs. On the new provisions including hospitalization, see Minutes of the Governors' Meetings, May 10, 1954, May 24, 1954, May 26, 1954, June 25, 1954, AAPS, roll 3.
164. The fourth-round negotiations are in Parkman to Department of State, CN-40417, April 30, 1954, NARA, RG 466, Entry 48, Box 15. For the final text of the agreement, see Agreement Made between the Representatives of the High Commissioners in Germany of the Signatory Powers of the London Agreement and the Charter of the International Military Tribunal Concerning Changes in the Regime of Spandau Prison, April 29, 1954, NARA, RG 466, Entry 48, Box 15. The final arrangements were made by the prison governors in September 1954. See Minutes of the Governors' Meeting, September 16, 1954 and Action to be taken in Event of Death of a Prisoner in Allied Prison Spandau, AAPS, roll 3.
165. Hoyer Millar to Bathurst with copy to Roberts, 166/1/80/54, April 29, 1954; AGSEC (54)283, May 3, 1954; Adenauer to Hoyer Millar, 204-515-01 d/2089/54, May 15, 1954, all in TNA, FO 371/109334.
166. Constantine von Neurath to Blankenhorn, BKA, June 15, 1954, BA-K, B 305, Bd. 158.
167. *SSD*, May 24, 1954.
168. BK/AHC(54)39, July 31, 1954, AMB/SlgD, AK 135/3. On the delay of Funk's surgery, see Knight to Dowling, CN-42065, June 16, 1954; Charles H. Owsley, Despatch No. 69, July 27, 1954, both in NARA, RG 466, Entry 10-A, Box 166.
169. Minutes of the Governors' Meeting, July 8, 1954, AAPS, roll 3.
170. Report by Mogilnikov, July 7, 1954, Spandau Governors' Official Correspondence File, AAPS, roll 21; HICOG Berlin to Department of State, July 16,1954, NARA, RG 466, Entry 48, Box 15.
171. *SSD*, July 8, 1954.
172. Minutes of the Governors' Meetings, July 15, 1954, July 23, 1954, AAPS, roll 3; Thomas D. McKiernan to U.S. High Commission, July 16, 1954, NARA, RG 466, Entry 10-A, Box 166.

173. BK/AHC(54)39, July 31, 1954, AMB/SlgD, AK 135/3.
174. See Jack Fishman, *The Seven Men of Spandau* (New York: Rinehart, 1954). For British discussion, see TNA, FO 371/109335. The August 15, 1954, issue of the West German magazine *Quick* also contained an article and smuggled photographs from Spandau including the burial site in the prison courtyard. Allied Kommandatura Berlin, Legal Committee, LEG/R(54)27, August 18, 1954, MAE-AOFAA, GMFB, 15/1, Folder: Modifications.
175. Minutes of the Governors' Meeting, July 15, 1954, AAPS, roll 3; HICOG Berlin to Department of State, July 16, 1954, NARA, RG 466, Entry 48, Box 15; Charles H. Owsley Despatch No. 69, July 27, 1954, NARA, RG 466, Entry 10-A, Box 166; De Margerie (Berlin) to French High Commission, No. 722/723, July 24, 1954, and François-Poncet to Quai d'Orsay, No. 707/710, August 13, 1954, MAE-AOFAA, GMFB 15/1, Folder: Modifications. See also the Commandants' recommendations in BK/AHC(54)39, AMB/SlgD, AK 135/3.
176. Parkman to Dowling, CN-31128, August 4, 1954, NARA, RG 466, Entry 10-A, Box 166.
177. *SSD*, September 2, 1954.
178. Minutes of the Governors' Meeting, September 2, 1954, AAPS, roll 3.
179. *SSD*, September 6, 1954; Minutes of the Governors' Meeting, September 9, 1954, AAPS, roll 3.
180. Minutes of the Governors' Meeting, September 9, 1954, AAPS, roll 3; Blankenhorn to German missions abroad, undated, 204/1078/54 E, BA-K, B 305, Bd. 158; *Die Welt*, September 30, 1954. Alabjev, thanks to this article, wanted to prohibit further visits from Winifred. Minutes of the Governors' Meetings, October 21, 1954, October 28, 1954, AAPS, roll 3.
181. Georgy Morev's recollections are in the Russian online magazine *Trud*, No. 074, April 22, 2004, http://www.trud.ru [accessed January 2006]. I am grateful to Arsen Djatej for this reference and translation.
182. Adenauer to Hoyer Millar as Chairman of the Allied High Commission, undated, 204-515-01 d/3631/54, BA-K, B 305, Bd. 158. See also TNA, FO 371/109335.
183. Parkman to Dowling, CN-31620, August 18, 1954, NARA, RG 466, Entry 10-A, Box 166; Owsley Despatch No. 95, August 16, 1954, NARA, RG 66, Entry 10-A, Box 169; De Margerie (Berlin) to French High Commission, No. 722/723, July 24, 1954 and François-Poncet to Quai d'Orsay, No. 707/710, August 13, 1954, MAE-AOFAA, GMFB 15/1, Folder: Modifications.
184. Owsley Despatch No. 95, August 16, 1954, NARA, RG 466, Entry 10-A, Box 169.
185. Memorandum from Referat 204, 204/1078/54 E, November 3, 1954, BA-K, B 305, Bd. 158.
186. *SSD*, November 4, 8, 1954.
187. *Manchester Guardian*, November 4, 1954; *Neue Züricher Zeitung*, November 5, 1954.
188. On this, see Khrushchev to Walter Ulbricht, July 14, 1955, SAPMO, DY 30 [Büro Ulbricht], Bd. 3749.
189. "Last Hours at Spandau," *The Times*, November 7, 1954.
190. AA, Dienststelle Berlin (Roedel) to AA, 209-210-84/54g, Br. Nr. 694, November 10, 1954; Botschaft der BRD, Den Haag, 515-00 Kontr. Nr. 3365, November 11, 1954, both in BA-K, B 305, Bd. 158.
191. *FAZ*, November 8, 1954; HICOG Bonn to Department of State, No. 1013, November 12, 1954, NARA, RG 59, Entry 1311, LF 59 D 609, Box 17.
192. Press Report of November 9, 1954, BA-K, B 305, Bd. 158.
193. Both pieces of correspondence were printed in "Von Neurath Freed," *The Times*, November 8, 1954.
194. Hausenstein (Paris) to AA, 200-00 I Tgb. Nr. 4557/54, November 12, 1954, BA-K, B 305, Bd. 158.
195. Botschaft der BRD Den Haag, 515-00 Kontr. Nr. 3365, November 11, 1954, BA-K, B 305, Bd. 158.
196. Diplomatische Vertretung der BRD in London to AA, 246-01, Nr. 22647/54, November 12, 1954, BA-K, B 305, Bd. 158.
197. Pfeiffer (Botschaft der BRD), 246-00 K. Nr. 4411/54, November 22, 1954, BA-K, B 305, Bd. 158.
198. Press Report of November 9, 1954, BA-K, B 305, Bd. 158.

199. HICOG Bonn to Department of State, No. 1013, November 12, 1954, NARA, RG 59, Entry 1311, LF 59 D 609, Box 17.
200. Hans Peter Mensing, ed., *Konrad Adenauer – Theodor Heuss: Unter vier Augen, Gespräche aus den Gründerjahren 1949–1959* (Berlin: Siedler, 1997), p. 363, n. 29.
201. See the article by Paul Sethe in *FAZ*, November 12, 1954.
202. Undated Blankenhorn circular 204/1078/54 E, BA-K, B 305, Bd. 158.
203. Heuss to Pen Zentrum deutscher Autoren im Ausland (London), December 9, 1954, BA-K 305, Bd.158. See also his comments to Adenauer in Hans-Peter Mensing, ed., *Theodor Heuss und Konrad Adenauer – Unserem Vaterlande zugute: Der Briefwechsel, 1948–1963* (Berlin: Seidler, 1989), pp. 197, 473.
204. Details on Raeder's release are in BA-K, B 305, Bd. 159; For Funk, see NARA, RG 59, Entry 1311, LF 59 D 609, Box 19; Chapter 4 and 5 in this book.
205. Heineman, *von Neurath*, p. 327, n. 95.

## CHAPTER FOUR. HITLER'S SUCCESSOR: A TALE OF TWO ADMIRALS

1. On naval construction under Raeder, see Jost Dülffer, *Weimar, Hitler und die Marine: Reichspolitik und Flottenbau 1920–1939* (Düsseldorf: Droste, 1973).
2. *TMWC*, v. 14, pp. 171ff, May 20, 1946.
3. Raeder presentation to Hitler, October 16, 1939, with Attachment of October 15, *TMWC*, v. 34, document 157-C, pp. 608–41.
4. Carl-Axel Gemzell, *Hitler, Raeder und Skandinavien: Der Kampf für einen maritimen Operationsplan* (Lund: Gleerup, 1965).
5. Summarized in Norman J. W. Goda, *Tomorrow the World: Hitler, Northwest Africa and the Path toward America* (College Station: Texas A&M University Press, 1998), pp. xx–xxi.
6. Norman J. W. Goda, "Black Marks: Hitler's Bribery of His Senior Military Officers during World War II," *Journal of Modern History* 72, No. 2 (2000): 413–52.
7. *TMWC*, 14, pp. 73–4, May 17, 1946, reference to document 653-D, *TMWC*, v. 35, pp. 310–14.
8. *TMWC*, v. 14, p. 161.
9. Taylor, *Anatomy*, pp. 252–3.
10. *TMWC*, v. 14, p. 96, May 17, 1946.
11. *TMWC*, v. 14, pp. 188–9, May 20, 1946.
12. *TMWC*, v. 14, pp. 198, 203, May 20, 1946, reference to document 157-C, *TMWC*, v. 34, pp. 608–41.
13. *TMWC*, v. 14, p. 206, May 20, 1946.
14. *TMWC*, v. 14, pp. 213–15, May 20, 1946.
15. Good accounts are in Peter Padfield, *Dönitz: The Last Führer* (New York: Harper & Row, 1984); Michael Salewski, *Die deutsche Seekriegsleitung*, v. 2: *1942–1945* (Frankfurt am Main: Bernard & Graefe, 1975).
16. Quoted in Padfield, *Dönitz*, p. 316.
17. *TMWC*, v. 35, p. 106.
18. *TMWC*, document 2878-PS, v. 31, pp. 250–1.
19. Quoted in Charles Thomas, *The German Navy in the Nazi Era* (Annapolis, MD: Naval Institute Press, 1990), p. 243.
20. Douglas C. Peifer, *The Three German Navies: Dissolution, Transition, and New Beginnings, 1945–1960* (Gainsville: University Press of Florida, 2002), pp. 15–16.
21. On the appointment, see David Grier, "The Appointment of Karl Dönitz as Hitler's Successor," in *The Impact of Nazism: New Perspectives on the Third Reich and Its Legacy*, ed. Alan Steinweis and Daniel E. Rogers (Lincoln: University of Nebraska Press, 2003), pp. 182–98.
22. British merchant crewmen killed at sea by the enemy in World War II numbered 30,248. U.S. merchant crewmen killed at sea numbered about 8,651, which statistically made the U.S. merchant marine the deadliest American service. On British casualties, see Stephen W. Roskill, *The War at Sea, 1939–1945*, vol. 3, pt. 2 (London: HMSO, 1961), p. 305. For U.S. casualties, see Robert M. Browning, *U.S. Merchant Vessel War Casualties of World War II*

(Annapolis, MD: Naval Institute Press, 1996); Arthur R. Moore, *A Careless Word – A Needless Sinking: A History of the Staggering Losses Suffered by the U.S. Merchant Marine, Both in Ships and Personnel during World War II* (King's Point, NY: American Merchant Marine Museum, 1983).

23. Jane Gilliland, "Submarines and Targets: Suggestions for New Codified Rules of Submarine Warfare" *Georgetown Law Journal* 73, No. 3 (1985): 975–1005. For the summary of the case, see Sprecher, *Inside the Nuremberg Trial*, v. 2, pp. 981–96.
24. On the *Athenia*, see *TMWC*, v. 13, pp. 390–1; Padfield, *Dönitz*, pp. 191–4. German and Italian submarines sank a total of 2,919 Allied and neutral ships, which in turn totaled nearly 14.4 million tons of shipping. See the appendices of Clay Blair, *Hitler's U-Boat War*, 2 vols. (New York; Random House, 1996-98).
25. *TMWC*, document 191-C, v. 34, pp. 776–8.
26. *TMWC*, document 021-C, v. 34, pp. 177–9.
27. *TMWC*, document 642-D, v. 35, pp. 267–70.
28. *TMWC*, document 423-D, v. 35, pp. 94–104.
29. *TMWC*, document 630-D, v. 35, pp. 216–18.
30. For Möhle, see *TMWC*, v. 5, pp. 233–6; *TMWC*, v. 25, p. 395. For Heisig, see *TMWC*, document 566-D, v. 35, pp. 160–2.
31. *TMWC*, document 158-C, v. 34, pp. 641–4. Padfield, *Dönitz*, pp. 252–6, discusses this trend in the context of the *Laconia* order.
32. Padfield, *Dönitz*, p. 436.
33. *TMWC*, v. 14, p. 267.
34. *TMWC*, v. 14, p. 292, May 10, 1946. See also John Cameron, ed., *Trial of Heinz Eck, August Hoffmann, Walter Weisspfennig, Hans Richard Lenz and Wolfgang Schwender (The Peleus Trial)* (London: Hodge, 1948).
35. *TMWC*, v. 13, p. 438, May 13, 1946.
36. *TMWC*, v. 13, p. 343, May 10, 1946.
37. *TMWC*, v. 13, pp. 335 ff, May 10, 1946, reference to document 526-PS.
38. *TMWC*, v. 13, p. 393.
39. *TMWC*, v. 18, pp. 26–8. Summary of Dönitz's defense in Taylor, *Anatomy*, 398–410.
40. The judgment is in *TMWC*, v. 1, pp. 313ff. See also Taylor, *Anatomy*, pp. 566–8.
41. *SSD*, February 4, 1949.
42. *SSD*, December 6, 1946, March 18, 1947, May 11, 1947, October 11, 1947, February 3, 1949.
43. *SSD*, December 11, 1951.
44. Hansen to McCloy, Kirkpatrick, and François-Poncet, November 1, 1950, BA-K, B 305, Bd. 159; "Ein Bitte für Raeder," *FAZ*, November 14, 1950.
45. On these issues, see Lyon to U.S. Embassy Bonn and Department of State, CN-40536, January 22, 1953; Samuel Reber to S. Houston Lay, January 21, 1953, both in NARA, RG 466, Entry 48, Box 14; Memorandum by von Trützschler, 515-01 E II Raeder/53, January 21, 1953; Allied High Commission for Germany to Adenauer, AGSEC(53)95, February 6, 1953, both in BA-K, B 305, Bd. 159; *Die Welt*, January 22, 1953.
46. *Die Welt*, September 23, 1953.
47. On Chichester and Hankey, *Hansard* (Lords), 5th Series, May 5, 1949, v. 162, c. 376ff. On Liddell Hart, see *FAZ*, March 13, 1951.
48. Erika Raeder to Fraulein Adenauer, May 22, 1952; Memorandum by Trützschler, 204-515-01 Raeder/54 E, February 19, 1954; Erika Raeder to Cecil B. Lyon, January 8, 1954; Erika Raeder to Semeonov, January 8, 1954, all in BA-K, B 305, Bd. 159. See also Hoyer Millar to FO, No. 58, January 21, 1954, TNA, FO 371/109330.
49. *Empire News*, November 29, 1953.
50. "Raeder wurde nichts geschenkt," *Wochenend*, January 23, 1954. See also the treatment of the Norway argument by chief editor Karl Silex in *Tagesspiegel*, April 21, 1955.
51. Winston Churchill, *The Second World War*, v. 1: *The Gathering Storm* (Boston: Houghton Mifflin, 1948), pp. 544–47, 600.
52. On the U.S assessment of Hansen, see Clare H. Timberlake (U.S. Consul General Hamburg) to Department of State, No. 268, January 20, 1953, NARA, RG 59, Entry 1311, LF 59 D 609, Box 17. On his comments concerning Raeder, see Hansen to McCloy, Kirkpatrick, and François-Poncet, November 1, 1950; Hansen to François-Poncet, November

14, 1950, both in BA-K, B 305, Bd. 159. See also "Ein Bitte für Raeder," *FAZ*, November 14, 1950.

53. François-Poncet to Hansen, November 4, 1950, BA-K, B 305, Bd. 159.
54. Boehm to Trygve Lie, April 12, 1951, BA-K, B 305, Bd. 159. Copies to Adenauer, Thomas Dehler (West German Minister of Justice), and all four high commissioners.
55. *Die Welt*, May 17, 1954.
56. Hansen to high commissioners, December 20, 1953, TNA, FO 371/109330.
57. "Gnadengesuch für Raeder und Dönitz," *Die Welt*, December 23, 1950.
58. Ostpreussische Landsmannschaft in der Interessengemeinschaft der Ostvertriebenen to Heuss, March 15, 1952, BA-K, B 305, Bd. 159.
59. Grier, "Admiral Karl Dönitz," pp. 190–1.
60. Frei, *Vergangenheitspolitik*, p. 330. For contemporary permutations, see Omer Bartov, "The Wehrmacht Exhibition Controversy: The Politics of Evidence," *Crimes of War: Guilt and Denial in the Twentieth Century*, eds. Omer Bartov, Atina Grossmann, and Mary Nolan (New York: The New Press), pp. 41–60.
61. *DzD*, Ser. II, v. 3, d. 402.
62. The Adenauer memorandum is enclosed in Conant to Dulles, No. 2201, January 11, 1954, NARA, RG 59, Entry 1311, LF 59 D 609, Box 17.
63. Minutes of the Governors' Meeting, August 2, 1947, AAPS, roll 2.
64. *SSD*, January 20, 1953; Speer to his children, February 19, 1953, BA-K, NL 1340, Sig. 136, Bd. 5.
65. On the March 1953 letter see Parkman (U.S. Mission Berlin) to Dowling, CN-30555, July 19, 1954, NARA, RG 466, Entry 10-A, Box 166. See also *SSD*, April 11, 1953, September 7, 1953.
66. See Parkman to secretary of state, No. 37, July 19, 1954, NARA, RG 59, Entry 1311, LF 59 D 609, Box 17.
67. Anthony Sedon, *Churchill's Indian Summer: The Conservative Government, 1951–55* (London: Hodder and Stroughton, 1981), pp. 386–7.
68. See the policy paper by Hancock, January 20, 1954, TNA, FO 371/109330.
69. Kirkpatrick to Sir Frank Roberts, January 22, 1954, TNA, FO 371/109330.
70. Roberts memorandum of January 21, 1954, TNA, FO 371/109330.
71. Bathurst to Hoyer Millar, L 15/8/21, April 12, 1954, TNA, FO 371/109333.
72. Hoyer Millar to Evans, Foreign Office, C 1661/69, April 14, 1954, TNA, FO 371/109333.
73. Minute by Evans, April 22, 1954, TNA, FO 371/109333.
74. *SSD*, January 20, 1953, April 9, 1954.
75. *SSD*, November 6, 1954, November 8, 1954.
76. Von der Lippe to von Trützschler, November 9, 1954, BA-K, B 305, Bd. 159.
77. "Und Spandau?," *FAZ*, July 25, 1955.
78. Karl Kühlenthal to AA, August 1, 1955, BA-K, B 305, Bd. 159.
79. Kranzbühler memorandum, January 5, 1955, TNA, LCO 2/4429.
80. Von Trützschler to Hallstein, June 25, 1955, BA-K, B 305, Bd. 155.
81. Kranzbühler to Conant (copies to other three ambassadors), May 5, 1955, BA-K, B 305, Bd. 155.
82. See especially Wolfgang Freiherr von Welck's telegram to Hallstein of July 20, 1955, which discusses von Welck's meeting with Hoyer Millar, BA-K, B 305, Bd. 159. See also Brentano to Conant, Hoyer Millar, and François-Poncet, July 21, 1955 (draft), 204-799/55, BA-K, B 305, Bd. 159.
83. Memorandum by Karl Hans Born, 204/799/55 for von Trützschler, June 21, 1955, BA-K, B 305, Bd. 155.
84. Von Trützschler to Hallstein, June 25, 1955, BA-K, B 305, Bd. 155.
85. Hallstein to Conant, Hoyer Millar, and François-Poncet, 204/799/55, May 20, 1955, BA-K, B 305, Bd. 155.
86. Hallstein to Dehler, 204-799/55, undated; von Trützschler to Hallstein, June 25, 1955, both in BA-K, B 305, Bd. 155.
87. Memorandum by Born, 204/799/55 for von Trützschler, June 21, 1955, BA-K, B 305, Bd. 155.
88. "Dönitz wird nicht entlassen," *Die Welt*, May 27, 1955.
89. Von Hassel to Adenauer, July 9, 1955, BA-K, B 305, Bd. 159.

90. *SSD*, November 26, 1954.
91. Kirkpatrick to G. P. Coldstream, January 14, 1955, TNA, LCO 2/4429.
92. Department of State to HICOG Bonn, No. 2286, February 28, 1955, NARA, RG 59, Entry 1311, LF 59 D 609, Box 17.
93. Linebaugh to John W. Auchincloss, November 4, 1955; Department of State to HICOG Bonn, No. 2336, March 4, 1955; Department of State to Embassies in London and Paris, CA-8436, June 2, 1955; Dillon (Paris) to Dulles, No. 5411, June 9, 1955, all in NARA, RG 59, Entry 1311, LF 59 D 609, Box 17.
94. Kirkpatrick to Coldstream, June 24, 1955; C. W. B. Rankin to A. M. Palliser, January 23, 1956, both in TNA, LCO 2/4429.
95. British Military Hospital to British Governor E. R. Vickers, February 1, 1955, May 13, 1955, May 25, 1955 and Secret report from Captain Protheroe, September 19, 1955, AAPS, roll 10.
96. Kranzbühler to Brentano, July 11, 1955, BA-K, B 305, Bd. 159.
97. Parkman to secretary of state, No. 724, May 11, 1955, NARA, RG 59, Entry 1311, LF 59 D 609, Box 17.
98. Conant to Department of State, No. 3609, May 24, 1955, NARA, RG 59, Entry 1311, LF 59 D 609, Box 17.
99. Von Welck to Hallstein, July 20, 1955, BA-K, B 305, Bd. 159.
100. Brentano said in late July that Bonn had still had no news since von Welck's visit to Hoyer Millar in June. See Brentano to Kranzbühler, 204/799 + 1079/55, July 30, 1955, BA-K, B 305, Bd. 155.
101. François-Poncet to Quai d'Orsay, No. 2878/81, July 23, 1955, and No. 2940/43, July 26, 1955, MAE-AOFAA, GMFB 15/4, Folder: Raeder.
102. Conant to Dulles, No. 299, July 26, 1955; Dulles to U.S. Embassy Bonn, No. 277, July 27, 1955; Aldrich (Paris) to Dulles, No. 330, July 27, 1955; Butterworth (London) to Dulles, No. 468, August 8, 1955, all in NARA, RG 59, Entry 1311, LF 59 D 609, Box 17.
103. Adenaur to Anita Diestel, July 22, 1955, BA-K, B 305, Bd. 159.
104. Deutsche Press-Agentur GmbH, Chefredaktion, Nr. 914–918, Inf. 914, June 14, 1955, BA-K, B 305, Bd. 155.
105. Kranzbühler to Adenauer, July 11, 1955, BA-K, B 305, Bd. 159.
106. Brentano to Kranzbühler, 204/799 + 1079/55, July 30, 1955, BA-K, B 305, Bd. 155.
107. Lynch to Department of State, No. 19, August 2, 1955, NARA, RG 59, Entry 1311, LF 59 D 609, Box 17. For similar comments by other naval officers see Peifer, *Three German Navies*, pp. 173–4.
108. Dowling to Dulles No. 617, August 23, 1955, NARA, RG 59, Entry 1311, LF 59 D 609, Box 17. Letters from each of the three powers were sent to Pushkin on August 26. See Conant to Pushkin (Copy), August 26, 1955, BA-K, B 305, Bd. 159.
109. Memorandum of September 25, 1955, BA-K, B 305, Bd. 159.
110. *Der Tag*, September 27, 1955.
111. Vermerk 204/1079/55, undated, BA-K, B 305, Bd. 159.
112. Kapitän zur See a.D. Heinz Bonatz (Chairman, Marine-Offizier-Hilfe) to Hallstein, December 9, 1955, BA-K, B 305, Bd. 155.
113. See for example *Chicago Daily Tribune*, September 30, 1955.
114. Note from Colonel R. H. Stevens, January 19, 1956 (the quote above is a paraphrase by Stevens) and C. W. B. Rankin to Stevens, January 25, 1956, TNA, LCO 2/4425.
115. Kranzbühler to Stevens, December 8, 1955, TNA, LCO 2/4429.
116. Paraphrased in Dowling to Dulles, No. 2352, January 18, 1956, NARA, RG 59, Entry 1311, LF 59 D 609, Box 17. See also A. M. Palliser to Rankin, January 25, 1956, TNA, FO 371/124690.
117. Palliser to Rankin, January 25, 1956; Minute by Harrison of January 25, 1956, TNA, FO 371/124690.
118. See Kirkpatrick's minute of March 7, 1956, on Hankey to Foreign Secretary Selwyn Lloyd, February 24, 1956, TNA, FO 371/124691.
119. Minutes of the Medical Board Meeting, February 29, 1956, and subsequent reports, AAPS, roll 10.
120. Bathurst to Foreign Office, No. 22021, February 15, 1956, TNA, FO/124690; Guffler to Department of State, Nos. 748, 749, February 14, 1956; Department of State to U.S.

Embassy Bonn, No. 2308, February 15, 1956, both in NARA, RG 59, Entry 1311, LF 59 D 609, Box 19.

121. Hoyer Millar to Foreign Office, No. 99, February 15, 1956, TNA, FO 371/124690.
122. Memorandum by C. M. Rose, February 16, 1956, TNA, FO 371/124690.
123. Conant to Dulles, No. 2831, February 17, 1956; Conant to Dulles, No. 2924, February 23, 1956, both in NARA, RG 59, Entry 1311, LF 59 D 609, Box 19.
124. Guffler to Dulles, No. 792, February 29, 1956, NARA, RG 59, Entry 1311, LF 59 D 609, Box 19.
125. Raeder to Adenauer, November 1, 1955, BA-K, B 305, Bd. 159. Raeder mentioned each Spandau prisoner by name with the exception of Albert Speer.
126. The possible illegality of the stripping of Raeder's honor was based on technicalities. See "Raeder Ehrenbürger Kiels?" *FAZ*, March 3, 1956; "Die Ehrenbürgerschaft Raeders," *FAZ*, March 6, 1956.
127. On Heuss, see "Die Ehrenbürgerschaft Raeders," *FAZ*, March 6, 1956. On Erika Raeder, see Memorandum by Dr. Born, Abteilung 2/20, Ref. 204/1079/56, March 13, 1956, BA-K, B 305, Bd. 159.
128. Vermerk Referat 204-204/1079/56, March 5, 1956, BA-K, B 305, Bd. 159.
129. For the press summary, see von Stechow (BRD Embassy Copenhagen) to AA, No. 286/56, March 14, 1956, BA-K, B 305, Bd. 159.
130. "Verzicht auf die Ehrenbürgerschaft," *FAZ*, April 17, 1956. On the honorary doctorate, see Memorandum by D. D. Brown (private secretary to Kirkpatrick), L 15/8/105, January 19, 1951, TNA, FO 1060/544.
131. "Verzicht auf die Ehrenbürgerschaft," *FAZ*, April 17, 1956. For Bonn's efforts in this direction, see Memorandum by Born, Ref 204/1079/56, March 13, 1956, BA-K, B 305, Bd. 159.
132. A copy is included in BA-K, B 305, Bd. 154. The Zenker affair is also covered in Dieter Krüger, "Das schwierige Erbe: Die Traditionsansprache des Kapitäns zur See Karl-Adolf Zenker 1956 und ihre parliamentarischen Folgen," in *Deutsche Marine im Wandel: Vom Symbol nationaler Einheit zum Instrument internationaler Sicherheit*, ed. Werner Rahn (Munich: Oldenbourg, 2005), pp. 549–64.
133. See the note from the City Council to Adenauer, January 29, 1954, BA-K, B 305, Bd. 154.
134. The confiscation affected Dönitz's property in Berlin-Dahlem. The West Berlin denazification chamber had begun proceedings in September 1951 of the Spandau prisoners who still held assets there (Dönitz, Speer, Funk, and von Schirach) with a view toward fines and property confiscation, but the Spandau prisoners were among roughly six thousand cases underway. The original decision concerning Dönitz's fine came on November 11, 1955, after which Dönitz was allowed a month to appeal. On the start of the proceedings, see Lyon to U.S. High Commission Bonn, CN-44839, March 20, 1952, NARA, RG 466, Entry 59, Box 25. See also the Order of Seizure dated November 28, 1955 in Dönitz's Personal File, AAPS, roll 12, and *FAZ*, January 17, 1956, January 19, 1956. In general, see Donald Abenheim, *Reforging the Iron Cross: The Search for Tradition in the West German Armed Forces* (Princeton, NJ: Princeton University Press, 1988), pp. 187ff.
135. Hoyer Millar to FO, No. 33, January 21, 1956, TNA, FO 371/124690.
136. On the issue of parliamentary control of the defense minister, see David Clay Large, *Germans to the Front: West German Rearmament in the Adenauer Era* (Chapel Hill: University of North Carolina Press, 1996), pp. 247–51.
137. Hoyer Millar to FO, No. 33, January 21, 1956, TNA, FO 371/124690.
138. *Große Anfrage der Fraktion SPD – Drucksache 2125*, February 10, 1956, BA-K, B 305, Bd. 156. See also *FAZ*, February 15, 1956.
139. Grewe to Hallstein, 204/799/56, March 6, 1956, BA-K, B 305, Bd. 155.
140. Heye to Hallstein, March 24, 1956; Heye to Hallstein, April 2, 1956, both in BA-K, B 305, Bd. 156.
141. Memorandum from Born to Grewe, March 6, 1956, 204/799/56, BA-K, B 305, Bd. 155.
142. Carstens to Hallstein, 204 (508)/799/56, April 6, 1956, BA-K, B 305, Bd. 155.
143. Grewe to Hallstein, 204/799/56, March 6, 1956, BA-K, B 305, Bd. 155.
144. On this issue, see Goda, "Black Marks," pp. 413–52.
145. Memorandum to Hallstein from Abt. 2 Referat 211, 508/1079/56, May 26, 1956; Hallstein to Blank, May 26, 1956, both in BA-K, B 305, Bd. 159.

146. Brentano to Bonatz, confidential draft, 508/799/56, May 1956, BA-K, B 305, Bd. 156.
147. See the memorandum from Carstens to Hallstein, Abt. 2 Ref.: 508 Dr. Born, 508/799/56, May 8, 1956, BA-K, B 305, Bd. 156.
148. Department of State memorandum of June 4, 1956, NARA, RG 59, Entry 1311, LF 59 D 609, Box 19.
149. On Dönitz's comment, see U.S. Mission, Berlin (Martin J. Hillenbrand, Chief, Political Affairs Division) to Department of State, No. 92, August 2, 1956, NARA, RG 59, Entry 1311, LF 59 D 609, Box 19. There are no records of this painting in the Bundesarchiv files, which are concerned with Hitler's gifts to his subordinates. Jonathan Petropoulos, *Art as Politics in the Third Reich* (Chapel Hill: University of North Carolina Press, 1996), p. 236, recounts that Speer presented Dönitz with the painting *Glazer Bergland* in 1943, but the painting to which Dönitz referred was probably not the same one. The correspondence from Speer to Dönitz is dated December of that year, and Dönitz's birthday was in September. Moreover, Dönitz detested Speer by the time he left Spandau, and it is unlikely that he would list a gift from Speer as one of the two worldly possessions that he would wish to recover. On the other hand, there are records of gifts from Hitler in the form of art to various administrators, party officials, and senior military officers, including the former Field Marshal August von Mackensen, Field Marshal Walther von Brauchitsch, Field Marshal Hugo Sperrle, and Raeder himself. See BA-B, R 43 II, Bd. 985, 985a, 1087a, and 1092. For art gifts from Hitler not included in these files including another painting to Raeder, see Petropoulos, *Art*, pp. 275–6.
150. Carstens to Hallstein, Abteilung 2 (Ref. 508: Dr. Born) 508/799/56, May 22, 1956; Memorandum from Hergt, Referat 508, 508/799/56, July 28, 1956, both in BA-K, B 305, Bd. 156.
151. Memorandum by Carstens, Abteilung 2, Ref 508, 508/799/56, August 29, 1956, BA-K, B 305, Bd. 156.
152. Memorandum by Hergt, Ref. 508, 508/799/56, August 3, 1956, BA-K, B 305, Bd. 156. A similarly cursory discussion was held between Grewe and the French chargé d'affaires, Roland de Margerie, the next day, August 4, 1956. See Memorandum by Dr. Schmidt-Dumont to Carstens, 508/799/56, August 8, 1956, BA-K, B 305, Bd. 156.
153. U.S. Mission, Berlin (Hillenbrand) to Department of State, No. 92, August 2, 1956, NARA, RG 59, Entry 1311, LF 59 D 609, Box 19.
154. Minute by D. J. McCarthy, August 16, 1956, TNA, FO 371/124692.
155. Edward H. Peck (Berlin) to E. J. W. Barnes (Bonn), August 31, 1956, TNA, FO 371/124692.
156. Minute by Barnett, September 5, 1956, TNA, FO 371/124692.
157. E. J. W. Barnes (Bonn) to Chester Martin Anderson (Western Department), September 10, 1956; Anderson to Barnes, No. WG1662/37, September 19, 1956; F. J. Leishman (Washington) to Anderson, 1661/21/56, September 10, 1956; Peck (Berlin) to British Embassy Bonn, September 10, 1956, all in TNA, FO 371/124692.
158. Guffler to Dulles, No. 228, September 14, 1956; Guffler to Dulles, No. 234, September 17, 1956; Guffler to Dulles, No. 254, September 25, 1956, all in NARA, RG 59, Entry 1311, LF 59 D 609, Box 19.
159. Minutes of the Governors' Meeting, September 29, 1956, AAPS, roll 4; Capt. Ralph A. George (U.S. governor Spandau) to U.S. commandant, Berlin, November 27, 1956, NARA, RG 466, Entry 48, Box 15; John Robey (political adviser, British Military Government in Berlin) to FO, No. 1661, October 2, 1956; Rome to FO, No. 206, September 27, 1956, both in TNA, FO 371/124692. On Soviet intransigence, see also Guffler to Dulles, No. 266, September 28, 1956; Guffler to Dulles, No. 276, September 29, 1956, both in NARA, RG 59, Entry 1311, LF 59 D 609, Box 19.
160. Rome to FO, No. 203, September 25, 1956; Rome to FO, No. 211, October 1, 1956, both in TNA, FO 371/124692.
161. Grewe to Dienststelle des AA in Berlin, September 26, 1956, BA-K, B 305, Bd. 156; Hoyer Millar to FO, No. 735, September 28, 1956, TNA, FO 371/124692.
162. Memorandum by Carstens, Abteilung 2, Referat 508, LR Hergt, 508/799/56, November 8, 1956, BA-K, B 306, Bd. 156; Peck to Barnes, No. 1661, undated, TNA, FO 371/124692.
163. On the details, see Memorandum by Rose, October 1, 1956; Robey to FO, No. 1661, October 2, 1956, both in TNA, FO 371/124692; George to U.S. commandant Berlin, November 27, 1956, NARA, RG 466, Entry 48, Box 15. See also the accounts in *Die Welt*,

2 October 1956; *Der Tag*, October 2, 1956; *Telegraf*, October 2, 1956; *Der Tagespiegel*, October 2, 1956; *Münchener Merkur*, October 2, 1956.

164. *Der Kurier*, October 5, 1956; *Der Tagesspiegel*, October 2, 1956; Peck to Barnes, No. 1661, undated, TNA, FO 371/124692.
165. Vickers admitted one and a half years later that he made the threat. See Guffler to Dulles, No. 1224, May 5, 1958, NARA, RG 59, Entry 1311, LF 59 D 609, Box 19.
166. Memorandum by Carstens, Abteilung 2, Referat 508, LR Hergt, 508/799/56, November 8, 1956, BA-K, B 305, Bd. 156.
167. *Die Welt*, October 2, 1956; *Münchener Merkur*, October 2, 1956.
168. Robey to FO, No. 1661, October 2, 1956, TNA, FO 371/124692.
169. Erich Raeder, *My Life*, trans. Henry W. Drexel (Annapolis, MD: Naval Institute Press, 1960 [1957]), pp. 182, 187.
170. Raeder, *My Life*, pp. 269–71.
171. Raeder, *My Life*, p. 287.
172. Raeder, *My Life*, pp. 300–13.
173. Raeder, *My Life*, p. 395.
174. Taylor, *Anatomy*, pp. 566–9, 593–4; *TMWC*, v. 1, pp. 310–15.
175. Karl Dönitz, *Memoirs: Ten Years and Twenty Days*, trans. R. H. Stevens (London: Weisenfeld & Nicolson, 1959), p. 307.
176. Dönitz, *Memoirs*, pp. 184, 307–9.
177. Dönitz, *Memoirs*, pp. 303ff.
178. Dönitz, *Memoirs*, p. 314.
179. Dönitz, *Memoirs*, p. 442.
180. On *Laconia*, see Dönitz, *Memoirs*, pp. 255ff; on Nuremberg, see pp. 52–3.
181. Karl Dönitz, *Mein wechselvolles Leben*, rev. ed. (Göttingen: Musterschmidt, 1975).
182. *SSD*, March 24, 1959.

## CHAPTER FIVE. THE FOILED ESCAPE: ALBERT SPEER'S TWENTY YEARS

1. Roughly half of Schwanenwerder's residents were Jewish before 1933, but the island was cleared of Jewish residents after 1936. A lot had been bought and reserved for Hitler as well. For the fate of Schwanenwerder's property, see Janin Reif, Horst Schumacher, and Lothar Uebel, *Schwanenwerder: Ein Inselparadies in Berlin* (Berlin: Nicolai, 2000).
2. The exchange with the Verwaltung der ehemaligen Reichsbahnvermögens, and Speer's attorney Hans Fläschner is in Speer Personal File, AAPS, roll 13. In 1953 Speer had lawyers transfer his assets to his wife and children to avoid confiscation. He got the idea when von Neurath told him in late 1952 that his own estate had been protected since the local authorities in Baden-Württemberg recognized the rights of his wife to half the estate while placing the confiscated half under the control of his daughter. Von Neurath's lawyer, Dr. Helmuth Fischinger, advised the Speers on this issue. See Speer's note to Rudolf Wolters of December 21, 1952 in BA-K, NL 1340/Sig. 95, and the correspondence of 1953 and 1956 in BA-K, NL 1340/Sig. 96; *SSD*, June 16, 1953. Denazification proceedings were opened in Berlin in September 1951 but were delayed thanks to Speer's imprisonment. At the time, Speer still held a piece of property in Berlin-Nikolassee valued at RM 64,000. Because he no longer owned the Schwanenwerder property, it was not mentioned. See BA-K, NL 1340/Sig. 94. Marie-Anne's arrival in New York is listed in *New York Times*, March 29, 1938, p. 16. I am grateful to Dr. Geoffrey Megargee of the United States Holocaust Memorial Museum for locating her whereabouts.
3. Gitta Sereny, *Albert Speer: His Battle with the Truth* (New York: Knopf, 1995), pp. 164–5, 176.
4. Albert Speer, *Inside the Third Reich*, trans. Richard Winston and Clara Winston (New York: Macmillan, 1970); Albert Speer, *Infiltration*, trans. Joachim Neugroschel (New York: Macmillan, 1981); and *SSD*.
5. The phrase is in Dan van der Vat, *The Good Nazi: The Life and Lies of Albert Speer* (New York: Houghton Mifflin, 1997), p. 96.
6. Joachim Fest, *Speer: The Final Verdict*, trans. Ewald Osers and Alexandra Dring (New York: Harcourt, 2001), pp. 3–4.

7. See for example *SSD*, September 4, 1965.
8. Wolters to Walter Rohland, November 5, 1975, ThyssenKrupp Konzernarchiv (Duisburg) [hereafter TKA], Nachlaß Walter Rohland, NRO/26.
9. Primarily Matthias Schmidt, *Albert Speer: The End of a Myth*, trans. Joachim Neugroschel (New York: St. Martin's, 1984). Also Sereny, *Albert Speer*; Van der Vat, *The Good Nazi.*
10. On the sanitization and restoration, see Sereny, *Albert Speer*, pp. 224–7.
11. Hitler's Berlin speech of December 4, 1930 to the National Socialist Student Federation, which argued for racial unity and idealism, attracted about five thousand people and is printed in Constantin Goschler, ed., *Hitler: Reden – Schriften – Anordnungen (Februar bis Januar 1933)*, v. 4, Teil 1 (Munich: K. G. Sauer, 1994), d. 37.
12. Traudl Junge, *Bis zur letzten Stunde: Hitlers Sekretärin erzählt ihr Leben* (Munich: Classen Verlag, 2002).
13. Jochen Thies, *Architekt der Weltherrschaft: Die Endziele Hitlers* (Düsseldorf: Droste, 1981); Jost Dülffer, Jochen Thies, and Josef Henke, *Hitlers Städte: Baupolitik im Dritten Reich – Eine Dokumentation* (Cologne: Bohlau, 1978).
14. Van der Vat, *The Good Nazi*, p. 100.
15. He also reported the insouciance of Berlin Mayor Julius Lippert to Heinrich Himmler. Schmidt, *Speer*, pp. 50–2.
16. Van der Vat, *The Good Nazi*, Chapter 5; Schmidt, *Speer,* Chapter 12; Michael Thad Allen, *The Business of Genocide: The SS, Slave Labor, and the Concentration Camps* (Chapel Hill: University of North Carolina Press, 2002), pp. 59–60.
17. Schmidt, *Speer*, pp. 182–8.
18. Susanne Willems, *Der entsiedelte Jude: Albert Speers Wohnungsmarktpolitik für den Berliner Hauptstadtbau* (Berlin: Edition Hentrich, 2002).
19. Speer took over the rest of Todt's offices in construction as well. The most thorough analysis of his work as minister for armaments is Militärgeschichtliches Forschungsamt, gen. eds. [hereafter MGFA], *Germany and the Second World War*, v. 5: *Organization and Mobilization of the German Sphere of Power*, pt. 2: *Wartime Administration, Economy, and Manpower Resources, 1942–1944/5* (Oxford: Clarendon Press, 2003), sec. 2.
20. Allen, *Business of Genocide*, pp. 173–7.
21. Schmidt, *Speer*, pp. 117–20; Allen, *Business of Genocide*, pp. 189ff.
22. MGFA, *Germany and the Second World War*, v. 5, pt. 1: *Wartime Administration, Economy, and Manpower Resources, 1939–1941* (Oxford: Clarendon Press, 2000), pp. 360–8.
23. See Susanne Willems's findings at http://www.wdr.de [accessed January 2006].
24. Wolters to Walter Rohland, November 5, 1975, TKA, NRO/26.
25. Van der Vat, *The Good Nazi*, p. 252.
26. *TMWC*, v. 16, p. 483.
27. *TMWC*, v. 16, pp. 432–3; Taylor, *Anatomy*, p. 448.
28. *TMWC*, v. 16, p. 457.
29. *TMWC*, v. 16, p. 441.
30. See Sauckel's directive for the recruitment of labor in occupied France, August 31, 1943, Document NI-449, NARA, RG 238, Entry 171, Box 7a.
31. *TMWC*, v. 16, pp. 483–92, 498.
32. Fest, *Final Verdict*, pp. 238ff. The decree is *TMWC*, v. 41, pp. 430–2.
33. Sereny, *Albert Speer*, p. 487.
34. Report by Oberbergrat Dr. Schensky, October 31, 1944, Document NI-296, NARA, RG 238, Entry 171, Box 4.
35. *TMWC*, v. 16, pp. 493–5. This myth is demolished by Schmidt, *Speer*, pp. 124ff; see also Van der Vat, *The Good Nazi*, pp. 278–9.
36. *TMWC*, v. 16, pp. 543, 549, 560–1.
37. *TMWC*, v. 16, pp. 520–1.
38. *TMWC*, v. 16, p. 535.
39. *TMWC*, v. 16, p. 563.
40. Taylor, *Anatomy*, pp. 450, 453–4.
41. Taylor, *Anatomy*, p. 563.
42. Wolters to Walter Rohland, November 5, 1975, TKA, NRO/26.
43. Van der Vat, *The Good Nazi*, pp. 96, 98–9, 247–8, 272, 359–61.

44. Sereny, *Albert Speer*, pp. 571–2.
45. Sereny, *Albert Speer*, pp. 616–18. The 25,000 items are mentioned in Wolters to Walter Rohland, November 5, 1975, TKA, NRO/26.
46. MGFA, *Germany and the Second World War*, v. 5, pt. 1, pp. 297–99, 379.
47. For biographical information, see Manfred Rasch, *Findbuch zum Nachlaß Walter Rohland (1898–1981) und zum Bestand Ruhr-Consulting GmbH* (Duisburg: ThyssenKrupp AG, 2001), pp. 3–63. On the aforementioned documents, United States, *Trials of War Criminals before the Nuernberg Military Tribunals under Control Council Law No. 10, Nuernberg, October 1946–April 1949* [hereafter *TWC-CC10*], v. 6 [Flick Case] (Washington, DC: U.S. Government Printing Office, 1952).
48. For the affidavit Rohland made at Nuremberg in February 1947, see NARA, RG 238, Entry 183, Box 120.
49. See Rohland's statement of May 24, 1945, in TKA, NRO/109; Rasch, *Rohland*, pp. 48–51.
50. Foreign Economic Administration, Supplementary Data for Biographical Report, NARA, RG 238, Entry 14, Box 40. For biographical information see also OSS, Research and Analysis Branch, Biographical Report in the same box.
51. For his movements between Dustbin and Nuremberg see NARA, RG 549, Entry 2223, Box 28. Rohland's activities there are in his daily diary from 1946, TKA, NRO/111.
52. *TWC-CC10*, v. 6 [Flick Case]; *TWC-CC10*, v. 9 [Krupp Case].
53. On Rohland, see Rasch, *Rohland*, pp. 54–5. In general, see S. Jonathan Wiesen, *West German Industry and the Challenge of the Nazi Past 1945–1955* (Chapel Hill: University of North Carolina Press, 2001).
54. Wiesen, *West German Industry*, pp. 224–5.
55. NARA, RG 549, Entry 2223, Box 29.
56. On trade, see Mommsen to Ambassador Alexander Smirnov, May 21, 1957, BA-K, NL 1340/Sig. 128, Bd. 3. In general, see Peter Kopf, *Die Mommsens: Von 1848 bis heute – die Geschichte einer Familie ist die Geschichte der Deutschen* (Hamburg: Europa Verlag, 2004), pp. 342–68; Karsten Rudolph, *Wirtschaftsdiplomatie im Kalten Krieg: Die Ostpolitik der westdeutschen Großindustrie 1945–1991* (Frankfurt am Main: Campus Verlag, 2004).
57. Quoted in Helmut Weihsmann, *Bauen unterm Hakenkreuz: Architektur des Untergangs* (Vienna: Promedia, 1998), p. 209. On the Niebelungen Bridge, see pp. 948, 955.
58. Speer to Margret, October 6, 1950, October 12, 1950, December 12, 1950, BA-K, NL 1340/Sig. 133, Bd. 2; Speer to Margret, December 2, 1951, BA-K, NL 1340/Sig. 134, Bd. 3; Speer to Margret, March 25, 1953, BA-K, NL 1340/Sig. 136, Bd. 5; Margret Speer to Winifred von Mackensen, October 29, 1950, BA-K, NL 1340/Sig. 107, Bd. 2.
59. Sereny, *Albert Speer*, pp. 616–18.
60. Speer to Margret, February 1949, BA-K, NL 1340/Sig. 132, Bd. 1. Thinking in 1950 he would be a desirable asset to the Soviets should war break out in Germany as it had in Korea, Speer urged Margret to escape west. The Soviets would try to kidnap his family in return for Speer's services, he warned, and he had no desire to work for them. "My entire sympathy," he told her, "belongs to the West. There is for us but one enemy – Communism." See Speer to Margret, June 21, 1950, and Speer to Margret, July 21, 1950, both in BA-K, NL 1340/Sig. 133, Bd. 2.
61. Speer to Margret, May 7, 1949, BA-K, NL 1340/Sig. 132, Bd. 1.
62. Speer to Margret, November 8, 1950, BA-K, NL 1340/Sig. 133, Bd. 2.
63. Speer to Margret, April 2, 1950; Speer to Margret, October 14, 1950; Speer to Margret, September 4, 1950, all in BA-K, NL 1340/Sig. 133, Bd. 2. On Trevor-Roper, see the September 4, 1950, letter and Hugh R. Trevor-Roper, *The Last Days of Hitler* (New York: Macmillan, 1947). At one point, Speer even tried to secure an affidavit from the thoroughly disgraced former head of the Vichy state, Marshal Henri Philippe Pétain, now serving the rest of his days in prison, to show "my friendly attitude toward the French."
64. Speer to Schütz, August 19, 1952, BA-K, NL 1340/Sig. 179.
65. Wolters to Margret Speer, February 14, 1951, BA-K, NL 318/Sig. 28. Also noted in Rohland's appointment book for 1951 in TKA, NRO/111.
66. Speer to Margret, June 21, 1950, BA-K, NL 1340/Sig. 133, Bd. 2. M.A.N. was in fact not a pro-Nazi company, having a Nazi party membership of but 4 percent. See Wiesen, *West German Industry*, p. 228; Paul Erker, *Industrie-Eliten in der NS-Zeit:*

*Anpassungsbereitschaft und Eigeninteresse von Unternehmern in der Rüstungs- und Kriegswirtschaft, 1936–1945* (Passau: Wissenschaftsverlag, 1994), p. 37. Haspel remained head of Daimler after the war despite his ruthless use of slave labor in meeting production targets. Neil Gregor, *Daimler-Benz in the Third Reich* (New Haven, CT: Yale University Press, 1998), pp. 191ff.

67. See the entries from June and July 1951, BA-K, NL 318/Sig. 32. On Rohland, see Wolters to Margret Speer, February 14, 1951, BA-K, NL 318/Sig. 28. For Margret's letters to various banks from 1950 to 1952, see BA-K, NL 1340/Sig. 96.
68. Kranzbühler to Kempf, September 11, 1951, BA-K, NL 318/Sig. 28.
69. Wolters to Margret Speer, October 9, 1951, BA-K, NL 318/Sig. 28.
70. Kranzbühler to Wolters, February 13, 1952, BA-K, NL 318/Sig. 28. See also Hans Speidel to Kranzbühler, February 23, 1952, BA-K, NL 318/Sig. 28.
71. Speer to his children, December 16, 1952, BA-K, NL 1340/Sig. 135, Bd. 4.
72. Speer to Margret, April 13, 1953. BA-K, NL 1340/Sig. 136, Bd. 5.
73. See the excellent accounts in van der Vat, *The Good Nazi*, Chapter 16, and Sereny, *Albert Speer*, pp. 120–1.
74. The letters are in BA-K, NL 1340/Sig. 136, Bd. 5, and are analyzed in Sereny, *Albert Speer*, pp. 631–2. See also Van der Vat, *The Good Nazi*, pp. 304–6, which ties the tone of Speer's reply to the beginning of his larger memoir effort in 1953.
75. Speer to Margret, June 23, 1951, BA-K, NL 1340/Sig. 134, Bd. 3.
76. Speer to Hilde, October 10, 1952, BA-K, NL 1340/Sig. 135, Bd. 4.
77. Speer to Margret, December 7, 1952, BA-K, NL 1340/Sig. 135, Bd. 4.
78. Speer to Hilde, June 23, 1952, October 10, 1952, BA-K, NL 1340/Sig. 135, Bd. 4.
79. Speer to Hilde, October 10, 1952, BA-K, NL 1340/Sig. 135, Bd. 4.
80. Speer to Hilde, November 12, 1952, BA-K, NL 1340/Sig. 135, Bd. 4.
81. Sereny, *Albert Speer*, p. 615.
82. Kempf to Wolters, February 22, 1954, BA-K, NL 1340/Sig. 98, Bd. 1.
83. Kempf to Fläschner, March 31, 1954, BA-K, NL 1340/Sig. 98, Bd. 1.
84. Kempf to Wolters, November 11, 1954, BA-K, NL 1340/Sig. 98, Bd. 1.
85. Referat 204, 204-515-01 d/2817/55, August 19, 1955, Entwurf für eine Erklärung des Herrn Bundeskanzlers zum Problem Spandau bei deutsch-sowjetischen Besprechungen in Moskau, BA-K, B 305, Bd. 154.
86. German Foreign Ministry figures of September 1955 in Anlage 2 to Memorandum by Born to the state secretary, 204-515 d/3081/55, August 31, 1955, BA-K, B 305, Bd. 54.
87. Wolters to Kempf, March 28, 1955, BA-K, NL 1340/Sig. 98, Bd. 1.
88. Kempf to Wolters, May 2, 1955, BA-K, NL 1340/Sig. 98, Bd. 1.
89. Speer hoped that Adenauer would not view Margret's reserve thus far as excessive pride, since, as he saw it, the other wives had a sizable head start. Speer to Margret, October 23, 1953, BA-K, NL 1340/Sig. 136, Bd. 5; Speer to Margret, January 28, 1954, BA-K, NL 1340/Sig. 137, Bd. 6
90. The copy to British High Commissioner Hoyer Millar is in TNA, FO 1060/520.
91. Bathurst memorandum of October 17, 1955 and J. W. P. Perkins (Bonn) to Bathurst, December 12, 1955, both in TNA, FO 1060/520.
92. The extensive medical evaluations of 1956 are in AAPS, roll 10. For the procedures of movement, see Minutes of the Governors' Meeting, August 10, 1956, AAPS, roll 4.
93. See the June–December correspondence on Funk's health in NARA, RG 59, Entry 1311, LF 59 D 609, Box 19, especially Guffler to secretary of state, No. 148, August 22, 1956. See also Minutes of the Governors' Meeting, February 8, 1957, AAPS, roll 4.
94. Hillenbrand to Department of State, No. 654, January 14, 1957, NARA, RG 59, Entry 1311, LF 59 D 609, Box 19.
95. *SSD*, December 27, 1956.
96. On Funk's release, see the British correspondence from January to May 1957 in TNA, FO 371/130852 and the U.S. records in NARA, RG 59, Entry 1311, LF 59 D 609, Box 19.
97. *SSD*, May 17, 1957.
98. Brochhagen, *Nach Nürnberg*, pp. 112–13, Chapter 8, 16.
99. Brentano to Steel, Bruce and Couve de Murville, April 23, 1957, BA-K, B 305, Bd. 152.
100. Memorandum of May 16, 1957, Referat 204, IR Hergt; Memorandum for Brentano, Referat 204, 204/916/57, October 30, 1957, BA-K, B 305, Bd. 152.

101. Brentano's note of November 14, 1957, is included in Bruce to secretary of state, No. 1600, November 21, 1957, NARA, RG 59, Entry 1311, LF 59 D 609, Box 19.
102. Department of State to U.S. Embassy Bonn, No. 2181, February 2, 1956, NARA, RG 59, Entry 1311, LF 59 D 609, Box 19.
103. O'Shaugnessy to Department of State, No. 2382, December 19, 1956; O'Shaugnessy to secretary of state, No. 754, August 28, 1956, both in NARA, RG 59, Entry 1311, LF 59 D 609, Box 19.
104. Dulles to Bruce, No. 1851, January 7, 1957, NARA, RG 59, Entry 1311, LF 59 D 609, Box 19.
105. On Funk's release, see the British correspondence from January to May 1957 in TNA, FO 371/130852, and the U.S. records in NARA, RG 59, Entry 1311, LF 59 D 609, Box 19.
106. The full American report is in Gufler to secretary of state, No. 312, September 9, 1957, NARA, RG 59, Entry 1311, LF 59 D 609, Box 19. For the others, see Hess Personal File, AAPS, roll 14.
107. For the Embassy, see Couve de Murville to Quai d'Orsay, No. 1690/92, MAE-AOFAA, GMFB 15/1, Folder: Liquidation éventuelle de la Prison de Spandau; French Berlin comment relayed in Hillenbrand to secretary of state, No. 70, July 22, 1957, NARA, RG 59, Entry 1311, LF 59 D 609, Box 19.
108. Gufler to secretary of state, No. 312, September 9, 1957, NARA, RG 59, Entry 1311, LF 59 D 609, Box 19.
109. *SSD*, August 10, 1957.
110. Couve de Murville to Pinaeu, May 3, 1957, MAE-AOFAA, GMFB 15/1, Folder: Liquidation éventuelle de la Prison de Spandau.
111. Couve de Murville to Pineau, November 4, 1957, MAE-AOFAA, GMFB 15/1, Folder: Liquidation éventuelle de la Prison de Spandau; U.S. Embassy Bonn to Department of State, No. 832, November 13, 1957, NARA, RG 59, Entry 1311, LF 59 D 609, Box 17.
112. On the reduction of service employees and warders, see the governors' minutes for April and November 1957, AAPS, roll 4; U.S. Mission Berlin to U.S. Embassy Bonn, G-191, January 16, 1960, NARA, RG 84, Entry 1006, Box 7, Folder: Spandau Allied Prison. The formal protocol of the deputy commandants dated November 19, 1957, is in MAE-AOFAA, GMFB 15/1, Folder: Liquidation éventuelle de la Prison de Spandau.
113. U.S. Embassy Bonn to Department of State, No. 832, November 13, 1957; Gufler (Berlin) to Department of State, No. 30, July 11, 1957; U.S. Embassy Bonn to Department of State, No. 832, November 13, 1957, all in NARA, RG 59, Entry 1311, LF 59 D 609, Box 17.
114. Bruce to secretary of state, No. 1885, December 13, 1957; Department of State to Bruce, No. 1708, December 27, 1957; Bruce to secretary of state, No. 2134, January 13, 1958, all in NARA, RG 59, Entry 1311, LF 59 D 609, Box 19. Also Burton (Bonn) note of January 9, 1958, TNA, FO 1042/42.
115. Peck to Barnes, January 10, 1958, TNA, FO 1042/42.
116. *FAZ*, January 8, 1958, reported in Geze (French Mission Berlin) to French Embassy Bonn, No. 14, February 8, 1958, MAE-AOFAA, GMFB 15/1, Folder: Liquidation éventuelle de la Prison de Spandau.
117. Note from Ledwidge to de Guenyveau, January 22, 1958, MAE-AOFAA, GMFB 15/1, File Liquidation éventuelle de la Prison de Spandau.
118. On Ledwidge's meeting, Berlin Telegram, No. 28, to British Embassy Bonn, January 22, 1958, TNA, FO 1042/42. See also Wilkinson to Peck, January 28, 1958, and Minute from Buxton to Barnes, February 7, 1958, in the same file.
119. Politburo Meeting, February 5, 1958, SAPMO, DY 30/J IV 2/2, Bd. 579.
120. Hope Harrison, *Driving the Soviets Up the Wall: Soviet-East German Relations, 1953–1961* (Princeton, NJ: Princeton University Press, 2003), pp. 99–100.
121. Ulbricht to Pushkin, May 11, 1956, SAPMO, DY 30 [Büro Ulbricht], Bd. 3496.
122. Ulbricht to Pushkin, May 11, 1956, SAPMO, DY 30 [Büro Ulbricht], Bd. 3496.
123. SAPMO, DY 30/IV A 2/2.028 [Büro Norden], Bd. 67.
124. Marc Trachtenberg, *A Constructed Peace: The Making of the European Settlement, 1945–1963* (Princeton, N.J: Princeton University Press, 1999), pp. 232–3.
125. MGFA, gen. eds., *Anfänge westdeutscher Sicherheitspolitik 1945–1956*, v. 3: *Die NATO-Option* (Munich: Oldenbourg, 1993), pp. 707–14.
126. MGFA, *Anfänge westdeutscher Sicherheitspolitik*, v. 3, pp. 716–17, 733.

127. Protocol No. 14/58, March 25, 1958, SAPMO, DY 30/J IV 2/2, Bd. 586, and the work protocol of same meeting in DY 30/J IV 2/2A, File 619. Adenauer had indeed made bold statements in the context of the parliamentary inquiry on the atomic issue in support of Strauss while elaborating the desire to achieve greater diplomatic and strategic freedom from the United States with the overall aim of bringing freedom to the seventeen million Germans in the "Soviet Zone" as part of the German "Volk." Germany (West), Bundestag, *Verhandlungen des deutschen Bundestages, Stenographische Berichte*, Bd. 40, (Bonn: Bonner Universitäts-Buchdruckerei Gebr. Scheur, 1958), pp. 1099ff.
128. Telegram No. 40 to British Embassy Bonn, February 8, 1958, TNA, FO 1042/42; Bruce to Department of State, No. 2527, February 13, 1958, NARA, RG 59, Entry 1311, LF 59 D 609, Box 19.
129. Ledwidge to Barnes, March 10, 1958 and Minute by Barnes, March 11, 1958, TNA, FO 1042/42. See also B. J. Garnett (External Department British Military Government) to Wilkinson (British Embassy Bonn), May 12, 1958, TNA, FO 1042/42.
130. Record of Bruce's conversation with Pervukhin, April 26, 1958, MAE-AOFAA, GMFB 15/1, Folder: Liquidation éventuelle de la Prison Spandau; Dulles to McCloy, July 15, 1958 and Bruce to Dulles, July 31, 1958, both in John J. McCloy Papers (Amherst College) [hereafter McCloy Papers], Series 14, Box GY2, Folder 9. See also Harry Schwartz to Department of State, May 6, 1958, NARA, RG 84, Entry 1006, Box 7, Folder: Spandau Allied Prison, and the memorandum of the discussion in the same folder.
131. *SSD*, November 17, 1957, April 4, 1958.
132. Wolters to Margret Speer, May 16, 1957, BA-K, NL 1340/Sig. 100, Bd. 3.
133. Speer to family, February 10, 1960, BA-K, NL 1340/Sig. 143, Bd. 12; Speer to Hilde, December 1963, BA-K, NL 1340/Sig. 146, Bd. 15. Speer's claim in his *Spandau Diaries* to have written the Red Cross on Hess's behalf is not borne out by any letters in his papers or in his personal file from Spandau Prison. *SSD*, November 23, 1960.
134. Wolters to Kempf, May 27, 1957, BA-K, NL 1340/Sig. 98, Bd. 1.
135. See Wolters to Herbert Rimpl, February 17, 1958 and Wolters to Rimpl, March 17, 1958, both in BA-K, NL 318/Sig. 31. On Schlieker's earlier visit with Undersecretary of State Robert Murphy in Washington, see also *SSD*, December 31, 1956. For coordination with Margret Speer, see the exchange between Mommsen and Margret Speer of May and June 1955, BA-K, NL 1340/Sig. 107, Bd. 2. On Offie's OPC work, see Michael Warner, "Origins of the Congress of Cultural Freedom, 1949-1950," *Studies in Intelligence* (CIA) 35, No. 5 (1995) (online declassified version), http://www.cia.gov/csi/studies/95unclass/Warner.html [accessed May 2006]; Peter Grose, *Operation Rollback: America's Secret War Behind the Iron Curtain* (Boston: Houghton Mifflin, 2000).
136. Mommsen to Pushkin, November 18, 1955, BA-K, NL 1340/Sig. 107, Bd. 2.
137. For the correspondence on the Smirnov meeting, see Mommsen to Margret Speer, May 24, 1957, BA-K, NL 1340/Sig. 107, Bd. 2; Wolters to Margret Speer, May 27, 1957, BA-K, NL 1340/Sig. 100, Bd. 3; Mommsen to Smirnov, May 21, 1957, BA-K, NL 1340, Sig. 128, Bd. 3.
138. Wolters to Kempf, December 17, 1957, Wolters to Kempf, December 23, 1957, BA-K, NL 1340/Sig. 98, Bd. 1.
139. Offie to Schlieker, December 4, 1957, BA-K, NL 1340/Sig. 127, Bd. 2.
140. Van der Vat, *The Good Nazi*, p. 302.
141. Wolters to Margret Speer, July 28, 1954, BA-K, NL 318/Sig. 29.
142. Wolters to Kempf, December 12, 1957, BA-K, NL 1340/Sig. 98, Bd. 1; Wolters to Margret Speer, January 16, 1958, BA-K, NL 1340/Sig 100, Bd. 3. On the argument for clemency, see the memorandum sent to Globke from Schütz, March 7, 1958, BA-K, NL 1340/Sig 105, Bd. 8.
143. Wolters to Hans Dustmann, February 1, 1958, BA-K, NL 318/Sig. 31.
144. Four thousand men and women from the concentration camps at Sachsenhausen and Ravensbrück helped build the complex. Weihsmann, *Bauen unterm Hakenkreuz*, pp. 730–4, 773–4.
145. Weihsmann, *Bauen unterm Hakenkreuz*, pp. 791–810.
146. Brigitte Jacob and Wolfgang Schäche, "Rimpl, Herbert," Grove Art Online, Oxford University Press, http://www.groveart.com [accessed July 2004].
147. The exchange is in BA-K, NL 318/Sig. 31. Totals are in the same file.

148. Speer to his family, July 10, 1958, BA-K, NL 1340/Sig. 141, Bd. 10.
149. Schütz to Wolters, March 28, 1958, BA-K, NL 1340/Sig. 100, Bd. 3.
150. Schütz to Globke, June 6, 1958, BA-K, NL 1340/Sig. 105, Bd. 8.
151. Schütz to Hilde Speer, June 6, 1958, Schütz to Wolters, August 11, 1958, BA-K, NL 1340/Sig. 105, Bd. 8; Schütz to Margret Speer, June 6, 1958, BA-K, NL 1340/Sig. 107, Bd. 2. See also Rohland's correspondence with Gustav Hilger, August 1958 in BA-K, NL 1340/Sig. 107, Bd. 2.
152. Couve de Murville to Quai d'Orsay, No. 1112/15, May 8, 1958, MAE-AOFAA, GMFB 17/4; U.S. Embassy Bonn to Department of State, No. 1995, May 6, 1958, enclosure 2, NARA, RG 59, Entry 1311, LF 59 D 609, Box 19; Bruce to Dulles, July 31, 1958, McCloy Papers, Series 14, Box GY2, Folder 9; U.S. Embassy Communique, received May 5, 1958; B. J. Garnett to Wilkinson, May 12, 1958; Wilkinson to Hancock, May 21, 1958; Memorandum by R. F. Stretton, July 14, 1958; Minute by Buxton, July 31, 1958, all in TNA, FO 1042/42.
153. Schütz to Wolters, August 11, 1958, BA-K, NL 1340/Sig. 105, Bd. 8. See also Schütz to Margret Speer, June 6, 1958, BA-K, NL 1340/Sig. 107, Bd. 2.
154. Mommsen to Kroll, August 15, 1958, BA-K, NL 1340/Sig. 121, Bd. 3.
155. Kroll to Mommsen, August 28, 1958, BA-K, NL 1340/Sig. 121, Bd. 3.
156. *SSD*, September 20, 1958.
157. Wolters to Hilde Speer, September 2, 1958, BA-K, NL 1340/Sig. 120, Bd. 2.
158. None are in PA-AA, Botschaft der BRD in Moskau, Bd. 4118–4119, which concern Berlin matters in the fall of 1958.
159. "Bonn verhändelt über Speer," *Die Welt*, October 13, 1958. The Soviet statement is in *Die Welt*, October 16, 1958. See analysis in Bruce to State, No. 225, October 13, 1958, NARA, RG 84, Entry 1006, Box 7, Folder: Spandau Allied Prison.
160. Reported in Chalvron (Berlin) to Quai d'Orsay, No. 301, October 16, 1958, MAE-AOFAA, GMFB 15/1, Folder: Liquidation éventuelle de la Prison de Spandau.
161. Minute by Stretton, September 29, 1948; Wilkinson to Anderson, No. 1661, October 2, 1958; Wilkinson to Anderson, No. 1661, October 13, 1959; Extract from Minutes of Quadripartite consultations in Bonn, October 15, 1958, all in TNA, FO 1042/42.
162. Soviet Foreign Ministry Note No. 222/3eo-frg, September 18, 1958, PA-AA, Botschaft der BRD in Moskau, Bd. 4118.
163. Adenauer's meeting with Smirnov is described in Knappstein to Kroll, No. 507, October 16, 1958, PA-AA, Botschaft der BRD Moskau, Bd. 4118. Kroll's meeting with Gromyko is described in Kroll's No. 737, October 18, 1958, in the same file. See also the Soviet aide mémoire of October 14, 1958 in the same file.
164. Hilde Speer's report on her conversation with Hans Gawlick of April 20, 1959, is in BA-K, NL 1340/Sig. 120, Bd. 2.
165. Offie to Schlieker, December 4, 1957, BA-K, NL 1340/Sig. 127, Bd. 2.
166. Wolters to Kempf, December 17, 1957; Wolters to Kempf, December 23, 1957, BA-K, NL 1340/Sig. 98, Bd. 1. Schlieker was also behind a major article series in the right-wing magazine *Quick* in February 1958, publication of which Schütz, who had been informed late, could not prevent. Wolters to Dietrich Kenneweg (*Quick* Editor), January 22, 1958, BA-K, NL 1340/Sig. 100, Bd. 3; Wolters to Kempf, February 12, 1958, BA-K, NL 1340/Sig. 98, Bd. 1. Speer noted too that the series would not help his cause because "Funk and his friends have been telling atrocity stories." *SSD*, April 4, 1958.
167. Offie to Schlieker, October 13, 1958, BA-K, NL 1340/Sig. 127, Bd. 2.
168. Wolters to Hilde Speer, October 21, 1958, and November 4, 1958, BA-K, NL 1340/Sig. 120, Bd. 2.
169. Harrison, *Driving the Soviets Up the Wall*, pp. 105ff. Actually, the postwar status of Berlin was not determined by the Potsdam agreement by rather by agreements reached at Yalta.
170. Brentano to all missions, Dipex No. 3, November 22, 1958, PA-AA, Botschaft der BRD in Moskau, Bd. 4118.
171. Soviet Foreign Ministry Note No. 200/3eo-FRG to BRD Embassy Moscow, November 27, 1958, PA-AA, Botschaft der BRD Moskau, Bd. 4119.
172. Aufzeichnung über eine Besprechung mit Mr. Pope, von der Britischen Botschaft Bonn, December 10, 1959, BA-K, B 305, Bd. 151; Memorandum by Herbert Northe, December 16, 1958, PA-AA, B 12, Bd. 185.

173. *SSD*, November 28, 1958, February 15, 1959.
174. Speer to Kempf, April 19, 1959, BA-K, NL 1340/Sig. 160, Bd. 8.
175. *Der Spiegel*, May 27, 1959.
176. On Soviet confidence on this point, Harrison, *Driving the Soviets Up the Wall*, pp. 121–4; Jack Schick, *The Berlin Crisis 1958–1962* (Philadelphia: University of Pennsylvania Press, 1971), p. 91.
177. See for example Kempf to Hilde Speer, November 25, 1958, BA-K, NL 1340/Sig. 119, Bd. 1.
178. Wolters to Kempf, December 23, 1957, BA-K, NL 1340/Sig. 98, Bd. 1; Schütz to Weitz, May 2, 1958, BA-K, NL 1340/Sig. 105, Bd. 8.
179. Memorandum by Gawlick, May 27, 1959, BA-K, B 305, Bd. 152.
180. See notes to this effect in TNA, FO 371/154293.
181. Weitz to Brentano, November 11, 1959, BA-K, B 305, Bd. 151.
182. Kempf to Heinz Lorenz, December 4, 1959, BA-K, NL 1340/Sig. 104, Bd. 7.
183. *SSD*, December 18, 1959, August 22, 1960, August 24, 1960. The last entry ruminates over Eichmann but uses Eichmann's case as a vehicle to remake the argument that Speer only understood gradually the meaning of Nazism. "Going over it all in Spandau, I have gradually understood completely that the man I served was not a well-meaning tribune of the masses, not the rebuilder of German grandeur, and also not the conqueror of a new German empire, but a pathological hater.... Perhaps I can forgive myself for everything else: having been his architect is excusable, and I could even justify my having served as his armaments minister. I can even conceive of a position in which a case could be made for the use of millions of prisoners of war and forced labor in industry.... But I have nothing to say for myself when a name like Eichmann's is mentioned."
184. Ritter to AA, Pol 503-80, December 16, 1959; Ritter to AA, Pol 503-80, December 17, 1959, both in BA-K, B 305, Bd. 151. On Hilde's preparation, see her exchanges with Annemarie Kempf from 1959, BA-K, NL 1340/Sig. 119, Bd. 1, and Wolters of the same year in BA-K, NL 1340/Sig. 120, Bd. 2.
185. *Die Welt*, September 27, 1959; *Frankfurter Neue Presse*, September 28, 1959. See also the November 8 lead story in the *Manchester Guardian*.
186. Roberts to George Coldstream, December 3, 1959, TNA, LCO 2/4429; Minute by Pridham, December 5, 1959, TNA, FO 371/146064.
187. Roberts to Coldstream, April 25, 1960, TNA, LCO 2/4429.
188. See more generally TNA, FO 371/146064.
189. Coldstream to Tompkins, December 10, 1959, TNA, FO 371/146064. Hilde Speer's report on the trip from December 2–14, 1959 to Wolters is in BA-K, NL 1340/Sig. 120, Bd. 2.
190. Speer to family, February 10, 1960, BA-K, NL 1340/Sig. 143, Bd. 12.
191. Wolters to Hilde Speer, November 5, 1959, BA-K, NL 1340/Sig. 120, Bd. 2.
192. Speer to family, February 10, 1960, BA-K, NL 1340/Sig. 143, Bd. 12.
193. Reference to letter in Abteilung 5, XXIV 396/60, April 7, 1960, BA-K, B 305, Bd. 151.
194. Hilde's report to Wolters of her trip to Paris from March 18–30, 1960 is in BA-K, NL 1340/Sig. 120, Bd. 2. See also Memorandum by Gawlick, ZRS-E 209/55, May 16, 1960, PA-AA, B 12, Bd. 185.
195. On German-British intentions and the summit, see Memorandum by Pridham, December 12, 1959; Minute by J. E. (John) Killick, December 14, 1959, TNA, FO 371/146064. See also Botschaft der BRD London to AA, December 16, 1959, BA-K, B 305, Bd. 151; Minute by Wilberforce, April 28, 1960, and Minute by Drinkall, April 28, 1960, both in TNA, FO 371/154293. On Pervukhin, Memorandum to Rumbold, February 17, 1960, TNA, FO 371/154293.
196. Botschaft der BRD London (Ritter) to AA, Pol. 503–80, December 16, 1959, BA-K, B 305, Bd. 151.
197. Aufzeichnung über die Berliner Besprechungen vom 17.12.59, BA-K, B 305, Bd. 151. On expectations, see Aufzeichnung über eine Besprechung mit Mr. Pope (by Wagner, representative of the German Red Cross, General Secretariat), December 10, 1959, BA-K, B 305, Bd. 151. Weitz discovered when visiting the Soviet Embassy in East Berlin that the Soviets were not as sanguine about Spandau as he had thought. Pervukhin did not even meet him, and the attaché Grimitzki blandly and incorrectly told him that Spandau was not the concern of the embassy.

198. Stretton to Pridham, December 23, 1959, and Minute by Pridham, January 4, 1960, TNA, FO 371/154293.
199. Referat 700, 700–83.60, March 22, 1960, BA-K, B 305, Bd. 151.
200. Botschaft der BRD London to AA, Pol 503-80, December 16, 1959, BA-K, B 305, Bd. 151; Memorandum by Reute, Referat 704, 704-82.08/94.29-56/60, January 12, 1960, PA-AA, B 12, Bd. 185.
201. Stretton to Wilberforce, No. 1661, April 29, 1960, TNA, FO 371/154293.
202. Memorandum by Reute, Referat 704, 704.82.08/94.29/56/60, January 12, 1960, BA-K, B 305, Bd. 151.
203. Memorandum by Reinkemeyer, Referat 704, 704-83.000/94.29-1289/60, October 18, 1960, PA-AA, B 12, Bd. 185.
204. Khruschchev to Adenauer, December 24, 1962, PA-AA, B 2, Bd. 145.
205. Brentano to Reuter, April 2, 1960, BA-K, B 305, Bd. 151. This letter was recalled and not sent.
206. Hans-Peter Schwarz, ed., *Konrad Adenauer – Reden 1917–1967: Eine Auswahl* (Stuttgart: Deutsche Verlags-Anstalt, 1975), pp. 409–10.
207. Brochhagen, *Nach Nürnberg*, pp. 284–5, 292–4.
208. Harrison, *Driving the Soviets Up the Wall*, pp. 161. On East German involvement, see Brochhagen, *Nach Nürnberg*, pp. 279–90.
209. For East German propaganda efforts concerning Globke, see SAPMO, DY 30/IV 2/2.028 [Büro Norden], Bd. 1, 2, 9, 21, 36.
210. Brochhagen, *Nach Nürnberg*, pp. 298–316. As Brentano had made clear to Adenauer, West Germany had "to distance itself definitively from these crimes on the occasion of this dreadful trial." Bonn publicly supported the trial and the ex post facto Israeli law on which it was based, but did not pay Eichmann's German lawyer Robert Servatius for fear of the headline "Bonn defends Eichmann." Brentano also sent an observer, though not one with an official government position, and he prepared Adenauer's television comments very carefully. On Adenauer's April trip to Washington to meet President John Kennedy for the first time and discuss Berlin, the chancellor was armed with answers to possible press inquiries about the Eichmann trial. Brochhagen, *Nach Nürnberg*, pp. 338, 340, 344. See also the materials on the Eichmann trial, Mengele, and the restitution payments in PA-AA, B 2, Bd. 82.
211. Brentano to Reuter, April 2, 1960, BA-K, B 305, Bd. 151. This letter was recalled and not sent.
212. Memorandum by von Forster, Referat 700, 700-81.15, June 2, 1960, BA-K, B 305, Bd. 151; Memorandum by von Forster, Referat 700, 700-84.29 VS-NfD, July 15, 1960, PA-AA, B 12, Bd. 185.
213. ZRS-XXIV 596/60, July 30, 1960, BA-K, B 305, Bd. 151.
214. Hilde's report to Wolters of her trip to Paris from March 18–30, 1960, is in BA-K, NL 1340/Sig. 120, Bd. 2.
215. Minute by Wilberforce, April 28, 1960; Minute by Drinkall, April 28, 1960, both in TNA, FO 371/154293. See also the records from June 1960 on this issue in PA-AA, B 12, Bd. 185.
216. Stretton to Wilberforce, April 29, 1960 and subsequent documents, TNA, FO 371/154293.
217. Fläschner to Hilde Speer, May 13, 1960, BA-K, NL 1340/Sig. 121, Bd. 3.
218. Hilde Speer to Karl Frank (former Finance Minister), December 21, 1960, BA-K, NL 1340/Sig. 121, Bd. 3. Same letter to General Hans Speidel.
219. Abteilung V, ZRS-XXIV-596/60, October 21, 1960; Abteilung V, ZRS-XXIV 596/60, December 12, 1960, both in BA-K, B 305, Bd. 151, also in PA-AA, B 12, Bd. 185. These memoranda mistakenly note that Speer was arrested by the Americans and von Schirach by the British.
220. ZRS-XXIV 596/60, November 9, 1960; ZRS-XXIV 596/60, December 1, 1960, both in BA-K, B 305, Bd. 151.
221. In general for 1961, see TNA, FO 1042/75; François Seydoux (French ambassador Bonn) to Quai d'Orsay, January 5, 1961, MAE-AOFAA, GMFB 15/4, Folder: Speer. On Mommsen, see Carstens to Mommsen, StS. 289/61, March 23, 1961, PA-AA, B 2, Bd. 82.
222. On the history of the liaison missions, see Dorothee Mußgnug, *Alliierte Militärmissionen in Deutschland, 1946–1990* (Berlin: Duncker & Humblot, 2001).

223. "Denial of Soviet Access to the Spandau Prison," November 7, 1961 (based on British study), NARA, RG 84, Entry 1006, Box 7, Folder: Spandau Allied Prison. The Western Allies had always maintained the position that they had observed all Four-Power agreements, and despite their walkout from the Kommandatura, the Soviet maintained the same argument.
224. Lieutenant Colonel Oscar Drake (U.S. governor, Spandau), to POL (Day), September 13, 1962, NARA, RG 84, Entry 1006, Box 7, Folder: Spandau Prison 1958–1963. In November 1961, there was talk of denying the Soviet access to Spandau, but only if the Soviets denied access to East Berlin to Allied missions and left the Berlin Air Safety Center.
225. David E. Murphy, Sergei Kondrashev, and George Bailey, *Battleground Berlin: CIA vs. KGB in the Cold War* (New Haven, CT: Yale University Press, 1997), pp. 392–3.
226. U.S. Mission Berlin to U.S. Embassy Bonn, November 28, 1962, NARA, RG 84, Entry 1006, Box 7, Folder: Spandau Prison 1958–1963; *SSD*, November 26, 1962.
227. Foreign Secretary Richard Butler to Ambassador Frank Roberts (Bonn), No. 471, December 17, 1963, TNA, FO 371/172201.
228. Alaric Searle, *Wehrmacht Generals, West German Society, and the Debate on Rearmament, 1949–1959* (Westport, CT: Praeger, 2003), pp. 246–56. In 1957, Schörner received a sentence of four and a half years but served only part, allegedly due to ill health. For the U.S. Army Counter Intelligence Corps assessment of Schörner's release by the Soviets, see NARA, RG 319, Entry 134-B, Box 542.
229. NARA, RG 263, Entry A1-86, Box 32, CIA Name File: Friedrich Panzinger.
230. NARA, RG 263, Entry ZZ-19, Box 1, File: Felfe, Heinz: KGB Exploitation.
231. Brewster Morris (U.S. Minister Berlin) to Department of State, CN-1170, June 29, 1962, NARA, RG 84, Entry 1006, Box 7, Folder: Spandau Prison 1958–1963. See also Seydoux to Quai d'Orsay, No. 2895/98, June 19, 1962 and his No. 3042–43, June 27, 1962, MAE-AOFAA, GBFB 15/4, Folder: Speer.
232. Carstens to Schröder, St.S./ 902/62, October 25, 1962, PA-AA, B 2, Bd. 82; Memorandum of Carsten's discussion with Smirnov, May 20, 1963, and Memorandum on Naumann and Sonntag, July 24, 1964, PA-AA, B 2, Bd. 145. See also PA-AA, B 2, Bd. 158 on this case. The students were ironically traded for the KGB penetration agent Heinz Felfe (arrested by the West German authorities in 1961) whose lapse in communication had led to the West German arrest of Pripolzev in the first place. See NARA, RG 263, Entry ZZ-18, Box 23, Name File: Heinz Felfe, vol. 4.
233. Discussion between Smirnov and Carstens, May 20, 1963, PA-AA, B 2, Bd. 145.
234. Secret memorandum by Stretton, March 26, 1958, TNA, FO 1042/42; *Hansard* (Commons), 5th Series, v. 585, c. 133–34, April 1, 1958 (written). On the divorce, see the Spandau Governors' Minutes for 1950, AAPS, roll 2; Schirach Personal File, AAPS, roll 12.
235. Klaus von Schirach to German Red Cross, January 1, 1963, BA-K, B 305, Bd. 152.
236. Minutes of Extraordinary Meeting, December 4, 1963, AAPS, roll 5; TNA, FO 371/172201.
237. See Speer's letters to Hilde and his son-in-law Ulf Schramm of December 1963 and January 1964, BA-K, NL 1340/Sig. 146–147, Bd. 15–16. Compare to *SSD*, December 4, 1963, December 6, 1963, December 9, 1963.
238. Butler to Roberts, No. 471, December 17, 1963, TNA, FO 371/172201; Christian Aumale (chargé d'affaires, Bonn) to Quai d'Orsay, No. 819/25, January 27, 1964, MAE-AOFAA, GMFB 17/4.
239. Julian Bullard (British Embassy Bonn) to Philip Mallet, December 13, 1963, TNA, FO 371/172201.
240. See the Rusk and Ball correspondence in NARA, RG 84, Entry 1006, Box 7, Folder: Spandau Prison 1958–1963.
241. Bullard to Foreign Office, January 28, 1964; Bullard to H. K. Mathews, British military governor, Berlin, February 3, 1964, TNA, FO 371/177995. The rumor about von Schirach might be attributable to comments he made to the Soviet female censor in Spandau, Margarita Nerucheva, known to the inmates by the sardonic nickname "Pretty Margret." *SSD*, November 13, 1961.
242. Text in TNA, FO 371/177995.
243. Trevelyan to FO, No. 1202, June 16, 1964, TNA, FO 371/177995. Deppner's acquittal of January 22, 1964 in Munich for ordering the shooting of sixty-five

Soviet POWs was indeed based on the assumption that Deppner was responding to atrocities against Germans on the Eastern Front. For French and West German comments, see French Embassy Bonn (Margerie) to Quai d'Orsay, No. 4247/49, June 17, 1964, MAE-AOFAA, GMFB, 17/4. The West Germans argued that the suspension of the Deppner case came from a lack of evidence sufficient to prove his guilt and not for the reasons given in the Soviet note.

244. Mommsen to Wolters, February 11, 1964, BA-K, NL 318/Sig. 31.
245. Speer to Hilde, November 2, 1963, November 29, 1963, BA-K, NL 1340/Sig. 146, Bd. 15. Compare with *SSD*, November 2, 1963, which notes that Schlabrendorff was to make a legal argument.
246. McCloy to Dulles, June 27, 1958; McCloy to Tyler, November 6, 1963, McCloy Papers, Series 14, GY2, Folder 9.
247. Neither London nor Paris had yet been notified of this scheme. See Meeting between Schlabrendorff, William Tyler (EUR), and Grover Penberthy (BTF), March 19, 1964, NARA, RG 84, Entry 1006, Box 7, Folder: Spandau Prison 1964. There is brief reference in *SSD*, April 4, 1964. On Tyler's public statement of March 8, 1963, see PA-AA, B 38-II A 1, Bd. 157.
248. Speer to Hilde, April 8, 1964, BA-K, NL 1340/Sig. 147, Bd. 16. On Powers, see Craig R. Whitney, *Spy Trader: Germany's Devil's Advocate and the Darkest Secrets of the Cold War* (New York: Times Books, 1993), pp. 27ff.
249. Speer to Margret (official) April 26, 1964; Speer to Hilde, June 7, 1964, BA-K, NL 1340/Sig. 147, Bd. 16. See also *SSD*, August 4, 1964.
250. Speer to Hilde, October 28, 1964, BA-K, NL 1340/Sig. 147, Bd. 16; Sereny, *Albert Speer*, pp. 659–61, 678.
251. Speer to Hilde, March 6, 1966, BA-K, NL 1340/Sig. 149, Bd. 18.
252. On the money, see BA-K, NL 318/Sig. 31. On Brandt and Hilde Speer, see van der Vat, *The Good Nazi*, pp. 324, 328. On Brandt's view of Speer, see Willy Brandt, *Errinerungen* (Frankfurt am Main: Propyläen, 1989), p 145. While governing mayor of Berlin in 1964, Brandt had made a case for Speer with Robert Kennedy, then the U.S. attorney general, arguing that he wished to be of help to the family and that Speer's release was more justified than the others. See John Calhoun (U.S. Mission Berlin) to Robert Creel (director, Office of German Affairs, Department of State), June 10, 1964, NARA, RG 84, Entry 1006, Box 7, Folder: Spandau Prison 1964.
253. Presse- und Informationsamt der Bundesregierung, Az. 210–4 IV, September 26, 1966, PA-AA, B 38, Bd. 157.
254. Sereny, *Albert Speer*, pp. 662-68, 710-17.

## CHAPTER SIX. "I REGRET NOTHING": THE PROBLEM OF RUDOLF HESS

1. On Kappler, see Robert Katz, *The Battle for Rome: The Germans, the Allies, the Partisans and the Pope, September 1943–June 1944* (New York: Simon and Schuster, 2003). On Reder, see Christian Ortner, *Am Beispiel Walter Reder: Die SS-Verbrechen in Marzabotto und ihre Bewältigung* (Vienna: DÖW, 1985). On selective memory, see Tony Judt, "The Past Is Another Country: Myth and Memory in Postwar Europe," in *The Politics of Retribution in Europe: World War II and Its Aftermath*, ed. István Deák, Jan T. Gross, and Tony Judt (Princeton, NJ: Princeton University Press, 2000), pp. 293–323. On the Dutch, see Berger to AA, No. 189, August 7, 1964, PA-AA, B 2, Bd. 158.
2. Churchill minute to Eden, Ser. M 561/52, December 5, 1952, TNA, PREM 11/793.
3. *FAZ*, July 12, 1973.
4. *The Times*, November 27, 1979. See also Peter Schupljak, "Wahrnehmung und Legenden: Das Bild von Rudolf Heß in sowjetischen Publikationen," in Kurt Pätzold and Manfred Weißbecker, *Rudolf Heß: Der Mann an Hitlers Seite* (Leipzig: Militzke, 1999), pp. 393–409.
5. Pätzold and Weißbecker, *Rudolf Heß*, pp. 33–54.
6. Ian Kershaw, *Hitler 1889–1936: Hubris* (New York: Norton, 1998), pp. 240–53.
7. Pätzold and Weißbecker, *Rudolf Heß*, pp. 54–6. On Hitler, see Kershaw, *Hitler 1889–1936*, pp. 240–50.

8. Dietrich Orlow, *The History of the Nazi Party*, 1919–1933 (Pittsburgh: University of Pittsburgh Press, 1969), pp. 150–1, 202; Gerhard L. Weinberg, ed., *Hitler's Second Book*, trans. Krista Smith (New York: Enigma, 2003), p. xiv.
9. Pätzold and Weißbecker, *Rudolf Heß*, pp. 63–4, 67.
10. Pätzold and Weißbecker, *Rudolf Heß*, pp. 71, 87.
11. *TMWC*, v. 7, pp. 121–4.
12. *TMWC*, v. 4, pp. 112–13. By September 1935, he also demanded consultation in the appointment of all civil servants. *TMWC*, v. 7, p. 127.
13. Pätzold and Weißbecker, *Rudolf Heß*, pp. 90–3, 102.
14. A consideration in Pätzold and Weißbecker, *Rudolf Heß*, pp. 156ff.
15. Text in Rudolf Hess, *Reden* (Munich: Eher, 1938), pp. 15–32. The speech is discussed in detail in Pätzold and Weißbecker, *Rudolf Heß*, pp. 122–5.
16. Pätzold and Weißbecker, *Rudolf Heß*, p. 190.
17. Pätzold and Weißbecker, *Rudolf Heß*, pp. 245–7.
18. *TMWC*, v. 7, pp. 128–9.
19. *TMWC*, v. 3, pp. 523–4; Pätzold and Weißbecker, *Rudolf Heß*, pp. 147–55; Peter Longerich, *Hitlers Stellvertreter: Führung der Partei und Kontrolle des Staatsapparates durch den Stab Heß und die Partei-Kanzlei Bormann* (Munich: K. G. Saur, 1992), pp. 93–9.
20. *TMWC*, v. 3, pp. 522–3; v. 7, pp. 129.
21. Pätzold and Weißbecker, *Rudolf Heß*, 216–18.
22. *TMWC*, v. 2, p. 339; v. 7, p. 128–34.
23. Gerhard L. Weinberg, ed., "National Socialist Organization and Foreign Policy Aims in 1927," *The Journal of Modern History* 36, No. 3 (December 1964): 428–33.
24. Pätzold and Weißbecker, *Rudolf Heß*, pp. 217–18.
25. Pätzold and Weißbecker, *Rudolf Heß*, p. 216
26. Pätzold and Weißbecker, *Rudolf Heß*, pp. 234–5.
27. *TMWC*, v. 3, pp. 574–86, v. 7, 134–37.
28. Max Domarus, ed., *Hitler: Speeches and Proclamations*, trans. Chris Wilcox and Mary Fran Gilbert (Wauconda, IL: Bolchazy-Carducci, 1992), v. 3, p. 2055.
29. Pätzold and Weißbecker, *Rudolf Heß*, pp. 259–60.
30. Roy Conyers Nesbit and Georges van Acker, *The Flight of Rudolf Hess: Myth and Reality* (Phoenix Mill: Sutton Publishing Ltd., 1999), pp. 32–69. To be used with more caution are Rainer F. Schmidt, *Rudolf Heß: Der Botengang eines Toren? Der Flug nach Großbritannien vom 10. Mai 1941* (Düsseldorf: Econ, 1997) and Peter Padfield, *Hess: Flight for the Führer* (London: Weidenfeld & Nicholson, 1991), both of whom argue that British intelligence lured Hess to Great Britain. To be used with maximum caution is John Costello, *Ten Days that Saved the West* (London: Bantam, 1991).
31. This Hess assumed to be true from his discussions with his friend Albrecht Haushofer, the son of Hess's mentor on geopolitics, Karl Haushofer. See James Douglas-Hamilton, "Hess and the Haushofers," in *Flight from Reality: Rudolf Hess and His Mission to Scotland, 1941*, ed. David Stafford (London: Pimlico, 2002), pp. 78–103.
32. For transcripts of the Kirkpatrick interviews see *TMWC*, v. 38, pp. 177–84; for Lord Simon, *TMWC*, v. 40, pp. 279–92.
33. On Hitler and Great Britain, see Gerhard Weinberg, *Germany, Hitler and World War II: Essays in German and World History* (New York: Cambridge University Press, 1996), pp. 85–94. On Hitler's reaction to the Hess flight, see Fröhlich, ed. *Tagebücher von Joseph Goebbels*, Teil I, Bd. 4, May 13–16, 1941.
34. The entire assessment in Rudolf Hess: The Report of British Observation and Findings May 10, 1941–October 8, 1945, Hess Personal File, AAPS, roll 14.
35. Quoted in Report of the Commission to examine Defendant Hess, *TMWC*, v. 1, pp. 159ff.
36. On Hess's period in England, see Nesbit and van Acker, *The Flight of Rudolf Hess*, pp. 70–80, 99–119.
37. See the editor's introduction and Lothar Kettenacker, "Mishandling a Spectacular Event: The Rudolf Hess Affair," in Stafford, ed., *Flight from Reality*, pp. 1–18, 19–37. See also Stalin's comments to Soviet Ambassador in London Ivan Maisky of October 19, 1942, in *UdSSR*, v. 1, d. 30 as well as d. 34, 35.
38. Schupljak, "Wahrnehmungen und Legenden," pp. 398ff; John Erickson, "Rudolf Hess: A Post-Soviet Postscript," in Stafford, ed., *Flight from Reality*, pp. 38–60.

39. Variations are based on Hugh Thomas, *The Murder of Rudolf Hess* (London: Hodder and Stoughton, 1979); Hugh Thomas, *Hess: A Tale of Two Murders* (London: Hodder and Stoughton, 1988). The argument was demolished in Le Tissier, *Farewell to Spandau*, pp. 44–5, 99–109, but reemerged in Lynn Picknett, Clive Prince, and Stephen Prior, *Double Standards: The Rudolf Hess Cover Up* (Boston: Little Brown, 2001).
40. *UdSSR*, v. 1, d. 34, 35; Kochavi, *Prelude to Nuremberg*, pp. 36–7; Overy, *Interrogations*, pp. 118, 575, n. 3.
41. Overy, *Interrogations*, pp. 406ff.
42. *TMWC*, v. 1, pp. 164–5.
43. *TMWC*, v. 2, p. 492–3.
44. Taylor, *Anatomy*, p. 178; *TMWC*, v. 2, p. 163.
45. Hess to Ilse, October 2, 1946, Ilse Hess, *Ein Schicksal in Briefen* (Leoni am Starnberger See: Druffel, 1971) [hereafter *Schicksal in Briefen*], pp. 114–15.
46. *SSD*, November 20, 1946. See also *SSD*, January 1, 1958. See also entries of December 27, 1949, April 20, 1950.
47. Quoted in Nesbit and van Acker, *The Flight of Rudolf Hess*, pp. 116–17.
48. *SSD*, January 1, 1948.
49. Sprecher, *Inside the Nuremberg Trial*, v. 2, pp. 787–9; "Stalin and the Nuremberg Trial," *Moscow News*, March 24, 1995.
50. *TMWC*, v. 17, pp. 550–4.
51. *TMWC*, v. 19, pp. 353ff.
52. *TMWC*, v. 19, pp. 358–67.
53. *TMWC*, v. 19, p. 378.
54. *TMWC*, v. 19, pp. 388, 391.
55. *TMWC*, v. 22, p. 367.
56. For his work on the statement, see Rudolf Hess: Progress Notes, entries of August 22, 23, 24, 1946, Hess Personal File, AAPS, roll 14; Hess to Ilse, September 2, 1946, *Schicksal in Briefen*, pp. 111–12. For the full Nuremberg statement, see NARA, RG 238, Entry 22, Box 2, Folder: Hess.
57. Taylor, *Anatomy*, p. 560.
58. *SSD*, April 24, 1947.
59. Chief Warder Log Book, July 18, 1947, AAPS, roll 22. On his complaints, see Hess Personal File, AAPS, roll 14; Hess Medical File, AAPS, roll 15.
60. This episode in W. A. E. Bullen to Chisholm, August 27, 1951, Hess Personal File, AAPS, roll 14.
61. *SSD*, April 9, 1950, December 20–25, 1950, June 17, 1952, July 21, 1956.
62. *SSD*, April 19, 1952.
63. *SSD*, June 14, 1952.
64. Minutes of the Governors' Meetings, June 16, 1952, September 3, 1953, AAPS, roll 3.
65. Hess Medical File, AAPS, roll 15.
66. Report by Maurice Walsh, Consultant in Neuropsychiatry, May 27, 1948, Hess Personal File, AAPS, roll 14; Report by Captain Robert I. Levy, Psychiatrist, U.S. Army Hospital, August 23, 1955, Hess Personal File, AAPS, roll 14. The report by Captain John Hitchcock, April 1964, Hess Medical File, AAPS, roll 15, found no psychosis but commented, "I believe he would suicide if the opportunity presented itself."
67. Chief Warder Log Book, June 13–15, 1952, AAPS, roll 23; A. S. Whitaker to Vickers, September 22, 1953, Hess Personal File, AAPS, roll 14; *SSD*, June 13–15, 1952.
68. On punishments, see Chief Warder Log Book, November 15–18, 1947, AAPS, roll 22. See also Minutes of the Governors' Meetings, October 20, 1947, November 6, 1947, December 18, 1947, January 9, 1948, February 24, 1949, January 11, 1951, AAPS, roll 2; June 15, 1952, September 23, 1953, AAPS, roll 3; October 29, 1955, January 12, 1956, February 7, 18, 1957, August 8, 1957, AAPS, roll 4; *SSD*, February 25, 1949, June 13, 1952, March 26, 1957.
69. Minutes of the Governors' Meeting, July 16, 1956, AAPS, roll 4. There was a similar incident in October of that year when Hess refused to clean a toilet. See the Minutes of the Governors' Meetings for that month, AAPS, roll 4.
70. Chief Warder Log Book, December 20, 1950, December 23, 1950, December 25, 1950, AAPS, roll 22; Chief Warder Log Book, February 2, 1952, AAPS, roll 23; Chief Warder

Log Book, July 7, 1956, AAPS, roll 24; *SSD*, February 25, 1949, December 20, 1950, December 23, 1950, December 25, 1950, May 2, 1955, July 17, 1956, March 26, 1957.

71. *SSD*, June 13, 1952, June 15, 1952, April 23, 1955, April 26, 1955, May 2, 1955; Minutes of the Governors' Meeting, September 3, 1953, AAPS, roll 3.
72. On weight, see Minutes of the Governors' Meeting, November 25, 1959, AAPS, roll 4. On the suicide attempt, see Note of November 25, 1959, Hess Medical File, AAPS, roll 15; *SSD*, November 27, 1959.
73. Hess Medical File, December 1959, AAPS, roll 15; *SSD*, November 27, 1959, December 11, 1959, July 10, 1960.
74. *SSD*, March 16, 1964, October 24, 1964, November 19, 1964.
75. *SSD*, December 25, 1963, February 10, 1965. Hess Medical File, April 2, 1945, AAPS, roll 5, notes lack of cramping pain for three months.
76. On Roberts's visit, see *AAP-BRD 1966*, v. 1, d. 9. On Ilse, see Hess to Ilse, *Schicksal in Briefen*, p. 594.
77. The chronology of the family efforts is in Wolf Rüdiger Hess, *Mein Vater Rudolf Heß: Englandflug und Gefangenschaft* (Munich: Langen Müller, 1984), pp. 353ff.
78. The petition to Waldheim is dated July 16, 1979, and is in NARA, RG 84, Entry 1006, Box 4 Folder: Hess and Spandau 1980–1982, General File 2. See also Gamal Badr (deputy director for research and studies) to Seidl, November 7, 1979, in the same folder.
79. NARA, RG 84, Entry 1006, Box 1, Folder: Plans (Spandau and Hess); NARA, RG 84, Entry 1006, Box 1, Folder: Admin. Case Hess vs. Land Berlin; NARA, RG 84, Entry 1006, Box 4, Folder: Hess and Spandau General 1979.
80. On the West German press, see the lengthy article by Ursula von Kardoff in *Süddeutsche Zeitung*, April 3, 1968, which vastly overestimated that four hundred soldiers and fifty warders were part of Hess's confinement, and that this "absurd and melodramatic act of atonement" cost the West German taxpayers DM 800,000 per year.
81. For the visit, see the notes of the British chief warder, November 20, 1964, Hess Personal File, AAPS, roll 14; *SSD*, November 18, 1964, February 7, 1965.
82. Minutes of the Governors' Meeting, April 26, 1967; Soviet Statement regarding the 1088th Directors' Meeting, May 9, 1967; Minutes of the Governors' Meeting, May 8, 1969, all in AAPS, roll 5; Minutes of the Governors' Meeting, October 26, 1973, AAPS, roll 6.
83. Stoessel to secretary of state, No. 14265, August 14, 1979, NARA, RG 84, Entry 1006, Box 4, Folder: Hess and Spandau General 1979.
84. Seidl was awarded the Bavarian Verdienstorden in 1968 and the Grosse Bundesverdienstkreuz in 1973 with star added in 1976.
85. Seidl to Strauss, April 23, 1957, PA-AA, B 83, Bd. 1465; Strauss to Brandt, December 22, 1966, PA-AA, B 83, Bd. 1466.
86. Gawlick to Seidl, January 3, 1961 and V4-ZRS-E 21–57, February 28, 1966, both in PA-AA, B 83, Bd. 1465.
87. For the petition, see Seidl to De Gaulle, Draft, April 6, 1966, PA-AA, B 83, Bd. 1465. The final petition is dated May 18, 1966, and is in PA-AA, B 83, Bd. 1466.
88. IA3–84.20–94.07, May 12, 1966, PA-AA, B 83, Bd. 1465.
89. V4-ZRS-E21/57, May 17, 1966, PA-AA, B 83, Bd. 1465.
90. PA-AA, B 83, Bd. 1466, passim.
91. David Gladstone (British Embassy Bonn) to D. A. T. Stafford (Western Department, FCO), No. 1661, August 18, 1967, TNA, FCO 33/296. De Gaulle, unlike Lyndon Johnson and British Prime Minister Harold Wilson, answered personally a humanitarian petition on Hess's behalf from West German Catholic and Evangelical Church leaders in February 1967 in order to maintain a positive image in West German church circles. See Martin J. Hillenbrand (U.S. Embassy Bonn) to Department of State, No. 9627, February 17, 1967 and subsequent documents, NARA, RG 84, Entry 1006, Box 8, Folder: Spandau Prison Jan–June 1967.
92. Hess's letters to Ilse in October 1946 at first disapproved of Seidl's clemency petition at Nuremberg as undignified, but after Hess discovered the defiant nature of the petition, which challenged the Tribunal itself, he approved. Hess to Ilse, October 13, 1946, December 28, 1946; *Schicksal in Briefen*, pp. 118–19.
93. *SSD*, August 18, 1965.

94. W. R. Hess, *Mein Vater Rudolf Heß*, p. 355.
95. Ilse Hess, *England–Nürnberg–Spandau* (Leoni an Starnberger See: Druffel, 1952); later reprinted in *Schicksal in Briefen.*
96. Hess to Ilse, September 2, 1946, October 2, 1946, March 10, 1947, *Schicksal in Briefen*, pp. 111–13, 114–15, 121–3.
97. Seidl to Gawlick, February 20, 1958, PA-AA, B 83, Bd. 1465 includes Ilse's petition of January 15.
98. Copy in PA-AA, B 83, Bd. 1465. See also Wolf Rüdiger Hess, *Hess – Weder Recht noch Menschlichkeit: Das Urteil von Nürnberg – Die Rache von Spandau – Eine Dokumentation* (Leoni am Starnberger See: Druffel, 1974), pp. 25ff .
99. Pätzold and Weißbecker, *Rudolf Heß*, p. 349. For the statements, see W. R. Hess, *Mein Vater Rudolf Heß*, pp. 385ff; *Sunday Express*, April 27, 1969, April 7, 1974; December 23, 1979 (for Taylor); *Bild am Sonntag*, April 10, 1977 (for Shawcross). See also Hartley Shawcross, *Life Sentence: The Memoirs of Lord Shawcross* (London: Constable, 1995), pp. 129–30.
100. Ads in *FAZ* May 7, 1981, October 3, 1981, May 6, 1982, October 7, 1982.
101. On the founding and various steps, see Pätzold and Weißbecker, *Rudolf Heß*, pp. 348–9; W. R. Hess, *Mein Vater Rudolf Heß*, pp. 356ff.
102. W. R. Hess, *Heß – Weder Recht noch Menschlichkeit*; W. R. Hess, *Mein Vater Rudolf Heß*.
103. W. R. Hess, "The Life and Death of My Father Rudolf Hess," presented by videotape to the Eleventh Conference of the Institute for Historical Review, 1992, http://www.ihr.org/jhr/v.13/v13n1p24_Hess.html [accessed June 2004].
104. Memorandum to the foreign minister, received August 22, 1967, PA-AA, B 83, Bd. 1466. See also the West German comments relayed in Kenneth Rush (U.S. ambassador Bonn) to secretary of state, No. 14349, October 31, 1969, NARA, RG 59, Entry 1613, Box 2108, Folder: Pol 27–12. On Kiesinger, who was a routine target of East German attacks, see Daniel E. Rogers, "The Chancellors of the Federal Republic of Germany and the Political Legacy of the Holocaust," in *The Impact of Nazism: New Perspectives on the Third Reich and Its Legacy*, eds. Alan Steinweis and Daniel E. Rogers (Lincoln: University of Nebraska Press, 2003), pp. 236–7.
105. The effort is covered in NARA, RG 84, Entry 1006, Box 8, Folder: Spandau Prison (Jan–June 1966).
106. Jean-Claude Winckler (French minister Berlin) to François Seydoux (French ambassador Bonn), No. 128/EU, March 6, 1965, MAE-AOFAA, GMFB 17/4.
107. Reasoning in U.S. Intra-Berlin Message No. 32 of January 29, 1966, MAE-AOFAA, GMFB, 17/4.
108. Text in U.S. Embassy Bonn to secretary of state, No. 1092, June 16, 1966, NARA, RG 84, Entry 1006, Box 8, Folder: Spandau Prison (Jan–June 1966). Abrassimov had in fact commented immediately in February 1966, after an informal British statement, that there could be no question of amnesty for Hess and that he doubted whether Hess had any health problems. See Carstens memorandum St.S. 375/66 VS-Vertr., February 23, 1966, PA-AA, B 2, Bd. 158. Another Allied attempt in August 1966 on the eve of Speer's and von Schirach's release met a similar refusal. On this attempt, see NARA, RG 59, Entry 1004, Prefix LR 16, Box 28.
109. George C. McGhee (U.S. ambassador Bonn) to Department of State, No. A-1098, March 15, 1968; Brewster Morris (U.S. minister Berlin) to secretary of state, No. 4381, June 13, 1969, both in NARA, RG 59, Entry 1004, Prefix LR 22, Box 28; Major General James Bowes-Lyon (commandant British sector Berlin) to British Embassy Bonn, No. 190, June 13, 1969, TNA, FO 1042/331; Sir Archibald Duncan Wilson (British ambassador Moscow) to FCO, 14/2, March 16, 1970, TNA, FCO 33/1164; *AAP-BRD 1968*, v. 1, d. 96. The NPD vote in state and federal elections from 1966 to 1968 is covered in Lee McGowan, *The Radical Right in Germany 1870 to the Present* (New York: Longman, 2002), pp. 156–8. The NPD's greatest success on the federal level came in 1969 with 1.42 million votes or 4.3 percent of the total. On the NPD in Berlin, see *AAP-BRD 1970*, v. 3, d. 593.
110. Le Tissier, *Farewell to Spandau*, p. 56, counts twenty-seven Allied appeals in all for Hess's release, with the British government participating in twenty-four. There were also thirteen solo British appeals on the ministerial level after 1970 alone.

111. Parliamentary pressure for an end to the Spandau regime, sporadic from 1966 to 1969, came mostly from John Biggs-Davidson and focused on the absurdity of the Spandau arrangement rather than real debate on Hess's guilt. See *Hansard* (Commons), v. 730, pp. 1234–5 (Oral Answers); v. 734, p. 104 (Written Answers); v. 735, p. 206 (Written Answers); v. 736, p. 170 (Written Answers); v. 750, pp. 161–2 (Written Answers); v. 757, p. 12 (Written Answers); v. 762–3, p. 21 (Oral Answers); v. 782, pp. 936–7 (Oral Answers).
112. TNA, FCO 33/295.
113. P. H. Gore-Booth Confidential Memorandum to foreign secretary, January 11, 1967, TNA, FCO 33/295.
114. H. T. Morgan (British Military Government Berlin) to Alan Campbell (head, Western Department, FCO), December 29, 1966; Frank Roberts to Gore-Booth, January 19, 1967; Roberts to Gore-Booth, February 9, 1967, all in TNA, FCO 33/295.
115. The most complete file on the subject is MAE-AOFAA, GMFB 17/2. See also AK Berlin, Legal Committee, LEG/R(66)12, July 1, 1966, NARA, RG 84, Entry 1006, Box 8, Folder: Spandau Prison (Jan–June 1966); Memorandum: "Transfer of Prisoner No. 7 (Hess) to the Hospital Building at Spandau Prison," October 21, 1966, AP/M(66)37, AAPS, roll 5. See also U.S. Mission Berlin (David Klein) to U.S. Embassy Bonn, A-418, September 25, 1969, NARA, RG 59, Entry 1613, Box 2108, Folder: Pol 27-12.
116. Winckler to Seydoux, No. 1825, September 29, 1966, MAE-AOFAA, GMFB 17/2.
117. Re-accommodation of Prisoner No. 7 (Rudolf Hess) in Old Hospital Building, Spandau Allied Prison, December 8, 1966, TNA, FCO 33/395. See also cost assessments in NARA, RG 84, Entry 1006, Box 8, Folder: Spandau Prison Jan–June 1967; Senator für Bundesangelegenheiten, Bevollmächtiger des Landes Berlin beim Bund to AA (Redenz, V/4 ZRS), -I/1–0352–01, December 9, 1966, PA-AA, B 83, Bd. 1466.
118. This he mentioned to the Allied commandants. See Winckler to Seydoux, No. 1452, July 10, 1966, MAE-AOFAA, GMFB 17/2.
119. Abteilung V, V 4 – ZRS – 22/66, September 26, 1966, PA-AA, B 83, Bd. 1466. On the June 1968 public statement by Hans-Günther Hoppe, the senator for justice, see also U.S. Mission Berlin (Klein), to U.S. Embassy Bonn, A-418, September 25, 1969, NARA, RG 59, Entry 1613, Box 2108, Folder: Pol 27-12. See also Minutes of the Medical Board Meetings, November 26, 1969–March 1970, AAPS, roll 11.
120. R. Hanbury-Tenison (British Embassy Bonn) to H. T. Morgan (Western Department, FCO), 14/1, June 12, 1968, TNA, FCO 33-297. Documents on Bonn's refusal are in PA-AA, B 38, Bd. 259.
121. Additional discussion in TNA, FO 1042/331; MAE-AOFAA, GMFB 17/2.
122. Special Meeting of November 19, 1969, AAPS, roll 5. Hess also refused preventive X-rays in the summer of 1967, and the governors had agreed on new procedures in September 1968 for the emergency movement of the prisoner to the British Military Hospital for procedures that could not be done in the prison. On the political implications of Hess's health problem of this time, see NARA, RG 59, Entry 1613, Box 2108, Folder: Pol 27-12.
123. See Hess's letter of January 10, 1970, in Bowes-Lyon to FCO and British Embassy Bonn, No. 26, January 17, 1970, TNA, FCO 33/1162.
124. For the whole of the Quadripartite Agreement of September 3, 1971, see Germany (West), Press and Information Office, *The Berlin Settlement: The Quadripartite Agreement on Berlin and the Security Arrangements* (Wiesbaden: Graphische Betrieb, 1972).
125. On British interest, see TNA, FCO 33/1161–1164, and Terence Prittie, "The Power and the Pity," *The Guardian*, January 24, 1970. On West German hopes, see Rush to secretary of state, No. 15345, November 28, 1969, NARA, RG 59, Entry 1004, Prefix LR 30, Box 28. West German public interest at this time was indeed smaller than public interest in Great Britain. See D. S. Broucher (British Military Government Berlin) to FCO, 14/1, October 6, 1970, TNA, FCO 33/1164, which comments, "It seems fair to say that the interest generated in the case of Hess has tended to be greater in the United Kingdom than in Germany itself."
126. Morris to secretary of state, No. 2033, November 28, 1969, NARA, RG 59, Entry 1613, Box 2108, Folder: Pol 27–12. On Soviet armament in 1970, see Nikolai Sysoev's account in "Victors: Guarding the Number Two Nazi," *Bratishka* (*Brotherhood: Journal for Members of Special Forces*), October 2004, http://www.bratishka.ru [accessed January 2006]. I am grateful to Arsen Djatej for this reference and translation.
127. Bowes-Lyon to British Embassy Bonn, No. 394, December 2, 1969, TNA, FO 1042/331.

128. Minutes of the Governors' Meeting, December 2, 1969, and Extraordinary Meeting of December 3, 1969, AAPS, roll 5. On the Soviet insistence that Hess return once he showed some improvement, see Minutes of the Medical Board Meetings, December 29, 1969, January 14, 1970, AAPS, roll 11.
129. Morris to secretary of state, No. 2087, December 19, 1969; Morris to secretary of state, No. 2070, December 11, 1969, both in NARA, RG 59, Entry 1613, Box 2108, Folder: Pol 27-12; West Berlin Priority Telegram No. 228 to FCO, December 30, 1969, TNA, FCO 1042/331.
130. Bowes-Lyon to British Embassy Bonn, No. 394, December 2, 1969, TNA, FO 1042/331.
131. Hess's requests that he visit his family with no observers in the room, that the visit last longer than the prescribed thirty minutes, and that they receive a Christmas dinner were rejected by the Soviets, but the governors did agree (this time) that Ilse and Wolf Rüdiger could visit together. See the materials in Hess Personal File, AAPS, roll 14; Minutes of the Governors' Meetings, December 11, 1969, December 18, 1969, AAPS, roll 5; Morris to secretary of state, December 30, 1969, NARA, RG 59, Entry 1613, Box 2108, Folder: Pol 27-12.
132. Rogers to U.S. Embassy Bonn, U.S. Mission Berlin, No. 198295, November 26, 1969; Rogers to U.S. Embassy Bonn, U.S. Mission Berlin, No. 200011, December 1, 1969; Morris to secretary of state, No. 2020, November 27, 1969, all in NARA, RG 59, Entry 1613, Box 2108, Folder: Pol 27-12.
133. Morris to secretary of state, No. 2034, November 28, 1969, NARA, RG 59, Entry 1613, Box 2108, Folder: Pol 27-12; Memorandum of Discussion at Spandau Prison Mess, December 1, 1967, NARA, RG 59, Entry 1004, Prefix LR 56, Box 28.
134. Morris to secretary of state, No. 2036, December 11, 1969, NARA, RG 59, Entry 1613, Box 2108, Folder: Pol 27-12; Minutes of the Governors' Meeting, December 4, 1968, December 11, 1969, AAPS, roll 5.
135. Rogers to U.S. Embassy Bonn, U.S. Mission Berlin, No. 207163, December 13, 1969, NARA, RG 59, Entry 1613, Box 2108, Folder: Pol 27-12; Charles N. Brower (assistant legal adviser for European affairs) to Martin J. Hillenbrand (assistant secretary for European affairs), undated, NARA, RG 59, Entry 1004, Prefix LR 50, Box 28.
136. Minutes of the Governors' Meetings, January 22, 1970, February 7, 1970, February 28, 1970, AAPS, roll 5.
137. British thinking recorded in TNA, FCO 33/1161, 1162, 1163, 1164. See also Rush to secretary of state, No. 293, January 13, 1970; Rogers to Rush, No. 6245, January 14, 1970, both in NARA, RG 59, Entry 1004, Prefixes LR 76 and LR 78, Box 28. On subjective British medical diagnoses, see Brower to David H. Small (legal adviser, U.S. Mission Berlin) and Donald Wehmeyer (political adviser, U.S. Embassy Bonn), January 16, 1970; Rush to secretary of state, No. 1303, February 5, 1970, both in NARA, RG 59, Entry 1004, Prefixes LR 82 and LR 96, Box 28. The property in question had technically been owned by the Soviet state since the 1920s.
138. George Thomson to Stewart, February 6, 1979, TNA, FCO 33/1163.
139. In general, see TNA, FCO 33/1162, 1163, 1164. See also Minutes of the Medical Board Meeting, February 25, 1970, AAPS, roll 11; Minutes of the Governors' Meeting, March 13, 1970, AAPS, roll 6. The new regulations of March 1970 are in AAPS, roll 1. On negotiations and the British tie of conditions for Hess to the cremation agreement, see Morris to U.S. Embassy Bonn, No. 247, February 14, 1970; Morris to U.S. Embassy Bonn, No. 361, March 5, 1970; Morris to secretary of state, No. 388, March 12, 1970, all in NARA, RG 59, Entry 1004, Prefix LR 105, LR 125, LR 126, Box 28; Bowes-Lyon to FCO, No. 70, March 9, 1970, TNA, FCO 33/1164.
140. See for example the tussle over tests for stomach cancer in August and September 1973. Hess had the tests in the British Military Hospital. TNA, FCO 33/2223.
141. Morris to U.S. Embassy Bonn, A-236, May 5, 1970, NARA, RG 59, Entry 1004, Prefix LR 132, Box 28.
142. Exposé de Michel Planet (French prison governor 1973–1987) to Jean-Pierre Brunet (French ambassador Bonn), September/October 1977, MAE-AOFAA, GMFB 239/1, Folder: Divers. This report sums up Hess's amenities to date.
143. Minutes of the Governors' Meetings, December 29, 1972, January 18, 1973, May 29, 1975, AAPS, roll 6; Prisoner's Daily Schedule, April 20, 1978 and Regulations dated June 7, 1977, AAPS, roll 1.

144. Exposé de Michel Planet to Jean-Pierre Brunet, September/October 1977, MAE-AOFAA, GMFB 239/1, Folder: Divers.
145. On visiting periods, see the discussions in TNA, FCO 33/1164; Minutes of the Governors' Meeting, December 27, 1973, AAPS, roll 6. On number of visits, see Pätzold and Weißbecker, *Rudolf Heß*, p. 354. On Dejev's comment, see Minutes of the Governors' Meeting, December 12, 1974, AAPS, roll 6.
146. Bird was fired for these indiscretions in January 1972. See Minutes of the Governors' Meeting, May 28, 1974, AAPS, roll 6. For his book, not used here, see Eugene Bird, *Prisoner Number 7, Rudolf Hess: The Thirty Years in Jail of Hitler's Deputy Führer* (New York: Viking, 1974).
147. See for example Minutes of the Governors' Meetings, January 24, 1974, February 8, 1974, AAPS, roll 6.
148. The inventory is in the U.S. Berlin Command report by Lieutenant Colonel Thomas J. Ambrose, April 26, 1972, NARA, RG 84, Entry 1006-A, Box 5.
149. The story of Eugene Bird is documented in Memorandum of Conversation, March 22, 1972, NARA, RG 59, Entry 1004, Prefix LR 149, 149A, Box 28.
150. Michel Planet mentioned Schuman's views on the subject in a loose note dated October 1979, "Deux problèmes subsistent en ce qui concerne Hess," in MAE-AOFAA, GBFB 233/6. On initial French reaction, see Morris to secretary of state, No. 5125, November 28, 1969; Morris to secretary of state, No. 737, May 8, 1970; Morris to Department of State, A-002, January 6, 1971, all in NARA, RG 59, Entry 1004, Prefix LR 52, LR 134, LR 137, LR 137A, Box 28; Arthur Hartman (U.S. Ambassador Paris) to secretary of state, No. 29292, September 19, 1979, NARA, RG 84, Entry 1006, Box 1, unnamed folder. See also David L. N. Goodchild (British Military Government Berlin) to FCO, 14/1, May 21, 1970, and 14/1, November 19, 1970, TNA, FO 33/1164, the latter of which describes the official French legal argument that since the 1954 burial arrangement was signed by the Higher Executive Authority (in the form of the Berlin Mission legal representatives), it could not be countermanded by their subordinates (the prison governors themselves). Schuman also argued that cremation against the family's will violated the 1966 UN International Convention on Civil and Political Rights.
151. Hartman to secretary of state, No. 29292, September 19, 1979, NARA, RG 84, Entry 1006, Box 1, unnamed folder.
152. U.S. Mission Berlin (James Nelson, U.S. political adviser Berlin) to secretary of state, No. 290, February 12, 1979, NARA, RG 84, Entry 1006, Box 3, Folder: Hess and Spandau General 1979.
153. See discussions in TNA, FCO 33/1164.
154. Martin J. Hillenbrand, (U.S. ambassador Bonn) to secretary of state, No. 10294, June 16, 1976, NARA, RG 84, Entry 1006, Box 1, Folder: Plans (Spandau and Hess).
155. This Soviet answer was to be seen as final. See Scott George (U.S. minister Berlin) to secretary of state, No. 1659, June 21, 1977; Stoessel to secretary of state, No. 1587, January 27, 1977; David Anderson (U.S. minister Berlin) to U.S. Embassy Bonn, No. 0047, January 8, 1979, all in NARA, RG 84, Entry 1006, Box 1, unnamed folder.
156. French Mission Berlin (Landy) to Quai d'Orsay, No. 152/53, February 24, 1979, MAE-AOFAA, GMFB 239/1, Folder: TG au Départ; U.S. Mission Berlin to secretary of state, No. 546, March 19, 1979, NARA, RG 84, Entry 1006, Box 3, Folder: Hess and Spandau General 1979.
157. French Mission Berlin (Gaschignard) to Quai d'Orsay, No. 97, April 23, 1981, MAE-AOFAA, GMFB, 239/1, Folder: TG au Départ.
158. Stoessel to secretary of state, No. 728, January 16, 1979, NARA, RG 84, Entry 1006, Box 1, unnamed folder.
159. Jeffrey James (British deputy political adviser Berlin) to Nelson (U.S. political adviser Berlin) and Perrin (French political adviser Berlin), Intra-Berlin Message No. 63, February 8, 1979; Nelson to secretary of state, No. 291, February 12, 1979, both in NARA, RG 84, Entry 1006, Box 1, unnamed folder.
160. Transcript of December 12, 1979, in NARA, RG 84, Entry 1006, Box 4, Folder: Hess and Spandau General 1979.
161. Sprecher, *Inside the Nuremberg Trial*, v. 2, pp. 1135ff.
162. For quotes, see "Protests and Hess Goes Back to Gaol," *The Times*, March 14, 1970; Airey Neave, *On Trial at Nuremberg* (Boston: Little Brown, 1978), p. 316.

163. On the April 1969 demonstration, see *Tagesspiegel*, April 27, 1969. For Wolf Rüdiger's visit to George Thomson (the chancellor of the Duchy of Lancaster) on January 5, 1970, see TNA, FCO 33/1161, 1162. On the visit to Washington, see Memorandum of Conversation, February 6, 1970, NARA, RG 59, Entry 1004, Prefix LR 98, Box 28. On the financing, see British Embassy Washington (Freeman) to FCO, No. 418, February 9, 1970, TNA, FCO 33/1163.
164. *Hansard* (Commons), v. 816, c. 17, April 26, 1971 (oral). For Neave's warnings, see Minute by Morgan, January 22, 1970; Stewart to British Missions in Bonn and Berlin, No. 40, February 5, 1970, both in TNA, FCO 33/1162. See also *Hansard* (Commons), v. 795, c. 26–8, February 2, 1970 (oral); v. 796, c. 148, February 18, 1970 (written); v. 797, c. 22, March 2, 1970 (oral); v. 808, c. 13, December 7, 1970 (written); v. 814, c. 12–13, March 22, 1971 (written); v. 845, c. 286, November 10, 1972 (written); v. 846, c. 109, November 14, 1972 (written); v. 872, c. 40, April 8, 1974 (written); and Le Tissier, *Farewell to Spandau*, p. 55. See also TNA, FCO 33/1564 and 1565 for Neave's correspondence with the Foreign Office.
165. See for example the AA Memorandum, II A 1–84.29, February 2, 1971, PA-AA, B 38, Bd. 345. As John Kenneth Drinkall, head of the FCO's Western Department, said of Neave's pressure in January 1971, "In the context of the Berlin talks the timing is entirely wrong.... I am, frankly, getting very fed up with Mr. Neave's persistent needling on this point." See his memorandum of January 21, 1971, TNA, FCO 33/1564.
166. Record of Rippon's lunch with the Soviet Ambassador, June 18, 1971, TNA, FCO 33/1564. See also the meeting between Foreign Secretary Alec Douglas-Home with Soviet Ambassador Mikhail Smirnovsky on May 4, 1971, in this file. See also British Intra-Berlin Message No. 680 of October 24, 1975, NARA, RG 84, Entry 1006-A, Box 4.
167. Record of the Conversation between Douglas-Home and Gromyko on July 4, 1973, TNA, FCO 33/2223.
168. See especially *Hansard* (Commons), v. 898, c. 205–14, October 20, 1975 (oral); v. 953, c. 985–96, July 7, 1978 (oral). The three volumes of letters, *England-Nürnberg-Spandau – Ein Schicksal in Briefen* (1952); *Gefangener des Friedens – Neue Briefe aus Spandau* (1955); and *Antwort aus Zelle Sieben – Briefwechsel mit dem Spandauer Gefangenen* (1967), are reprinted in the single volume *Schicksal in Briefen*.
169. The meeting of October 10 was originally to be with Douglas-Home, who became ill at the last moment. Lord Balniel took Douglas-Home's place. On October 12, Hess met with Anthony Royle. The meetings were in part to appease Neave and the parliamentary lobby. See TNA, FCO 33/2224. The article in question is "Freiheit für meinen Vater!" *Der Freiwillige* (October 1973), pp. 4–7.
170. W. R. Hess, *Mein Vater Rudolf Heß*, pp. 357–61.
171. Information on these movements in PA-AA, B 38, Bd. 345.
172. Sir Duncan Wilson (British ambassador Moscow) to FCO, No. 13, January 7, 1970, and No. 20, January 8, 1970, TNA, FCO 33/1161. See also the comments on Moscow Radio of that month in TNA, FCO 33/1162.
173. See the examples of June 1971 triggered by Neave's efforts in TNA, FCO 33/1564.
174. Report from Botschaft der BRD Moscow, Nr. 2202/71, July 7, 1971, PA-AA, B 38, Bd. 345.
175. W. R. Hess, *Mein Vater Rudolf Heß*, pp. 11–19; Le Tissier, *Farwell to Spandau*, pp. 55–6.
176. George to U.S. Embassy Bonn and secretary of state, No. 1277, June 22, 1976, NARA, RG 84, Entry 1006, Box 1, Folder: Plans (Spandau and Hess).
177. See for example Kissinger to U.S. Embassy Bonn and Mission Berlin, No. 20972, January 28, 1976, NARA, RG 84, Entry 1006, Box 1, Folder: Plans (Spandau and Hess); Vance to U.S. Embassies Paris, Bonn, London, Moscow, No. 245914, September 19, 1979, NARA, RG 84, Entry 1006, Box 1, unnamed folder; Stoessel to secretary of state, No. 3496, February 27, 1979, NARA, RG 84, Entry 1006, Box 3, Folder: Hess and Spandau General 1979.
178. Urology Note and Opinion on Prisoner Number 7, September 8, 1979, AAPS, roll 11.
179. Made clear in a long discussion with the British doctors, "Interview to Obtain Operation Consent," September 12, 1979, AAPS, roll 11.
180. All the above including text of Hess letter in Anderson to secretary of state, No. 2017, September 11, 1979, NARA, RG 84, Entry 1006, Box 4, Folder: Hess and Spandau General

1979. Hess also tried to send this statement to Seidl and Wolf Rüdiger. See Hess Personal File, AAPS, roll 14.

181. Vance to U.S. Embassy Bonn, No. 240469, September 13, 1979, NARA, RG 84, Entry 1006, Box 4, Folder: Hess and Spandau General 1979. Hess continued to refuse the surgery, but medical reports at the end of 1980 and 1981 described him in reasonably good spirits, appearing "younger than his present age of 86" with a good appetite despite his long standing mysterious abdominal cramps, and exercising outdoors despite the cold weather. Report on the State of Health of Prisoner No. 7, December 23, 1980; Report on the State of the Health of Prisoner No. 7, February 5, 1981, both in AAPS, roll 11.

182. Exposé de Michel Planet to Jean-Pierre Brunet, September/October 1977, MAE-AOFAA, GMFB 239/1, Folder: Divers.

183. Minutes of the Governors' Meeting, September 25, 1979, AAPS, roll 9.

184. Anderson to secretary of state, No. 2147, September 26, 1979, NARA, RG 84, Entry 1006, Box 4, Folder: Hess and Spandau General 1979.

185. Department of State Draft Cable (undated) to U.S. Embassy Bonn, NARA, RG 59, Entry 1004, Prefix LR 214, Box 28; Anderson to secretary of state, No. 2025, September 12, 1979, NARA, RG 84, Entry 1006, Box 4, Folder: Hess and Spandau General 1979; British Intra-Berlin Message No. 592 of November 4, 1980, NARA, RG 84, Entry 1006, Box 4, Folder: Hess and Spandau 1980–1982, General File 3. For the statements by Seidl and Wolf Rüdiger, see Hess Personal File, AAPS, roll 14.

186. Alan Burner (British Embassy Bonn) to FCO, April 19, 1973, TNA, FCO 33/2223; Peter Semler (deputy political adviser, U.S. Mission Berlin) to George, July 15, 1975, NARA, RG 84, Entry 1006, Box 1, Folder: Plans (Spandau and Hess).

187. Minutes of the Governors' Meeting, February 23, 1977, AAPS, roll 8.

188. Exposé de Michel Planet to Jean-Pierre Brunet, September/October 1977, MAE-AOFAA, GMFB 239/1, Folder: Divers.

189. George to secretary of state, No. 569, February 25, 1977; Stoessel to secretary of state, No. 3432, February 25, 1977; U.S. Mission Berlin to secretary of state, No. 581, February 26, 1977; George to secretary of state, No. 598, March 1, 1977, all in NARA, RG 84, Entry 1006, Box 10, Folder: Spandau Prison and Hess, 1977.

190. Stoessel to secretary of state, No. 4244, March 9, 1977; Vance to U.S. Embassy Bonn, No. 59153, March 17, 1977; Stoessel to secretary of state, No. 4886, March 18, 1977; Vance to U.S. Mission Berlin, No. 76344, April 6, 1977, all in NARA, RG 84, Entry 1006, Box 10, Folder: Spandau Prison and Hess, 1977.

191. U.S. Embassy Bonn to secretary of state, No. 10773, June 15, 1978 (information from von Braunmühl, the BRD liaison to Allied embassies), NARA, RG 84, Entry 1006, Box 3, Folder: Hess and Spandau General 1978. Scheel had also raised Hess with the Head of the Supreme Soviet in Moscow, Nikolai Podgorny, in November 1975 and had written to the four heads of state in July 1977 (Queen Elisabeth II, President Carter, and President Giscard d'Estaing replied personally); and he would again write the Allied heads of state in March 1979. For reasons yet to be discovered, the West German Federal President's office under Scheel maintained close contact with Wolf Rüdiger on these efforts, which complicated the efforts if nothing else. Wolf Rüdiger learned from Scheel the Soviet statements about his father's lack of remorse, which triggered efforts by Scheel and Wolf to set up a private meeting in Spandau wherein Wolf Rüdiger would apparently induce his father to say he was sorry for the past. See Memorandum for Zbigniew Brzezinski, August 5, 1977, NARA, RG 59, Entry 1004, Prefix LR 212, Box 28; Stoessel to secretary of state, No. 6508, April 10, 1978, NARA, RG 84, Entry 1006, Box 3, Folder: Hess and Spandau General 1978. On the 1979 effort, see NARA, RG 84, Entry 1006, Box 3, Folder: Hess and Spandau General 1979 and specifically Warren Christopher (deputy secretary of state) to U.S. Embassy Bonn No. 92850, April 13, 1979, in that folder.

192. Christopher to U.S. Embassy Bonn, No. 150183, June 13, 1978, NARA, RG 84, Entry 1006, Box 3, Folder: Hess and Spandau General 1978. On the Soviet reply in London, see British Intra-Berlin Message No. 54 of February 5, 1979, NARA, RG 84, Entry 1006, Box 3, Folder: Hess and Spandau General 1979.

193. Thatcher had Seidl informed to this effect on December 21, 1979. See letter text in W. R. Hess, *Mein Vater Rudolf Heß*, p. 428.

194. On this attempt, see Anderson to secretary of state, No. 2419, October 25, 1979; Vance to U.S. Embassy Bonn, U.S. Mission Berlin, No. 254607, October 16, 1979, both in NARA, RG 84, Entry 1006, Box 4, Folder: Hess and Spandau General 1979. On the approach in New York, see U.S. Embassy Bonn (Woessner) to secretary of state, No. 16845, September 20, 1979 in the same folder. French Foreign Minister Jean François-Poncet raised Hess with Gromyko in New York, but Carrington's meeting with Gromyko there went so badly that Carrington did not mention Hess.
195. Vance to U.S. Embassies Paris, Bonn, London, Moscow, No. 245914, September 19, 1979, NARA, RG 84, Entry 1006, Box 1, unnamed folder.
196. Dufour to Brunet, No. 1450, January 4, 1980, MAE-AOFAA, GMFB/239/1, Folder: Telegrammes de Paris; Anderson to secretary of state, No. 12065, January 12, 1981, NARA, RG 84, Entry 1006, Hess Files, Box 4.
197. Transcript of December 12, 1979 in NARA, RG 84, Entry 1006, Box 4, Folder: Hess and Spandau General 1979.
198. Stéphane Chmelewski (French deputy political adviser Berlin), French Intra-Berlin Message No. 36 of January 30, 1979, MAE-AOFAA, GMFB 239/1, Folder: Intra-Berlin.
199. John C. Kornblum (U.S. deputy political adviser Berlin) to French and British deputy political advisers (Chmelewsky and James), Intra-Berlin Communication No. 463 of September 11, 1980, NARA, RG 84, Entry 1006, Box 1, unnamed folder.
200. Eagleburger to Haig, June 30, 1981; U.S. Embassy Rome to secretary of state, No. 10658, May 4, 1981, both in NARA, RG 84, Entry 1006, Box 1, unnamed folder.
201. Haig to U.S. Embassy Paris, No. 105183, April 24, 1981, NARA, RG 84, Entry 1006, Box 1, unnamed folder.
202. Eagleburger to Haig, June 30, 1981; U.S. Embassy Rome to secretary of state, No. 10658, May 4, 1981, both in NARA, RG 84, Entry 1006, Box 1, unnamed folder.
203. Haig to Carrington, July 6, 1981, NARA, RG 84, Entry 1006, Box 1, unnamed folder.
204. Carrington to Haig, November 19, 1981, NARA, RG 84, Entry 1006, Box 1, unnamed folder.
205. On the April 2, 1982, meeting, see Nelson Ledsky (U.S. minister Berlin) to U.S. Embassy Bonn and secretary of state, No. 773, April 5, 1982, NARA, RG 84, Entry 1006, Box 1, unnamed folder, which includes the text of the Allied proposal.
206. *New York Times*, January 7, 1981. On the Soviet response, see U.S. Embassy Bonn to secretary of state, No. 8286, April 16, 1982, NARA, RG 84, Entry 1006, Box 1, unnamed folder. See also Abrassimov's comments in *Süddeutsche Zeitung*, February 10, 1981.
207. See MAE-AOFAA, GMFB 17/1, Folder: Médaille, which includes the protocol of the meeting at the West German Embassy in Moscow and the official Soviet statement.
208. Ledsky to secretary of state, No. 863, April 19, 1982, NARA, RG 84, Entry 1006, Box 1, unnamed folder.
209. Ledsky to secretary of state, U.S. Embassy Bonn, No. 1241, June 2, 1982; Ledsky to secretary of state and U.S. Embassy Bonn, No. 1325, July 14, 1982; Ernie Nagy (U.S. political adviser Berlin) to Michael Wood (British political adviser Berlin) and Auchere (French political adviser Berlin), Intra-Berlin Communication No. 261, June 23, 1982, all in NARA, RG 84, Entry 1006, Box 1, Folder: Pol 27-12A; Wood to Nagy and Fabbri (acting French political adviser), Intra-Berlin Message No. 319, July 21, 1982, NARA, RG 84, Entry 1006, Box 1, Folder: Plans (Spandau and Hess).
210. Burns to secretary of state, No. 14693, July 8, 1982; Haig to U.S. Embassy Bonn, No. 127730, May 11, 1982, both in NARA, RG 84, Entry 1006, Box 1, Folder: Pol 27-12A.
211. On the Schmidt letter, see NARA, RG 84, Entry 1006, Box 2, Folder: Pol 27-12A, passim.
212. Hess to Ilse, September 1982, NARA, RG 84, Entry 1006, Box 2, Folder: Pol 27-12A.
213. John Byerly (U.S. legal adviser Berlin) to Richard Hoover (EUR/CE), Department of State, July 2, 1982, NARA, RG 84, Entry 1006, Box 4.
214. Report on the State of Health of Prisoner No. 7, September 30, 1982, AAPS, roll 11. Hess was in the hospital from September 15 to September 27, 1982.
215. Byerly memorandum of September 1982, NARA, RG 84, Entry 1006, Box 2, Folder: Pol 27-12A.
216. Protocol, October 1, 1982, NARA, RG 84, Entry 1006, Box 1, Folder: Plans (Spandau and Hess). Also see AAPS, roll 1; MAE-AOFAA, GMFB 233/2.

217. For text of Wolf Rüdiger's pledge, see AAPS, roll 1. Kosobrodov insisted that the family not receive a copy of the Protocol. See British Intra-Berlin Message No. 406, October 6, 1982, MAE-AOFAA, GMFB 239/1, Folder: Intra-Berlin.
218. Memorandum by Taylor, October 7, 1982, NARA, RG 84, Entry 1006, Box 2, Folder: Pol 27-12A; Burns to secretary of state, No. 15017, June 13, 1983, NARA, RG 84, Entry 1006, Box 2, Folder: Hess and Spandau 1983–1985.
219. Ledsky to secretary of state, No. 1498, May 15, 1984; British Intra-Berlin Message No. 152 of April 18, 1983, NARA, RG 84, Entry 1006, Box 5, File: Hess and Spandau 1983–1985, General File 2.
220. Real deterioration began in the summer of 1986 with recurrent episodes of tachycardia, which prompted the bringing of an EKG monitor into the prison and discussions regarding a pacemaker. Hess stopped his regular exercise in March 1987, and by that month a heart specialist reported that "he looks his age." Hess also had increasing prostate problems in his last year – he requested a catheter in March 1987 – but he was no longer a good surgical risk. His eyesight began to degenerate in 1984, and by his last year, despite new spectacle prescriptions, he had great difficulty reading. See the Medical Officers' discussions from 1983 to 1987, AAPS, roll 11; Medical Report on Allied Prisoner No. 7, March 1, 1987, AAPS, roll 9.
221. Le Tissier, *Farewell to Spandau*, p. 58.
222. See the procedures as designed in March 1987 in AAPS, roll 9.
223. Meetings were in Bonn in May 1973, Bad Godesberg in December 1974, Neustadt in April 1975, Munich in May 1975, Essen in October 1975, Hamburg in November 1975, Bonn in May 1976, Wiesbaden in November 1976, Augsburg in May 1981 (for the fortieth anniversary of the flight).
224. McGowan, *The Radical Right in Germany*, pp. 155ff.
225. John C. Kornblum (U.S. Minister Berlin) to secretary of state, No. 3796, December 19, 1985, NARA, RG 84, Entry 1006, Box 5, Folder: Hess and Spandau 1983–1985, General File 2. On the Hess Congress, see also *Tageszeitung*, November 29, 1985.
226. Report by Michel Planet, May 13, 1986, MAE-AOFAA, GMFB 238/7, Folder: Articles de presse.
227. NARA, RG 84, Entry 1006, Box 5, Folder: Hess and Spandau 1986, passim. NARA, RG 84, Entry 1006, Box 6, Folder: Hess and Spandau 1987. On the bombing, see Le Tissier, *Farewell to Spandau*, pp. 63–5 and MAE-AOFAA, GMFB 238/7. The full report of November 6, 1986, and the note of October 23 are in AAPS, roll 8.
228. U.S. Mission Berlin to secretary of state, No. 1354, April 29, 1986, NARA, RG 84, Entry 1006, Box 5, Folder: Hess and Spandau 1986; U.S. Mission Berlin to secretary of state, No. 2874, August 19, 1987, NARA, RG 84, Entry 1006, Box 6, Folder: Hess and Spandau: Suicide 1987.
229. On Kappler and the Breda prisoners, see Scheel's discussion with Kießling, the President of the Verband der Heimkehrer, Kriegsgefangenen und Vermißten-Angehörigen Deutschlands, November 2, 1971, PA-AA, B 38, Bd. 345. See also *AAP-BRD 1971*, v. 1, d. 104, 114; *AAP-BRD 1973*, v. 3, d. 365.
230. Kenneth Rush to secretary of state, No. 14349, October 31, 1969, RG 59, Entry 1613, Box 2108, Folder: Pol. 27–12. On the Bundestag questions see *Verhandlungen des deutschen Bundestages*, Bd. 70, May 9, 1969, pp. 12869–71 and May 14, 1971. Private inquiries from Bundestag members and State Parliament inquiries from 1970 and 1971 can be found in PA-AA, B 38, Bd. 345. On Brandt, Anlage zu II A 1-84.20/0-2213/69 geh., November 27, 1969, PA-AA, B 38, Bd. 345 and subsequent documents reflecting the Soviet mood. On Scheel's reluctance to raise Spandau with Falin, see Scheel to Fritz Baier, July 1971, PA-AA, B 38, Bd. 345.
231. LR I Zenter to Gruner & Jahr GmbH, April 20, 1971, PA-AA, B 38, Bd. 345.
232. What the British Embassy knew of this is in PRO, FCO 33/2223.
233. Rogers, "The Chancellors of the Federal Republic," p. 242. See also Jochen Thies, *Helmut Schmidts Rückzug von der Macht: Das Ende der Ära Schmidt aus nächster Nahe* (Stuttgart: Bonn Aktuel, 1988), p. 196.
234. U.S. Embassy Bonn (Woessner) to secretary of state, No. 12668, August 8, 1980; Stoessel to secretary of state, No. 12668, July 5, 1980, both in NARA, RG 84, Entry 1006, Box 1, unnamed folder.

235. Burns to secretary of state, No. 24051, December 7, 1981, both in NARA, RG 84, Entry 1006, Box 1, unnamed folder.
236. Documents in NARA, RG 84, Entry 1006, Box 4, Folder: Hess and Spandau 1980–1982, General File 3.
237. *Verhandlungen des deutschen Bundestages*, Bd. 123, December 15, 1982, p. 8820.
238. On the effort with Andropov, see Kohl to Wolf Rüdiger Hess printed in W. R. Hess, *Mein Vater Rudolf Heß*, pp. 438–9.
239. Herf, *Divided Memory*, pp. 360–3.
240. Text in Schultz to U.S. Embassy Bonn, No. 92585, March 29, 1984, NARA, RG 84, Entry 1006, Box 5, Folder: Hess and Spandau 1983–1985, General File 2. This misstep came after Kohl, in a letter to Wolf Rüdiger of November 1983, said that the government could only work for Hess's freedom on humanitarian grounds. See W. R. Hess, *Mein Vater Rudolf Heß*, p. 269. Kohl made another public appeal in August 1986 arguing that mercy did not imply a pardon and that Hess's release would be an act of humanity. See *FAZ*, August 2, 1986.
241. Text in Burns to secretary of state, No. 12115, May 8, 1984, NARA, RG 84, Entry 1006, Box 5, Folder: Hess and Spandau 1983–1985, General File 2.
242. All summarized in NARA, RG 84, Entry 1006, Box 5, Folder: Hess and Spandau 1983–1985, General File 2. On *Izvestia*, see Arthur Hartman (U.S. ambassador Moscow) to secretary of state, No. 4680, April 16, 1984, NARA, RG 84, Entry 1006, Box 5, Folder: Hess and Spandau 1983–1985, General File 2.
243. U.S. Intra-Berlin Communication, No. 160, May 15, 1984, NARA, RG 84, Entry 1006, Box 5, Folder: Hess and Spandau 1983–1985, General File 2. The Soviet replies to London and Paris are contained in the same folder.
244. Herf, *Divided Memory*, pp. 354–9.
245. MacGinnis to Ledsky, June 4, 1982, and enclosure of MacGinnis discussion with von Weizsäcker, NARA, RG 84, Entry 1006, Box 1, Folder: Plans (Spandau and Hess).
246. Richard von Weizsäcker, *From Weimar to the Wall: My Life in German Politics*, trans. Ruth Hein (New York: Broadway Books, 1999), p. 284.
247. Kornblum to secretary of state, No. 3863, December 27, 1985, NARA, RG 84, Entry 1006, Box 5, Folder: Hess and Spandau 1983–1985, General File 2.
248. Hess to Spandau prison governors, November 11, 1980, September 17, 1984, May 23, 1986, Hess Personal File, AAPS, roll 14. On the latter request, see Minutes of the Governors' Meeting, June 23, 1986, AAPS, roll 8.
249. Hess to Spandau prison governors, March 25, 1987, June 24, 1987, AAPS, roll 9.
250. Minutes of the Governors' Meeting, June 27, 1986, AAPS, roll 8.
251. On Chernykh's suggestion that Gabel be watched more closely, see Planet to French Embassy Bonn, No. 173/POL, May 3, 1985, MAE-AOFAA, GMFB 238/7, Folder: Prison de Spandau – Sécurité. The papers, which consist of a hodgepodge of menus, reading notes, musings, and Hess's final statement to history, are in Hess Personal File, AAPS, roll 14. The seizure of the papers by Chernykh is described in Kornblum to Department of State, No. 2371, July 30, 1986, NARA, RG 84, Entry 1006, Box 5, Folder: Hess and Spandau 1986. See also Minutes of the Governors' Meeting, July 4, 1986, AAPS, roll 8. In an unfortunate coincidence, Gabel had been nominated for the Federal German Distinguished Service medal by von Weizsäcker himself only a month before and would receive the award in August 1986. There was no evidence von Weizsäcker knew of Gabel's smuggling, but the award was connected with Gabel's overall service at Spandau. On Gabel's sympathies with Hess and the Hess family as well as his denial that he was smuggling, see Charles Gabel, *Conversations interdites avec Rudolf Hess 1977–1986* (Paris: Plon, 1988), July 16, 1986.
252. Taylor, *Anatomy*, p. 536. Copies of the handwritten outline are in NARA, RG 238, Entry 20, Box 2, Folder: Hess.
253. Rudolf Hess, Progress Notes August 12, 1946–September 1, 1946 (by Lieutenant Colonel William H. Dunn, Nuremberg prison psychiatrist), Hess Personal File, AAPS, roll 14.
254. For the full text (two parts of more than twenty-four typed pages each) and the cover sheet mentioning Mosley, see NARA, RG 238, Entry 20, Box 2, Folder: Hess. I am grateful to Robert Wolfe of the National Archives and Records Administration for information on the odyssey of these papers.

255. On July 7, 1986, Hess asked the governors to return the report, which had been hidden in a jacket pocket in his closet. He said it was a study that went to the question of his guilt, and that he had planned to submit it to the governors when it was complete and typed. He hoped, he said, that it could be sent to Mikhail Gorbachev. The request was not honored. See Hess to the prison governors, July 7, 1986, and July 17, 1986; Minutes of the Governors' Meetings, July 10, 1986 and July 25, 1986, all in AAPS, roll 8.

## BURIALS: AN EPILOGUE

1. The last attempt, predicated on Jordan's supposed impoliteness to Hess, was Hess to Darold Keane, April 4, 1987; Hess to prison governors, May 12, 1987, both in AAPS, roll 9. The governors' refusal to fire Jordan is in Minutes of the Governors' Meeting, May 1, 1987, AAPS, roll 9. The incident forms the basis of later conspiracy theories that Jordan had murdered Hess. See the Jean-Pax Mefret article in *Figaro*, April 1, 1989.
2. The sequence is in Tony Le Tissier, *Farewell to Spandau* (Leatherhead: Ashfort, Buchnan and Enright, 1994), pp. 72–4. See also the forty-nine-page investigation by the British Special Investigations Branch in NARA, RG 84, Entry 1006, Box 3, Folder: Hess and Spandau 1987 [hereafter SIB report]. A copy of the suicide note is in AAPS, roll 9.
3. Cameron's report in AAPS, roll 9.
4. SIB report, passim. On the note, see U.S. Mission Berlin to Department of State, No. 2861, August 18, 1987, NARA, RG 84, Entry 1006, Box 7, Folder: Spandau General 1987. On the handover of the note, see Le Tissier, *Farewell to Spandau*, pp. 79–83. On the Soviet proposals, see MAE-AOFAA, GMFB 238/7, Folder: Sécurité.
5. U.S. Mission Berlin (James Williams, political adviser) to secretary of state, No. 2875, August 19, 1987, NARA, RG 84, Entry 1006, Box 7, Folder: Rudolf Hess, Suicide 8/17/87.
6. Report available at http://www.rudolfhess.org [accessed June 2004].
7. NARA, RG 84, Entry 1006, Box 3, Folder: Hess and Spandau 1987, passim on press. On the second autopsy and Seidl specifically, see U.S. Embassy Bonn to Department of State, No. 26033, August 24, 1987, NARA, RG 84, Entry 1006, Box 7, Folder: Rudolf Hess Suicide 8/17/87.
8. U.S. Mission Berlin (Williams) to secretary of state, No. 2909, August 21, 1987, NARA, RG 84, Entry 1006, Box 7, Folder: Rudolf Hess, Suicide 8/17/87.
9. Minutes of the Governors' Meetings, August 17, 1987, August 18, 1987, AAPS, roll 9.
10. Le Tissier, *Farewell to Spandau*, p. 75; U.S. Mission Berlin (Williams) to Department of State, No. 2861, August 18, 1987, NARA, RG 84, Entry 1006, Box 7, Folder: Spandau General 1987.
11. U.S. Mission Berlin (Williams) to secretary of state, No. 2861, August 18, 1987, NARA, RG 84, Entry 1006, Box 7, Folder: Rudolf Hess, Suicide 8/17/87; Minutes of the Governors' Meeting, August 18, 1987 (1855 hrs), AAPS, roll 9.
12. Minutes of the Governors' Meeting, August 19, 1987, AAPS, roll 9.
13. Yves Pagniez (French ambassador Moscow) to Quai d'Orsay, No. 3093, August 19, 1987, MAE-AOFAA, GMFB 264/1, Folder: Moscou.
14. "Hess's Private Cell of Torture," *Daily Express*, August 18, 1987.
15. Former Sturmbannführer Walter Kruger of the 1st SS Panzer Corps, quoted in *Daily Telegraph*, August 18, 1987.
16. *Berliner Morgenpost*, August 19, 1987.
17. Minutes of the Governors' Meeting, August 18, 1987 (1230 hrs), August 20, August 21, 1987, AAPS, roll 9.
18. Minutes of the Governors' Meeting, August 28, 1987, AAPS, roll 9.
19. U.S. Mission Berlin (Williams) to secretary of state, No. 2909, August 21, 1987, NARA, RG 84, Entry 1006, Box 7, Folder: Rudolf Hess, Suicide 8/17/87.
20. Minutes of the Governors' Meeting, September 15, 1987, AAPS, roll 9.
21. "Nazi Vigil as Hess Dies Alone," *Daily Express*, August 18, 1987; *Tageszeitung*, August 19, 1987 counted fewer than one hundred.
22. Pätzold and Weißbecker, *Rudolf Heß*, pp. 359–61.
23. Le Tissier, *Farewell to Spandau*, pp. 84–6.
24. Pätzold and Weißbecker, *Rudolf Heß*, pp. 357–9.

25. Wolf Rüdiger Hess, ed. *Rudolf Heß: Briefe 1908–1933* (Munich: Langen-Müller, 1990).
26. Wolf Rüdiger Hess, *Mord an Rudolf Heß? Der geheimnisvolle Tod meines Vaters in Spandau* (Leoni am Starnberger See: Druffel, 1989); Wolf Rüdiger Hess, *Ich bereue nichts*, 3rd ed. (Graz: Leopold Stocker Verlag, 1998).
27. Le Tissier, *Farewell to Spandau*, p. 106.
28. Anderson (U.S. minister Berlin) to secretary of state, No. 950, April 24, 1981, NARA, RG 84, Entry 1006, Box 1, unnamed folder.
29. U.S. Embassy Bonn (Woessner) to secretary of state, No. 1509, January 26, 1981 and James to Chmelewsky and Kornblum, January 29, 1981, both in NARA, RG 84, Entry 1006, Box 1, Folder: Plans (Spandau and Hess).
30. Goodchild to FCO, 14/1, May 29, 1970, TNA, FCO 33/1164.
31. Abrassimov's comment was April 4, 1978. See George to secretary of state, No. 773, April 5, 1978, NARA, RG 84, Entry 1006, Box 1, unnamed folder. On the French assessment, Brunet to Jean Francois-Poncet, 1270/EU, November 23, 1979, MAE-AOFAA, GMFB 239/1, Folder: TG de Bonn; and Perrin to Quai d'Orsay, No. 75/79, January 26, 1979, MAE-AOFAA, GMFB 239/1, Folder: TG au Depart.
32. U.S. Intra-Berlin Communication, No. 58, February 9, 1982, MAE-AOFAA, GMFB 239/1, Folder: Intra-Berlin.
33. "Planning Paper: The Closure of Spandau Prison," original version authored by British FCO from February 1979 in MAE-AOFAA, GMFB 239/1, Folder: Divers. The 1981 version based on further Embassy discussions in Bonn, is in NARA, RG 84, Entry 1006, Box 1, Folder: Plans (Spandau and Hess).
34. The closest legal authority was British Military Government Sector Ordinance 202 of December 30, 1949, which stated that former Reich and Prussian state property located in the British sector was transferred to the City of Berlin as trustee for any future German state recognized by the British occupation authorities as being appropriate for final ownership. Article 2(b) of that ordinance excepted from it any property temporarily used or occupied by the occupation authorities in the British sector of Berlin. The final disposition of this property "will be dealt with in accordance with the decisions of the Occupation Authorities in the British Sector of Berlin." And with Hess's death, the quadripartite status of the prison would cease to apply. For explanation, see David H. Small to Charles N. Brower, March 10, 1970, NARA, RG 84, Entry 1006-A, Box 1. See also the extensive considerations saved in MAE-AOFAA, GMFB 239/1 (Avenir de la prison de Spandau).
35. Peter Semler (deputy political adviser, U.S. Mission Berlin) to Robert K. German (political officer, U.S. Embassy Bonn), October 19, 1976, NARA, RG 84, Entry 1006, Box 1, Folder: Plans (Spandau and Hess).
36. "Planning Paper: The Closure of Spandau Prison," British version from 1981 based on Embassy discussions in Bonn, NARA, RG 84, Entry 1006, Box 1, Folder: Plans (Spandau and Hess).
37. Nelson C. Ledsky (U.S. Minister Berlin) to secretary of state, No. 1032, May 5, 1982, NARA, RG 84, Entry 1006, Box 1, Folder: Pol 27–12A.
38. MacGinnis to Ledsky, June 4, 1982, and MacGinnis to Ledsky, July 22, 1982, each with enclosures of discussions with von Weizsäcker, NARA, RG 84, Entry 1006, Box 1, Folder: Plans (Spandau and Hess).
39. NARA, RG 84, Entry 1006, Box 5, Folder: Hess and Spandau 1983–1985, General File 2.
40. French Intra-Berlin Message No. 260, August 17, 1984; U.S. Intra-Berlin Message No. 291, August 20, 1984, both in MAE-AOFAA, GMFB 238/7. CBS News made a request in 1981 and the BBC made one in 1983. British Intra-Berlin Message No. 191, July 22, 1983, MAE-AOFAA, GMBF, 238/7.
41. British Intra-Berlin Message No. 147, April 11, 1986, NARA, RG 84, Entry 1006, Box 5, Folder: Hess and Spandau 1986.
42. British Intra-Berlin Message No. 396, September 4, 1987, NARA, RG 84, Entry 1006, Box 6, Folder: Hess and Spandau: Suicide 1987.
43. Harry Gilmore (U.S. Minister Berlin) to secretary of state, No. 3046, September 8, 1987; British Intra-Berlin Message No. 398, September 8, 1987, both in NARA, RG 84, Entry 1006, Box 3, Folder: Hess and Spandau 1987.
44. Text in U.S. Mission Berlin to secretary of state, No. 2861, August 18, 1987, NARA, RG 84, Entry 1006, Box 7, Folder: Spandau General 1987.

45. Gilmore to secretary of state, No. 2940, August 25, 1987, NARA, RG 84, Entry 1006, Box 3, Folder: Hess and Spandau 1987.
46. British Intra-Berlin Message No. 391, September 1, 1987, NARA, RG 84, Entry 1006, Box 3, Folder: Hess and Spandau 1987.
47. British Intra-Berlin Message No. 305, August 26, 1987, NARA, RG 84, Entry 1006, Box 3, Folder: Hess and Spandau 1987 and passim. See also Minutes of the Governors' Meeting, September 18, 1987, AAPS, roll 9.
48. Minutes of the Governors' Meeting, August 31, 1987, AAPS, roll 9.
49. Le Tissier, *Farewell to Spandau*, pp. 88–9.
50. Minutes of the Governors' Meeting, August 25, 1987, AAPS, roll 9.
51. Minutes of the Governors' Meeting, September 29, 1987, AAPS, roll 9.
52. Le Tissier, *Farewell to Spandau*, pp. 90–1, Minutes of the Governors' Meeting, September 25, 1987, AAPS, roll 9.
53. Gilmore to secretary of state, No. 3046, September 8, 1987, NARA, RG 84, Entry 1006, Box 3, Folder: Hess and Spandau 1987; Le Tissier, *Farewell to Spandau*, p. 88; Minutes of the Governors' Meetings, September 2, 1987, September 3, 1987, AAPS, roll 9.
54. Gilmore to secretary of state, No. 3046, September 8, 1987; U.S. Mission Berlin to secretary of state, No. 3160, September 16, 1987, both in NARA, RG 84, Entry 1006, Box 3, Folder: Hess and Spandau 1987; Gilmore to secretary of state, No. 3578, October 26, 1987, NARA, RG 84, Entry 1006-A, Box 1, Folder: Hess/Spandau — Theft/Archives/Death.
55. Minutes of the Governors' Meeting, January 6, 1987, AAPS, roll 9.
56. "Die Planierraupe sollte die Errinerung eineben," *FAZ*, July 17, 1997.
57. Gitta Sereny, *The Healing Wound: Experiences and Reflections on Germany, 1938–2001* (New York: Norton, 2000), pp. 271, 285.
58. On the theft, see Minutes of the Governors' Meeting, August 29, 1986, AAPS, roll 8; GOC HQ Berlin British Sector Report of January 26, 1987, NARA, RG 84, Entry 1006, Box 6, Folder: Hess and Spandau 1987. See also NARA, RG 84, Entry 1006, Box 6, Folder: Hess and Spandau:1988–1989; Le Tissier, *Farewell to Spandau*, pp. 63ff.
59. Kommandatura discussions concerning leaks to *Quick* (August 18, 1954 issue) and to *Stern* (May 14, 1967 issue) are in AMB/SlgD, AK 135/3. See also the records in NARA, RG 84, Entry 1006-A, Box 2, Folder: 1986; Kornblum to secretary of state, No. 2371, July 30, 1986, NARA, RG 84, Entry 1006, Box 5, Folder: Hess and Spandau 1986; MAE-AOFAA, GMFB 238/7, Folder: Prison de Spandau – Sécurité; Minutes of the Governors' Meeting, August 29, 1986, AAPS, roll 8; Le Tissier, *Farewell to Spandau*, p. 63.
60. The comment came after the article of January 3, 1985 in *Bunte*, "Der einsamste Mensch der Welt," which contained smuggled photographs of Hess. Chernykh said that if the prison were in the Communist bloc he would have located the culprit in no time. This leak also occasioned his call for the prison's division into sealed security zones and the installation of a closed circuit surveillance system. Planet to French Embassy Bonn, No. 16/Pol., January 11, 198[4], MAE-AOFAA, GMFB 238/7, Folder: Prison de Spandau – Sécurité. Chernykh's apoplectic response to the theft of Hess's property can be found in the same folder. A further article in *Bunte*, "Gnadenlos," appeared in the May 12, 1986, issue, and the July 11, 1986, article in *Quick*, "Beim Lesen muß ich tief durchatmen," contained information on Hess's health.

# Bibliography

ARCHIVES

*United States*

- National Archives and Records Administration (College Park, Maryland)

  RG 59 – Records of the Department of State
  Cited Entries:
  - Entry 1004 – Select Documents Released under the Nazi War Crimes and Imperial Japanese Government Disclosure Acts, 1923–1999
  - Entry 1311 – Records of the Assistant Legal Adviser for European Affairs; Subject Files of the Assistant Legal Adviser for European Affairs Relating to Germany and Austria,1945–1960, Lot File 59 D 609
  - Entry 1368 – Records of the Legal Adviser Relating to War Crimes; Country Files, 1943–1950, Lot File 61 D 33
  - Entry 1494-I – Office of the Legal Adviser; Division of United Nations Affairs, 1945–1959, Lot File 62 D 205
  - Entry 1613 – Subject Numeric Files: Central Foreign Policy Files, 1967–1969

  RG 84 – Records of Foreign Service Posts of the Department of State
  Cited Entries:
  - Entry 1006 – Germany, Berlin Mission, Political Section, Hess Files, Group 50
  - Entry 1006-A – Germany, Berlin Mission, Political Section, Hess Files, Group 18
  - Entry 1015 – Germany; Records of the U.S. Mission, Berlin; Allied Komandatura Secretariat; Miscellaneous Papers and Files, Group 37 A, 1945–1990
  - Entry 1016 – Records of the U.S. Mission, Berlin; Allied Kommandatura Secretariat; Subject Files, Group 6, 1945–1990
  - Berlin Mission, Records Relating to Spandau Prison, 1947–1987, Microfilm Publication A3352

  RG 238 – National Archives Collection of World War II War Crimes Records
  Cited Entries:
  - Entry 14 – United States Counsel for the Prosecution of Axis Criminality; German Dossiers
  - Entry 20 – Office of the Chief of Counsel for War Crimes, Attwood Collection
  - Entry 22 – Office of the Chief of Counsel for War Crimes, Records Received from the Collection of Colonel F. C. Teich

- Entry 33 – Office of the Chief of Counsel for War Crimes; Evidence Division; Library Section; Records Relating to Military Tribunal Case 6
- Entry 69 – Miscellaneous Unidentified Records
- Entry 171 – Office of the Chief of Counsel for War Crimes; Executive Counsel; Documentation Branch; Nuernberg, Industrialists (NI) Series
- Entry 183 – Office of the Chief of Counsel for War Crimes; Executive Counsel; Evidence Division; Interrogation Branch; Interrogations and Summaries of Interrogations of Defendants and Witnesses

RG 260 – Records of United States Occupation Headquarters, World War II, Office of Military Government, U.S. Zone (Germany) (OMGUS)
Cited Entries:

- Entry 22 – Records of the Executive Office; Records of the Chief of Staff; Records Maintained for Military Governor, Lieutenant General Lucius D. Clay, 1945–1949
- Entry 23 – Records of the Executive Office; Records of the Chief of Staff; Correspondence and Other Records Maintained by Major General Frank Keating, Assistant Deputy Military Governor, 1946–1947
- Entry 31 – Records of the Office of Adjutant General; Records Created by the Office of Adjutant General; Allied Control Directives and Related Records, 1945–1949
- Entry 139 – Records of the Executive Office; Records of the Control Office; Records of the Historical Division; Records Relating to the Office of Military Government, Berlin Sector; Subject Files, 1945–1949
- Entry 1790 – Records of the U.S. Element of Inter-Allied Organizations; Records of the U.S. Element, Allied Control Authority, General Records, 1945–1949
- Entry 1792 – Records of the U.S. Element of Inter-Allied Organizations; Records of the U.S. Element, Allied Control Authority; Records of the Control Council (CONL), General Records, 1945–1948
- Entry 1796 – Records of the U.S. Element of Inter-Allied Organizations; Records of the U.S. Element, Allied Control Authority; Records of the U.S. Element of the Coordinating Committee (CORC), Verbatim Minutes, 1945–1948
- Entry 1797 – Records of the U.S. Element of Inter-Allied Organizations; Records of the U.S. Element, Allied Control Authority; Records of the U.S. Element of the Coordinating Committee (CORC), Minutes of Meetings, 1945–1948
- Entry 1806 – Records of the U.S. Element of Inter-Allied Organizations; Records of the U.S. Element, Allied Control Authority; Records of U.S. Elements of other ACA Organizations; Records of the Legal Directorate, General Records, 1945–1948
- Entry 1954 – Records of U.S. Elements of Inter-Allied Organizations; Records of the U.S. Element of the Tripartite Control Office; Records of the U.S. Element of the Tripartite Secretariat, Records of Meetings,1948–1949
- Entry 1955 – Records of U.S. Elements of Inter-Allied Organizations; Records of the U.S. Element of the Tripartite Control Office; Records of the U.S. Element of the Tripartite Secretariat, General Records, 1948–1949

RG 263 – Records of the Central Intelligence Agency
Cited Entries:

- Entry A1-86 – First Release of Name Files under the Nazi War Crimes and Japanese Imperial Government Disclosure Acts, 1923–1999

- Entry ZZ-18 – Second Release of Name Files under the Nazi War Crimes and Japanese Imperial Government Disclosure Acts, 1936–2000
- Entry ZZ-19 – Second Release of Subject Files under the Nazi War Crimes and Japanese Imperial Government Disclosure Acts, 1946–2003

RG 319 – Records of the Army Staff
Cited Entries:
- Entry 134-B – Assistant Chief of Staff, G-2, Intelligence; Army Intelligence and Security Command; Records of the Investigative Records Repository; Security Classified Intelligence and Investigative Dossiers – Personal Name Files, 1939–1976

RG 466 – Records of the U.S. High Commissioner in Germany
Cited Entries:
- Entry 10-A – Office of the U.S. High Commissioner for Germany; Bonn; Executive Director; Security Segregated General Records, 1949–1952
- Entry 16-B – Office of the Executive Secretary; Miscellaneous Files Relating to Berlin
- Entry 48 – Prisons Division; Security Segregated Records of the Prisons Division, 1945–1957
- Entry 49 – Prisons Division; General Records of the Prisons Division, 1945–1957
- Entry 59 – U.S. Secretary; Allied High Commission; General Records (Subject Files), 1949–1952

RG 549 – Records of the U.S. Army Headquarters Europe
Cited Entries:
- Entry 2223 – Records of the Judge Advocate General, War Crimes Branch; Index to War Crimes Case Files, 1946–1947

- Amherst College Library, Archives and Special Collections

  Papers of John J. McCloy


## *Great Britain*


- The National Archives (Kew)

  FO – Records of the Foreign Office
  - FO 371 – Political Department, General Correspondence 1906–1966
  - FO 936 – Control Office for Germany and Austria and Foreign Office, German Section: Establishments: Files, 1947–1957
  - FO 945 – Control Office for Germany and Austria and Foreign Office, German Section: General Department, 1943–1948
  - FO 1005 – Control Commission for Germany (British Element), Records Library, 1943–1959
  - FO 1008 – Office of the United Kingdom High Commissioner for Germany, 1950–1955
  - FO 1012 – Control Office for Germany and Austria and Foreign Office: Control Commission for Germany (British Element), Berlin: Records, 1944–1952
  - FO 1032 – Economic and Industrial Planning Staff and Control Office for Germany and Austria and Successor: Control Commission for Germany (British Element), Military Sections and Headquarters Secretariat: Registered Files, 1942–1952

- FO 1042 – Embassy, Bonn, West Germany: General Correspondence,1954–1972
- FO 1049 – Control Office for Germany and Austria and Foreign Office: Control Commission for Germany (British Element), Political Division, 1943–1951
- FO 1060 – Records of the Foreign Office, Control Office for Germany and Austria and Foreign Office: Control Commission for Germany (British Element), Legal Division, and UK High Commission, Legal Division: Correspondence, Case Files and Court Registers, 1944–1958

FCO – Records of the Foreign and Commonwealth Office

- FCO 33 – Western Department and Western European Department: Registered Files, 1967–1975
- FCO 90 – Office of the Deputy Commandant, British Military Government, Berlin: Registered Files, 1972–1978

LCO – Records of the Lord Chancellor's Office

- LCO 2 – Registered Files, 1850–1984

PREM – Records of the Prime Minister's Office

- PREM 11 – Prime Minister's Office: Correspondence and Papers, 1951–1964

### *France*

- Ministère des Affaires étrangères, Bureau des Archives de l'occupation française en Allemagne et Autriche (Colmar)

GMFB – Gouvernement militaire français de Berlin
HC – Cabinet du Haut-Commissariat de la République française en Allemagne
GFCC – Groupe français au Conseil de Contrôle
KI – Kommandatura interalliée de Berlin

### *Germany*

- Allied Museum Berlin

Sammlung Dokumenten

- Bundesarchiv Berlin

R 43 – Reichskanzlei
DP 1 – Ministerium der Justiz (DDR)
DP 3 – Generalstaatsanwalt der DDR
DP 2 – Oberstes Gericht der DDR

- Bundesarchiv, Koblenz

B 136 – Bundeskanzleramt
B 141 – Bundesjustizministerium
B 305 – Zentrale Rechtsschutzstelle
NL 318 – Nachlaß Rudolf Wolters
NL 1340 – Nachlaß Albert Speer

- Politisches Archiv des Auswärtigen Amtes, Berlin

B 2 – Büro Staatssekretäre
B 10 – Politische Abteilung 2
B 12 – Abteilung 7, Ostabteilung
B 38 – Referat IIA1 (Wiedervereinigung, Berlinfragen)
B 83 – Referat 503/V4, Strafrecht

B 86 – Referat 506/507/V7, Kriegsfolgen
Botschaft der BRD in Moskau

- Stiftung Archiv der Parteien und Massenorganisationen der DDR im Bundesarchiv (Berlin)

  DY 3 – Demokratischer Blok – Verbindungdbüro
  DY 6 – Nationalrat der Nationalfront
  DY 30 – Sozialistische Einheitspartei Deutschlands
  NY 4036 – Nachlaß Wilhelm Pieck
  NY 4182 – Nachlaß Walter Ulbricht

- Landesarchiv Berlin

  B Rep 35 – British Military Government, Legal Branch
  B Rep 59 – Strafvollzugsamt/Justizvolzugsamt Berlin
  B Rep 62 – Gefängnis Tiergarten/Abwicklungsstelle Strafgefängnis Spandau

- Landeskirchliches Archiv (Stuttgart)

  D 1 – Nachlaß Landesbischof Wurm

- ThyssenKrupp Konzernarchiv (Duisburg)

  NRO – Nachlaß Walter Rohland

## NEWSPAPERS AND MAGAZINES

*Berlin Observer*
*Berliner Morgenpost*
*Berliner Zeitung*
*Bild*
*Bild am Sonntag*
*Bonner Rundschau*
*Bratishka*
*Bunte*
*Chicago Daily Tribune*
*Daily Express*
*Daily Mail*
*Daily Mirror*
*Daily Telegraph*
*Der Freiwillige*
*Der Kurier*
*Der Morgen*
*Der Spiegel*
*Der Tag*
*Der Tagesspiegel*
*Die Welt*
*Empire News*
*Figaro*
*Frankfurter Allgemeine Zeitung*
*Frankfurter Neue Presse*
*General-Anzeiger*
*Izvestia*
*La Lanterne*
*Le Monde*
*Manchester Guardian (The Guardian* after 1959)
*Moscow News*
*Münchener Merkur*
*Nationalzeitung*
*Neue Zeit*
*Neue Zeitung*
*Neue Züricher Zeitung*
*Neues Deutschland*
*Newsweek*
*Pravda*
*Quick*
*Revue*
*Stars and Stripes*
*Stern*
*Süddeutsche Zeitung*
*Sunday Express*
*Tagesspiegel*
*Tageszeitung*
*Täglische Rundschau*
*Telegraf*
*The Guardian*
*The New York Times*
*The Times*
*Trud* (Russia)
*Yorkshire Post*
*Völkischer Beobachter*
*Wochenend*

## PUBLISHED OFFICIAL DOCUMENTARY AND REFERENCE SETS

Birke, Adolf E., Hans Booms, and Otto Merker, eds. *Akten der britischen Militärregierung, Sachinventar 1945–1955*. 11 vols. London: Deutsches Historisches Institut, 1993.

Baumgartner, Gabrielle, and Dieter Hebig. *Biographisches Handbuch der SBZ/DDR 1945–1990*. 2 vols. Munich: Oldenbourg, 1996.

Commission de Publication des Documents diplomatiques français/Institut Historique Allemand, *Les Rapports Mensuels d'André François-Poncet, Haut-Commissaire française en Allemagne 1949–1955*. 2 vols. Paris: Imprimerie Nationale, 1996.

France. Ministère des Affaires étrangères. *Documents diplomatiques français, 1945*. 2 vols. and Annex. Paris: Imprimerie Nationale, 1996–2000.

France. Ministère des Affaires étrangères. *Documents diplomatiques français, 1946*. 2 vols. and Annex. Paris: Imprimerie Nationale, 1996–2004.

Germany (East). Deutsches Institut für Zeitgeschichte. *Dokumente zur Außenpolitik der Regierung der Deutschen Demokratischen Republik*. 10 vols. Berlin (East): Staatsverlag, 1954–1963.

Germany (East). Deutsches Institut für Zeitgeschichte. *Dokumente zur Außenpolitik der Deutschen Demokratischen Republik*. 22 vols. Berlin (East): Rütten & Loening, 1965–1988.

Germany (East). Deutsches Institut für Zeitgeschichte. *Dokumente zur Deutschlandpolitik der Sowjetunion*. 3 vols. Berlin: Rütten & Loening, 1957–1968.

Germany (West). Forschungsinstitut der deutschen Gesellschaft für auswärtige Politik. *Dokumente zur Berlin Frage*. 2 vols. Munich: Oldenbourg, 1962–1987.

Germany (West). Auswärtiges Amt. *Akten zur auswärtigen Politik der Bundesrepublik Deutschland-Adenauer und die Hohen Kommissare*. 2 vols. Munich: Oldenbourg, 1989–1990.

Germany (West). Auswärtiges Amt. *Akten zur auswärtigen Politik der Bundesrepublik Deutschland 1949/50*. Munich: Oldenbourg, 1997.

Germany (West). Auswärtiges Amt. *Akten zur auswärtigen Politik der Bundesrepublik Deutschland 1951*. Munich: Oldenbourg, 1999.

Germany (West). Auswärtiges Amt. *Akten zur auswärtigen Politik der Bundesrepublik Deutschland 1952*. Munich: Oldenbourg, 2000.

Germany (West). Auswärtiges Amt. *Akten zur auswärtigen Politik der Bundesrepublik Deutschland 1953*. 2 vols. Munich: Oldenbourg, 2001.

Germany (West). Auswärtiges Amt. *Akten zur auswärtigen Politik der Bundesrepublik Deutschland 1963*. 3 vols. Munich: Oldenbourg, 1994.

Germany (West). Auswärtiges Amt. *Akten zur auswärtigen Politik der Bundesrepublik Deutschland 1964*. 2 vols. Munich: Oldenbourg, 1995.

Germany (West). Auswärtiges Amt. *Akten zur auswärtigen Politik der Bundesrepublik Deutschland 1965*. 3 vols. Munich: Oldenbourg, 1996.

Germany (West). Auswärtiges Amt. *Akten zur auswärtigen Politik der Bundesrepublik Deutschland 1966*. 2 vols. Munich: Oldenbourg, 1997.

Germany (West). Auswärtiges Amt. *Akten zur auswärtigen Politik der Bundesrepublik Deutschland 1967*. 3 vols. Munich: Oldenbourg, 1998.

Germany (West). Auswärtiges Amt. *Akten zur auswärtigen Politik der Bundesrepublik Deutschland 1968*. 2 vols. Munich: Oldenbourg, 1999.

Germany (West). Auswärtiges Amt. *Akten zur auswärtigen Politik der Bundesrepublik Deutschland 1969*. 2 vols. Munich: Oldenbourg, 2000.

Germany (West). Auswärtiges Amt. *Akten zur auswärtigen Politik der Bundesrepublik Deutschland 1970*. 3 vols. Munich: Oldenbourg, 2001.

Germany (West). Auswärtiges Amt. *Akten zur auswärtigen Politik der Bundesrepublik Deutschland 1971*. 3 vols. Munich: Oldenbourg, 2002.

Germany (West). Auswärtiges Amt. *Akten zur auswärtigen Politik der Bundesrepublik Deutschland 1972*. 3 vols. Munich: Oldenbourg, 2003.

Germany (West). Auswärtiges Amt. *Akten zur auswärtigen Politik der Bundesrepublik Deutschland 1973*. 3 vols. Munich: Oldenbourg, 2004.

Germany (West). Bundesministerium des Innern. *Dokumente zur Deutschlandpolitik*. Series II–VI. Munich: Oldenbourg, 1961–2005.

Germany (West). Bundestag. *Verhandlungen des deutschen Bundestages. Stenographische Berichte*. (1.–11. Wahlperiode) Bonn: Bonner Universitäts-Buchdruckerei Gebr. Scheur, 1950–1988.

Great Britain. Parliament. House of Commons. *Parliamentary Debates (Hansard): Official Report*. 5th Series. London: H. M. Stationery Office, 1909–1981.

Great Britain. Parliament. House of Commons. *Parliamentary Debates (Hansard): Official Report*. 6th Series. London: H. M. Stationery Office, 1981–.

Great Britain. Parliament. House of Lords. *Parliamentary Debates (Hansard): Official Report*. 5th Series. London: H. M. Stationery Office, 1909–.

International Military Tribunal. *Trial of the Major War Criminals before the International Military Tribunal, Nuremberg, 14 November 1945–1 October 1946*. 42 vols. Nuremberg: International Military Tribunal, 1949.

Laufer, Jochen P., and Georgij P. Kynin, *Die UdSSR und die deutsche Frage, 1941–1948: Dokumente aus dem Archiv für Außenpolitik der Russischen Föderation*. 3 vols. Berlin: Duncker und Humblot, 2004.

Lohmann, Walter, and Hans H. Hildebrand. *Die deutsche Kriegsmarine*. 3 vols. Bad Nauheim: Padzon, 1956.

Merritt, Anna J., and Richard L. Merritt. *Public Opinion in Occupied Germany: The OMGUS Surveys, 1945–1949*. Urbana: University of Illinois Press, 1970.

Merritt, Anna J., and Richard L. Merritt. *Public Opinion in Semisovereign Germany: The HICOG Surveys, 1949–1955*. Urbana: University of Illinois Press, 1980.

Möller, Horst, and Klaus Hildebrand, gen. eds. *Die Bundesrepublik Deutschland und Frankreich: Dokumente 1949–1963*. 3 vols. Munich: K. G. Saur, 1997.

Rasch, Manfred. *Findbuch zum Nachlaß Walter Rohland (1898–1981) und zum Bestand Ruhr-Consulting GmbH*. Duisburg: ThyssenKrupp AG, 2001.

Salewski, Michael. "Von Raeder zu Dönitz: Der Wechsel im Oberbefehl der Kriegsmarine 1943." *Militärgeschichtliche Mitteilungen* 14 (1973): 101–46.

Scherstjanoi, Elke, ed. *Das SKK-Statut: Zur Geschichte der sowjetischen Kontrollkommission in Deutschland 1949 bis 1953 – Eine Dokumentation*. Munich: K. G. Saur, 1998.

Smith, Bradley F. *The American Road to Nuremberg: The Documentary Record, 1944–1945*. Stanford, CA: Hoover Institution Press, 1982.

Smith, Jean Edward, ed. *The Papers of General Lucius D. Clay: Germany 1945–1949*. 2 vols. Bloomington: Indiana University Press, 1974.

Tuturow, Norman, ed. *War Crimes, War Criminals, and War Crimes Trials: An Annotated Bibliography and Source Book* (New York: Greenwood, 1986).

United States. Department of State. *Foreign Relations of the United States: The Conference of Berlin (The Potsdam Conference), 1945*. 2 vols. Washington, DC: U.S. Government Printing Office, 1960.

United States. Department of State. *Foreign Relations of the United States – 1947*. vol. 2: *Council of Foreign Ministers – Germany and Austria*. Washington, DC: U.S. Government Printing Office, 1972.

United States. Department of State. *Foreign Relations of the United States – 1948*. vol. 2: *Germany and Austria*. Washington, DC: U.S. Government Printing Office, 1973.

United States. Department of State. *Foreign Relations of the United States – 1949*. vol. 3: *Council of Foreign Ministers: Germany and Austria*. Washington, DC: U.S. Government Printing Office, 1974.

United States. Department of State. *Foreign Relations of the United States – 1950*. vol. 3: *European Security and the German Question*. Washington, DC: U.S. Government Printing Office, 1982.

United States. Department of State. *Foreign Relations of the United States – 1952–1954*. vol. 7: *Germany and Austria*. Washington, DC: U.S. Government Printing Office, 1986.

United States. Department of State. *Foreign Relations of the United States – 1958–1960*. vols. 8–9: *The Berlin Crisis*. Washington, DC: U.S. Government Printing Office, 1993.

United States. Department of State. *Foreign Relations of the United States – 1961–1963*. vols. 14–15: *Berlin Crisis*. Washington, DC: U.S. Government Printing Office, 1994.

United States. Department of State. *Foreign Relations of the United States – 1964–1968*. vol. 15: *Berlin, Germany*. Washington, DC: U.S. Government Printing Office, 1999.

United States. Office of the United States Chief of Counsel for Prosecution of Axis Criminality. *Nazi Conspiracy and Aggression*. 8 vols. Washington, DC: U.S. Government Printing Office, 1946.

United States. *Trials of War Criminals before the Nuernberg Military Tribunals under Control Council Law No. 10, Nuernberg, October 1946–April 1949*. 13 vols. Washington, DC: U.S. Government Printing Office, 1949–1953.

Vogel, Walter, and Christoph Weisz. *Akten zur Vorgeschichte der Bundesrepublik Deutschland*. Reprint ed. 5 vols. Munich: Oldenbourg, 1989.

Weisz, Christoph, ed. *OMGUS Handbuch: Die amerikanische Militärregierung in Deutschland 1945–1949*, 2nd ed. Munich: Oldenbourg, 1995.

## MEMOIRS, SPEECHES, LETTERS, AND SECONDARY SOURCES

Abenheim, Donald. *Reforging the Iron Cross: The Search for Tradition in the West German Armed Forces*. Princeton, NJ: Princeton University Press, 1988.

Abrassimow, Pjotr A. *300 Meter von Brandenburger Tor: Errinerungen eines Botschafters*. Berlin (East): Quadriger, 1985.

Abrassimow, Pjotr A. *Westberlin – gestern und heute*. Berlin (East): Staatsverlag, 1981.

Acheson, Dean. *Present at the Creation: My Years in the State Department*. New York: Norton, 1969.

Adenauer, Konrad. *Briefe*. 5 vols. Berlin: Siedler, 1984–2004.

Adenauer, Konrad. *Errinerungen*. 4 vols. Stuttgart: Deutsche Verlags-Anstalt, 1964–1968.

Adenauer, Konrad. *Teegespräche*. 4 vols. Berlin: Siedler, 1984–1992.

Adomeit, Hannes. *Imperial Overstretch: Germany in Soviet Strategy from Stalin to Gorbachev*. Baden-Baden: Nomos Verlagsgesellschaft, 1998.

Ahonen, Pertti. "The Expellee Organizations and West German Ostpolitik, 1949–1969." Ph.D. Dissertation, Yale University, 1999.

Ahonen, Pertti. "Franz-Josef Strauss and the German Nuclear Question, 1956–1962," *Journal of Strategic Studies* 18, No. 2 (1995): 25–51.

Alderman, Sidney F. "Negotiating on War Crimes Prosecutions, 1945." In *Negotiating with the Russians*, eds. Raymond Dennett and Joseph E. Johnson. Boston: World Peace Foundation, 1951.

Allen, Michael Thad. *The Business of Genocide: The SS, Slave Labor, and the Concentration Camps*. Chapel Hill: University of North Carolina Press, 2002.

Amos, Heike. *Die Westpolitik der SED 1948/49–1961*. Berlin: Akademie Verlag, 2000.

Andrus, Burton C. *The Infamous of Nuremberg*. London: Leslie Frewin, 1969.

Arendt, Hannah. *Eichmann in Jerusalem: A Report on the Banality of Evil*. New York: Viking, 1963.

Assmann, Aleida, and Ute Frevert. *Geschichtsvergessenheit/Geschichtsversessenheit: Vom Umgang mit deutschen Vergangenheiten nach 1945*. Stuttgart: Deutsche Verlags-Anstalt, 1999.

Ausland, John C. *Kennedy, Khrushchev, and the Berlin-Cuba Crisis, 1961–64*. Oslo: Scandinavian University Press, 1996.

Baird, Jay. *To Die for Germany: Heroes in the Nazi Pantheon*. Bloomington: Indiana University Press, 1990.

Baring, Arnulf, ed. *Sehr veehrter Herr Bundeskanzler!: Heinrich von Brentano im Briefwechsel mit Konrad Adenauer*. Hamburg: Hoffmann Campe, 1974.

Bartov, Omer. "The Wehrmacht Exhibition Controversy: The Politics of Evidence." In *Crimes of War: Guilt and Denial in the Twentieth Century*, eds. Omer Bartov, Atina Grossmann, and Mary Nolan, 41–60. New York: The New Press, 2002.

Bass, Gary Jonathan. *Stay the Hand of Vengeance: The Politics of War Crimes Tribunals*. Princeton, NJ: Princeton University Press, 2000.

Bethge, Eberhard, and Ronald C. D. Jasper, eds. *An der Schwelle zum gespaltenen Europa: Der Briefwechsel zwischen George Bell und Gerhard Leibholz 1939–1951*. Stuttgart: Kreuz-Verlag, 1974.

Biddle, Francis. *In Brief Authority*. Garden City, NY: Doubleday, 1962.

Bird, Eugene. *Prisoner Number 7, Rudolf Hess: The Thirty Years in Jail of Hitler's Deputy Führer*. New York: Viking, 1974.

Blair, Clay. *Hitler's U-Boat War*. 2 vols. New York: Random House, 1996–98.

Blankenhorn, Herbert. *Verständnis und Verständigung: Blätter eines politischen Tagebuch 1949–1979*. Frankfurt am Main: Propyläen, 1980.

Bloxham, Donald. "The Genocidal Past in Western Germany and the Experience of Occupation, 1945–6," *European History Quarterly* 34, No. 4 (2004): 305–36.

Bloxham, Donald. *Genocide on Trial: War Crimes Trials and the Formation of Holocaust History and Memory*. New York: Oxford University Press, 2001.

Bloxham, Donald. "Punishing German Soldiers during the Cold War: The Case of Erich von Manstein," *Patterns of Prejudice* 33, No. 4 (1999): 25–45.

Bonwetsch, Bernd, and Alexei Filitow. "Chruschtschow und der Mauerbau: Die Gipfelkonferenz der Warschauer-Pakt-Staaten vom 3.–5. August 1961," *Vierteljehrshefte für Zeitgeschichte* 48: (2000): 155–98.

Bosch, William J. *Judgment on Nuremberg: American Attitudes toward the Major German War-Crime Trials*. Chapel Hill: University of North Carolina Press, 1970.

Bower, Tom. *Blind Eye to Murder: Britain, America and the Purging of Nazi Germany – A Pledge Betrayed*. London: Granada, 1983.

Boyle, Peter G., ed. *The Churchill-Eisenhower Correspondence, 1953–1955*. Chapel Hill: University of North Carolina Press, 1990.

Brandt, Willy. *Errinerungen*. Frankfurt am Main: Propyläen, 1989.

Briggs, Asa. *The Channel Islands: Occupation and Liberation*. London: B. T. Batsford, 1995.

Brochhagen, Ulrich. *Nach Nürnberg: Vergangenheitsbewältigung und Westintegration in der Ära Adenauer*. Hamburg: Junius, 1994.

Browning, Robert M. *U.S. Merchant Vessel War Casualties of World War II*. Annapolis MD: Naval Institute Press, 1996.

Bunting, Madeleine. *The Model Occupation: The Channel Islands under German Rule, 1940–1945*. London: Harper Collins, 1996.

Buruma, Ian. *The Wages of Guilt: Memories of War in Germany and Japan*. New York: Farrar, Strauss, and Giraux, 1994.

Buscher, Frank M. *The U.S. War Crimes Trial Program in Germany, 1946–1955*. Westport, CT: Greenwood Press, 1989.

Calvocoressi, Peter. *Fall Out: World War II and the Shaping of Postwar Europe*. New York: Longman, 1997.

Cameron, John ed. *Trial of Heinz Eck, August Hoffmann, Walter Weisspfennig, Hans Richard Lenz and Wolfgang Schwender (The Peleus Trial)*. London: Hodge, 1948.

Carrington, Peter Lord. *Reflecting on Things Past*. New York: Harper and Row, 1988.

Carstens, Karl. *Erinnerungen und Erfahrungen*. Edited by Kai von Jena and Reinhard Schmoeckel. Boppard am Rhein: Boldt, 1994.

Churchill, Winston S. *The Second World War*. 6 vols. Boston: Houghton Mifflin, 1948–1953.

Clay, Lucius D. *Decision in Germany*. New York: Doubleday, 1950.

Conant, James. *My Several Lives: Memoirs of a Social Inventor*. New York: Harper and Row, 1970.

Connelly, Mark. *We Can Take It!: Britain and the Memory of the Second World War*. New York: Longman, 2004.

Costello, John. *Ten Days that Saved the West*. London: Bantam, 1991.

Dastrup, Boyd L. *Crusade in Nuremberg: Military Occupation 1945–1949*. Westport, CT: Greenwood Press, 1985.

Dewhurst, Claude H. *Close Contact*. Boston: Houghton Mifflin, 1954.

Domarus, Max, ed. *Hitler: Speeches and Proclamations*. Translated by Chris Wilcox and Mary Fran Gilbert. 4 vols. Wauconda, IL: Bolchazy-Carducci, 1990–1992.

Dönitz, Karl. *Memoirs: Ten Years and Twenty Days*. Translated by R. H. Stevens. London: Weisenfeld & Nicolson, 1959.

Dönitz, Karl. *Mein wechselvolles Leben*. Revised ed. Göttingen: Musterschmidt, 1975.

Döscher, Hans- Jürgen. *Verschworene Gesellschaft: Das Auswärtige Amt unter Adenauer zwischen Neubeginn und Kontinuität*. Berlin: Akademie Verlag, 1995.

Douglas, Lawrence. *The Memory of Judgment: Making Law and History in the Trials of the Holocaust*. New Haven, CT: Yale University Press, 2001.

Douglas, Sholto (Lord Douglas of Kirtleside). *Combat and Command: The Story of an Airman in Two World Wars*. New York: Simon and Schuster, 1963.

Douglas-Hamilton, James. "Hess and the Haushofers." In *Flight from Reality: Rudolf Hess and His Mission to Scotland, 1941*, ed. David Stafford, 78–103. London: Pimlico, 2002.

Dubiel, Helmut. *Niemand ist frei von der Geschichte: Die nationalsozialistische Herrschaft in den Debatten des deutschen Bundestages*. Munich: C. Hanser, 1999.

Dülffer, Jost. *Weimar, Hitler und die Marine: Reichspolitik und Flottenbau 1920–1939*. Düsseldorf: Droste, 1973.

Dülffer, Jost, Jochen Thies, and Josef Henke. *Hitlers Städte: Baupolitik im Dritten Reich – Eine Dokumentation*. Cologne: Bohlau, 1978.

Dzhirkvelov, Ilya. *Secret Servant: My Life with the KGB and the Soviet Elite*. London: Collins, 1987.

Eden, Anthony. *Full Circle*. Boston: Houghton Mifflin, 1960.

Eisenberg, Carolyn Woods. *Drawing the Line: The American Decision to Divide Germany*. New York: Cambridge University Press, 1996.

Erickson, John. "Rudolf Hess: A Post-Soviet Postscript." In *Flight from Reality: Rudolf Hess and His Mission to Scotland, 1941*, ed. David Stafford, 38–61. London: Pimlico, 2002.

Erker, Paul. *Industrie-Eliten in der NS-Zeit: Anpassungsbereitschaft und Eigeninteresse von Unternehmern in der Rüstungs– und Kriegswirtschaft, 1936–1945*. Passau: Wissenschaftsverlag, 1994.

Ermarth, Michael, ed. *America and the Shaping of German Society, 1945–1955*. Providence, RI: Berg, 1993.

Farmer, Sarah. *Martyred Village: Commemorating the 1944 Massacre at Oradour-Sur-Glane*. Berkeley: University of California Press, 1999.

Felken, Detlef. *Dulles und Deutschland: Die amerikanische Deutschlandpolitik, 1952–1959*. Berlin: Bouvier, 1993.

Fest, Joachim. *Speer: The Final Verdict*. Translated by Ewald Osers and Alexandra Dring. New York: Harcourt, 2001.

Fishman, Jack. *Long Knives and Short Memories: The Spandau Prison Story*. New York: Richardson & Steirman, 1987.

Fishman, Jack. *The Seven Men of Spandau*. New York: Rinehart, 1954.

Foschepoth, Josef, and Rolf Steininger, eds. *Die britische Deutschland- und Besatzungspolitik 1945–1949: Eine Veröffentlichung des Deutschen Historischen Instituts London*. Paderborn: Schöningh, 1985.

François-Poncet, André. *De Versailles à Potsdam: La France et le problème allemande contemporain, 1919–1945*. Paris: Flammarion, 1948.

Frei, Norbert. *Adenauer's Germany and the Nazi Past: The Politics of Amnesty and Integration*. Translated by Joel Golb. New York: Columbia University Press, 2002.

Frei, Norbert. *Karrieren im Zweilicht: Hitlers Eliten nach 1945*. Frankfurt am Main: Campus Verlag, 2001.

Frei, Norbert. *Vergangenheitspolitik: Die Anfänge der Bundesrepublik und die NS-Vergangenheit*. Munich: Beck, 1996.

Fröhlich, Elke, ed. *Die Tagebücher von Joseph Goebbels*. Teil I: *Sämtliche Fragmente*. 15 vols. Munich: K. G. Sauer, 1987–2004.

Fulbrook, Mary. *German National Identity after the Holocaust*. Cambridge: Blackwell, 1999.

Gabel, Charles A. *Conversations interdites avec Rudolf Hess 1977–1986*. Paris: Plon, 1988.

Gellately, Robert, ed. *The Nuremberg Interviews* (Conducted by Leon Goldensohn). New York: Knopf, 2004.

Gemzell, Carl-Axel. *Hitler, Raeder und Skandinavien: Der Kampf für einen maritimen Operationsplan*. Lund: Gleerup, 1965.

Geraghty, Tony. *BRIXMIS: The Untold Exploits of Britain's Most Daring Cold War Spy Mission*. London: Harper Collins, 1997.

Gerlach, Wolfgang. *And the Witnesses Were Silent: The Confessing Church and the Persecution of the Jews*. Lincoln: University of Nebraska Press, 2000.

Germany (West). Press and Information Office. *The Berlin Settlement: The Quadripartite Agreement on Berlin and the Security Arrangements*. Wiesbaden: Graphische Betrieb, 1972.

Gilbert, G. M. *Nuremberg Diary*. New York: Farrar, Strauss & Co., 1947.

Gilbert, Martin. *Winston S. Churchill*, vol. 7: *Never Despair 1945–1965*. Boston: Houghton Mifflin, 1988.

Gilliland, Jane. "Submarines and Targets: Suggestions for New Codified Rules of Submarine Warfare," *Georgetown Law Journal* 73, No. 3 (1985): 975–1005.

Ginsburgs, George. *Moscow's Road to Nuremberg: The Soviet Background of the Trial*. The Hague: Martinus Nijhoff, 1996.

Ginsburgs, George, and V. N. Kudriavtsev, eds. *The Nuremberg Trial and International Law*. Boston: Martinus Nijhoff, 1990.

Goda, Norman J. W. "Black Marks: Hitler's Bribery of His Senior Military Officers during World War II," *Journal of Modern History* 72, No. 2 (2000): 413–52.

Goda, Norman J. W. "Justice and Politics in Karl Dönitz's Release from Spandau." In *The Impact of Nazism: New Perspectives on the Third Reich and Its Legacy*, eds. Alan Steinweis and Daniel E. Rogers, 199–214. Lincoln: University of Nebraska Press, 2003.

Goda, Norman J. W. *Tomorrow the World: Hitler, Northwest Africa and the Path Toward America*. College Station: Texas A&M University Press, 1998.

Golytsyn, Anatoly. *New Lies for Old: The Communist Strategy of Deception and Disinformation*. New York: Dodd Mead, 1984.

Goschler, Constantin, ed. *Hitler: Reden – Schriften – Anordnungen (Februar bis Januar 1933)*, v. 4, Teil 1. Munich: K. G. Sauer, 1994.

Granieri, Ronald. *The Ambivalent Alliance: Konrad Adenauer, the CDU/CSU, and the West 1949–1966*. New York: Berghahn Books, 2002.

Grathwol, Robert P., and Donita M. Moorhus. *American Forces in Berlin 1945–1994: Cold War Outpost*. Washington, DC: Department of Defense, 1994.

Grathwol, Robert P., and Donita M. Moorhus. *Berlin and the American Military: A Cold War Chronicle*, 2nd ed. New York: New York University Press, 1999.

Gregor, Neil. *Daimler-Benz in the Third Reich*. New Haven, CT: Yale University Press, 1998.

Grier, David. "The Appointment of Karl Dönitz as Hitler's Successor." In *The Impact of Nazism: New Perspectives on the Third Reich and Its Legacy*, eds. Alan Steinweis and Daniel E. Rogers, 182–98. Lincoln: University of Nebraska Press, 2003.

Grose, Peter. *Operation Rollback: America's Secret War Behind the Iron Curtain*. Boston: Houghton Mifflin, 2000.

Gromyko, Andrei. *Memoirs*. Translated by Harold Shukman. New York: Doubleday, 1990.

Hankey, Lord Maurice. *Politics, Trials and Errors*. Chicago: Henry Regnery Co., 1950.

Harrison, Hope. *Driving the Soviets Up the Wall: Soviet-East German Relations, 1953–1961*. Princeton, NJ: Princeton University Press, 2003.

Hartrich, Edwin. *The Fourth and Richest Reich*. London: Macmillan, 1980.

Heineman, John L. *Hitler's First Foreign Minister: Constantin Freiherr von Neurath, Diplomat and Statesman*. Berkeley: University of California Press, 1979.

Hendry, I. D., and M. C. Wood. *The Legal Status of Berlin*. Cambridge: Grotius, 1987.

Herf, Jeffrey. *Divided Memory: The Nazi Past in the Two Germanys*. Cambridge, MA: Harvard University Press, 1996.

Hess, Ilse. *Antwort aus Zelle Sieben – Briefweschsel mit dem Spandauer Gefangenen*. Leoni am Starnberger See: Druffel, 1967.

Hess, Ilse. *Ein Schicksal in Briefen*. Leoni am Starnberger See: Druffel, 1971.

Hess, Ilse, *England – Nürnberg – Spandau*. Leoni am Starnberger See: Druffel, 1952.

Hess, Ilse. *Gefangener des Friedens – Neue Briefe aus Spandau*. Leoni am Starnberger See: Druffel, 1954.

Hess, Rudolf. *Reden*. Munich: Eher, 1938.

Hess, Wolf Rüdiger. *Hess – Weder Recht noch Menschlichkeit: Das Urteil von Nürnberg – Die Rache von Spandau – Eine Dokumentation*. Leoni am Starnberger See: Druffel, 1974.

Hess, Wolf Rüdiger. *Ich bereue nichts*. 3rd ed. Graz: Leopold Stocker Verlag, 1998.

Hess, Wolf Rüdiger. "The Life and Death of My Father Rudolf Hess," presented by videotape to the Eleventh Conference of the Institute for Historical Review, 1992 [accessed June 2004], http://www.ihr.org/jhr/v.13/v13n1p24˙Hess.html.

Hess, Wolf Rüdiger. *Mein Vater Rudolf Heß: Englandflug und Gefangenschaft* Munich: Langen Müller, 1984.

Hess, Wolf Rüdiger. *Mord an Rudolf Heß? Der geheimnisvolle Tod meines Vaters in Spandau*. Leoni am Starnberger See: Druffel, 1989.

Hess, Wolf Rüdiger, ed. *Rudolf Hess: Briefe, 1908–1933*. Munich: Langen Müller, 1987.

Hilger, Andreas, Ute Schmidt, and Günther Wagenleher, eds. *Sowjetische Militärtribunale*. Bd. 1. *Die Verteilung deutscher Kriegsgefangener 1941–1953*. Cologne: Böhlau Verlag, 2001.

Hillenbrand, Martin J. *Fragments of Our Time: Memoirs of a Diplomat*. Athens: University of Georgia Press, 1998.

Hoffman, J. H. "German Field Marshals as War Criminals? A British Embarrassment," *Journal of Contemporary History* 23, No. 1 (1988): 17–35.

Holloway, David. *The Soviet Union and the Arms Race*. New Haven, CT: Yale University Press, 1983.

Howley, Frank. *Berlin Command*. New York: Putnam, 1950.

Jacob, Brigitte, and Wolfgang Schäche. "Rimpl, Herbert." In Grove Art Online, Oxford University Press [accessed July 2004], http://www.groveart.com.

Jasper, Donald C. D. *George Bell: Bishop of Chichester*. London: Oxford University Press, 1967.

Judt, Tony. "The Past is Another Country: Myth and Memory in Postwar Europe." In *The Politics of Retribution in Europe: World War II and Its Aftermath*, eds. István Deák, Jan T. Gross, and Tony Judt, 293–323. Princeton, NJ: Princeton University Press, 2000.

Junge, Traudl. *Bis zur letzten Stunde: Hitlers Sekretärin erzählt ihr Leben*. Munich: Classen Verlag, 2002.

Karner, Stefan, ed. *Gefangen in Russland: Die Beiträge des Symposions auf der Schalleburg, 1995*. Graz: Ludwig Boltzmann-Institut für Kriegsfolgen-Forschung, 1995.

Katz, Robert. *The Battle for Rome: The Germans, the Allies, the Partisans and the Pope, September 1943–June 1944*. New York: Simon and Schuster, 2003.

Keithly, David M. *Breakthrough in the Ostpolitik: The 1971 Quadripartite Agreement*. Boulder, CO: Westview Press, 1983.

Kelley, Douglas M. *22 Cells at Nuremberg*. New York: Greenberg, 1947.

Kershaw, Ian. *Hitler 1889–1936: Hubris*. New York: Norton, 1998.

Kershaw, Ian. *Hitler 1936–1945: Nemesis*. New York: Norton, 2000.

Kettenacker, Lothar. "Mishandling a Spectacular Event: The Rudolf Hess Affair." In *Flight from Reality: Rudolf Hess and His Mission to Scotland, 1941*, ed. David Stafford, 19–37. London: Pimlico, 2002.

Kilmuir, Earl of (Sir David Maxwell Fyfe). *Political Adventure: The Memoirs of the Earl of Kilmuir*. London: Weidenfeld & Nicolson.

Kipp, Yvonne. *Eden, Adenauer und die deutsche Frage: Britische Deutschlandpolitik im internationalen Spannungsfeld 1951–1957*. Paderborn: Schöningh, 2002.

Kirkpatrick, Ivone. *The Inner Circle: Memoirs of Sir Ivone Kirkpatrick*. London: Macmillan, 1959.

Klemperer, Klemens von. *German Resistance against Hitler: The Search for Allies Abroad 1938–1945*. Oxford: Clarendon Press, 1992.

Kochavi, Arieh J. "The Moscow Declaration, the Kharkov Trial and the Question of Policy towards War Criminals in the Second World War," *History* 76, No. 3 (1991): 401–17.

Kochavi, Arieh J. *Prelude to Nuremberg: Allied War Crimes Policy and the Question of Punishment*. Chapel Hill: University of North Carolina Press, 1998.

König, Helmut. *Die Zukunft der Vergangenheit: Der Nationalsozialismus im politischen Bewußtsein der Bundesrepublik*. Frankfurt am Main: Fischer, 2003.

Kopf, Peter. *Die Mommsens: Von 1848 bis heute – die Geschichte einer Familie ist die Geschichte der Deutschen*. Hamburg: Europa Verlag, 2004.

Kosthorst, Daniel. *Brentano und die deutsche Einheit: Die Deutschland- und Ostpolitik des Außenministers im Kabinett Adenauers 1955–1961*. Düsseldorf: Droste, 1993.

Krieger, Wolfgang. *Lucius D. Clay und die amerikanische Deutschlandpolitik 1945–1949*. Stuttgart: Klett-Cotta, 1987.

Krüger, Dieter. "Das schwierige Erbe: Die Traditionsansprache des Kapitäns zur See Karl-Adolf Zenker 1956 und ihre parliamentarischen Folgen." In *Deutsche Marine im Wandel: Vom Symbol nationaler Einheit zum Instrument internationaler Sicherheit*, ed. Werner Rahn, 549–64. Munich: Oldenbourg, 2005.

Kunze, Gerhard. *Grenzerfahrungen: Kontakte und Verhandlungen zwischen dem Land Berlin und der DDR 1949–1989*. Berlin: Akademie Verlag, 1999.

KZ-Gedenkstätte Vaihingen/Enz. *Das Konzentrationslager "Wiesengrund": Vom Arbeitslager zum Sterbelager*, 4th ed. Vaihingen/Enz: IPA Verlag, 2002.

Large, David Clay. *Germans to the Front: West German Rearmament in the Adenauer Era*. Chapel Hill: University of North Carolina Press, 1996.

Larres, Klaus. *Churchill's Cold War: The Politics of Personal Diplomacy*. New Haven, CT: Yale University Press, 2002.

Lawson, Tom. "Constructing a Christian History of Nazism: Anglicanism and the Memory of the Holocaust, 1945–49," *History and Memory* 16, No. 21 (2004): 146–76.

Lemke, Michael. *Die Berlinkrise 1958 bis 1963. Interessen und Handlungsspielräume der SED im Ost-West Konflikt.* Berlin: Akademie Verlag, 1995.

Le Tissier, Tony. *Farewell to Spandau.* Leatherhead: Ashford, Buchnan and Enright, 1994.

Liddell Hart, Basil. *The Other Side of the Hill: Germany's Generals, Their Rise and Fall, With Their Own Account of Military Events.* London: Cassell, 1948.

Lockenour, Jay. *Soldiers as Citizens: Former Wehrmacht Officers in the Federal Republic of Germany, 1945–1955.* Lincoln: University of Nebraska Press, 2001.

Longerich, Peter. *Hitlers Stellvertreter: Führung der Partei und Kontrolle des Staatsapparates durch den Stab Heß und die Partei-Kanzlei Bormann.* Munich: K. G. Saur, 1992.

Mahncke, Dieter. *Berlin in geteilten Deutschland.* Munich: Oldenbourg, 1973.

Marks, Sally. "The Myth of Reparations," *Central European History* 11, No. 3 (1978): 231–55.

Marrus, Michael. "The Holocaust at Nuremberg," *Yad Vashem Studies* 26 (1998): 5–41.

Marrus, Michael. *The Nuremberg War Crimes Trial 1945–1946: A Documentary History.* Boston: Bedford, 1997.

Marshall, Barbara. *The Origins of Postwar German Politics.* London: Croom and Helm, 1988.

Mastny, Vojtech. *The Cold War and Soviet Insecurity: The Stalin Years.* New York: Oxford University Press, 1996.

McAdams, A. James. *Germany Divided: From the Wall to Reunification.* Princeton, NJ: Princeton University Press, 1993.

McAdams, A. James, ed. *Transitional Justice and the Rule of Law in New Democracies.* Notre Dame, IN: University of Notre Dame Press, 1997.

McGowan, Lee. *The Radical Right in Germany 1870 to the Present.* New York: Longman, 2002.

Mensing, Hans Peter, ed. *Konrad Adenauer – Theodor Heuss: Unter vier Augen. Gespräche aus den Gründerjahren 1949–1959.* Berlin: Siedler, 1997.

Mensing, Hans-Peter, ed. *Theodor Heuss und Konrad Adenauer: Unserem Vaterland zugute. Der Briefwechsel, 1948–1963.* Berlin: Seidler, 1989.

Merseburger, Peter. *Willy Brandt 1913–1992: Visionär und Realist.* Stuttgart: Deutsche Velags-Anstalt, 2002.

Michaelis, Meier. *Mussolini and the Jews: German-Italian Relations and the Jewish Question in Italy, 1922–1945.* London: Clarendon Press, 1978.

Militärgeschichtliches Forschungsamt, gen. eds. *Anfänge westdeutscher Sicherheitspolitik 1945–1956*, vol. 3: *Die NATO-Option.* Munich: Oldenbourg, 1993.

Militärgeschichtliches Forschungsamt, gen. eds. *Germany and the Second World War*, vol. 5: *Organization and Mobilization of the German Sphere of Power.* Parts 1 and 2. Oxford: Clarendon Press, 2000–2003.

Miller, Judith. *One by One by One: Facing the Holocaust.* New York: Simon and Shuster, 1990.

Moeller, Robert G. *War Stories: The Search for a Usable Past in the Federal Republic of Germany.* Berkeley: University of California Press, 2001.

Moisel, Claudia. *Frankreich und die deutschen Kriegsverbrecher: Politik und Praxis der Strafverfolgung nach dem zweiten Weltkrieg.* Göttingen: Wallstein, 2004.

Moore, Arthur R. *A Careless Word – A Needless Sinking: A History of the Staggering Losses Suffered by the U.S. Merchant Marine, Both in Ships and Personnel during World War II*. King's Point, NY: American Merchant Marine Museum, 1983.

Morina, Christina. "Instructed Silence, Constructed Memory: The SED and the Return of German Prisoners of War as 'War Criminals' from the Soviet Union to East Germany, 1950–1956," *Contemporary European History* 13, No. 3 (2004): 323–43.

Müller, Klaus-Dieter, Konstantin Nikischkin, and Günther Wagenlehner, eds. *Die Tragödie der Gefangenschaft in Deutschland und in der Sowjetunion 1941–1956*. Cologne: Bohlau, 1998.

Murphy, David E., Sergei Kondrashev, and George Bailey. *Battleground Berlin: CIA vs. KGB in the Cold War*. New Haven, CT: Yale University Press, 1997.

Mußgnug, Dorothee. *Alliierte Militärmissionen in Deutschland 1946–1990*. Berlin: Duncker & Humblot, 2001.

Naftali, Timothy, Norman J.W. Goda, Richard Breitman, and Robert Wolfe. "The Mystery of Heinrich Müller: New Evidence from the CIA," *Holocaust and Genocide Studies* 15, No. 3 (2001): 453–67.

Naimark, Norman M. *The Russians in Germany: A History of the Soviet Zone of Occupation, 1945–1949*. Cambridge, MA: Belknap Press of Harvard University Press, 1995.

Neave, Airey. *On Trial at Nuremberg*. Boston: Little Brown, 1978.

Nerucheva, Margarita. "Vozmezdie [Retribution]," *Sibirskie Ogni [Siberian Lights]*, No. 2 (2000) [accessed January 2006], http://sibogni.ru/archive/2/215.

Nesbit, Roy Conyer, and Georges van Acker. *The Flight of Rudolf Hess: Myth and Reality*. Phoenix Mill: Sutton Publishing, 1999.

Ninkovich, Frank. *Germany and the United States: The Transformation of the German Question since 1945*. Boston: Twayne, 1988.

Niven, Bill. *Facing the Nazi Past: United Germany and the Legacy of the Third Reich*. London: Routledge, 2002.

Nolan, Mary. "Germans as Victims During the Second World War: Air Wars, Memory Wars," *Central European History* 38, No. 1 (2005): 7–40.

Orlow, Dietrich. *The History of the Nazi Party, 1919–1933*. Pittsburgh: University of Pittsburgh Press, 1969.

Ortner, Christian. *Am Beispiel Walter Reder: Die SS-Verbrechen in Marzabotto und ihre "Bewältigung."* Vienna: DÖW, 1985.

Osiel, Mark. *Mass Atrocity, Collective Memory, and the Law*. New Brunswick, NJ: Transaction, 1997.

Overy, Richard. *Interrogations: The Nazi Elite in Allied Hands, 1945*. New York: Viking, 2001.

Padfield, Peter. *Dönitz: The Last Führer*. New York: Harper and Row, 1984.

Padfield, Peter. *Hess: Flight for the Führer*. London: Weidenfeld & Nicolson, 1991.

Parish, Scott D., and Mikhail M. Narinsky. "New Evidence on the Soviet Rejection of the Marshall Plan, 1947: Two Reports," Cold War International History Project Working Paper No. 9. Washington, DC: Woodrow Wilson Center, 1994.

Pätzold, Kurt, and Manfred Weißbecker. *Rudolf Heß: Der Mann an Hitlers Seite*. Leipzig: Militzke Verlag, 1999.

Peifer, Douglas C. *The Three German Navies: Dissolution, Transition, and New Beginnings, 1945–1960*. Gainsville: University Press of Florida, 2002.

Pendaries, Yveline. *Les procès de Rastatt (1946–1954): Le jugement des crimes de guerre en zone française d'occupation en Allemagne*. Berne: Lang, 1995.

Persico, Joseph E. *Nuremberg: Infamy on Trial*. New York: Viking, 1994.

Petropoulos, Jonathan. *Art as Politics in the Third Reich*. Chapel Hill: University of North Carolina Press, 1996.

Picknett, Lynn, Clive Prince, and Stephen Prior. *Double Standards: The Rudolf Hess Cover Up*. Boston: Little Brown, 2001.

Pittman, Avril, ed. *From Ostpolitik to Reunification: West German-Soviet Political Relations since 1974*. New York: Cambridge University Press, 1992.

Poltorak, A. I. *The Nuremberg Epilogue*. Translated by David Skvirsky. Moscow: Progress Publishers, 1971.

Prusin, Alexander Victor. "Fascist Criminals to the Gallows!: The Holocaust and Soviet War Crimes Trials, December 1945–February 1946," *Holocaust and Genocide Studies* 17, No. 1 (2003): 1–30.

Raeder, Erich. *Mein Leben*. 2 vols. Tübingen-Neckar: Schlichtenmayer, 1956–1957.

Raeder, Erich. *My Life*. Translated by Henry W. Drexel. Annapolis, MD: Naval Institute Press, 1960.

Reichel,Peter. *Vergangenheitsbewältigung in Deutschland: Die Auseinandersetzung mit der NS-Diktatur von 1945 bis heute*. Munich: Beck, 2001.

Reif, Janin, Horst Schumacher, and Lothar Uebel. *Schwanenwerder: Ein Inselparadies in Berlin*. Berlin: Nicolai, 2000.

Roberts, Frank. *Dealing with Dictators: The Destruction and Revival of Europe 1930–1970*. London: Weidenfeld and Nicolson, 1991.

Rogers, Daniel E. "The Chancellors of the Federal Republic of Germany and the Political Legacy of the Holocaust." In *The Impact of Nazism: New Perspectives on the Third Reich and Its Legacy*, eds. Alan Steinweis and Daniel E. Rogers, 231–47. Lincoln: University of Nebraska Press, 2003.

Rogers, Daniel E. *Politics after Hitler: The Western Allies and the German Party System*. New York: New York University Press, 1995.

Rohland, Walter. *Bewegte Zeiten: Errinerungen eines Eisenhüttenmannes*. Stuttgart: Seewald, 1978.

Roskill, Stephen W. *The War at Sea, 1939–1945*. 3 vols. London: HMSO, 1957–1961.

Rückerl, Adalbert. *The Investigation of Nazi Crimes, 1945–1978: A Documentation*. Translated by Derek Rutter. Hamden, CT: Archon Books, 1980.

Rudolph, Karsten. *Wirtschaftsdiplomatie im Kalten Krieg: Die Ostpolitik der westdeutschen Großindustrie 1945–1991*. Frankfurt am Main: Campus Verlag, 2004.

Rupieper, Hermann-Josef. *Der besetzte Verbündete: Die amerikanische Deutschlandpolitik 1949–1955*. Opladen: Westdeutscher Verlag, 1991.

Salewski, Michael. *Die deutsche Seekriegsleitung*. 3 vols. Frankfurt am Main: Bernard & Graefe, 1970–1975.

Schechter, Jerrold L., and Peter S. Deriabin. *The Spy Who Saved the World: How a Soviet Colonel Changed the Course of the Cold War*. New York: Scribners, 1992.

Schick, Jack. *The Berlin Crisis 1958–1962*. Philadelphia: University of Pennsylvania Press, 1971.

Schirach, Baldur von. *Ich glaubte an Hitler*. Hamburg: Mosaik, 1967.

Schmidt, Matthias. *Albert Speer: The End of a Myth*. Translated by Joachim Neugroschel. New York: St. Martin's, 1984.

Schmidt, Rainer F. *Rudolf Heß: Der Botengang eines Toren? Der Flug nach Großbritannien vom 10. Mai 1941*. Düsseldorf: Econ, 1997.

Schöllgen, Gregor. *Willy Brandt: Die Biographie*. Berlin: Propyläen, 2001.

Schunk, Sharif Regina. "Ostpolitik and German Public Opinion, 1964–1972: A Study of Political Attitudes and Political Change in the Federal Republic of Germany," Ph.D. Dissertation, American University, 1974.

Schupljak, Peter. "Wahrnehmung und Legenden: Das Bild von Rudolf Hess in sowjetischen Publikationen." In *Rudolf Hess: Der Mann an Hitlers Seite*, by Kurt Pätzold and Manfred Weißbecker, 393–409. Leipzig: Militzke, 1999.

Schwartz, Thomas Alan. *America's Germany: John J. McCloy and the Federal Republic of Germany*. Cambridge, MA: Harvard University Press, 1991.

Schwartz, Thomas Alan. "John J. McCloy and the Landsberg Cases." In *American Policy and the Reconstruction of West Germany, 1945–1955*, eds. Jeffry Diefendorf, Axel Frohn, and Hermann-Josef Rupieper, 433–53. New York: Cambridge University Press, 1993.

Schwartz, Hans-Peter. *Geschichte der Bundesrepublik Deutschland*, Bd. 2: *Die Ära Adenauer 1949–1957*. Stuttgart: Deutsche Verlags-Anstalt, 1981.

Schwarz, Hans-Peter, ed. *Konrad Adenauer – Reden 1917–1967: Eine Auswahl*. Stuttgart: Deutsche Verlags-Anstalt, 1975.

Schwarz, Hans-Peter. *Konrad Adenauer: A German Politician in the Age of War, Revolution and Reconstruction*. 2 vols. Translated by Louise Wilmot. Providence, RI: Berghahn, 1995.

Schwarzmüller, Theo. *Zwischen Kaiser und "Führer": Generalfeldmarschall August von Mackensen. Eine politische Biographie*. Paderborn: Schöningh, 1999.

Searle, Alaric. "A Very Special Relationship: Basil Liddell Hart, Wehrmacht Generals, and the Debate on West German Rearmament," *War in History* 5, No. 3 (1998): 327–57.

Searle, Alaric. *Wehrmacht Generals, West German Society, and the Debate on Rearmament, 1949–1959*. Westport, CT: Praeger, 2003.

Seidl, Alfred. *Der Fall Rudolf Hess: Dokumentation des Verteidigers*. Munich: Universitas, 1984.

Seldon, Anthony. *Churchill's Indian Summer: The Conservative Government, 1951–1955*. London: Hodder and Stroughton, 1981.

Semjonow, Wladimir S. *Von Stalin bis Gorbatschow: Ein halbes Jahrhundert in diplomatischer Mission 1939–1991*. Berlin: Nicolai, 1995.

Sereny, Gitta. *Albert Speer: His Battle with the Truth*. New York: Knopf, 1995.

Sereny, Gitta. *The Healing Wound: Experiences and Reflections on Germany, 1938–2001*. New York: Norton, 2000.

Shawcross, Sir Hartley. *Life Sentence: The Memoirs of Lord Shawcross*. London: Constable, 1995.

Smith, Bradley F. *Reaching Judgment at Nuremberg*. New York: Basic Books, 1977.

Smith, Bradley F. *The Road to Nuremberg*. New York: Basic Book, 1981.

Smith, Jean Edward. *Lucius D. Clay: An American Life*. New York: Holt, 1990.

Speer, Albert. *Infiltration*. Translated by Joachim Neugroschel. New York: Macmillan, 1981.

Speer, Albert. *Inside the Third Reich*. Translated by Richard Winston and Clara Winston. New York: Macmillan, 1970.

Speer, Albert. *Spandau: The Secret Diaries*. Translated by Richard Winston and Clara Winston. New York: Macmillan, 1976.

Sprecher, Drexel. *Inside the Nuremberg Trial: A Prosecutor's Comprehensive Account*. 2 vols. Lanham, MD: University Press of America, 1999.

Stafford, David, ed. *Flight from Reality: Rudolf Hess and His Mission to Scotland, 1941*. London: Pimlico, 2002.

Steinert, Marlis. *Capitulation 1945*. Translated by Richard Barry. New York: Walker, 1969.

Steininger, Rolf. *The German Question: The Stalin Note of 1952 and the Problem of Reunification*. Translated by Jane T. Hedges. Edited by Marc Cioc. New York: Columbia University Press, 1990.

Storey, Robert G. *The Final Judgment? Pearl Harbor to Nuremberg*. San Francisco: Naylor, 1966.

Sutterlin, James S., and David Klein. *Berlin: From Symbol of Confrontation to Keystone of Stability*. New York: Praeger, 1989.

Sykes, Christopher. *Nancy: The Life of Lady Astor*. London: Collins, 1972.

Taylor, Telford. *Anatomy of the Nuremberg Trials: A Personal Memoir*. New York: Knopf, 1992.

Tent, James. *Mission on the Rhine: Reeducation and Denazification in American-Occupied Germany*. Chicago: University of Chicago Press, 1982.

Teschke, John P. *Hitler's Legacy: West Germany Confronts the Aftermath of the Third Reich*. New York: Peter Lang, 1999.

Thies, Jochen. *Architekt der Weltherrschaft: Die "Endziele" Hitlers*. Düsseldorf: Droste, 1981.

Thies, Jochen. *Helmut Schmidts Rückzug von der Macht: Das Ende der Ära Schmidt aus nächster Nähe*. Stuttgart: Bonn Aktuel, 1988.

Thomas, Charles. *The German Navy in the Nazi Era*. Annapolis, MD: Naval Institute Press, 1990.

Thomas, Hugh. *The Murder of Rudolf Hess*. London: Hodder and Stoughton, 1979.

Thomas, Hugh. *Hess: A Tale of Two Murders*. London: Hodder and Stoughton, 1988.

Trachtenberg, Marc. *A Constructed Peace: The Making of the European Settlement, 1945–1963*. Princeton, NJ: Princeton University Press, 1999.

Trainin, A. N. *Hitlerite Responsibility under Criminal Law*. Translated by A. Rothstein. London: Hutchinson, 1945.

Trevor-Roper, Hugh R. *The Last Days of Hitler*. New York: Macmillan, 1947.

Tusa, Ann, and John Tusa. *The Nuremberg Trial*. London: Macmillan, 1983.

Van der Vat, Dan. *The Good Nazi: The Life and Lies of Albert Speer*. New York: Houghton Mifflin, 1997.

Vercel, Michel C. *Les rescapés de Nuremberg: les "seigneurs de la guerre" après le verdict*. Paris: Édicions Albin Michel, 1966.

Vollnhals, Clemens, ed. *Entnazifizierung: Politische Säuberung und Rehabilitierung in den vier Besatzungszonen, 1945–1949*. Munich: Deutscher Taschenbuch Verlag, 1991.

Wachsmann, Nikolaus. *Hitler's Prisons: Legal Terror in Nazi Germany*. New Haven, CT: Yale University Press, 2003.

Warner, Michael. "Origins of the Congress of Cultural Freedom, 1949–1950," *Studies in Intelligence* 38, No. 5 (1995) (online declassified version) [accessed April 2006], http://www.cia.gov/csi/studies/95unclass/Warner.html.

Weihsmann, Helmut. *Bauen unterm Hakenkreuz: Architektur des Untergangs*. Vienna: Promedia, 1998.

Weinberg, Gerhard L. *The Foreign Policy of Hitler's Germany*. 2 vols. Reprint ed. Atlantic Highlands, NJ: Humanities Press, 1994.

Weinberg, Gerhard L. *Germany, Hitler and World War II: Essays in German and World History*. New York: Cambridge University Press, 1996.

Weinberg, Gerhard L., ed. *Hitler's Second Book*. Translated by Krista Smith. New York: Enigma, 2003.

Weinberg, Gerhard L., ed. "National Socialist Organization and Foreign Policy Aims in 1927," *The Journal of Modern History* 36, No. 3 (1964): 428–33.

Weinke, Annette. *Die Verfolgung von NS-Tätern im geteilten Deutschland: Vergangenheitsbewältigungen 1949–1959*. Paderborn: Schöningh, 2002.

Weizsäcker, Richard von. *From Weimar to the Wall: My Life in German Politics*. Translated by Ruth Hein. New York: Broadway Books, 1999.

West, Rebecca. *A Train of Powder*. New York: Viking, 1965.

Whitney, Craig R. *Spy Trader: Germany's Devil's Advocate and the Darkest Secrets of the Cold War*. New York: Times Books, 1993.

Wiesen, S. Jonathan. *West German Industry and the Challenge of the Nazi Past 1945–1955*. Chapel Hill, NC: University of North Carolina Press, 2001.

Willems, Susanne. *Der entsiedelte Jude: Albert Speers Wohnungsmarktpolitik für den Berliner Hauptstadtbau*. Berlin: Edition Hentrich, 2002.

Willis, F. Roy. *The French in Germany 1945–1949*. Stanford, CA: Stanford University Press, 1962.

Wise, David. *Molehunt: The Secret Search for Traitors that Shattered the CIA*. New York: Random House, 1992.

Wolfrum, Edgar. *Französische Besatzungspolitik und deutsche Sozialdemokratie: Politische Neuansätze in der "vergessenen Zone" bis zur Bildung des Südweststaates 1945–1952*. Düsseldorf: Droste, 1991.

Wyden, Peter. *Wall: The Inside Story of Divided Berlin*. New York: Simon and Schuster, 1989.

Wynecken, Jon David K. "Memory as Diplomatic Leverage: Bishop Theophil Wurm and War Crimes Trials, 1948–1952." Paper presented at German Studies Association, Annual Meeting, September 30, 2004.

Zarusky, Jürgen, ed. *Die Stalin-Note vom 10. März 1952: Neue Quellen und Analysen*. Munich: Oldenbourg, 2002.

Zucotti, Susan. *Under His Very Windows: The Vatican and the Holocaust in Italy*. New Haven, CT: Yale University Press, 2000.

# Index